A HISTORY
OF
INDIAN PHILOSOPHY

A HISTORY
OF
INDIAN PHILOSOPHY

BY

SURENDRANATH DASGUPTA

VOLUME IV
INDIAN PLURALISM

CAMBRIDGE
AT THE UNIVERSITY PRESS
1955

PUBLISHED BY
THE SYNDICS OF THE CAMBRIDGE UNIVERSITY PRESS
London Office: Bentley House, N.W. 1
American Branch: New York
Agents for Canada, India, and Pakistan: Macmillan

First Edition 1949
Reprinted 1955

First printed in Great Britain at the University Press, Cambridge
Reprinted by offset-litho by
Percy Lund Humphries & Co. Ltd., Bradford

TO THE SACRED AND BLESSED MEMORY OF

THE LATE MAHĀTMĀ

MOHANDAS KARAMCHAND GANDHI,

THE POET

RABINDRANATH TAGORE,

and those martyrs and patriots who have
died or worked
for the liberation and elevation of
India

THIS HUMBLE WORK, WHICH SEEKS TO DISCOVER
INDIA AT ITS BEST AND HIGHEST, IS
DEDICATED WITH SINCEREST
REVERENCE AND
HUMILITY

PREFACE

THE third volume of the present series was published in 1940. The manuscript of the fourth volume was largely ready at that time and it would have been possible to send it for publication at least by 1942. But the second world-war commenced in 1939 and although the Cambridge University Press was prepared to accept the manuscript even during war-time, the despatch of the manuscript from Calcutta to Cambridge and the transmission of proofs to and fro between England and India appeared to me to be too risky. In 1945, after retiring from the Chair of Philosophy in the Calcutta University, I came to England. But shortly after my arrival here I fell ill, and it was during this period of illness that I revised the manuscript and offered it to the University Press. This explains the unexpected delay between the publication of the third volume and the present one. The promises held out in the preface to the third volume, regarding the subjects to be treated in the present volume, have been faithfully carried out. But I am not equally confident now about the prospects of bringing out the fifth volume. I am growing in age and have been in failing health for long years. The physical and mental strain of preparing a work of this nature and of seeing it through the Press is considerable, and I do not know if I shall be able to stand such a strain in future. But I am still collecting the materials for the fifth volume and hope that I may be able to see it published in my life-time.

The present volume deals with the philosophy of the *Bhāgavata-purāṇa*, the philosophy of Madhva and his followers, the philosophy of Vallabha and the philosophy of the Gauḍīya school of Vaiṣṇavism. So far as I know, nothing important has yet been published on the philosophy of the *Bhāgavata-purāṇa* and that of Vallabha. Two important works by Mr Nāgarāja Śarmā of Madras and by Professor Helmuth von Glasenapp on the philosophy of Madhva have been published in English and German respectively. But so far nothing has appeared about the philosophy of the great teachers of the Madhva school such as Jaya-tīrtha and Vyāsa-tīrtha. Very little is known about the great controversy between the eminent followers of the Madhva school of thought and of the followers of the

Śaṅkara school of Vedānta. In my opinion Jaya-tīrtha and Vyāsa-tīrtha present the highest dialectical skill in Indian thought. There is a general belief amongst many that monism of Śaṅkara presents the final phase of Indian thought. The realistic and dualistic thought of the Sāṃkhya and the *yoga* had undergone a compromise with monism both in the Purāṇas and in the hands of the later writers. But the readers of the present volume who will be introduced to the philosophy of Jaya-tīrtha and particularly of Vyāsa-tīrtha will realize the strength and uncompromising impressiveness of the dualistic position. The logical skill and depth of acute dialectical thinking shown by Vyāsa-tīrtha stands almost unrivalled in the whole field of Indian thought. Much more could have been written on the system of Madhva logic as explained in the *Tarka-tāṇdava* of Vyāsa-tīrtha. In this great work Vyāsa-tīrtha has challenged almost every logical definition that appears in the *Tattva-cintāmani* of Gaṅgeśa, which forms the bed-rock of the new school of Nyāya logic. But this could have been properly done only in a separate work on the Madhva logic. Of the controversy between the monists of the Śaṅkara school and the dualists of the Madhva school, most people are ignorant of the Madhva side of the case, though there are many who may be familiar with the monistic point of view. It is hoped that the treatment of the philosophy of Madhva and his followers undertaken in the present volume will give new light to students of Indian thought and will present many new aspects of dialectical logic hitherto undiscovered in Indian or European thought.

The treatment of the philosophy of Vallabha which is called *viśuddhādvaita* or pure monism, presents a new aspect of monism and also gives us a philosophical analysis of the emotion of devotion. Though readers of Indian philosophy may be familiar with the name of Vallabha, there are but few who are acquainted with the important contributions of the members of his school.

I have not devoted much space to the philosophy of the *Bhāgavata-purāṇa*. Much of its philosophical views had already been anticipated in the treatment of the Sāṃkhya, *yoga* and the Vedānta. As regards the position of God and His relation to the world the outlook of the *Bhāgavata-purāṇa* is rather ambiguous. The *Bhāgavata-purāṇa* has therefore been referred to for support by the Madhvas, Vallabhas and thinkers of the Gauḍīya school.

The Gauḍīya school seems to make the *Bhāgavata-purāṇa* the fundamental source of its inspiration.

The chief exponent of the Gauḍīya school of thought is Caitanya. He, however, was a religious devotee and very little is known of his teachings. He did not produce any literary or philosophical work. But there were some excellent men of letters and philosophers among his disciples and their disciples. The treatment of the Gauḍīya school of Vaiṣṇavism thus gives a brief exposition of the views of Rūpa Gosvāmī, Jīva Gosvāmī and Baladeva Vidyābhūṣaṇa. Dr S. K. De has contributed a number of important articles on the position of Jīva Gosvāmī, though it does not seem that he cared to put an emphasis on the philosophical perspective.

In writing the present volume I have been able to use the huge amount of published materials in Sanskrit as well as a number of rare manuscripts which I collected from South India on my journeys there on various occasions.

My best thanks are due to my old friend, Dr F. W. Thomas, who, in spite of his advanced age and many important pre-occupations, took the trouble to revise some portions of the manuscript and of revising and correcting the proofs, with so much care and industry. But for his help the imperfections of the present work would have been much greater. I also have to thank Dr E. J. Thomas for the many occasional helps that I received from him from the time of the first inception of the present series. My best thanks are also due to my wife, Mrs Surama Dasgupta, M.A., Ph.D. (Cal. et Cantab), Śāstrī, for the constant help that I received from her in the writing of the book and also in many other works connected with its publication. I am also grateful to Dr Satindra Kumar Mukherjee, M.A., Ph.D., my former pupil, for the help that I received from him when I was preparing the manuscript some years ago. I wish also to thank the Syndics of the University Press for undertaking the publication of this volume at a time when the Press was handicapped by heavy pressure of work, and by great difficulties of production.

SURENDRANATH DASGUPTA

Trinity College, Cambridge
August, 1948

CONTENTS

CHAPTER XXIV

THE BHĀGAVATA PURĀṆA

CHAPTER XXV

MADHVA AND HIS SCHOOL

CHAPTER XXVI

MADHVA'S INTERPRETATION OF THE *BRAHMA-SŪTRAS*

CHAPTER XXVII

A GENERAL REVIEW OF THE PHILOSOPHY OF MADHVA

CHAPTER XXVIII

MADHVA LOGIC

CHAPTER XXIX

CONTROVERSY BETWEEN THE DUALISTS AND THE MONISTS

CHAPTER XXX

CONTROVERSY BETWEEN THE DUALISTS AND THE MONISTS (*cont.*)

CHAPTER XXXI

THE PHILOSOPHY OF VALLABHA

CHAPTER XXXII
CAITANYA AND HIS FOLLOWERS

CHAPTER XXXIII
THE PHILOSOPHY OF JĪVA GOSVĀMĪ AND BALADEVA VIDYĀBHŪṢAṆA, FOLLOWERS OF CAITANYA

CHAPTER XXIV

THE *BHĀGAVATA-PURĀṆA*

The Bhāgavata-purāṇa.

THE *Bhāgavata-purāṇa* shares with the *Bhagavad-gītā* a unique position in the devotional literature of India. It cannot however claim the same antiquity: before the tenth century A.D. no references to it have been discovered by the present writer. Even Rāmānuja (born in A.D. 1017) had not mentioned its name or made any quotations from it. But by the time of Madhva the work had become famous: one of the principal works of Madhva (thirteenth century A.D.) is called the *Bhāgavata-tātparya*, in which he deals with the principal ideas of the *Bhāgavata-purāṇa*, and lays emphasis on them so far as they support his views. The thoughts of the *Bhāgavata-purāṇa* are loftily poetic, but the style is more difficult. The present writer is of opinion that it must have been composed by a Southerner, as it makes references to the Āḷvārs, who have probably never been referred to by any writer in Northern or Upper India. The *Bhāgavata-purāṇa*, however, was so much appreciated that immediately commentaries were written upon it. Some of these commentaries are:

Amṛta-raṅgiṇī, *Ātmapriyā*, *Kṛṣṇa-padī*, *Caitanya-candrikā*, *Jaya-maṅgalā*, *Tattva-pradīpikā*, *Tātparya-candrikā*, *Tātparya-dīpikā*, *Bhagavallīlā-cintāmaṇi*, *Rasa-mañjarī*, *Śukapakṣīyā Prabodhinī*, a *ṭīkā* by Janārdana Bhaṭṭa, a *ṭīka* by Narahari, *Prakāśa* by Śrīnivasa, *Tattva-dīpikā* by Kalyāṇa Rāya, a *ṭīkā* by Kṛṣṇa Bhaṭṭa, a *ṭīkā* by Kaura Sādhu, a *ṭīkā* by Gopāla Cakravartī, *Anvaya-bodhinī* by Cūḍāmaṇi Cakravartī, *Bhāva-prakāśikā* by Narasiṃhācārya, a *ṭīkā* by Yadupati, *Subodhinī* by Vallabhācārya, *Pada-ratnāvalī* by Vijayadhvaja-tīrtha, a *ṭīkā* by Viṭṭhala Dīkṣita, *Sārārtha-darśinī* by Viśvanātha Cakravartī, a *ṭīkā* by Viṣṇusvāmin, *Bhāgavata-candrikā* by Vīrarāghava, *Bhāvārtha-dīpikā* by Śivarāma, *Bhāvārtha-dīpikā* by Śrīdhara-svāmī, *Sneha-pūraṇī* by Keśavadāsa, a *ṭīkā* by Śrīvāsā-cārya, a *ṭīkā* by Satyābhinava-tīrtha, a *ṭīkā* by Sudarśana Sūri, a *ṭīkā* by Braja-bhūṣaṇa, *Bhāgavata-purāṇārka-prabhā* by Hari-bhānu, *Bhāgavata-purāṇa-prathama-śloka-ṭīkā* by Jayarāma and

Madhusūdana Sarasvatī, *Pañcama-skandha-ṭīkā* by Vallabhācārya, *Subodhinī* by Bālakṛṣṇa Yati, *Vaiṣṇava-toṣiṇī* by Sanātana Gosvāmī, *Budharañjinī* by Vāsudeva, *Nibandha-prakāśa* by Viṭṭhala Dīkṣita, *Anukramaṇikā* by Vallabhācārya, *Ekādaśa-skandha-tātparya-candrikā* by Brahmānanda, *Anukramaṇikā* by Vopadeva. Many other works also have been written on the diverse subjects of the *Bhāgavata-purāṇa* and some have also summarized it. Some of these works are by Rāmānanda-tīrtha, Priyādāsa, Viśveśvara, Puruṣottama, Śrīnātha, Vṛndāvana Gosvāmī, Viṣṇu Purī and Sanātana.

Dharma.

The word *dharma*, ordinarily translated as "religion" or "virtue," is used in very different senses in the different schools and religious traditions of Indian thought. It will be useful to deal with some of the more important of these notions before the reader is introduced to the notion of *dharma* as explained in the *Bhāgavata-purāṇa*. The *Mīmāṃsā-sūtra* begins with an enquiry regarding the nature of *dharma*, and defines it as that good which is determinable only by the Vedic commands.[1] According to Śabara's and Kumārila's interpretation, the good that is called *dharma* means the Vedic sacrifices that lead to good results—the attainment of Heaven and the like. The fact that the Vedic sacrifices may bring about desirable results of various kinds can neither be perceived by the senses nor inferred from other known data: it can be known only from the testimony of the Vedic commands and directions. *Dharma*, therefore, means both the good results attainable by the Vedic sacrifices and the sacrifices themselves, and, as such, it is determinable only by the Vedic injunctions. Desirable results which are attained by rational and prudent actions are not *dharma*: for by definition *dharma* means only those desirable results which are attainable by operations which are performed strictly in accordance with Vedic injunctions. But in the Vedas are described various kinds of sacrifices by the performance of which one may take revenge on his enemies by destroying them or causing grievous injuries of various kinds to them, but action causing injury to any fellow-being is undesirable, and such action cannot be *dharma*.

[1] *athāto dharma-jijñāsā. Mīmāṃsā-sūtra*, I. I. I.
codanā-lakṣano'rtho dharmaḥ. Ibid. I. I. 2.

Dharma in this sense has nothing to do with God, or with ordinary or customary morality, or any kind of mystical or religious fervour as we understand it now. It simply means Vedic rituals and the good results that are supposed to follow from their performances; it has but little religious or moral application; and such a *dharma* can only be known through scriptural injunctions[1]. It contains however just a little germ of the idea of non-injury, inasmuch as the performance of rituals for injuring others is not included within its content. *Dharma* also definitely rules out all kinds of emotion, mystic feeling, and exercise of intellect or thought of any description, and merely presupposes a strict loyalty to external scriptural commands; there is not the slightest trace here of any internal spiritual law, or rational will, or loyalty to God's will. The scriptural command however is categorically imperative in some cases, whereas in others it is only conditionally imperative, i.e. conditioned by one's desire for certain good things. Kumārila, in interpreting this idea, says that any substance (*dravya*), action (*kriyā*) or quality (*guṇa*) which may be utilized to produce happiness, by a particular kind of manipulation of them in accordance with Vedic commands, is called *dharma*[2]. Though these substances, qualities etc. may be perceived by the senses yet the fact that their manipulation in a particular ritualistic manner will produce happiness for the per-

[1] *ya eva śreyas-karaḥ, sa eva dharma-śabdena ucyate; katham avagamyatām; yo hi yāgam anutiṣṭhati, taṃ dhārmika iti samācakṣate; yaśca yasya kartā sa tena vyapadiśyate; yathā pāvakaḥ, lāvaka iti. tena yaḥ puruṣaṃ niḥśreyasena saṃyunakti, sa dharma-śabdena ucyate...ko'rthah—yo niḥśreyasāya jyotiṣṭomādiḥ. ko'narthaḥ—yaḥ pratyavāyāyaḥ.* *Śabara-bhāṣya* on *Mīmāṃsā-sūtra*, I. I. 2.

Prabhākara however gives a different interpretation of this rule, and suggests that it means that every mandate of the Vedas is always binding, and is called *dharma* even when by following it we may be led to actions which are injurious to other people:

tataḥ sarvasya vedārthasya kāryatvam arthatvaṃ ca vidhīyata iti śyenādi-niyogānām api arthatvaṃ syāt.

Śāstra-dīpikā, p. 17, Nirṇaya-sāgara Press, Bombay, 1915.

Kumārila, further interpreting it, says that an action (performed according to the Vedic commands) which produces happiness and does not immediately or remotely produce unhappiness is called *dharma*.

[2] *phalaṃ tāvad adharmo'sya śyenādeḥ sampradhāryate*
yadā yeneṣṭa-siddhiḥ syād anuṣṭhānānubandhinī
tasya dharmatvam ucyeta tataḥ śyenādi-varjanam
yadā tu codanā-gamyaḥ kāryākāryānapekṣayā
dharmaḥ prīti-nimittaṃ syāt tadā śyene'pi dharmatā
yadā tvaprīti-hetur yaḥ sākṣād vyavahito'pi vā
so'dharmaś codanātaḥ syāt tadā śyene'py adharmatā.

Śloka-vārttika, on *sūtra* 2, *śloka* 270–273.

former can be known only by Vedic injunctions; and it is only with regard to this knowledge that the *dharma* is dependent on the Vedas[1]. Doing an injury to one's enemy may immediately give one happiness, but by its nature it is bound to produce unhappiness in the future, since it is prohibited by the Vedic injunctions. [But injury to the life of animals in the performance of sacrifices does not produce any sin, and must be regarded as being included within *dharma*.]

On the other hand, there are actions performed with the motive of injuring one's enemies, which are not *commanded* by the Vedas, but the methods of whose performance are *described* in the Vedas only in the case of those who are actuated by such bad motives: these actions alone are called *adharma*. Thus not all injury to life is regarded as sinful, but only such as is prohibited by the Vedas: whereas those injuries that are recommended by the Vedas are not to be regarded as sin (*adharma*) but as virtue (*dharma*). By nature there are certain powers abiding in certain substances, actions or qualities which make them sinful or virtuous, but which are sinful and which can only be known by the dictates of the scriptures[2]. *Dharma* and *adharma* are thus objective characters of things, actions, etc., the nature of which is only revealed by the scriptures. It has already been noted above that Prabhākara gave an entirely different meaning of *dharma*. With him *dharma* means the transcendental product (*apūrva*) of the performance of Vedic rituals which remains in existence long after the action is completed and produces the proper good and bad effects at the proper time[3].

The *smṛti* literature is supposed to have the Vedas as its sources, and therefore it is to be regarded as authoritative; even when its contents cannot be traced in the Vedas it is inferred that such Vedic

1 *dravya-kriyā-guṇādīnāṃ dharmatvaṃ sthāpayiṣyate*
teṣām aindriyakatve'pi na tādrūpyeṇa dharmatā
śreyaḥ-sādhanatā hy eṣāṃ nityaṃ vedāt pratīyate
tādrūpyeṇa ca dharmatvaṃ tasmān nendriya-gocaraḥ.
Śloka-vārttika, sūtra 2. 13, 14.

2 *dharmādharmārthibhir nityaṃ mṛgyau vidhi-niṣedhakau*
kvacid asyā niṣiddhatvāc chaktiḥ śāstreṇa bodhitā...
vidyamānā hi kathyante śaktayo dravya-karmaṇām
tad eva cedaṃ karmeti śāstram evānudhāvatā.
Ibid. 249, 251.

3 *na hi jyotiṣṭomādi-yāgasyāpi dharmatvam asti, apūrvasya dharmatvābhyupagamāt. Śāstra-dīpikā*, p. 33, Bombay, 1915.

texts must have existed[1]. It is only when the *smṛti* is directly contradicted by the Vedas in any particular injunction or statement of fact that the former is to be regarded as invalid. The *smṛti* works are therefore generally regarded as a continuation of the Vedas, though as a matter of fact the *smṛti* works, written at different times at a later age, introduce many new concepts and many new ideals; in some of the *smṛtis*, however, the teachings of the *Purāṇas* and *Smṛtis* are regarded as possessing a lower status than those of the Vedas[2]. On the relation of the *Smṛtis* and the Vedas there are at least two different views. The first view is that, if the *Smṛtis* come into conflict with the Vedas, then the *smṛti* texts should be so interpreted as to agree with the purport of the Vedic texts; and, if that is not possible, then the *smṛti* texts should be regarded as invalid. Others hold that the conflicting *smṛti* text should be regarded as invalid. Mitra Miśra, commenting on the above two views of the Śavara and Bhaṭṭa schools, says that, on the first view, it may be suspected that the author of the conflicting *smṛti* texts is not free from errors, and as such even those non-conflicting *smṛti* texts which cannot be traced in the Vedas may be doubted as erroneous. On the second view, however, *smṛti* is regarded as valid, since no one can guarantee that the non-conflicting texts which are not traceable to the Vedas are really non-existent in the Vedas. Even in the case of irreconcilably conflicting texts, the *smṛti* directions, though in conflict with the Vedic ones, may be regarded as optionally valid[3]. The Vedic idea of *dharma* excludes from its concept all that can be known to be beneficial, to the performer or to others, through experience or observation; it restricts itself wholly to those ritualistic actions, the good effects of which cannot be known by experience, but can only be known through Vedic commands[4]. Thus the digging of wells, etc., is directly known by experience to be of public good (*paropakārāya*) and therefore is not *dharma*. Thus nothing that is *dṛṣṭārtha*, i.e. no action, the

[1] *virodhe tvanapekṣyaṃ syād asati hyanumānam.* *Mīmāṃsā-sūtra*, I. 3. 3.

[2] *ataḥ sa paramo dharmo yo vedād avagamyate*
avaraḥ sa tu vijñeyo yaḥ purāṇadiṣu smṛtaḥ
tathā ca vaidiko dharmo mukhya utkṛṣṭatvāt, smārtaḥ anukalpaḥ apakṛṣṭatvāt.
Vyāsa-smṛti as quoted in *Vīramitrodaya-paribhāṣāprakāśa*, p. 29.

[3] See *Vīramitrodaya*, Vol. I, pp. 28, 29.

[4] *tathā pratyupasthita-niyamānām ācārāṇāṃ dṛṣṭārthatvād eva prāmāṇyam... prapās taḍāgāni ca paropakārāya na dharmāya ity evā'vagamyate.*
Śabara-bhāṣya on *Mīmāṃsā-sūtra*, I. 3. 2.

beneficial effects of which may be known through experience, can be called *dharma*. The *Aṅgiraḥ smṛti* echoes this idea when it says that, excepting efforts for attaining self-knowledge, whatever one does out of his own personal desire or wish is like child's play and unnecessary[1].

Many of the important *Smṛtis* however seem to extend the limits of the concept of *dharma* much further than the pure Vedic commands. As Manu's work is based entirely on the purport of the Vedas, he is regarded as the greatest of all *smṛti* writers; whatever *smṛti* is in conflict with Manu's writings is invalid[2]. Manu defines *dharma* as that which is always followed by the learned who are devoid of attachment and antipathy, and that to which the heart assents[3]. In another place Manu says that *dharma* is of four kinds; the observance of the Vedic injunctions, of the injunctions of *smṛti*, the following of the customary practices of good people, and the performance of such actions as may produce mental satisfaction (*ātmanas tuṣṭiḥ*) to the performer[4]. But the commentators are very unwilling to admit any such extension of the content and meaning of *dharma*. Thus Medhātithi (9th century), one of the oldest commentators, remarks that *dharma* as following the Vedic injunctions is beginningless; only the Vedic scholars can be said to know *dharma*, and it is impossible that there should be other sources from which the nature of *dharma* could be known. Other customs and habits and disciplines of life which pass as religious practices are introduced by ignorant persons of bad character (*mūrkha-duḥśīla-puruṣa-pravarttitaḥ*): they remain in fashion for a time and then die out. Such religious practices are often adopted out of greed (*lobhān mantra-tantrādiṣu pravarttate*)[5]. The wise and the good are

[1] *svābhiprāya-kṛtaṃ karma yatkiṃcij jñāna-varjitam*
krīḍā-karmeva bālānāṃ tat-sarvaṃ niṣ-prayojanam.
Vīramitrodaya-paribhāṣāprakāśa, p. 11.

[2] *vedārthopanibandhṛtvāt prādhānyaṃ hi manoḥ smṛtam*
manvartha-viparītā tu yā smṛtiḥ sā na praśaṣyate.
Bṛhaspati quoted in *Vīramitrodaya*, *ibid.* p. 27.

[3] *vidvadbhiḥ sevitaḥ sadbhir nityam adveṣa-rāgibhiḥ*
hṛdayenābhyanujñāto yo dharmas taṃ nibodhata.
Manu-saṃhitā, II. 1.

[4] *vedo'khilo dharma-mūlaṃ smṛti-śīle ca tadvidām*
ācāraś caiva sādhūnām ātmanas tuṣṭir eva ca. *Ibid.* II. 6.

[5] Medhātithi says that such practices as those of besmearing the body with ashes, carrying human skulls, going about naked or wearing yellow robes, are adopted by worthless people as a means of living. *Ibid.* II. 1.

only those who know the injunctions of the Vedas, who carry them into practice out of reverence for the law, and who are not led astray into following non-Vedic practices out of greed or antipathy to others. And, though a man might be tempted in his mind to perform many actions for his sense-gratification, real contentment of the heart can come only through the performance of Vedic deeds[1]. Consistently with his own mode of interpretation Medhātithi discards not only the Buddhists and the Jains as being outside the true Vedic *dharma*, but also the followers of Pañcarātra (i.e. the Bhāgavatas) and the Pāśupatas as well, who believed in the authority of the authors of these systems and in the greatness of particular gods of their own choice. He held that their teachings are directly contrary to the mandates of the Vedas: and as an illustration he points out that the Bhāgavatas considered all kinds of injury to living beings to be sinful, which directly contradicts the Vedic injunction to sacrifice animals at particular sacrifices. Injury to living beings is not in itself sinful: only such injury is sinful as is prohibited by the Vedic injunctions. So the customs and practices of all systems of religion which are not based on the teachings of the Vedas are to be discarded as not conforming to *dharma*. In interpreting the phrase *smṛti-śīle ca tad-vidām*, Medhātithi says that the word *śīla* (which is ordinarily translated as "character") is to be taken here to mean that concentration which enables the mind to remember the right purports of the Vedic injunctions[2]. By customary duties (*ācāra*) Medhātithi means only such duties as are currently practised by those who strictly follow the Vedic duties, but regarding which no Vedic or *smṛti* texts are available. He supposes that minor auspices and other rituals which are ordinarily

[1] In interpreting the meaning of the word *hṛdaya* (heart) in the phrase *hṛdayena abhyanujñāta* Medhātithi says that the word *hṛdaya* may mean "mind" (*manas, antar-hṛdaya-varttīni buddhyādi-tattvāni*); on this supposition he would hold that contentment of mind could only come through following the Vedic courses of duties. But, dissatisfied apparently with this meaning, he thinks that *hṛdaya* might also mean the memorized content of the Vedas (*hṛdayaṃ vedaḥ, sa hy adhīto bhāvanā-rūpeṇa hṛdaya-sthito hṛdayam*). This seems to mean that a Vedic scholar is instinctively, as it were, led to actions which are virtuous, because in choosing his course of conduct he is unconsciously guided by his Vedic studies. A man may be prompted to action by his own inclination, by the example of great men, or by the commands of the Vedas; but in whichever way he may be so prompted, if his actions are to conform to *dharma*, they must ultimately conform to Vedic courses of duties.

[2] *samādhiḥ śīlam ucyate...yac cetaso'nya-viṣaya-vyākṣepa-parihāreṇa śāstrārtha-nirūpaṇa-pravaṇatā tac chīlam ucyate.* Medhātithi's commentary, II. 6.

performed by the people of the Vedic circle have also ultimately originated from the Vedic injunctions. Similarly it is only the feeling of self-contentment of those persons who are habituated to work in accordance with the Vedas that can be regarded as indicating the path of *dharma*. It simply means that the instinctive inclination of the true adherents of the Vedas may be relied on as indicating that those actions to which their minds are inclined must be consistent with the Vedic injunctions, and must therefore conform to *dharma*. Other commentators however take a more liberal view of the meaning of the words *śīla*, *ātmanas tuṣṭi* and *hṛdayena abhyanujñāta*. Thus Govindarāja explains the last phrase as meaning "absence of doubt" (*antaḥ-karaṇa-cikitsā-śūnya*), and Nārāyaṇa goes so far as to say that, unless the heart approves of the action, it cannot be right: Rāmānanda says that, when there is any doubt regarding two conflicting texts, one should act in a way that satisfies his own mind. The word *śīla* has been interpreted as "character" (*vṛtta* or *caritra*) by Rāmānanda in his *Manvartha-candrikā* and as dissociation of attachment and antipathy by Govindarāja: Kullūka takes it according to Hārīta's definition of *śīla* as involving the qualities of non-injury to others, absence of jealousy, mildness, friendliness, gratefulness, mercy, peace, etc. Self-satisfaction can in practice discern the nature of *dharma*, but only when there are no specified texts to determine it. Thus, though the other later commentators are slightly more liberal than Medhātithi, they all seem to interpret the slight concession that Manu had seemed to make to right character and self-contentment or conscience as constituent elements of *dharma*, more or less on Medhātithi's line, as meaning nothing more than loyalty to scriptural injunctions.

It has been pointed out that Medhātithi definitely ruled out the Pañcarātra and the Pāśupata systems as heretical and therefore invalid for inculcating the nature of *dharma*. But in later times these too came to be regarded as Vedic schools and therefore their instructions also were regarded as so authoritative that they could not be challenged on rational grounds[1].

[1] Thus *Yogi-yājñavalkya* says: *Sāṃkhyaṃ yogaḥ pañca-rātraṃ vedāḥ pāśupataṃ tathā ati-pramāṇānyetāni hetubhir na virodhayet*, quoted in *Vīra-mitrodaya*, p. 20, but not found in the printed text, Bombay. This *Yogi-yājña-valkya* is a work on *yoga* and the other a work on *smṛti*, and it is the former text

It is however a relief to find that in some of the later *Smṛtis* the notion of *dharma* was extended to morality in general and to some of the cardinal virtues. Thus Bṛhaspati counts kindness (*dayā*, meaning a feeling of duty to save a friend or foe from troubles), patience (*kṣamā*, meaning fortitude in all kinds of difficulty), the qualities of appreciating others' virtues and absence of elation at others' faults (*anasūyā*), purity (*śauca*, meaning avoidance of vices, association with the good and strict adherence to one's caste duties), avoidance of vigorous asceticism (*sannyāsa*), performance of approved actions and avoidance of disapproved ones (*maṅgala*), regular charity even from small resources (*akārpaṇya*), contentment with what little one may have and want of jealousy at others' prosperity (*aspṛhā*), as constituting the universal *dharma* for all[1]. Viṣṇu counts patience (*kṣamā*), truthfulness for the good of all beings (*satya*), mind-control (*dama*), purity (*śauca* as defined above), making of gifts (*dāna*), sense-control (*indriya-saṃyama*), non-injury (*ahiṃsā*), proper attendance to teachers (*guru-śuśrūṣā*), pilgrimage, kindness (*dayā*), straightforwardness (*ārjava*), want of covetousness, adoration of gods and Brahmins, as constituting universal *dharma*. Devala considers purity (*śauca*), gifts (*dāna*), asceticism of the body (*tapas*), faith (*śraddhā*), attendance to teachers (*guru-sevā*), patience (*kṣamā*), mercifulness in the sense of pity for others' sufferings, showing friendliness as if these were one's own (*dayā*), acquirement of knowledge, Vedic or non-Vedic (*vijñāna*), mind-control and body-control (*vinaya*), truthfulness (*satya*), as constituting the totality of all *dharmas* (*dharma-samuccaya*). Yājñavalkya speaks of *ahiṃsā*, *satya*, *asteya* (avoidance of stealing), *śauca*, *indriya-nigraha* (sense-control), *dāna*, *dama*, *dayā*, and *kṣānti* as constituting universal *dharma* for all. The *Mahābhārata* counts truthfulness (*satya*), steadiness in one's caste duties (*tapas* as *sva-dharma-vartitva*), purity (*śauca*), con-

that has been printed. The present writer has no knowledge whether the latter text has been published anywhere.

Viṣṇudharmottara also speaks of Pañcarātra and Pāśupata as means of enquiry into Brahman:

sāṃkhyaṃ yogaḥ pañcarātraṃ vedāḥ pāśupataṃ
tathā kṛtānta-pañcakaṃ viddhi brahmaṇaḥ parimārgaṇe. *Ibid.* p. 22.

But Mitra Miśra on the same page distinguishes between Pāśupata as a Vedic *āgama* and as a non-Vedic *āgama*. Similarly there was a Vedic and non-Vedic Pañcarātra too. *Ibid.* p. 23.

[1] *Ibid.* pp. 32–4.

tentment, meaning sex-restriction to one's own wife and also cessation from sense-attractions (*viṣaya-tyāga*), shame at the commission of evil deeds (*hrī*), patience as capacity in bearing hardships (*kṣamā*), evenness of mind (*ārjava*), philosophic knowledge of reality (*jñāna*), peace of mind (*śama* as *citta-praśāntatā*), desire to do good to others (*dayā*), meditation, meaning withdrawal of the mind from all sense objects (*dhyāna* as *nirviṣaya*), as universal *dharmas*. Yājñavalkya says that the highest of all *dharmas* is self-knowledge through *yoga*.

These universal *dharmas* are to be distinguished from the special *dharmas* of the different castes, of the different stages of life (*āśrama*), or under different conditions. We have thus three stages in the development of the concept of *dharma*, i.e. *dharma* as the duty of following the Vedic injunctions, *dharma* as moral virtues of non-injury, truthfulness, self-control etc., *dharma* as self-knowledge through *yoga*.

But the *Bhāgavata* presents a new aspect of the notion of *dharma*. *Dharma* according to the *Bhāgavata* consists in the worship of God without any ulterior motive—a worship performed with a perfect sincerity of heart by men who are kindly disposed towards all, and who have freed themselves from all feelings of jealousy. This worship involves the knowledge of the absolute, as a natural consequence of the realization of the worshipfulness of the spirit, and naturally leads to supreme bliss[1]. The passage under discussion does not directly refer to the worship of God as a characteristic of the definition of *dharma* as interpreted by Śrīdhara[2]. The *dharma* consists of absolute sincerity—absolute cessation of the spirit from all motives, pretensions and extraneous associations of every description: and it is assumed that, when the spirit is freed from all such extraneous impurities, the natural condition of the spirit is its natural *dharma*. This *dharma* is therefore not a thing that is to be attained or achieved as an external acquirement, but it is man's own nature, which manifests itself as soon as the impurities are removed. The fundamental condition of *dharma* is not therefore something positive but negative, consisting of the dissociation (*projjhita*) of extraneous elements (*kitava*). For, as soon as the extraneous elements are wiped out, the spirit shows itself in its own

[1] *Bhāgavata-purāṇa*, I. I. 2, interpreted according to Śrīdhara's exposition.

[2] *komalam īśvarārādhana-lakṣaṇo dharmo nirūpyate*. Śrīdhara's comment on the above passage.

true nature, and then its relation to absolute truth and absolute good is self-evident: the normal realization of this relationship is what is called *dharma* or worship of God, or what Śrīdhara calls the tender worshipfulness towards God. The primary qualifications needed for a person to make a start towards a true realization of the nature of *dharma* in himself are, that he should have no jealousy towards others, and that he should have a natural feeling of friendliness towards all beings. The implications of this concept of *dharma* in the *Bhāgavata*, which breaks new ground in the history of the development of the notion of *dharma* in Indian Philosophy, are many, and an attempt will be made in the subsequent sections to elucidate them. That this dissociation from all extraneous elements ultimately means motiveless and natural flow of devotion to God by which the spirit attains supreme contentment, and that it is supreme *dharma*, is very definitely stated in I. 2. 6: If anything which does not produce devotion to God can be called *dharma*, such a *dharma* is mere fruitless labour[1]. For the fruits of *dharma* as defined by the Vedic injunctions may lead only to pleasurable consequences which are transitory. The real *dharma* is that which through devotion to God leads ultimately to self-knowledge, and as such *dharma* cannot be identified with mere gain or fulfilment of desires. Thus *dharma* as supreme devotion to God is superior to the Vedic definition of *dharma*, which can produce only sense-gratification of various kinds.

Brahman, Paramātman, Bhagavat and Parameśvara.

The opening verse of the *Bhāgavata* is an adoration of the ultimate (*param*) truth (*satya*). The word *para* however is explained by Śrīdhara as meaning God (*parameśvara*). The essential (*svarūpa*) definitive nature of God is said to be truth (*satya*). Truth is used here in the sense of reality; and it is held that by virtue of this supreme reality even the false creation appears as real, and that on account of this abiding reality the entire world of appearance attains its character of reality. Just as illusory appearances (e.g. silver) appear as real through partaking of the real character of the real object (e.g. the conch-shell) or the substratum of the illusion, so in this world-appearance all appears as real on account of the underlying reality of God. The fact that the world is produced from

[1] *Ibid.* I. 2. 7.

God, is sustained in Him and is ultimately dissolved in Him, is but an inessential description of an accidental phenomenon which does not reveal the real nature of God.

God is called by different names, e.g. Brahman, Paramātman and Bhagavat, but, by whatever name He may be called, His pure essence consists of pure formless consciousness (*arūpasya cidātmanaḥ*)[1]. He creates the world by His *māyā*-power, consisting of the three *guṇas*. Underlying the varied creations of *māyā*, He exists as the one abiding principle of reality which bestows upon them their semblance of reality. The *māyā* represents only His external power, through which He creates the world with Himself as its underlying substratum. But in His own true nature the *māyā* is subdued, and as such He is in His pure loneliness as pure consciousness. Śrīdhara in his commentary points out that God has two powers called *vidyā-śakti* and *avidyā-śakti*. By His *vidyā-śakti* God controls His own *māyā-śakti* in His own true nature as eternal pure bliss, as omniscient and omnipotent. The *jīva* or the individual soul can attain salvation only through right knowledge obtained through devotion. On this point Śrīdhara tries to corroborate his views by quotations from Viṣṇusvāmin, who holds that Īśvara a being, intelligence, and bliss (*saccid-ānanda īśvara*) is pervaded with blissful intelligence (*hlādinī samvit*), and that the *māyā* is under his control and that his difference from individual souls consists in the fact of their being under the control of *māyā*. The individual souls are wrapped up in their own ignorance and are therefore always suffering from afflictions (*kleśa*)[2]. God in His own nature as pure consciousness transcends the limits of *māyā* and *prakṛti* and exists in and for Himself in absolute loneliness; and it is this same God that dispenses all the good and bad fruits of virtue and vice in men under the influence of *māyā*[3]. That God in His own true

[1] *Bhāgavata-purāṇa*, I. 3. 30.

[2] *Ibid.* I. 7. 6 (Śrīdhara's comment):

tad uktaṃ viṣṇu-svāminā
hlādinyā saṃvidāśliṣṭaḥ sac-cid-ānanda īśvaraḥ
svāvidyā-saṃvṛto jīvaḥ saṃkleśa-nikarākaraḥ
tathā sa īśo yad-vaśe māyā sa jīvo yas tayārditaḥ, etc.

Jīva quotes the same passage and locates it in *Sarvajña-śukti Ṣaṭ-sandarbha*, p. 191.

[3] *tvam ādyaḥ puruṣaḥ sākṣād īśvaraḥ prakṛteḥ paraḥ*
māyāṃ vyudasya cic-chaktyā kaivalye sthita ātmani
sa eva jīva-lokasya māyā-mohita-cetaso
vidhatse svena vīryeṇa śreyo dharmādi-lakṣaṇam. *Ibid.* I. 7. 23, 24.

nature is pure consciousness and absolutely devoid of all duality and all distinctions is emphasized again and again in numerous passages in the *Bhāgavata*. In this He is ultimate and transcendent from all: the individual souls also lie dormant, and in this stage all the *guṇa* reals exist only in their potential forms; and it is by His own power that He rouses the *prakṛti* which is His *māyā* by which the individual souls are being always led into the experience of diverse names and forms. God in His own nature is therefore to be regarded as absolutely formless pure consciousness; by His power of consciousness (*cic-chakti*) He holds the individual souls within Him and by His power of materiality He spreads out the illusion of the material world and connects it with the former for their diverse experiences [1].

It is thus seen that God is admitted to have three distinct powers, the inner power as forming His essence (*antaraṅga-svarūpa-śakti*), the external power (*bahiraṅga-śakti*) as *māyā* and the power by which the individual souls are manifested. This conception however may seem to contradict the view already explained that Brahman is one undifferentiated consciousness. But the interpreters reconcile the two views by the supposition that from the ultimate point of view there is no distinction or difference between "power" and "possessor of power" (*śakti* and *śaktimān*). There is only one reality, which manifests itself both as power and possessor of power [2]. When this one ultimate reality is looked at as the possessor of power, it is called God; when, however, emphasis is laid on the power, it is called the great power which is mythologically represented as Mahā lakṣmī [3]. Thus the terms Brahman, Bhagavat and Paramatman are used for the same identical reality according as the emphasis is laid on the unity or differencelessness, the possessor of power, or the transcendent person. The *antar-aṅga*, or the essential power, contains within it the threefold powers of bliss (*hlādinī*), being (*sandhinī*) and consciousness (*saṃvit*), of which the two latter are regarded as an elaboration or evolution or

[1] *anantāvyakta-rūpeṇa yenedam akhilaṃ tatam*
cid-acic-chakti-yuktāya tasmai bhagavate namaḥ.
Bhāgavata, VII. 3. 34.

[2] *atha ekam eva svarūpaṃ śaktitvena śaktimattvena ca virājati.*
Ṣaṭ-sandarbha, p. 188 (Śyāmalāl Gosvāmī's edition).

[3] *yasya śakteḥ svarūpa-bhūtatvaṃ nirūpitaṃ tac-chaktimattva-prādhānyena virājamānam bhagavat-saṃjñām āpnoti tac ca vyākhyātam; tad eva ca śaktitva-prādhānyena virājamānaṃ lakṣmī-saṃjñām āpnoti. Ibid.*

manifestation of the former (the *hlādinī* power, or bliss). This threefold power is also called *cic-chakti* or *ātma-māyā* (essential *māyā*), and, as such, is to be distinguished from God's external power of *māyā* (*bahiraṅga-māyā*), by which He creates the world. His other power, by which He holds the individual souls (which are but parts of Himself) within Himself and yet within the grasp and influence of His external power of *māyā*, is technically called *taṭastha-śakti*. The individual souls are thus to be regarded as the parts of God as well as manifestations of one of His special powers (*taṭastha-śakti*). Though the individual souls are thus contained in God as His power, they are in no way identical with Him, but are held distinct from Him as being the manifestations of one of His powers. The unity or oneness (*advaya-tattva*) consists in the facts that the ultimate reality is self-sufficient, wholly independent, and standing by itself; and that there is no other entity, whether similar (e.g. the individual souls) or dissimilar to it (e.g. the matrix of the world, the *prakṛti*), which is like it; for both the *prakṛti* and the *jīvas* depend upon God for their existence, as they are but manifestations of His power. God exists alone with His powers, and without Him the world and the souls would be impossible[1]. The nature of His reality consists in the fact that it is of the nature of ultimate bliss (*parama-sukha-rūpatva*), the ultimate object of all desires (*parama-puruṣārthatā*) and eternal (*nitya*). It is this ultimate eternal reality which has formed the content of all Vedānta teachings. Thus the *Bhāgavata-purāṇa* points out that it is this reality which is the cause of the production, maintenance and destruction of all; it is this that continues the same in deep sleep, dreams and in conscious life; it is this that enlivens the body, senses, life and mind, yet in itself it is without any cause. It is neither born, nor grows, nor decays, nor dies, yet it presides over all changes as the one constant factor—as pure consciousness; and even in deep sleep, when all the senses have ceased to operate, its own self-same experience continues to be just the same[2].

Now this reality is called Brahman by some, Bhagavat by some and Paramātman by others. When this reality, which is of the nature

[1] *advayatvaṃ ca asya svayaṃ-siddha-tādṛśātādṛśa-tattvāntarābhāvāt sva-śaktyeka-sahāyatvāt, paramāśrayaṃ taṃ vinā tāsām asiddhatvāc ca.*
Tattva-sandarbha, p. 37.

[2] *Bhāgavata-purāṇa*, XI. 3. 35–39.

of pure bliss, is experienced by sages as being identical with their own selves, and when their minds are unable to grasp its nature as possessing diverse powers, and when no distinction between itself and its powers is realized, it is called Brahman. In such experiences this reality is only grasped in a general featureless way in its abstractness[1]. But when this reality is realized by the devotees in its true nature as being possessed of diverse powers in their distinction from the former, He is called by the name Bhagavat. In this it is the pure bliss which is the substance or the possessor, and all the other powers are but its qualities. So, when the reality is conceived in its fulness in all its proper relations, it is called Bhagavat: whereas, when it is conceived without its specific relations and in its abstract character, it is called Brahman[2]. So far as this distinction between the concepts of Brahman and Bhagavat is concerned it is all right. But in this system philosophy is superseded at this point by mythology. Mythologically Kṛṣṇa or the lord Bhagavān is described in the *Purāṇas* as occupying His throne in the transcendent Heaven (*Vaikuṇṭha*) in His resplendent robes, surrounded by His associates. This transcendent Heaven (*Vaikuṇṭha*) is non-spatial and non-temporal; it is the manifestation of the essential powers (*svarūpa-śakti*) of God, and as such it is not constituted of the *guṇas* which form the substance of our spatio-temporal world. Since it is non-spatial and non-temporal, it is just as true to say that God exists in *Vaikuṇṭha* as to say that He Himself is *Vaikuṇṭha*. Those who believed in this school of religion were so much obsessed with the importance of mythological stories and representations that they regarded God Himself as having particular forms, dress, ornaments, associates etc. They failed to think that these representations could be interpreted mythically, allegorically or otherwise. They regarded all these intensely anthropomorphic descriptions as being literally true. But such admissions would involve the irrefutable criticism that a God with hands, feet,

[1] *tad ekam eva akhaṇḍānanda-rūpaṃ tattvaṃ...parama-haṃsānāṃ sādhana-vaśāt tādātmyam anupapamyaṃ satyām api tadīya-svarūpa-śakti-vaicitryāṃ tad-grahaṇa-sāmarthye cetasi yathā sāmānyato lakṣitaṃ tathaiva sphurad vā tad-vad eva avivikta-śakti-śaktimattābhedatayā pratipādyamānaṃ vā brahmeti śabdyate.* *Ṣaṭ-sandarbha*, pp. 49–50.

[2] *evaṃ ca ānanda-mātraṃ viśeṣyaṃ samastāḥ śaktayaḥ viśeṣaṇāni viśiṣṭo bhagavān ityāyātam. tathā caivaṃ vaiśiṣṭye prāpte pūrṇāvirbhāvatvena akhaṇḍa-tattva-rūpo'sau bhagavān brahma tu sphuṭam aprakaṭita-vaiśiṣṭyākāratvena tasyaiva asamyag-āvirbhāvaḥ.* *Ibid.* p. 50.

and dress would be destructible. To avoid this criticism they held that God's forms, abode, etc., were constituted of non-spatial and non-temporal elements of His non-material essential power. But forms involve spatial notions, and non-spatial forms would mean non-spatial space. They had practically no reply to such criticism, and the only way in which they sought to avoid it was by asserting that the essential nature of God's powers were unthinkable (*acintya*) by us, and that the nature of God's forms which were the manifestations of this essential power could not therefore be criticized by us on logical grounds, but must be accepted as true on the authoritative evidence of the *Purāṇas*.

This notion of the supra-logical, incomprehensible or unthinkable (*acintya*) is freely used in this school to explain all difficult situations in its creeds, dogmas, and doctrines. *Acintya* is that which is to be unavoidably accepted for explaining facts, but which cannot stand the scrutiny of logic (*tarkāsahaṃ yaj-jñānaṃ kāryānyathānupapatti-pramāṇakam*), and which can account for all happenings that may be deemed incomprehensible or impossible (*durghaṭa-ghaṭakatvam*). How the formless Brahman may be associated with the three powers by which it can stay unchanged in itself and yet create the world by its external power of *māyā* or uphold the individual souls by its other power is a problem which it is attempted to explain by this concept of incomprehensibility (*acintya*)[1]. The *māyā* which is the manifestation of the external power of God is defined in the *Bhāgavata* as that which cannot manifest itself except through the ultimate reality, and which yet does not appear in it, i.e. *māyā* is that which has no existence without Brahman and which, nevertheless, has no existence in Brahman[2]. This *māyā* has two functions, viz. that with which it blinds the individual souls, called *jīva-māyā*, and the other by which the world transformations take place, called the *guṇa-māyā*.

Jīva Gosvāmī argues in his *Sarva-saṃvādinī*, which is a sort of a running commentary on *Tattva-sandarbha*, that the followers of Śaṅkara consider ultimate reality to be pure consciousness, one and

[1] In the *Viṣṇu-purāṇa* these three powers are called *parā*, *avidyā-karma-saṃjñā* and *kṣetrajñākhya*. This *parā māyā* or the *svarūpa-śakti* is also sometimes called *yoga-māyā*.

[2] *ṛte'rthaṃ yat pratīyeta na pratīyeta cātmani*
tad vidyād ātmano māyāṃ yathābhāso yathā tamaḥ.
Bhāgavata, II. 9. 33.

undifferentiated. There exists no other entity similar or dissimilar to it, and it is this fact that constitutes its infinitude and its reality. According to them such a reality cannot have any separate power or even any power which may be regarded as its essence (*svarūpa-bhūta-śakti*). For, if such a power were different from reality, it could not be its identical essence; and if it were not different from reality, it could not be regarded as being its power. If such an essential power, as distinct from reality, be admitted, such a power must be of the same nature as reality (i.e. of the nature of pure consciousness); and this would make it impossible to conceive of this power as contributing God's diverse manifestations, His transcendent forms, abode and the like, which are admitted to be the principal creed of the Vaiṣṇavas. But against the views of the followers of Śaṅkara it may be urged that even they have to admit that the Brahman has some power by which the world-appearance is manifested; if the world is wholly a creation of *māyā* and Brahman has nothing to do in it, there is no good in admitting its existence, and the *māyā* would be all in all. This power cannot be different in nature from the reality that possesses it, and, since the nescience or *avidyā* cannot exist without Brahman, it is an additional proof that the *avidyā* is also one of his powers. The power of any entity always exists in it as its own self even when it is not manifested. If it is argued that the Brahman is self-shining and that it does not require any power, it may be replied that the very reason by virtue of which it is self-shining may be regarded as its power. In this way Jīva follows some of the fundamental points in Rāmānuja's argument in favour of the doctrine that ultimate reality, the Brahman, is not formless and qualityless, but a qualified being, having its powers and qualities. In attempting to prove this view Jīva follows briefly the central argument of Rāmānuja. But Jīva introduces the notion that the relation of the qualities and powers of ultimate reality is supra-logical, inexplainable on logical grounds, and that therefore in a mysterious manner the powers are different from reality and yet one with it; so that in spite of the manifestation of ultimate reality as concrete God with human forms, dress etc., He is, at the same time, unchanged in His own changeless existence as Brahman. The introduction of the mystic formula of incomprehensibility seems to discharge the Vaiṣṇavas of this school from all responsibility of logically explaining their dogmas and creeds, and, thus uncontrolled, they descend from the domain of reason to the domain of the *purāṇic* faith of a mythological character.

In describing the special excellences of God, Jīva follows Rāmānuja in holding that He has none of the evil qualities that are found in the world, but possesses all the excellent characters that we can conceive of. In the light of the concept of incomprehensibility (*acintya*) all these excellent characters are regarded as somehow manifestations of His essential power and therefore identical with Him. The introduction of the supra-logical concept of *acintya* enables Jīva and other interpreters of the *Bhāgavata* of his school to indulge in eclecticism more freely than could otherwise have been possible; and thus it is that, though Jīva follows Rāmānuja in admitting ultimate reality to be qualified, he can in the same breath assert that ultimate reality is formless and characterless. Thus he says that, though the followers of Rāmānuja do not accept the view of Brahman as characterless, yet admission of characters naturally presupposes the admission of the characterless also[1]. The idea of introducing the concept of the supra-logical in order to reconcile the different scriptural texts which describe reality as characterless (*nirviśeṣa*), qualified (*viśiṣṭa*) and many, can be traced to the introduction of the concept of *viśeṣa* in the philosophy of Madhva, already described in a previous chapter, by which Madhva tried to reconcile the concept of monism with that of plurality. The Bengal school of Vaiṣṇavism, introduced by Caitanya, is based principally on the *Bhāgavata-purāṇa*, and of the many writers of this school only two are prominent as authors of philosophical treatises, Baladeva Vidyābhūṣaṇa and Jīva Gosvāmī. Of these Baladeva has again and again referred to the indebtedness of this school to the philosophy of Madhva, and to the initiation of Caitanya as an ascetic by a follower of the Madhva school of Vaiṣṇavism. Though he was a junior contemporary of Jīva Gosvāmī and a commentator of the latter's *Tattva-sandarbha*, yet he often reverts to Madhva's doctrine of *viśeṣa* in reconciling the monistic position with the positions of qualified monism and pluralism. Had he adhered to Jīva's concept of the supra-logical, the

[1] *yadyapi śrī-Rāmānujīyair nirviśeṣaṃ brahma na manyate tathāpi saviśeṣaṃ manyamānair viśeṣātiriktaṃ mantavyam eva.*

Jīva's *Sarva-saṃvādinī*, p. 74 (Nityasvarūpa Brahmacārī's edition).

concept of *viśeṣa* would have been entirely unnecessary. Baladeva, however, uses not only the concept of *viśeṣa*, but also the concept of the supra-logical (*acintya*), and he characterizes the concept of *viśeṣa* as being itself the concept of the supra-logical. Thus in his *Siddhānta-ratna* he says that the qualities of consciousness, bliss, etc., do not differ from the nature of Brahman, and yet Brahman is consistently described as possessing these different qualities because of the supra-logical functions of *viśeṣa* (*acintya-viśeṣa-mahimnā*). This assertion does not involve the doctrine that reality is from a particular point of view different from its qualities and from another point of view identical with them (*na caivaṃ bhedabhedau syātām*), and the only solution of the difficulty is to assume the doctrine of the supra-logical (*tasmād avicintyataiva śaraṇam*). In this connection Baladeva further says that the doctrine of *viśeṣa* must be accepted as something which even in the absence of difference can explain the phenomena of difference[1]. This concept of *viśeṣa*, however, is to be applied only in reconciling the simultaneous plurality and unity of ultimate reality. But so far as the relation between reality and individual souls is concerned, their difference is well known, and therefore the application of the principle of *viśeṣa* would be unjustifiable. The principle of *viśeṣa* is, however, applied not only in reconciling the unity of Brahman with the plurality of his qualities and powers, but also with his divine body, divine dress, his divine abode and the like, so that though these appear to be different from him they are at the same time identical with him[2].

Speaking on the same topic, Jīva holds that God Viṣṇu's power of consciousness (*cic-chakti*) is identical with His own essence. When this essence is on the way to produce effects, it is called power (*sva-rūpam eva kāryyonmukhaṃ śakti-śabdena uktam*). Now this special state of reality cannot be regarded as different from it, and can have no separate existence from it, since it can never be regarded (*cintayituṃ aśakyatvād*) as different from the essence of reality; since moreover difference itself cannot be regarded as being in any way different, the difference between the power and its possessor is unthinkable, incomprehensible and supra-logical. This view is not that of Rāmānuja and his followers, who regard the

[1] *Siddhānta-ratna*, pp. 17–22 (Benares, 1924).

[2] *tathā ca vigrahādeḥ sva-rupānatireke'pi viśeṣād eva bheda-vyavahāraḥ. Ibid.* p. 26.

power as different from its possessor; yet, since they also believe that God's powers are essentially contained in Him, there is a good deal of similarity between the Rāmānuja school and the Bengal school of Vaiṣṇavism[1]. Arguing against the followers of Śaṅkara, Jīva says that even in the Upaniṣad passage on pure consciousness, bliss, the Brahman (*vijñānam ānandaṃ Brahma*), the consciousness and the bliss cannot be identical, for then the two words would be mere repetition; they cannot be different, for then Brahman would have two conflicting qualities within himself. If the two words *vijñāna* and *ānanda* mean the negation of ignorance and of sorrow, then these two negations, being two different entities, are co-existent in Brahman. If the two negations mean one entity, how can one entity be the negation of two different things? If it is said that only agreeable consciousness is called bliss, then again the quality of agreeableness stands out as a separate quality. Even if these words stood merely as negations of ignorance or sorrow, then these also would be specific characters; if it is urged that these are not specific characters, but represent only special potencies (*yogyatā*) by virtue of which ignorance and sorrow are negated, then nonetheless those special potencies would be special characters. Thus the theory that ultimate reality is characterless is false. The characters of Brahman are identically the same as his powers, and these are all identical with his own self.

On the subject of the nature of self, Jīva says that individual selves are not pure consciousness, but entities which are characterized by self-consciousness as "ego" or "I." Individual souls are on no account to be regarded as being identical with God or Paramātman, and each individual self is different from every other[2]. These individual souls are of atomic size and therefore partless. The atomic self resides in the heart, whence it pervades the whole body by its quality of consciousness, just as sandal paste pervades the whole neighbourhood by its sweet smell. Just so, individual selves are atomic, but they pervade the bodies in which they are located by their power of consciousness. Consciousness is called a quality of the self because it is always dependent on that and serves its purpose (*nitya-tad-āśrayatva-tac-cheṣatva-nibandhanaḥ*)[3]. Again,

[1] *Sarva-saṃvādinī*, pp. 29, 30.
[2] *tasmāt prati-kṣetraṃ bhinna eva jīvaḥ. Ibid.* p. 87.
[3] *Ibid.* p. 94.

consciousness, being thus dependent on the self, expands and contracts in order to pervade the different bodies in which it may be operating at the time. Being thus different from God, individual selves, even in emancipation, remain separate and distinct. They are thus produced from the highest self (Paramātman or God), and they are always under His absolute control and pervaded by Him. It is on this account that God is called Paramātman as distinguished from individual souls (*ātman*). They are like rays emanating from Him and are therefore always entirely dependent on Him and cannot exist without Him[1]. They are also regarded as God's disengaged power (*taṭastha-śakti*), because, though they are God's power, yet they are in a way disengaged and separately situated from Him, and therefore they are under the delusion of God's other power, *māyā*, which has no influence on God Himself; and therefore, though individual selves are suffering under the blinding operation of ignorance (*avidyā*), the highest self (paramātman) is absolutely untouched by them. As individual souls are the powers of God, they are sometimes spoken of as identical with Him and sometimes as different from Him. Of these individual selves some are always naturally devoted to God, and others are dominated by ignorance and are turned away from Him; it is the latter that are the denizens of this world and suffer rebirth.

Māyā, the external power (*bahiraṅga-śakti*) has two functions, creative (*nimitta*) and passive (*upādāna*); of these, time (*kāla*), destiny (*daiva*), and actions (*karma*) represent the former, and the three *guṇas* the latter. Individual selves contain within them as integral parts elements of both these functions of *māyā*. The creative function of *māyā* has again two modes, which operate either for the bondage or for the liberation of man. This creative *māyā* also typifies the cosmic knowledge of God, His will and His creative operation[3]. Knowledge of God is also regarded as twofold —that which is His own self-knowledge and which forms a part of His essential power (*svarūpa-śakti*), and that which is turned

[1] *tadīya-raśmi-sthānīyatve'pi nitya-tad-āśrayitvāt, tadvyatirekeṇa vyatirekāt.* *Ṣaṭ-sandarbha*, p. 233.

[2] *tad evaṃ śaktitve'pi anyatvam asya taṭasthatvāt, taṭasthatvaṃ ca māyā-śakty-atītatvāt, asya avidyā-parābhavādi-rūpeṇa doṣeṇa paramātmano lopā-bhāvāc ca.* *Ibid.* p. 234.

[3] *nimittāṃśa-rūpayā māyākhyayaiva prasiddhā śaktis tridhā dṛśyate jñāne-cchā-kriyā-rūpatvena.* *Ibid.* p. 244.

towards cosmical operation for the good of the individual selves. It is this cosmic knowledge of God that falls within the creative function of His power of *māyā*. This cosmic knowledge is again twofold—that which abides in God as His omniscience, His desire of creation, and his effort of creation (otherwise called time (*kāla*)); and that which He passes over to individual selves as their desire for enjoyment or liberation from their works (*karma*), etc.; these in their turn are regarded as their ignorance (*avidyā*) and wisdom (*vidyā*)[1]. *Māyā* according to this view does not mean ignorance, but power of manifold creation (*mīyate vicitraṃ nirmiyata anayā iti vicitrārtha-kara-śakti-vacitvam eva*), and therefore the world is to be regarded as a transformation of Paramātman (*paramātma-pariṇāma eva*)[2]. By the supra-logical power of God, He remains unchanged in Himself and is yet transformed into the manifold creations of the world. According to Jīva, *pariṇāma* does not mean the transformation of reality (*na tattvasya pariṇāma*), but a real transformation (*tattvato pariṇāmaḥ*)[3]. The manifestation of God in Himself in His own essential power (*svarūpa-śakti*) remains however always untouched by His transformations through His supra-logical *māyā* power unto the world. This does not mean that God has two distinct forms, but merely that what appears contradictory to our ordinary reason may yet be a transcendental fact; and in the transcendental order of things there is no contradiction in supposing God as unchanged and as at the same time changeable by the operation of His two distinct powers. *Māyā* in this system is not something unreal or illusory, but represents the creative power of God, including His omniscience and omnipotence, the entire material substance of the world in the form of the collocation and combination of the *guṇas*, and also the totality of human experience for good and for evil in all its diverse individual centres of expression. But in spite of all these transformations and manifestations of Himself through His supra-logical power of *māyā*, He remains entirely complete and unchanged in the manifestations of His supra-logical essential power. On the one side we have God as the creator and upholder of the universe, and on the other we have the God of religion, the object of the mystic raptures of His

[1] *Ṣaṭ-sandarbha*, p. 244. [2] *Ibid.* p. 247.
[3] *tattvato'nyathā-bhāvaḥ pariṇāma ityeva lakṣaṇaṃ na tu tattvasya.* *Sarva-saṃvādinī*, p. 121.

devotees. The world is produced by the *māyā* power of God and is therefore not identical with Him. The gross and the impure selves and the world, all that is conscious and unconscious, the cause and the subtle pure element of the self—none of them are different from God, because the subtler ones are of the nature of His power, and the grosser ones are the modification or effects of His power; and though the world is one with Him, yet the defects and impurities of the world do not affect Him in the least, for in spite of these transformations He is untouched by them; such is the supra-logical character of His power[1].

Jīva then proceeds to show that the ultimate substance of the gross physical world, of the five elements and their modifications, is none other than the highest self, Paramātman or God. There is nothing in gross physical objects which can explain their appearance of unity as concrete wholes. For these wholes cannot be wholes in the same sense as forests made up of trees; these latter, indeed, cannot properly be called wholes, for, if one pulls a tree, the forest is not pulled; whereas in the case of a concrete object, when one pulls at one end, the object itself is pulled. If it is argued that there is a whole distinct from the parts, then its relation to the latter would be incomprehensible, for it is never experienced as entirely different from the parts; if the whole is supposed to be connected with each of the parts, then even a finger may be felt as a whole body; if it is supposed that a whole exists in parts only, in parts, then the same difficulty will again arise, and there will be a vicious infinite. So no concrete whole as distinct from the parts can be admitted to exist, and for the same reason the separate concrete existence of the elements may be denied. If the existence of wholes is denied in this way, then the existence of parts must also be denied; for, if there are no wholes, then there cannot be any parts, since it is only the wholes that are directly experienced, and parts are only admitted to account for the experience of the wholes. So the only assumption that remains is that God is the ultimate substance. Jīva refers to the *Bhāgavata-purāṇa*, III. 6. 1–3, which seems to hold that the discrete elements of God's own powers form the twenty-three Sāṃkhya categories, which are combined and united into wholes through the element of time, which is but another name for His transcendent effort. The curious doctrine here put forth is

[1] *Ibid.* p. 251.

rather very new in the history of Indian philosophy, though it is unfortunate that it has not been further developed here. It seems to maintain that the discrete elements of the substantial part (*upādānāṃśa*) of *māyā* derive their appearance of reality from God, and that through God's *élan* or activity as time these elements are held together and produce the notion of wholes, since there is no other whole than God. How time is responsible for the combination of atoms into molecules and of molecules into wholes is not explained.

Kapila's philosophy in the Bhāgavata-purāṇa.

The *Bhāgavata-purāṇa* gives an account of Sāṃkhya which is somewhat different from the account that can be got from the classical Sāṃkhya works. There is one beginningless qualityless *puruṣa*, which shines forth as all the individual souls, self-shining, which transcends the sphere of the *prakṛti*[1]. It is this *puruṣa* that playfully (*līlayā*) accepts the *prakṛti* that approaches it of its own accord; it is this *puruṣa* that is probably regarded as Īśvara or God[2]. He however, having perceived the *prakṛti* as producing diverse kinds of creation out of its own stuff, was Himself blinded (*vimūḍha*) by the veiling power of ignorance (*jñāna-gūhaya*) of this *prakṛti*[3]. By a false imposition the *puruṣa* conceives itself to be the agent in the changes that take place by the natural movement of the *guṇas* of *prakṛti*; and hence it exposes itself to births and rebirths and becomes bound by the laws of *karma*. In reality the *prakṛti* itself is the cause and agent of all its own self-abiding effects, and *puruṣa* is only the passive enjoyer of all pleasures and pains. In describing the evolution of the categories we have the five gross elements or *mahābhūtas*, the five *tanmātras*, the ten senses and the microcosm (*antarātmaka*)—consisting of *manas*, *buddhi*, *ahaṃkāra* and *citta*.

1 *anādir ātmā puruṣo nirguṇaḥ prakṛteḥ paraḥ*
pratyag-dhāmā svayaṃ-jyotir viśvaṃ yena samanvitam.
Bhāgavata-purāṇa, III. 26. 3.

2 *ayam īśvara ity ucyate. Subodhinī* commentary on *ibid.*

3 *Subodhinī* points out here that in this state, in which the *puruṣa* blinds himself, he is called *jīva*. Vijaya-dhvajī, however, takes it in the sense that the transcendent *puruṣa* or *īśvara* which had accepted the *prakṛti* as its own thus blinds the individual souls through it. Śrīdhara says that there are two kinds of *puruṣa*, *īśvara* and *jīva*; and, further, that according to its blinding power (*āvaraṇa-śakti*) and creative power (*vikṣepa-śakti*) *prakṛti* is twofold; and that *puruṣa* also is twofold, according as it behaves as individual souls or as God.

In addition to these there is the twenty-fifth category, called time (*kāla*), which some regard as a separate category, not as an evolute of *prakṛti*, but as the transcendental effort of *puruṣa* (used in the sense of God)[1]. It is said that God manifests Himself in man internally, as his inner self, as the controller of all his experiences, and externally, as time in the manifold objects of experience. Thus there are twenty-five categories if time, individual soul, and God are taken as one; if time is taken separately and God and *puruṣa* are taken as one, there are twenty-six categories; and if all the three are taken separately, there are twenty-seven categories[2]. It is the *puruṣa* which is to be taken as being under the influence of *prakṛti* and as free of it in its transcendent capacity as God (in an implicit manner). It is by the influence of time (*kāla*) that the equilibrium of the *guṇas* in the *prakṛti* is disturbed and that their natural transformations take place; and through the direction of laws of *karma* superintended by God the category of *mahat* is evolved[2]. It is curious that, though *mahat* is mentioned as a stage of *prakṛti*, it is only regarded as a creative state (*vṛtti*) or *prakṛti*, and not as a separate category. In another passage in the *Bhāgavata* it is said that in the beginning God was alone in Himself with His own dormant powers, and not finding anything through which He could reflect Himself and realize Himself, He disturbed the equilibrium of His *māyā* power through the functioning of time and through His own self (*puruṣa*), impregnating it with consciousness; and thus the process of creation started through the transformations of the *prakṛti*[3]. In another passage the question is raised how, if God is free in Himself, can He put Himself in bondage to *māyā*; and the reply given is that in reality there is no bondage of God, but, just as in dreams a man may perceive his own head to be struck off his body, or may perceive his own reflection shaking in water on account of its ripples, so it is but the reflection of God that appears as individual souls suffering bondage to world-experiences. It follows therefore, according to this view, that individual souls are illusory creations, and that both they and their world-experience must consequently be false[4]. In another passage which immediately

[1] *prabhavaṃ pauruṣaṃ prāhuḥ kālam eke yato' bhayam. Ibid.* III. 26. 16.

[2] *Prakṛti* is not included in this enumeration; if it were, there would be twenty-eight categories.

[3] *Ibid.* II. 5. 22, 23.

[4] *Ibid.* III. 5. 22–27.

follows the previous one it is definitely stated that the world only appears in consciousness, but that in reality it does not exist[1]. It is clear that these passages of the *Bhāgavata* distinctly contradict the interpretation of its philosophy given by Jīva in the previous section, as they deny the reality of individual souls and the reality of world-appearance.[2] But this is just what we may expect if we remember that the *Bhāgavata* is a collection of accretions from different hands at different times and not a systematic whole. If the Sāṃkhya theory described in II. 5, III. 5, III. 7 and III. 26 be interpreted consistently, then the result is that there are two fundamental categories, God and His own *māyā*, the *prakṛti*; that God, in His desire to realize Himself, reflects Himself in the *prakṛti*, which is but His own power, and it is through this impregnation of Himself in His own power that He appears as individual souls suffering the bondage of *prakṛti*; it is again through this impregnation of Himself that *prakṛti* is enlivened by consciousness; and then, through His creative effort, which is designated as time, the equilibrium of the *guṇas* of *prakṛti* is disturbed, the transformatory movement is set up in the *prakṛti*, and the categories are evolved.

In a passage in the fifth chapter (V. 12. 6–9) the existence of wholes is definitely described as illusory. There are no entities but the partless atoms, and even these atoms are imaginary constructions without which it would not be possible to conceive of wholes. All our conceptions of the external world start with atoms, and all that we see or feel gradually grows through a series of accretions. This growth in accretion is not a real growth, but is only an application of the time-sense. Time is therefore co-pervasive with the universe. The conception of an atom is but the conception of the smallest moment, and the entire conception of wholes of atoms as developing into dyad molecules, grosser specks and so on is nothing but advancing temporal construction and the growing combination of time-moments. The ultimate reality underlying all these changes is one all-pervasive unchanging whole, which through the activity of time appears as moments and their accretions (corresponding to atoms and their combinations)[3]. Time is

[1] *Bhāgavata-purāṇa*, III. 7. 9–12.

[2] *arthābhāvaṃ viniścitya pratītasyāpi nātmanaḥ. Ibid.* III. 7. 18.
anātmanaḥ prapañcasya pratītasyāpi arthābhāvam artho'tra nāsti kintu pratīti-mātram. (Śrīdhara's comment on *Bhāgavata*, III. 7. 18).

[3] *Ibid.* III. 11. 1–5.

thus not a product of *prakṛti* but the transcendent activity of God, through which the unmanifested *prakṛti* is transformed into the gross world and by which all the discrete entities appear as wholes[1]. In God this time exists as His inherent power of activity. It has been pointed out in the last section how Jīva considered time to be the active element of the *māyā* and the *guṇas* the passive element.

The first category evolved from the *prakṛti* is *mahat*, which contains the germs of the entire universe; it is pure translucent *sattva* (also called *citta* and *Vāsudeva* according to the terminology of the Bhāgavata cult). From the category of *mahat* the threefold *ahaṃkāra*, viz. *vaikārika*, *taijasa* and *tāmasa*, was produced. In the terminology this *ahaṃkāra* is called *Saṃkarṣaṇa*. All activity, instrumentality and transformatory character as effect is to be attributed to this *ahaṃkāra*. The category of *manas* is produced from the *vaikārika ahaṃkāra*, and it is called *Aniruddha* in the terminology of the Bhāgavata cult. The Bhāgavata cult here described believed in three *vyūhas* of *Vāmadeva*, *Saṃkarṣaṇa* and *Aniruddha*, and therefore there is no mention here of the production of the *Pradyumna-vyūha*. *Pradyumna* in this view stands for desire; desires are but functions of the category of *manas* and not a separate category[2]. From the *taijasa-ahaṃkāra* the category of *buddhi* is evolved. It is by the functions of this category that the functioning of the senses, the cognition of objects, doubts, errors, determinateness, memory and sleep are to be explained[3]. Both the conative and cognitive senses are produced from the *taijasa-ahaṃkāra*. From the *tāmasa-ahaṃkāra* the sound-potential (*śabda-tanmātra*) is produced, and from it the element of *ākāśa* is produced. From the element of *ākāśa* the heat-light-potential (*rūpa-tanmātra*) is produced, and from that the element of light, and so on.

The *puruṣa* is immersed in the *prakṛti*, but nevertheless, being unchangeable, qualityless and absolutely passive, it is not in any way touched by the qualities of *prakṛti*. It has already been pointed

[1] This view of time is different from the *yoga* view of time as moments (as explained by Vijñāna-bhikṣu in his *Yoga-vārttika*, III. 51). There a moment is described as the movement of a *guṇa* particle through a space of its own dimension, and the eternity of time is definitely denied. Time in that view can only be the discrete moments.

[2] *Ibid.* III. 26. 27. *yasya manasaḥ saṅkalpa-vikalpābhyāṃ kāma-sambhavo varttata iti kāma-rūpā vṛttilakṣaṇatvena uktā na tu pradyumna-vyūhotpattiḥ tasya saṅkalpādi-kāryatvābhāvāt.* (Śrīdhara's comment on the above.)

[3] Those who believe in four *vyūhas* call this the *pradyumna-vyūha*.

out that the influence of the *prakṛti* is limited to the image of *puruṣa* in the *prakṛti*, and that, being reflected in the *prakṛti*, the one *puruṣa* throws a shadow of infinite selves. These selves are deluded by egoism and consider themselves to be active agents, and, though there are no real births and rebirths, yet they continue to suffer the bondage of the *saṃsāra* cycle like a man who suffers from bad dreams.

Those who wish to be emancipated should therefore steadily practise disinclination from worldly joys and keen devotion. They should take to the path of self-control, make their minds free of enmity to all beings, practise equality, sex-control and silence, should remain contented with anything that comes in their way, and should have a firm devotion to God. When they leave their false self-love and egoism and can realize the truth about *prakṛti* and *puruṣa*, viz. that the latter is the unconditioned and underlying reality of all, as the one Sun which creates illusions like its reflections in the water; when they understand that the real self, the ultimate reality, is always experienced as the underlying being which manifests our biological, sensory and psychical personality or egohood, and that this reality is realized in deep dreamless sleep (when this egohood temporarily ceases to exist), they attain their real emancipation[1]. The well-known *yoga* accessories mentioned by Patañjali, such as non-injury, truthfulness, non-stealing, contentment with the bare necessities of life, purity, study, patience, control of the senses, are also regarded as a necessary preparation for self-advancement. The practice of postures (*āsana*), breath-control (*prāṇāyāma*), and that of holding the mind steadily on particular objects of concentration, are also advised as methods of purifying the mind. When the mind is thus purified and concentration practised, one should think of God and His great qualities[2]. Devotion to God is regarded as the second means of attaining right knowledge and wisdom about the oneness of the ultimate and the relation between the *prakṛti* and the illusory individual selves. Thus it is said that, when one meditates upon the beautiful transcendent and resplendent form of Hari and is intoxicated with love for Him, one's heart melts through devotion, through excess of emotion one's hair stands on end, and one floats in tears of excessive delight through yearning after God; it is thus that the hook of the

[1] *Bhāgavata-purāṇa*, III. 27. [2] *Ibid.* III. 28.

mind is dislodged from the sense-objects to which it was attached[1]. When through such excess of emotion one's mind becomes disinclined to all other objects, and thus there is no object of meditation, the mind is destroyed like a flame extinguished, and the self, returning from the conditions imposed upon it by the transformations of the *guṇas*, finds itself to be one with the transcendent and the highest self[2]. Devotion is said to be of four kinds, *sāttvika*, *rājasa*, *tāmasa* and *nirguṇa*. Those who want God's grace and are devoted to Him in order to satisfy their personal jealousy, pride or enmity are called *tāmasa*, those who seek Him for the attainment of power, fame, etc. are called *rājasa*, and those who are devoted to Him or who renounce all their *karmas* and their fruits to Him through a sense of religious duty or for the washing away of their sins are called *sāttvika*. But those who are naturally inclined towards Him without any reason save deep attachment, and who would not desire anything but the bliss of serving Him as His servants, it is they who may be said to possess the *nirguṇa* devotion (*bhakti*). But this *nirguṇa* devotion must manifest itself in realizing God as pervading all beings: devotees of this type would consider all beings as their friends, and with them there is no difference between a friend and a foe. No one can claim to possess this high devotion merely by external adorations of God; he must also serve all humanity as a friend and brother[3]. Thus either by *yoga* methods of self-purification and concentration of the mind on God and His super-excellent qualities, or by a natural love for Him, one may attain the ultimate wisdom, that the one reality is God and that individual selves and their experiences are but mere reflections in *prakṛti* and its transformations.

It may however be pointed out that even the first method of *yoga*

[1] *evaṃ harau bhagavati prati-labdha-bhāvo*
bhaktyā dravad-hṛdaya utpulakaḥ pramodāt
autkaṇṭhya-vāṣpa-kalayā muhur ardyamānas
tac cāpi citta-baḍiśaṃ śanakair viyuṅkte. *Ibid.* III. 28. 34.

[2] *muktāśrayaṃ yan nirviṣayaṃ viraktam*
nirvāṇam ṛcchati manaḥ sahasā yathā'rciḥ
ātmānam atra puruṣo'vyavadhānam ekam
anvīkṣa'e prati-nivṛtta-guṇa-pravāhaḥ. *Ibid.* III. 28. 35.

[3] *yo māṃ sarveṣu bhūteṣu śāntam ātmānam īśvaram*
hitvā'rcāṃ bhajate mauḍhyād bhasmany eva juhoti saḥ
aham uccāvacair dravyaiḥ kriyayotpannayā'naghe
naiva tuṣye'rcito'rcāyāṃ bhūta-grāmāvamāninaḥ.
Ibid. III. 29. 22, 24.

is associated with some kind of *bhakti* or devotion, as it involves meditation upon God and the blissful feeling associated with it. The word *yoga* is not used in this connection in Patañjali's technical sense (from the root *yuj samādhau*), but in the more general sense of *yoga* (*yoga* as "connection," from the root *yujir yoge*). Though this system involves most of the accessories of *yoga* for the purification of mind and as preparation for concentration, yet the ultimate aim is the realization of unity of the phenomenal self with God, which is entirely different from the *yoga* of Patañjali. So, as this *yoga* essentially aims at a unification with God through meditation upon Him, it may also be called a sort of *bhakti-yoga*, though it in its turn is different from the other *bhakti-yoga*, in which all the purposes of *yoga* discipline are served by an excess of emotion for God[1].

Kapila has been described as an incarnation of God, and the philosophy that is attributed to him in the *Bhāgavata* forms the dominant philosophy contained therein. All through the *Bhāgavata* the philosophy of theistic Sāṃkhya as described by Kapila is again and again repeated in different passages in different contents. Its difference from the classical Sāṃkhya as expounded by Īśvarakṛṣṇa or by Patañjali and Vyāsa is too patent to need explanation at any length. In the *Bhāgavata*, XI. 22 a reference is made to different schools of Sāṃkhya which count their ultimate categories as three, four, five, six, seven, nine, eleven, thirteen, fifteen, sixteen, seventeen, twenty-five and twenty-six, and it is asked how these differences of view can be reconciled. The reply is that these differences do not involve a real difference of Sāṃkhya thought; it is held that the difference is due to the inclusion of some of the categories within others (*parasparānupraveśāt tattvānām*); for instance, some of the effect categories are included within the cause categories, or some categories are identified from particular considerations. Thus, when one thinks that the *puruṣa*, being always under the influence of beginningless ignorance (*anādyavidyā-yuktasya*), cannot by itself attain the knowledge of ultimate reality, it becomes necessary to conceive the existence of a super-person, different from it, who could grant such knowledge; according to

1 *yataḥ sandhāryamānāyāṃ yogino bhakti-lakṣaṇaḥ*
āśu sampadyate yoga āśrayaṃ bhadram īkṣataḥ.
Bhāgavata-purāṇa, II. I. 21.

this view there would be twenty-six categories. But, when one thinks that there is not the slightest difference between the *puruṣa* (or the individual soul) and God, the conception of the latter as separate from the former becomes quite unnecessary; on this view there would be only twenty-five categories. Again, those who reckon nine categories do so by counting *puruṣa*, *prakṛti*, *mahat*, *ahaṃkāra* and the five *tanmātras*. In this view knowledge (*jñāna*) is regarded as a transformation of the *guṇas*, and (*prakṛti* being nothing more than the equilibrium of the *guṇas*) knowledge may also be regarded as identical with *prakṛti*; similarly actions are to be regarded as being only transformations of *rajas* and ignorance as transformation of *tamas*. Time (*kāla*) is not regarded here as a separate category, but as the cause of the co-operative movement of the *guṇas*, and nature (*svabhāva*) is identified with the *mahat-tattva*. The cognitive senses are here included within the cognitive substance of *sattva*, the conative senses within the *rajas*, and the cognitions of touch, taste, etc. are regarded as the fields of the manifestations of the senses and not as separate categories. Those who reckon eleven categories take the cognitive and conative senses as two additional categories and, considering the sensations of touch, taste, etc. as being manifestations of the senses, naturally ignore their claim to be considered as categories. In another view *prakṛti*, which is moved into activity by the influence of *puruṣa*, is regarded as different from it, and thus there are the two categories of *puruṣa* and *prakṛti*, then are the five *tanmātras*, the transcendental seer and the phenomenal self; thus there are nine categories in all. Upon the view that there are six categories, only the five elements and the transcendent self are admitted. Those who hold that there are only four categories admit only the three categories of light-heat (*tejas*), water and earth, and accept the transcendent self as the fourth. Those who hold that there are seventeen categories admit the five *tanmātras*, five elements and five senses, *manas* and the self. Those who hold that there are sixteen categories identify *manas* with the self. Those who hold that there are thirteen categories admit the five elements (which are identified with the *tanmātras*), the five senses, *manas*, and the transcendent and the phenomenal selves. Those who admit only eleven categories accept only the five elements, five senses and the self. There are others, again, who admit eight *prakṛtis* and the *puruṣa*, and thus reduce the number to nine. The eclectic spirit of the *Bhāgavata* tried to reconcile the conflicting accounts of the Sāṃkhya categories by explaining away the differences; but to an impartial observer these differences are sometimes fundamental, and at least it is evident that, though these different lines of thought may all be called in some sense Sāṃkhya, they signify the existence of a good deal of independent thinking, the exact value of which, however, cannot be determined for want of detailed and accurate information regarding the development of these schools[1].

The fundamental difference of the Bhāgavata school of Sāṃkhya from that of the classical Sāṃkhya is that it admits one *puruṣa* as the real all-pervading soul, which is the real seer of all our experiences and the basic universal being that underlies all things of this universe. The individual phenomenal selves appear as real entities only by the delusive confusion of the universal *puruṣa* with the transformations of the *prakṛti* and by the consequent false attribution of the movements and phenomena of the *prakṛti* to this universal *puruṣa*. The false individual selves arise out of such false attribution and there is thus produced the phenomenon of birth and rebirth, though there is no association of the *prakṛti* with the universal *puruṣa*. All our world-experiences are mere illusions, like dreams, and are due to mental misconceptions. The emphasis on the illusory character of the world is very much stronger in the passages that are found in the *Bhāgavata*, XI. 22 than in the passages that deal with Kapila's philosophy of Sāṃkhya just described; and though the two treatments may not be interpreted as radically different, yet the monistic tendency which regards all worldly experiences as illusory is so remarkably stressed that it very nearly destroys the realistic note which is a special feature of the Sāṃkhya schools of thought[2].

[1] In Aśvaghoṣa's *Buddha-carita* there is an account of Sāṃkhya which counts *prakṛti* and *vikāra*. Of these *prakṛti* consists of eight categories—the five elements, egoism (*ahaṃkāra*), *buddhi* and *avyakta*, and the *vikāra* consists of seventeen categories—the five cognitive and the five conative senses, *manas*, *buddhi* and the five kinds of sense-knowledge. In addition to these there is a category of *kṣetrajña* or self or *ātman*.

[2] *yathā mano-ratha-dhiyo viṣayānubhavo mṛṣā*
svapna-dṛṣṭāś ca dāśārha tathā saṃsāra ātmanaḥ
arthe hy avidyamāne'pi saṃsṛtir na nivartate
dhyāyato viṣayān asya svapne'narthāgamo yathā.
Bhāgavata, XI. 22. 55, 56.

In xi. 13 this monistic interpretation or rather this monistic transformation of Sāṃkhya reaches its culmination; it is held that ultimate reality is one, and that all differences are but mere differences of name and form. Whatever may be perceived by the senses, spoken by words or conceived in thought is but the one reality, the Brahman. The *guṇas* are the product of mind and the mind of the *guṇas*, and it is these two illusory entities that form the person; but one should learn that both of them are unreal and that the only reality, on which both of them are imposed, is Brahman. Waking experiences, dreams, and dreamless sleep are all functions of the mind; the true self is the pure seer (*sākṣin*), which is entirely different from them. So long as the notion of the "many" is not removed by philosophical reasonings, the ignorant person is simply dreaming in all his waking states, just as one feels oneself awake in one's dreams. Since there is nothing else but the self, and since all else is mere illusion like dreams, all worldly laws, purposes, aims and works are necessarily equally false. One should observe that we have the notion of the identity of our selves, in our wakeful and dream experiences and in our experiences of dreamless deep sleep, and one should agree that all these experiences in all these three stages of life do not really exist, they are all but the manifestations of *māyā* on the ultimate reality, the Brahman; and thus by such inferences and considerations one should remove all one's attachments and cut asunder all one's fetters by the sword of knowledge. One should regard the entire world and its experiences as nothing more than the imagination of the mind—a mere appearance which is manifested and lost; all experiences are but *māyā* and the only underlying reality is pure consciousness. Thus it is through right knowledge that true emancipation comes, though the body may hold on so long as the fruits of *karma* are not exhausted through pleasurable and painful experiences. And this is said to be the secret truth of Sāṃkhya and Yoga. It may generally appear rather surprising to find such an extreme idealistic monism in the *Bhāgavata*, but there are numerous passages which show that an extreme form of idealism recurs now and then as one of the principal lines of thought in the *Bhāgavata*[1].

The first adoration verse is probably the most important passage in the *Bhāgavata*. And even in this passage it is said (in one of its

[1] *Ibid.* xi. 13.

prominent and direct interpretations) that the creation through *guṇas* is false and that yet, on account of the all-pervading reality that underlies it, it appears as real; that the production, maintenance and destruction of the universe all proceed from the ultimate reality, Brahman, and that it is through the light of this reality that all darkness vanishes[1]. In another passage, in VI. 4. 29–32, it is said that Brahman is beyond the *guṇas*, and that whatever may be produced in the world, or as the world, has Brahman for its ground and cause, and that He alone is true; and that both the atheistic Sāṃkhya and the theistic Yoga agree in admitting Him as the ultimate reality.

It was pointed out in a previous section that according to Jīva the *māyā* had two parts, formative and constitutive, and it was the latter that was identified with *prakṛti* or the three *guṇas*. But this *māyā* was regarded as an external power of God as distinguished from His essential power. The *Viṣṇu-purāṇa*, however, does not seem to make any such distinction; it says that the great Lord manifests Himself through His playful activity as *prakṛti*, *puruṣa*, the manifold world and time, but yet it considers the *prakṛti* and the *puruṣa* to be different from the essential nature of the Lord, and time as that which holds these two together and impels them for the creational forms[2]. Thus, since time is the cause which connects the *prakṛti* and the *puruṣa*, it exists even when all creational modes have shrunk back into the *prakṛti* in the great dissolution. When the *guṇas* are in equilibrium, the *prakṛti* and the *puruṣa* remain disconnected, and it is then that the element of time proceeds out of the Lord and connects the two together[3]. But the *prakṛti* in both its unmanifested and manifested forms or its contraction and dilation (*saṃkoca-vikāsābhyām*) is a part of God's nature; so in disturbing the equilibrium of *prakṛti* it is God who disturbs His

[1] *janmādyasya yato'nvayād itarataś cārtheṣv abhijñaḥ svarāṭ*
tene brahma hṛdā ya ādikavaye muhyanti yat sūrayaḥ.
tejo-vāri-mṛdāṃ yathā vinimayo yatra trisargo'mṛṣā
dhāmnā svena sadā nirasta-kuhakaṃ satyaṃ paraṃ dhīmahi.
Bhāgavata, I. 1. 1.

[2] *vyaktaṃ viṣṇus tathāvyaktaṃ puruṣaḥ kāla eva ca.*
krīḍato bālakasyeva ceṣṭāṃ tasya niśāmaya.
viṣṇoḥ svarūpāt parato hi te'nye rūpe pradhānaṃ puruṣaś ca viprās
tasyaiva te'nyena dhṛte viyukte rūpādi yat tad dvija kāla-saṃjñam.
Viṣṇu-purāṇa, I. 2. 18, 24.

[3] *guṇa-sāmye tatas tasmin pṛthak puṃsi vyavasthite*
kāla-svarūpa-rūpaṃ tad viṣṇor maitreya vartate. *Ibid.* 27.

own nature (*sa eva kṣobhako brahman kṣobhyaś ca puruṣottamah*), and this He does through the instrumentality of time. Through His will He penetrates into the *prakṛti* and the *puruṣa*, and sets off the creative operation of the *prakṛti*, though this operation of the will does not involve any notion of ordinary physical activity[1]. Time is thus regarded as the spiritual influence of God, by which the *prakṛti* is moved though He remains unmoved Himself. From *prakṛti* there is the threefold evolution of *mahat* (*sāttvika*, *rājasa* and *tāmasa*) by a process of differentiation and development of heterogeneity[2]. By the same process the differentiation of *mahat* into *vaikārika*, *taijasa* and *bhūtādi* takes place as integrated within the *mahat* as integrated within the *prakṛti*[3]. Being similarly integrated in the *mahat*, the *bhūtādi* is further differentiated into the *tanmātric* stage and produces first the sound-potential (*śabda-tanmātra*). From the *śabda-tanmātra* the element of *ākāśa* was produced from the relevant matter of *bhūtādi*; this *śabda-tanmātra* and *ākāśa* was further integrated in *bhūtādi* and in this integrated state the element of *ākāśa* transformed itself into the touch-potential (*sparśa-tanmātra*); then from this touch-potential air was produced by its transformation (through accretion from *bhūtādi*). Then in association of the integration of the element of *ākāśa* and *śabda-tanmātra* with the touch-potential (*sparśa-tanmātra*) the element of air produced the heat-light-potential (*rūpa-tanmātra*) in the medium of the *bhūtādi*, and from that the element of heat-light was produced by an accretion from *bhūtādi*. Again in association of the integration of touch-potential, the element of air and the heat-light-potential, the element of heat-light transformed itself into the taste-potential in the medium of the *bhūtadi*, and in a similar way water was produced by an accretion from the *bhūtādi*. Again, from the integration of taste-potential, heat-light potential and water, the smell-potential was produced by a transformation of the element of water in the medium of the *bhūtādi*, and out of this smell-potential in integration with the above the element of earth was produced by an accretion from *bhūtādi*. Out of the

[1] *pradhānaṃ puruṣaṃ cāpi praviśyātmecchayā hariḥ*
kṣobhayāmāsa saṃprāpte sarga-kālevyayāvyayau. *Ibid*. 29.

[2] This view of the evolution of three different kinds of *mahat* is peculiar to the *Viṣṇu-purāṇa*, which is different from the classical Sāṃkhya.

[3] This second stage is in agreement with the doctrine of Sāṃkhya as explained in the *Vyāsa-bhāṣya* on the *Yoga-sūtra*, II. 19 of Patañjali.

taijasa-ahaṃkāra the ten conative and cognitive senses were produced, and *manas* was produced out of the *vaikārika-ahaṃkāra*. The five *tanmātras* are called the unspecialized modifications (*aviśeṣa*), and the senses and the gross elements are regarded as fully specialized modifications (*viśeṣa*)[1].

It will appear from the above and also from what has already been said in the chapter on the Kapila and Patañjala school of Sāṃkhya in the first volume of the present work that the system of Sāṃkhya had undergone many changes in the hands of various writers at different times. But it is difficult to guess which of these can be genuinely attributed to Kapila. In the absence of any proof to the contrary it may be assumed that the account of Sāṃkhya attributed to Kapila in the *Bhāgavata* may generally be believed to be true. But Īśvarakṛṣṇa also gives us an account of what can be called the classical Sāṃkhya in his *Sāṃkhya-kārikā*, which he says was first taught by Kapila to Āsuri and by him to Pañcaśikha, and that his account of Sāṃkhya was a summary of what was contained in the *Ṣaṣṭi-tantra* with the exception of the polemical portions and fables; also that he himself was instructed in the traditional school of Sāṃkhya as carried down from Āsuri through generations of teachers and pupils. But the *Bhāgavata* account of Kapila's Sāṃkhya materially differs from the Sāṃkhya of the *Sāṃkhya-kārikā*, for, while the former is definitely theistic, the latter is at least tacitly atheistic, for it is absolutely silent about God; apparently God has no place in this system. But the theistic Sāṃkhya as described in the *Bhāgavata*, which is of course quite different and distinct from the theistic Sāṃkhya of Patañjali and *Vyāsa-bhāṣya*, is not an isolated instance which can easily be ignored; for most of the *Purāṇas* which have a Vaiṣṇava tradition behind them generally agree in all essential features with the theistic element of the Kapila Sāṃkhya of the *Bhāgavata*, and some of the important Pañcarātra *āgamas* also in some ways support it. Thus the *Ahirbudhnya-saṃhitā* describes the Sāṃkhya system as that which believes the *prakṛti* to be the cause of the manifold world and that this *prakṛti* is moved into creative transformations through the

[1] *Viṣṇu-purāṇa*, I. 2. See also Dr Sir B. N. Seal's interpretation of this passage in P. C. Ray's *Hindu Chemistry*, Vol. II, pp. 90–5.

The same verses occur in the *Padma-purāṇa* (*Svarga-khaṇḍa*) regarding the evolution of the Sāṃkhya categories.

influence of time by the will of Lord Viṣṇu. There is but one *puruṣa*, who is the sum-total of all *puruṣas* and who is absolutely changeless (*kūṭastha*); there is the *prakṛti*, constituted of the three *guṇas* in equilibrium; and there is also the element of time (*kāla*), through which by the will of the Lord (*viṣṇu-saṃkalpa-coditāt*) the *puruṣa* and the *prakṛti* are connected and the creative movement of the *prakṛti* set up. The *puruṣa*, *prakṛti* and *kāla* are in their turn but special manifestations of Lord Viṣṇu[1]. The evolution of the gross elements is also described here as being directly from their respective *tanmātras*. It also believes that the powers of the Lord are supra-logical (*acintya*), and therefore cannot be contested on purely formal grounds of reason or logical principles of self-contradiction. It holds however the rather unique view that from time the *sattva-guṇa* springs into being and from *sattva rajas* and from *rajas tamas*, and it also gives a different interpretation of the *vyūha* doctrine—but these have already been discussed in the chapter on the Pañcarātra philosophy. The *Ahirbudhnya*, however, ascribes this Sāṃkhya philosophy to Kapila (the incarnation of Viṣṇu) who wrote the *Ṣaṣṭi-tantra*, and it also enumerates the names of the chapters or *tantras* of this work[2]. The work is divided into two books; in the first book there is one chapter (*tantra*) on Brahman, one on *puruṣa*, three on power (*śakti*), destiny (*niyati*) and time (*kāla*), three on the *guṇas*, one on the changeless (*akṣara*), one on *prāṇa* and one on the agent (*kartṛ*), one on the Lord, five on cognition, five on actions, five on *tanmātras* and five on the five gross elements; thus altogether there are thirty-two chapters in the first book. In the second book there are twenty-eight chapters—five on duties, one on experience, one on character, five on afflictions, three on the *pramāṇas*, one on illusions, one on *dharma*, one on disinclination, one on miraculous powers, one on *guṇa*, one on *liṅga* or signs, one on perception, one on Vedic performances, one on sorrow, one on final achievement, one on removal of passions, one on customs and one on emancipation[3]. Thus we have a theistic

[1] *puruṣaś caiva kālaś ca guṇaś ceti tridhocyate*
bhūtiḥ śuddhetarā viṣṇoḥ.... *Ahirbudhnya-saṃhitā*, VI. 8.

[2] *sāṃkhya-rūpeṇa saṃkalpo vaiṣṇavaḥ kapilād ṛṣeḥ*
udito yādṛśaḥ pūrvaṃ tādṛśaṃ śṛṇu me'khilam
ṣaṣṭi-bhedaṃ smṛtaṃ tantraṃ sāṃkhyaṃ nāma mahāmune
prākṛtaṃ vaikṛtaṃ ceti maṇḍale dve samāsataḥ. *Ibid.* XII. 19.

[3] *Ibid.* XII. 20–30.

and an atheistic account of Sāṃkhya, both alleged to be based on the *Ṣaṣṭi-tantra Śāstra*, both described as the philosophy of Kapila and both derived from authoritative ancient texts. Not only does the *Bhāgavata* refer to Kapila as an incarnation of God, but many of the Pañcarātra texts also allude to him as an incarnation of God Viṣṇu; the *Mahābhārata* describes him as Bhagavān Hari and Viṣṇu (III. 47. 18), with Vasudeva (III. 107. 31) and with Kṛṣṇa, and also describes him as a great *ṛsi* who reduced the sons of Sagara into ashes by his wrath. In the *Bhagavad-gītā* also Kṛṣṇa says that of the seers he is the sage Kapila (x. 26), but in the *Mahābhārata* (III. 220. 21) Kapila is identified with the Fourth Fire. A sage Kapila is also mentioned in the *Śvetāśvatara Upaniṣad* (v. 2), and Śaṅkara says in the commentary on the *Brahma-sūtra* that this Kapila must be different from the Kapila (who reduced the sons of Sagara to ashes) and the Kapila who wrote the Sāṃkhya philosophy cannot be ascertained. Thus we have at least three Kapilas, the Kapila who reduced the sons of Sagara into ashes, and who is regarded by the *Mahābhārata* as an incarnation or manifestation of Viṣṇu, Hari or Kṛṣṇa, a Kapila who is regarded as an incarnation of Fire, and the Upaniṣadic sage Kapila, who is regarded there as mature in wisdom. The first two are definitely reputed to be authors of Sāṃkhya philosophy, and Nīlakaṇṭha, the commentator on the *Mahābhārata*, says that it is Kapila (= the incarnation of Fire) who was the author of the atheistic Sāṃkhya[1]. In the *Mahābhārata* (XII. 350. 5) it is said that the sage Kapila based his Sāṃkhya philosophy on the doctrine that it is the one *puruṣa*, the great Nārāyaṇa, who in himself is absolutely qualityless and untouched by all worldly conditions and is yet the superintendent of all phenomenal selves associated with their subtle and gross bodies, and is the ultimate ground of all the cognitional and sense-experiences enjoyed by them, the absolute and ultimate reality which appears as the subjective and the objective world and yet behaves as the cosmic creator and ruler in his four-fold personality as Vāsudeva, Saṃkarṣaṇa, Aniruddha and Pradyumna[2]. Before examining other accounts of Sāṃkhya as found in the *Mahābhārata* we may point out that Pañcaśikha himself was not only called Kapileya from his sucking the breasts of a woman called

[1] Nīlakaṇṭha's commentary on the *Mahābhārata*, III. 220. 21.

[2] See the *Mahābhārata*, XII. 351. See also the commentary of Nīlakaṇṭha on it.

Kapilā while an infant, but was also called *Paramarṣi* Kapila[1]. It seems practically certain that there had been a number of pantheistic, theistic and atheistic varieties of Sāṃkhya. Since the *Ahirbudhnya-saṃhitā* gives the names of the chapters of the *Ṣaṣṭi-tantra*, it is almost certain that the author had seen this work, and that his account of Sāṃkhya is in the main in agreement with it. The table of subjects enumerated shows that the work contained a chapter on Brahman, *puruṣa*, *śakti* (power), *niyati* (destiny), and *kāla* (time), and it is these elements that occur in the *Ahirbudhnya* account of Sāṃkhya. It therefore seems very probable that the *Ahirbudhnya* account of Sāṃkhya is largely faithful to the *Ṣaṣṭi-tantra*. We know that the Sāṃkhya philosophy of Kapila had begun to change its form in some of its most important features, and it is quite probable that it had changed considerably by the time it was traditionally carried to Īśvarakṛṣṇa. It might still have been regarded as containing the essential instructions of the *Ṣaṣṭi-tantra* and yet be very different from it; there is no proof that Īśvarakṛṣṇa had a chance of reading this original *Ṣaṣṭi-tantra*, and it is reasonable to suppose that he had access only to a later version of it or to a revised compendium supposed to be based on it; it may be that the *Ṣaṣṭi-tantra*, being an ancient work, was probably so loosely worded that it was possible to get different interpretations from it —like the *Brahma-sūtra* of Bādarāyaṇa—or even that there were two *Ṣaṣṭi-tantras*[2].

[1] *yam āhuḥ Kāpilaṃ sāṃkhyaṃ paramarṣim prajāpatim*. *Ibid*. XII. 218. 9.

This Pañcaśikha is also described as *pañca-rātra-viśārada*, well-versed in the *pañca-rātra* rites.

[2] In the *Māṭhara-vṛtti* of Māṭharācārya on the *Sāṃkhya-kārikā* of Īśvarakṛṣṇa it is said that *Ṣaṣṭi-tantra* means a *tantra* or work dealing with sixty subjects and not a work containing sixty chapters (*tantryante vyutpādyante padārthā iti tantram*). These sixty subjects are: five *viparyayas* or errors, twenty-eight defects (*aśakti*), nine false satisfactions (*tuṣṭi*), and eight miraculous achievements (*siddhi*)—altogether fifty items (*kārikā* 47)—the other ten subjects being the existence of *prakṛti* as proved by five reasons (called the category of *astitva*), its oneness (*ekatva*), its teleological relation to *puruṣas* (*arthavattva* and *pārārthya*), the plurality of the *puruṣas* (*bahutva*), the maintenance of the body even after *jīvan-mukti* (*sthiti*), association and dissociation of *prakṛti* with *puruṣa* (*yoga* and *viyoga*), difference of *prakṛti* and *puruṣa* (*anyatva*), and final cessation of *prakṛti* (*nivṛtti*). Māṭhara quotes a *Kārikā* enumerating the latter ten subjects: *astitvam, ekatvam, arthavattvam, pārārthyam, anyatvam, arthanivṛttiḥ, yogo viyogo, bahavaḥ pumāṃsaḥ, sthitiḥ, śarīrasya viśeṣa-vṛttiḥ*. *Māṭhara-vṛtti*, 72.

This enumeration, however, seems to be entirely arbitrary, and apparently there is nothing to show that the *Ṣaṣṭi-tantra* was so called because it treated of these sixty subjects.

According to the interpretation of the *Ahirbudhnya-saṃhitā* God or Īśvara is above all, and then there is the category of the unchangeable, the Brahman (consisting of the sum-total of the *puruṣas*), the *prakṛti* as the equilibrium of the *guṇas*, and time (*kāla*), as has already been explained[1]. Time is regarded as the element that combines the *prakṛti* with the *puruṣas*. It is said that the *prakṛti*, the *puruṣas* and time are the materials which are led to their respective works in producing the manifold universe by the development of the categories through the will-movement of God (*Sudarśana*).[2] It is thus one unchangeable *puruṣa* that appears as the many individuals or parts of the Lord Viṣṇu or Īśvara[3]. The will of Īśvara, otherwise called *Sudarśana* or *saṃkalpa*, which is regarded as a vibratory (*parispanda*) thought movement (*jñāna-mūla-kriyātma*), is the dynamic cause of the differentiation of *prakṛti* into the categories (*mahat* and the rest). Time is not identified here with this power, but is regarded as a separate entity, an instrument through which the power acts. Yet this "time" has to be regarded as of a transcendental nature, co-existent with *puruṣa* and *prakṛti*, and distinguished from "time" as moments or their aggregates, which is regarded as the *tamas* aspect of the category of *mahat*. The *sattva* aspect of the *mahat* manifests itself as definite understanding (*buddhir adhyavasāyinī*), and the *rajas* aspect as life-activity (*prāṇa*). The *sattva* aspect of *mahat* as *buddhi* also manifests itself as virtue, wisdom, miraculous powers and as disinclination from worldly joys (*vairāgya*), and the *tamas* aspect as vice (*adharma*), ignorance, attachment and weakness. In the category of *mahat* the general sense-power is generated, by which objects are discerned as cognitional modes; the ego (*ahaṃkāra*) is also generated in the *mahat*, involving the notion of integrating all experience which

1 *anyūnānatiriktaṃ yad guṇa-sāmyaṃ tamomayaṃ*
tat sāṃkhyair jagato mūlaṃ prakṛtiś ceti kathyate.
kramāvatīrṇo yas tatra catur-manu-yugaḥ pumān
samaṣṭiḥ puruṣo yoniḥ sa kūṭastha itīryate
yat tat kālamayaṃ tattvaṃ jagataḥ samprakālanaṃ
sa tayoḥ kāryam āsthāya saṃyojaka-vibhājakaḥ.
Ahirbudhnya-saṃhitā, VII. 1–3.

2 *mṛt-piṇḍī-bhūtam etat tu kālādi-tritayaṃ mune*
viṣṇoḥ sudarśanenaiva sva-sva-kārya-praconditaṃ
mahadādi-pṛthivyanta-tattva-vargopapādakam. *Ibid.* 4.

3 *kūṭastho yaḥ purā proktaḥ pumān vyomnaḥ parād adhaḥ*
mānavo devatādyāś ca tad-vyaṣṭaya itīritāḥ.
jīva-bhedā mune sarve viṣṇu-bhūty-aṃśa-kalpitāḥ. *Ibid.* 58.

belongs to a person (*abhimāna*) as a cognizer and enjoyer of all experiences. The implication seems to be that the category of *mahat* manifests itself as the sense-faculties and the person who behaves as the cognizer, because these are the modes through which thought must interpret itself in order to realize its own nature as thought. The *sāttvika* aspect of the *ahaṃkāra* is called *vaikārika*, the *rājasa* character *taijasa* and the *tāmasa* aspect *bhūtādi*. It is well to point out here that this account greatly differs from the classical Sāṃkhya in this respect, that the sense-power is here generated prior to *ahaṃkāra* and not from *ahaṃkāra*, and that, while the evolution of *ahaṃkāra* is regarded as the evolution of a separate category by the thought-movement of God, the sense-power is regarded only as modes or aspects of *buddhi* or *mahat* and not as separate categories. The only sense-faculty that is evolved through the thought-activity of God out of *ahaṃkāra* is *manas*, the reflective sense (*cintanātmakam ahaṃkārikam indriyam*). From the *tamas* aspect of *ahaṃkāra* as *bhūtādi* the infra-atomic sound-potential (*śabda-tanmātra*) is produced and from this the element of *ākāśa*. *Ākāśa* here is supposed to be of two kinds, as the maintainer of sound and as manifesting vacuity, unoccupation or porosity (*avakāśa-pradāyi*). From the *vaikārika ahaṃkāra* the organs of hearing and speech are produced as categories through the thought-activity of God. In a similar manner the infra-atomic touch-potential (*sparśa-tanmātra*) is produced from the *bhūtādi*, and from this again air, as that which dries up, propels, moves and conglomerates, is produced; again, through the thought-activity of God the organ of touch and the active organ of grasping are produced, and in a similar manner the infra-atomic heat-light-potential (*rūpa-tanmātra*) is produced from *bhūtādi* and from that the element of heat-light; from the *vaikārika* also the visual organ and the conative organs of the two feet are produced, from the *bhūtādi* the infra-atomic taste-potential (*rasa-mātra*) is produced and from it water, and from the *vaikārika ahaṃkāra* the organ of taste and the genitals are produced; from the *bhūtādi* true infra-atomic smell-potential (*gandha-mātra*) is produced, and from it earth; from the *vaikārika-ahaṃkāra* the organs of smell and of excretion are produced. Will, energy, and the five kinds of bio-motor activities (*prāṇa*) are produced jointly from *manas*, *ahaṃkāra* and *buddhi*. The power (*śakti*) of Hari or Viṣṇu or Īśvara is one, but it is not a physical power, a power that involves mechanical movement, but it is in a sense homogeneous with God, and is of the nature of pure self-determined thought (*svacchanda-cinmaya*); it is not however thought in the ordinary sense of thought—with particular contents and object—but it is thought in potentiality, thought that is to realize itself in subject-object forms, manifesting itself as a spiritual thought movement (*jñāna-mūla-kriyātma*). It is this spiritual movement of that which by self-diremption splits itself up (*dvidhā-bhāvam ṛcchati*) as the thought of God (*saṃkalpa*), the determiner (*bhāvaka*) and the passive objectivity (*bhāvya*) called the *prakṛti*, and it is through the former that the latter developed and differentiated itself into the categories mentioned above. What is meant by the vibratory movement of the thought of God is simply its unobstructed character, its character of all potentiality for actuality without any obstruction. It is the pure unobstructed flow of God's thought-power that is regarded as His will, idea or thought (*sudarśanatā*)[1]. The *prakṛti* is thus as much spiritual as God's thought; it represents merely objectivity and the content of the thought of God, and it only has an opportunity of behaving as an independent category of materiality when by the self-diremption of God's power the thought-energy requires an objective through which it can realize itself.

In another chapter of the *Ahirbudhnya-saṃhitā* it is said that the power in its original state may be conceived to be pure stillness (*staimitya-rūpa*) or pure vacuity (*śūnyatva-rūpiṇī*), and it is out of its own indescribable spontaneity that it begins to set itself in motion[2]. It is this spontaneity, which springs out of itself and is its own, that is described as the thought of God or its self-diremptin activity, its desire for being many. All creation proceeds out of this spontaneity; creation is not to be described as an event which happened at a particular time, but it is the eternal spontaneity of this power of God that reveals itself as eternal creation, as eternal and continuous self-manifestation[3]. Whatever is described as movement (*kriyā*), energy (*vīrya*), self-completeness (*tejas*) or strength (*bala*) or God are but different aspects of this power. The strength

1 *avyāghātas tu yas tasya sā sudarśanatā mune*
jñāna-mūla-kriyātmāsau svacchaḥ svacchanda-cinmayaḥ.
Ahirbudhnya-saṃhita, VII. 67.

2 *svātantryād eva kasmāccit kvacit sonmeṣam ṛcchati. Ibid.* V. 4.

3 *satataṃ kurvato jagat. Ibid.* II. 59.

(*bala*) of God consists in the fact that He is never tired or fatigued in spite of His eternal and continuous operation of creation; His energy (*vīrya*) consists in this, that, though His own power is split up as the material on which His power acts, He does not suffer any change on that account[1]. His lustre of self-completeness (*tejas*) consists in this, that He does not await the help of any instrument of any kind for His creative operations[2]: and it is the self-spontaneity of this power that is described as His agency (*kartṛtva*) as the creator of the world. God is described as being both of the nature of pure consciousness and of the nature of power. It is the all-pervasive consciousness of Himself that constitutes the omniscience of God, and, when this stillness of omniscience and self-complete steady consciousness as pure differenceless vacuity dirempts itself and pulsates into the creative operation, it is called His power. It is on this account that the power (*śakti*) of God is described as thought-movement (*jñāna-mūla-kriyātmaka*). This power or consciousness may be regarded both as a part of God, and therefore one with Him, and also as His specific character or quality; it is this power which dirempts itself as consciousness and its object (*cetya-cetana*), as time and all that is measured by time (*kalya-kāla*), as manifest and unmanifest (*vyaktāvyakta*), as the enjoyer and that which is enjoyed (*bhoktṛ-bhogya*), as the body and that which is embodied (*deha-dehin*)[3]. The conception of *puruṣa* seems to indicate the view of a conglomeration of the individual selves into a colony or association of individual selves, like the honeycomb of the bees[4]. They are regarded as unchangeable in themselves (*kūṭastha*), but yet they are covered over with the dusty impurities of beginningless root-desires (*vāsanā*), and thus, though pure in themselves, they may be also regarded as impure[5]. In themselves they are absolutely unaffected by any kind of affliction, and, being parts of God's nature, are omniscient and eternally emancipated beings. These *puruṣas* are, however, through the will of God or rather of necessity through the creative operation of His power, differently affected by ignorance

1 *tasyopādāna-bhāve'pi vikāra-viraho hi yaḥ*
vīryaṃ nāma guṇaḥ so'yam acyutatvāparāhvayam. *Ibid.* II. 60.

2 *sahakāry-anapekṣā yā tat tejaḥ samudāhṛtam.* *Ibid.* II. 61.

3 *Ibid.* V. 6–12.

4 *sarvātmanāṃ samaṣṭir yā kośo madhu-kṛtām iva.* *Ibid.* VI. 33.

5 *śuddhyaśuddhimayo bhāvo bhūteḥ sa puruṣaḥ smṛtaḥ*
anādi-vāsanā-reṇu-kuṇṭhitair ātmabhiś citaḥ. *Ibid.* VI. 34.

(*avidyā*), which makes them subject to various kinds of affliction, and, as a result thereof, their own natures are hidden from themselves and they appear to be undergoing all kinds of virtuous and sinful experiences of pleasures and pains; and, being thus affected, they are first associated with the creative power (*śakti*) of God, and then, as this power first evolves itself into its first category of time as the all-determining necessity (*niyati*), they become associated with it; and then, as the third movement posits itself as all-grasping time, they become associated with that category, and then, as the *sattva-guṇas* gradually evolve from *kāla*, the *rājasa guṇas* from *sattva* and the *tāmasa guṇas* from *rajas*, the colony of *puruṣas* is associated first with *sattva*, then with *rajas* and then with *tamas*. When all the *guṇas* are evolved, though the three *guṇas* are then all disturbed for further creative operation, they are not disturbed in all their parts; there are some parts of the *guṇa* conglomeration which are in equilibrium with one another; and it is this state of equilibrium of the *guṇas* that is called *prakṛti*[1]. The account of the evolution of the various categories from the creative will of God up to the *prakṛti* does not occur in the seventh chapter of the *Ahirbudhnya*, which is definitely described as the Sāṃkhya philosophy of Kapila; it is only a Pañcarātra account given to supplement that of the Sāṃkhya, which starts from the evolution of the categories from the *prakṛti* —the equilibrium of the *guṇas*. According to the Pañcarātra account of the *Ahirbudhnya-saṃhitā* the colony or the honeycomb of the *puruṣas* thus forms a primal element, which is associated with the self-evolving energy of God from the first moment of its movement, continues to be so associated with each of the evolving stadiums of categories up to the evolution of the *prakṛti*, and later on with all the other categories that are evolved from the *prakṛti*. In the account of Kapila Sāṃkhya as found in the *Ahirbudhnya-saṃhitā* this conglomeration of the *puruṣas* is admitted to be the changeless category that is associated with the evolution of the categories and descends gradually through the successive stages of their evolution until we come to the complete human stage with the evolution of the different senses and the gross elements. Unlike the account of *puruṣa* that is found in the classical Sāṃkhya

1 *codyamāne'pi sṛṣṭyartham pūrṇaṃ guṇa-yugaṃ tadā*
aṃśataḥ sāmyam āyāti viṣṇu-saṃkalpa-coditam.
Ahirbudhnya-saṃhitā, VI. 62.

treatises, which regards the *puruṣas* as being absolutely untouched by the instinctive root-desires (*vāsanā*) and the afflictions, it considers (like the Jains) that the *puruṣas* are coated with the impurities of *vāsanās* and *kleśas*, though in themselves they are essentially pure; again, the classical Sāṃkhya considers that the *vāsanās* are produced in a beginningless way, through *karma*, through an endless series of births and rebirths, whereas the Pañcarātra holds that different *puruṣas* are originally associated with different *vāsanās* according to the will of God. Unlike the account of the classical Sāṃkhya, where the *vāsanās* are regarded as a part of *prakṛti* as *buddhi* or *citta*, in this it is an original extraneous impurity of the *puruṣas*. It is probable, however, that this account of *vāsanās* and their original association with the *puruṣas* through the will of God did not form any part of the philosophy of Kapila's *Ṣaṣṭi-tantra*, but was a supplementary doctrine introduced by the author of the *Ahirbudhnya*, as it is not mentioned in the seventh chapter of the work, which is definitely devoted to the account of Sāṃkhya.

The Sāṃkhya thought described in the *Gītā* has been explained in the second volume of the present work, and it will be seen that, though the *Gītā* account is unsystematic and nebulous, with significant details missing, it is essentially theistic and intimately associated with this *Ahirbudhnya* account of Kapila Sāṃkhya; and as such is fundamentally different from the classical Sāṃkhya of the *Sāṃkhya-kārikā*.

In Chapter 22 of the 11th book of the *Bhāgavata* a reference is made to various schools of Sāṃkhya admitting different categories of being or evolutes[1]. Thus some Sāṃkhyists admitted nine categories, some eleven, some five, some twenty-six, some twenty-five, some seven, some six, some four, some seventeen, some sixteen and some thirteen. Uddhava requested Lord Kṛṣṇa to reconcile these diverse opposing views. In reply Lord Kṛṣṇa said that the different enumeration of the categories is due to the varying kinds of subsumption of the lower categories into the higher or by the omission of the higher ones, i.e. by ignoring some of the effect entities (as

1 *kati tattvāni viśveśa saṃkhyātāny ṛṣibhiḥ prabho*
nava-ekādaśa-pañca-trīṇy atha tvam iha śuśruma
kecit ṣaḍviṃśatiṃ prāhur apare pañcaviṃśatiṃ
saptaike nava-ṣaṭ kecic catvāry ekādaśāpare
kecit saptadaśa prāhuḥ ṣoḍaśaike trayodaśa. Ślokas 1, 2.

being already contained in the cause) or by ignoring some of the successive causal entities (as being present in the effect)[1]. Thus, there may be systems of Sāṃkhya schools where the *tanmātras* are not counted or where the gross elements are not counted as categories. The explanation in all such cases is to be found in the principle that some thinkers did not wish to count the *tanmātras*, as they are already contained in the gross elements (*ghaṭe mṛdvat*); whereas others did not count the gross elements, as these were but evolutes in the *tanmātras* (*mṛdi ghaṭavat*). But there are differences of opinion not only as regards the evolutionary categories of *prakṛti*, but also as regards the souls or the *puruṣas* and God. Thus there are twenty-four evolutionary categories (including *prakṛti*); *puruṣa* is counted as the twenty-fifth category, and according to the theistic Sāṃkhya God or Īśvara is counted as the twenty-sixth. It may be objected that the above principle of reconciliation of the diverse counting of categories by subsuming the effect under the cause, or by ignoring the former, cannot apply here. The theistic Sāṃkhya admits Īśvara on the ground that there must be some being who should communicate self-knowledge to individual souls, as they cannot, by themselves, attain it. If on such a view the theistic school of twenty-six categories is regarded as valid, the other school of twenty-five categories becomes irreconcilable. To this the reply is that there is no intrinsic difference in the nature of *puruṣa* and Īśvara, as they are both of the nature of pure consciousness. The objection that even on the above supposition the self-knowledge communicated by Īśvara has to be counted as a separate category is invalid, for self-knowledge, being knowledge, is only the heightening of the *sattva* quality of the *prakṛti* and as such falls within *prakṛti* itself. Knowledge is not a quality of the *puruṣa*, but of the *prakṛti*. The state of equilibrium in which the *guṇas* are not specifically manifested is called *prakṛti*. An upsetting of the equilibrium leads to the manifestation of the *guṇas*, which have, therefore, to be regarded as attributes of the *prakṛti*. The *puruṣa*, not being an agent, cannot possess knowledge as an attribute of its own. So, all activity being due to *rajas* and all ignorance being due to *tamas*, activity and ignorance are also to be regarded as con-

[1] *anupraveśaṃ darśayati ekasminnapīti pūrvasmin kāraṇabhūte tattve sūkṣma-rūpeṇa praviṣṭāni mṛdi ghaṭavat. aparasmin kārya-tattve kāraṇa-tattvāni anugatatvena praviṣṭāni ghaṭe mṛdvat.* Śrīdhara's commentary on *śloka* 8.

stituents of *prakṛti*. Time (*kāla*) also is to be identified as God, because it is by the agency of God that the *guṇas* combine, that He is regarded as the cause of the combination of the *guṇas*. The view which regards *kāla* as the cause of the combination of the *guṇas* is grounded on this fact, and it is for that reason that in the scriptures *kāla* has been regarded as the name of Īśvara. As everything proceeds from the category of *mahat*, that itself is called *svabhāva* or nature. Thus the two apparently conflicting views that *kāla* and *svabhāva* are to be regarded as the ultimate causes of the world may well be reconciled with the Sāṃkhya according to the above interpretation.

The school of Sāṃkhya which reckons nine categories counts merely *puruṣa*, *prakṛti*, *mahat*, *ahaṃkāra* and the five elements. Those who reckon eleven count the five cognitive and conative senses and the *manas* only. Those who reckon five categories count the five sense objects only. Those who reckon seven count the five sense-objects, the soul and God. Those who reckon six include within them the five sense-objects and the *puruṣa*. There are others, however, who regard earth, water, fire and the soul as four categories. Others take the five sense-objects, the eleven sense-organs and the *puruṣa* as categories. By excluding *manas* some hold that there are only sixteen categories. Others take the five sense-objects, the five cognitive senses, *manas*, soul and God, and thus arrive at the thirteen categories. Others take the five sense-objects, the five cognitive senses and the sense as the eleven categories. Others count *prakṛti*, *mahat*, *ahaṃkāra*, the five *tanmātras* and the *puruṣa* as the nine categories.

It is regrettable that apart from a reference to the above schools of Sāṃkhya and the attempts at their reconciliation found in the *Bhāgavata*, it is not possible to trace these doctrines to the original works, which must have long preceded the period of the composition of the *Bhāgavata*. The *Bhāgavata* is interested in the theistic Sāṃkhya doctrine, as has already been shown, and attempts to reconcile the conflicting schools of Sāṃkhya as being substantially one school of thought. It further holds that the *prakṛti* and its manifestations are produced through the operation of the diverse power of the *māyā* of Īśvara. At the time of dissolution (*pralaya*) God remains in absolute identity with Himself, and the *guṇas*, which are the various manifestations of His *māyā* power, remain in equilibrium—a state in which all His energies are sleeping as it were. By His own inherent energy He breaks the equilibrium of His sleeping energy and sets Himself to the work of the creation—the *prakṛti* with its evolutes—and thereby associates them with *jīvas*, which are merely His parts, and which thus are deluding the dualistic experience of the world, which they enjoy and for which they suffer; and He also shows them the right way by instructing them through the Vedas[1]. The self in its transcendent nature is pure experience and as such is devoid of and is absolutely unassociated with any kind of objective form. The association of objectivity and of content is as illusory as creations in dreams, and must be regarded as products of *māyā*[2].

Puruṣa as pure experience (*anubhava-svarūpa*) is to be differentiated and comprehended as different from passing mental states, as the content of the waking, dream and dreamless stages by the method of agreement and difference (*anvaya-vyatireka*). For, through the contents of experience in the various constituents involved in the mental states, that which remains constant, like a thread in a garland of pearls, is the pure experiencer, the self. Self is therefore to be regarded as different from the contents of the mental states which it illuminates[3].

[1] *sa vai kilāyaṃ puruṣaḥ purātano*
ya eka āsīd aviśeṣa ātmani
agre guṇebhyo jagad-ātmanīśvare
nimīlitātman niśi supta-śaktiṣu
sa eva bhūyo nijavīrya-choditaṃ
sva-jīva-māyāṃ prakṛtiṃ sisṛkṣatīm
anāma-rūpātmani rūpa-nāmanī
vidhitsamāno'nusasāra śāstrakṛt.
Bhāgavata, I. 10. 21, 22.

[2] *ātma-māyām ṛte rājan parasyānubhavātmanaḥ*
na ghaṭetārthasambandhaḥ svapnadraṣṭur ivāñjasā.
Ibid. II. 9. 1.

Illusion or *māyā* is defined as that which manifests non-existent objects but is not manifested itself.
ṛte'rthaṃ yat pratīyeta na pratīyeta cātmani
tad vidyād ātmano māyāṃ yathābhāso tathā tamaḥ.
Ibid. II. 9. 33.

[3] *anvaya-vyatirekeṇa vivekena satātmanā*
sarga-sthāna-samāmnāyair vimṛśadbhir asatvaraiḥ
budher jāgaraṇaṃ svapnaḥ suṣuptir iti vṛttayaḥ
tā yenaivānubhūyante so'dhyakṣaḥ puruṣaḥ paraḥ.
Ibid. VII. 7. 24, 25.

Eschatology.

In the *Bhāgavata-purāṇa*, III. 32, it is held that those who perform sacrifices and make offerings to gods and forefathers pass after death to the lunar world, from which they return to earth again. Those, however, who follow their own duties and surrender all their actions to gods, pure in mind and heart and unattached to worldly things, pass after death to the solar sphere and thence to the Universal Being Who is the cause of the world. Those, however, who are obsessed with the notion of duality pass into the nature of qualified Brahman, and are then born again in the world in accordance with their past deeds. Those again who lead an ordinary life of desires and make offerings to their forefathers have first to go by the southern way of smoky path to the land of the forefathers, and are again born in the line of their own progenies.

In XI. 22. 37, however, we find a more rational view. It is said there that the *manas* of men is permeated by their deeds and their causes, and it is this *manas* that passes from one body to another. The *ātman*, the soul, follows this *manas*. Śrīdhara, the well-known commentator on the *Bhāgavata-purāṇa*, regards *manas* here as the *liṅga-śarīra*, and holds that the self follows the *manas* infested by egoism. The *Bhāgavata-purāṇa* further holds that through the destiny of *karma* the *manas* meditates over the things seen and heard and gradually loses its memory with regard to them. This *manas* entering into another body thus ceases to remember all the experiences of the previous bodies and thus death may be defined as absolute forgetfulness (*mṛtyuratyanta-vismṛtiḥ*, XI. 22. 39). Birth is regarded as the acceptance of new experiences. Śrīdhara points out that this takes place with the cessation of the functioning of egoism with reference to the experiences of past bodies and the extension of the function of egoism with reference to the experiences of the new body. Just as one does not remember one's dreams, so one ceases to remember one's past experiences, and this is conditioned by death. At birth the self that was always existent appears to be born anew. By identifying the self with the body one divides one's experiences as internal and external. As a matter of fact the body is being continually destroyed and generated, but such changes, being of a subtle nature, are overlooked. Just as there cannot be the same flame in two moments, or one flowing river in two different moments, so the body also is different in two different moments, though on account of our ignorance we suppose that the same body is passing through various stages and conditions. But in reality no one is born and no one dies through the agency of *karma*. It is all a panorama of illusions, just as the fire, as heat, exists eternally and yet appears to be burning in association with logs of wood. All the phenomena of birth, infancy, youth, old age and death as different stages of the body are but mere fancies. They are but stages of primal matter, the *prakṛti*, which are regarded through illusion as different stages of our life. One notices the death of one's father and the birth of a son and so may speak of the destruction and generation of bodies, but no one experiences that the experiencer himself undergoes birth and death. The self thus is entirely different from the body. It is only through inability to distinguish properly between the two that one becomes attached to sense-objects and seems to pass through the cycle of birth and death. Just as a man seeing another man dance or sing imitates his action, so does the *puruṣa*, which has no movement of itself, seem to imitate the qualities of *buddhi* in the operation of these movements. Again, just as when one looks at the images of trees in flowing water, the trees themselves seem to be many, so does the self regard itself as implicated in the movement of the *prakṛti*. This gives us the world-experience and the experience of the cycles of birth and death, though none of them really exists. Thus we see that the *Bhāgavata-purāṇa* agrees with the general Sāṃkhya and the Vedānta view regarding birth and death. It no doubt accepts the ordinary view of the Upaniṣads that a man, like a caterpillar, does not leave one body without accepting another at the same time (*Bhāgavata-purāṇa*, X. I. 38–44); but at the same time it holds that such birth and re-birth are due to one's own illusion or *māyā*.

CHAPTER XXV

MADHVA AND HIS SCHOOL

Madhva's Life.

BHANDARKAR in *Vaiṣṇavism, Śaivaism and Minor Religious Systems* says that in the *Mahābhārata-tātparya-nirṇaya*, Madhva has given the date of his birth as *Kali* 4300. The *Kali* age, according to Bhāskarācārya, begins with the year 3101 B.C. The date of Madhva's birth would thus be A.D. 1199 or 1121 *śaka*. Bhandarkar says that, as some use the current year of an era and some the past, the *śaka* era 1121 may be regarded as equivalent to 1119. But the present writer has not been able to discover it in the only printed edition of the text of *Mahābhārata-tātparya-nirṇaya* (1833 *śaka*, published by T. R. Kṛṣṇācārya). Bhandarkar, however, approaches the problem by another path also. He says that the list preserved in several of the Maṭhas gives the date of Madhva as *śaka* 1119, and, as Madhva lived for 79 years, the date of his birth was 1040 *śaka*. Bhandarkar, however, regards *śaka* 1119 as the date of his birth, and not of his death as given in the Maṭha list. He says that the inscription in the Kūrmeśvara temple at Śrīkūrma is in a Tāluka of the Ganjam district in which Narahari-tīrtha is represented to have constructed a temple and placed in it an idol of Narasiṃha dated *śaka* 1203 (*Epigraphica Indica*, Vol. VI, p. 260). The first person therein mentioned is Puruṣottama-tīrtha, who is the same as Acyutaprekṣa, then his pupil Ānanda-tīrtha, then Narahari-tīrtha, the pupil of Ānanda-tīrtha. Narahari-tīrtha was probably the same as Narasiṃha, the ruler of the Tāluk mentioned above, from *śaka* 1191 to 1225. He is mentioned in inscriptions at Śrīkūrman bearing the date *śaka* 1215, which is represented as the eighteenth year of the king's reign. He was Narasiṃha II, who was panegyrized in the *Ekāvalī*. From other inscriptions we get Narahari's date as between 1186 and 1212 *śaka*. These records confirm the tradition that Narahari-tīrtha was sent to Orissa by Ānanda-tīrtha. Now Narahari-tīrtha's active period ranged between 1186 to 1215. His teacher Madhva could not have died in *śaka* 1119, i.e. sixty-seven years before him. Bhandarkar therefore takes 1119 (as mentioned in the Maṭha list) as the date of the birth of Madhva, not as the date of his death. This date of Madhva's birth, *śaka* 1119 or A.D. 1197, has been accepted by Grierson and Krisnasvami Aiyar, and has not so far been challenged.

We have no authentic information about the life of Madhva. All that we can know of him has to be culled from the legendary and semi-mythical lives of Madhva, called the *Madhva-vijaya*, and the *Maṇi-mañjarī* of Nārāyaṇa Bhaṭṭa, son of Trivikrama, who was an actual disciple of Madhva. Some information can also be gathered from the adoration hymn of Trivikrama Paṇḍita. Madhva seems to have been a born enemy of Śaṅkara. In the *Maṇi-mañjarī*, Nārāyaṇa Bhaṭṭa gives a fanciful story of a demon, Maṇimat, who interpreted the Vedānta. Maṇimat was born as a widow's bastard, and therefore he was called Śaṅkara; with the blessing of Śiva he mastered the *śāṣtras* at Saurāṣṭra, invented the doctrine of *sūrya-mārga*, and was welcomed by persons of demoralized temperament. He really taught Buddhism under the cloak of Vedānta. He regarded Brahman as identified with Sūrya. He seduced the wife of his Brahmin host, and used to make converts by his magic arts. When he died, he asked his disciples to kill Satyaprajña, the true teacher of the Vedānta; the followers of Śaṅkara were tyrannical people who burnt down monasteries, destroyed cattle and killed women and children. They converted Prajñā-tīrtha, their chief opponent, by force. The disciples of Prajñā-tīrtha, however, were secretly attached to the true Vedāntic doctrine, and they made one of their disciples thoroughly learned in the Vedic scriptures. Acyutaprekṣa, the teacher of Madhva, was a disciple of this true type of teachers, who originated from Satyaprajña, the true Vedic teacher, contemporary with Śaṅkara.

Madhva was an incarnation of Vāyu for the purpose of destroying the false doctrines of Śaṅkara, which were more like the doctrines of the Lokāyatas, Jainas and Pāśupatas, but were more obnoxious and injurious.

Madhva was the son of Madhyageha Bhaṭṭa, who lived in the city of Rajatapīṭha, near Udipi, which is about 40 miles west of Śṛṅgeri, where there was a celebrated *maṭha* of Śaṃkara. Udipi is even now the chief centre of Madhvism in South Kanara. The ancient name of the country, which now comprises Dharwar, the North and the South Kanara, and the western part of the State of Mysore, was Tuluva (modern Tulu), which is mostly inhabited by the Madhvas. Grierson, writing in 1915, says that there are about 70,000 Madhvas in the locality. Elsewhere they are more distributed. It must, however, be noted that from the South of Hyderabad to Mangalore, that is, the whole of the North and the South Kanara, may also be regarded as the most important centre of Vīra-Śaivism, which will be dealt with in the fifth volume of the present work. The village of Rajatapīṭha, where Madhva was born, may probably be identified with the modern Kalyāṇapura. He was a disciple of Acyutaprekṣa, and received the name of Pūrṇaprajña at the time of initiation and later on another name, Ānanda-tīrtha; he is known by both these names. He at first studied the views of Śaṅkara, but soon developed his own system of thought, which was directly opposed to that of Śaṅkara. He refuted twenty-one *Bhāṣyas* which were written by other teachers who preceded him; and Śeṣa, the disciple of Chalāri-nṛsiṃhācārya, the commentator on the *Madhva-vijaya* of Nārāyaṇa Bhaṭṭa, enumerates the designations of these commentators on the *Brahma-sūtra* as follows; Bhāratīvijaya; Saṃvidānanda; Brahmaghoṣa; Śatānanda; Vāgbhaṭa; Vijaya; Rudra Bhaṭṭa; Vāmana; Yādavaprakāśa; Rāmānuja; Bhartṛprapañca; Draviḍa; Brahmadatta; Bhāskara; Piśāca; Vṛittikāra; Vijaya Bhaṭṭa; Viṣṇukrānta; Vādīndra; Mādhavadeśaka; Śaṅkara. Even in Rajatapīṭhapura he once defeated a great scholar of the Śaṅkara school who came to visit Madhva's teacher Acyutaprekṣa. He then went to the South with Acyutaprekṣa and arrived at the city of Viṣṇumaṅgala[1]. From here he went southwards and arrived at Anantapura (modern Trivandrum). Here he had a long fight with the Śaṅkarites of the Śṛṅgeri monastery. Thence he proceeded to Dhanuṣkoṭi and Rāmeśvaram, and offered his adoration to Viṣṇu. He defeated on the way there many opponents and stayed in Rāmeśvaram for four months, after which he came back to Udipi. Having thus established himself in the South as a leader of a new faith, Madhva started on a tour to North India, and, crossing the Ganges, went to Hardwar, and thence to Badarikā, where he met Vyāsa. He was here asked by Vyāsa to write a commentary on the *Brahma-sūtra* repudiating the false *Bhāṣya* of Śaṅkara. He then returned to Udipi, converting many Śaṅkarites on the way, such as Śobhana Bhaṭṭa and others residing near the banks of the Godāvarī[2]. He at last converted Acyutaprekṣa to his own doctrines. In the

[1] *Madhva-viyaya*, v. 30.

[2] *Ibid.* IX. 17.

eleventh and the thirteenth chapters of the *Madhva-vijaya* we read the story of the persecution of Madhva by Padma-tīrtha, the head of the Śṛṅgeri monastery, who tried his best to obstruct the progress of the new faith initiated by Madhva and even stole away Madhva's books, which were, however, returned to him through the intercession of the local Prince Jayasiṃha of Viṣṇumaṅgala; the faith continued to grow, and Trivirama Paṇḍita, the father of Nārāyaṇa Bhaṭṭa, the author of *Maṇi-mañjarī* and *Madhva-vijaya*, and many other important persons were converted to the Madhva faith. In his last years Madhva again made a pilgrimage to the North and is said to have rejoined Vyāsa, and to be still staying with him. He is said to have lived for seventy-nine years and probably died in 1198 *śaka* or A.D. 1276. He was known by various names, such as Pūrṇaprajña, Ānanda-tīrtha, Nandī-tīrtha and Vāsudeva[1].

The treatment of the philosophy of Madhva which is to follow was written in 1930; and so the present writer had no opportunity of diving into Mr Śarmā's excellent work which appeared some time ago, when the manuscript of the present work was ready for the Press. Padmanābhasura's *Madhva-siddhānta-sāra* contains a treatment of Madhva's doctrines in an epitomized form. Madhva wrote thirty-seven works. These are enumerated below[2];

(1) *The Ṛg-bhāṣya* a commentary to the *Ṛg-veda*, I. 1–40; (2) The *Krama-nirṇaya*, a discussion on the proper reading and

[1] A few works in English have appeared on Madhva. The earliest accounts are contained in "Account of the Madhva Gooroos" collected by Major MacKenzie, 24 August 1800, printed on pp. 33 ff. of the "Characters" in the *Asiatic Annual Register*, 1804 (London, 1806); H. H. Wilson's "Sketch of the religious sects of the Hindus," reprinted from Vols. XVI and XVII of *Asiatic Researches*, London, 1861, I, pp. 139 ff.; Krishnaswami Aiyar's *Śrī Madhva and Madhvaism*, Madras; R. G. Bhandarkar's *Vaiṣṇavism, Śaivaism and Minor Religious Systems*; *Bombay Gazetteer*, Vol. XXII, "Dharwar," Bombay, 1884; G. Venkoba Rao's "A sketch of the History of the Maddhva Āchāryas," beginning in *Indian Antiquary*, XLIII (1914), and C. M. Padmanābhacārya's *Life of Madhvācārya*. S. Subba Rao has a complete translation of the commentary of Śrī Madhvācārya on the *Brahma-sūtra* and a translation in English of the *Bhagavad-gītā* with the commentary according to Śrī Madhvācārya's *Bhāṣya*. The preface of this *Bhagavad-gītā* contains an account of Madhva's life from an orthodox point of view. There is also P. Ramchandra Roo's *The Brahma Sutras*, translated literally according to the commentary of Śrī Madhvācārya (Sanskrit, Kumbakonam, 1902); G. A. Grierson has a very interesting article on Madhva in the *Encyclopaedia of Religion and Ethics*, Vol. VIII; Mr Nāgarāja Śarmā has recently published a recondite monograph on the philosophy of Madhva.

[2] See Helmuth von Glasenapp's *Madhvas Philosophie des Vishṇu-Glaubens*, p. 13.

order of the *Aitareya-Brāhmaṇa*, IV. 1–4, *Aitareya-Āraṇyaka*, IV. 1, and the Vedic hymns cited therein; (3) The *Aitareya-upaniṣad-bhāṣya*; (4) The *Bṛhadāraṇyaka-upaniṣad-bhāṣya*; (5) *Chāndogya-upaniṣad-bhāṣya*; (6) *Taittirīya-upaniṣad-bhāṣya*; (7) *Īśāvāsya-upaniṣad-bhāṣya*; (8) *Kāṭhaka-upaniṣad-bhāṣya*; (9) *Muṇḍaka-upaniṣad-bhāṣya*; (10) *Māṇḍūkya-upaniṣad-bhāṣya*; (11) *Praśnopaniṣad-bhāṣya*; (12) *Kenopaniṣad-bhāṣya*; (13) *Mahābhārata-tātparya-nirṇaya*; (14) *Bhagavad-gītā-bhāṣya*; (15) *Bhagavad-gītā-tātparya-nirṇaya*; (16) *Bhāgavata-tātparya-nirṇaya*; (17) *Brahma-sūtra-bhāṣya*; (18) *Brahma-sūtrānubhāṣya*; (19) *Brahma-sūtrānuvyākhyāna*; (20) *Brahma-sūtrānuvyākhyāna-nirṇaya*; (21) *Pramāṇa-lakṣaṇa*; (22) *Kathā-lakṣaṇa*; (23) *Upādhi-khaṇḍana*; (24) *Māyāvāda-khaṇḍana*; (25) *Prapañca-mithyātānumāna-khaṇḍana*; (26) *Tattvoddyota;* (27) *Tattva-viveka;* (28) *Tattva-saṃkhyāna;* (29) *Viṣṇu-tattva-nirṇaya;* (30) *Tantra-sāra-saṃgraha;* (31) *Kṛṣṇāmṛta-mahārṇava;* (32) *Yati-praṇava-kalpa;* (33) *Sadacāra-smṛti;* (34) *Jayantī-nirṇaya* or the *Jayantī-kalpa;* (35) *Yamaka-bhārata;* (36) *Nṛsiṃha-nakha-stotra;* (37) *Dvādaśa-stotra.*

In the list given in the *Grantha-mālikā-stotra* of Jaya-tīrtha we have *Sannyāsa-paddhati* instead of *Brahma-sūtrānuvyākhyā-nyāya-nirṇaya.* The *Catalogus Catalogorum* of Aufrecht refers to the report on the search for Sanskrit Manuscripts in the Bombay Presidency during the year 1882–3 by R. G. Bhandarkar, and enumerates a number of other books which are not mentioned in the *Grantha-mālikā-stotra.* These are as follows:

Ātmajñāna-pradeśa-ṭīkā, Ātmopadeśa-ṭīkā, Ārya-stotra, Upadeśasahasra-ṭīkā, Upaniṣat-prasthāna, Aitareyopaniṣad-bhāṣya-tippanī, Kāṭhakopaniṣad-bhāṣya-ṭippanī, Kenopaniṣad-bhāṣya-ṭippanī, Kauṣītakyupaniṣad-bhāṣya-ṭippanī, Khapuṣpa-ṭīkā, Guru-stuti, Govinda-bhāṣya-pīṭhaka, Govindāṣṭaka-ṭīkā, Gauḍapādīya-bhāṣya-ṭīkā, Chāndogyopaniṣad-bhāṣya-ṭippanī, Taittirīyopaniṣad-bhāṣya-ṭippanī, Taittirīya-śruti-vārttika-ṭīkā, Tripuṭīprakaraṇa-ṭīkā, Nārāyaṇopaniṣad-bhāṣya-ṭippanī, Nyāya-vivaraṇa, Pañcīkaraṇa-prakriyā-vivaraṇa, Praśnopaniṣad-bhāṣya-ṭippanī, Bṛhajjābālopaniṣad-bhāṣya, Bṛhadāraṇyaka-bhāṣya-ṭippanī, Bṛhadāraṇyaka-vārttika-ṭīkā, Brahma-sūtra-bhāṣya-ṭīkā, Brahma-sūtra-bhāṣya-nirṇaya, Brahmānanda, Bhakti-rasāyana, Bhagavad-gītā-prasthāna, Bhagavad-gītā-bhāṣya-vivecana, Māṇḍūkyopaniṣad-bhāṣya-ṭippanī, Mita-bhāṣiṇī, Rāmottara-tāpanīya-bhāṣya, Vākyasudhā-ṭīkā, Viṣṇusaha-

sranāma-bhāṣya, *Vedānta-vārttika*, *Śaṅkara-vijaya*, *Śaṅkarācārya-avatāra-kathā*, *Śataśloka-ṭīkā*, *Saṃhitopaniṣad-bhāṣya*, *Saṃhitopaniṣad-bhāṣya-ṭippanī*, *Ṣaṭtattva*, *Sadācāra-stuti-stotra*, *Smṛti-vivaraṇa*, *Smṛti-sāra-samuccaya*, *Svarūpa-nirṇaya-ṭīkā*, *Harimīḍe-stotra-ṭīkā*.

Succession List of Madhva Gurus.

Bhandarkar in his search for Sanskrit MSS. in 1882–3 gives the names of teachers with the dates of their deaths. Thus Ānanda-tīrtha or Madhva was succeeded by Padmanābha-tīrtha 1126 *śaka*, and he by Narahari-tīrtha 1135 *śaka*; Mādhava-tīrtha 1152; Akṣobhya-tīrtha 1169; Jaya-tīrtha 1190; Vidyādhirāja-tīrtha 1254; Kavīndra-tīrtha 1261; Vāgīśa-tīrtha 1265; Rāmachandra-tīrtha 1298; Vidyānidhi-tīrtha 1306; Raghunātha-tīrtha 1364; Raghuvarya-tīrtha 1419; Raghūttama-tīrtha 1457; Vedavyāsa-tīrtha 1481; Vidyādhīśa-tīrtha 1493; Vedanidhi-tīrtha 1497; Satyavrata-tīrtha 1560; Satyanidhi-tīrtha 1582; Satyanātha-tīrtha 1595; Satyābhinava-tīrtha 1628; Satyapūrṇa-tīrtha 1648; Satyavijaya-tīrtha 1661; Satyapriya-tīrtha 1666; Satyabodha-tīrtha 1705; Satyasannidhāna-tīrtha 1716; Satyavara-tīrtha 1719; Satyadhāma-tīrtha 1752; Satyasāra-tīrtha 1763; Satyaparāyaṇa-tīrtha 1785; Satyakāma-tīrtha 1793; Satyeṣṭi-tīrtha 1794; Satyaparāyaṇa-tīrtha 1801; Satyavit-tīrtha was living in 1882, when the *Search for Sanskrit MSS.* was being written. Thus we have a list of thirty-five Gurus, including Madhva, from 1198 *śaka* (the year of the death of Madhva) to Satyavit-tīrtha, who was living in *śaka* 1804 or A.D. 1882. This list was drawn up in consonance with the two lists procured at Belgaum and Poona. It is largely at variance with the list given in the introduction to the commentary on the *Brahma-sūtra* by Baladeva. Baladeva gives the list as follows:

Madhva, Padmanābha, Nṛhari, Mādhava, Akṣobhya, Jaya-tīrtha, Jñānasiṃha, Dayānidhi, Vidyānidhi, Rājendra, Jayadharma, Puruṣottama-tīrtha, Brahmāṇḍa-tīrtha, Vyāsa-tīrtha, Lakṣmīpati, Mādhavendra, Īśvara. Īśvara was a teacher of Caitanya. We see that the list given by Baladeva is right as far as Jaya-tīrtha; but after Jaya-tīrtha the list given by Baladeva is in total discrepancy with the two lists from the Madhva Maṭhas in Belgaum and Poona. Under the circumstances we are unable to accept the list of Gurus given by Baladeva, which has many other discrepancies into details whereof we need not enter.

Important Madhva Works.

The *Mahābhārata-tātparya-nirṇaya*. This work of Madhva consists of thirty-two chapters and is written in verse. In the first chapter Madhva begins with a very brief summary of his views. He says there that the four Vedas, the *Pañcarātras*, the *Mahābhārata*, the original *Rāmāyaṇa*, and the *Brahma-sūtras* are the only authoritative scriptural texts, and that anything that contradicts them is to be regarded as invalid. The *Vaiṣṇava Purāṇas*, being essentially nothing more than an elaboration of the *Pañcarātras*, should also be regarded as valid scriptures. The *smṛti* literature of Manu and others is valid in so far as it does not come into conflict with the teachings of the Vedas, the *Mahābhārata*, the *Pañcarātras* and the *Vaiṣṇava Purāṇas*[1]. Other *śāstras* such as those of Buddhism were made by Viṣṇu to confuse the *Asuras*, and Śiva also produced the *Śaiva Śāstra* for the same object at the command of Viṣṇu. All the *śāstras* that speak of the unity of the self with Brahman either in the present life or at liberation are false. Viṣṇu is the true Lord, and is also called Nārāyaṇa or Vāsudeva. The process of the world is real and is always associated with five-fold differences, viz. that between the self and God, between the selves themselves, between matter and God, between matter and matter, and between matter and self[2]. It is only the gods and the best men that may attain salvation through knowledge and grace of God; ordinary men pass through cycles of births and rebirths, and the worst are cursed in hell. Neither the demons nor those who are eternally liberated have to go through a cycle of birth and rebirth. The demons cannot

[1] *ṛg-ādayaś catvāraḥ pañca-rātraṃ ca bhāratam*
mūla-rāmāyaṇam Brahma-sūtram mānaṃ svataḥ smṛtam.
Mahābhārata-tātparya-nirṇaya, I. 30.
a-viruddhaṃ tu yat tv asya pramāṇaṃ tac ca nānyathā
etad-viruddhaṃ yat tu syān na tan mānaṃ kathañcana
vaiṣṇavāni purāṇāni pāñcarātrātmakatvataḥ
pramāṇāny evam manvādyāḥ smṛtayo'py anukūlataḥ.
Ibid. I. 31–32.

[2] *jagat-pravāhaḥ satyo'yaṃ pañca-bheda-samanvitaḥ*
jīveśayor bhidā caiva jīva-bhedaḥ paras-param
jaḍeśayor jaḍānāṃ ca jaḍa-jīva-bhidā tathā
pañca bhedā ime nityāḥ sarvāvasthāsu nityaśaḥ
muktānāṃ ca na hīyante tāratamyaṃ ca sarvadā.
Ibid. I. 69–71.

under any circumstances attain salvation. The theory of eternal damnation is thus found only in Madhva, and in no other system of Indian philosophy. Men can attain salvation when they worship God as being associated with all good qualities and as being blissful and omniscient. Even in the state of liberation there are individual differences between the selves, and the perfect and desireless (*niṣkāma*) worship of God is the only means of salvation. It is only through devotion (*bhakti*) that there can be liberation; even the emancipated enjoy the eternal flow of pleasure through devotion; *bhakti*, or devotion, is here defined as an affection with the full consciousness of the greatness of the object of devotion[1], and it is regarded as the universal solvent. Even the performance of all religious duties cannot save a man from hell, but *bhakti* can save a man even if he commits the worst sin. Without *bhakti* even the best religious performances turn into sin, and with *bhakti* even the worst sins do not affect a man. God is pleased only with *bhakti* and nothing else, and He alone can give salvation.

In the second chapter Madhva says that in the *Mahābhārata-tātparya-nirṇaya* he tries to summarize the essential teachings of the *Mahābhārata*, the text of which in his time had become thoroughly corrupt; and that, difficult as the *Mahābhārata* itself is, it had become still more difficult to get to the root of it from these corrupt texts. He further says that in order to arrive at the correct reading he had procured the text of the *Mahābhārata* from various countries and that it is only by comparison of these different texts that he made his attempt to formulate its essential teachings in consonance with the teachings of other *śāstras* and the Vedas[2]. According to Madhva the *Mahābhārata* is an allegory, which shows a struggle between good and evil; the good representing the Pāṇḍavas, and the evil representing the sons of Dhṛtarāṣṭra. The object of the *Mahābhārata* is to show the greatness of Viṣṇu. Madhva does not follow the order of the story as given in the *Mahābhārata*, he omits most of the incidental episodes, and supplements the story with others culled from other *Purāṇas* and

[1] *bhaktyarthāny akhilāny eva bhaktir mokṣāya kevalā*
muktānam api bhaktir hi nityānanda-sva-rūpiṇī
jñāna-pūrva-para-sneho nityo bhaktir itīryate.
Mahābhārata-tātparya-nirṇaya, I. 106–7.

[2] *śāstrāntarāṇi sañjānan vedāṃś cāsya prasādataḥ*
deśe deśe tathā granthān dṛṣṭvā caiva pṛthagvidhān. *Ibid.* II. 7.

the *Rāmāyaṇa*. Thus he gives a summary of the *Rāmāyaṇa* and also the story of Kṛṣṇa in the *Bhāgavata-purāṇa* as being a part of the *Mahābhārata*. In his treatment of the general story also he insists on the super-excellence of Bhīma and Kṛṣṇa.

There are several commentaries on this work of Madhva, viz., that by Janārdana Bhaṭṭa, called the *Padārtha-dīpikā;* by Varadarāja, called the *Mahāsubodhinī* or the *Prakāśa;* by Vādirājasvāmī; by Viṭṭhalācārya-sūnu; by Vyāsa-tīrtha; the *Durghaṭārthaprakāśikā*, by Satyābhinava Yati: the *Mahābhārata-tātparya-nirṇaya-vyākhyā* (called also the *Padārthadīpikā*); the *Mahābhārata-tātparya-nirṇaya-vyākhyā* (called also *Bhāvacandrikā*), by Śrīnivāsa; and the *Mahābhārata-tātparya-nirṇayānukramaṇikā*, which is a small work giving a general summary of the work in verse. There were also other commentaries by Kṛṣṇācārya, Lakṣmaṇa Siṃha and Jayakhaṇḍin Siṃha.

In the *Bhāgavata-tātparya-nirṇaya* Madhva selects some of the important verses from the twelve *skandhas* of the *Bhāgavata-purāṇa*, and adds short annotations with the selected verses from the selected chapters of each of the *skandhas*. These are not continuous, and many of the chapters are sometimes dropped altogether; they are also brief, and made in such a manner that his own dualistic view may appear to be the right interpretation of the *Bhāgavata*. He sometimes supports his views by reference to the other *Purāṇas*, and in conclusion he gives a short summary of his view as representing the true view of the *Bhāgavata*. The *Bhāgavata-tātparya-nirṇaya* is commented upon by various writers; some of the commentaries are *Bhāgavata-tātparya-vyākhyā* (called also *Tātparya-bodhinī*), *Bhāgavata-tātparya-nirṇaya-vyākhyā-vivaraṇa*, *Bhāgavata-tātparya-nirṇaya-vyākhyā-prabodhinī*, *Bhāgavata-tātparya-nirṇaya-vyākhyā-padya-ratnāvalī*, *Bhāgavata-tātparya-nirṇaya-vyākhyā-prakāśa*, by Śrīnivāsa (a brief work in prose), and *Bhāgavata-tātparya-nirṇaya-ṭīkā*, by Jadupati, Chalāri and Vedagarbhanārāyanācārya.

The *Gītā-tātparya* of Madhva is a work in prose and verse, giving a summary of the essence of the *Gītā* as understood by Madhva. It is a continuous summary of all the eighteen chapters of the *Gītā* in serial order. The summary, however, often quotes verses from the *Gītā*, which, however, are sometimes interrupted by small prose texts serving as links, sometimes of an explanatory nature, sometimes referring to *purāṇic* and other texts in support of Madhva's interpretations, and sometimes introducing the context and the purpose of the verses of the *Gītā*—they sometimes introduce also discussions in prose against the monistic interpretation of the *Gītā* by Śaṅkara. The *Tātparya*, a work of about 1450 *granthas*, is commented upon by the famous Madhva author Jayatīrtha; the commentary is called *Bhagavad-gītā-tātparya-nirṇaya-vyākhyā* or *Nyāya-dīpikā*. This *Nyāya-dīpikā* was commented upon by Viṭṭhala-suta-śrīnivāsācārya or Tāmraparṇī-śrīnivāsācārya in a work called *Tātparya-dīpikā-vyākhyā-nyāya-dīpa-kiraṇāvalī*. The *Bhagavadgītā-tātparya* had at least two other commentaries, the *Tātparya-ṭippanī*, by Padmanābha-tīrtha, and the *Nyāya-dīpa-bhāva-prakāśa*, by Satyaprajña-bhikṣu. In addition to this Madhva wrote also a work styled *Gītā-bhāṣya*, in which he takes up the important *ślokas*, chapter by chapter, and in the course of commenting on them discusses many important problems of a controversial nature. Thus, following Kumārila, he says that it is because the *śāstra* is *aparijñeya* (of transcendent origin) that there is an absolute validity of the *śāstras*. Regarding the performance of *karmas* he says that they are to be performed because of the injunctions of the *śāstras*, without any desire for fruit. The only desires that should not be abandoned are for greater knowledge and a greater rise of *bhakti;* even if the *karmas* do not produce any fruit, they will at least produce the satisfaction of the Lord, because in following the injunctions of the *śāstras* the individual has obeyed the commands of God. He also controverts the Śaṅkara-view of monism, and says that, if God reflects Himself in men, the reflection cannot be identified with the original. The so-called *upādhi* or condition is supposed to make the difference between the Brahman and the individual. It is not also correct to say that, as water mixes with water, so also the individual at the time of salvation meets with God and there is no difference between them; for even when water mixes with water, there is difference, which explains the greater accumulation of water. So, in the state of salvation, the individual only comes closer to God, but never loses his personality. His state of *mokṣa* is said to be the most desirable because here one is divested of all sorrowful experiences, and has nothing to desire for oneself. It is in accordance with the difference in personality of different individuals; the state of salvation differs with each person. The common element in the state of salvation is the fact that no emancipated person has to suffer any painful experience. Madhva also takes great pains to show that Nārāyaṇa or Viṣṇu is the greatest or the highest Lord. In dealing with the third chapter he says that in the beginningless world even one *karma* may lead to many births and the accumulated store of *karmas* could never have yielded their full fruits to any person; therefore, even if one does not do any *karma*, he cannot escape the fruits which are in store for him as the result of his past *karmas;* consequently no good can be attained by the non-performance of *karma*. It is only the *karma* performed without any motive or desire that associates with knowledge and leads to salvation; so the non-performance of *karma* can never lead to salvation by itself. Madhva repudiates the idea that salvation can be attained by death in holy places, as the latter can only be attained by knowledge of Brahman. One is forced to perform the *karmas* by the force of one's internal *saṃskāras* or sub-conscious tendencies. It is unnecessary to show in further detail that in this way Madhva interprets the *Gītā* in support of his own doctrines; and he also often tries to show that the view propounded by him is in consonance with the teachings of other *Purāṇas* and the Upaniṣads. There is a number of works on Madhva's interpretation of the *Gītā: Gītārtha-saṃgraha* by Rāghavendra, *Gītā-vivṛti* by Rāghavendra Yati, *Gītā-vivṛti* by Vidyadhiraja Bhaṭṭopadhyaya, and *Prameya-dīpikā* by Jaya-tīrtha, which has a further commentary on it, called *Bhāva-prakāśa*. Madhva wrote another commentary on the *Brahma-sūtra*, the *Brahma-sūtra-bhāṣya*. It is a small work of about 2500 *granthas*, and the commentary is brief and suggestive[1]. He wrote also another work, the *Anubhāṣya*, which is a brief summary of the main contents and purport of the *Brahma-sūtra*. This has also a number of commentaries, by Jaya-tīrtha, Ananta Bhaṭṭa, Chalāri-nṛsiṃha, Rāghavendra-tīrtha and Śeṣācārya. There is also a work called *Adhikaraṇārtha-saṃgraha*, by Padmanābhācārya. The *Brahma-sūtra-bhāṣya* of Ānanda-tīrtha has a commentary by Jaya-tīrtha, called *Tattva-prakāśikā*. This has a number of commentaries: the *Tātparya-prakāśikā-bhāva-bodha* and the *Tātparya-prakāśikā-gata-nyāya-vivaraṇa* by Raghūttama Yati, and *Bhāva-dīpikā* or *Tattva-prakāśikā-ṭippaṇī*, the *Tantra-dīpikā*,

[1] A verse containing thirty-two letters is called a *grantha*.

by Rāghavendra Yati, *Tātparya-candrikā*, by Vyāsa-tīrtha, which had other commentaries, viz. the *Tātparya-candrikā-prakāśa* by Keśava Yati, *Tātparya-candrikā-nyāya-vivaraṇa* by Timmannācārya (or Timmapura-raghunāthācārya), and *Tātparya-candrikodāharaṇa-nyāya-vivaraṇa*. Besides these the *Tattva-prakāśikā* had other commentaries; the *Abhinava-candrikā* by Satyanātha Yati, one by Śrīnivāsa called *Tattva-prakāśikā-vākyārtha-mañjarī*, and also the *Vākyārtha-muktāvalī* by the same author. The *Tātparya-candrikā* had another commentary, by Gururāja, and the *Tattva-prakāśikā* had another, the *Tantra-dīpikā*. The *Bhāṣya* of Madhva was also commented upon by Jagannātha Yati (the *Bhāṣya-dīpikā*), by Viṭṭhala-suta-śrīnivāsa (the *Bhāṣya-ṭippaṇī-prameya-muktāvalī*), by Vādiraja (the *Gurvartha-dīpikā*), by Tāmraparṇī-śrīnivāsa, and by Sumatīndra-tīrtha. There are also two others, the *Brahma-sūtra-bhāṣyārtha-saṃgraha* and the *Brahma-sūtrārtha*. The *Anubhāṣya* of Madhva was commented upon by Nṛsiṃha, Jaya-tīrtha, Ananta Bhaṭṭa, Chalāri-nṛsiṃha, Rāghavendra-tīrtha and Śeṣācārya. Further, Madhva wrote another work on the *Brahma-sūtra* called the *Anuvyākhyāna*. This was commented upon by Jaya-tīrtha in his *Pañjikā* and *Nyāya-sudhā*, and also by Jadupati and Śrīnivāsa-tīrtha. There is also another commentary on it, called *Brahma-sūtrānuvyākhyāna-nyāya-saṃbandha-dīpikā*. Of these the *Nyāya-sudhā* of Jaya-tīrtha is an exceedingly recondite work of great excellence. *Anuvyākhyāna* is commented upon by Raghūttama in his *Nyāya-sūtra-nibandha-pradīpa* and also in his *Anuvyākhyāna-ṭīkā*. The *Nyāya-sudhā* itself was commented on by several writers. Thus we have commentaries by Śrīnivāsa-tīrtha, Jadupati, Viṭṭhala-sutānanda-tīrtha, by Keśava Bhaṭṭa (the *Śeṣa-vākyārtha-candrikā*), by Rāmacandra-tīrtha, Kuṇḍalagirisūri, Vidyādhīśa, Timmannārya, Vādirāja, and Rāghavendra Yati. We have also the *Nyāyasudhopanyāsa*, by Śrīpadarāja. The *Anuvyākhyāna* is a small work in verse which follows chapter by chapter the essential logical position of all the *Brahma-sūtras*. Madhva says there that in rendering the interpretations he followed the trustworthy scriptural texts—the Vedas—and also logical reasoning[1]. He further says in the introduction that it is for the purpose of clearing his views in a proper manner that

[1] *ātma-vākyatayā tena śruti-mūlatayā tathā*
yukti-mūlatayā caiva prāmāṇyaṃ trividhaṃ mahat.
Anuvyākhyāna, I. I.

he writes the *Anuvyākhyāna*, though he had already written a *bhāṣya* on the *Brahma-sūtra*. He says in the first chapter that the Oṃkāra which designates the Brahman and which is also the purport of Gāyatrī is also the purport of all the Vedas and one should seek to know it. Those who seek to know the Brahman please God by such an endeavour, and by His grace are emancipated. The existence of all things, actions, time, character and selves depends upon God, and they may cease to exist at His will. God gives knowledge to the ignorant and salvation to the wise. The source of all bliss for the emancipated person is God Himself. All bondage is real, for it is perceived as such; nor is there any means by which one can prove the falsity of bondage, for if there were any proofs of its falsity, the proofs must be existent, and that would destroy the monistic view. The mere one cannot split itself into proof and the object of proof. So all experiences should be regarded as real. That which we find in consonance with practical behaviour should be regarded as real. The monists assert that there are three kinds of existence, but they cannot adduce any proofs. If the universe were really non-existent, how could it affect anybody's interests in a perverse manner? Brahman cannot be regarded as being only pure "being," and the world-appearance cannot be regarded as false, for it is never negated in experience. If this world is to be known as different from pure non-being or the non-existent, then the non-existent has also to be known, which is impossible. It has been suggested that illusion is an example of non-existence, viz., the appearance of a thing as that which it is not. This virtually amounts to the assertion that appearance consists only of a being which does not exist, and this is also said to be indefinable. But such a position leads to a vicious infinite, because the reality of many entities has to depend on another and that on another and so on. Existence of a thing depends upon that which is not being negated, and its not being negated depends upon further experience and so on. Moreover, if the pure differenceless entity is self-luminous, how can it be covered by *ajñāna*? Again, unless it is possible to prove the existence of *ajñāna*, the existence of falsehood as a category cannot be proved. It is needless, however, for us to follow the whole argument of the *Anuvyākhyāna*, as it will be dealt with in other forms as elaborated by Vyāsa-tīrtha in his *Nyāyāmṛta* in controversy with the *Advaita-siddhi*.

Madhva also wrote a *Pramāṇa-lakṣaṇa*, *Kathā-lakṣaṇa*, *Mithyātvānumāna-khaṇḍana*, *Upādhi-khaṇḍana*, *Māyā-vāda-khaṇḍana*, *Tattva-saṃkhyāna*, *Tattvoddyota*, *Tattva-viveka*, *Viṣṇu-tattva-nirṇaya*, *Karma-nirṇaya*[1]. The *Pramāṇa-lakṣaṇa* has a number of commentaries: *Nyāya-kalpalatā*, by Jaya-tīrtha, *Sannyāya-dīpikā*, and others by Keśava-tīrtha, Pāṇḍuraṅga, Padmanābha-tīrtha, and Caṇḍakeśava. The *Nyāya-kalpalatā* of Jaya-tīrtha is a work of 1450 *granthas*; it has a commentary called *Nyāya-kalpalatā-vyākhyā*, by two other authors. One of them is a pupil of Vidyādhīśa Yati, but nothing is known about the author of the other work. There are also two other commentaries, the *Prabodhinī* and the *Nyāya-mañjarī*, by Caṇḍakeśavācārya. Other works relating to the same subject (the Madhva logic) are the *Nyāya-muktāvalī*, by Rāghavendra Yati, *Nyāya-mauktikā-mālā*, by Vijayīndra, and *Nyāya-ratnāvalī*, by Vādiraja. Jaya-tīrtha himself wrote a work called *Pramāṇa-paddhati*, which has a large number of commentaries (by Ananta Bhaṭṭa, Vedeśa-bhikṣu, Vijayīndra, Viṭṭhala Bhaṭṭa, Satyanātha Yati, Nṛsiṃha-tīrtha, Rāghavendra-tīrtha, Nārāyaṇa Bhaṭṭa, Janārdana Bhaṭṭa, and two others by unknown authors, the *Bhāva-dīpa* and the *Padārtha-candrikā*). The *Kathā-lakṣaṇa* of Madhva was commented on by Padmanābha-tīrtha, Keśava Bhaṭṭāraka, and Jaya-tīrtha. The *Mithyātvānumāna-khaṇḍana* of Madhva has at least four commentaries, by Jaya-tīrtha, the fourth being the *Mandāra-mañjarī*. The *Upādhi-khaṇḍana* has at least three commentaries, by Jaya-tīrtha, Ananta Bhaṭṭa and Śrīnivāsa-tīrtha. Both Śrīnivāsa-tīrtha and Padmanābha-tīrtha wrote commentaries on Jaya-tīrtha's commentary named *Upādhi-khaṇḍana-vyākhyā-vivaraṇa*. The *Māyā-vāda-khaṇḍana* of Madhva was commented upon by Jaya-tīrtha, Śrīnivāsa-tīrtha, Vyāsa-tīrtha, Keśavamiśra, Ananta Bhaṭṭa and Padmanābha-tīrtha. The *Tattva-saṃkhyāna* of Madhva was commented upon by Jaya-tīrtha, Śrīnivāsa-tīrtha, Ananta Bhaṭṭa, Veṅkaṭādrisūri, Satyaprajña Yati, Satyaprajña-tīrtha, Maudgala Narasiṃhācārya, Timmannācārya, Gururāja and Yadupati. The commentary of Jaya-tīrtha, the *Tattva-saṃkhyāna-vivaraṇa*, was commented upon by Satya-dharma Yati (*Satya-dharma-ṭippana*). The *Tattvoddyota* of Madhva

[1] These ten works of Madhva are called the *daśaprakaraṇa*. Sometimes, however, the *Mithyātvānumāna-khaṇḍana* is replaced by *Ṛgveda-brahma-pañcikā*.

was commented upon by Jaya-tīrtha, Yadupati, Vedeśa-bhikṣu, Padmanābha-tīrtha, Śrīnivāsa-tīrtha, Narapaṇḍita, Rāghavendra-tīrtha, Vijayīndra, Gururāja (or Keśava Bhaṭṭāraka). The *Tattva-viveka* of Madhva was commented upon by Jaya-tīrtha, Ananta Bhaṭṭa and Śrīnivāsa-tīrtha.

In the *Kathā-lakṣaṇa*, Madhva tries to give an estimate of the nature of various wholesome discussions (*vāda*) as distinguished from unwholesome discussions (wrangling, *vitaṇḍā*). *Vāda* is discussion between the teacher and the pupil for the elucidation of different problems or between two or more pupils who are interested in the discovery of truth by reasoning. When this discussion, however, takes place through egotism, through a spirit of emulation, for the sake of victory through controversy, or for the attainment of fame, the discussion is called *jalpa*. Unwholesome discussion, *vitaṇḍā*, is undertaken for the purpose of discrediting the true points of view by specious argument. There may be one or more presidents (*praśnika*) in a discussion, but such a person or persons should be strictly impartial. All discussions must be validly based, on the scriptural texts, and these should not be wrongly interpreted by specious argument[1]. The *Kathā-lakṣaṇa* of Madhva seems to have been based on a work called *Brahma-tarka*. The nature of *vāda*, *jalpa*, and *vitaṇḍā* according to the Nyāya philosophy has already been treated in the first volume of the present work[2].

It is unnecessary to enter into the *Prapañca-mithyātvānumāna-khaṇḍana*, *Upādhi-khaṇḍana* and *Māyāvāda-khaṇḍana*, because the main subject-matter of these tracts has been dealt with in our treatment of Vyāsa-tīrtha's *Nyāyāmṛta* in controversy with the *Advaita-siddhi*.

The *Tattva-saṃkhyāna* is a small tract of eleven verses which relates in brief some of the important tenets of Madhva's doctrines. Thus it says that there are two categories—the independent and the dependent; Viṣṇu alone is independent. The category of the dependent is of two kinds—the existent and the non-existent. The non-existent or the negation is of three kinds—negation before production (*prāgabhāva*), negation by destruction (*dhvaṃsā-*

[1] Mr Nāgarāja Śarma has summarized the contents of the *Kathā-lakṣaṇa*, utilizing the materials of the commentators Jaya-tīrtha, Rāghavendrasvāmi and Vedeśa-tīrtha, in the *Reign of Realism*.

[2] On the subject of the nature of *kathā* and the conditions of disputation see also *Khaṇḍana-khaṇḍa-khādya*, pp. 20 ff., Benares, 1914.

bhāva), and universal negation (*atyantābhāva*). The existents are again conscious or unconscious. The conscious entities are again twofold, those who are associated with sorrows and those who are not so. Those who are associated with sorrows are again twofold, viz., those who are emancipated and those who are in sorrow. Those who are in sorrow are again twofold, viz., those who are worthy of salvation and those who are not. There are others who are not worthy of salvation at any time. The worst men, the demons, the *rākṣasas* and the *piśācas* are not worthy of salvation at any time. Of these there are two kinds, viz., those who are already damned in hell and those who pursue the course of *saṃsāra* but are doomed to hell. The unconscious entities are again threefold, the eternal, the non-eternal, and the partly eternal and partly non-eternal. The Vedas alone are eternal. The sacred literature of the *Purāṇas*, time and *prakṛti* are both eternal and non-eternal; for, when in essence the teachings of the *Purāṇas* are eternal, time and *prakṛti* are eternal; in their evolution they are non-eternal. The non-eternal again is twofold—the created and the uncreated (*saṃsliṣṭa* and *asaṃsliṣṭa*). The uncreated ones are *mahat*, *aham*, *buddhi*, *manas*, the senses, the *tanmātras* and the five *bhūtis*. The world and all that exists in the world are created. Creation really means being prompted into activities, and as such the created entities undergo various stages: God alone is the inward mover of all things and all changes. The *Tattva-viveka* of Madhva is as small a work as the *Tattva-saṃkhyāna*, consisting only of a dozen *granthas*, and deals more or less with the same subject: it is therefore unnecessary to give a general summary of its contents.

The *Tattvoddyota*, however, is a somewhat longer work in verse and prose. It starts with a question, whether there is a difference between the emancipated souls, and Madhva says that the emancipated souls are different from God because they had been emancipated at a particular time. They cannot be both different and non-different from God, for that would be meaningless. The concept of *anirvacanīya* of the Vedāntists has no illustration to support it. Madhva takes pains to refute the theory of *anirvacanīya* with the help of scriptural texts, and he holds that the so-called falsity of the Śaṅkarites cannot be supported by perception, inference or implication. There is no reason to think that the world-appearances as such cannot be negated[1]. He further says that, if everything in the world were false, then the allegation that the world would be contradicted in experience would also be false. If the contradiction of the world be false, then virtually it amounts to saying that the world-experience is never contradicted. If it is said that the world-appearance is different from being and if the predicate "being" means the class-concept of being, then it is a virtual admission of a plurality of existents, without which the class-concept of being is impossible. If however the predicate "being" means pure being, then, since such a pure "being" is only Brahman, its difference from the world would be an intelligible proposition, and it would not prove the so-called *anirvacanīya*. It is said that falsity is that which is different from both being and non-being, and that would virtually amount to saying that that which is not different is alone true[2]. On such a supposition the plurality of causes or of effects or the diversities of grounds in inferences must all be discarded as false, and knowledge would be false. Knowledge implies diversity; for the knower, the knowledge and the object of knowledge cannot be the same. Again, it is wrong to hold that ignorance rests in the object of knowledge or the Brahman; for the ignorance always belongs to the knowledge. If on the occasion of knowledge it is held that the ignorance belonging to the objects is removed, then, the ignorance being removed in the object by one person's knowledge of it, all persons should be able to know the object. If any knowing of the jug means that the ignorance resting in the jug is removed, then, the ignorance being removed, the jug should be known even by persons who are not present here[3]. Again, if by the knowledge of any object the ignorance resting in another object be removed, then by the knowledge of the jug the ignorance in other objects could be removed.

Again, a material object is that which never can be a knower.

[1] *na ca bādhyaṃ jagad ity atra kiñcin mānam.*
Tattvoddyota, p. 242.

[2] *sad-vilakṣaṇatvam a-sad-vilakṣaṇatvaṃ ca mithyā ity a-vilakṣaṇam eva satyaṃ syāt.* *Ibid.* p. 242(*a*).

[3] *nahi jñāna-jñeyayor ekākāratā nahi*
ajñasya ghaṭāśrayatvaṃ brahmāśrayatvaṃ vā
asti; puṃgatam eva hi tamojñānena
nivartate; viṣayāśrayaṃced ajñanaṃ
nivartate tarhi ekena jñātasya ghaṭasya
anyair ajñātatvaṃ na syāt. *Ibid.* p. 242.

For that reason the self, as a knower, can never be regarded as material. But according to the monists the *ātman* which is equalized with Brahman, being without any quality, can never be a knower, and, if it cannot be a knower, it must be of the nature of a material object, which is impossible. Also the self, or the *ātman*, cannot be a false knower, for the category of falsehood as the indefinable (or *anirvacanīya*) has already been refuted. If materiality means non-luminousness (*aprakāśatva*), then we have to admit that the self, which is differenceless, is unable to illumine itself or anything else; and thus the self would be non-luminous. The self cannot illumine itself, because then it would itself be the subject and object of its work of illumination, which is impossible. The other objects, being false (according to the monists), cannot be illuminated either. If they are no objects and if they are only false, they cannot be illuminated. Thus the monists fail to explain the nature of the self-luminousness of Brahman. Again, the argument that things which are limited in time and space are false does not hold either; for time and the *prakṛti* are not limited by time and space, and therefore they cannot be regarded as false, as the monists wish to think. Again, if it *did* hold, things which are limited by their own nature and character would consequently be false. Thus, the selves would be false, since they are different from one another in their character.

Moreover, the world is perceived as true and real, and there is no one who has experienced it to be false (the perception of the smallness of the sun or of the moon is an illusion, due to the distance from which they are seen; such conditions do not hold regarding the world as we perceive it). There is no reason which supports the view that the world is the product of ignorance. Again, the analogy of a magician and his magic is inapplicable to the world; for the magician does not perceive his magic creation, nor is he deluded by it. But in the case under discussion God (the Īśvara) perceives His own creation. Therefore the world cannot be regarded as magic or *māyā*; for God perceives everything directly. Thus, from whatever point of view one may discuss the doctrine of *māyā*, one finds it untenable, and there are no proofs which can support it.

Madhva further holds that in the *Brahma-sūtra*, Book II, not only are various other philosophies refuted but that even the monistic doctrine has been refuted. The refutation of Buddhism is in reality also a refutation of the monists, who are in reality nothing but crypto-Buddhists or Buddhists in disguise[1]. The *śūnyavādi* Buddhists hold that truth is of two kinds, that which is *saṃvṛta*, or of limited or practical importance only, and that which is *paramārtha*, or ultimately real. If one truly discusses the nature of things, there is no reality, and what is perceived as real is only an appearance. What is called the *pāramārthika* reality means only the cessation of all appearance[2]. There is no difference between the qualityless Brahman and the *śūnya* of the Buddhists. The qualityless Brahman is self-luminous and eternal; the *śūnya* of the Buddhists is unknowable by mind or speech, and is also differenceless, self-luminous, and eternal. It is opposed to materiality, to practicality, to pain and suffering, and to cessation and the defects of bondage[3]. It is not actually a real-positive entity, though it supports all positive appearance; and, though in itself it is eternal, from the practical point of view it appears in manifold characters. It is neither existent nor non-existent, neither good, nor bad—it is not a thing which one should either leave aside or take, for it is the eternal *śūnya*[4]. It may be observed in this connection that the monists also do not believe in the reality of the characters of being and non-being, because the Brahman is devoid of all characters and qualities. Like *śūnya* of the Buddhists, it is unspeakable, though it is referred to by all words, and it is unknowable, though all knowledge refers to it. Neither the Śaṅkarites nor the Śūnyavādins believe in the category of being or positivity as characters. The

[1] *na ca nir-viśeṣa-brahma-vādinaḥ śunyāt kaś cid viśeṣaḥ,*
tasya nirviśeṣaṃ svayaṃbhūtaṃ nirlepam ajarāmaraṃ
śūnyaṃ tattvaṃ vijñeyaṃ manovācām agocaram.
Tattvoddyota, p. 243(*a*).

[2] *satyaṃ ca dvividhaṃ proktaṃ saṃvṛtam pāramarthikaṃ*
saṃvṛtaṃ vyavahāryaṃ syān nirvṛtaṃ pāramārthikaṃ
vicāryamānena satyañ cāpi pratīyate yasya tat saṃvṛtaṃ jñānaṃ vyavahāra-padañ ca yat. *Ibid.* p. 243(*a*).

[3] *nir-viśeṣaṃ svayaṃ bhūtaṃ nirlepam ajarāmaraṃ*
śūnyaṃ tattvam avijñeyaṃ manovācām agocaraṃ
jāḍya-saṃvṛti-duḥkhānta-pūrva-doṣa-virodhi yat
nitya-bhāvanayā bhātaṃ tad bhāvaṃ yogināṃ nayet
bhāvārtha-pratiyogitvaṃ bhāvatvaṃ vā na tattvata
viśvākārañca saṃvṛtya yasya tat padam akṣayam.
Ibid. p. 243(*a*).

[4] *nāsya sattvam asattvaṃ vā na doṣo guṇa eva vā*
heyopādeya-rahitaṃ tac chūnyaṃ padam akṣayam.
Ibid. p. 243.

Śūnyavādin does not regard the *śūnya* or the void as a character. The view of the Śaṅkarites, therefore, is entirely different from belief in a personal God, endowed with characters and qualities (which is the general purport of all valid scriptural texts). If the Brahman be void of all characters, it is beyond all determination. The monists think that the Brahman is absoluteless, differenceless, and this precludes them from resorting to any argument in support of their view; for all arguments presuppose relativity and difference. In the absence of any valid argument, and in the face of practical experience of the reality of the world, there is indeed nothing which can establish the monistic view. All arguments that would prove the falsity of the world will fall within the world-appearance and be themselves false. If all selves were identical, then there would be no difference between the emancipated and the un-emancipated ones. If it is held that all difference is due to ignorance, then God, who has no ignorance, would perceive Himself as one with all individual selves, and thus share their sufferings; but the scriptural text of the *Gītā* definitely shows that God perceives Himself as different from ordinary individual selves. The experience of suffering cannot also be due to *upādhi* (or condition) which may act as a limit; for in spite of diversity of conditions the experiencer remains the same. Moreover, since God is free from all conditions, the difference of conditions ought not to prevent Him from perceiving His equality with all beings in sharing their sufferings. Those also who hold that there is only one individual and that all misconceptions are due to Him are wrong; for at his death there should be cessation of the differences. There is also no proof in support of the view that all notion of difference and the appearance of the world is due to the misconception of only one individual. Thus there are no proofs in support of the monistic view as held by the Śaṅkarites. It is therefore time that the upholders of the *māyā* doctrine should flee, now that the omniscient Lord is coming to tear asunder the darkness of specious arguments and false interpretations of spiritual texts[1].

The *Karma-nirṇaya* of Madhva deals with the nature of *karma* or scriptural duties, which forms the subject-matter of the

[1] *palāyadhvaṃ palāyadhvaṃ tvarayā māyi-dānavāḥ*
sarvajño harir āyāti tarkāgama-darāribhid.
Tattvoddyota, p. 245 (*a*).

Pūrva-mīmāṃsā. The *Pūrva-mīmāṃsā* not only practically ignores the existence of God but also denies it. Madhva was himself a great believer in a personal God and therefore wished to interpret the Mīmāṃsā in an authentic manner. He held that the various gods, e.g., Indra or Agni, stood for Viṣṇu or Nārāyaṇa. The *Pūrva-mīmāṃsā* was satisfied with providing for heaven as the object of all performance of sacrifices, but with Madhva the ultimate goal was true knowledge and the attainment of emancipation through the grace of God. He disliked the idea that the scriptural sacrifices are to be performed with the object of attaining heaven, and he emphasized his notion that they should be performed without any motive; with him they should be performed merely because they are religious injunctions or the commands of God. He further held that it is only by such motiveless performance of actions that the mind could be purified for the attainment of the grace of God. The motiveless performance of sacrifices is therefore in a way preliminary and accessory to the attainment of wisdom and the grace of God.

Thus, as usual, Madhva tries to refute the argument of the monists against the possibility of possession by God of infinite attributes and in favour of a differenceless Brahma. He further says that the texts such as *satyam*, *jñānam*, *anantam*, *Brahma*, which apparently inspires a qualityless Brahman, are to be subordinated to other texts which are of a dualistic nature. Proceeding by way of inference, he says that the world, being of the nature of an effect, must have an intelligent cause—a maker—and this maker is God. The maker of this world must necessarily be associated with omniscience and omnipotence. Madhva cites the evidence of the *Bhāgavata-purāṇa* in favour of a *saguṇa* Brahma, a Brahma associated with qualities. Where the texts refer to Brahman as *nirguṇa*, the idea is that the Brahman is not associated with any bad qualities. Also the Brahman cannot be devoid of all determination, *viśeṣa*; the denial of determination is itself a determination, and as such would have to be denied by the monists; and this would necessarily lead to the affirmation of the determination. Madhva then resorts to his old arguments against *māyā*, *mithyā*, and *anirvacanīya*, and points out that the logic of excluded middle would rule out the possibility of a category which is neither *sat* nor *asat*. There is really no instance of a so-called *anirvacanīya*. An illusion, after it is contradicted, is sometimes pointed out as an instance of *anirvacanīya*, but this is wholly wrong; for in the case of an illusion something was actually perceived by the senses but interpreted wrongly. The fact that something was actually in contact with the visual sense is undisputed; and, when the illusion is contradicted, the contradiction means the discovery that an object which was believed to be there is not there. The object that was erroneously perceived—e.g., a snake—was a real object, but it did not exist where it was thought to exist. To say that the illusion is false (*mithyā*) only means that the object illusorily perceived does not exist there. The mere fact that an object was illusorily perceived cannot mean that it was really existent; and nevertheless its non-existence was contradicted; so it was neither existent nor non-existent. The only legitimate point of view is that the illusorily perceived object did not exist while it was perceived, i.e. it was *asat*. The rope which was perceived as "snake" is later on contradicted, when the perception of "snake" disappears; but the world as such has never been found to disappear. Thus there is no similarity between the perception of the world and the perception of the illusory snake. Moreover that which is *anirvacanīya* is so called because it is hard to describe it on account of its uniqueness, but that does not prove that it is a category which is neither existent nor non-existent. Though it may be sufficiently described, still one may not exhaust its description. A jar is different from a cloth and also different from the merely chimerical hare's horn, viz., a jar is different from an existent cloth and a non-existent hare's horn; but that does not make a jar *anirvacanīya*, or false. The jar as shown above is *sadasad-vilakṣaṇa*, but it is not on that account non-existent.

Again, the meaning of the phrase *sadasad-vilakṣaṇa* is very vague. In the first place, if it means the conception of a difference (*bheda*), then the meaning is inconsistent. The monists hold that only the Brahman exists, and therefore, if the difference between the existent and the non-existent exists, there will be dualism. But in reply it may be held that the affirmation of dualism is only possible as a lower degree of reality which is called the *vyāvahārika*. The meaning of this word is not clear. It cannot mean a category which is different from both being and non-being, since such a category is logically invalid. If it means only conditional being, then even the conception of the highest reality is conditioned by human knowledge, and is therefore conditional (*vyāvahārika*); and the application of the term to illusory perception or normal perception alone is doubtful. In the second place, the term *sadasad-vilakṣaṇa* also cannot mean identity between the Brahman and the world; for such identity is open to contradiction. The monists can therefore affirm neither the reality of difference nor the reality of absolute identity between the world and Brahman.

The view of the monists that there are different degrees of reality, and that there is identity between them in essence and difference only in appearance, cannot be established, unless the truth of degrees of reality can be established. They hold that the world (which has an inferior degree of reality) is superimposed on the Brahman, or that Brahman has manifested Himself as the world; but such an expression is invalid if there is absolute identity between the world and the Brahman. The phrase "absolute identity" would be merely a tautology, and the scriptural texts so interpreted would be tautological. The monists argue that even identical expressions have *satyaṃ jñānaṃ anantam*, and are not tautological, because they serve to exclude their negatives. To style Brahman "*satya*" or "*jñāna*" means that Brahman is not *asatya* and *ajñāna*. But such an interpretation would destroy their contention that all the scriptural epithets have an *akhaṇḍārtha*, i.e., refer to one differenceless Brahman; for according to their own interpretation the scriptural epithets do not have only one significance (viz., the affirmation of pure differenceless being), but also the negation of other qualities; and in that case the final significance of all scriptural epithets as referring to the differenceless Brahman is contradicted. Again, the *anirvacanīyatā* of the world depends upon a false analysis of illusion; and so the statement that the differencelessness of Brahman depends on the very illusoriness of the world is not established by any monist by any valid argument. The difference between the world-appearance and Brahman cannot be regarded by the monists as ultimately real; for in that case "difference" is a category having a co-existent reality with Brahman. Again, the concept of difference between the existent and the non-existent requires classification; and, unless this is done, the mere assertion that the world-appearance is both identical with and different from Brahman would have no meaning.

That which is different from the non-existent is existent and that which is different from the existent is non-existent or chimerical. The non-existent has no determination; for it cannot be known by any means, and as such its difference from the existent cannot be known either, since to know the difference between two entities one must know the two entities fully. No one can argue about whether the hare's horn is different or not different from a tree. Again, if *sat* or "existent" means the ultimately differenceless real, then, since such a difference has no character in it, it is not possible to form any concept of its difference from any other thing. Thus it is not possible to form any concept of anything which is different from the existent and also from the non-existent; if the world is different from the non-existent, it must be real; and if the world is different from the existent, it must be the hare's horn. The law of excluded middle again rules out the existence of anything which is neither existent nor non-existent; in a pair of contradictory judgments one must be right. Thus the reality of Brahman is endowed with all qualities and as a creator and sustainer of the world He cannot be denied.

Madhva then contends with the Prabhākaras, who hold that the ultimate import of propositions must lead to the performance of an action. If that were the case, the Vedic propositions would never have any import implying the reality of Brahman; for Brahman cannot be the object of the activity of man. Madhva holds that the purpose of all Vedic texts is the glorification of God; and, further, that what is effected by activity among finite human beings is already pre-established with infinite God. All actions imply *iṣṭasādhanatā* (pleasurable motive) and not mere activity. Nothing will be put into action by any man which is distinctly injurious to him. If the chief emphasis of all actions thus be *iṣṭasādhanatā*, then the assertion of the Mīmāmṣā school, that the import of all possibilities is *kāryatā*, is false; *iṣṭasādhanatā* includes *kāryatā*. The supreme *iṣṭasādhanatā* of all actions is the attainment of emancipation through the grace of God. It is therefore necessary that all sacrificial actions should be performed with devotion, since it is by devotional worship alone that one can attain the grace of God. The *Karma-nirṇaya* is a small work of less than 400 *granthas*.

In the *Viṣṇu-tattva-nirṇaya*, a work of about 600 *granthas*,

Madhva discusses a number of important problems. He declares that the Vedas, the *Mahābhārata*, the *Pañcarātras*, the *Rāmāyaṇa*, the *Viṣṇu-purāṇa* and all other sacred literature that follows them are to be regarded as valid scriptures (*sad-āgama*). All other texts that run counter to them are to be counted as bad scriptures (*dur-āgama*), and by following them one cannot know the real nature of God. It is neither by perception nor by inference that one can know God; it is only by the Vedas that one can know the nature of God. The Vedas are not produced by any human being (*apauru-ṣeya*); unless the transcendental origin of the Vedas is admitted, there can be no absolute validity of religious duties; all ethical and religious duties will be relative. No human commands can give the assurance of absence of ignorance or absence of false know-ledge; nor can it be supposed that these commands proceed from an omniscient being, for the existence of an omniscient being can-not be known apart from the scriptures. It will be too much to suppose that such an omniscient being is not interested in deceiving us. But, on the other hand, if the Vedas are regarded as not having emanated from any person, we are not forced to make any other supposition; the impersonal origin of the Vedas is valid in itself, because we do not know of any one who has written them. Their utterances are different from other utterances of an ordinary nature, because we know the authors of the latter. The Vedas exist in their own nature and have been revealed only to the sages, and their validity does not depend on anything else; for, unless this is ad-mitted, we can have no absolute criterion of validity and there will be infinite regress. Their validity does not depend on any reasoning; for good reasoning can only show that the process of thought is devoid of logical defects, and cannot by itself establish validity for anything. Since the Vedas are impersonal, the question of the absence of logical defects does not arise. All validity is self-evident; it is non-validity which is proved by later experience. Nor can it be said that the words of Vedic utterances of one syllable are pro-duced at the time of utterance; for in that case they would be recognized as known before. Such recognition cannot be due to similarity; for in that case all recognitions would have to be con-sidered as cases of similarity, which would lead us to the Buddhist view; recognitions are to be considered as illusory. Thus the self-validity of the Vedas has to be accepted as the absolute determinant of all important problems[1]. These Vedas were originally perceived by God; He imparted them to sages, who at the beginning of each creation, remembered the instructions of their previous birth. The alphabets and words are also eternal, as they are always apparent in the mind of the eternal God; so, though the syllables appear in the *ākāśa*, and though the Vedas consist of a conglomeration of them, the Vedas are eternal. The Mīmāṃsā view that the acquirement of words is associated with activity is wrong; for words and their meanings are already definitely settled, and it is only by physical gestures that meanings are acquired by individual people. The purpose of a proposition is finished when it indicates its meaning, and the validity of the proposition is in the realization of such a meaning. While one is acquainted with such a meaning and finds that the direction involved in it, if pursued, will be profitable, one works accordingly, but when one finds it to be injurious one desists from it. All grammars and lexicons are based on the relation already existent between words and their meanings, and no action is implied therein.

All the scriptures refer to Nārāyaṇa as omniscient and the creator of all things. It is wrong to suppose that the scriptures declare the identity of the individual selves with God; for there is no proof for such an assertion.

The existence of God cannot be proved by any inference; for inference of equal force can be adduced against the existence of God. If it is urged that the world, being an effect, must have a creator or maker just as a jug has a potter for its maker, then it may also be urged on the contrary that the world is without any maker, like the self; if it is urged that the self is not an effect and that therefore the counter-argument does not stand, then it may also be urged that all makers have bodies, and since He has no body, God cannot be a creator. Thus the existence of God can only be proved on the testimony of the scriptures, and they hold that God is different from the individual selves. If any scriptural texts seem to indicate the identity of God and self or of God and the world, this will be contradicted by perceptual experience and inference, and consequently the monistic interpretations of these texts would

[1] *vijñeyaṃ paramaṃ Brahma jñāpikā paramā śrutiḥ*
anādi-nityā sā tac ca vinā tāṃ na ca gamyate.
Viṣṇu-tattva-vinirṇaya, p. 206.

be invalid. Now the scriptures cannot suggest anything which is directly contradicted by experience; for, if experience be invalid, then the experience of the validity of the scriptures will also become invalid. The teaching of the scriptures gains additional strength by its consonance with what is perceived by other *pramāṇas*; and, since all the *pramāṇas* point to the reality of diversity, the monistic interpretation of the scriptural texts cannot be accepted as true. When any particular experience is contradicted by a number of other *pramāṇas*, that experience is thereby rendered invalid. It is in this manner that the falsity of the conch-shell-silver is attested What was perceived as silver at a distance was contradicted on closer inspection and by the contact of the hand, and for that reason the conch-shell-silver perceived at a distance is regarded as invalid. An experience which is contradicted by a large number of other *pramāṇas* is by reason of that very fact to be regarded as defective[1]. The comparative value of evidence can be calculated either by its quantity or its quality[2]. There are two classes of qualitative proofs, viz., that which is relative (*upajīvaka*) and that which is independent (*upajīvya*); of these the latter must be regarded as the stronger. Perception and inference are independent sources of evidence, and may therefore be regarded as *upajīvya*, while the scriptural texts are dependent on perception and inference, and are therefore to be regarded as *upajīvaka*. Valid perception precedes inference and is superior to it, for the inference has to depend on perception; thus, if there is a flat contradiction between the scriptural texts and what is universally perceived by all, the scriptural texts have to be so explained that there may not be any such contradiction. By its own nature as a support of all evidence, perception or direct experience, being the *upajīvya*, has a stronger claim to validity[3]. Of the two classes of texts, viz., those which are monistic and those which are dualistic, the latter is supported by perceptual evidence. If it is urged that the purpose of the *śruti*

[1] *bahu-pramāṇa-viruddhānāṃ doṣajanyatva-niyamāt; doṣa-janyatvaṃ ca balavat-pramāṇa-virodhād eva jñāyate.*

aduṣṭam indriyaṃ tv akṣaṃ tarko'duṣṭas tathānumā
āgamo'duṣṭavākyaṃ ca tādṛk cānubhavaḥ smṛtaḥ
balavat-pramāṇataś caiva jñeyā doṣā na cānyathā. *Ibid.* p. 262*a* (4).

[2] *dvi-vidham balavatvañ ca bahutvāc ca svabhāvataḥ.* *Ibid.*

[3] Madhva here states the different kinds of *pramāṇas* according to *Brahmatarka*. The account of the *pramāṇas* is dealt with in a separate section.

texts is to transcend perception and that it is by perception alone that we realize pure being, then it follows that the dualistic texts, which contradict ordinary perception, are to be regarded as more valid on the very ground that they transcend perception. So, whichever way we look at it, the superiority of the duality texts cannot be denied. Again, when a particular fact is supported by many evidences that strengthens the validity of that fact. The fact that God is different from the individual and the world, is attested by many evidences and as such it cannot be challenged; and the final and ultimate import of all the Vedic texts is the declaration of the fact that Lord Viṣṇu is the highest of all. It is only by the knowledge of the greatness and goodness of God that one can be devoted to Him, and it is by devotion to God and by His grace that one can attain emancipation, which is the highest object of life. Thus it is through the declaration of God and His goodness that the *śruti* serves to attain this for us.

No one can have any attachment to anything with which he feels himself identical. A king does not love his rival; rather he would try to inflict defeat on him by attacking him; but the same king would give away his all to one who praised him. Most of the ascriptions of the texts endow God with various qualities and powers which would be unexplainable on monistic lines. So Madhva urges that the ultimate aim of all *śruti* and *smṛti* texts is to speak of the superexcellence of Viṣṇu, the supreme Lord.

But his opponents argue that ascription or affirmation of qualities to reality depends upon the concept of difference; the concept of difference again depends upon the separate existence of the quality and the qualified. Unless there are two entities, there is no conception of difference; and, unless there is a conception of difference, there cannot be a conception of separate entities. Thus these two conceptions are related to each other in a circular manner and are therefore logically invalid[1]. Madhva in reply says that the above argument is invalid, because things are in themselves of the nature of difference. It is wrong to argue that differences are meaningless because they can only be realized with reference to

[1] *na ca viśeṣaṇa-viśeṣyatayā bheda-siddhiḥ, viśeṣaṇa-viśeṣya-bhāvaś ca bhedāpekṣaḥ dharmi-pratiyogy-apekṣayā bheda-siddhir bhedāpekṣaṃ ca dharmi-pratiyogitvam ity anyonyāśrayatayā bhedasyāyuktiḥ. Viṣṇu-tattva-vinirṇaya*, p. 264.

certain objects; for, just as unity has a separate meaning, so the difference is also realized by itself. It is wrong to think that first we have the notion of the differing objects in themselves in their unity and that then the differences are realized; to perceive the object is to perceive the difference. Difference is as simple and analysable as unity. Unity is also a simple notion, yet it can be expressed in the form of a relation of identity—such as that of Brahman and individual self, as the monists say. In the same way difference is a simple notion, though it may be expressed as subsisting between two entities. It is true that in cases of doubt and illusion our notion of difference is arrested, but so it is also in the case of our notion of unity. For to perceive an object is not to perceive its unity or identity; to perceive objects is to perceive their uniqueness, and it is this uniqueness which constitutes difference[1]. The expression "its difference" signifies the very uniqueness of the nature of the thing; for, had it not been so, then the perception of the object would not have led us to realize its separateness and difference from others. If such a difference was not realized with the very perception of the object, then one might easily have confused oneself with a jug or with a piece of cloth; but such a confusion never occurs, the reason being that the jug, as soon as it is perceived, is perceived as different from all other things. Difference therefore is realized as the very nature of things that are perceived; doubts occur only in those cases where there is some similarity, while in most other cases the difference of an entity from other entities is realized with the very perception of the entity. Just as, when a number of lights are seen at a glance, they are all known in a general manner, so difference is also known in a general manner, though the particular difference of the object from any other specific object may not be realized immediately upon perception. When a number of articles is perceived, we also perceive at once that each article is different, though the specific difference of each article from the other may not be realized at once. We conclude therefore that perception of difference is dependent upon a prior perception of multiplicity as a series of units upon which the notion

[1] *padārtha-sva-rūpatvād bhedasya na ca dharmi-pratiyogy-apekṣayā bhedasya svarūpatvam aikyavat-svarūpasyaiva tathātvāt, sva-rūpa-siddhā vai tad asiddhiś ca jīveśvaraikyaṃ vadataḥ siddhaiva, bhedas tu sva-rūpa-darśana eva siddhiḥ, prāyaḥ sarvato vilakṣaṇaṃ hi padārtha-sva-rūpaṃ dṛśyate. Ibid.*

of difference is superimposed. That in the perception of each entity its specific nature and uniqueness is perceived cannot be denied even by the Vedāntists, even by the monists, who regard each entity as being different from the Brahman. Thus the circular reasoning with which the monists associate the perception of difference is a fallacy and is untenable. If an object in the very revelation of its nature did not also reveal its special difference or uniqueness, then the perception of all things would be identical. Moreover each difference has its own unique character; the difference from a jug is not the same as the difference from a cloth. Thus the perception of difference cannot be challenged as invalid; to say that what is perceived in a valid manner is false is a denial of experience, and is invalid. The illusory perception of the conch-shell silver is regarded as illusory only because it is contradicted by a stronger perceptual experience. No syllogistic reasoning has the power to challenge the correctness of valid perceptual experience. No dialectical reasoning can prove the invalidity of direct and immediate experience. Upon this reasoning all arguments denying the differences of things are contradicted by the scriptural texts, by perception and by other arguments; the arguments of those who challenge the reality of difference are absolutely specious in their nature. It is idle to say that in reality there is no difference though such difference may be realized in our ordinary practical experience (*vyāvahārika*). It has already been demonstrated that falsehood defined as that which is different from both the existent and the non-existent is meaningless. To attempt to deny the non-existent because it is unworthy of experience is meaningless; for, whether it was or was not experienced, there would be no need to deny it. The difference of anything from the non-existent would not be known without the knowledge of the non-existent. The appearance of the silver in the conch-shell cannot be described as something different from the existent and the non-existent; for the silver appearance is regarded as non-existent in the conch-shell; it cannot be argued that, since such an appearance was realized, therefore it could not have been non-existent. The perception of the non-existent as the existent is the perception of one thing as another: it is of the nature of illusion. It cannot be said that the non-existent cannot be perceived even in illusion; for it is admitted by the monists that the *anirvacanīya*, which has no real existence, can be perceived. Nor can it be held that such a perception is itself *anirvacanīya* (or indefinable); for in that case we should have a vicious infinite, since the first *anirvacanīya* has to depend on the second and that on the third and so on. If the silver appearance was in reality *anirvacanīya* by nature, it would have been perceived as such, and that would have destroyed the illusion; for, if the silver-appearance was known at the time of perception as being *anirvacanīya* (or indefinable), no one would have failed to realize that he was experiencing an illusion. The word *mithyā*, "false", does not in reality mean *anirvacanīya*; it should mean non-existence. Now there cannot be anything which is neither existent nor non-existent; everyone perceives that either things are existent or they are not; no one has perceived anything which is neither existent nor non-existent. Thus the supposition of the so-called *anirvacanīya* and that of the perception of the non-existent are alike invalid; the perception of difference is valid, and the monistic claim falls to the ground.

The scriptures also assert difference between the individual selves and the Brahman; if even the scriptural texts are false, then it is idle to preach monism on scriptural grounds. It is on scriptural grounds that we have to admit that Brahman is the greatest and the highest; for the purport of all the valid scriptures tends to such an assertion—yet no one can for a moment think that he is one with Brahman; no one feels "I am omniscient, I am omnipotent, I am devoid of all sorrows and all defects"; on the contrary our common experience is just the opposite, and it cannot be false, for there is no proof of its falsity. The scriptures themselves never declare the identity of the self with the Brahman; the so called identity text (*tat tvam asi*, "That art thou") is proclaimed with illustrations which all point to a dualistic view. The illustration in the context of every "identity" (or monistic) text shows its real purport, viz., that it asserts the difference between Brahman and the selves. When it is said that, when one is known, everything is known, the meaning is that the chief object of knowledge is one, or that one alone is the cause; it does not mean that other things are false. For, if that one alone were the truth and everything else were false, then we should expect the knowledge of all falsehood to be derived from the knowledge of the truth, which is impossible (*nahi satya-jñānena mithyā-jñānam bhavati*). It cannot be said that the knowledge of the conch-shell leads to a knowledge of the silver; for the two awarenesses are different. It is only by knowing "this is not silver" that one knows the conch-shell; so long as one knows the silver (which is false), one does not know the conch-shell (which is true). By knowing an entity one does not know the negation of the entity. The knowledge of the non-existence of an entity is preceded by the knowledge of its existence elsewhere. It is customary for people to speak of other things as being known when the most important and the most essential thing is known; when one knows the principal men of a village, one may say that one knows the village. When one knows the father, one may say that he knows the son; "O! I know him, he is the son of so and so, he is known to me"; from one's knowledge of one person one may affirm the knowledge of other persons like him; by knowing one woman one may say "O! I know women." It is on the basis of such instances that the scriptural texts affirm that by the knowledge of one everything else is known. There is no reason for saying that such affirmations declare the falsity of all other things except Brahman. When the texts assert that by knowing one lump of earth one knows all earthen-wares, the idea is that of similarity, since surely not all earthen-wares are *made* out of one lump of earth; the text does not say that by knowing earth we know all earthen-wares; what it does say is that by knowing one lump of earth we know all earthen-wares. It is the similarity between one lump of earth and all other earthen-wares that justifies the text. The word "*vācārambhaṇam*" does not mean falsehood, generated by words, for in that case the word *nāmadheya* would be inapplicable. We conclude that the scriptures nowhere declare the falsehood of the world; on the contrary, they abound in condemnation of the view that the world is false[1].

The highest self, the Brahman, is absolutely independent, omniscient, omnipotent and blissful, whereas the ordinary self, though similar to Him in character, is always under His control, knows little and has little power. It is wrong to suppose that self is one but appears as many because of a false *upādhi* or condition,

[1] *asatyam apratiṣṭhaṃ te jagad āhur anīśvaram*
a-paras-para-sambhūtaṃ kim anyat kāma-haitukam
etāṃ dṛṣṭim avaṣṭabhya naṣṭātmāno'lpa-buddhayaḥ.
Gītā, XVI. 8. 9, as quoted by Madhva.

and impossible to conceive that the self could be misconceived as not-self. The so-called creation of illusory appearance by magic, in imitation of real things, is only possible because real things exist; it is on the basis of real things that unreal illusions appear. Dreams also occur on the basis of real experiences which are imitated in them. Dream creations can take place only through the functioning of the subconscious impressions (*vāsanā*); but there is no reason to suppose that the world as such, which is never contradicted and which is truly experienced, is illusory, like dream creations. Moreover the Lord is omniscient and self-luminous, and it is not possible that He should be covered by ignorance. If it is argued that the one Brahman appears as many through a condition (or *upādhi*) and that He passes through the cycles of birth and rebirth, then, since these cycles are never-ending, Brahman will never be free from them and He will never have emancipation because His association with *upādhi* will be permanent. It is no defence to say that the pure Brahman cannot have any bondage through conditions; that which is already associated with *upādhi* or condition cannot require a further condition for associating the previous condition with it; for that will lead to a vicious infinite. Again, the thesis of the existence of a false *upādhi* can be proved only if there is a proof for the existence of ignorance as an entity; if there is no ignorance, there cannot be any falsehood. Again, as *upādhi* cannot exist without ignorance, nor ignorance without *upādhi*, this would involve a vicious circle. According to the hypothesis omniscience can be affirmed only of that which is unassociated with a false *upādhi*; so that, if the pure Brahman is itself associated with ignorance, there can never be emancipation; for then the ignorance will be its own nature, from which it cannot dissociate itself. Moreover, such a permanent existence of ignorance would naturally lead to a dualism of the Brahman and ignorance. If it is held that it is by the *ajñāna* of the *jīva* (soul) that the false appearance of the world is possible, then it may be pointed out that there is a vicious circle here also; for without the pre-existence of *ajñāna* there is no *jīva*, and without *jīva* there cannot be *ajñāna*; without *ajñāna* there is no *upādhi*, and without *upādhi* there is no *ajñāna*. Nor can it be held that it is the pure Brahman that appears as ignorant through illusion; for, unless *ajñāna* is established, there cannot be illusion, and, unless there is illusion, there cannot be *ajñāna*. From another point of view too it may be urged that the monists support an impossible proposition in saying that, when all the individuals are emancipated, the Brahman will be emancipated, since the living units or the souls are far more numerous than even the atoms; on the tip of an atom there may be millions of living units, and it is impossible to conceive that they should all attain salvation through the knowledge of Brahman. It also cannot be said that there is nothing to be surprised at the logical certainty of falsehood; for it must be a very strong argument against our opponent, that they cannot prove the falsehood of all things which are immediately and directly perceived; and, unless such proofs are available, things that are perceived through direct experience cannot be ignored. We all know that we are always enjoying the objects of the world in our experience, and in view of this fact how can we say that there is no difference between an experience and the object experienced? When we perceive our food, how can we say that there is no food? A perceptual experience can be discarded only when it is known that the conditions of perception were such as to vitiate its validity. We perceive a thing from a distance; we may mistrust it in certain respects, since we know that when we perceive a thing at a distance the object appears small and blurred; but, unless the possibility of such distorting conditions can be proved, no perception can be regarded as invalid. Moreover, the defects of a perception can also be discovered by a maturer perception. The falsehood of the world has never been proved as defective by any argument whatever. Moreover the experience of knowledge, ignorance, pleasure and pain cannot be contradicted; so it has to be admitted that the experience of the world is true, and, being true, it cannot be negated; therefore it is impossible to have such an emancipation as is desired by the monists. If that which is directly experienced can be negated merely by specious arguments without the testimony of a stronger experience, then even the perception of the self could be regarded as false. There is no lack of specious arguments about the existence of the self; for one may quite well argue that, since everything is false, the experience of the self also is false, and there is no reason why we should distinguish the existence of other things from the experience of the self, since as experience they are of the same order. It will be an insupportable assumption that the experience of the self belongs to a different order, wherefore its falsity cannot be affirmed. Nor is it possible to affirm that all illusions occur on the basis of self-experience; for, in order to assert that, one must first prove that the experience of the self is not illusory, while all other experiences are so—which is exactly the point contested by the Madhvas. If it is urged that illogicality only shows that the experience is false, then it may also be urged that the illogicality or the inexplicable nature of the experience of the self in association with the objective experience only proves the falsity of the experience of the self and can lead to nothing; for the monists urge that all experiences may be mere semblances of experience, being only products of *avidyā*. The *avidyā* itself is regarded as inexplicable, and all reality is supposed to depend not on experience, but on the logical arguments; in which case one may as well say that objects are the real seers and the subject that which is seen. One may say too that there may be false appearances without a seer; the illogicality or inexplicability of the situation is nothing to shy at, since the *māyā* is illogical and inexplicable; a fact which makes it impossible to indicate in what manner it will create confusion. Creating confusion is its sole function, and therefore one may say that either there are appearances without any seer, illusions without a basis, or that the objects are the so-called seers and the self, the so-called seer, is in reality nothing but an object.

Again, if all differences are regarded as mere false appearances due to *upādhi*, why should there not on the same analogy be experience of reality? Though feelings of pleasure and pain appear in different limbs of one person, yet the experiencer is felt as the same. Why should not experiences in different bodies or persons be felt as belonging to the same individual?—the analogy is the same. In spite of the difference of *upādhis* (such as the difference between the limbs of one person), there is the feeling of one experiencer; so in the different *upādhis* of the bodies of more than one person there may be the appearance of one experiencer. And again, the destruction of one *upādhi* cannot liberate the Brahman or the self; for the Brahman is associated with other *upādhis* and is suffering bondage all the same.

Again, one may ask whether the *upādhi* covers the whole of the Brahman or a part of it. The Brahman cannot be conceived as made up of parts; if the association of *upādhi* were due to another *upādhi*, then there would be a vicious infinite. Again, since the Brahman is all-pervading, there cannot be any difference through *upādhi*, and no conception of a part of the Brahman is possible; *upādhi* is possible only of things that are limited by time or place. Again, for the same reason experiences through different *upādhis* must be of one and the same Brahman, and in that case there ought to be the appearance of one experience through all the different bodies, just as the experience of pleasure and pain in the different limbs of a person are attributed to him alone.

Again, the pure Brahman cannot pass through cycles of births and rebirths, because it is pure. Then the birth, rebirth and bondage of the monists must be of Brahman as associated with *upādhi* and *māyā*. Now the question is: is the Brahman associated with *māyā* different from pure Brahman or identical with it? If it be identical with pure Brahman, then it cannot suffer bondage. If it is not identical, then the question is whether it is eternal or non-eternal: if it is not eternal, then it will be destroyed, and there will be no emancipation; if it is eternal, then one has to admit that the *māyā* and Brahman remain eternally associated, which virtually means the ultimate reality of two entities. If it is urged that Brahman in pure essence is one, though He appears as many in association with the *upādhi*, the simple reply is that, if the pure essence can be associated with *upādhi*, the essence in itself cannot be regarded as pure. To say that the *upādhi* is false is meaningless, because the concepts of falsehood and *upādhi* are mutually interdependent. Nor can it be said that this is due to beginningless *karma*; for, unless the plurality of the *upādhis* can be proved, the plurality of the *karma* cannot be proved either, as the two concepts are interdependent. So the monistic view is contradicted by all our means of knowledge; and all the *śruti* texts support the pluralistic view. Both the *māyā* and the Brahman are incapable of description on a monistic view; it is difficult too to realize how the Brahman or the monist can express Himself; for, if He is one and there is no activity, He ought not to be able to express Himself. If He cannot express Himself to others who do not exist, He cannot express Himself to Himself either; for self-action is impossible (*na ca svenāpi jñeyatvam tair ucyate kartṛ-karma-virodhāt*). There cannot be any knowledge without a knower; the knowledge that is devoid of the knower and the known is empty and void, since none of us has experienced any knowledge where there is no knowledge and the knower.

The *Viṣṇu-tattva-nirṇaya* of Madhva had a comment called the *Viṣṇu-tattva-nirṇaya-ṭīkā* by Jaya-tīrtha, *Viṣṇu-tattva-nirṇaya-ṭīkā-ṭippaṇī* by Keśavasvāmin, *Viṣṇu-tattva-nirṇaya-ṭippaṇī* by Śrīnivāsa and Padmanābha-tīrtha, *Bhaktabodha* by Raghūttama; it had also another commentary, called *Viṣṇu-tattva-nirṇaya-ṭīkopanyāsa*. Besides these there were independent works on the lines of *Viṣṇu-tattva-nirṇaya* called *Viṣṇu-tattva-nirṇaya-vākyārtha* and Vanamālī Miśra's *Viṣṇu-tattva-prahāsa*[1].

The *Nyāya-vivaraṇa* of Madhva is a work of more than six hundred granthas, which deals with the logical connection of the different chapters of the *Brahma-sūtra*. A number of commentaries was written on it, by Viṭṭhala-sutānanda-tīrtha, Mudgalānanda-tīrtha, and Raghūttama; Jaya-tīrtha also wrote on it the *Nyāya-vivaraṇa-pañjikā*. Rāghavendra, Vijayīndra and Vādirāja wrote respectively *Nyāya-muktāvalī*, *Nyāya-mauktikamālā*, and *Nyāya-ratnāvalī*, on the lines of Madhva's *Nyāya-vivaraṇa*. Madhva wrote it after he had finished his *Bhāṣya*, *Anubhāṣya* and *Anuvyākhyāna;* it is needless for us to follow the work in detail, but we may briefly indicate Madhva's manner of approach. He says that the *Brahma-sūtra* was written in order to discredit the monistic interpretations of the Upaniṣads. Thus with the monist Brahman cannot be a subject of enquiry, because He is self-luminous; in opposition to this view the *Brahma-sūtra* starts with the thesis that Brahman, being the supreme person who is full of all qualities, can hardly be known by our finite minds. There is then a natural enquiry regarding the extent of the greatness of the supreme being, and in the second *sūtra* it is shown that Brahman cannot be identical with the individual selves, because He is the source from which the world has come into being and it is He who supports the world also. In the third *sūtra* we learn that the Brahman-causality of the world cannot be known except through scripture; in the fourth we read that the scriptures from which we can know the Brahman cannot be any other than the Upaniṣads. In this way, all through his first chapter, Madhva tries to show that, if we interpret the doubtful *śruti* texts on the basis of those whose meanings are clear and definite, we find that they too declare the superiority and transcendence of the supreme Lord. The same process of reconciling the *śruti* texts with

[1] *ato jñātṛ-jñeyābhāvāt jñānam api śūnyataiva; ataḥ śūnya-vādān na kaścid viśeṣaḥ; na ca jñātṛ-jñeya-rahitaṃ jñānaṃ kvacid dṛṣṭam.* *Op. cit.* p. 275 (17).

the idea of showing the transcendence of God over individual selves goes on through the remaining chapters of the first book. In dealing with the fourth book Madhva discusses his pet view that not all persons can be liberated, since only a few can be worthy of liberation[1]. He further says that God must be worshipped continually by chanting His excellent qualities every day. The scriptural duties as well as meditation (*dhyāna*) and its accessories (postures, etc.) are to be carried out; without meditation there cannot be a direct intuition of God[2]. It cannot be urged that with the rise of knowledge all *karmas* are destroyed and salvation comes by itself; for knowledge can remove only the unripe (*aprārabdha*) *karmas*. The fruit of the *prārabdha* or ripe *karmas* has to be enjoyed till they are exhausted. Thus Madhva favours the doctrine of *jīvanmukti*. Though it has been said that the rise of true knowledge removes the *aprārabdha karmas*, yet the real agency belongs to God; when the true knowledge rises in a man, God is pleased, and He destroys the unripe *karmas*[3]. At the time of death all wise persons pass on to fire and from there to *vāyu*, which takes them to Brahman, since it is only through *vāyu* that one can approach Brahman. Those who return to the world pass through smoke; and there are others who because of their sinful character pass on to the lowest world. Even in the state of salvation the emancipated beings enjoy devotion as pure bliss.

The *Tantra-sāra-saṃgraha* of Madhva is a work of four chapters on ritual, which deals with the methods of worshipping Viṣṇu by the use of mantras; and various processes of ritualistic worship are described. It is commented upon by Chalāri-nṛsiṃhācārya, Chalāri-śeṣācārya, Raghunātha Yati and Śrīnivāsācārya. Jaya-tīrtha wrote in verse a small work called *Tantra-sārokta-pūjāvidhi*; Śrīnivāsācārya also wrote a small work on the same lines, the *Tantra-sāra-mantroddhāra*.

Madhva wrote also another small work, called *Sadācāra-smṛti*, in forty verses; this too is a work on rituals, describing the normal duties of a good *vaiṣṇava* There is a commentary by Droṇācārya (*Sadācāra-smṛti-vyākhyā*).

[1] *mahā-phalatvāt sarveṣām aśaktyā eva upapannatvāt; anyathā sarva-puruṣāśakyasyaiva sādhanatayā sarvēṣām mokṣāpatteḥ.* *Nyāya-vivaraṇa*, p. 16(*a*).

[2] *dhyānaṃ vinā aparokṣa-jñānākhya-viśeṣa-kāryānupapatteḥ.* *Ibid.*

[3] *karmāṇi kṣapayed viṣṇur aprārabdhāni vidyayā*
prārabdhāni tu bhogena kṣapayan svaṃ padaṃ nayet. *Ibid.* 16.

He wrote also another small work, called *Kṛṣṇāmṛta-mahārṇava.* The present writer has not been able to trace any commentary on it. It consists of two hundred and forty-two verses, describing the forms of worshipping Viṣṇu, and emphasizes the indispensable necessity of continual meditation on the super-excellent nature of God and of worshipping Him; it speaks also of repentance and meditation on God's name as a way of expiation of sins. Madhva further says that in this present Kali age *bhakti* of God is the only way to emancipation. Meditation on God alone can remove all sins[1]; no ablutions, no asceticism are necessary for those who meditate on God; the name of God is the only instrument for removing sins. So the whole of the *Kṛṣnāmṛta-mahārṇava* describes the glory of God, as well as the methods of worshipping Him; and, further, the duties of the good *vaiṣṇavas* during the important *tithis.*

Madhva wrote another small work, the *Dvādaśa-stotra,* consisting of about one hundred and thirty verses. No commentary on this has been traced by the present writer.

He wrote also another very small work, in two verses, the *Narasiṃha-nakha-stotra,* and another, the *Yamaka-bhārata,* of eighty-one verses. This latter was commented upon by Yadupati and Timmaṇṇa Bhaṭṭa; and in it Madhva describes the story of Kṛṣṇa in brief, including the episodes of Vṛndāvana and that of Hastināpur in association with the Pāṇḍavas.

He wrote also the *Ṛg-bhāṣya,* i.e., a commentary on some selected verses of the *Ṛg-veda,* which was commented upon by Jaya-tīrtha, Śrīnivāsā-tīrtha, Veṅkaṭa, Chalāri-nṛsiṃhācārya, Rāghavendra, Keśavācārya, Lakṣmīnārāyaṇa and Satyanātha Yati. Two anonymous works are known to the present writer which were written on the lines of the *Ṛg-bhāṣya;* they are *Ṛg-artha-cūḍāmaṇi* and *Ṛg-arthoddhāra.* Rāghvendra Yati also wrote a work on the same lines, called *Ṛg-artha-mañjarī.* Madhva's commentary on the *Īṣoponiṣat* was commented on by Jaya-tīrtha, Śrīnivāsa-tīrtha, Raghunātha Yati, Nṛsiṃhācārya and Satyaprajña Yati, and Rāghavendra-tīrtha wrote a separate work on *Īśa, Kena, Kaṭha, Praśna, Muṇḍaka* and *Māṇḍūkya Upaniṣads,* which follows Madhva's line of interpretation of these Upaniṣads. Madhva's

[1] *smaraṇād eva kṛṣṇasya pāpasaṃghaṭṭapañjaraḥ*
śatadhā bhedam āyāti girir vajrāhato yathā.
Kṛṣṇāmṛta-mahārṇava, verse 46.

commentary on the *Aitareyopaniṣad* was commented upon by Tāmraparṇī Śrīnivāsa, Jaya-tīrtha, Viśveśvara-tīrtha and Nārāyaṇa-tīrtha; and Narasiṃha Yati wrote a separate treatise, the *Aitareyopaniṣad-khaṇḍārtha*, on which a commentary, the *Khaṇḍārtha-prakāśa*, was written by Śrīnivāsa-tīrtha. The *Kaṭhopaniṣad-bhāṣya* of Madhva was commented upon by Vedeśa. Vyāsa-tīrtha wrote a commentary, the *Kenopaniṣad-bhāṣya-ṭīkā*, on Madhva's *Kenopaniṣad-bhāṣya*, while Rāghavendra-tīrtha wrote a separate work (the *Kenopaniṣad-khaṇḍārtha*). The *Chāndogyopaniṣad-bhāṣya* of Madhva was commented upon by Vyāsa-tīrtha; Vedeśa and Rāghavendra-tīrtha wrote a separate work, the *Chāndogyopaniṣad-khaṇḍārtha*. The *Talavakāra-bhāṣya* of Madhva had the following commentaries: the *Talavakāra-bhāṣya-ṭīkā*, by Vyāsa-tīrtha, and *Talabavāra-ṭippanī*, by Vedeśa-bhikṣu; Nṛsiṃha-bhikṣu wrote the *Talavakāra-khaṇḍārtha-prakāśikā*. The *Praśnopaniṣad-bhāṣya* of Madhva was commented upon by Jaya-tīrtha in the *Praśnopaniṣad-bhāṣya-ṭīkā*, which had two commentaries, the *Praśnopaniṣad-bhāṣya-ṭīkā-ṭippana* by Śrīnivāsa-tīrtha. The *Bṛhadāraṇyaka-bhāṣya* of Madhva had commentaries (*Bṛhadāraṇyaka-bhāṣya-ṭīkā*) by Raghūttama, Vyāsa-tīrtha and Śrīnivāsa-tīrtha, and Raghūttama Yati wrote a separate work on it, called the *Bṛhadāraṇyaka-bhāva-bodha*. The *Māṇḍūkyopaniṣad-bhāṣya* of Madhva had two commentaries on it, by Vyāsa-tīrtha and Kṛṣṇācārya, and Rāghavendra Yati wrote a separate work on it, the *Māṇḍūkya-khaṇḍārtha*. The *Muṇḍakopaniṣad-bhāṣya* of Madhva has the following commentaries: the *Muṇḍakopaniṣad-bhāṣya-ṭīkā* by Vyāsa-tīrtha and Nārāyaṇa-tīrtha; *Muṇḍakopaniṣad-bhāṣya-ṭīkā-ṭippanī* by Kṛṣṇācārya; and *Muṇḍakopaniṣad-bhāṣya-vyākhyā* by Nṛsiṃha-bhikṣu.

Teachers and Writers of the Madhva School.

Historical enquiry about the Madhvas was probably first started by Kṛṣṇasvāmī Ayer, with a paper in which he tried to solve the question of the age of Madhva[1]: but he was not in a position to utilize the archaeological data as was done by H. Kṛṣṇa Śāstrī[2]. The conclusions at which he arrived were in some

[1] *Madhvācārya, a Short Historical Sketch*, by C. N. Kṛṣṇasvāmī Ayer, M.A.
[2] See his article, *Epigraphica Indica*, vol. VI, pp. 260–8.

cases against the records of the Madhva *maṭhas*, and the Madhva-Siddhānta Unnāhinī Sabhā, which is annually held at a place near Tirupati, took serious objections to his statements; Subba Rao, in the introduction to his translation of the *Gītā-bhāṣya* of Madhva, severely criticized Kṛṣṇa Śāstrī for his orthodox bias, stating that he was not posted in all the facts of the question[1]. Later on C. M. Padmanābhācārya also tried to deal with the subject, utilizing the epigraphical data, but only partially[2]; his book deals with all the central facts of Madhva's life according to the traditional accounts.

We have already dealt with the outline of Madhva's life. Madhva, on his way from Badarikāśram to South India, had met Satya-tīrtha and had journeyed together with him through the Vaṅga and Kaliṅga countries. In the Telugu country Madhva was challenged by Śobhana Bhaṭṭa, a famous monist, who was defeated and converted to Madhva faith. This Śobhana Bhaṭṭa was then styled Padmanābha-tīrtha. Madhva had dispute with another scholar who was a prime minister in the Kaliṅga country; he too was converted by Madhva, and was called Narahari-tīrtha. In the meantime the Kaliṅga king had died, leaving an infant son, and Narahari-tīrtha was asked to take charge of the child and administer the state on his behalf. At the instance of Madhva Narahari carried on the regency for twelve years and brought out for him the images of Rāma and Sītā which were in the treasury of the Kaliṅga kingdom. Madhva at one time had a hot discussion leading to a dispute with Padma-tīrtha, a prominent monist of the locality, who, upon being defeated, fled, carrying with him the library of Madhva; at the intercession, however, of a local chieftain, Jayasiṃha, the books were restored. Later on Madhva defeated another monist, Trivikrama Paṇḍita, who became converted to the Madhva faith, and wrote the *Madhva-vijaya*. After the death of Madhva Padmanābha-tīrtha became pontiff and was succeeded by Narahari-tīrtha; we have already given the list of the pontiffs in succession, with their approximate dates as far as they are available from the list of the Madhva *gurus* in the Madhva *maṭhas* of the South. In an article on the outline history of the Madhvācāryas

[1] See *The Bhagavadgītā*, by Subba Rao, M.A., printed at the Minerva Press, Madras.

[2] *The Life of Madhvācārya*, by C. M. Padmanābhācārya, printed at the Progressive Press, Madras.

G. Venkoba Rao gives the following chronology of the principal facts of Madhva's life: birth of Madhva, *śaka* 1118; assumption of holy orders, *śaka* 1128; tour to the South; pilgrimage to Badari; conversion of Śobhana Bhaṭṭa, Śyāmaśāstrī and Govinda Bhaṭṭa; second tour to Badari; beginning of Narahari's regency, *śaka* 1186; end of Narahari's regency, *śaka* 1197; death of Madhvācārya and accession of Padmanābha, *śaka* 1197: death of Padmanābha-tīrtha, *śaka* 1204; Narahari's pontificate, *śaka* 1204–5.

Grierson, in his article on the *Madva-charita* in the *Encyclopaedia of Religion and Ethics* (vol. VIII), thinks that the influence of Christianity on Madhvism is very apparent; he says that Madhva's birth-place was either in the ancient city of Kalyānapura or close to it. Kalyānapura has always been reputed one of the earliest Christian settlements in India; these Christians were Nestorians. Again, among the legends described in Nārāyaṇa's *Madhva-vijaya* there is one which holds that the spirit of the deity Ananteśvara appeared to a Brahman and made him a messenger of good news to proclaim that the kingdom of Heaven was at hand. The child, Madhva, was being led through a forest by his parents when their passage was obstructed by evil spirits, who, being rebuked by Madhva, fled away. The child Madhva was at one time missed by his parents at the age of five and he was found teaching the way to worship Viṣṇu according to the *śāstras*. In his tour in the Southern districts Madhva is said to have increased the store of food to meet the needs of his followers. In his Northern tour he walked over water without wetting his feet, and on another occasion he pacified the angry sea by his stern look. From these miracles attributed to him, and from the facts that there is great similarity between the *bhakti* doctrine of Madhva and the devotionalism of the Christians, and that Madhva flourished in a place where there were Christians, Grierson thinks that Madhvaism had an element of Christian influence. The fact also that according to Madhva salvation can be secured only through the intermediary of the wind god *Vāyu* has been interpreted in favour of the above thesis. I think, however, that there is not sufficient ground in these arguments for tracing a Christian influence on Madhva. The doctrine of *bhakti* is very old, and can be traced in a fairly developed form even in some of the Vedic and Upaniṣadic verses, the *Gītā*, the *Mahābhārata* and the earlier *Purāṇas*. There may have been some Christians in

Kalyānapura, but there is no evidence that they were of such importance as to influence the orthodox faith of Madhva. He, like all other teachers, urges again and again that his doctrines are based on the Vedas, the *Gītā*, the *Pañcarātras* and the *Mahābhārata*; nor do we find any account of discussion between Madhva and the Christians; and he is never reported to have been a polyglot or to have had access to Christian literature. Though occasionally *vāyu* is accepted as an intermediary, yet the main emphasis is on the grace of God, depending upon the knowledge of God; there is not the slightest trace of any Trinity doctrine in Madhva's school of thought. Thus the suggestion of a probable Christian influence seems to be very far-fetched. Burnell, however, supports the idea in his paper in *The Indian Antiquary*, 1873–4; but Garbe considers it probable that Kalyānapura might have been another Kalyāna, in the north of Bombay, while Grierson thinks that it must have been the Kalyāna in Udipi, which is close to Malabar.

Burnell again points out that before the beginning of the ninth century some Persians had settled at Manigrama, and he further suggests that these Persians were Manicheans. But Burnell's view was successfully controverted by Collins, though he could not deny the possibility that "Manigrama" was derived from the name Manes (*mani*). Grierson supports the idea of Burnell, and co-relates it with the peculiar story of Maṇimat, the demon supposed to have been born as Śaṅkara, a fabulous account of whom is given in the *Maṇimañjarī* of Nārāyaṇa. It cannot be denied that the introduction of the story of Maṇimat is rather peculiar, as Maṇimat plays a very unimportant part as the opponent of Bhīma in the *Mahābhārata;* but there is practically nothing in the philosophy or theology of Śaṅkara, which is a form of dualism wherein two principles are acknowledged, one light (God) and the other darkness.

Padmanābha-tīrtha succeeded Madhva in the pontificate in A.D. 1197 and died in 1204; he wrote a commentary on the *Anuvyākhāna*, the *Ṣaṇnyāya-ratnāvalī*. Narahari-tīrtha, who is said to have been a personal disciple of Madhva, held the pontificate from 1204 to 1213[1]; he wrote a *ṭippanī* on the *Brahma-sūtra-bhāṣya* of Madhva. We do not know of any work by Mādhava-tīrtha, the next pontiff

[1] For a discussion on Narahari's career and date see *Epigraphica Indica*, vol. VI, p. 206, etc.

(1213–30). Akṣobhya-tīrtha held the pontificate from 1230 to 1247, and then Jaya-tīrtha from 1247 to 1268. It is held by some that he was a pupil not only of Akṣobhya-tīrtha, but also of Padmanābha-tīrtha[1]; he was the most distinguished writer of the Madhva school, and composed many commentaries of a very recondite character, e.g., *Ṛg-bhāṣya-ṭīkā* on Madhva's *Ṛg-bhāṣya*, *Vyākhyāna-vivaraṇa* on Madhva's *Īśopaniṣad-bhāṣya*, *Praśnopaniṣad-bhāṣya-ṭīkā*, *Prameya-dīpikā* on the *Gītā-bhāṣya*, *Nyāya-dīpikā* on the *Gītā-tātparya-nirṇaya*, and *Tattva-prakāśikā* on the *Brahma-sūtra-bhāṣya*. His most learned and incisive work, however, is his *Nyāya-sudhā*, which is a commentary on the *Anuvyākhyāna* of Madhva; it is a big work. He begins by referring to Akṣobhya-tīrtha as his teacher. The work forms the principal source-book of most of the writers of the Madhva school; it was commented upon by Rāghavendra Yati in a work called *Nyāya-sudhā-parimala*. C. M. Padmanābhacārya says of the *Nyāya-sudhā* that in the whole range of Sanskrit literature a more masterly commentary is unknown.

Rāmānuja and Madhva.

We know that the system of Madhva, being a defence of dualism and pluralism, regarded Śaṅkara and his followers as its principal opponents, and therefore directed its strongest criticism against them. Madhva flourished in the thirteenth century, and by that time many of the principal exponents of monism, like Vācaspati, Prakāśātman, Sureśvara and others, had written scholarly treatises in support of the monistic philosophy of Śaṅkara. Madhva and his followers, Jaya-tīrtha, Vyāsa-tīrtha and others, did their best to refute the monistic arguments for the falsity of the world, and to establish the reality and the plurality of the world and the difference between self and Brahman, which latter was conceived as a personal God. They in their turn were attacked by other writers of the Śaṅkara school, and we have a long history of attacks and counter-attacks between the members of these two important schools of thought. But readers may naturally be curious about the relation between the school of Madhva and the school of Rāmānuja. Madhva himself says little or nothing

[1] Helmuth von Glasenapp, *Madhva's Philosophie des Vishṇu-Glaubens*, 1923, p. 52.

which may be interpreted as a direct attack upon his predecessor Rāmānuja; but in later times there is evidence of recondite disputes between the followers of the Rāmānuja school and those of the Madhva. For instance, Parakāla Yati, in the sixteenth century, wrote *Vijayīndra-parājaya*, which is evidently a treatise containing refutations of some of the most important doctrines of the Madhva philosophy. It seems desirable to give a short account of this treatise, which is rare and available only in a manuscript form.

Parakāla Yati takes his views from Veṅkaṭa's *Tattva-muktā-kalāpa*, and often quotes verses from it in support of his own views. His attack is made upon Madhva's view which discards the Rāmānuja division of categories (*dravya*, "substance," and *adravya*, "non-substance") and his view of the qualities as constituents of the substance; and this forms the subject-matter of the first two sections of the *Vijayīndra-parājaya*.

In describing Madhva's position upon the question of difference between substance and qualities, the writer says that the Madhvas think that the expression "the blue jug" is justified by the fact that the "blueness" enters into the "sufficient description" of the jug and has no separate existence from it. It is wrong, they say, to affirm that the qualities of the jug stood apart from the jug and entered into it at any particular moment; the conception of the jug carries with it all of its qualities, and these have no separate existence, that is, they are *a-pṛthak-siddha* from the jug. Parakāla Yati points out that, since we know that the unqualified jug assumes a blue colour by heat, the blue colour may be regarded as different from the jug[1]. The qualities, colour etc., have the substance as their support, and they may flow into it or not according to circumstances or conditions. It cannot be said that the determining condition for the influx of qualities is nothing but the nature of the substance, consisting of inseparability from the qualities; for the possibility of such an inseparable association is the matter under dispute and cannot therefore be taken as granted; moreover, the existence of an *upādhi* is relevant only when the entities are different and when the association of the *hetu* with the *sādhya* is true only under certain

[1] *ghaṭe pākena nailyam utpannam ityananyathā-siddha-pratyakṣaṃ ca tatra pramāṇaṃ kiñca rūpādi svādhikaraṇād bhinnaṃ svāśraye sphāre asya āgamopādhi-dharmatvāt. Vijayīndra-parājaya*, p. 3 (MS.).

circumstances; in which case these circumstances are called the determining condition of association (*upādhi*)[1].

But, if the Madhvas argue that even the Rāmānujas admit the inseparable nature of substance and qualities, to this the reply would be that according to Rāmānuja *a-pṛthak-siddhatva* or "inseparability" only means that at the time of the union (of the quality and the substance) the constituent elements cannot be separated[2]. The mere fact that the expression "blue jug" apparently means the identity of the blueness and the jug without any qualifying suffix denoting "possession" should not be regarded as actually testifying to the identity of "blue" and the jug. The Madhvas themselves do not regard the blueness and jugness as the same and so they have to admit that blueness somehow qualifies the jug. Such an admission would repudiate their own theory[3]. If blueness as something different from blue be associated with lotus-ness, then the admission of the fact that, when the words blue and lotus are used adjectivally and substantively with the same suffix, they mean one and the same identical thing is by itself no sound logic. If they are understood as different, then one is substance and the other is not.

As a matter of fact our perceptual experience discloses a qualified character of all substances and qualities. No true follower of the Upaniṣads can believe that perception reveals the pure indeterminate nature of being. If no distinction can be made out between characters and substances, then it will not be possible to distinguish one substance from another; for one substance is distinguished from another only by reason of their characters.

Moreover, the distinction between substance and qualities is evident from other *pramāṇas* also. Thus a blind man can dispute about the touch-feeling of an object, but he cannot do so about the colour. So the colour and touch-feeling have to be regarded as distinct from the object itself. Moreover, we speak of a jug as having colour, but we do not say that a jug *is* colour. So it must be

[1] *na ceha apṛthak-siddhatvam upādhistasya sādhyarūpatve*
sādhana-vyāpakatvād bheda-ghaṭito hi vyāpya-vyāpaka-bhāvaḥ.
Vijayīndra-parājaya.

[2] *rūpāder madīyam apṛthak-siddhatvaṃ saṃsaktaṃ paṭe anyatra netum aśakyatvam eva. tac ca tadrūpābhāve'pi rūpāntareṇa dharma-sattayā avirodhitayā na pṛthaksiddhatvena virudhyate. Ibid.*

[3] *tasya tvayā'pi akhaṇḍārthatvānabhyupagamāt viśiṣṭārthatve tvad-abhimata-siddheḥ. Ibid.* p. 4.

admitted that a denial on Madhva lines of the classification of categories as *dravya* and *adravya* is illogical; it must be held that the *adravya*, though entirely different from *dravya*, remains in association with it and expresses its nature as characters of qualities. Parakāla Yati then takes up a number of Upaniṣad passages and tries to show that, if distinction of qualities and substances is not admitted, then most of the *śruti* texts are inadmissible.

There are some Madhvas who hold that there is both difference and identity, and that even with careful observation the *dravya* and the *adravya* cannot be distinguished, and therefore no distinction can be made between *dravya* and *adravya* as the Rāmānujas make. To this Parakāla Yati replies that the rule that determines the reality of anything must be based upon the principle of non-contradiction and then unconditional invariability[1]. The expression "blue jug," wherein the "jugness" and "blueness" may appear in one, may be contradicted by other equally valid expressions, such as "blueness in jug," "blue-coloured jug," and it would thus be ineffective to determine the nature of reality merely by following the indication of the expression "blue jug", which may show an apparent identity between the blue and the jug. The very fact that the jug appears as qualified shows that it has a distinction in the quality that qualifies it. Nor can it be said that because a particular colour is always associated with a particular substance that colour and substance are one and the same; for a conch-shell associated with white colour may also sometimes appear as yellow. Moreover, when one substance carries with it many qualities, it cannot be regarded as being at the same time identical with all the manifold qualities[2]. The distinction of substances on the basis of qualities will also be erroneous, if, like qualities, the special natures of the substances be themselves naturally different[3]. If a thing can be at the same time identical with many qualities, then that involves acceptance of the Jaina view of *saptabhaṅgī*. Thus, from whatever point of view the Madhva attempt to refute the classification of *dravya* and *adravya* is examined, it is found to be faulty and invalid.

[1] *yastu abādhito nānyathā-siddhaś ca pratyayaḥ sa evārthaṃ vyavasthāpayati. Ibid*, p. 30.

[2] *kiñca paraspara-bhinnair guṇair ekasya guṇinaḥ abhedo'pi na ghaṭate iti tad-abhedopajīvanena ity uktir api ayuktā.... Ibid.* p. 33.

[3] *guṇagata-bheda-vyavahāro nir-nibandhanaśca syāt yadi guṇavat guṇidharma-viśeṣah svata eva syāt. Ibid.*

One of the important doctrines in which Madhva differs from others is that the experience in emancipation is not the same with all saints or emancipated persons. This view is supported by some of the *Purāṇas* and also accepted by the Vaiṣṇavas of the Gauḍīya school; but the Rāmānujas as well as the Śaṅkarites were strongly against it, and therefore the followers of the Rāmānuja school criticized Madhva strongly on this point. Thus Śrīnivāsa Ācārya wrote a separate *prakaraṇa* work called *Ānanda-tāratamya-khaṇḍana*. But a much longer and more critical attempt in this direction was made by Parakāla Yati in the fourth chapter of his *Viyajīndra-parājaya*. Both these works exist in manuscript.

In the fourth chapter of the fourth book of the *Brahma-sūtra* the question of how the emancipated ones enjoy their experience after emancipation is discussed. It is said here that it is by entering into the nature of the supreme Lord that the emancipated beings participate in the blissful experiences by their mere desire (*saṃkalpa*). There are however others who hold that the emancipated enjoy the blissful experiences directly through themselves, through their bodies, as mere attempts of intelligence. It is because in the emancipated state one is entitled to all kinds of blissful experiences that one can regard it as a state of *summum bonum* or the highest good. But the emancipated persons cannot have all the enjoyable experiences that the supreme Lord has; each individual soul is limited by his own rights and abilities, within which alone his desires may be rewarded with spontaneous fruition. Thus each emancipated person is entitled to certain types of enjoyment, limited by his own capacity and rights.

Again, in the third chapter of the third book of the *Brahma-sūtra* different types of worship are prescribed for different people: and such a difference of worship must necessarily mean difference in the attainment of fruits also. Thus it must be admitted that in the state of emancipation there are grades of enjoyment, experienced by emancipated persons of different orders.

This view is challenged by the Rāmānujas, who refer to the textual quotations of the Upaniṣads. The passages in the *Brahmā-nanda-vallī* of the *Taittirīya Upaniṣad*, where different kinds of pleasures are associated with men, *gandharvas* and other beings, are not to be interpreted as different kinds of pleasures enjoyed by different kinds of emancipated beings. According to the Rāmānuja view individuals in an unemancipated state are under the complete control of the supreme Lord. But in the emancipated state, when they become free, they are all in harmony with God and share and participate in all His joys; they are parts of Him. The emancipated person is like a good wife who has no separate will from her husband and enjoys with her husband all that he does or feels. Thus the emancipated souls, being completely associated with God, enjoy and participate in all His joys: and there cannot be any degrees of enjoyment among the different emancipated persons[1]. Sense-enjoyment, however, is not possible, as such enjoyment of Brahman at the time of emancipation would have to be the experience of the nature of Brahman, and Brahman Himself also has the self-realizing experience; this enjoyment, therefore, being only of the nature of the self-realizing experience of Brahman, cannot have any degrees or grades in it. The enjoyment of ordinary men, being of a sensuous nature, is only the contraction and expansion of their intelligence, and is therefore distinguishable into higher or lower, greater or smaller grades or degrees of enjoyment. The Madhvas think that in the stage of emancipation there are many diverse kinds of experiences, and consequently that there are degrees or grades of enjoyment associated with such experience in accordance with the capacity of the saint; but all the scriptural texts indicate that at the time of salvation one has the experience of the nature of Brahman, and, if this were admitted, there could not possibly be degrees or grades in emancipation.

In the fifth chapter Parakāla Yati, continuing the discussion, says that there is no difference in the enjoyment attained at emancipation on the ground that the methods of approaching God may be different with different persons; for, however different the methods may be, the results attained are the same, viz., the realization of the nature of Brahman. There may be some beings who are capable of greater *bhakti* or devotion and some who are capable of less, but that does not make any difference in the attainment of the final

1 *pāratantryaṃ pare puṃsi prāpya nirgata-bandhanaḥ*
svātantryam utulaṃ prāpya tenaiva saha modate

iti muktāḥ svadehātyaye karma-nāśāc ca svatantraśeṣ atvena śarīratayā bhoktur brahmaṇa eva icchām anusṛtya svānuṣaṅgika-tulya-bhoga-phalaka-tad-bhaktyaivo-pakaraṇa-bhūtāḥ yathā patnī-vyāpārādayaḥ patyur evaṃ muktānāṃ śāstra-siddhāḥ parasparavyāpārā api brahmaṇa eva sarvaśarīrakatayā śarīriṇy eva śarīra-bhoga-nyāyāt. *Vijayīndra-parājaya*, p. 43.

mukti, and, *mukti* being the same for all, its enjoyment must also be the same. The analogy of the different kinds of sacrifices leading to different results does not apply to this case; for these sacrifices are performed by external means and therefore their results may be different; but emancipation is attained by spiritual means, viz., *bhakti*. The argument that the bliss of the emancipated, being the bliss of an individual self, cannot be of the same nature is not valid either; for in the emancipated state the individuals enjoy the bliss of the realization of Brahman, which is homogeneous and ubiquitous. It is wrong too to argue that the bliss of the emancipated, being like the bliss that we experience in our worldly lives, must be capable of degrees of enjoyment. The argument that, since we have a sufficient description or definition of Brahman in regarding it as superlatively blissful, individuals cannot in the same sense be regarded as superlatively blissful, is invalid; for, since the Brahman is limitless (*ananta*), it will be wrong to limit it by such a definition as the above, since it is inapplicable to Him. The question of its conflict with the individuals who are superlatively blissful in the state of emancipation does not arise. It is also wrong to say that the bliss of Brahman, being possessed by Brahman, cannot be enjoyed by anybody else, since enjoyment (*bhoga*) really means favourable experience; the wife may thus enjoy the good qualities of her husband, the teacher of his pupil, the parents of their son. The emancipated person realizes the identity of Brahman in himself, and this realization of the nature of Brahman in himself is bliss in the superlative degree. It does not imply any decrease of qualities of Brahman, but it means that in realizing the qualities in oneself one may find supreme bliss[1].

[1] *yady atra tadīyatvena taccheṣatvaṃ tarhi rājapuruṣa-bhogye rājñi vyabhicāraḥ, bhogo hi svānukūlatva-prakāraka-sākṣātkāraḥ tadviṣayatvam eva bhogyatvam, tac ca dāsam prati svāmini śiṣyaṃ praty ācārye putraṃ prati mātarai pitari ca sarvānubhava-siddham. Vijayīndra-parājaya*, p. 124.

CHAPTER XXVI

MADHVA'S INTERPRETATION OF THE *BRAHMA-SŪTRAS*

MADHVA not only wrote a *Bhāṣya* on the *Brahma-sūtras*, but also described the main points of his views regarding the purport of the *Brahma-sūtras* in a work called the *Anuvyākhyāna*. Jaya-tīrtha wrote a commentary on the *Bhāṣya* of Madhva, known as *Tattva-prakāśikā*. Vyāsa Yati wrote another commentary on the *Tattva-prakāśikā*, the *Tātparya-candrikā*, in which he draws attention to and refutes the views of the Vedānta writers of other schools of interpretation and particularly of the Śaṅkara school[1]. Rāghavendra Yati wrote a commentary on the *Tātparya-candrikā*, the *Candrikā-prakāśa*. Keśava Bhaṭṭāraka, a pupil of Vidyādhīśa, wrote another commentary on it, the *Candrikā-vākyārtha-vivṛti*, but it extends only to the first book. Rāghavendra Yati wrote another commentary on the *Tattva-prakāśikā*, the *Bhāva-dīpikā*, in which he answered the criticisms of his opponents and explained the topics in a simpler manner. In the present section I shall try to trace the interpretation of the *Brahma-sūtras* by Madhva in the light of these commentaries, noting its difference from the interpretation of Śaṅkara and his commentators. There are, of course, several other commentaries on the *Brahma-sūtra-bhāṣya* and its first commentaries, as also on the *Anuvyākhyāna*. Thus Trivikrama Paṇḍitācārya wrote a commentary, the *Tattva-pradīpikā*, on Madhva's *Bhāṣya*. Nṛsiṃha wrote a *Bhāva-prakāśa* and Vijayīndra Yati a *Nyāyādhva-dīpikā* thereon. Again, on the *Tattva-prakāśikā* of Jaya-tīrtha there are at least five other commentaries, e.g., *Bhāva-candrikā*, *Tattva-prakāśikā-bhāva-bodha*, *Tattva-prakāśikā-gata-nyāya-vivaraṇa*, *Nyāya-mauktikā-mālā* and *Prameya-muktāvalī* by Narasiṃha, Raghūttama Yati, Vijayīndra Yati and Śrīnivāsa. On the *Tātparya-candrikā* there are at least two other commentaries, by Timmanācārya and Vijayīndra Yati, called *Candrikā-nyāya-vivaraṇa* and *Candrikādarpaṇa-nyāya-vivaraṇa*. On the *Anuvyākhyāna* there is the *Nyāya-sudhā* of Jaya-tīrtha and *Sudhā*

[1] See Helmuth von Glasenapp's *Madhva's Philosophie des Vishṇu-Glaubens*, Bonn and Leipzig, 1923, pp. 51–64.

of Vijayīndra Yati; and on the *Nyāya-sudhā* there is a number of commentaries such as that by Nārāyaṇa, *Nyāya-sudhā-ṭippanī* by Yadupati, *Vākyārtha-candrikā* by Vidyādhirāja, and the commentary by Śrīnivāsa-tīrtha[1].

Interpretation of Brahma-sūtra I. I. I.

In commenting on the first *sūtra* of Bādarāyaṇa's *Brahma-sūtra* (*athāto brahma-jijñāsā*, "now therefore Brahma-enquiry"), Śaṅkara holds that the word "now" (*atha* in Sanskrit) does not refer to any indispensable necessity for previous ritualistic performances of Vedic observances in accordance with Vedic injunctions as interpreted by the Mīmāṃsā canons, but that it refers only to the previous possession of moral qualifications, such as self-control, etc., after which one becomes fit for the study of Vedānta. The word "therefore" refers to the reason, consisting in the fact that the knowledge of Brahman alone brings about the superior painless state of all-blessedness, and justifies the enquiry of Brahman. As Brahman is the self, and as the self stands immediately revealed in all our perceptions, Brahman is also always directly known to us. But, as there are divergences of opinion regarding the nature of self, there is scope for Brahma-enquiry. So, though by the general knowledge of self, Brahman is known, the enquiry is necessary for the special knowledge of Brahman or the nature of self.

Madhva explains the reason (*ataḥ*) for Brahma-enquiry as being the grace of the Lord Viṣṇu—as greater favours from the Lord Viṣṇu can be acquired only by proper knowledge of Him, Brahma-enquiry, as a source of Brahma-knowledge, is indispensable for securing His favours. Brahma-enquiry is due to the grace of the great Lord; for He alone is the mover of all our mental states[2]. There are, according to Madhva, three stages of fitness for the study of Vedānta. A studious person devoted to the Lord Viṣṇu is in the third, a person endowed with the sixfold moral qualifications of self-control, etc., is in the second, and the person who is solely attached to the Lord and, considering the whole world to be

[1] See Helmuth von Glasenapp's *Madhva's Philosophie des Vishṇu-Glaubens*, Bonn and Leipzig, 1923, pp. 51–64.

[2] *atha-śabdasyātaḥ-śabdo hetv-arthe samudīritaḥ.*
parasya brahmaṇo Viṣṇoḥ prasādād iti vā bhavet.
sa hi sarva-mano-vṛtti-prerakaḥ samudāhṛtaḥ.
Brahma-sūtra-bhāṣya, I. I. I.

transitory, is wholly unattached to it, is in the first stage of fitness[1]. Again, the performance of the Vedic observances can entitle us only to the inferior grace of the Lord, listening to the scriptural texts to a little higher degree of grace; but the highest grace of the Lord, leading to *mukti*, can be secured only through knowledge[2]. Right knowledge can be secured only through listening to scriptural texts (*śravaṇa*), reflection (*manana*), meditation (*nididhyāsana*) and devotion (*bhakti*); no one acquires right knowledge without these. The word "Brahman", Madhva holds, means the great Lord Viṣṇu. One of the most important points which Madhva wishes to emphasize against Śaṅkara in regard to the first *sūtra*, as he brings out clearly in his *Nyāya-vivaraṇa*, consists in his belief that even the root meaning of Brahman means "the great" or "endowed with all qualities of perfection", and hence it cannot be identified with the imperfect individual souls, since we know from the Upaniṣads that the world sprang forth from it[3]. Our object in getting ourselves employed in Brahma-enquiry is the attainment of knowledge of Viṣṇu as the all-perfect One, from whom we imperfect beings are in a sense so different; Lord Viṣṇu will be pleased by this our knowledge of Him, and He will release us from our bondage. In the *Anuvyākhyāna* Madhva tries to emphasize the fact that our bondage is real, and that the release is also real, as effected by the grace of the Lord Viṣṇu. Madhva argues that, if sorrow, pain, etc.—all that constitutes bondage—were false and unreal, there would be some proof (*pramāṇa*) by which this is established. If such a proof exists, the system naturally becomes dualistic. The form-less and differenceless Brahman (according to Śaṅkara's view) cannot itself participate in any demonstration of proof. Also the falsehood of the world-appearance cannot be defined as that which is contradicted by knowledge (*jñāna-bādhyatva*); for, if the concept of Brahman is pure and differenceless intelligence, it cannot involve within it the notion that it is different from the world-appearance (*anyathātva*) or that it negates it, which is necessary if the Brahma-knowledge is said to

1 *Ibid.*

2 *karmaṇātrādhamaḥ proktaḥ*
prasādaḥ śravaṇādibhir
madhyamo jñāna-sampattyā
prasādas tūttamo mataḥ. Ibid.

3 *Brahma-śabdena pūrṇa-guṇatvoktenānubhava-siddhālpaguṇo jīvābhedaḥ.*
Nyāya-vivaraṇa of Madhva, I. I. I.

contradict the world-appearance. When the Brahman is considered to stand always self-revealed, what is the *ajñāna* of Śaṅkara going to hide? If it is said that it hides the false differences of an objective world, then a further difficulty arises—that the false differences owe their existence to *ajñāna*, but, in order that *ajñāna* might hide them, they must be proved to have a separate existence independent of *ajñāna*, so that it may hide them. Here is then a clear case of a vicious circle; the very name *ajñāna* shows that it can yield no knowledge of itself and it is therefore false; but even then such a false entity cannot have any existence, as the want of knowledge and *ajñāna* are so related that we have either a vicious infinite (*anavasthā*) or a vicious circle (*anyonyāśraya*); for in any specific case ignorance of any entity is due to its *ajñāna*, and that *ajñāna* is due to a particular ignorance, and so on. Śaṅkara's interpretation thus being false, it is clear that our sorrow and bondage are real, and the Vedas do not hold that the Brahman and the individual souls are identical—for such an explanation would openly contradict our experience[1].

The *Tātparya-candrikā*, a recondite commentary by Vyāsa Yati on the *Tattva-prakāśikā* of Jaya-tīrtha, not only explains the purport of the *Bhāṣya* of Madhva, but always refers to and tries to refute the views of opponents on most of the disputed points[2]. It raises a few important philosophical problems, in which it criticizes the views of the followers of Śaṅkara—Vācaspati, Prakāśātman and others—which could hardly be overlooked. Thus it refers to the point raised by Vācaspati in his *Bhāmatī*, a commentary on the *Bhāṣya* of Śaṅkara, viz., that there is no validity in the objection that there is no necessity of any Brahma-enquiry on the ground that the individual soul, which is identical with Brahman, is directly and immediately experienced by us, and that even the extinction of nescience (*avidyā*) cannot be considered as the desired end, since, though the self is always experienced as self revealed, such an experience does not remove the *avidyā*; and that, since the notion of the ego is implied even in studying and understanding Vedāntic

1 *satyatvāt tena duḥkhādeḥ pratyakṣeṇa virodhataḥ*
na brahmatvaṃ vaded vedo jīvasya hi kathaṃcana.
Anuvyākhyāna, I. I. I.

2 *prati-sūtraṃ prakāśyeta ghaṭanāghaṭane mayā*
svīyānya-pakṣayoḥ samyag vidāṃkurvantu sūrayaḥ.
Op. cit. verse 10.

texts, the Vedāntic passages which seem to describe Brahman as the pure identity of subject-objectless intelligence, being and blessedness, have to be otherwise explained to suit our ordinary experience. For it is certain that the self-revealed Vedānta passages denote the Brahman of the above description, and, since these cannot have any other meaning, our so-called experience, which may easily be subject to error, has to be disbelieved. The result arrived at according to the *Bhāmatī* then is that the unmistakable purport of the Vedānta texts is the differenceless reality, the Brahman, and that, since this pure Brahman is not directly revealed in experience (*śuddho na bhāti*), an enquiry regarding the nature of pure Brahman is justified[1].

The objection which Vyāsa-tīrtha raises against the above view of Vācaspati is that, if in our ordinary experience the "pure" does not reveal itself, what could this mean? Does it mean that that which does not reveal itself is a difference from the body, the negation of our character as doer and enjoyer, or non-difference between Brahman and *ātman*, or the negation of mere duality? But is this non-revealing entity different from the self? If so, then it is contrary to the general monistic Vedāntic conclusion; and, if it is urged that the existence of a negative entity will not involve a sacrifice of the monistic principle, it can be pointed out that such a view of negation has already been refuted in the work called *Nyāyāmṛta*. If such a non-revealing entity is false, then it cannot for the scriptures be the subject of instruction. If, again, it is held that it is the self (*ātman*) that does not reveal itself in experience, then this can be held only in the sense that *ātman* has two parts, that one part is revealed while the other is not, and that there is some imaginary or supposed difference (*kalpita-bheda*) between the two, such that, though the self is revealed (*gṛhīta*), its non-revealing (*abhāsamāna*) part (*aṃśa*) does not seem to have been revealed and experienced (*agṛhīta iva bhāti*). But, if even this is the case, it is acknowledged that there is no real difference between any two supposed parts of the self; the non-appearing part must be endowed with an unreal and illusory difference (*kalpita-bheda*), and no Vedānta can undertake the task of instructing in the nature of such an illusory and non-appearing self. The non-appearing part may be either real or unreal; if it is unreal, as it must be on such a supposition, it cannot

[1] *Ibid.* pp. 15–17.

be an object of the Vedānta to instruct about its nature. For, if the illusory non-appearing remains even when the self is known, this illusion can never break; for all illusory images break with the true knowledge of the locus or the support (*adhiṣṭhāna*) of such illusions (e.g. with the knowledge of the conch-shell the illusory image of silver vanishes)[1]. Moreover, the *ātman* is self-revealed, and so it cannot be said that it does not appear in experience as self-revealed (*svaprakāśatvena bhāvayogāt*). If it is argued that, though self-revealed, yet it may be covered by *avidyā*, the answer to such an objection is that, if the *avidyā* could cover the revelation of the self, the *avidyā* itself and its products such as pain, sorrow, etc., could not be revealed by it; for it is acknowledged that the revelation of these is effected by the self-revealing self[2]. It is also evident that intelligence (*cit*) or the being self-revealed (*sphuratī*) cannot also remain not-revealed (*asphuratī*). Nor can it be held that, though pure intelligence is itself in its purity self-revealed (*sva-prakāśa*), yet, since it is opposed to *ajñāna* only through the mental states (*vṛtti*) and not by itself, and since ordinarily there is no *vṛtti* for itself, it can lie covered by the *ajñāna* and, being thus hidden in spite of its self-revealing character, can become a fit subject of enquiry. Such a supposition is not true; for, if the pure intelligence is not opposed to nescience (*ajñāna*), the sorrow, etc. which are directly known by pure intelligence should have remained covered by *ajñāna*. The view is that pleasure, pain, etc. cannot be considered to have a reality even while they are not perceived. A mental state or *vṛtti* of the form of an object is only possible when the object is already existent; for according to Vedānta epistemology the *antaḥkaraṇa* or mind must rush out through the senses and get itself transformed into the form of the object, and for this the object must exist previously; but feelings such as pleasure, pain, etc., have no existence except when they are felt; and, if it is said that a *vṛtti* is necessary to apprehend it, then it must be admitted to have a previous objective existence, which is impossible[3]. It must be admitted, therefore, that feelings are directly known by

[1] *adhiṣṭhāna-jñānasyaiva bhrama-virodhitayā tasmin saty api bheda-bhramasya tan-nimittakāgṛhītāropasya vā abhyupagame nirvartakāntarasyābhāvāt tad-anivṛtti-prasaṅgāt. yad uktam abhāsamāno'ṃśa ātmātiriktaś cet satyo mithyā vā iti tatra mithyā-bhūta iti brūmaḥ. Candrikā-vākyārtha-vivṛti*, p. 18.

[2] *sva-prakāśasyāpi avidyā-vaśād abhāne avidyāder duḥkhādeś ca prakāśo na syāt, tasya caitanyaprakāśādhīnaprakāśāc copagamāt. Tātparya-candrikā*, p. 19.

[3] *sukhāder jñātaikasattvābhāvāpātāt. Op. cit.* p. 20.

pure intelligence, without the intervention of a *vṛtti* or mind-state, and that would be impossible if the *cit* had no opposition of *ajñāna*; for then the *cit* by itself would always have remained hidden, and there could not have been any apprehension of pain, etc.[1] Another point also arises in this connection in our consideration of the theory of perception of ordinary objects according to the Śaṅkara school of Vedānta. For it is held there that even in the mind-states corresponding to the perception of objects (such as "this jug") there is the revelation of pure intelligence as qualified by the mind-state-form of a jug; but if this is so, if our perception of jug means only the shining of pure intelligence (*cit*) with the mind-state-form of a jug added to it, then it cannot be denied that this complex percept necessarily involves the self-revelation of pure intelligence[2].

Further, it cannot be suggested that there is an appearance of an element of non-self (*anātman*) and that this justifies our enquiry; for, if this non-self shines forth as an extraneous and additional entity along with the self-revealing intelligence, then, since that does not interfere with the revelation of this pure intelligence, there is no occasion for such an enquiry. It is evident that this non-self cannot appear as identical (*tādātmya*) with the self; for, when the pure intelligence shines as such, there is no room for the appearance of any element of non-self in this manner (*adhiṣṭhāne tattvataḥ sphuratī anātmāropāyogāc ca*). An analogy has been put forth by Vācaspati in his *Bhāmatī*, where he wishes to suggest that, just as the various primary musical tones, though intuitively apprehended in our ordinary untutored musical perception, can only be properly manifested by a close study of musical science (*gandharva-śāstra*), so the true Brahma-knowledge can dawn only after the mind is prepared by realizing the purport of the Vedānta texts and their discussions, and so, though in the first instance in our ordinary experience there is the manifestation of the self-revealing *cit*, yet the Brahma-enquiry is needed for the fuller realization of the nature of Brahman. But this analogy does not apply; for in the case of our knowledge of music it is possible to have a general apprehension which becomes gradually more and more differenti-

[1] *sva-rūpa-cito'jñāna-virodhitve tad-vedye duḥkhādāv ajñāna-prasaṅgāt.* *Candrikā*, p. 20.

[2] *tvan-mate ayaṃ ghaṭa ityādy-aparokṣa-vṛtterapi ghaṭādyavacchinna-cid-viṣayatvāc ca. Ibid.*

ated and specially manifested with the close study of the musical science; but in the case of our knowledge of Brahman, the self-revealing intelligence, the self, this is not possible; for it is absolutely homogeneous, simple and differenceless—it is not possible to have a general and a special knowledge. It is the flash of simple self-revelation, absolutely without content, and so there cannot be any greater or lesser knowledge. For the very same reason there is no truth in the assertion contained in the *Bhāmatī*, that, though by a right understanding of the great Vedāntic text "that art thou" one may understand one's identity with Brahman, yet owing to the objections of disputants there may be doubt about Brahman which might justify a Brahma-enquiry. For, when the simple contentless pure intelligence is once known, how can there be any room for doubt? So, since the pure monistic interpretations of certain Upaniṣad texts are directly contradicted by ordinary experience, some other kinds of suitable interpretations have to be made which will be in consonance with our direct experience.

The general result of all these subtle discussions is that the Saṅkara point of view (that we are all identical with Brahma, the self-revealing *cit*) is not correct; for, had it been so, this self-revealing must be always immediately and directly known to us, and hence there would have been no occasion for the Brahma-enquiry; for, if the Brahman or the self is always directly known to us, there is no need for enquiry about it. As against the Śaṅkara point of view, the Madhva point of view is that the individual souls are never identical with Brahman; the various ordinary concepts of life are also real, the world is also real, and therefore no right knowledge can destroy these notions. If we were identical with Brahman, there would be no necessity for any Brahma-enquiry; it is only because we are not identical with Brahman that His nature is a fit subject of enquiry, because it is only by such knowledge that we can qualify ourselves for receiving His favour and grace, and through these attain emancipation. If the self is identical with Brahman, then, such a self being always self-revealed, there is no need of enquiry for determining the meaning of the Brahma part (*Brahma-kāṇḍa*) of the Vedas, as there is for determining the meaning of the *karma* part (*karma-kāṇḍa*) of the Vedas; for the meaning of the *Brahma-kāṇḍa* does not depend on anything else for its right comprehension (*dharmavad brahma-*

kāṇḍārthasyātmanaḥ paraprakāśyatvābhāvāt)[1]. Though such a Brahman is always self-revealed in our experience, yet, since by the realization of such a Brahman we are not in any way nearer to liberation (*mokṣa*), no benefit can be gained by this Brahma-enquiry. So the explanations of this *sūtra*, as given by Śaṅkara, are quite out of place. By Brahman is meant here the fullness of qualities (*guṇa-pūrtti*), which is therefore different from *jīva*, which is felt as imperfect and deficient in qualities (*apūrṇa*)[2].

Madhva also disapproves of the view of Śaṅkara that Brahma-enquiry must be preceded by the distinction of eternal and non-eternal substances, disinclination from enjoyments of this life or of the other life, the sixfold means of salvation, such as self-control, etc., and desire for liberation. For, if we follow the *Bhāmatī*, and the eternal (*nitya*) and not-eternal (*anitya*) be understood as truth and falsehood, and their distinction, the right comprehension of Brahman, as the truth, and everything else as false (*brahmaiva satyam anyad anṛtam iti vivekaḥ*), then it may very well be objected that this requirement is almost the ultimate thing that can be attained—and, if this is already realized, what is the use of Brahma-enquiry? Or, if the self is understood as *nitya* and the non-self as *anitya*, then again, if this distinction is once realized, the non-self vanishes for good and there is no need to employ ourselves in discussions on the nature of Self. The explanation of the *Pañca-pādikā-vivaraṇa* is that the word *nityānitya-viveka* means the comprehension that the result of *Brahma*-knowledge is indestructible, whereas the result of *karma*, etc. is destructible (*dhvaṃsa-pratiyogi*). But this is not justifiable either; for the appearance of silver in the conch-shell being always non-existent (*atyantābhāva*), the word "destructible" is hardly applicable to it. If it is said that in reality the conch-shell-silver is non-existent (*pāramārthikatvā-kāreṇa atyantābhāvaḥ*), but in its manifested form it may be said to be destroyed (*svarūpeṇa tu dhvaṃsaḥ*), this is not possible either; for no definite meaning can be attached to the word "in reality" (*pāramārthika*), which is explained as being "non-contradiction" (*abādhyatva*); "non-contradiction" means "in reality"; and thus we have an argument in a circle (*anyonyāśraya*). Brahma, being

[1] *Tātparya-candrikā*, p. 36.

[2] *jijñāsya-brahma-śabdena guṇa-pūrty-abhidhāyinā*
apūrṇatvenānubhūtāj jīvād bhinnaṃ pratīyate. *Ibid.* p. 46.

formless (*nirākāra*), might itself be considered as non-existent (*atyantābhāva-pratiyogitvasya nirākāre brahmaṇy api saṃbhavāt*)[1].

Again, if, as the *Vivaraṇa* has it, even sense-objects (*viṣaya*) serve only to manifest pleasure, which is but the essence of self (*ātma-svarūpa*), then there is no reason why the enjoyment of sense-objects should be considered different from the enjoyment of liberation. Again, the desire for liberation is also considered as a necessary requirement. But whose is this desire for liberation (*mumukṣutva*)? It cannot belong to the entity denoted by ego (*aham-artha*); for this entity does not remain in liberation (*aham-arthasya muktāv ananvayāt*). It cannot be of the pure intelligence (*cit*); for that cannot have any desire. Thus the interpretations of the word "now" (*atha*), the first word of the *sūtra*, were objected to by the thinkers of the Madhva school. Their own interpretation, in accordance with the *Bhāṣya* of Madhva as further elaborated by Jaya-tīrtha, Vyāsa-tīrtha, Rāghavendra Yati and others, is that the word *atha* has, on the one hand, an auspicious influence, and is also a name of Nārāyaṇa[2]. The other meaning of the word *atha* is that the enquiry is possible only after the desired fitness (*adhikārānantaryārthaḥ*)[3]. But this fitness for Brahma-enquiry is somewhat different from that demanded by the Śaṅkara school, the views of which I have already criticized from the Madhva point of view. Madhva and his followers dispense with the qualifications of *nityānitya-vastu-viveka*, and they also hold that desire for liberation must be illogical, if one follows the interpretation of Śaṅkara, which identifies *jīva* and Brahman. The mere desire for liberation is not enough either; for the *sūtras* themselves deny the right of Brahma-enquiry to the Śūdras[4]. So, though any one filled with the desire for liberation may engage himself in Brahma-enquiry, this ought properly to be done only by those who have studied the Upaniṣads with devotion, and who also possess the proper moral qualities of self-control, etc. and are disinclined to ordinary mundane enjoyments[5].

[1] *Tātparya-candrikā*, p. 69.

[2] *evaṃ ca atha-śabdo maṅgalārtha iti bhāṣyasya atha-śabdo vighnotsāraṇa-sādhāraṇakaram ātmakānanuṣṭheya-viṣṇu-smaraṇāthaśabdoccāraṇarūpa-maṅgala-prayojanakaḥ praśastarūpānanuṣṭheya-rūpa-viṣṇv-abhidhāyakaś ca iti artha-dvayaṃ draṣṭavyam. Ibid.* p. 77. The same view is also expressed in the *Tattva-pradīpa*, a commentary on Madhva's *Bhāṣya* by Trivikrama Paṇḍitācārya.

[3] *Anubhāṣya*.

[4] *Brahma-sūtra*, I. 3. 34–8.

[5] *mukti-yogyatva-bhakti-pūrvakādhyayana-śama-damādi-vairāgya-saṃpatti-rūpādhikārārpaṇena*, etc. *Tattva-prakāśikā-bhāva-dīpikā*, p. 12.

The word "therefore" (*ataḥ*) in the *sūtra* means "through the grace or kindness of the Lord Viṣṇu"; for without His grace the bondage of the world, which is real, cannot be broken or liberation attained. Jaya-tīrtha in his *Nyāya-sudhā* on the *Anuvyākhyāna* of Madhva here anticipates an objection, viz., since liberation can be attained in the natural course through right knowledge, as explained by Śaṅkara and his followers on the one hand and the *Nyāya-sūtra* on the other, what is the usefulness of the intervention of Īśvara for producing liberation? All sorrow is due to the darkness of ignorance, and, once there is the light of knowledge, this darkness is removed, and it cannot therefore wait for the grace of any supposed Lord[1]. The simplest answer to such an objection, as given in the *Nyāya-sudhā*, is that, the bondage being real, mere knowledge is not sufficient to remove it. The value of knowledge consists in this, that its acquirement pleases the Lord and He, being pleased, favours us by His grace so as to remove the bondage[2].

The word "Brahman" (which according to Śaṅkara is derived from the root *bṛhati-*, "to exceed" (*atiśayana*), and means eternity, purity and intelligence) means according to the Madhva school the person in whom there is the fullness of qualities (*bṛhanto hy asmin guṇāḥ*). The argument that acceptance of the difference of Brahman and the souls would make Brahman limited is not sound; for the objects of the world are not considered to be identical with Brahman nor yet as limiting the infinitude of Brahman; and the same sort of answer can serve in accepting the infinitude of Brahman as well as in accepting His difference from the souls[3]. The infinitude of Brahman should not therefore be considered only in the negative

[1] *tathā ca jñāna-svabhāva-labhyāyāṃ muktau kim īśvara-prasādena; na hi andhakāra-nibandhana-duḥkha-nivṛttaye pradīpam upādadānāḥ kasyacit prabhoḥ prasādam apekṣante. Nyāya-sudhā*, p. 18.

[2] The *Tattva-prakāśikā* says that the letter *a* means Viṣṇu, and *ataḥ* therefore means through the grace of Viṣṇu: *akāra-vācyād viṣṇos tat-prasādāt*, p. 4. The *Bhāmatī*, however, following Śaṅkara, explains the word *ataḥ* as meaning "since the Vedas themselves say that the fruits of sacrifices are short-lived, whereas the fruits of Brahma-knowledge are indestructible and eternal". So that through the Vedas we have disinclination from mundane and heavenly joys (*ihāmutra-phala-bhoga-virāgaḥ*), and these through Brahma-enquiry. But the *Candrikā* points out that such a connection with *vairāgya*, as signified by *ataḥ*, is remote and, moreover, the connection with *vairāgya* was already expressed by the word *atha*.

[3] *Tātparya-ṭīkā*, pp. 89–93.

way, as not being limited by difference, but as being fullness in time, space and qualities; for otherwise even the Buddhist momentary knowledge would have to be considered as equal to Brahman, since it is limited neither by time nor by space[1].

Coming to the formation of the compound Brahma-enquiry (*brahma-jijñāsā*), the *Candrikā* points out that neither Śaṅkara nor his followers are justified in explaining Brahman as being in the objective case with reference to the verb implied in "enquiry" (*jijñāsā*); for Brahma—being pure and absolute intelligence, open only to direct intuition—cannot be the fit object of any enquiry which involves discussions and arguments[2]. But, of course, in the Madhva view there cannot be any objection to Brahma being taken as the object of enquiry. According to both the *Nyāya-sudhā* and the *Tātparya-candrikā* the word "enquiry" (*jijñāsā*) in Brahma-enquiry (*brahma-jijñāsā*) means directly (*rūḍhi*) argumentative reasoning (*manana*) and not desire to know, as the followers of Śaṅkara would suggest[3]. The object of Brahma-enquiry involving reasoned discussions is the determination of the nature of Brahman, whether He possesses the full perception of all qualities, or has only some qualities, or whether He has no qualities at all[4].

Not only did the followers of Madhva try to refute almost all the points of the interpretation of this *sūtra* by Śaṅkara and his followers, but Madhva in his *Anuvyākhyāna*, as interpreted in the *Nyāya-sudhā* and *Nyāya-sudhā-parimala*, raised many other important points for consideration, which seem to strike the position of Śaṅkara at its very root. A detailed enumeration of these discussions cannot be given within the scope of a single chapter like the present; and I can refer to some only of the important points. Thus the very possibility of illusion, as described by Śaṅkara, is challenged by Jaya-tīrtha, following the *Anuvyākhyāna*.

[1] *bauddhābhimata-kṣaṇika-vijñānāder api vastutaḥ kālādy abhāvena aparicchinnatva-prasaṅgāc ca; tasmād deśataḥ kālataś caiva guṇataś cāpi pūrṇatā brahmatā, na tu bhedasya rāhityaṃ brahmateṣyate. Tātparya-ṭīkā*, p. 94.

[2] *para-pakṣe vicāra-janya-jñāna-karmaṇo brahmaṇo vicāra-karmatvāyogāt, aparokṣa-vṛtti-vyāpyasya phala-vyāpyatva-niyamāc ca. Ibid.* p. 95.

[3] The *Bhāmatī*, however, holds that the primary meaning of the word *jijñāsā* is "desire to know"; but, since desire to know can only be with reference to an object which is not definitely known (*jñātum icchā hi saṇdigdha-viṣaye nirṇayāya bhavati*), it means by implication reasoned discussion (*vicāra*), which is necessary for coming to any decided conclusion.

[4] *tasmād vedāntādinā'pāta-pratīte brahmaṇi saguṇa-nirguṇālpaguṇatvādinā vipratipatter jijñāsyatvam. Tātparya-candrikā*, p. 109.

He says that the individual is by nature free in himself in all his works and enjoyments, and is dependent only on God. That such an individual should feel at any time that he was being determined by some other agent is certainly due to ignorance (*avidyā*)[1]. Ignorance, so far as it may be said to be existent as such in the self, has real being (*avidyādikaṃ ca svarūpeṇātma-saṃbandhitvena sad eva*). So the intellect (*buddhi*), the senses, the body and external sense-objects (*viṣaya*) are really existent in themselves under the control of God; but, when through ignorance they are conceived as parts of my self, there is error and illusion (*avidyādi-vaśād ātmīyatayā adhyāsyante*). The error does not consist in their not having any existence; on the contrary, they are truly existent entities, and sorrow is one of their characteristics. The error consists in the fact that what belongs distinctly to them is considered as belonging to an individual self. When through ignorance such a false identification takes place, the individual thinks himself to be under their influence and seems to suffer the changes which actually belong to them; and, being thus subject to passions and antipathy, suffers rebirth and cannot get himself absolutely released except by the worship of God. Those who believe in the *māyā* doctrine, like Śaṅkara and his followers, however, hold that the sorrow does not exist in itself and is false in its very nature (*duḥkhādikaṃ svarūpeṇāpi mithyā*). Śaṅkara says that we falsely identify the self with the non-self in various ways; that may be true, but how does that fact prove that non-self is false? It may have real existence and yet there may be its false identification with the self through ignorance. If the very fact that this non-self is being falsely identified with the self renders it false, then the false identification, on the other side, of the self with the non-self ought to prove that the self also is false[2]. As the selves, which are bound, are real, so the sense-objects, etc., which bind them, are also real; their false identification through ignorance is the chain of bondage, and this also is

[1] *tasya parāyattatvāvabhāso'vidyā-nimittako bhramaḥ. Nyāya-sudhā*, p. 26.

[2] *atra hi pramātṛ-pramāṇa-prameya-kartṛ-karma-kārya-bhoktṛ-bhoga-lakṣaṇa-vyavahāra-trayasya śarirendriyadiṣu ahaṃ-mamādhyasa-puraḥsaratva-pradarśanena vyavahāra-kārya-liṅgakam anumānam vyavahārānyathānupapattir vā adhyāse pramāṇam uktam. na cānenāntaḥkaraṇa-śarīrendriya-viṣayāṇāṃ tad-dharmāṇāṃ duhkhādīnāṃ ca mithyātvaṃ sidhyati svarūpa-satām api tādātmya-tatsambandhitvābhyām āropeṇaiva vyavahāropapatter. na ca āropitatvamātreṇa mithyātvam; ātmano'pi antaḥkaraṇādiṣu āropitatvena mithyātva-prasaṅgāt.* *Ibid.*

real, and can be removed only through knowledge by the grace of God.

The idea suggested by the Śaṅkara school, that the notion of an individual as free agent or as one enjoying his experiences is inherent in the ego (*ahaṃ-kāra*), and is simply associated with the self, is also incorrect; for the notion of ego (*ahaṃ-kāra*) really belongs to the self and it is present as such even during deep sleep (*suṣupti*), when nothing else shines forth excepting the self, and we know that the experience of this state is "I sleep happily". This notion "I," or the ego, therefore belongs to the self[1].

If everything is false, then the very scriptures by which Śaṅkara would seek to prove it would be false. The answer to such an objection, as given by Śaṅkarites, is that even that which is false may serve to show its own falsehood and the truth of something else, just as in the case of acquired perception, e.g. in the case of *surabhi-candana*, "fragrant sandal," the sense of sight may reveal the smell as well as the colour. But the counter-reply to this answer naturally raises the question whether the false scriptures or other proofs are really existent or not; if they are, then unqualified monism fails; for their existence would necessarily mean dualism. If, on the other hand, they do not exist at all, then they cannot prove anything. The answer of Śaṅkara, that even the false can prove the true, just as a line (a unit) by the side of zeros might signify various numbers, is incorrect; for the line is like the alphabet signs in a word and like them can recall the number for which it is conventionally accepted (*saṅketita*), and is therefore not false (*rekhāpi varṇe padām-īva arthe saṅketite taṃ smārayatīti no kiṃcid atra mithyā asti*)[2].

Nor can it be maintained that the bondage of sorrow, etc. is not real; for it is felt to be so through the direct testimony of the experience of the spirit (*sākṣin*)[3]. Its unreality or falsehood cannot be proved by the opponent; for with him truth is differenceless (*nirviśeṣa*): but any attempt to prove anything involves duality between that which is to be proved and that whereby it is to be

[1] *ahaṃ-pratyayasya ātma-viṣayatvāt. Nyāya-sudhā*, p. 27. It also distinguishes two words of the same form, *aham*, though one is an *avyaya* word and the other the nominative singular of the word *asmad*. It is the former that is used to denote an evolutionary product of *prakṛti*, whereas the latter denotes the self.

[2] Several other examples of this type furnished by Śaṅkara and his followers are here given and refuted in the same manner.

[3] *duḥkhādi-bandha-satyatāyāṃ sākṣi-pratyakṣam eva upanyastam. Ibid.* p. 30.

proved, and that a differenceless entity may be the proof cannot be established by the differenceless entity itself; for this would involve a vicious circle. If the world were false, then all proofs whereby this could be established would also by the same statement be false; and how then could the statement itself be proved?

As has just been said, the opponents, since they also enter into discussions, must admit the validity of the means of proof (*pramāṇa* or *vyavahṛti*); for without these there cannot be any discussion (*kathā*); and, if the proofs are admitted as valid, then what is proved by them as valid (*prameya* or *vyāvahārika*) is also valid[1]. In this connection Jaya-tīrtha raises the points contained in the preliminary part of the *Khaṇḍana-khaṇḍa-khādya* of Śrīharṣa, where he says that it is, of course, true that no discussions are preceded by an open non-acceptance of the reality of logical proofs, but neither is it necessary to accept the validity of any proof before beginning any discussion. Those who begin any discussion do so without any previous forethought on the subject; they simply do not pay any attention to the ultimate existence or non-existence of all proofs, but simply begin a discussion as if such a question did not need any enquiry at the time[2]. In a discussion what is necessary is the temporary agreement (*samaya-bandha*) or the acceptance for the purpose of the discussion of certain canons of argument and proofs; for that alone is sufficient for it. It is not necessary in these cases that one should go into the very nature of the validity or invalidity, existence or non-existence of the proofs themselves[3]. So even without accepting the ultimate existence and validity of the *pramāṇas* it is possible to carry on a discussion, simply through a temporary mutual acceptance of them as if they did exist and were valid. So it is wrong to say that those who do not believe in their existence cannot legitimately enter into a proper discussion. After referring to the above method of safeguarding the interests of the upholders of the *māyā* doctrine, Jaya-tīrtha says that, whatever may be mutual agreement in a discussion, it remains an undeniable fact

[1] *vyavahārikaṃ vyavahāra-viṣayo duḥkhādi. Ibid.* p. 31.

[2] *na brūmo vayaṃ na santi pramāṇādīni iti svīkṛtya kathārabhyeti kiṃ nāma santi na santi pramāṇādīni ityasyāṃ cintāyāṃ udāsīnaiḥ yathā svīkṛtya tāni bhavatā vyavahriyante tathā vyavahāribhir eva kathā pravartyatām. Ibid.* p. 32.

[3] *tac ca vyavahāra-niyama-bandhād eva...sa ca pramāṇena tarkeṇa ca vyavahartavyam ityādi-rūpaḥ; na ca pramāṇādīnāṃ sattāpi ittham eva tubhyam aṅgīkartum ucitā, tādṛśa-vyavahāra-niyama-mātreṇaiva kathā-pravṛtteḥ. Ibid.*

that, if the proofs do not exist, nothing at all can be proved by such non-existing entities. Either the *pramāṇas* exist or they do not; there is no middle course. If they are not admitted to be existent, they cannot prove anything. You cannot say that you will be indifferent with regard to the existence or non-existence of *pramāṇas* and still carry on a discussion merely as a passive debater; for our very form of thought is such that they have either to be admitted as existent or not. You cannot continue to suspend your judgment regarding their existence or non-existence and still deal with them in carrying a discussion[1]. You may not have thought of it before starting the discussion; but, when you are carrying on a discussion, the position is such that it is easy to raise the point, and then you are bound to admit it or to give up the discussion. Dealing with the *pramāṇas* by mutual agreement necessarily means a previous admission of their existence[2].

The Śaṅkarites generally speak of three kinds of being, real (*pāramārthika*), apparent (*vyāvahārika*) and illusory (*prātibhāsika*). This apparent being of world-appearance (*jagat-prapañca*) is neither existent nor non-existent (*sad-asad-vilakṣaṇa*). The scriptures call this false, because it is not existent; and yet, since it is not absolutely non-existent, the proofs, etc. which are held within its conception can demonstrate its own falsehood and the absolute character of the real[3]. Such a supposition would indeed seem to have some force, if it could be proved that the world-appearance is neither existent nor non-existent; which cannot be done, since non-existence is nothing but the simple negation of existence (*tasya sattvābhāvāvya tirekāt*). So that which is different from existent must be non-existent, and that which is different from non-existent must be existent; there is no middle way. Even the scriptures do not maintain that the world-appearance has a character which is different from what is existent and what is non-existent (*sad-asad-vilakṣaṇa*).

With regard to the question what may be the meaning of the

[1] *sattvāsattve vihāya pramāṇa-svarūpasya buddhau āropayitum aśakyatvena udāsīnasya tat-svīkārānupapatteḥ. Nyāya-sudhā*, p. 34.

[2] *pramāṇair vyavahartavyam iti ca niyama-bandhanaṃ pramā-karaṇa-bhāvasya niyamāntarbhāvān niyata-pūrva-sattva-rūpaṃ karaṇatvam pramāṇānām anādāya na paryavasyati. Ibid.* p. 34.

[3] *tatra vyāvahārikasya prapañcasya sad-asad-vilakṣaṇasya sad-vilakṣaṇatvād upapannaṃ śrutyādinā mithyātva-samarthanam asad-vilakṣaṇatvāt tad-antar-gatasya pramāṇādeḥ sādhakatvaṃ ca iti. Ibid.* p. 35.

phrase "different from existents" (*sad-vilakṣaṇa*), after suggesting numerous meanings and their refutations, Jaya-tīrtha suggests an alternative interpretation, that the phrase might mean "difference (*vailakṣaṇya*) from existence in general (*sattā-sāmānya*)". But surely this cannot be accepted by the opponent; for the acceptance of one general existence would imply the acceptance of different existents, from which the abstraction can be made[1]. This cannot be accepted by a Śaṅkarite, and, as for himself, he does not accept any general existence apart from the individual existents (*dravyādy-atirikta-sattva-sāmānyasyaiva anaṅgīkārāt*). The Śaṅkarites say that the indefinable nature of this world-appearance is apparent from the fact that it is ultimately destructible by right knowledge and that this world-appearance is destructible by right knowledge and that this world-appearance is destructible is admitted even by the Madhvas. To this objection Jaya-tīrtha replies that, when the Madhvas say that the world is destroyed by the Lord, it is in the same sense in which a jug is reduced to dust by the stroke of a heavy club[2]. But even such a destruction, in our view, is not possible with regard to *prakṛti*; and this destruction is entirely different from what a Śaṅkarite would understand by the cessation (*bādha*) through knowledge (*jñāna*). For that, as Prakāśātman writes in his *Vivaraṇa*, means that the nescience (*ajñāna*) ceases with all its effects through knowledge (*ajñānasya sva-kāryeṇa vartamānena pravilīnena vā saha jñānena nivṛttir bādhaḥ*). Cessation (*bādha*), according to the Madhvas, proceeds through right knowledge (*samyag-jñāna*) regarding something about which there was a different knowledge (*anyathā-jñāna*). The existence of any such category as "different-from-existent and non-existent" (*sad-asad-vilakṣaṇa*) cannot be defined as corresponding to that which ceases through right knowledge; only that which you falsely know about anything can cease through right knowledge: the example of conch-shell-silver does not prove anything; for we do not admit that there is anything like conch-shell-silver which existed and was destroyed through right knowledge, since in fact it never existed at all. Not only in the case of conch-shell-silver, but in the case of the

[1] *sattā-sāmānyāṅgikāre ca sad-bhedo durvāra eva; na hy ekāśrayaṃ sāmānyam asti. Ibid.* p. 38.

[2] *mudgara-prahārādinā ghaṭasyeva īśvarasya jñānecchā-prayatna-vyāpārair vināśa eva. Ibid.* p. 39.

ākāśa, etc., too, the assertion that it is *sad-asad-vilakṣaṇa* is utterly wrong; for, being eternal, it can never cease.

Error or illusion consists in knowing a thing differently from what it is (*anyathā-vijñānam eva bhrāntiḥ*). Now conch-shell-silver is a simple case of *anyathā-vijñāna* or *anyathā-khyāti*, and there is nothing here of *sad-asad-vilakṣaṇatva* or *jñāna-nivartyatva* (possibility of being removed by knowledge); for it does not exist. It may be objected that, if it did not exist, one could not have the notion (*pratīti*) of it: no one can have any notion of that which does not exist; but the conch-shell-silver is to all appearance directly perceived. The answer to this is that even the opponent does not admit that there is any such concomitance that what does not exist cannot yield any notion of it; for when the opponent speaks of anything as being *asad-vilakṣaṇa*, i.e. different-from-the-non-existent, he must have a notion of what is non-existent; for, if any one is to know anything (e.g., a jug) as being different from some other thing (e.g., a piece of cloth), then, previously to this, in order to know this difference he must have known what that thing (a jug) is[1]. This again raises the epistemological problem, whether it is possible to have knowledge of the non-existent. Thus it may be asked whether the sentence "There are horns on the head of the man" conveys any meaning; and, if it does, whether it is of any existing or of a non-existing entity. It cannot be the first; for then we should have actually seen the horns; there must be notion of the non-existent entity of the horn, and so it has to be admitted that we can know non-existent entities. It cannot be said that this is not non-existent, but only that it is indefinable (*anirvacanīya*); for, if even entities like the hare's horn or man's horn should not be regarded as non-existent, then from what is it intended to distinguish conch-shell-silver? for *asad-vilakṣaṇa* must be admitted to have some meaning; *asat* cannot mean "indefinable"; for in that case conch-shell-silver, which is described as being different from *asat*, would be definable[2]. Not only can the non-existent be the object of knowledge, but it can also be the subject or the object of a verb. Thus, when it is said "the jug is being produced, *ghaṭo jāyate*," this refers

[1] *yo yadvilakṣaṇaṁ pratyeti sa tat-pratītimān yathā ghaṭa-vilakṣaṇaḥ paṭa iti pratītimān devadatto ghaṭa-pratītimān ityanumānāt. Nyāya-sudhā*, p. 57.

[2] *nirupākhyād iti cet tarhi tad-vailakṣaṇyaṁ nāma sopākhyānatvam eva. Ibid.* p. 58.

to the non-existent jug, as being the subject of the verb "to be produced, *jāyate*"; for it will be shown later that Śaṅkara's theory of the previous or simultaneous existence of effects, even before the causal operation (*sat-kārya-vāda*), is false. Therefore, since the non-existent may be known, the objection that conch-shell-silver cannot be non-existent, because it is known, is invalid.

But a further objection is raised, that, while it is not denied that the non-existent may be known, it *is* denied that the non-existent cannot appear as directly perceived and as existent (*aparokṣatayā sattvena ca*); as if one should find horns on the head of a man, as he finds them on the head of a cow. But in the case of the conch-shell-silver what is perceived is directly perceived as existent; so the conch-shell-silver must be non-existent. In answer to this the following may be urged: those who do not regard conch-shell-silver as non-existent, but as indefinable (*anirvacanīya*), have to accept the appearance of identity of "this" and the silver (*idaṃ-rajatayoḥ*). Illusion, according to these Śaṅkarites, is the appearance of something in that which is not so (*atasmiṃs tad iti pratyaya iti*). This is not, of course, *anyathā-khyāti* (a different appearance from the real); for the basis of the illusion (*adhiṣṭhāna*, as the conch-shell of the illusory silver) is not here false in itself, but only false in its appearance as silvery or associated with a false appearance (*saṃsṛṣṭa-rūpa*); but the illusory appearance (*adhyāsta*) is false both in itself (*svarūpa*) and also as associated with the object before the observer; this is admitted by the holders of the *māyā* doctrine. The holders of the *anyathā-khyāti* view of illusion think that both the conch-shell and the silver are real, only the appearances of identity of conch-shell with silver and of silver with conch-shell are false[1]. This appearance of the false or the non-existent is both immediate (*aparokṣa*), as is well known to experience, and endowed with real existence; for otherwise no one could be moved by it (*sattvenā-pratītāu pravṛttyanupapatteś ca*). Until the illusion is broken this association of the non-existent silver with the "this" does not differ in the least from the perception of real silver before the observer. The opponents would say that this is not a false and non-existent association (*anyathātvaṃ yady asat syāt*), as the Madhvas hold; but it is difficult to understand what they can mean by such an objec-

[1] *anyathā-khyāti-vādibhir adhiṣṭhānāropyayor ubhayor api saṃsṛṣṭa-rūpeṇaiva asattvaṃ svarūpeṇa tu sattvam ity aṅgīkṛtam. Ibid.* p. 58.

tion; for such an association of silver with the conch-shell cannot be real (*sat*), since, if it was so, why should it appear only in the case of illusions (*bhrānti*), where the first perception is contradicted, as in "this is not silver"? Again, those who think that in the case of illusion the silver is indefinable (*anirvacanīya*) may be asked what is the nature of that which appears as indefinable. Does it appear as non-existent or as illusory? It cannot be so; for then no one would trouble about it and try to pick it up, knowing it to be non-existent or illusory. So it has to be admitted that it appears as existent. This agrees with our experience of the illusion ("this silver"). The mere notion of silver is not enough to draw us towards it, apart from our notion of it as existing. But this has no real existence, since then it cannot be indefinable; if this is non-existent, then it has to be admitted that the non-existent appears in immediate perceptual experience and as endowed with existence. The opponents however may point out that this is not a right analysis of the situation as they understand it. For in their view the true "this" in the conch-shell and its association with silver is as indefinable as the indefinable silver itself, and so the silver in the appearance of silver is indefinable, and so their mutual connection also is indefinable. It is the reality in the conch-shell that becomes indefinably associated with the silver. The answer to this is that such a view is open to the serious defect of what is known as the vicious infinite (*anavasthā*). For, when it is said that the mutual association (*saṃsarga*) of "thisness" and "silverness" and the association of the reality of the conch-shell with the silver are both indefinable, it may be asked what exactly is meant by calling them indefinable. It is not of the nature of ordinary phenomenal experience (*vyāvahārika*); for the illusory silver is not of any ordinary use. If it is illusory (*prātibhāsika*), does it appear to be so or does it appear as if it was of the nature of ordinary phenomenal experience? If it did appear as illusory, no one would be deluded by it, when he knows it to be illusory, and he would not trouble to stoop down to pick it up. If it did appear as if it was of the nature of ordinary phenomenal experience, then it could not be really so; for then it could not be illusory. If it was not so and still appeared to be so, then the old point, that the non-existent can appear to immediate perception as existent, has to be admitted. If this appearance of silver as being of the nature of an object of ordinary phenomenal experience is itself considered as being indefinable, then the same sorts of questions may again be asked about it, and the series will be infinite; this would be a true case of a vicious infinite, and not like the harmless infinite of the seed and the shoot; for here, unless the previous series is satisfactorily taken as giving a definite solution, the succeeding series cannot be solved, and that again depends in a similar way on another, and that on another and so on, and so no solution is possible at any stage[1]. Therefore the old view that even the unreal and the non-existent may appear as the real and the existent has to be accepted; and the world-appearance should not be considered as indefinable (*anirvacanīya*).

Interpretation of Brahma-sūtra I. I. 2.

The literal translation of the second *sūtra*, *janmādy asya yataḥ*, is "from which production, etc., of this". The purport of Śaṅkara's commentary on this *sūtra* may briefly be stated as follows: "Production, etc." means production, existence and destruction. Production, existence and destruction of this world-appearance, which is so great, so orderly and so diversified, is from that ultimate cause, God (Īśvara); and neither the *paramāṇus* nor the inanimate *prakṛti* can be its cause. This rule is not intended to stand as an inference in favour of the existence of God, but is merely the description of the purport of the Upaniṣad texts on the nature of Brahman[2]; for the ultimate grasp of the nature of Brahman, which is beyond the range of our sense-organs, can only come through the right comprehension of the meaning of Upaniṣad texts.

Jaya-tīrtha, in commenting on the *Bhāṣya* of Madhva and the *Anuvyākhyāna*, follows Madhva in explaining this *sūtra* as a definition (*lakṣaṇa*) of Brahman, intended to differentiate Him from beings of His class, viz., the souls (*jīva*), and inanimate objects, which belong to a different class. The idea is that that from which the production, etc., of the world takes place is Brahman, and there are important *śruti* texts which say that the world was produced from Brahman[3]. It has already been pointed out that by "pro-

[1] *Nyāya-sudhā*, p. 59.

[2] *janmādi-sūtraṃ nānumānopanyāsārthaṃ kiṃ tarhi vedānta-vākya-pradarśanārtham.*

[3] Jaya-tīrtha refers to another interpretation of the *sūtra* as *janma ādyasya hiraṇyagarbhasya yatas tad brahma.* The *Tātparya-candrikā* discusses the points of view raised in the *Nyāya-sudhā* and elsewhere with regard to the meaning of

duced, etc." in the *sūtra* Śaṅkara understood production (*sṛṣṭi*), existence (*sthiti*) and destruction (*laya* or *bhaṅga*), and he there reconciled the six stages of existent things (*bhāva-vika*) referred to by Yāska in the *Nirukta*, such as being produced, to continue to exist, to grow, to change, to decay and to be destroyed, as being included within the three stages referred to by him; for growth and change are included within production (*janma*), and decay is included within destruction. Madhva, however, includes eight different categories in the term "production, etc."; these with him are production (*sṛṣṭi*), existence (*sthiti*), destruction (*saṃhāra*), control (*niyama*), knowledge (*jñāna*), ignorance (*ajñāna*), bondage (*bandha*) and release (*mokṣa*)[1]. The existence of all these qualities implies the fullness of qualities signified by the name Brahman. That single being in whom all the above-mentioned eightfold qualities exist is called Brahman.

Generally two kinds of definitions are distinguished from each other, viz., essential (*svarūpa-lakṣaṇa*) and accidental (*taṭastha-lakṣaṇa*). Prakāśātman, the writer of the *Pañca-pādikā-vivaraṇa*, speaks of this definition of Brahman as being of the latter type, since it is only in association with *māyā* that Brahman can be said to be the cause of the production, etc., of the world-appearance. In itself

Brahman as referred to by the word *yataḥ*. *Bṛha*, a constituent of the word *brahman*, has several technical meanings (*rūḍhi*), such as *jāti* (class-notion), *jīva*, *Kamalāsana* or *Brahmā*. But the word is not used here in its technical sense, but in the etymological sense, which signifies the entity in which there is a fullness of qualities; for it is only in this sense that the Upaniṣad texts alluded to in connection with this *sūtra* and the previous one become significant. Again, on the basis of other texts, which speak of Him (from which everything is produced) as lying in the ocean, Brahman here means Viṣṇu (as in the *Samākhya-śruti*, *dyāvāpṛthivī paraṃ mama yonir apsu antaḥ samudre*), because it is only in Him that there is the fullness of all qualities. This characteristic would not apply to any of the other technical (*rūḍhi*) senses, such as *jāti* or *jīva*; and so it is that, though the *rūḍhi* sense is stronger than the etymological sense (*yaugika*), yet the latter has preference here: *brahma-śabdasya jīve rūḍhatve'pi bādhaka-sadbhāvāt tad brahma iti śruty-uktaṃ brahma viṣṇur eva* (*Tattva-prakāśikā*). It may also be added that, according to the *Tattva-prakāśikā*, *Tātparya-candrikā* and other Madhva works, it is held that, though ordinarily *brahma* has the technical sense of *jīva*, yet with scholars the word always has the technical meaning of Viṣṇu. Thus a distinction is drawn between the ordinary technical sense (*rūḍhi*) and the technical sense with scholars (*vidvad-rūḍhi*), and preference is given to the latter: *viduṣāṃ brahma-śabdena viṣṇu-vyakti-pratīteḥ* (*Tātparya-candrikā*, p. 120).

[1] *Anubhāṣya* of Madhva or *Brahma-sūtra*, I. I. 2. Madhva quotes for his authority a passage from the *Skanda-purāṇa*:

utpatti-sthiti-saṃhāra-niyatir jñānam āvṛtiḥ
bandha-mokṣaṃ ca puruṣād yasmāt sa harir ekarāṭ.

it is of the nature of pure bliss (*ānanda*), which is also identical in its nature with pure knowledge[1]. Madhva and his followers, however, consider the characteristics mentioned in the *sūtra* as essential and do not think that the essences of *ānanda* and *jīva* are in any sense anything else but qualities, in which case they would not be essences identical with Brahman, as would be required by what may be called a *svarūpa-lakṣaṇa*; for *ānanda* is as much a characteristic as any other characteristic is, and, if *ānanda* could be regarded as a defining essence, then the characteristic of being the cause of the world might also be regarded as a defining essence[2]. If His being the cause involves qualities unessential to Himself, then in His purity He could neither be *ānanda*, whether as a class notion, as a desirable feeling (*anukūla-vedanā*), as being the dearest one (*parama-premāspada*), or as being opposed to sorrow; for, if these be the nature of *ānanda*, it must by its very nature be associated with inessential traits (*sopādhikatvāt*). So knowledge also must express something and must therefore by its very nature be connected with something outside of itself (*artha-prakāśātmakatvena sopādhikam eva*); for knowledge is inseparably connected with the knower and the known (*jñānasya jñātṛ-jñeya-sāpekṣatvāt*). It has been urged in the *Pañca-pādikā-vivaraṇa* that the knowledge which forms the essential defining characteristic of Brahman is all-illuminating revelation which is not in any way conditioned by its being dependent on, or its being inseparably connected with, objects[3]. But the fact that it can reveal everything implies possession of power, and this power is necessarily connected with the object with reference to which it is effective. Moreover, if any power can be considered as being an essential defining characteristic, then the power of producing the world and of affecting it in other ways (as referred to in the *sūtra*) might also be considered as an essential defining characteristic[4]. The objection, that the essence (*svarūpa*) of anything cannot be expressed by a reference to anything other than itself, is not valid; for a thing wholly unrelated

[1] *Pañca-pādikā-vivaraṇa*, pp. 222–3.

[2] *ānandaṃ lakṣaṇam iti cet tarhi jagat-kāraṇaṃ lakṣaṇam astu.*
Tātparyā-candrikā, p. 140.

[3] *anena sarvajña-śabdena sarvāvabhāsa-kṣamaṃ vijñapti-mātram ādityādi-prakāśavad aviṣayopādhikaṃ vijñānam eva brahma-svarūpa-lakṣaṇam.*
Pañca-pādikā-vivaraṇa, p. 210.

[4] *sāmarthyasya śakti-rūpatvād, viṣaya-nirūpyatvāc ca, jagaj-jananādi-sāmarthyasyaiva svarūpa-lakṣaṇatvopapatteś ca.* *Tātparya-candrikā*, p. 141.

to, and devoid of all reference to, any other thing cannot be known (*svarūpasya sva-vedyatvāt*). It is further held by the opponents that an accidental defining characteristic like that of the Brahman being the cause of the world (*taṭastha-lakṣaṇa*)—as, for example, indicating a house by a temporary association, as that of a crow sitting on the roof of it—is not an inherent and intrinsic characteristic (*ananvayī*), whereas an essential characteristic like *ānanda* is an inherent and intrinsic constituent (*kāryānvayī*) of the thing. But such an objection cannot rule out the causality, etc., of Brahman as being inessential; for we want to know Brahman in its essence as the cause or *kāraṇa* of the world, as much as by any other characteristic. The essential feature of Brahman is its fullness of qualities, as the ultimate cause of production, etc., and these are in no sense less essential than His nature as *ānanda*. Like the power of burning in fire, these powers of world-creation, etc., are coextensive with the essence of Brahman. It is indeed surprising, says Vyāsa-tīrtha, that the Śaṅkarites should enter into any long discussion with regard to the distinction of essential and accidental definitions; for all definitions mean the making known of object by its distinctive characteristics such as are well known[1]. But, as the Śaṅkarites believe in absolutely unqualified Brahman, how do they undertake to define it? All definitions must proceed through the means of known qualities[2]. Whether a definition (*lakṣaṇa*) be *svarūpa* or *taṭastha*, it must proceed by way of enumerating distinctive characteristic qualities; and, as the Brahman of the opponents has no qualities, it cannot be defined at all.

Rāmānuja in his interpretation of this *sūtra* asserted that the characteristic qualities and powers of Brahman referred to in the *sūtra* belong to Brahman as He is immanent; but the Upaniṣads also define Him in His essential characteristic features, as transcendent, by speaking of Him as being truth, knowledge, the infinite (*satyaṃ jñānam anantaṃ brahma*); and this distinguishes Him from the souls and inanimate objects, which also are held within Him. But Vyāsa-tīrtha points out that Madhva has by implication denied this in his *Anuvyākhyāna*, where he distinctly asserted the causality of

[1] *prasiddhasya asādhāraṇa-dharmasya lakṣaṇatvena*; also *asādhāraṇa-dharmo hi lakṣaṇam parikīrtyate. Tātparya-candrikā*, pp. 140, 143.

[2] *svarūpaṃ vā taṭasthaṃ vā lakṣaṇaṃ bhedakaṃ mataṃ*
sajātīyād vijātiyāt tac-cādvaiti-mate katham. Ibid. p. 143.

Brahman as its own intrinsic constitutive definition[1]. Vyāsa-tīrtha says that in defence of the Rāmānuja point of view it may be urged that, as a special form of a jug would differentiate it from all other things, yet its possession of smell constitutes its nature as earth, so, though causality, etc., differentiate Brahman from others, yet it is His nature as truth, knowledge and infinite that really differentiates Him from souls and inanimate objects. But Vyāsa-tīrtha contends that this is wrong, since the special form of a jug differentiates it from cloth, etc., and not from earth; an earthen jug is itself earth; but the special form which distinguishes an earthen jug from other objects (such as cloth, etc.) also by that very fact shows that it belongs to a class different from them. Here also the causality which differentiates Brahman from souls, etc., also shows that He is different in nature from them. So the fact that Brahman is the ultimate cause of production, etc., constitutes its essential defining characteristic. He, Brahman, not only possesses these qualities, but in reality His qualities are infinite, and their possession forms His defining characteristic (*ananta-guṇa-sattvam eva brahmano lakṣaṇam*)[2].

The two principal Vedānta texts by which the Śaṅkarites seek to establish their theory of absolute monism (*advaita*) are "that art thou" (*tat tvam asi*) and "Brahma is truth, knowledge, infinite" (*satyaṃ jñānam anantam brahma*). Now Madhva urges that, since these may also be otherwise interpreted directly (*mukhyārtha*) on the basis of difference, it is not proper to explain them on the basis of non-difference with an indirect and distant meaning (*lakṣaṇa*)[3]. The *Nyāya-sudhā* points out that with the monistic interpretation the difficulty arises, how to identify the qualityless (*nirguṇa*) with the qualified (*saguṇa*), as in the case of the souls; the qualityless is indeterminable by itself (*nirguṇa syaiva nirūpayitum aśakyatvāt*)[4]. If this *nirguṇa brahma* were entirely different from the *saguṇa* Brahma or Īśvara acknowledged by the Śaṅkarites, then there would be a duality; if the relation is held to be indefinable (*anirvacanīya*),

[1] *asyodbhavādi-hetutvaṃ sākṣād eva sva-lakṣaṇam. Op. cit.*

[2] *Nyāya-sudhā*, p. 107.

[3] *bhedenaiva tu mukhyārtha-sambhave lakṣaṇaṃ kutaḥ. Anuvyākhyāna*, p. 5. *nanu abhedam upādāya sūtra-lakṣaṇaṃ vā āśrayaṇīya-bhedam upādāya mukhya-vṛttir na iti sandihyate; vayaṃ tu brūmaḥ, dvitīya eva pakṣaḥ śreyān. Nyāya-sudhā*, p. 101.

[4] *Ibid.* p. 102.

then the criticisms against the indefinable suggested in the first *sūtra* apply to it[1]. If, however, it is urged that the unity or identity referred to in the above passages is with regard to the Brahman as pure self-revealing intelligence and the same element as forming the principal reality of *jīva*, then it becomes difficult to understand how the Upaniṣads can have the presumption of revealing the self-revealing intelligence[2]. Moreover, it may be objected that, if the Brahman is nothing else but pure intelligence, then its "unity" with *jīva* as taught by the Upaniṣads, being different from Brahman, is false; for "unity" is not pure intelligence, and, if unity is false, then duality becomes true. If the "unity" was identical with pure intelligence, then with the self-shining of pure intelligence there would be the self-shining of "unity" too, and even for expressing the "unity" it would not be necessary to take the help of the Upaniṣads or of anything else.

Another question of importance arises in connection with the attribution of the epithets "truth," "knowledge," "infinite" to Brahman. Is Brahman, to whom all these qualities are attributed, a simple unity in Himself, or is He a complex of many qualities, truth, knowledge, infinite, etc., which have different connotations and are not synonymous? Pure intelligence (*caitanya*) is one, but these epithets are many. How can we conceive the one *caitanya* to coexist in itself with the many attributes which are said to belong to it? How is the plurality of these attributes to be implied in the unity of the one[3]? To this the answer that Madhva gives in his *Anuvyākhyāna*, which is further explained by Jaya-tīrtha, is that it has to be admitted that in the unity of Brahman there is some special virtue (*atiśaya*) which represents difference and serves its purpose; there is no other way of solving the difficulty, and this is the only solution left (*gaty-antarābhāvād arthāpattyā*). This special virtue, which serves to hold and reconcile plurality without sacrificing its

[1] In such Upaniṣad passages as *sākṣī cet kevalo nirguṇaś ca* (*Śvet.* VI. 11) the word *nirguṇa*, "qualityless," could be given a modified meaning, in view of the fact that the strict direct meaning is not possible even in the context of the sentence; for in the very passage itself the *brahman* is said to be not only *nirguṇa*, but *sākṣī* (direct perceiver) also, and this is evidently a *guṇa*. It is not possible to attribute a *guṇa* and to call it *nirguṇa* at the same time. *Nyāya-sudhā*, p. 102.

[2] *svaprakāśa-caitanyātmakaṃ ca śāstra-pratipādyaṃ ceti vyāhatam.* *Ibid.* p. 103.

[3] *caitanyam ekaṃ satyatvādīny anekāni iti saṃkhyā-vailakṣaṇyam ityādi-bhedakāryāṇi cāvagamyante.* *Ibid.* p. 106.

unity, is called by the Madhvas *viśeṣa*; this *viśeṣa* exists not only in Brahman, but in all other things. Thus, for example, a cloth is not different from its whiteness, since both of them form one indissoluble whole. So it has to be admitted that there is in cloth such a special virtue, a *viśeṣa*, by which it remains one with itself and yet shows the plurality of qualities with which it is sure to form a whole. These *viśeṣas* are infinite in number in the infinite number of objects, though there is no intrinsic difference in the nature of these *viśeṣas*. Each whole or unity may be said to possess as many *viśeṣas* as there are qualities through which it expresses itself, and each of these *viśeṣas* is different from the others according to the difference of the quality with which it is associated; but these *viśeṣas* are not considered as requiring other *viśeṣas* for their connection with the thing, and so there is no vicious infinite (*anavasthā*). So there is not only one *viśeṣa* in each thing, but there are as many *viśeṣas* as there are different qualities unified with it[1].

The result attained by the first two *sūtras*, then, is that Brahman, as defined by the second *sūtra*, is the object of enquiry for those who seek release.

Interpretation of Brahma-sūtra I. I. 3–4.

Śaṅkara gives two interpretations of this *sūtra*, *śāstra-yonitvāt* ("because of its being scripture-cause"), expounding the compound "scripture-cause" in two ways, first, as "the cause of the scriptures," secondly as "that of which the scripture is the cause or source of revelation or *pramāṇa*." The force of the first meaning is that Brahman is omniscient not only as being the cause of the production, etc., of the world, but also as being the cause of the revelation of the Vedas, since no one but an omniscient being could be the source of the Vedas, which are the greatest repository of knowledge unfathomable by human intellect. The second meaning suggests that it is the Vedas only which can prove to us that Brahman is the cause of the production, etc., of the world[2].

[1] *tepy ukta-lakṣaṇa-viśeṣā aśeṣato'pi vastuṣu pratyekam anantāḥ santy ato nokta-doṣāvakāśaḥ; ananta iti upalakṣaṇam; yatra yāvanto vyavahārās tatra tāvanto viśeṣa iti jñātavyam. Ibid.* p. 106.

It may be noted in this connection that the Madhvas were more or less forced to this position of accepting the *viśeṣas*, as they could not accept the *samavāya* relation of the *Nyāya-vaiśeṣika*, which is rejected by the *Brahma-sūtras*.

[2] *śāstrād eva pramāṇāj jagato janmādi-kāraṇam brahma adhigamyate.*
Bhāṣya of Śaṅkara, I. I. 3.

The Madhvas accept the second meaning and object to the first, on the ground that His being the source of the Vedas does not in any way add anything to His omniscience beyond what was implied in His being the cause of the production, etc., of the world, as described in the first *sūtra*[1]. The commentators on Madhva's *Bhāṣya* and *Anuvyākhyāna*, Jaya-tīrtha, Vyāsa-tīrtha and others, following Madhva's explicit statements, argue in detail that the word "scripture" (*śāstra*) in the *sūtra* means the Vedas *Ṛk*, *Sāman*, *Yajus* and *Atharva*, and not the *Śaiva āgamas*, which hold that Śiva is the cause of the production, etc., of the world[2]. The Madhva commentators try to emphasize the fact that inference by itself is helpless to prove Brahman to be the cause of the production, etc., of the world.

Sūtra I. I. 4. Śaṅkara here supposes a *mīmāṁsā* objection that the Vedas cannot have for their purport the establishing of Brahman, since they are always interested in orders and prohibitions with reference to some kind of action. He refutes it by saying that a proper textual study of the Upaniṣads shows that their principal purport is the establishing of pure Brahman, and that it has no connection whatever with the performance of any action.

Madhva holds that this *sūtra* (*tat tu samanvayāt*, "that however through proper relationing") means that it is intended to indicate that all the scriptures (*śāstra*) agree in holding Viṣṇu as Brahman and the ultimate cause, and not Śiva or any other gods, as held by

[1] *kathaṃ ca ananta-padārthakasya prapañcasya kartṛtvena na sphuṭaṃ tad-eka-deśa-veda-kāraṇatvena sphuṭībhaviṣyati sarvajñam.* Jaya-tīrtha further argues that there is no such concomitance whereby from the authorship of the Vedas omniscience can be inferred. Again, if the authorship of the Vedas means the literary composition representing facts known by sense experience or inference, it must be admitted that the Vedas have been composed like any other ordinary book (*pauruṣeya*); and, if the authorship means only utterance like that by a teacher, that may not mean even a thorough knowledge of the contents of the Vedas. *Nyāya-sudhā*, pp. 111, 112.

[2] The other scriptures which the Madhvas admitted as authoritative are the *Pañcarātra*, *Mahābhārata* and *Rāmāyaṇa* and not the *Sāṃkhya*, *Yoga* or *Pāśupata*. Thus Madhva says in his *Bhāṣya: Ṛg-yajuḥ-sāmātharvaś ca bhārataṃ pañca-rātrakam, mūla-rāmāyaṇaṃ caiva śāstrāṇīty abhidhīyate.* Whatever else agrees with these has to be accepted as valid, and the other so-called scriptures have to be rejected. The *Pañcarātra* and the Vedas are in thorough agreement, and therefore the word *śāstra* in the *sūtra* refers to the *Pañcarātra*; so that by declaring the validity of the *Pañcarātra* alone the Vedas, which agree with it, are also accepted as valid, but everything else which is in disagreement with it is rejected. Thus Madhva says in his *bhāṣya* on this *sūtra*: *veda-pañcarātrayor aikyābhiprāyeṇa pañca-rātrasyaiva prāmāṇyam uktam.*

others. The *mīmāṃsā* objection and Śaṅkara's own views are, of course, all rejected on grounds similar to those already dealt with in the first *sūtra*[1].

A general review of the other important topics of the Brahma-sūtras.

On the topic (*adhikaraṇa*) contained in *sūtras* 5–11 Śaṅkara suggests the following argument against the supposed Sāṃkhya claim that the ultimate causality is attributed in the Upaniṣads to *prakṛti* and not to Brahman: he says that *prakṛti* is foreign to the Upaniṣads; for they speak of perceiving (*īkṣater nāśabdam*)[2], and perceiving can only be true of an intelligent agent. Brahman being all-revealing eternal intelligence, omniscience and perceiving (*īkṣati*) can very well be attributed to it. The word "perceiving" (*īkṣati*) of the text cannot be otherwise explained; for its reference to an intelligent agent is further emphasized by its being called *ātman* (self), a word whose application to conscious agents is well known[3]; and we are certain that the word *ātman* cannot mean *prakṛti*; for the instruction of liberation is given to it[4]. Moreover, the whole chapter ends in the same vein, and there is no further correction of the sense in which the *ātman*, etc., have been used, as might have been the case, if this *ātman* had been rejected later on as bearing a meaning irrelevant to the teaching of release[5]. Moreover, the cause referred to in the above passages is also spoken of in the same textual connection as being the last place of dissolution, to which everything returns[6]. Moreover, there is in all Vedānta texts[7] a complete agreement in regard to such an interpretation, and there are also explicit statements of the Upaniṣads (*śrutatvāc ca Brahma-sūtra*, I. I. II), which declare an Īśvara to be the ultimate cause of the world[8]. So according to Śaṅkara the purport of this topic is that according to these *sūtras* Brahman is the ultimate cause and not *prakṛti*.

[1] See *Tātparya-candrikā* (on I. I. 4), pp. 201–4.

[2] The Upaniṣad passage referred to is *tad aikṣata bahu syām*, etc. *Chāndogya*, VI. 2. 3.

[3] *gauṇaś cet nātma-śabdāt, Brahma-sūtra*, I. I. 6; see also *anena jīvena ātmanā anupraviśya* (*Chāndogya*, VI. 3. 2).

[4] *tan-niṣṭhasya mokṣopadeśāt. Ibid.* I. I. 7; also text referred to. *Chāndogya*, VI. 14. 2.

[5] *heyatva-vacanāc ca. Ibid.* I. I. 8.

[6] *svāpyayāt, ibid.* I. I. 9; also *Chāndogya*, VI. 8. I.

[7] *gati-sāmānyāt. Ibid.* I. I. 10.

[8] *Śvetāśvatara*, VI. 9.

Madhva and his followers do not find any reference to a refutation of the Sāṃkhya doctrine, but a simple assertion of the fact that Brahman is not undescribed by the *śāstras*, because they themselves enjoin that He should be perceived[1]. Unless Brahman could be described by the *śāstras*, there would be no meaning in their reference to the possibility of discussing it. This refers to the highest soul, Brahman, and not only to the lower and qualified soul, because it is said that liberation depends on it, and it is also said that the final return of all things in the great dissolution takes place in it; the *nirguṇa* Brahman is also definitely described in the Upaniṣad texts.

On the sixth topic (*sūtras* 12–19) Śaṅkara tries to prove, by a comparison of the several passages from the *Taittirīya Upaniṣad* and the supposed objections from the other Upaniṣads, that the word "blissful," *ānandamaya* (in *Taittirīya*, II. 5) refers to the supreme soul or Brahman; Madhva and his followers contend that the word *ānandamaya* refers to Viṣṇu and to him alone, and not to any other deity. All the other *sūtras* of this *adhikaraṇa* are explained as giving contextual references and reasons in support of this interpretation[2].

[1] *Brahma-sūtra*, I. I. 5. This is quite a different interpretation of the rule and surely not less cogent. The objection raised against Śaṅkara's interpretation is that his reference to the Sāṃkhya as being foreign to the Vedas (*aśabda*) is not accepted by the adherents of the Sāṃkhya, and there are certainly passages in the Upaniṣads (e.g. *Śvet*. IV. 51) which have to be taken as distinct references to the Sāṃkhya. Moreover, if Brahman could not be grasped and described by any of the *pramāṇas*, there would be hardly any proof of its existence; it would be like the hare's horn.

[2] The *Nyāya-sudhā* points out that Śaṅkara's commentary is based on an untenable hypothesis that two kinds of Brahman are referred to in the Upaniṣads, Brahman as under the cover of *avidyā*, and as pure Brahman. Of the Upaniṣad passages (those which refer to the former), some are said to be for purposes of worship and consequent material advantage (*upāsanāni abhyudayārthāni*), some for attaining gradually the progressive stages towards liberation (*krama-muktyarthāni*), etc. Jayatīrtha says that this theory is wholly wrong, since it is quite unwarrantable to hold that Brahman is of two kinds (*brahmaṇo dvairūpyasya aprāmāṇikatvāt*); for all the Vedānta texts refer to Nārāyaṇa, the repository of all qualities, but some describe him as being endowed with omniscience, omnipotence, all-controlling power, beauty, etc., some with the negative qualities of being devoid of sin, sorrow, ordinary elemental bodies (*prākṛta-bhāntikara-vigraha-rahitatva*), and others describe Him as unspeakable and beyond speech and thought (to show His deep and mysterious character); others again leave out all the qualities and describe Him as the one, and yet others as the soul of all (*sarvātmaka*); but these are all but different descriptions of the supreme person Viṣṇu (*parama-puruṣa*), and do not in any way refer to two different kinds of Brahman. It is only through a misconception (that Brahman has only a unitary

On the seventh topic (*sūtras* 20, 21) Śaṅkara discusses the meaning of a passage (*Chāndogya*, I. 6. 6, 7, 8), and comes to the conclusion that the person referred to as being in the orb of the sun and the eye is supreme Brahman. But Madhva refers to a quite different passage and quite a different relation of contexts; and he holds that the indwelling person referred to in that passage is Nārāyaṇa, the supreme lord[1]. On the eighth topic (*sūtra* 22) Śaṅkara discusses *Chāndogya*, I. 9. 1, and concludes that the word *ākāśa* there does not mean elemental *ākāśa*, but supreme Brahman. Madhva also takes the same passage as being indicated by the *sūtra* and comes to the same conclusion; but with him supreme Brahman always means Viṣṇu. On the ninth topic (*sūtra* 23) Śaṅkara discusses *Chāndogya*, I. 11. 4, 5, and concludes that the word *prāṇa* there is used to denote Brahman and not the ordinary *prāṇa*, which is a modification of *vāyu*. Madhva, however, comes to the same conclusion with reference to the use of the word *prāṇa* in another passage of the *Taittirīya Āraṇyaka*[2]. On the tenth topic (*sūtras* 24–27) Śaṅkara discusses *Chāndogya*, III. 13. 7, and concludes that the word *jyotiḥ* there means Brahman and not ordinary light. Madhva does not discuss this topic in the *Anuvyākhyāna*; in his *Bhāṣya* he comes to the same conclusion, but with reference to a quite different text. The 25th *sūtra*, which according to Śaṅkara belongs to the tenth topic, is considered by Madhva as forming a separate topic, where the word *chandas*, meaning *gāyattrī* (*Chāndogya*, III. 12. 1, *gāyattrī vā idaṃ sarvaṃ bhūtam*, "*gāyattrī* is all this"), means Viṣṇu and not the metre of that name or the combination of letters forming that metre. The next and last topic of the first chapter of the first book (*sūtras* 28–31) is explained by Śaṅkara as referring to the *Kauśītaki* passage III. 1. 2, 3, where the word *prāṇa* is said by him to refer to Brahman, and not to any air current. Madhva, however, takes this topic in reference to a

nature) that these have been so interpreted by Śaṅkara, who had no previous teachers who knew the Vedas to guide him (*tato vyākula-buddhayo guru-sampradāya-vikalā aśruta-veda-vyākhyātāraḥ sarvatrāpi veda-rūpatām anusandadhānā vedaṃ chindanti*). *Nyāya-sudhā*, p. 124.

[1] According to Madhva doubt occurs in regard to the following passage of the *Taittirīya*, whether the word *antaḥ-praviṣṭa* in it refers to the supreme self or to some other being: *antaḥ-praviṣṭaṃ kartāram etam antaś candramasi manasā carantaṃ sahaiva santaṃ na vijānanti devāḥ*. *Taittirīya Āraṇyaka*, III. 11. 5.

[2] *tad vai tvaṃ prāṇo' bhavaḥ; mahān bhagati; prajāpateḥ; bhujaḥ kariṣyamāṇaḥ; yaddevān prāṇayanneveti. Ibid.*

number of other passages occurring in the *Aitareya*, where the word *prāṇa* occurs, and holds that textual comparisons show that the word in those passages refers to Viṣṇu and not to ordinary air currents, or souls, etc.

The second chapter of the first book has altogether seven topics or subjects of discussion according to both Śaṅkara and Madhva. On the first topic Madhva, referring to certain Vedic passages, seeks to establish that they refer to Nārāyaṇa as the culmination of the fullness of all qualities[1]. Though He is capable of rousing all the powers of all objects even from a distance, yet He in a sportive way (*līlayā*) is present everywhere and presides over the budding energies of all objects. It is further pointed out that the succeeding passages distinguish the all-pervading Brahman from *jīvas*, or souls, by putting the former in the accusative and the latter in the nominative case in such a way that there ought not to be any doubt that the references to the qualities of all-pervadingness, etc., are to Brahman and not to the *jīvas*[2]. Śaṅkara, however, refers to an altogether different text (*Chāndogya*, III. 14. 1) as hinted at by the topic and concludes, after a discussion of textual comparisons, that the passage alludes to Īśvara and not to *jīva*. On the second topic Madhva raises with reference to *Bṛhad-āraṇyaka*, I. 2. 5, the doubt whether the "eats" (*atti*) refers to the destructive agency of Viṣṇu or of Aditi, and decides in favour of the former, and states that Viṣṇu is also often called by the name Aditi[3]. Śaṅkara, how-

[1] *Aitareya-Āraṇyaka*, III. 2. 3.

[2] *Ibid.*

[3] Some interesting points on this topic are here noted by Jaya-tīrtha in his *Nyāya-sudhā* on the *Anuvyākhyāna*. Thus Jaya-tīrtha says that an objection may be made that God, being the producer and the destroyer of the universe, is consequently eternal, but actions (*kriyā*) are non-eternal: and how then can the two contradictory qualities reside in God (*nityānityayoḥ katham abhedaḥ syāt*)? The answer to the objection is that even actions in God are static (*na kevalam īśvaraḥ sthiraḥ api tu sa tadīya-viśeṣa-dharmo'pi kṛyā-rūpaḥ sthiraḥ*); and this is not impossible, since there is no proof that all actions must be of a vibratory (*parispanda*) nature (which may not exist in God). Again, there can be no objection to admitting vibrations to be eternally existing in God. As motion or action can as a result of continuous existence for many moments produce contacts and so forth, so eternally existing motion or action could produce contacts and separations at particular moments (*yathā aneka-kāla-vartiny api kriyā kadācit saṃyogādi ārabhate na yāvat sattvam, tathā nityāpi kadācit saṃyogādy ārabhatāṃ ko virodhaḥ*). All actions exist eternally in God in potential form as *śakti*, and it is only when this is actualized (*vyakti*) that real transformations of energy and performance of work happen (*śakti-rūpeṇa sthiraḥ sa yadā vyajyate, tadā vyavahārālambanam*); actuality is but a condition or special state of potential power (*vyakti-śabdena śakter eva avasthāviśeṣasya vivakṣitatvāt*). In this connection Jaya-tīrtha

ever, holds that the topic relates to *Kaṭha*, I. 2. 24, and concludes that the "eater" there alluded to is Īśvara and not *jīva* or *agni*[1]. The third topic relates according to both Madhva and Śaṅkara to *Kaṭha*, I. 3. 1, and the dual agents alluded to there are according to Madhva two forms of Īśvara, while according to Śaṅkara they are *jīva* and Īśvara. Madhva wishes to lay stress on what he thinks the most important point in relation to this topic, viz., that *brahma* and *jīva* are, upon the cumulative evidence of the Upaniṣad texts, entirely distinct[2]. On the fourth topic Madhva alludes to a passage in *Chāndogya*, IV. 15, where a doubt seems to arise about the identity of the person who is there alluded to as being seen in the eye, i.e., whether this person is fire (*agni*) or Viṣṇu, and Madhva concludes on textual grounds that it is Viṣṇu[3]. Śaṅkara also alludes to the same passage here; he comes to a similar conclusion, and holds that the person referred to is Īśvara. The fifth topic is said, according to both Śaṅkara and Madhva, to allude to *Bṛhad-āraṇyaka*, III. 7. 1. 2, where an inner controller (*antar-yāmin*) of the world is referred to, and it is concluded that this inner controller is Viṣṇu (Īśvara according to Śaṅkara) or *jīva*. One of the *sūtras* of this topic (*śarīraś-cobhaye'pi hi bhedenainam adhīyate*) points out clearly that in both recensions of the *Bṛhad-āraṇyaka*, III. 7. 22 (the Kaṇvas and the Mādhyandinas), the soul (*śārīra*) is distinctly said to be different from the inner controller. Śaṅkara could not ignore this; but he, of course, thinks that the difference is due to the fact that the *jīva* is limited by the limitation of *ajñāna*, as the unlimited *ākāśa* is by a jug (*ghaṭākāśavad upādhi-paricchinnatvāt*). Vyāsa-tīrtha, in his *Tātparya-candrikā*, makes this an occasion for a severe criticism of the adherents of the theory of Advaita Vedānta.

also indulges in a long argument and discussion to prove that *karma* or actions are directly perceived and not merely inferred (*pratyakṣāśritaṃ karma pratyakṣam eva*).

[1] The *Tātparya-candrikā* objects to Śaṅkara's interpretation, pointing out that the word *carācara* in the *sūtra* is not mentioned in the text referred to, and the word *odana* in the text ought to mean destruction (*saṃhārya*). Madhva quotes the *Skanda* and *Brahma-vaivarta purāṇas* in support of his view.

[2] Madhva quotes in support of his view *Brahma-purāṇa, Paiṅgi-śruti, Bhāllaveya-śruti*, etc. Śaṅkara, however, seems to be fighting with an opponent (*ākṣeptṛ*) who held that the dual agents alluded to in the passage cannot be either *buddhi* and *jīva* or Jīva and Īśvara.

[3] Jaya-tīrtha, in his *Nyāya-sudhā* on this topic, points out that the quality that we possess of being controlled by God and the necessity that He should always remain as the controller have also been so ordained by God.

He says that, if, in spite of such manifest declarations of duality, these *sūtras* are otherwise explained, then even the Buddhists may be considered to be making a right interpretation of the *sūtras*, if they explain their purport to be the unreality of everything except the *śūnya* ("the Void"). The Buddhists make their opposition from outside the Vedas, but the holders of the *māyā* doctrine do it from within the Vedas and are therefore the more dangerous[1]. The sixth topic is said to relate to the *Muṇḍaka*, I. I. 6 (according to both Madhva and Śaṅkara), and it is held by both that *bhūta-yoni* there and *akṣara* in *Muṇḍaka*, I. I. 7, refer to Viṣṇu (Īśvara according to Śaṅkara) and not to *prakṛti* or *jīva*. In *sūtra* 26 (*rūpopanyāsāc ca*) of this topic Śaṅkara first tries to refute a previous interpretation of it, attributed to Vṛttikāra, who is supposed to hold here (on the ground of the contents of the *Muṇḍaka* passages (II. I. 4) immediately following it) the view that Īśvara has for His self the entire changing universe (*sarva-vikārātmakaṁ rūpaṁ upanyasyamānaṁ paśyāmaḥ*). With reference to *sūtra* 21 of this topic, Vyāsatīrtha points out in his *Tātparya-candrikā* that, in opposing the supposition that, since only inanimate things can be the cause of other immediate things, it is only *prakṛti* that can be the cause of this immediate world; Vācaspati points out that in the occurrence of illusions through illusory superimpositions without real change (*vivarta*) there is no condition that there should be any similarity between the basis of illusion (*adhiṣṭhāna*) and the illusion imposed (*āropya*) on it. There is nothing to prevent illusions taking place through the perceiver's mental deficiencies, his ignorance or passions, without any similarity. The world is an illusory imposition on Brahman, the pure and unchangeable:

vivartas tu prapañco'yam brahmaṇo pariṇāmiṇaḥ
anādi-sādhanodbhūto na sārūpyam apekṣate.

Vyāsa-tīrtha, of course, cannot agree to this interpretation of Śaṅkara, and tries to argue on the basis of other Upaniṣad texts,

[1] *advaitibhir vyākriyate kathaṃ vā dvaitadūṣaṇaṃ sūtrayatāṃ savsiddhānta-tyāgaṃ vinaiva tu yadi mithyārthavādīni sūtraṇītyeva kartavyaṃ, sūtra-vyākhyā tarhi veda-bādhya-mithyātva-bodhako bauddhāgamo'pi vedasya vyākḥyā-rūpaḥ prasajyate, bauddho'pi brahma-sūtraṃ vyākhyāyate yathā tathā bhavamiva mithyaiṣo'rthaḥ kiṃtu tattvaṃ śūnyameveti kīrttayet, asad-vetyādivcanaṃ tasya syāt tattva-vedakaṃ. svoktaṃ śrutibhiḥ sūtre yatnena sādhitaṃ mithyārthatāṃ kathaṃ brūyāt sūtrāṇāṃ bhāṣyakṛt svyaṃ. saugatā veda-bāhyā hi vedāprāmāṇya-vādinaḥ, avaidikā iti jñātvā vaidikaiḥ parivarjitāḥ. vedān praviśya vedānām aprāmāṇyaṃ prasādhayan māyī tu yatnatas tyajyaḥ.*

and also on the analogy of creation given there as of a spider (and not of the rope-snake, as would be the case with *vivarta*), that it should be admitted that the qualified Viṣṇu is referred to here[1]. The seventh topic is said to relate to *Chāndogya*, V. 11, and the doubt arises whether the word *Vaiśvānara* used there refers to fire or to Viṣṇu; Madhva, upon a comparison of contextual passages, decides in favour of the latter (Śaṅkara prefers Īśvara)[2].

The first topic of the third chapter of the first book is said to allude to *Muṇḍaka*, II. 11. 5, and it is held by Madhva that the "abode of Heaven and earth" (*dyu-bhv-ādy-āyatana*) refers to Viṣṇu and not to Rudra. Śaṅkara holds that it signifies Īśvara and not *prakṛti*, *vāyu* or *jīva*[3]. The second topic is said to relate to certain passages in the *Chāndogya* (such as VII. 23, 24, VII. 15, 1, etc.), where *prāṇa* is described as great, and the conclusions of Madhva and Śaṅkara respectively are that *prāṇa* here means Viṣṇu and Īśvara. The third topic is said to relate to *Bṛhad-āraṇyaka*, III. 8, 7, 8, where the word *akṣara* is said to mean Viṣṇu according to Madhva and Brahman according to Śaṅkara, not "alphabetic sign," which also is ordinarily meant by that word. The fourth topic alludes, according to Madhva, to *Chāndogya*, VI. 2. 1, and it is held that the word *sat*, there used, denotes Viṣṇu and not *prakṛti*, as the word *aikṣata* ("perceived") occurs in the same context. With Śaṅkara the topic alludes to *Praśna*, V. 2, 5. This is opposed by Vyāsa-tīrtha in his *Tātparya-candrikā* on textual grounds[4]. The fifth topic is said to allude to *Chāndogya*, VIII. 1. 1, and the word *ākāśa* there used is said to refer to Viṣṇu[5]. The sixth topic is said to relate to the *Muṇḍaka*, and the light there alluded to is said to be the light of *brahman* and not some other light or soul. The seventh topic is

[1] Jaya-tīrtha discusses on this topic, in accordance with the discussions of the *Anuvyākhyāna*, the reality of negative qualifications, and argues that negation, as otherness from, has a full substantive force. Thus such qualifications of Brahman as *adṛśya*, etc., are real qualities of Him.

[2] With reference to rule 26 of this topic (I. 2. 26) Śaṅkara notes a different reading (*puruṣavidham api cainam adhīyate*) for that which he accepts (*puruṣam api cainam adhīyate*). The former, however, is the reading accepted by Madhva.

[3] In the concluding portions of the first rule of this topic Śaṅkara refers to the views of some other interpreter as *apara aha*. It is hard to identify him; no clue is given by any of the commentators on Śaṅkara.

[4] *Tātparya-candrikā*, pp. 610–12. In the first rule of this topic Śaṅkara quotes the view of some other interpreter, which he tries to refute.

[5] In *sūtra* 19 of this topic a different interpretation of *Chāndogya*, VIII. 11, by some other interpreter is referred to by Śaṅkara. He also refers in this *sūtra* to more than one interpretation of the *Brahma-sūtra*.

said to allude to *Kaṭha*, II. 4. 13, and Madhva holds that the word "Lord" (Īśvara), there used, signifies not air, but Viṣṇu. Śaṅkara, however, thinks that the difficulty is with regard to another word of the sentence, viz., *puruṣa*, which according to him means Īśvara and not *jīva*. The eighth topic purports to establish that even the gods are entitled to higher knowledge. The tenth topic is said to allude to *Kaṭha*, II. 6. 2, and it is held that the *prāṇa*, which is there referred to as shaking the world, is neither thunder nor wind, but God. The eleventh topic, according to Madhva, alludes to *Bṛhad-āraṇyaka*, IV. 3. 7, and it is held that the word *jyotih* used there refers to Viṣṇu and not to Jīva. Śaṅkara, however, thinks that the topic alludes to *Chāndogya*, VIII. 12. 3, and maintains that the word *jyotih* used there means Brahman and not the disc of the Sun. The twelfth topic is said to allude to *Chāndogya*, VIII. 14. 1, and *ākāśa*, as there used, is said to refer to Viṣṇu according to Madhva and to Brahman according to Śaṅkara. The thirteenth topic, according to Madhva, alludes to *Bṛhad-āraṇyaka*, IV. 3. 15, and it is held that *asaṅga* ("untouched") in this passage refers to Viṣṇu and not to Jīva. Śaṅkara, however, thinks that the allusion is to *Bṛhad-āraṇyaka*, IV. 3. 7, and that *vijñānamaya* ("of the nature of consciousness") refers to Brahman and not to Jīva.

The fourth chapter of the first book is divided into seven topics. Of these the first topic discusses the possible meaning of *avyakta* in *Kaṭha*, I. 3. 11, and Śaṅkara holds that it means "human body," while Madhva says that it means Viṣṇu and not the *prakṛti* of the Sāṃkhya[1]. The second topic, containing three *sūtras*, is supposed to allude to *Śvetāśvatara*, IV. 5, according to Śaṅkara, who holds that it refers to the material principles of fire, water and earth and not to

[1] The word *avyakta*, ordinarily used to denote *prakṛti* on account of its subtleness of nature, can very aptly be used to denote Brahman, who is the subtlest of all and who by virtue of that subtlety is the ultimate support (*āśraya*) of *prakṛti*. Śaṅkara's interpretation of *avyakta* as the subtle material causes of the body is untenable; for, if the direct meaning of *avyakta* is forsaken, then there is nothing to object to in its referring to the *prakṛti* of the Sāṃkhya. The supposed Sāṃkhya argument—that the assertion contained in the passage under discussion (that *avyakta* is superior (*parā*) to *mahat* and *puruṣa* is superior to *avyakta*) can be true only if by *avyakta prakṛti* is meant here—is not true; for since all qualities of *prakṛti* are dependent on God, attributes which could be applied to *prakṛti* could also be applied to God its master (*pradhānādigata-parāvaratvādi-dharmāṇāṃ bhagavad-adhīnatvāt*). *Tāttva-prakāśikā*, p. 67.

In this topic the *sūtra*, *vadatīti cen na prājño hi prakaraṇāt* (I. 4. 5), as read by Śaṅkara, is split up by Madhva into two *sūtras*, *vadatīti cen na prājño hi* and *prakaraṇāt*, which are counted as I. 4. 5 and I. 4. 6 respectively.

prakṛti[1]; according to Madhva it is more an extension of the previous topic for the purpose of emphasizing the fact that, like many other words (*camasa*, etc.), *avyakta* here means Viṣṇu and not *prakṛti*.

With Madhva, however, the second topic begins with *sūtra* I. 4. 9, and not with I. 4. 8 as with Śaṅkara. With Madhva the second topic is restricted to I. 4. 9 and I. 4. 10, and it alludes to a passage beginning *vasante vasante jyotiṣā yaja*, which is regarded by others as alluding to the *Jyotiṣṭoma* sacrifice; Madhva holds that the word *jyotiṣ* here used does not refer to the *Jyotiṣṭoma* sacrifice, but to Viṣṇu. The third topic with both Madhva and Śaṅkara consists of *sūtras* 12, 13 and 14, and they both allude here to the same passage, viz., *Bṛhad-āraṇyaka*, IV. 4. 17; Śaṅkara thinks that it refers to the five *vāyus*, not to the twenty-five categories of the Sāṃkhya, but Madhva holds that it refers to Viṣṇu. He has been called "five" (*pañca-janāḥ*), possibly on account of the existence of five important qualities, such as of seeing (*cakṣuṣṭva*), of life (*prāṇatva*), etc. The fourth topic according to Śaṅkara conveys the view that, though there are many apparently contradictory statements in the Upaniṣads, there is no dispute or contradiction regarding the nature of the creator. Madhva, however, holds that the topic purports to establish that all the names, such as *ākāśa*, *vāyu*, etc., of things from which creation is said to have been made, refer to Viṣṇu. Madhva contends that the purport of the *Samanvaya-sūtra* (I. 1. 4) is that all words in the Upaniṣads refer to Viṣṇu and Viṣṇu alone, and it is in accordance with such a contention that these words (*ākāśa*, etc.), which seem to have a different meaning, should prove to refer to Viṣṇu and Viṣṇu alone. These proofs are, of course, almost always of a textual character. Thus, in support of this contention Madhva here quotes *Bṛhad-āraṇyaka*, III. 7. 12, etc. The fifth topic, consisting of I. 4. 16 (I. 4. 15 according to Śaṅkara), 23 (I. 4. 24 according to Śaṅkara) according to Madhva, is to the effect that there is no difficulty in the fact that words which in the Upaniṣads are intended to mean Viṣṇu are seen to have in ordinary linguistic usage quite different meanings. Śaṅkara, however, counts the topic from I. 4. 15–18 and holds that it alludes to *Kauśītaki Brāhmaṇa*, IV. 19, and that the being who is there sought to be known is not Jīva, but Īśvara; this is opposed by Vyāsa Yati in his

[1] *ajam ekam lohita-śukla-kṛṣṇam*, etc. *Śvetāśvatara*, IV. 5.

Tātparya-candrikā on grounds of *sūtra* context, which according to him does not justify a reference to the meanings of passages after the concluding remarks made shortly before in this very chapter[1]. The sixth topic, consisting with Śaṅkara of I. 4. 19–22, alludes to *Bṛhād-āraṇyaka*, IV. 5. 6 and concludes that *ātman* there refers to Brahman and not to *jīva* enduring the cycles of *saṃsāra*. Madhva, however, thinks that the sixth topic (I. 4. 24–28) concludes after textual discussions that even those words, such as *prakṛti*, etc., which are of the feminine gender, denote Viṣṇu; for, since out of Viṣṇu everything is produced, there cannot be any objection to words of feminine gender being applied to him. With Śaṅkara, however, the seventh topic begins with I. 4. 23–27 (Śaṅkara's numbering), and in this he tries to prove that Brahman is not only the instrumental cause, but also the material cause (*upādāna-kāraṇa*) of the world. To this the obvious Madhva objections are that, if the material cause and the instrumental cause of the universe could be identical, that could also have been the case with regard to a jug; one could assume that the potter and the mud are identical. Stray objections are also taken against the *Bhāmatī*, which supposes that material cause here means "the basis of illusion" (*bhramādhiṣṭhāna*). Śaṅkara, however, has an eighth topic, consisting of only the last *sūtra* of I. 4, which corresponds to the seventh topic of Madhva. Madhva holds that the import of this topic is that such words as *asat* ("non-existent") or *śūnya* also denote Viṣṇu, since it is by His will that non-existence or even the hare's horn is what it is. Śaṅkara, however, holds that the topic means that so far the attempts at refutation were directed against the Sāṃkhya doctrine only, because this had some resemblance to the Vedānta doctrines, in that it agreed that cause and effect were identical and also in that it was partly accepted by some lawgivers, for instance Devala and others—while the other philosophical doctrines such as the Nyāya, Vaiśeṣika, etc., which are very remote from the Vedānta, do not require any refutation at all.

The first chapter of the second book contains thirteen topics. The whole chapter is devoted to refuting all objections from the point of view of the accepted works of other schools of thinkers. Madhva holds that the first topic is intended to refute the objections

[1] *Tātparya-candrikā*, p. 821. Other objections also are made to Śaṅkara's interpretation of this topic.

of other schools of believers, such as the Pāśupata, etc., who deny that Viṣṇu is the ultimate cause of the world[1]. But these views have no validity, since these teachings are not in consonance with the teaching of the Vedas; all such doctrines are devoid of validity. The Vedas are not found to lend any support to the traditional canonical writings (*smṛti*) known as the *Pañcarātra* or to those of the Pāśupatas or of the Yoga, except in certain parts only. Śaṅkara, however, takes this topic as refuting the opinion that the Vedic texts are to be explained in consonance with the Sāṃkhya views on the ground that the Sāṃkhya represents some traditional canonical writings deserving of our respect; if models of interpretation were taken from the Sāṃkhya, that would come into conflict with other canonical writings such as Manu, the *Gītā*, etc., which deserve even greater respect than the Sāṃkhya. That the Sāṃkhya is entitled to respect is due to the fact that it is said to represent Kapila's view; but there is no proof that this Kapila is the great sage praised in the Upaniṣads; and, if this is not so, the Sāṃkhya's claim to respect vanishes.

The second topic of Madhva (third of Śankara) is supposed by him to import that no one could, on account of the unfruitfulness of certain Vedic sacrifices in certain cases, doubt the validity of the Vedas, as one could the validity of the Pāśupata texts; for the Vedas are eternal and uncreated and, as such, are different from other texts. The authority of the Vedas has to be accepted on their own account and is independent of reference to any other text[2]. If under the circumstances, in spite of the proper performance of any sacrifice, the desired results are not seen to follow, that must be explained as being due to some defects in the performance[3]. The

[1] According to Madhva the topic consists of the first three *sūtras*, while Śaṅkara has one topic for the first two *sūtras* and another for the third *sūtra* (*etena yogaḥ pratyuktaḥ*), and the latter merely asserts that the arguments given in the first topic against the Sāṁkhya refute the Yoga also.

[2] Madhva mentions here the following text as being alone self-valid, quoting it from the *Bhaviṣyat-purāṇa* in his *Bhāṣya* (II. I. 5).

ṛg-yajuṣ-sāmātharvāś ca mūla-rāmāyaṇaṃ tathā
bhāratam pañca-rātram ca veda ity eva śabditaḥ
purāṇāni ca yānīha vaiṣṇavā nivido, viduḥ
svataḥ-prāmāṇyam eteṣāṃ nātra kiṁcid vicāryate.

[3] There is not only a discrepancy in the division of topics, and the order of *sūtras*, between Madhva and Śaṅkara, but also addition of a new *sūtra* in Madhva's reading of the text of the *Brahma-sūtras*. Thus the second topic with Madhva consists of the fourth and the fifth *sūtras* only, and the third topic of the sixth and the seventh *sūtras*. But the fifth *sūtra* is the sixth in the Śaṅkara's text and the

main points of the third topic of Śaṅkara (*sūtras* 4–12) are as follows: It may be objected that the unconscious and impure world could not have been produced from the pure Brahman of the pure intelligence, and that this difference of the world as impure is also accepted in the Vedas; but this is not a valid objection; for the Upaniṣads admit that even inanimate objects like fire, earth, etc., are presided over by conscious agents or deities; and such examples as the production of hair, nails, etc., from conscious agents and of living insects from inanimate cow-dung, etc., show that it is not impossible that the unconscious world should be produced from Brahman, particularly when that is so stated in the Upaniṣads. There cannot be objection that this would damage the doctrine of coexistence or pre-existence of effects (*sat-kārya-vāda*); for the reality of the world, both in the present state and even before its production, consists of nothing but its nature as Brahman. In the state of dissolution everything returns to Brahman, and at each creation it all joins the world cycle, except the emancipated ones, as in the awakened state after dreams; and such returns of the world into Brahman cannot make the latter impure, just as a magician is not affected by his magic creations or just as the earth-forms of jug, etc., cannot affect their material, earth, when they are reduced thereto. Moreover, such objections would apply also to the objectors, the Sāṃkhyas. But, since these difficult problems which cannot be settled by experience cannot be solved by inference—for, however strongly any inference is based, a clever logician may still find fault with it—we have to depend here entirely on Vedic texts.

The third topic of Madhva (*sūtras* 6, 7) is supposed to raise the objection that the Vedas are not trustworthy, because they make impossible statements, e.g., that the earth spoke (*mṛd abravīt*); the objection is refuted by the answer that references to such conscious actions are with regard to their presiding deities (*abhimāni-devatā*). The fourth topic of Madhva (*sūtras* 8–13) is intended to refute other supposed impossible assertions of the Vedas, such as that concerning the production from non-existence (*asat*); it is held that,

sixth of Madhva is the fifth of Śaṅkara. The seventh *sūtra* of Madhva is altogether absent in Śaṅkara's text. The third topic of Śaṅkara consists of *sūtras* 4–11. But the topics of Madhva are as follows: second topic, *sūtras* 4, 5; third topic, *sūtras* 5, 6, 7; fourth topic, *sūtras* 8–13, the thirteenth being the twelfth of Śaṅkara's text. Śaṅkara has for his fourth topic this *sūtra* alone.

if it is urged as an answer that there may be some kind of non-existence from which on the strength of Vedic assertions production is possible (though it is well-known that production is impossible from all kinds of non-existence, e.g., a hare's horn), yet in that case the state of dissolution (*pralaya*) would be a state of absolute non-existence (*sarvā sattva*), and that is impossible, since all productions are known to proceed from previous states of existence and all destructions must end in some residue[1]. The answer given to these objections is that these questions cannot be decided merely by argument, which can be utilized to justify all sorts of conclusions. Śaṅkara's fourth topic consists of only the twelfth *sūtra*, which says that the objections of other schools of thought which are not generally accepted may similarly be disregarded.

The fifth topic of Śaṅkara (*sūtra* II. I. 13) is supposed by him to signify that the objection that the enjoyer and the enjoyable cannot be identified, and that therefore in a similar way Brahman cannot be considered as the material cause of the world, cannot hold, since, in spite of identity, there may still be apparent differences due to certain supposed limitations, just as, in spite of the identity of the sea and the waves, there are points of view from which they may be considered different. According to Madhva, however, this topic means that those texts which speak of the union of *jīva* with Brahman are to be understood after the analogy of ordinary mixing of water with water; here, though the water is indistinguishably mixed, in the sense that the two cannot be separated, still the two have not become one, since there has been an excess in quantity at least. By this it is suggested that, though the *jīva* may be inseparably lost in Brahman, yet there must be at least some difference between them, such that there cannot be anything like perfect union of the one with the other[2].

The sixth topic, consisting of the same *sūtras* in Śaṅkara and Madhva (*sūtras* 14–20), is supposed by Śaṅkara to affirm the identity of cause and effect, Brahman and the world, and to hold that the apparent differences are positively disproved by scriptural texts and arguments. Śaṅkara holds that *Chāndogya*, VI. I. I,

[1] *sata utpattiḥ saśeṣa-vināśaś ca hi loke dṛṣṭaḥ*. *Madhva-bhāṣya*, II. I. 10.

[2] It is pointed out by Vyāsa-tīrtha that Śaṅkara's interpretation is wrong, both with regard to the supposed opponent's view (*pūrva-pakṣa*) and as regards the answer (*siddhānta*). The illustration of the sea and the waves and foam (*phena-taraṅga-nyāya*) is hardly allowable on the *vivarta* view. *Tātparya-candrikā*, p. 872.

definitely asserts the identity of Brahman with the world after the analogy of clay, which alone is considered to be real in all its modifications as jug, etc. So Brahman (like clay) alone is real and the world is considered to be its product (like jug, etc.). There are many Upaniṣad texts which reprove those who affirm the many as real. But this again contradicts ordinary experience, and the only compromise possible is that the many of the world have existence only so long as they appear, but, when once the Brahma-knowledge is attained, this unreal appearance vanishes like dream-experiences on awaking. But even from this unreal experience of the world and from the scriptures true Brahma-knowledge can be attained; for even through unreal fears real death might occur. The practical world (*vyāvahārika*) of ordinary experience exists only so long as the identity of the self with Brahman is not realized; but, once this is done, the unreal appearance of the world vanishes. The identity of cause and effect is also seen from the fact that it is only when the material cause (e.g. clay) exists that the effect (e.g. *ghaṭa*) exists, and the effects also ultimately return to the cause. Various other reasons are also adduced in II. I. 18 in favour of the *sat-kārya-vāda*. Madhva, however, takes the topic in quite a different way. Brahman creates the world by Himself, without any help from independent instruments or other accessories; for all the accessories and instruments are dependent upon Him for their power. Arguing against Śaṅkara's interpretation, Vyāsa-tīrtha says that the unreal world cannot be identified with Brahman (*anṛtasya viśvasya satya-brahmābhedāyogāt*). Moreover, *abheda* cannot be taken in the sense in which the *Bhāmatī* takes it, namely, as meaning not "identity", but simply "want of difference"; for want of difference and identity are the same thing (*bhedābhāve abhedadhranūyāt*). Moreover, if there is no difference (*bheda*), then one cannot be called true and the other false (*bhedābhāve satyānṛta-vyavasthāyogāc ca*). The better course therefore is to admit both difference and non-difference. It cannot be said that *ananyatva* ("no-other-ness") is the same as imposition on Brahman (*brahmaṇy āropitatvam*). What Vyāsa-tīrtha wants to convey by all this is that, even if the Upaniṣads proclaim the identity of Brahman and the world, not only does such an identity go against Śaṅkara's accepted thesis that the world is unreal and untrue and hence cannot be identified with Brahman, but his explanation that "identity" means illusory imposition (*āropa*) is unacceptable, since no one thinks the conch-shell to be identical with its illusory imposed silver. There are no grounds for holding that knowledge of the basis should necessarily involve knowledge of the imposed, and so the former cannot be considered as the essence of the latter; and the knowledge of earth does not remove the knowledge of jug, etc., nor does knowledge of earth imply knowledge of its form as jug[1]. Jaya-tīrtha in his *Nyāya-sudhā* on this topic formulates the causal doctrine of the Madhva school as being *bhedābheda* theory, which means that effect is in some ways identical with cause and in other ways different. Thus it opposes both the extremes—the complete difference of cause and effect as in Nyāya, and their complete identity as in Śaṅkara or the Sāṃkhya. He argues that, if the effect were already existing identical with the cause, then that also would be existent previously in its cause, and so on till the original root cause is reached. Now, since the root cause is never produced or destroyed, there could be no production or destruction of ordinary things, such as cloth, jug, etc., and there could be no difference between eternal entities, such as soul, etc., and non-eternal entities, such as jug, etc., and causal operations also would be useless. Moreover, if the effect (e.g., cloth) is previously existent in the cause (e.g., threads), it ought to be perceptible; if the existence of anything which is in no way perceptible has to be accepted, then even the existence of a hare's horn has to be admitted. If the effect (e.g., cloth) were already existent, then it could not be produced now; the effect, again, is largely different from the cause; for, even when the effect is destroyed, the cause remains; the causes are many, the effect is one; and the utility, appearance, etc., of them both also widely vary. It is urged sometimes that production of the effect means its manifestation (*vyakti*) and its destruction means cessation of manifestation (*avyakti*). This manifestation and non-manifestation would then mean perception (*upalabdhi*) and non-perception (*anupalabdhi*). That would mean that whatever is perceived at a particular time is produced at that time. If the effect were previously existent, why was it not perceived at that time? In case everything must exist, if it is to appear as produced, then it may be asked whether the manifestation (*abhivyakti*) was also existent before the appearance

[1] *mṛt-tattva-jñāne'pi tat-saṃsthāna-viśeṣatva-rūpa-ghaṭatvā-jñānena ghaṭas tattvato na jñāta iti vyavahārāt. Tātparya-candrikā*, p. 879.

of the effect; if so, then it ought to have been visible at the time; if the manifestation also requires another manifestation and that another, then there is infinite regress. The point of view of causal conception accepted by Jaya-tīrtha is that, if the cause of production exists, there is production, and if sufficient cause of destruction exists, there is destruction. A hare's horn is not produced, because there is not a sufficient cause for its production, and *ātman* is not destroyed, because there is not a sufficient cause for its destruction[1].

The seventh topic with Śaṅkara (*sūtras* 21–23) is said to answer the objection that, if Brahman and *jīva* are identical, then it is curious that Brahman should make Himself subject to old age, death, etc., or imprison Himself in the prison-house of this body, by pointing out that the creator and the individual souls are not one and the same, since the latter represent only conditional existence, due to ignorance; so the same Brahman has two different forms of existence, as Brahman and as *jīva*. According to Madhva the topic is intended to introduce a discussion in favour of Īśvara being the creator, as against the view that individuals themselves are the creators. According to him this topic consists of *sūtras* 21–26; with Śaṅkara, however, of *sūtras* 24 and 25, which according to him mean that, on account of the existence of diverse powers, it is possible that from one Brahman there should be the diversified creation. Again, *sūtras* 26–28 form according to Śaṅkara the ninth topic, which purports to establish that it is possible that the world should be produced from the bodiless Brahman. The eighth topic begins with Madhva from the 28th *sūtra*, as counted by him, and extends to the 32nd. According to Madhva the object of this topic is to refute the arguments urged against the all-creatorship of Viṣṇu. Thus it refutes the objections that, if Brahman worked without any instrument, His whole being might be involved even in creating a single straw, etc. Everything is possible in God, who possesses diverse kinds of power. According to Śaṅkara *sūtras* 30, 31, forming the tenth topic, maintain that Brahman possesses all powers and can perform everything without the aid of any sense organs. *Sūtras* 33 and 34 (32 and 33 of Śaṅkara's counting) form a new topic, which maintains that, though all His wishes are always fulfilled, yet He

[1] *yasya ca vināśa-kāraṇaṃ vidyate tat sad api nirudhyate, na ca khara-viṣāṇa-janmani ātmavināśe vā kāraṇam asti iti tayor janana-vināśābhāvaḥ.*
Nyāya-sudhā, p. 302.

creates this world only in play for the good of all beings. The same is also here the purport of Śaṅkara's interpretation of this topic. The tenth topic, consisting of *sūtras* 34–36, is said to maintain that the rewards and punishments bestowed by God upon human beings are regulated by Him in accordance with the virtuous and sinful deeds performed by them, and that He does so out of His own sweet will to keep Himself firm in His principle of justice, and therefore He cannot be said to be in any way controlled in His actions by the *karma* of human beings, nor can He be accused of partiality or cruelty to anyone. The same is also the purport of Śaṅkara's interpretation of this topic. The chapter ends with the affirmation that the fact of Viṣṇu's being the fullness of all good qualities (*sadā-prāpta-sarva-sad-guṇam*) is absolutely unimpeachable.

In the second chapter of the second book, which is devoted to the refutation of the views of other systems of Indian thought, Madhva and Śaṅkara are largely in agreement. It is only in connexion with the twelfth topic, which Śaṅkara interprets as a refutation of the views of the Bhāgavata school, that there is any real divergence of opinion. For Madhva and his followers try to justify the authority of the *Pañcarātra* and interpret the topic accordingly, while Śaṅkara interprets it as a refutation of the Bhāgavata school.

The third chapter of the second book begins with a topic introducing a discussion of the possibility of the production of *ākāśa*, since two opposite sets of Upaniṣad texts are available on the subject. Madhva's followers distinguish two kinds of *ākāśa*, *ākāśa* as pure vacuity and *ākāśa* as element; according to them it is only the latter that is referred to in the Upaniṣad texts as being produced, while the former is described as eternal. The second, third, fourth, fifth and sixth topics relate to the production of air, the being (*sat*) or Brahman, fire and earth, and it is held that Brahman alone is originless and that everything else has come out of Him. These topics are almost the same in Śaṅkara and Madhva. The seventh topic maintains according to Madhva that Viṣṇu is not only the creator, but also the destroyer of the world. According to Śaṅkara, however, this topic asserts that the successive production of the elements from one another is due not to their own productive power, but to the productive power of God Himself. The eighth topic holds that the destruction of elements takes place in an order inverse to that in which they were produced. Madhva accepts the same meaning of the topic. The ninth topic, according to Madhva, discusses whether it is true that all cases of destruction must be in inverse order to their production, and it is decided in the affirmative; the objection that, since *vijñāna* is produced from *manas* and yet the latter is destroyed first, these two must be considered as exceptions, is not correct, since in reality *vijñāna* is not produced out of *manas*. *Manas* has two senses, as "category" and as "inner organ" (*antaḥkaraṇa*), and the word *vijñāna* also means "category" and "understanding" (*avabodha*). Where *vijñāna* is said to rise from *manas*, it is used only in a general way, in the sense of understanding as arising from grasping (*ālocana*); Śaṅkara, however, interprets this topic as consisting only of the 16th *sūtra* (while Madhva takes the 15th and 16th *sūtras* from this topic), asserting that the production of the sense faculties does not disturb the order of the production of the elements. The tenth topic of Madhva, the 17th *sūtra*, is supposed to hold that there cannot be any destruction of Viṣṇu. With Śaṅkara this topic, the 16th *sūtra*, is said to hold that birth and death can be spoken of only with regard to body and not with regard to the soul. The eleventh topic (the 17th *sūtra* with Śaṅkara) means that the birth of *jīva* is true only in a special sense, since in reality *jīva* has neither birth nor death. The eleventh topic, consisting of the 18th and 19th *sūtras*, gives according to Madhva the view that the individual souls have all been produced from God. According to Madhva the twelfth topic (*sūtras* 20–27) deals with the measure of *jīvas*. The topic gives, according to him, the view that the *jīva* is atomic in size and not all-pervading. Being in one place, it can vitalize the whole body, just as a lamp can illuminate a room by its light, which is a quality of the lamp; for a substance may be pervading by virtue of its quality[1]. The thirteenth topic (27th *sūtra*), according to Madhva, is supposed to affirm the plurality of souls. The fourteenth topic (*sūtras* 28, 29) demonstrates that Brahman and *jīva* are different. The fifteenth topic of Madhva shows that, though the souls are produced from God, yet they are not destructible. The souls are like reflections from the Brahman, and they therefore must persist as long as the Brahman remains and

[1] A discussion is raised here by Jaya-tīrtha regarding the nature of light, and it is held that light is of the nature of a quality and not a substance.

must therefore be eternal. The conditions (*upādhi*) through which these reflections are possible are twofold, external (*bāhya*) and essential (*svarūpa*). The external condition is destroyed, but not the essential one[1]. The souls are thus at once one with the Brahman and different; they depend on God for their existence and are similar to Him in nature. The sixteenth topic seeks to establish the nature of souls as consciousness and pure bliss, which are however revealed in their fullness only in the state of emancipation by the grace of God, while in our ordinary states these are veiled, as it were by ignorance (*avidyā*)[2]. The seventeenth topic seeks to reconcile the freedom of action of the *jīva* with the ultimate agency of God. It is God who makes the *jīvas* work in accordance with their past *karmas*, which are beginningless (*anādi*). Thus, though God makes all *jīvas* perform all their works, He is guided in His directorship by their previous *karmas*. The eighteenth topic seeks to establish that, though the *jīvas* are parts of God, they are not parts in the same sense as the part-incarnations, the fish-incarnation, etc., are; for the latter are parts of essential nature (*svarūpāṁśa*), whereas the former are not parts of an essential nature (*jīvānām asvarūpāṁśatvam*); for, though parts, they are different from God. The nineteenth topic asserts that the *jīvas* are but reflections of God.

With Śaṅkara, however, these *sūtras* yield quite different interpretations. Thus the twelfth topic (*sūtra* 18) is supposed to assert that even in deep sleep there is consciousness, and the circumstance that nothing is known in this state is due to the fact that there is no object of which there could be any knowledge (*viṣayābhāvād iyam acetayamānatā na caitanyābhāvāt*). The thirteenth topic (*sūtras* 19–32) discusses upon his view the question whether, in accordance with the texts which speak of the going out of self, the self should be regarded as atomic, or whether it should be regarded as all-pervasive; and he decides in favour of the latter, because of its being identical with Brahman. The fourteenth topic (*sūtras* 33–39), after considering the possible agency of mind, senses, etc., denies them and decides in favour of the agency of soul, and holds that the

[1] *jīvopādhir dvidhā proktaḥ svarūpaṃ bāhya eva ca,*
bāhyopādhir layaṃ yāti muktāv anyasya tu sthitiḥ.
Tattva-prakāśikā, p. 119.

[2] *evaṃ jīva-svarūpatvena mukteḥ pūrvam api sato jñānānanden īśvara-prasādenābhivyakti-nimittena ānandī bhavati; prāg anabhivyaktatvena anubhavābhāva-prasaṅgāt. Ibid.* p. 120.

buddhi and the senses are only instruments and accessories. Yet in the fifteenth topic (*sūtra* 40) Śaṅkara tries to establish this agency of the self, not as real, but as illusory in presence of the conditions of the sense-organs, intellect, etc. (*upādhi-dharmādhyāsenaiva ātmanaḥ kartṛtvaṃ na svābhāvikam*). Upon the sixteenth topic (*sūtras* 41–42) Śaṅkara tries to establish the fact that God helps persons to perform their actions in accordance with their previous *karma*. The seventeenth topic (*sūtras* 43–53) is interpreted by Śaṅkara as stating the view that the difference between the selves themselves and between them and Brahman can be understood only by a reference to the analogy of reflection, spatial limitations or the like; for in reality they are one, and it is only through the presence of the limiting conditions that they appear to be different.

In the fourth chapter of the first book the first topic of both Śaṅkara and Madhva describes the origin of the *prāṇas* from Brahman[1]. The second topic of Madhva, containing the 3rd *sūtra* of Śaṅkara's reading, describes the origin of *manas* from Brahman. The 4th *sūtra*, forming the third topic of Madhva, holds the view that speech (*vāk*) also is produced from Brahman, though we sometimes hear it spoken of as eternal, when it is applied to the Vedas. The 5th and the 6th *sūtras*, forming the fourth topic, discuss the purports of various texts regarding the number of the *prāṇas*, and hold the view that they are twelve in number. The fifth topic of Madhva, consisting of the 7th *sūtra*, states the view that the *prāṇas* are atomic by nature and not all-pervasive, and that hence there cannot be any objection to the idea of their being produced from Brahman. The *sūtras* 8 and 9, forming the sixth topic, show the production of *prāṇas* from Brahman. The *sūtras* 10 and 11, forming the seventh topic, show that even the principal (*mukhya*) *prāṇa* is dependent on Brahman for its production and existence. In the eighth topic, consisting of the 12th *sūtra*, it is held that the modifications (*vṛtti*) of the principal *prāṇa* are like servants, so their functions are also in reality derived from Brahman. The ninth topic, consisting of the 13th *sūtra*, repeats textual proofs of the atomic character of *prāṇa*. The tenth topic, consisting of *sūtras* 14–

[1] This topic consists according to Śaṅkara of only four *sūtras*, and according to Madhva of the first three *sūtras*. Of these the third *sūtra* (*pratijñānuparodhāc ca*) happens to be absent in Śaṅkara's reading of the *Brahma-sūtras*.

16, states the view that the senses are instruments of Brahman, though in a remote way they may also be regarded as instruments of the *jīva*. The eleventh topic, consisting of the 17th to the 19th *sūtras*, states the view that all the other twelve *prāṇas*, excepting the thirteenth or the principal (*mukhya*) *prāṇa*, are so many senses. The difference between these and the principal *prāṇa* consists in this, that the work of these other *prāṇas*, though depending principally on Brahman, also depends on the effort of *jīva* (*iśvara-paravaśā hi indriyāṇāṃ pravṛttir jīva-prayatnāpekṣaiva*), but the functioning of the *mukhya prāṇa* does not in any way depend on the individual souls (*mukhyaprāṇasya pravṛttir na puruṣa-prayatnāpekṣayā*). The twelfth topic (20th *sūtra*) shows that all our bodies also are derived from Brahman. The last topic (21st *sūtra*) instils the view that our bodies are made up not of one element, but of five elements.

According to Śaṅkara, however, the chapter is to be divided into nine topics, of which the first has already been described. The second topic (*sūtras* 5–6) holds the view that there are eleven senses, and not seven only as some hold, after the analogy of seven *prāṇas*. The third topic (7th *sūtra*) states that the senses are not all-pervasive, as the adherents of Sāṃkhya hold, but are atomic by nature. The fourth topic (8th *sūtra*) states that the *mukhya prāṇa* is a modification of Brahman, like any other *prāṇa*. The fifth topic (*sūtras* 9–12) states that *prāṇa* is not simply *vāyu*, but a subjective modification of it in the fivefold form, and its general function cannot be properly explained by reference to the individual actions of the separate *prāṇas*, like the movement of a cage by a concerted effort of each one of the birds encaged therein; for the actions of the *prāṇas* do not seem to be in any way concerted. As there are five states of mind, desire, imagination, etc., so the five *prāṇas* are but modifications of the principal *prāṇa*. The sixth topic (13th *sūtra*) states that this principal *prāṇa* is atomic by nature. The seventh topic (*sūtras* 14–16) states that the *prāṇas* in their functioning are presided over by certain deities for their movement and yet these can only be for the enjoyment of the *jīvas*. The eighth topic (*sūtras* 17–19) states that the senses (conative and cognitive) are different categories (*tattvāntara*) from the principal *prāṇa*. The ninth topic (*sūtras* 20–22) states that the *jīva* is not the creator, who is Īśvara.

CHAPTER XXVII

A GENERAL REVIEW OF THE PHILOSOPHY OF MADHVA

Ontology.

THE philosophy of Madhva admits the categories, viz., substance (*dravya*), quality (*guṇa*), action (*karma*), class-character (*sāmānya*), particularity (*viśeṣa*), qualified (*viśiṣṭa*) whole (*aṃśī*), power (*śakti*), similarity (*sādṛśya*) and negation (*abhāva*)[1]. *Dravya* is defined as the material cause (*upādāna-kāraṇa*)[2]. A *dravya* is a material cause with reference to evolutionary changes (*pariṇāma*) and manifestation (*abhivyakti*) or to both. Thus the world is subject to evolutionary changes, whereas God or souls can only be manifested or made known, but cannot undergo any evolutionary change; again, ignorance (*avidyā*) may be said to undergo evolutionary changes and to be the object of manifestation as well. The substances are said to be twenty, viz., the highest self or God (*paramātman*), *Lakṣmī*, souls (*jīva*), unmanifested vacuity (*avyākṛtākāśa*), *prakṛti*, the three *guṇas*, *mahat*, *ahaṃkāra*, *buddhi*, *manas*, the senses (*indriya*), the elements (*bhūta*), the element-potentials (*mātra*), ignorance (*avidyā*), speech-sounds (*varṇa*), darkness (*andha-kāra*), root-impressions (or tendencies) (*vāsanā*), time (*kāla*), reflection (*pratibimba*).

The qualities of Madhva are of the same nature as those of the Vaiśeṣika; but the inclusion of mental qualities, such as self-control

[1] In the *Tattva-saṃkhyāna* (p. 10) it is said that reality (*tattva*) is twofold, independent (*svatantra*) and dependent (*asvatantra*), and elsewhere in the *Bhāṣya* it is said that there are four categories (*padārtha*), viz., God, *prakṛti*, soul (*jīva*) and matter (*jaḍa*):

īśvaraḥ prakṛtir jīvo jaḍaṃ ceti catuṣṭayaṃ
padārthānāṃ sannidhānāt tatreśo viṣṇurucyate.

But the present division of Madhva's philosophy, as admitting of ten categories, is made in view of similar kinds of division and classification used by the Vaiśeṣika and others.

[2] There is another definition of *dravya*, when it is defined as the object of a competitive race in the second canto of *Bhāgavata-tātparya*, also referred to in the *Madhva-siddhānta-sāra*. Thus it is said: *dravyaṃ tu dravaṇa-prāpyaṃ dvayor vivadamānayoḥ pūrvaṃ vegābhisambandhādākāśas tu, pradeśataḥ*. But this does not seem to have been further elaborated. It is hardly justifiable to seek any philosophical sense in this fanciful etymological meaning.

(*śama*), mercy (*kṛpā*), endurance (*titikṣā*), strength (*bala*), fear (*bhaya*), shame (*lajjā*), sagacity (*gāmbhīrya*), beauty (*saundarya*), heroism (*śaurya*), liberality (*audārya*), etc., is considered indispensable, and so the qualities include not only the twenty-four qualities of the syncretist Vaiśeṣika, but many more.

Actions (*karma*) are those which directly or indirectly lead to merit (*puṇya*) or demerit (*pāpa*). There are no actions which are morally absolutely indifferent; even upward motion and the like —which may be considered as indifferent (*udāsīna*) *karmas*—are indirectly the causes of merit or demerit. *Karmas* are generally divided into three classes, as *vihita*, i.e., enjoined by the *śāstra*, *niṣiddha*, prohibited by it, and *udāsīna*, not contemplated by it or indifferent. The latter is of the nature of vibration (*pariṣpanda*), and this is not of five kinds alone, as the Vaiśeṣika supposes, but of many other kinds[1]. Actions of creation, destruction, etc., in God are eternal in Him and form His essence (*svarūpa-bhūtāḥ*); the contradictory actions of creation and destruction may abide in Him, provided that, when one is in the actual form, the other is in the potential form[2]. Actions in non-eternal things are non-eternal and can be directly perceived by the senses.

The next question is regarding *jāti*, or universals, which are considered by the Nyāya-Vaiśeṣika as one and immutable. These are considered in the Madhva school as eternal only in eternal substances like the *jīvas*, whereas in non-eternal substances they are considered to be destructible and limited specifically to the individuals where they occur. There are in destructible individuals no such universals, which last even when the individuals are destroyed. An objection is raised that, if the existence of permanent universals is not agreed to, then the difficulty of comprehending concomitance (*vyāpti*) would be insurmountable, and hence inference would be impossible. The answer that is given on the side of Madhva is that inference is possible on the basis of similarity (*sādṛśya*), and that the acceptance of immutable universals is not

[1] The syncretistic Vaiśeṣika view, that action is of five kinds, is described here; for it is held that the Vaiśeṣika view that by simple rectilineal motion (*gamana*), circular motion (*bhramaṇa*) or other kinds of motion could be got, is strongly objected to, because circular motion is not a species of rectilinear motion; and hence the Vaiśeṣika classification of *karma* into five classes is also held to be inadequate.

[2] *sṛṣṭi-kāle sṛṣṭi-kriyā vyakty-ātmanā vartate, anyadā tu śakty-ātmanā, evaṃ saṃhāra-kriyāpi.* *Madhva-siddhānta-sāra*, p. 4.

necessary for that purpose; and this also applies to the comprehension of the meaning of words: when certain objects are pointed out as having any particular name, that name can be extended to other individuals which are extremely similar to the previous objects which were originally associated with that name[1]. A difference is also drawn between *jāti* ("universal") and *upādhi* ("limiting condition") in this, that the latter is said to be that which depends for its comprehension upon the comprehension of some other primary notion, while the former is that whose comprehension is direct and does not depend upon the comprehension of some other notion[2]. Thus the universal of cow (*gotva*) is known immediately and directly, whereas the notion of the universal of "cognizability" (*prameyatva*) can only be known through the previous knowledge of those things which are objects of knowledge. So the universal of cognizability is said to be *upādhi*, and the former *jāti*. It is further objected that, if objections are taken against an immutable universal existing in all individuals of a class at one and the same time, then the same objection may be taken against the acceptance of similarity, which must be supposed to exist at one time in a number of individuals. The answer to this is that the relation of similarity between two or three individuals is viewed in Madhva philosophy as existing uniformly between the number of individuals so related, but not completely in any one of them. When two or three terms which are said to be similar exist, the relation of similarity is like a dyadic or triadic relation subsisting between the terms in mutual dependence[3]; the relation of similarity existing between a number of terms is therefore not one, but many, according as the relation is noted from the point of view of one or the other of the terms. The similarity of A to B is different from the similarity of B to A, and so forth (*bhinnābhinnaṃ sādṛśyam iti siddham*).

[1] *anugata-dharmaṃ vināpi sādṛśyena sarvatra vyāpty-ādi-graha-sambhavāt, ayaṃ dhūmaḥ etat-sadṛśaś ca vahni-vyāpya ity evaṃ-krameṇa vyāpti-grahah,* "even without the basis of the existence of identical characteristics, comprehension of *vyāpti* is possible on the basis of similarity, e.g., 'This is smoke and entities similar to these are associated with fire, etc.'" *Madhva-siddhānta-sāra*, p. 6.

[2] *itara-nirūpaṇādhīna-nirūpaṇakatvam upādhi-lakṣaṇam* and *anya-nirūpaṇādhīna-nirūpaṇatvaṃ jātitvam. Ibid.* p. 7.

[3] *eka-nirūpitāparādhikaraṇa-vṛttitvena tri-vikrama-nyāyena tat-svīkārāt, pratiyogitvānuyogitvādivat. Ibid.* p. 6.

We next come to the doctrine of specific particulars (*viśeṣa*) in the Madhva school. It supposes that every substance is made up of an infinite number of particulars associated with each and every quality that it may be supposed to possess. Thus, when the question arises regarding the relation of qualities to their substances (e.g., the relation of colour, etc., to a jug) if any quality was identical with the substance, then the destruction of it would mean destruction of the substance, and the words denoting the substance and the quality would mutually mean each other; but that is not so, and this difficulty can be solved only on the supposition that there are specific particulars corresponding as the basis to each one of the qualities. As to the exact relation of these to their substance there are divergences of view, some holding that they are identical with the substance (*abheda*), others that they are different (*bheda*), and others that they are both identical and different (*bhedābheda*). Whatever view regarding the relation of the qualities to the substance is accepted, the doctrine of specific particulars (*viśeṣa*) has to be accepted, to escape the contradiction. Thus *viśeṣas* in each substance are numberless, corresponding to the view-points or qualities intended to be explained; but there are no further *viśeṣas* for each *viśeṣa*, as that would lead to an infinite regress. For a satisfactory explanation of the diverse external qualities of God it is necessary to admit eternal *viśeṣas* in Him. In order to explain the possibility of a connection of the continuous eternal space or vacuity (*ākāśa*) with finite objects like jug, etc. it is necessary to admit the existence of *viśeṣas* in *ākāśa*[1]. It will be seen from the above that the acceptance of *viśeṣas* becomes necessary only in those cases where the unity and difference of two entities, such as the substance and the qualities or the like, cannot otherwise be satisfactorily explained. For these cases the doctrine of *viśeṣas* introduces some supposed particulars, or parts, to which the association of the quality could be referred, without referring to the whole substance for such association. But this does not apply to the existence of *viśeṣa* in the atoms; for the atoms can very well be admitted to have parts, and the contact with other atoms can thus be very easily explained without the assumption of any *viśeṣa*. An atom may be admitted to be the smallest unit in comparison with

[1] *ato gaganādi-vibhu-dravyasya ghaṭādinā saṃyoga-tadabhāvobhaya-nirvāhako viśeṣo'nanya-gatyā svīkaraṇīyaḥ*. *Ibid.* p. 9.

everything else: but that is no reason why it should not be admitted to be bigger than its own parts. If the atoms had not parts, they could not be held to combine on all their ten sides[1]. So the Vaiśeṣika view, admitting *viśeṣas* in atoms, has to be rejected. It is well worth remembering here that the Vaiśeṣikas held that there were among the atoms of even the same *bhūta*, and also among the souls, such specific differences that these could be distinguished from one another by the *yogins*. These final differences, existing in the atoms themselves, are called *viśeṣas* by the Kaṇāda school of thinkers. This conception of *viśeṣa* and its utility is different from the conception of *viśeṣa* in the Madhva school[2].

Samavāya, or the relation of inherence accepted in the Nyāya-Vaiśeṣika school, is discarded in the system of Madhva on almost the same grounds as in Śaṅkara's *Bhāṣya* on the *Brahma-sūtras*. The view is that the appearance of the cause in the effect and of the qualities in the substance is manifestly of the nature of a relation and, as this relation is not contact (*saṃyoga*), it must be a separate relation, viz., the relation of inherence (*samavāya*). But in the same way *samavāya* (e.g., in the sentence *iha tantuṣu paṭa-samavāyaḥ*) itself may have the appearance of existing in something else in some relation, and hence may be in need of further relations to relate it. If without any such series of relations a relation of inherence can be related in the manner of a quality and a substance, then that sort of relatedness or qualifiedness (*viśiṣṭatā*) may serve all the purposes of *samavāya*. This brings us to the acceptance of "related" or "qualified" as a category separate and distinct from the categories of quality (*guṇa*) and substance (*dravya*) and the relation involved between the two[3]. So also the whole (*aṃśī*) is not either the relations or the parts or both, but a separate category by itself.

Power (*śakti*), as a separate category, exists in four forms: (i) as mysterious—*acintya-śakti*—as in God, (ii) causal power

[1] *anyāpekṣayā paramāṇutve'pi svāvayavāpekṣayā mahattvopapatteḥ:...kiṁ ca paramāṇor avayavānaṅgīkāre tasya daśadikṣv abhisaṁbandho na syāt. Madhva-siddhānta-sāra*, p. 10.

[2] *asmad-viśiṣṭānāṃ yogināṃ nityeṣu tulyākṛti-guṇa-kriyeṣu paramāṇuṣu muktātmasu ca anya-nimittāsaṃbhavād yebhyo nimittebhyaḥ pratyādhāraṃ vilakṣaṇo'yaṃ vilakṣaṇo'yam iti pratyaya-vyāvṛittiḥ, deśa-kāla-viprakarṣe ca paramāṇau sa evāyam iti pratyabhijñānaṃ ca bhavati te antyā viśeṣāḥ.*
Praśasta-pāda-bhāṣya, pp. 321–2.

[3] *viśiṣṭaṃ viśeṣaṇa-viśeṣya-tatsambandhātiriktam avaśyam aṅgīkartavyam. Madhva-siddhānta-sāra*, p. 11.

(*kāraṇa-śakti* or *sahaja-śakti*), which naturally exists in things and by virtue of which they can produce all sorts of changes, (iii) a power brought about by a new operation in a thing called the *ādheya-śakti*, as in an idol through the ritual operations of the installation ceremony (*pratiṣṭhā*), and (iv) the significant power of words (*pada-śakti*). Negation is said to be of three kinds: (i) the negation preceding a production (*prāg-abhāva*), (ii) that following destruction (*dhvaṃsābhāva*), (iii) as otherness (*anyonyābhāva*), e.g., there is the negation of a jug in a pot and of a pot in a jug: this is therefore the same as differences, which are considered as the essence of all things[1]. When things are destroyed, their differences are also destroyed. But the five differences between God and souls, between souls themselves, between inanimate objects themselves, between them and God, and between them and the souls, are all eternal; for the differences in eternal things are eternal and in non-eternal things non-eternal[2]. The fourth kind of negation, *atyantābhāva*, is the non-existence belonging to impossible entities like the hare's horn.

God, or Paramātman, is in this system considered as the fullness of infinite qualities. He is the author of creation, maintenance, destruction, control, knowledge, bondage, salvation, and hiding (*āvṛti*). He is omniscient, and all words in their most pervading and primary sense refer to Him. He is different from all material objects, souls and *prakṛti*, and has for His body knowledge and bliss, and is wholly independent and one, though He may have diverse forms (as in *Vāsudeva*, *Pradyumna*, etc.); all such forms of Him are the full manifestation of all His qualities.

The souls (*jīva*) are naturally tainted with defects of ignorance, sorrow, fear, etc., and they are subject to cycles of transformation. They are infinite in number. They are of three kinds, viz., those who are fit for emancipation (*mukti-yogya*), e.g., gods such as Brahmā, Vāyu, etc., or sages, like Nārada, etc., or like the ancestors (*pitṛ*), or kings like Ambarīśa, or advanced men; these advanced

[1] *bhedas tu sarva-vastūnāṃ svarūpaṃ naijam avyayam.* *Ibid.* p. 20.

[2] Jaya-tīrtha, however, in his *Nyāya-sudhā*, I. 4. 6 (*adhikaraṇa*, p. 222), holds that differences (whether in eternal or in non-eternal things) are always eternal: *na ca kadāpi padārthānām anyonya-tādātmyam asti iti anityānām api bhedo nitya eva ity āhuḥ.* Padmanābha-tīrtha also in his *San-nyāya-ratnāvalī* or *Anuvyākhyāna* holds exactly the same view on the same topic (I. 4. 6): *vināśino'pi ghaṭāder dharma-rūpo bhedaḥ para-vādy-abhyupagataghaṭatvādi-jātivan nityo'-bhyupagantavyaḥ.*

souls think of God as being, bliss, knowledge and *ātman*. It is only the second class of souls that are subject to transmigration and suffer the pleasures of Heaven and the sufferings of Earth and Hell. There is a third class of beings, the demons, ghosts and the like. Each one of these souls is different from every other soul, and even in emancipation the souls differ from one another in their respective merits, qualifications, desires, etc.

Next comes the consideration of unmanifested space (*avyākṛta ākāśo dig-rūpaḥ*), which remains the same in creation and destruction. This is, of course, different from *ākāśa* as element, otherwise called *bhūtākāśa*, which is a product of the *tāmasa* ego and is limited. *Ākāśa* as space is vacuity and eternal[1].

Prakṛti also is accepted in the Madhva system as the material cause of the material world[2]. Time is a direct product of it, and all else is produced through the series of changes which it undergoes through the categories of *mahat*, etc. *Prakṛti* is accepted here as a substance (*dravya*)[3] and is recognized in the Madhva system as what is called *māyā*, a consort of God, though it is called impure (*doṣa-yukta*) and material (*jaḍa*), evolving (*pariṇāminī*), though under the full control of God, and may thus be regarded almost as His will or strength (*Harer icchāthavā balam*). This *prakṛti* is to the world the cause of all bondage (*jagabhandhātmikā*)[4]. The subtle bodies (*liṅga-śarīra*) of all living beings are formed out of the stuff of this *prakṛti*. It is also the source of the three *guṇas* (*guṇa-trayādy-upādāna-bhūta*). It is held that during the time of the great creation *prakṛti* alone existed and nothing else. At that time God out of His creative desire produced from *prakṛti* in three masses *sattva*, *rajas* and *tamas*[5]. It is said that *rajas* is double of *tamas* and *sattva* is double of *rajas*. *Sattva* exists by itself in its pure form: *rajas* and *tamas* are always mixed with each other and with *sattva*. Thus *sattva* exists not only in this pure form, but also as an element in the mixed *rajas* variety and *tamas* variety. In the mixed *rajas* there are for each part of *rajas* a hundred parts of *sattva* and one hundredth part of *tamas*. In the *tamas* mixture there are for

[1] *bhūtākāśātiriktāyā deśa-kāla-paricchinnāyās tārkikādy-abhimata-diśā evāsmākam avyākṛtākāśatvāt. Tātparya-candrikā*, II. 3. 1 (p. 932). Also *Nyāya-sudhā*, II. 3. 1.

[2] *sākṣāt paramparayā vā viśvopādānaṃ prakṛtiḥ. Padārtha-saṃgraha*, 93.

[3] *Nyāya-sudhā* and *San-nyāya-ratnāvalī* on the *Anuvyākhyāna*, II. 1.6 (p. 21).

[4] *Bhāgavata-tātparya*, III. 10. 9 (p. 29). [5] *Madhva-siddhānta-sāra*, p. 36.

each part of *tamas* ten parts of *sattva* and one-tenth part of *rajas*. At the time of the world-dissolution (*vilaya*) ten parts return to *sattva* and one part to *rajas* with one part in *tamas*. The evolution of the *mahat-tattva* takes place immediately after the production of the three *guṇas*, when the entire amount of the produced *rajas* becomes mixed with *tamas*; the *mahat-tattva* is constituted of three parts of *rajas* and one part of *tamas*. With reference to the later derivatives this *mahat-tattva* is called *sattva*[1]. In the category *ahaṃkāra* (that which is derived immediately after *mahat*) there is for every ten parts of *sattva* one part of *rajas* and a tenth part of *tamas*. From the *sattva* of the *tamas* part of it the *manas*, etc., are produced, out of the *rajas* part of it the senses are produced, and out of the *tamas* the elements are produced. They are at first manifested as *tan-mātras*, or the powers inherent in and manifested in the elements. As *ahaṃkāra* contains within it the materials for a threefold development, it is called *vaikārika*, *taijasa* and *tāmasa* accordingly. In the *Tattva-saṃkhyāna* *buddhi-tattva* and *manas-tattva* are said to be two categories evolving in succession from *ahaṃkāra*. The twenty-four categories counted from *mahat* are in this enumeration *mahat*, *ahaṃkāra*, *buddhi*, *manas*, the ten *indriyas* (senses), the five *tan-mātras* and the five *bhūtas*[2]. As *buddhi* is of two kinds, viz., *buddhi* as category and *buddhi* as knowledge, so *manas* is also regarded as being of two kinds, *manas* as category and *manas* as sense-organ. As sense-organ, it is both eternal and non-eternal; it is eternal in God, Lakṣmī, Brahmā and all other souls,

[1] *Bhāgavata-tātparya*, III. 14, by Madhvācārya. In this passage the original *sattva* is spoken of as being the deity *Śrī*, the original *rajas* as *Bhū*, and the original *tamas* as *Durgā*, and the deity which has for her root all the three is called *Mahā-lakṣmī*. The Lord *Janārdana* is beyond the *guṇas* and their roots.

[2] There seems to be a divergence of opinion regarding the place of the evolution of *buddhi-tattva*. The view just given is found in the *Tattva-saṃkhyāna* (p. 41): *asaṃsṛṣṭam mahān ahaṁ buddhir manaḥ khāni daśa mātra-bhūtāni pañca ca*, and supported in its commentary by Satyadharma Yatī. This is also in consonance with *Kaṭha*, I. 3. 10. But in the passage quoted from Madhva's *Bhāṣya* in the *Madhva-siddhānta-sāra* it is said that the *vijñāna-tattva* (probably the same as *buddhi-tattva*) arises from the *mahat-tattva*, that from it again there is *manas*, and from *manas* the senses, etc.:

vijñāna-tattvaṃ mahataḥ samutpannaṁ caturmukhāt,
vijñāna-tattvāc ca mano manas-tattvācca khādikam.

The way in which Padmanābha Sūri tries to solve the difficulty in his *Padārtha-saṃgraha* is that the *buddhi-tattva* springs directly from the *mahat-tattva*, but that it grows in association with *taijasa ahaṃkāra* (*taijasāhaṃkāreṇa upacita*). This explains the precedence of *ahaṃkāra* as given in the *Tattva-saṃkhyāna*. *Buddhi*, of course, is of two kinds, as knowledge (*jñāna-rūpa*) and as category (*tattva*).

as their own essence (*svarūpa-bhūtam*) or self. The non-eternal *manas*, as belonging to God, *brahma*, individual souls, etc., is of five kinds; *manas*, *buddhi*, *ahaṃkāra*, *citta* and *cetana*, which may also be regarded as the *vṛttis* or functions of *manas*. Of these *manas* is said to be that to which is due imagination (*saṃkalpa*) and doubt (*vikalpa*); *buddhi* is that to which is due the function of coming to any decision (*niścayātmikā buddhi*); *ahaṃkāra* is that through the functioning of which the unreal is thought of as real (*asvarūpe svarūpa-matiḥ*), and the cause of memory is *citta*. The senses are twelve, including five cognitive, five conative, *manas* and the *sākṣīndriya*, as *buddhi* is included within *manas*. The senses are considered from two points of view, viz., from the point of view of their predominantly *tejas* materials, and as being sense-organs. In their aspects as certain sorts produced in course of the evolution of their materials they are destructible; but as sense-organs they are eternal in God and in all living beings. As regards the bodily seats of these organs, these are destructible in the case of all destructible beings. The internal sense of intuition (*sākṣī*) can directly perceive pleasure and pain, ignorance, time and space. The sense-data of sounds, colours, etc., appearing through their respective sense-organs, are directly perceived by this sense of intuition. All things that transcend the domain of the senses are intuited by the sense of intuition (*sākṣī*), either as known or unknown. To consider the *sākṣi-jñāna* as a special source of intuitive knowledge, indispensable particularly for the perception of time and space, is indeed one of the important special features of Madhva's system. In Śaṅkara Vedānta *sākṣī* stands as the inextinguishable *brahma*-light, which can be veiled by *ajñāna*, though *ajñāna* itself is manifested in its true nature, ignorance, by the *sākṣī*[1]. Madhva holds that it is through the intuitive sense of *sākṣī*

[1] *yat-prasādād avidyādi sphuraty eva divā-niśam tam apy*
apahnute'vidyā nājñānasyāsti duṣkaram.
Advaita-brahma-siddhi, p. 312.

As this work also notices, there are in *Śaṅkara Vedānta* four views on the status of *sākṣī*. Thus the *Tattva-śuddhi* holds that it is the light of Brahman, appearing as if it were in the *jīva*; the *Tattva-pradīpikā* holds that it is Īśvara manifesting Himself in all individual souls; the *Vedānta-kaumudī* holds that it is but a form of Īśvara, a neutral entity which remains the same in all operations of the *jīva* and is of direct and immediate perception, but is also the nescience (*avidyā*) which veils it. The *Kūṭastha-dīpa* considers it to be an unchangeable light of pure intelligence in *jīva*, which remains the same under all conditions and is hence called *sākṣī*.

that an individual observes the validity of his sense-knowledge and of his own self as the ego (*aham*). Our perception of self, on this view, is not due to the activity of mind or to mental perception (*manonubhava*); for, had it been so, one might as a result of mind activity or mental functioning have doubted his own self; but this never happens, and so it has to be admitted that the perception of self is due to some other intuitive sense called *sākṣī*. *Sākṣī* thus always leads us to unerring and certain truths, whereas, wherever in knowledge there is a discriminating process and a chance of error, it is said to be due to mental perception[1].

The *tan-mātras* are accepted in Madhvaism as the subtler materials of the five grosser elements (*bhūtas*). It must be noted that the categories of *ahaṃkāra* and *buddhi* are considered as being a kind of subtle material stuff, capable of being understood as quantities having definite quantitative measurements (*parimāṇa*)[2].

Ignorance (*avidyā*) is a negative substance (*dravya*), which by God's will veils the natural intelligence of us all[3]. But there is no one common *avidyā* which appears in different individuals; the *avidyā* of one individual is altogether different from the *avidyā* of another individual. As such, it seems to denote our individual ignorance and not a generalized entity such as is found in most of the Indian systems; thus each person has a specific (*prātisviki*) *avidyā* of his own.

Time (*kāla*) is coexistent with all-pervading space (*avyākṛta ākāśa*), and it is made directly from *prakṛti* stuff having a more primeval existence than any of the derived kinds[4]. It exists in itself

[1] *yat kvacid vyabhicāri syāt darśanaṃ mānasaṃ hi tat. Anuvyākhyana. evaṃ sa devadatto gauro na vā paramāṇuḥ gurutvādhikaraṇam na vā iti saṃśayo mānasah. Madhva-siddhānta-sāra*, p. 44.

[2] *Manu-bṛhaspaty-ādayas tu ahaṃkārāt parimāṇato hīnena buddhi-tattvena svocita-parimāṇena parimita-deśa-paryantam avasthitam viṣṇuṃ paśyanti soma-sūryaṁ tu buddhi-tattvāt parimāṇato hīnena manas-tatvena parimita-deśa-paryantaṃ avasthitaṁ viṣṇuṃ paśyataḥ varuṇādayas tu ākāśa-vāyv-ādi-bhūtaiḥ krameṇa parimāṇato daśāhīnaiḥ parimita-deśa-paryantam avasthitaṃ viṣṇuṃ yogyatānusāreṇa paśyanti.*

San-nyāya-ratnāvalī and *Madhva-siddhānta-sāra*, p. 49.

[3] *ataḥ parameśvara eva sattvādi-guṇamay-āvidyāvirodhitvena avidyayā svādhīnayā prakṛtyā acintyādbhutayā svaśaktyā jīvasya sva-prakāśam api svarūpa-caitanyam apy ācchādayati. Nyāya-sudhā* on the topic of *jijñāsa*.

[4] The objection that, if time is made out of *prakṛti* stuff, from whence would *mahat*, etc., be evolved, is not valid; for it is only from some parts of *prakṛti* that time is evolved, while it is from other parts that the categories are evolved: *sarvatra vyāptānāṁ katipaya-prakṛti-sūkṣmāṇāṃ kālopādānatvam, katipayānāṃ mahad-ādy-upādānatvaṃ katipayānāṃ ca mūla-rūpeṇa avasthānam. Madhva-siddhānta-sāra*, p. 64.

(*sva-gata*) and is, like space, the vehicle (*ādhāra*) of everything else, and it is also the common cause of the production of all objects.

Darkness (*andhakāra*) is also considered as a separate substance and not as mere negation of light. A new conception of *pratibimba* ("reflection") is introduced to denote the *jīvas*, who cannot have any existence apart from the existence of God and who cannot behave in any way independent of His will, and, being conscious entities, having will and feeling, are essentially similar to him; though reflections, they are not destructible like ordinary reflections in mirrors, but are eternal (*pratibimbas tu bimbāvinābhūta-sat-sadṛśaḥ*)[1].

The system of Madhva admits the qualities (*guṇa*) more or less in the same way as the Nyāya-Vaiśeṣika does; the points of difference are hardly ever of any philosophical importance. Those which deserve to be mentioned will be referred to in the succeeding sections.

Pramāṇas (ways of valid knowledge).

Pramāṇa is defined as that which makes an object of knowledge cognizable as it is in itself (*yathārthaṃ pramāṇam*)[2]. The function of *pramāṇa* consists both in making an entity object of knowledge through the production of knowledge (*jñāna-jananad vāva jñeyatā-sampādakatvena*), either directly (*sākṣāt*) or indirectly (*asākṣāt*)[3]. There are two functions in a *pramāṇa*, viz. (1) to render an entity an object of knowledge (*jñeya-viṣayīkaraṇa*) and (2) to make it cognizable (*jñeyatā-saṃpādana*)[3]. So far as the function of making an entity an object of knowledge is concerned, all *pramāṇas* directly perform it; it is only with reference to the second function that there is the distinction between the two kinds of *pramāṇas*, *kevala* and *anu*, such that it is only the former that performs it directly and only the latter that performs it indirectly (*paraṃparā-krama*)[4]. These two functions also distinguish a *pramāṇa* from the *pramātā* ("subject") and the *prameya* ("object"), since neither the subject

[1] *Padārtha-saṃgraha*, 193.

[2] Madhva's definition of *pramāṇa* in his *Pramāṇa-lakṣaṇa* is elaborated by Jaya-tīrtha in his *Pramāṇa-paddhati* as *jñeyam anatikramya vartamānaṃ yathāvasthitam eva jñeyaṃ yad viṣayīkaroti nānyathā tat pramāṇam* (p. 8).

[3] *Jaya-tīrtha-vijaya-ṭippaṇī* on the *Pramāṇa-paddhati* by Janārdana.

[4] *Ibid.* Also *kevalaṃ viṣayasya jñeyatvaṃ jñānam upādhitayā karaṇaṃ tu taj-janakatayā saṃpādayanti ity etāvantaṃ viśeṣam āśritya kevalānu-pramāṇa-bhedaḥ samarthitaḥ. Nyāya-sudhā*, II. 1. 2 (p. 249).

nor the object can be called the instrumental causes of knowledge, though they may in some sense be admitted as causes, and they do not cause an entity to be an object of knowledge either. Our knowledge does not in any way modify an object of knowledge, but an entity becomes known when knowledge of it is produced. Truth, by which is understood exact agreement of knowledge with its object, belongs properly to knowledge alone (*jñānasyaiva mukhyato yāthārthyam*). The instruments of knowledge can be called true (*yathārtha*) only in an indirect manner, on the ground of their producing true knowledge (*yathārtha-jñāna-janaka yathārtha*)[1]. But yet the definition properly applies to the instruments as well, since they are also *yathārtha* in the sense that they are also directed to the object, just as knowledge of it is. So far as they are directed towards the right object of which we have right knowledge, their scope of activity is in agreement with the scope or extent of the object of knowledge. So it is clear that *pramāṇa* is twofold: *pramāṇa* as true knowledge (*kevala pramāṇa*) and *pramāṇa* as instrument (*sādhana*) of knowledge (*anu pramāṇa*). This *kevala pramāṇa* is again twofold, as consciousness (*caitanya*) and as states (*vṛtti*). This consciousness is described by Jaya-tīrtha as superior, middling and inferior (*uttama-madhyamādhama*), as right, mixed, and wrong; the *vṛtti* is also threefold, as perception, inference, and scriptures (*āgama*). The *anu pramāṇa* also is threefold, as perception, inference and scriptures. A question arises, whether the term *pramāṇa* could be applied to any right knowledge which happens to be right only by accident (*kākatālīya*) and not attained by the proper process of right knowledge. Thus, for example, by a mere guess one might say that there are five shillings in one's friend's pocket, and this knowledge might really agree with the fact that one's friend has five shillings in his pocket; but, though this knowledge is right, it cannot be called *pramāṇa*; for this is not due to the speaker's own certain knowledge, since he had only guessed, which is only a form of doubt (*vaktur jñānasya saṃśayatvena aprasaṅgāt*)[2]. This also applies to the case where one makes an inference on the basis of a misperceived *hetu*, e.g., the inference of fire from steam or vapour mistaken for smoke.

The value of this definition of *pramāṇa* as agreement with objects of knowledge (*yathārtha*) is to be found in the fact that it

[1] *Ibid.* [2] *Ibid.* p. 250.

includes memory (*smṛti*) of previous valid experience as valid, whereas most of the other systems of Indian philosophy are disposed so to form their definition as purposely to exclude the right of memory to be counted as *pramāṇa*[1]. Śālikanātha's argument, as given in his *Prakaraṇa-pañcikā*, on the rejection of memory from the definition of *pramāṇa* is based on the fact that memory is knowledge produced only by the impressions of previous knowledge (*pūrva-vijñāna-saṃskāra-mātrajaṃ jñānam*); as such, it depends only on previous knowledge and necessarily refers to past experience, and cannot therefore refer independently to the ascertainment of the nature of objects[2]. He excludes recognition (*pratyabhijñā*) from memory, as recognition includes in its data of origin direct sense contact; and he also excludes the case of a series of perceptions of the same object (*dhārā-vāhika jñāna*); for though it involves memory, it also involves direct sense contact, but the exclusion of memory from the definition of *pramāṇa* applies only to pure memory, unassociated with sense contact. The idea is that that which depends on or is produced only by previous knowledge does not directly contribute to our knowledge and is hence not *pramāṇa*.

The reason why Jaya-tīrtha urges the inclusion of memory is that memory may also agree with an object of knowledge and hence may rightly be called *pramāṇa*. It may be that, while I am remembering an object, it may not still be there or it may have ceased to exist, but that does not affect the validity of memory as *pramāṇa*, since the object did exist at the time of previous experience referred to by memory, though it may not be existing at the time when the memory is produced. If it is argued that, since the object is not in the same condition at the time of memory as it was at the time of experience, memory is not valid, in that case all knowledge about past and future by inference or scriptures would be invalid, since the past and future events inferred might not exist at the time of

[1] Here Jaya-tīrtha refers to the definitions of the Mīmāṃsā as *anadhigatārtha-gantṛ pramāṇam* and as *anubhūtiḥ pramāṇam*. The first refers to Kumārila's definition and the second to that of Prabhākara. Kumārila defines *pramāṇa* (as found in the *Codanā-sūtra* 80, *Śloka-vārttika*) as firm knowledge (*dṛḍhaṃ vijñānam*) produced (*utpannam*) and unassociated with other knowledge (*nāpi jñānāntareṇa saṃvādam ṛcchati*). The second definition is that of Prabhākara as quoted in Śālikanātha's *Prakaraṇa-pañcikā*, p. 42: *pramāṇam anubhūtiḥ*.

[2] *smṛtir hi tad-ity-upajāyamānā prācīṃ pratītim anurudhyamānā na svātantryeṇa arthaṃ paricchinatti iti na pramāṇam. Prakaraṇa-pañcikā*, p. 42.

experience. If it is argued that the object of previous knowledge changes its state and so cannot in its entirety be referred to as the object of memory, then that destroys the validity of all *pramāṇas*; for nothing can be made an object of all the *pramāṇas* in its entirety. Also it cannot be objected that, if the thing does not change its state, then memory should grasp it as an entity which has not changed its state. This is not valid either; for memory does not grasp an object as if it had not changed its state, but as "it was so at that time" (*tadāsan tadṛśa iti*). Memory is absolutely indifferent with regard to the question whether an object has changed its state or not. Since memory agrees with real objective facts it has to be considered valid, and it is the special feature of the present definition that it includes memory as a valid definition, which is not done in other systems. The validity of memory as a *pramāṇa* is proved by the fact that people resort to it as valid knowledge in all their dealings, and only right knowledge is referred to by men (*loka-vyavahāra*). There is no way of establishing the validity of the *pramāṇas* of perception, etc., except the ultimate testimony of universal human experience[1].

Moreover, even the validity of the sacred writings of Manu is based on the remembered purport of the Vedas, and thence they are called *smṛti*[2]. Again, the argument that memory has no validity because it does not bring us any fruit (*niṣphalā*) is not right; for the validity depends on correctness of correspondence and not on fruitfulness. Want of validity (*aprāmāṇya*) is made evident through the defect of the organs or the resulting contradiction (*bādhaka-pratyaya*). It may also be noted that memory is not absolutely fruitless; thus the memory of happy things is pleasant and strengthens the root impressions also (*saṃskāra-patana*). Again, it is argued that that alone could be called *pramāṇa* which involves the knowledge of something new, and that therefore memory, which does not involve new knowledge, cannot be counted as *pramāṇa*. If it is required that an object of knowledge should be *pramāṇa*, then the eternal entities about which there cannot be any new knowledge cannot be the objects of *pramāṇa*. If the require-

[1] *na hy asti pratyakṣādi-prāmāṇya-sādhakam anyad loka-vyavahārāt. Nyāya-sudhā*, II. I. 2 *adhikaraṇa*, p. 251.

[2] *te hi śrutyādinānubhūtārthaṃ smṛtvā tat-pratipādakaṃ grantham āracayati. Ibid.* p. 252.

ment of new knowledge is not considered to refer to objects of knowledge, but only to the method or process of knowledge, then the knowledge involved in continuous perception of an object (*dhārāvāhika jñāna*) could not be considered as *pramāṇa*. The Buddhists might, of course, answer that each new moment a new object is produced which is perceived; the Sāṃkhya might hold that at each new moment all objects suffer a new change or *pariṇāma*; but what would the Mīmāṃsaka say? With him the object (e.g., the jug) remains the same at all successive moments. If it is argued that in the knowledge of an object abiding in and through successive moments we have at each particular moment a new element of time involved in it and this may constitute a newness of knowledge in spite of the fact that the object of knowledge has been abiding all through the moments, the same may be argued in favour of memory; for it manifests objects in the present and has reference to the experience as having happened in the past (*smṛtir api vartamāna-tat-kālatayā anubhūtam artham atīta-kālatayā avagāhate*). Jaya-tīrtha maintains that it is not possible to show any necessary connection between *prāmāṇya* (validity), and the requirement that the object should be previously unacquired (*anadhigatārtha*) either through association (*sāhacārya*), or through that and the want of any contradictory instance; for on the first ground many other things associated with *prāmāṇya* would have to be claimed to be *anadhigata*, which they are not, and the second ground does not apply at least in the case of continuous knowledge (*dhārā-vāhika jñāna*). For in the case of continuous knowledge successive moments are regarded as *pramāṇa* in spite of there being in them no new knowledge.

If it is objected "how could it be the function of *pramāṇa* to make an already-known object known to us" (*adhigatam evārtham adhigamayatā pramāṇena piṣṭaṃ piṣṭaṃ syāt*), what does the objection really mean? It cannot mean that in regard to a known object no further cognition can arise; for neither is knowledge opposed to knowledge, nor is want of knowledge a part of the conditions which produce knowledge. The objection to the rise of a second knowledge of a known object on the ground of fruitlessness has already been answered. Nor can it be said that a *pramāṇa* should not be dependent on anything else or on any other knowledge; for that objection would also apply to inference, which is admitted by all to be a *pramāṇa*. So *pramāṇa* should be so defined that memory may be included within it. Chaḷari-śeṣācārya quotes an unidentified scriptural text in support of the inclusion of memory in *pramāṇa*[1]. Jaya-tīrtha, in a brief statement of the positive considerations which according to him support the inclusion of memory in *pramāṇa*, says that memory is true (*yathārtha*). When an object appears in consciousness to have a definite character in a particular time and at a particular place and has actually that character at that time and at that place, then this knowledge is true or *yathārtha*. Now memory gives us exactly this sort of knowledge; "it was so there at that time." It is not the fact that at that time it was not so. Memory is directly produced by the *manas*, and the impressions (*saṃskāra*) represent its mode of contact with the object. It is through the impressions that mind comes in contact with specific objects (*saṃskāras tu manasas tad-artha-sannikarṣa-rūpa eva*). It may be objected that, the object referred to by memory having undergone many changes and ceased in the interval to exist in its old state, the present memory cannot take hold of its object; the answer is that the objection would have some force if *manas*, unaided by any other instrument, were expected to do it; but this is not so. Just as the sense-organs, which are operative only in the present, may yet perform the operation of recognition through the help of the impressions (*saṃskāra*), so the *manas* also may be admitted to refer by the help of the impressions to an object which has changed its previous state[2].

The conception of *pramāṇa* is considered a subject of great importance in Indian philosophy. The word *pramāṇa* is used principally in two different senses, (i) as a valid mental act, as distinguished from the invalid or illusory cognitions; (ii) as the instruments or the collocations of circumstances which produce knowledge. Some account of *pramāṇa* in the latter sense has already been given in Vol. I, pp. 330–2. The conflicting opinions regarding the interpretation of *pramāṇa* as instruments of know-

[1] *smṛtiḥ pratyakṣam aitihyam anumānacatuṣṭayaṁ*
praṃāṇam iti vijñeyaṃ dharmādy-arthe mumukṣubhiḥ.
Pramāṇa-candrikā, p. 4.

[2] *saṃskāra-sahakṛtam manaḥ ananubhūtām api nivṛtta-pūrvāvasthāṃ viṣayī-kurvat smaraṇam janayet iti ko doṣaḥ; vartamāna-viṣayāṇi api indriyāṇi sahakāri-sāmarthyāt kālāntara-sambandhitām api gocarayanti; yathā saṁskāra-sahakṛtāni soyam ity atīta-vartamānatva-viśiṣṭaviṣayapratyabhijñā-sādhanāni prākṛtendri-yāṇi mano-vṛtti-jñānaṁ janayanti.* *Pramāṇa-paddhati*, p. 24.

ledge is due to the fact that diverse systems of philosophy hold different views regarding the nature and origin of knowledge. Thus the Nyāya defines *pramāṇa* as the collocation of causes which produces knowledge (*upalabdhi* or *pramā*). The causes of memory are excluded from *pramāṇa* simply on verbal grounds, namely that people use the word *smṛti* (memory) to denote knowledge produced merely from impressions (*saṃskāra-mātra-janmanaḥ*) and distinguish it from *pramā*, or right knowledge, which agrees with its objects[1].

The Jains, however, consider the indication of the object as revealed to us (*arthopadarśakatva*) as *pramā*, and in this they differ from the Buddhist view which defines *pramā* as the actual getting of the object (*artha-prāpakatva*). The Jains hold that the actual getting of the object is a result of *pravṛtti*, or effort to get it, and not of *pramāṇa*[2]. Though through an effort undertaken at the time of the occurrence of knowledge and in accordance with it one may attain the object, yet the function of *jñāna* consists only in the indication of the object as revealed by it[3]. *Pramā* is therefore according to the Jains equivalent to *svārtha-paricchitti*, or the outlining of the object, and the immediate instrument of it, or *pramāṇa*, is the subjective inner flash of knowledge, leading to such objective *artha-paricchitti*, or determination of objects[4]. Of course *svārtha-paricchitti* appears to be only a function of *jñāna* and thus in a sense identical with it, and in that way *pramāṇa* is identical with *jñāna*. But it is because the objective reference is considered

[1] *pramā-sādhanaṃ hi pramāṇaṃ na ca smṛtiḥ pramā lokādhīnāvadhāraṇo hi śabdārtha-sambandhaḥ. lokaś ca saṃskāra-mātra-janmanaḥ smṛter anyām upalabdhim arthāvyābhicāriṇīṃ pramām ācaṣṭe tasmāt tad-dhetuḥ pramāṇam iti na smṛti-hetu-prasaṅgaḥ. Tātparya-ṭīkā*, p. 14.

[2] *pravṛtti-mūlā tūpādeyārtha-prāptir na pramāṇādhīnā tasyāḥ puruṣecchādhīna-pravṛtti-prabhavatvāt. Prameya-kamala-mārtaṇḍa*, p. 7.

[3] *yady apy anekasmāt jñāna-kṣaṇāt pravṛttau artha-prāptiṣ tathāpi paryālocyamānam artha-pradarśakatvam eva jñānasya prāpakatvaṃ nānyat. Ibid.*

The reflection made here against the Buddhists is hardly fair; for by *pravartakatva* they also mean *pradarśakatva*, though they think that the series of activities meant by *pramāṇa-vyāpāra* is finally concluded when the object is actually got. The idea or *vijñāna* only shows the object, and, when the object is shown, the effort is initiated and the object is got. The actual getting of the object is important only in this sense, that it finally determines whether the idea is correct or not; for when the object which corresponds exactly to the idea is got the idea can be said to be correct. *Nyāya-bindu-ṭīkā*, pp. 3, 4.

[4] *anya-nirapekṣatayā svārtha-paricchittisādhakatamatvād jñānam eva pramāṇam. Prameya-kamala-mārtaṇḍa*, p. 5.

here to be the essence of *pramā*, that *jñāna*, or the inner revelation of knowledge, is regarded as its instrument or *pramāṇa* and the external physical instruments or accessories to the production of knowledge noted by the Nyāya are discarded. It is the self-revelation of knowledge that leads immediately to the objective reference and objective determination, and the collocation of other accessories (*sākalya* or *sāmagrī*) can lead to it only through knowledge[1]. Knowledge alone can therefore be regarded as the most direct and immediately preceding instrument (*sādhakatama*). For similar reasons the Jains reject the Sāṃkhya view of *pramāṇa* as the functioning of the senses (*aindriya-vṛtti*) and the Prabhākara view of *pramāṇa* as the operation of the knower in the knowing process beneath the conscious level[2].

It is interesting to note in this connection that the Buddhist view on this point, as explained by Dharmottara, came nearer the Jain view by identifying *pramāṇa* and *pramāṇa-phala* in *jñāna* ("knowledge"). Thus by *pramāṇa* Dharmottara understands the similarity of the idea to the object, arising out of the latter's influence, and the idea or *jñāna* is called the *pramāṇa-phala*, though the similarity of the idea to the object giving rise to it is not different from the idea itself[3]. The similarity is called here *pramāṇa*, because it is by virtue of this similarity that the reference to the particular object of experience is possible; the knowledge of blue is possibly only by virtue of the similarity of the idea to the blue.

The Madhva definition of *pramāṇa* as *yathārthaṃ pramāṇam* means that by which an object is made known as it is. The instrument which produces it may be external sense-contact and the like, called here the *anupramāṇa* corresponding to the *sāmagrī* of the Nyāya, and the exercise of the intuitive function of the intuitive sense (*kevala pramāṇa*) of *sākṣī*, which is identical with self. Thus it combines in a way the subjective view of Prabhākara and the Jains and the objective view of the Nyāya.

[1] For other Jain arguments in refutation of the *sāmagrī* theory of *pramāṇa* in the Nyāya see *Prameya-kamala-mārtaṇḍa*, pp. 2–4.

[2] *etenendriya-vṛttiḥ pramāṇam ity abhidadhānaḥ sāṃkhyaḥ pratyākhyātaḥ... etena Prabhākaro'py artha-tathātva-prakāśako jñātṛ-vyāpāro'jñāna-rūpo'pi pramāṇam iti pratipādayan prativyūḍhaḥ patipattavyaḥ. Ibid.* p. 6.

[3] *yadi tarhi jñānam pramiti-rūpatvāt pramāṇa-phalam kiṁ tarhi pramāṇam ity āha; arthena saha yat sārupyaṃ sādṛśyam asya jñānasya tat pramāṇam iha... nanu ca jñānād avyatiriktaṃ sādṛśyam: tathā ca sati tad eva jñānaṃ pramāṇam tad eva pramāṇa-phalam. Nyāya-bindu-ṭīkā*, p. 18.

Svataḥ-prāmāṇya (self-validity of knowledge).

In the system of Madhva the doctrine of self-validity (*svataḥ-prāmāṇya*) means the consideration of any knowledge as valid by the intuitive agent (*sākṣī*) which experiences that knowledge without being hindered by any defects or any other sources of obstruction[1]. The *sākṣī* is an intelligent and conscious perceiver which can intuitively perceive space and distance, and when the distance is such as to create a suspicion that its defect may have affected the nature of perception, the intelligent intuitive agent suspends its judgment for fear of error, and we have then what is called doubt (*saṃsáya*)[2]. Vyāsa Yati, in his *Tarka-tāṇḍava*, expresses the idea in the language of the commentator of the *Tattva-nirṇaya* by saying that it is the *sākṣī* that is capable of comprehending both the knowledge and its validity, and even when obstructed it still retains its power, but does not exercise it[3]. When there is an illusion of validity (*prāmāṇya-bhrama*), the *sākṣī* remains inactive and the *manas*, being affected by its passions of attachment, etc., makes a mis-perception, and the result is an illusory perception. The operation of the *sākṣī* comprehending the validity of its knowledge is only possible when there is no obstruction through which its operation may be interfered with by the illusory perceptions of *manas*. Thus, though there may be doubts and illusions, yet it is impossible that the *sākṣī*, experiencing knowledge, should not at the same time observe its validity also, in all its normal operations when there are no defects; otherwise there would be no certainty anywhere. So the disturbing influence, wherever that may be, affects the natural power (*sahaja śakti*) of the *sākṣī*, and the doubts and illusory perceptions are created in that case by the *manas*. But,

[1] *doṣādy-apratiruddhena jñāna-grāhaka-sākṣiṇā*
svatastvaṃ jñānamānatvanirṇīti-niyamo hi naḥ.
Yukti-mallikā, I. 311.

[2] *yato dūratva-doṣeṇa sva-gṛhītena kuṇṭhitaḥ,*
na niścinoti prāmāṇyaṃ tatra jñāna-grahe'pi sva deśa-stha-viprakarśo hi dūratvaṃ
sa ca sākṣiṇāvagra hītuṃ śakyate yasmād ākāśavyākṛto hyasau.
Ibid. I. 313, 314.

[3] *sākṣyeṇa jñānaṃ tat-prāmāṇyaṃ ca viṣayīkartuṃ kṣamaḥ, kintu pratibaddho jñānamātraṃ gṛhītvā tat-prāmāṇya-grahaṇāya na kramate.* *Tarka-tāṇḍava*, p. 7.
Rāghavendra-tīrtha, in commenting on this, writes: *prāmāṇyasya sahaja-śakti-viṣayatvaṃ pratibandha-sthale yogyatā asti.*

wherever there are no distracting influences at work, the *sākṣī* comprehends knowledge and also its validity[1].

The problem of self-validity of knowledge in Mīmāṃsā and Vedānta has already been briefly discussed in the first volume of the present work[2]. A distinction is made between the way in which the notion that any knowledge is valid arises in us or is cognized by us (*svataḥ-prāmāṇya-jñapti*) and we become aware of the validity of our awareness, and the way in which such validity arises by itself from considerations of the nature of objective grounds (*svataḥ-prāmāṇyotpatti*). The former relates to the subjective and spontaneous intuitive belief that our perceptions or inferences are true; the latter relates to the theory which objectively upholds the view that the conditions which have given rise to knowledge also by its very production certify its truth. The word *prāmāṇya* in *svataḥ-prāmāṇya* is used in the sense of *pramātva* or true certainty.

According to the difference of epistemological position the nature of the subjective apperception of the validity of our knowledge differs. Thus, the followers of Prabhākara regard knowledge as self-luminous, meaning thereby that any moment of the revelation of knowledge involves with it the revelation of the object and the subject of knowledge. Any form of awareness (*jñāna-grāhaka*), such as "I am aware of the jug," would according to this view carry with it also the certainty that such awareness is also true, independent of anything else (*jñāna-grāhakātiriktānapekṣatvam*). The followers of Kumārila, however, regard knowledge (*jñāna*) as something transcendent and non-sensible (*atīndriya*) which can only be inferred by a mental state of cognition (*jñātatā*), such as "I am aware of the jug," and on this view, since the mental state is the only thing cognized, knowledge is inferred from it and the validity attaching to it can be known only as a result of such inference. Since there is a particular form of awareness (*jñātatā*) there must be valid knowledge. The validity attaching to knowledge can only be apparent, when there is an inference; it is, therefore, dependent on an inference made by reason of the awareness (*jñātatā*) of the particular form (*yāvat-svāśrayānumiti-grāhyatvam*).

[1] *manasā kvacid apramāyām api prāmāṇya-graheṇa sarvatra tenaiva prāmāṇya-grahaṇe asvarasa-prasaṅgena pramā-rūpeṣu gṛhīta-tat-tat-prāmāṇye asvarasya niyamena yathārthasya prāmāṇya-grāhakasya sākṣiṇo avaśyam apekṣitatvāt. Bhāva-vilāsinī*, p. 50 (by Surottama-tīrtha on *Yukti-mallikā*).

[2] *A History of Indian Philosophy*, Vol. I, pp. 268 n., 372–5, 484.

The analysis of the situation produced when we know an object as it appears consists on this view in this, that it distinguishes knowledge as a permanent unit which in association with the proper sense-contact, etc., produces the particular kinds of awareness involving specific and individual objectivity (*viṣayatā* or *karmatā*), such as "I know a jug." In this view objectivity, being the product of knowledge, cannot be identified with knowledge. It should be noted that, objectivity (*viṣayatā*) remaining the same (e.g., "a jug on the ground" is not the same as "ground on the jug," though the objectivity of the connected jug and ground is the same), there may be important differences in the nature of such objectivity through a difference of relations. In such cases the view held is that objectivity is different from knowledge; knowledge is the invariant (*nitya*) entity; objectivity remaining the same, a difference of relations (*prakāratā*) may give rise to a difference in the nature of awareness (*jñātatā*); each *jñātatā* or awareness means therefore each specific objectivity with its specific relations; it is only this *jñātatā* that is directly and immediately perceived. Knowledge is therefore a transcendent entity which cannot be intuited (*atīndriya*), but can only be inferred as a factor conditioning the awareness. The rise of an awareness gives rise to the notion of its validity and the validity of knowledge (*jñāna*) which has conditioned it[1]. The necessity of admitting a transcendent existence of *jñāna*, apart from the varying states of awareness, is due probably to the desire to provide a permanent subjective force, *jñāna*, which, remaining identical with itself, may ultimately determine all states of awareness. Another important Mīmāṁsā exponent, Murāri Miśra, thinks that the objective knowledge (e.g., knowledge of a jug) is followed by the subjective self-consciousness, associating the knowledge of the object with the self (*anuvyavasāya*), and it is this *anuvyavasāya* which determines the final form of knowledge resulting in the intuition of its own validity[2]. A general definition to

[1] *Bhāṭṭa-cintāmaṇi*, by Gāgā Bhaṭṭa, pp. 16–18. The inference, however, as Mathurānātha points out in his commentary on the *Tattva-cintāmaṇi* on *prāmāṇya-vāda* (p. 144), is not of the form, as *iyaṃ jñātatā ghaṭatvavati ghaṭatva-prakāraka-jñāna-janyā ghaṭatvavati ghaṭatva-prakāraka-jñātatātvāt*, but as *ahaṃ jñānavān jñātatāvattvāt*.

[2] *jñānasyātīndriyatayā pratyakṣā-saṃbhavena sva-janya-jñātatā-liṅgakānumiti-sāmagrī sva-niṣṭha-prāmāṇya-niścayitā iti Bhāṭṭāḥ; jñātatā ca jñāta iti pratīti-siddho jñānoajanya-viṣaya-samavetaḥ prākaṭyāparanāmā atirikta-padārthaviśeṣaḥ.* Mathurānātha on *Pramāṇa-vāda-rahasya* of the *Tattva-cintāmaṇi*, p. 126 (Asiatic Society's edition).

cover all these three types of *svataḥ-prāmāṇya* of Prabhākara, Kumārila Bhaṭṭa and Murāri Miśra is given by Gaṅgeśa in his *Tattva-cintāmaṇi* as follows: the validity of any knowledge (except in the case where a knowledge is known to be false, e.g., this knowledge of silver is false) is communicated by the entire system of collocations giving rise to that knowledge and by that alone[1]. Vyāsa-tīrtha, in discussing the value of this definition, points out several defects in its wording and criticizes it by saying that the condition imposed, that the knowledge should be communicated by the same system of collocating circumstances that produces the validity, is defective in defining the *svataḥ-prāmāṇya* position, since the condition is fulfilled even on the *parataḥ-prāmāṇya* theory; for there also the conditioning circumstances which communicate to us the validity of any knowledge are the same which make the rise of knowledge possible[2]. The definition of self-validity proposed by Vyāsa-tīrtha agrees with the second alternative definition given by Gaṅgeśa in his *Tattva-cintāmaṇi*: it dispenses with the necessity of admitting the collocating circumstances or conditions as producing knowledge; it defines self-validity of knowledge as that characteristic of it which is not grasped by any knowledge having for its object the matter of which the validity is grasped, i.e., the same knowledge which grasps an object does in the same act, without entering into any further mediate process, grasp its validity as well[3]. It will be seen that such a view is different from that of the Bhāṭṭa and Miśra views of self-validity; for on the Bhāṭṭa view self-validity is affirmed of knowledge which can be inferred only and not directly taken with a specific awareness (as "I know this jug"), and in the Miśra view self-validity is affirmed only as a result of *anuvyavasāya*, associating the cognition with the self (as "I know")[4].

[1] *tad-aprāmāṇya-grāhaka-yāvaj-jñāna-grāhaka-sāmagrī-grāhyatvam. Ibid.* p. 122. The *jñāna-grāhaka-sāmagrī* is, however, different with the three Mīmāṃsā views, viz., self-luminous knowledge in the case of Prabhākara, inference in the case of Bhāṭṭas and self-consciousness as *anuvyavasāya* in the case of Murāri Miśra.

[2] *tathā ca yāvati prāmāṇyaviṣayikā sāmagrī tad-grāhyatvaṃ svatastvam ity uktaṃ syat; tathā ca etādṛśasvatastvasya paratastvapakṣayā sattvāt siddhasādhanam. Tarka-tāṇḍava*, p. 12.

[3] *taj-jñāna-viṣayaka-jñānājanya-jñāna-viṣayatvam eva svatastvam. Tarka-tāṇḍava*, p. 15, and *Tattva-cintāmaṇi*, p. 122.

[4] The above definition of *svataḥ-prāmāṇya*, agreed to by Vyāsa-tīrtha, has been given in the *Tattva-cintāmaṇi* as a definition in which there is a general agreement in the views of the three schools of Mīmāṃsā (*mata-traya-sādhāraṇa*); it involves a special interpretation of the word *jñāna-viṣaya* in *taj-jñāna-viṣayaka* as *jñānānubandhi-viṣayatāśraya* (see Mathurānātha's commentary, p. 144).

Vyāsa-tīrtha emphasizes the view that in the absence of faults and doubts (*doṣa-śaṅkādinā anāskanditaḥ*) the subjective realization of an objective fact carries validity with it. He points out that it is not correct to say that sense-contact with a larger surface of the object can be regarded as the cause why the knowledge so produced is considered as valid; for it is well known that in spite of such sense-contact there may be error, if there are the defects (*doṣa*) which render mal-observation possible. So it is better to hold that the validity of knowledge arises from the datum of knowledge (*jñāna-sāmagrī*) itself. Sense-contact is useful only when there are doubts and other obstructions in the production of knowledge; but it does not by itself produce validity of knowledge[1]. Even the absence of defects is not the cause of the validity of knowledge; for the absence of defects is only a negative factor, which is no doubt necessary, but is not by any means the constitutive element of the positive realization of self-validity, which proceeds immediately and directly from the datum of knowledge[2]. Even in spite of the presence of defects there might by chance be true knowledge[3]. All illusory knowledge, however, is due to the presence of defects (*doṣa*); for in that case the object of which a knowledge is produced is not before us, and there is no actual sense contact with it. So the followers of Madhva hold the theory of *parataḥ-aprāmāṇya*, which in their view means that all cases of invalid knowledge are due to sources (namely *doṣas* or defects) other than the datum of knowledge[4]. Vādirāja points out in this connection in his *Yukti-mallikā* that the absence of defect, being a qualifying characteristic of the datum of knowledge, cannot by itself be regarded as an independent cause of right knowledge. In most cases of perception under normal conditions we have right knowledge, and it is only in special circumstances that there comes doubt and the necessity of scrutiny is realized. If in every step of knowledge there were doubt regarding its validity, then there would be an infinite regress (*anavasthā*), and hence we could never feel the validity and certainty of any knowledge[5]. Vyāsa-tīrtha also emphasizes the infinite regress on any

[1] *Tarka-tāṇḍava*, pp. 83–90.

[2] *doṣābhāvasyāpekṣitatve' pi pramā-janana-śaktiḥ sahāyā*. *Ibid.* p. 88.

[3] *uktaṃ hi Viṣṇu-tattva-nirṇaya-ṭikāyāṁ doṣābhāvo'pi na prāmāṇya-kāraṇam, yādṛcchika-saṁvādādiṣu saty api doṣe pramā-jñānodayāt*. *Ibid.* p. 89.

[4] *Ibid.* p. 98. Also *Viṣṇu-tattva-nirṇaya*, p. 2.

[5] *Yukti-mallikā*, *śl.* 343–70 and *Bhāva-vilāsinī* of Surottama-tīrtha on the same.

view like that of the Nyāya, where the validity of knowledge has to be determined by subsequent tests from without (*paratastvā-numāna*). He points out that the realization of the validity of our knowledge leads us to action (*prāmāṇya-niścayasya pravart-akatvam*)[1]. But, if the validity of each knowledge has to be tested by another, we have naturally an infinite regress[2]. The self-conscious self (*sākṣī*), however, knows its states, its pleasures and pains directly and immediately, and there is no possibility of doubt in such cases of undoubted self-validity of knowledge.

Illusion and Doubt.

The above discussion of self-validity of knowledge naturally leads us to enquire concerning the Madhva theory of illusion and the way in which it refutes the other theories of illusion accepted by other schools of Indian Philosophy. Illusion is in Madhva's system of Philosophy knowing of an object in a manner different from what it is (*anyathā-vijñānam eva bhrāntiḥ*), and the contradiction (*bādha*) of illusion consists in the knowing of the illusory form as false through the rise of the right knowledge (*samyag-jñāna*). What this means is that this illusion is a knowledge in which one entity appears as another; that which is non-existent appears as existent, and that which is existent appears as non-existent[3]. The illusions are produced by the senses affected by the defects. The defects do not only obstruct; they can also cause a wrong representation of the object, so they are not only responsible for non-observation, but also for mal-observation. Now the point arises that that alone can be an object of knowledge which can in some way affect its production; in an illusory knowledge of silver in respect of conch-shell, the silver, being non-existent, cannot have any part in producing the knowledge and therefore cannot be an object of knowledge. To this Jaya-tīrtha replies that even a non-existent entity may be an object of knowledge; we all infer past events and refer things to persons who have long ceased to exist. In such cases the non-existent entities may be said not to have produced the knowledge, but to have determined (*nirūpaka*) it[4]. Such determination, it may be held, does not presuppose the immediate existence of that entity, since it may well be considered as

[1] *Tarka-tāṇḍava*, pp. 41–6.
[2] *Ibid.* pp. 46–50.
[3] *Nyāya-sudhā*, p. 46.
[4] *Ibid.* p. 48.

limited to the idea, concept or knowledge produced, without having reference to the presence or existence of any corresponding objective entity. It may be objected that in the case of the visual perception of an object, it is definite that it is produced by the object through sense-contact; but in the case of illusion of silver in the conch-shell the silver is really absent, and therefore it cannot have any sense-contact, and consequently no visual perception of it is possible. The answer given to this objection is that it is the affected visual organ that, being in contact with conch-shell, causes the rise of a cognition representing it as a piece of silver which did not exist at all[1]. It ought not to be argued, says Jaya-tīrtha, that, if there can be knowledge without an object, then no knowledge can be trustworthy; for as a rule knowledge is self-valid (*autsargikaṃ jñānānāṃ prāmāṇyam*). The self-conscious agent (*sākṣī*) perceives and certifies to itself the validity of the mental states without the mediation of any other process or agent. This direct certitude or "belief as true," realized by ourselves in our capacities as conscious perceivers in every case where the knowledge produced is not affected or influenced by defects which cause mal-observation and non-observation, is what is understood as the self-validity of knowledge[2]. In the case of an illusory perception (e.g., of a piece of conch-shell as silver) there is an appearance of one thing as another, and that this is so is directly perceived or felt (*anubhava*); had it not been that a piece of conch-shell was perceived as silver, why should a man who sought silver stoop to pick up the conch-shell? The illusory perception of silver does not differ in appearance from a case of a real perception of silver.

Jaya-tīrtha, in arguing against the Mīmāṃsā view of illusion of conch-shell-silver as consisting of the memory of silver and the perception of conch-shell and the inability to distinguish between them, says that the appearance of silver in such cases has none of the characteristics of memory, and the activity generated by this false belief cannot be explained merely by the supposition of a non-distinction of difference between a memory-image and a visual percept. A mere negation involving the non-distinction of two entities cannot lead anyone to any definite choice. Moreover, if one

[1] *śuktikā-sannikṛṣṭaṃ duṣṭam indriyaṃ tam eva atyantāsadrajatātmena avagrāhamānam jñānaṃ janayati. Nyāya-sudhā*, p. 48.

[2] *Ibid.* p. 48.

is conscious of the memory-image as what it is and of the percept as what it is, then how is it that their difference is not realized?

Against the explanation of illusion by the Śaṅkara school Jaya-tīrtha urges that the view that conch-shell-silver is indescribable or indefinite (*anirvācya*) is also not correct, for such an indescribable character would mean that it is neither existent, nor non-existent, nor neither existent-nor-existent. Of these the first and the last alternatives are accepted on the Madhva view also. The second view cannot be correct; for it cannot be denied that even the non-existent silver did appear to us as being before us. It can be replied that such an appearance was due to the presence of the defect; for that which was non-existent could not be the object of knowledge, and, as the followers of Śaṅkara think that the knowledge of the locus (*adhiṣṭhāna*), the "this," is a true mental state, how can any defect interfere?[1] If it is indescribable, why should conch-shell-silver appear as existent at the time of perception and non-existent later on, and why should it not appear as indescribable at any time? Moreover, the Śaṅkarite will find it immensely difficult to explain what non-existence is.

Vādirāja points out in his *Yukti-mallikā* that in ordinary perception the eye comes into contact with an entity, the "this" before it, which may be regarded as the substantive (*viśeṣya*), and by grasping the substantive, the entity, its character as "jug" is also grasped, because the one is associated in a relation of identity with the other. But in illusory perception the character "silver" is not associated with the substantive "this," and hence through sense-contact with the "this," the conch-shell, the silver cannot be known; and hence such illusory knowledge can only be explained by supposing it to be due to the presence of defects. So the data of knowledge (*jñāna-sāmagrī*) in the case of right knowledge and illusory knowledge are different; in the case of the former we have the ordinary datum of knowledge, whereas in the case of the latter we have an extraneous influence, namely that of *doṣa*. And absence of *doṣa*, being but the natural characteristic of any datum of knowledge, cannot be regarded as an extraneous cause of right knowledge[2].

[1] *māyā-vādi-mate adhiṣṭhāna-jñānasya antaḥkaraṇa-vṛttitvena satyatvān na doṣa-janyatvam. Ibid.* p. 55.

[2] *Yukti-mallikā, Guṇa-saurabha, ślokas* 460–500.

Right knowledge, it should be observed, is distinguished from two other kinds of knowledge, namely illusory knowledge (*viparyaya*) and doubt (*saṃśaya*), by virtue of the fact that it alone can lead to a definite and settled action[1]. Some say that doubt may be considered to be of five kinds[2]. The first is due to the observation of common characteristics of two objects; thus, finding an object at some distance to be as high as a man, one might be led to remember both the stump of a tree and a man, and, not being able to distinguish the special features of each, viz., the holes, the rough and hard surface, etc. (in the case of the tree) and the movement of the head, hands and feet (in the case of a man), one would naturally doubt "is it the stump of a tree, or a man?" Again, seeing that the special characteristic (*asādhārano dharma*) of *ākāśa* is sound, one might doubt if sound (*śabda*) is eternal as sound. Again, seeing that followers of Sāṃkhya and Vaiśeṣika quarrel (*vipratipatti*) regarding the physical nature (*bhautikatva*) of the senses, there may be doubt whether the senses are physical or not. Again, when after digging a well we find (*upalabdhi*) water, there may be a doubt whether the water was already there and only manifested by the digging operation, or whether it was non-existent but produced by the digging operation. Again there may be a rumour that a ghost resides in a certain tree, but, when we go to it and do not see (*anupalabdhi*) it, there may be a doubt whether the ghost really was there and was not seen by reason of its power of rendering itself invisible, or whether it did not exist at all in the tree. Others, however, include the fourth and the fifth views, those of finding and not finding (*upalabdhi* and *anupalabdhi*), within the first type, viz., that of the

[1] *avadhāraṇatvaṃ ca niṣkampa-pravṛtti-janana-yogyatvam.* Janārdana's *Jaya-tīrtha-vijaya* (a commentary on the *Pramāṇa-paddhati*), p. 10.

[2] Vātsyāyana, in interpreting *Nyāya-sūtra*, I. I. 23, thinks that doubt is of five kinds, viz., through *samāna-dharma*, *aneka-dharma*, *vipratipatti*, *upalabdhi* and *anupalabdhi*, the first two being objective occurrences of common and uncommon features, and the last two subjective conditions of presence and absence of knowledge. The examples as given by him are the same as have been given below. Uddyotakara, however, interprets the above rule to refer only to the first three types of doubt, viz., *samāna-dharmopapatti*, *aneka-dharmopapatti* and *vipratipatti* (*Nyāya-vārttika*, pp. 87, 96–9). Kaṇāda, in his *Vaiśeṣika-sūtras*, (II. II. 17, 18, 19, 20) speaks of doubt as being of two kinds, internal (e.g., when anyone doubts whether the predictions of the astrologer, which were found true in some cases and false in others, are likely to be correct in any particular case) and external (e.g., when one doubts whether a stump before him is a tree or a man). External doubt is again of two kinds, (i) when the object is seen in totality, and (ii) when a part of it only is seen. *Nyāya-kandalī*, pp. 175–6.

perception of common characteristics (*sādhāraṇa dharma*), and thus hold that there are only three kinds of doubt[1]. Jaya-tīrtha, however, thinks that the other two varieties, that of the special characteristics (*asadhāraṇa dharma*) and that of conflicting views (*vipratipatti*) may also be included in the first type; for a special characteristic cannot by itself lead to the remembering of two objects leading to doubt. To know that sound is the special characteristic of *ākāśa* is not to remember any two objects between which there may be doubt, and doubt must be preceded by the remembering of two objects. Common characteristics may either be positive or negative. Thus space (*ākāśa*) has a set of characteristics which are not to be found in eternal things and a set of characteristics which are not to be found in non-eternal things (*nitya-vyāvṛttatva-viśiṣṭam ākāśa-guṇatvam* and *anitya-vyāvṛttatva-viśiṣṭam ākāśa-guṇatvam*). There may be doubt whether sound, which is a special characteristic of *ākāśa*, is one of those qualities which the *ākāśa* has in common with eternal things or with non-eternal things. Thus, this doubt also is to be classed with doubts of the first type, viz., that of the perception of common features. The followers of Madhva, by virtue of their theory of specific particulars (*viśeṣa*), can agree to the existence of two opposite sets of qualities in a thing. So, in the case of conflicting views (*vipratipatti*) also, the doubt may be said to rise through perception of the common qualities in physical and non-physical objects, so that one might very well doubt whether the senses, on account of certain qualities which they have in common with physical objects, are physical or whether, on account of the other qualities which they have in common with non-physical objects, are non-physical. So on Madhva's system doubt is of one kind only. Jaya-tīrtha says that the followers of the Vaiśeṣika think that apart from doubt and illusion (*viparyaya*) there are two kinds of false knowledge, viz., uncertainty (*anadhyavasāya*) and dreams. Uncertainty is different from doubt; for it is not an oscillation between two entities, but between an infinite number of possibilities, e.g., what is this tree called? Jaya-tīrtha says that uncertainty in such cases cannot be called knowledge at all; it is a mere enquiry (*saṃjñā-viṣayaṃ jijñāsā-mātraṃ*): thus, though I know that this tree is different from many other trees

[1] This is Uddyotakara's view of *Nyāya-sūtra*, I. I. 23, as has been mentioned before.

which I know, I still do not know its name and enquire about it. Most dreams are due to sub-conscious memory impressions and so far as these are there they are not false; the error consists in our conceiving these, which are mere memory images, as actually existing objectively at the time; and this part is therefore to be considered as illusion (*viparyaya*). Probability (*saṃbhāvanā*, also called *ūha*) is also to be considered as a kind of doubt, in which the chance of one of the entities is greater than that of the other (e.g., "it is very probable that that is the man who was standing outside the house")[1].

It is evident from the above that doubt is here considered only as a mental state of oscillation; its importance in stimulating philosophical enquiry and investigation, its relations to scepticism and criticism are wholly missed. The classifications of Vātsyāyana, Uddyotakara and Kaṇāda are of hardly any philosophical importance. This being so, it is much better to take doubt in the way in which Jaya-tīrtha has done.

Defence of Pluralism (Bheda)[2].

The difference between God and the individual (*jīva*) is perceived on our side by us and on God's side by Him. We know we are different from Him, and He knows that He is different from us; for, even though we may not perceive God, we may perceive our difference in relation to Him; the perception of difference does not necessarily mean that that from which the difference is perceived should also be perceived; thus even without perceiving a ghost one can say that he knows that a pillar is not a ghost[3].

Again, the difference of the individuals from Brahman can also be argued by inference, on the ground that the individuals are objects of sorrow and suffering, which the Brahman is not[4]. And, since the Brahman and the individuals are permanent eternal entities, their mutual difference from each other is also eternal and real. It is argued that the suffering of sorrow belongs to the limited

[1] *Pramāṇa-paddhati*, pp. 10–13; also *Jaya-tīrtha-vijaya* thereon.

[2] The materials of this section are taken from Vyāsa-tīrtha's *Bhedojjīvana* and the *Vyākhyā-śarkarā* of Śrīnivāsa.

[3] *sapratiyogika-padārtha-pratyakṣe na pratiyogi-pratyakṣaṃ tantram... stambhaḥ piśāco na ity ādau vyabhicārāt. Bhedojjīvana*, p. 13.

[4] *jīvo brahma-pratiyogika-dharmi-sattā-samāna-sattāka-bhedādhikaraṇaṃ brahmaṇyanusaṃhita-duḥkhānusaṃdhātṛtvād vyatirekeṇa brahmavat. Ibid.* p. 15.

soul and not to the pure consciousness; it is this pure consciousness which is the individual (*jīva*), and, since the suffering exists only so long as there is limitation, the difference ultimately vanishes when the limitation vanishes, and cannot therefore be real. But the Madhvas do not consider such individuals, limited in nature, to be false, and hence the difference depending on their nature is also not false. There being an eternal and real difference between the nature of the individuals and that of God, namely that the former suffer pain while the latter does not, the two can never be identical. The individual souls are but instances of the class-concept "soulhood," which is again a sub-concept of substance, and that of being. Though the souls have not the qualities of substances, such as colour, etc., yet they have at least the numerical qualities of one, two, three, etc. If this is once established, then that would at once differentiate this view from the Śaṅkara view of self as pure self-shining consciousness, leading to differenceless monism. The self as a class-concept would imply similarity between the different selves which are the instances or constituents of the concept, as well as difference among them (insomuch as each particular self is a separate individual numerically different from all other selves and also from God). The supposition of the adherents of the Śaṅkara school is that there is no intrinsic difference among the selves, and that the apparent difference is due to the limitations of the immediately influencing entity, the minds or *antahkaraṇas*, which is reflected in the selves and produces a seeming difference in the nature of the selves, though no such difference really exists; but Vyāsa-tīrtha urges that the truth is the other way, and it is the differences of the selves that really distinguish the minds and bodies associated with them. It is because of the intrinsic difference that exists between two individual selves that their bodies and minds are distinguished from each other. The Upaniṣads also are in favour of the view that God is different from the individual souls, and the attempt to prove a monistic purport of the Upaniṣad texts, Vyāsa-tīrtha tries to demonstrate, may well be proved a failure[1].

This defence of difference appears, however, to be weak when compared with the refutations of difference by Citsukha in his *Tattva-pradīpikā*, Nṛsimhāśrama muni in his *Bheda-dhikkāra*, and

[1] He refers to the Upaniṣad text *dvā suparṇā*, etc.

others. Citsukha goes directly into the concept of difference and all the different possible ways of conceiving it: difference as the nature of things (*svarūpa*), difference as mutual negation (*anyonyābhāva*, e.g., the jug is not cloth, the cloth is not a jug), difference as distinctness (*pṛthaktva*), difference as separateness of qualities (*vaidharmya*), and difference as manifested in the variety of categories, each of which has its own separate definition (*bhinna-lakṣaṇa-yogitva-bheda*); but Vyāsa-tīrtha does not make any attempt squarely to meet these arguments. A typical example of how the notion of difference is refuted by these writers has already been given in the first volume of the present work[1].

[1] *A History of Indian Philosophy*, Vol. I, p. 462.

CHAPTER XXVIII

MADHVA LOGIC

Perception.

Pramāṇa has already been defined as true correspondence with objects, and it has also been mentioned that it is divided into two kinds, *kevala-pramāṇa* and *anu-pramāṇa*. *Kevala-pramāṇa* is that by which direct and immediate intuition of objects of cognition is made; in fact it is both the intuitive process and the intuition. Four kinds of such direct intuition are admitted in the Madhva school of thought, viz., God's intuition, intuition of His consort *Lakṣmī*, intuition of sages (Yogins), intuition of ordinary persons[1]. God's intuition is always correct, independent (*svatantram*), beginningless and eternal, perfectly clear and has its scope or field everywhere (*sarvārtha-viṣayakam*). *Lakṣmī*'s intuition is dependent on Īśvara and inferior in clearness to His knowledge; it is equally beginningless, eternal, and correct, and has for its object everything except the entire extent of God Himself.

The specially efficient knowledge attained by *yoga* is that which belongs to Yogins: these are of three kinds. The first is of those straight sages (*ṛju-yogin*) who deserve Brahmahood. Excepting that this kind knows Īśvara and *Lakṣmī* only partially, it knows everything; this knowledge increases with the increase of *yoga*, until *mukti* is attained. These sages know of God more than other individual souls can do. Next to these comes the knowledge of Gods (*tāttvika-yogi-jñānaṃ*); it is inferior in scope to the knowledge of Yogins. Next comes the knowledge of ordinary persons, and of these also there are three classes in a descending order of merit; first, those that deserve liberation, secondly those that suffer rebirth, thirdly those who are in a still lower state of existence. *Pramāṇa* as intuition (*kevala*) is to be distinguished from *anu-pramāṇa*, as means of such intuition, which may be of three kinds, perception, inference, and testimony of the scriptures (*āgama*). The contact of any faultless sense-organ with a faultless object.

[1] *īśvara-jñānaṃ lakṣmī-jñānaṃ yogi-jñānaṃ ayogi-jñānaṃ ceti. Nyāya-paddhati*, p. 16.

Objects become faulty through excessive remoteness, excessive nearness, excessive smallness, intervening obstruction, being mixed up with things similar to them, being manifested, and being similar to other things (*sādṛśya*). Cognitive senses are of two kinds, the intuitive faculty of the cognitive agent which is identical with himself, and the ordinary cognitive senses of smell, taste, eye, touch, ear and *manas*; by the power of the intuitive faculty are perceived the self and its qualities, ignorance, *manas* and its faculties, and all sense-knowledge, pleasure, pain, etc., time and space[1]. The visual organ is supposed to perceive large objects having colour, and *manas* is the superintendent of all sense-organs and the faculty of memory. The faults of *manas*, in consequence of which errors are committed, are the passions and attachments, and those of the other senses are diseases like jaundice, etc., and the distracting influence of intervening medium, such as glass, etc. The ordinary cognitive senses produce the states of *manas*. The sense-organs are like so many instruments which have contact with the objects of cognition. The intuitive faculty also by virtue of its functions (existing as identical with itself and yet separately by virtue of *viśeṣa*) may be considered to be in contact. The verdict of intuitive faculty need not necessarily always be objectively valid, though it is always capable of correctly intuiting the contents of sense-observations. In God and Yogins it is both subjectivity and objectivity in agreement with facts; in ordinary persons it may or may not in any particular case be in agreement with the objective parts, or, in other words, its contents may or may not correspond to objective facts, but it is always correct in intuiting what is brought to it by the senses[2].

Jaya-tīrtha dispenses with the necessity of sixfold contact as advocated by the followers of the Nyāya[3]. This has to be so, because the *samavāya* relation is not admitted in the system of Madhva, nor is it admitted that there is any difference between things and their qualities (*guṇa-guṇy-abheda*). Sense-contact therefore takes place according to Jaya-tīrtha as one event; on the one

[1] *indriya-śabdena jñānendriyaṃ gṛhyate, tad dvi-vidhaṃ, pramātṛ-svarūpaṃ prākṛtaṃ ca tatra svarūpendriyaṃ sākṣīty ucyate; tasya viṣaya ātma-svarūpaṃ tad-dharmaḥ avidyā-manas-tad-vṛttayaḥ bāhyendriya-jñāna-sukhādayaḥ kālavyākṛtākāśaś ca. Pramāṇa-paddhati*, p. 22.

[2] *Ibid.* p. 26.

[3] See *A History of Indian Philosophy*, Vol. I (first edition), p. 334.

hand, because there is no difference between qualities and things, on the other because the self and its qualities are directly perceived by the intuitive entity and there is no necessity of admitting the contact of *manas*, and hence no need to admit a sixfold contact as is proposed by the followers of the Nyāya.

Again, we know that the Nyāya draws a distinction between indeterminate (*nirvikalpa*) and determinate (*savikalpa*) knowledge; according to this system, indeterminate knowledge means the simple cognition of the object in itself without any of the eightfold conceptual determinations as regards substance-concept (*dravya-vikalpo yathā daṇḍī*), as "the possessor of a stick," as regards quality-concept (*guṇa-vikalpo yathā śuklaḥ*), as "white", as regards action-concept (*kriyā-vikalpo yathā gacchati*), as "he goes", as regards class-concept (*jāti-vikalpo yathā gauḥ*), as "cow", as regards ultimately distinguishing characteristic (*viśeṣa-vikalpo yathā viśiṣṭaḥ paramāṇuḥ*), as "the atoms have ultimate characteristics by virtue of which the sages can distinguish one atom from another", as regards the concept of relation of inseparable inherence (*samavāya-vikalpo yathā paṭa-samavāyavantās tantavaḥ*), as "the threads in a piece of cloth", as regards the concept of name (*nāma-vikalpo yathā Devadatta*), as "the man Devadatta", as regards the concept of negation (*abhāva-vikalpo yathā ghaṭābhāvavad bhū-talam*), as in "there is no jug on the ground". But Jaya-tīrtha says that none of these distinctions between determinate and indeterminate perceptions can be accepted, as they are based on the assumption of the two categories of specific ultimate characteristics (*viśeṣa*) and the relation of inseparable inherence (*samavāya*), both of which are invalid. The name of a percept is also known by memory operating at a later moment, and the negation of an entity is known to depend on the memory of the entity itself. Though not all these concepts are produced at the first moment of perception, yet, since some of the concepts, such as substance, quality, action, etc., are grasped at the first moment of perception, there is no reason to suppose the existence of indeterminate perception (*nirvikalpa pratyakṣa*). All perception is determinate. The Nyāya view that the feeling of usefulness of an object or of its being undesirable is the result of perception is not correct: for these are obtained by inference[1]. When a man avoids

[1] *Nyāya-mañjarī*, pp. 67–71.

a thorn, it is because of his past experience that he judges that it would cause him pain; when he turns to something which is desirable, it is from the inference of the experience of it as having felt desirable in the past.

Inference (Anumāna).

The cause of inference is a faultless reason (through which by virtue of its association anything can be ascertained). The nature of this association or concomitance is described by Jaya-tīrtha as being inseparable concomitance (*avinābhāva*). Vyāsa-tīrtha urges in the *Tarka-tāṇḍava* that this inseparable concomitance ought really to mean contradiction of experience leading to inadmissible assumption or implication (*anupapatti*). When anything experienced in a particular space-time relation must be invalid except on the assumption of some other thing, in some other space-time relation, it must be admitted that such a particular relation subsisting between the two is a relation of concomitance (*vyāpti*), leading to the inference of the latter through the former[1].

Vyāsa-tīrtha urges that this view of inference has also been supported by Madhva in his *Pramāṇa-lakṣaṇa*, where he says that the residual method (*pariśeṣa*) is the essential method in all cases of valid inference[2]. Reduction to absurdity in regard to any valid experience is what necessitates the supposition in an act of inference.[3] Jaya-tīrtha in his *Pramāṇa-paddhati* has indeed defined concomitance (*vyāpti*) as inseparability (*avinā-bhāva*); this inseparable concomitance cannot be described as being in all cases agreement in absence, i.e., the absence of the reason, *hetu*, in all cases of the absence of the *probandum* (*sādhya*), or the inferred entity; for there are cases where, in spite of the absence of such negative instances, inference is possible, e.g., sound is expressible on account of its being an object of knowledge; now here no such negative instance is available where there would be no expression; hence in such cases of impossible-negative (*kevalānvayi*) inferences the above definition of concomitance, which

[1] *yad-deśa-kāla-saṃbaddhasya yasya yad-deśa-kāla-saṃbaddhena yena vinānupapattis tasyiva tena saha vyāptiḥ. Tarka-tāṇḍava* (MS., p. 1).

[2] *pariśeṣo'rthāpattir anumānam ity aviśeṣaḥ. Pramāṇa-lakṣaṇa* and *Pramāṇa-lakṣaṇa-ṭīkā*, p. 27.

[3] *anumānam api āvaśyakānupapattyaiva gamakam. Tarka-tāṇḍava* (MS., p. 2).

requires the existence of negative instances for the ascertainment of concomitance, would not apply. Also no kind of spatial association of the reason and consequence (*sādhya*) can be urged as being an indispensable condition of concomitance: for there can be the inference of rain in the upper part of a country from perceiving a rise of water in the river in the lower part, and there is no spatial contiguity between the reason and consequence. So the main point in concomitance determining inference is the reduction of an incontrovertible experience into an impossibility, which necessitates the assumption of the inferred entity. It is this which has also been described as the law of unconditional and invariable association (*sāhacarya-niyama*). In the well-known example of fire and smoke what is described as the unconditional and invariable coexistence of the absence of smoke in all cases of the absence of fire is also a case of *reductio ad absurdum* (*anupapatti*). It would apply with equal force in the cases of impossible-negatives (*kevalānvayi*); for there also the impossible absence of the consequence would render the reason absurd; and hence the assumption of the consequence is necessary.

Vyāsa-tīrtha refutes at great length the definition of inference given by Gaṅgeśa in his *Tattva-cintāmaṇi*, where he explains concomitance as the coexistence of consequence and reason as qualified by the fact of the absence of the latter in each case of the absence of the former. Had it not been for the fact that in inferences of the type of impossible-negatives (*kevalānvayi*) no negative instances are available where we might have been acquainted with cases of absence of the consequence being also cases of absence of the reason (*sādhyābhāvavad-avṛttitvam*), Gaṅgeśa would have been glad to define concomitance (*vyapti*) as unconditional and invariable non-existence of the reason in all cases of the non-existence of the consequence (*sādhyābhāvavad-avṛttitvam*). But owing to the above difficulty Gaṅgeśa was forced to define concomitance as coexistence (*sāmānādhikaraṇya*) of the consequence and reason where the reason is also qualified as the repository of the negation of all possible conditions which could invalidate its unconditional and invariable relation to the consequence (*sādhya*)[1]. The insight of Gaṅgeśa in formulating such a definition consists in this, that he

[1] *pratiyogy-asamānādhikaraṇa-yat-samānādhikaraṇātyantābhāva-pratiyogitāvacchedakāvacchinnaṃ yan na bhavati tena samaṃ tasya sāmānādhikaraṇyaṃ vyāptiḥ. Tattva-cintāmaṇi*, Part II, p. 100 (ed. 1888, *Bibliotheca Indica*).

thinks that universal existence of the reason in case of the consequence is alone sufficient for an inference of the latter from the former, provided that the reason is pure and unmixed by the presence of any other entity. It is the presence of other entities mixed with the reason that may invalidate its universal coexistence with the consequence; so, if that could be eliminated, then mere universal existence of the reason in cases of the consequence would be sufficient to establish a relation of concomitance between the former and the latter.

Vyāsa-tīrtha, however, points out that the existence of the reason in cases of the consequence is not universally valid in all cases of inference. Thus in the inference of rain in the upper regions from perceiving a rise of water in the river in the lower regions there is no spatial coexistence of the reason in the consequence; so also in the inference that the constellation *Rohiṇī* will shortly rise in the east because the constellation *Kṛttikā* has already risen. In all such cases and in all cases of inference the view of *reductio ad absurdum* (*anupapatti*) can always define concomitance in the best possible way and therefore can also serve as the best ground for all kinds of inference, including the class known as impossible-negatives (*kevalānvayi*). For in the example given of that class, "this is expressible because it is an object of knowledge", we can argue that the denial of non-expressibility is a necessary postulate for the validity of the incontrovertible experience of its being an object of knowledge[1]. An objection may be raised that, non-expressibility being as fictitious an entity as a round square, there would be no meaning in further denying it. To this Vyāsa-tīrtha's reply is that negation may apply even to the fictitious and the non-existent (*aprāmāṇika*)[2].

It is evident that this view of concomitance is a later development of theory by Vyāsa-tīrtha. For Jaya-tīrtha, in his *Pramāṇa-paddhati*, describes concomitance as being inseparable existence (*avinābhāva*), which he explains as invariable coexistence (*sāha-carya-niyama*) and also as invariable relation (*avyabhicaritaḥ saṃbandhaḥ*)[3]. Janārdana, however, in his commentary on the

[1] *idaṃ vācyaṃ jñeyatvāt kevalānvayi anumānam.*

[2] *tatra sādhyābhāvasya asattvād eva sādhyābhāve sati sādhanasya yopapattis tad-abhāva-rūpānupapatteḥ sattvāt; manmate'prāmāṇikasyāpi niṣedha-prati-yogitvāt. Tarka-tāṇḍava* (MS., p. 6).

[3] *Pramāṇa-paddhati*, p. 30.

Pramāṇa-paddhati, holds that this *sāhacarya-niyama* of Jaya-tīrtha must be interpreted to mean the *reductio ad absurdum* of Vyāsa-tīrtha; otherwise it would be evident to all that his view of concomitance has been intended by the above definition of Jaya-tīrtha; and he supports his view by pointing out that both in the *Pramāṇa-lakṣaṇa* and in his commentary on the *Pramāṇa-lakṣaṇa* Jaya-tīrtha has included inference by residues (*pariśeṣa*) and implication (*arthāpatti*) within inference, as he thought that the methods of these are practically methods of inference itself[1]. But this only proves that *pariśeṣa* and *arthāpatti* are also kinds of inference and not that the method of *anupapatti* involved in them should be regarded as being the only possible form of inference. Had he thought this to be so, he would certainly have mentioned it and would not have limited his definition of concomitance to invariable coexistence (*sāhacarya-niyama*). Chaḷari-śeṣācārya, who faithfully follows the footprints of Jaya-tīrtha, often repeating his language also, explains this invariable coexistence of Jaya-tīrtha as "where there is smoke, there is fire"; but he remarks that this invariable coexistence means only the existence of an invariable relation of the reason to the consequence (*atra sāhacaryaṁ hetoḥ sādhyena saṃbandha-mātraṃ vivakṣitam*), and not merely existence in the same place (*sāmānādhikaraṇya*). Coexistence therefore is said to mean here unfailing relation to the consequence (*avyabhicarita-sādhya-saṁbandho vyāptiḥ*), and this is *vyāpti*[2]. He also refers to Gaṅgeśa's definition of *vyāpti*, noted above, and points out that this definition of *vyāpti* would be inapplicable in those instances of inference where there is no spatial coexistence (e.g., the inference of rain in the upper regions from the rise of water in the river in the lower regions)[3]. He points out on the strength of such instances that concomitance cannot be defined as coexistence (*sāmānādhikaraṇya*), but is an unfailing relation which may hold between a cause and an effect existing in different places. On the strength of these instances Chaḷari-śeṣācārya argues in favour of concomitance without co-

[1] *anupapatter vyāptitvaṃ ca pramāṇa-lakṣaṇe pariśeṣārthāpattiḥ anumā-viśeṣa ity atrārthāpattir iva anumānam api āvaśyakānupapattyaiva gamakam ity uktatvāt.* *Tarka-tāṇḍava* (MS., pp. 1–2). Also *Pramāṇa-lakṣaṇa-ṭīkā*, pp. 5–7.

[2] Cf. Gaṅgeśa's alternative definition of *vyāpti* in the section on *Viśeṣa-vyāpti: yat-saṃbandhitāvacchedaka-rūpavattvaṃ yasya tasya sā vyāptiḥ. Tattva-cintāmaṇi*, Part II, p. 156.

[3] *na tu samāṇādhikaraṇyam eva. Pramāṇa-candrikā*, p. 8*a*.

existence (*vyadhikaraṇa-vyāpti*) as being possible, and therefore advocates the dropping of the coexistence as a necessary condition of concomitance. Vyāsa-tīrtha seems to have profited by these remarks and, instead of remaining content with "unfailing relation" of Chaḷari-śeṣācārya, explained this "unfailing relation" as being the definite relation of *reductio ad absurdum* (*anupapatti*)[1].

Tarka (Ratiocination).

The determining oscillation constituent in a mental process leading to inference is called *tarka* or *ūha*[2]. Gautama, in his *Nyāya-sūtra*, describes it as being ratiocination with a view to knowledge of truth, involving attempt at determination of any fact as possessing a particular character, based on a proper enquiry regarding the cause of such a determination. Thus there is a desire to know the truth about the nature of selves as knowers. Are they produced or are they uncreated? If they were created, they would suffer destruction, like all created things, and would not suffer or enjoy the fruits of their own deeds. If they are uncreated, they may very well continue to exist for ever to suffer or enjoy the fruits of their deeds and undergo rebirth. So the self which undergoes rebirth and enjoys or suffers the fruits of all its deeds must necessarily be uncreated[3]. Vātsyāyana says that *tarka* is neither included within the accepted *pramāṇas* nor is it a separate *pramāṇa*, but is a

[1] *Pramāṇa-candrikā*, pp. 8*a*, 9

[2] *ūhatvaṃ ca mānasatva-vyāpyo jāti-viśeṣaḥ "tarkayāmi" ity anubhava-siddhaḥ. Viśvanātha-vṛtti*, I, p. 40.

Tarka is used in the sense of *ūha* by Jayanta also in the *Nyāya-mañjarī*, p. 586. Jayanta says that its function as *ūha* consists in weakening the chances of the weak alternative, thereby strengthening the probability of the stronger alternative and so helping the generation of a valid knowledge of the certainty of the latter alternative. The meaning of *tarka* here must be distinguished from the meaning "inference" (*anumāna*), which it has in *Brahma-sūtra*, II. I. 12 (*tarkā-pratiṣṭhānāt*...), and also from its use as the science of logic (*ānvīkṣikī*), one of the fourteen subjects of learning (*vidyā-sthāna*). *Yājñavalkya-smṛti*, I. 3; also *Nyāya-mañjarī*, pp. 3–4. *Ūha* is with Sāṃkhya a quality of *buddhi* and with the Mīmāṃsakas it is a process of application of recognized linguistic maxims for the determination of the sense of words or of sentences (*yuktyā prayoga-nirūpaṇam ūhaḥ*), *ibid.* p. 588. Here *ūha* is used practically in the sense of "inference" and is such a *pramāṇa*. But here in the *Nyāya ūha* or *tarka* stands between right knowledge and doubt. Thus Jayanta says: *tad eṣa mīmāṃsaka-kalpyamāno nohaḥ pramāṇa-vyatirekam eti pramāṇa-sandehadaśāntarālavartī tu tarkaḥ kathito'tra śāstre* (p. 590).

[3] *Nyāya-sūtra*, I. I. 40 and Vātsyāyana's *Vṛtti* on it.

process which helps the *pramāṇas* to the determination of true knowledge[1]. Keśava Miśra, in his *Tarka-bhāṣya*, is inclined to include it under doubt[2]. But Annam Bhaṭṭa, in his *Tarka-dīpikā*, says that, though *tarka* should properly be counted under false knowledge (*viparyaya*), yet, since it helps the *pramāṇas*, it should be separately counted[3]. The usefulness of *tarka* in inference consists in assuring the mind of the absence of any cases of failure of existence of the reason in the consequence and thereby helping the formation of the notation of the concomitance of the reason and the consequence[4]. Viśvanātha says that *tarka* clears away the doubts regarding the possible cases of failure (*vyabhicāra*) of the reason (e.g., if smoke existed in any instance where there was no fire, then fire would not be the cause of smoke), and thereby renders the knowledge of concomitance infallible and so helps the work of inference not in a direct, but in an indirect way (*pāraṁparayā*)[5]. Viśvanātha further adds that such a *tarka* is of five kinds, namely consideration of the fallacy of self-dependence (*ātmāśraya*, e.g., if the knowledge of this jug is produced by the knowledge of this jug, then it should be different from it), mutual dependence (*anyonyāśraya*, e.g., if this jug is the object of the knowledge as produced by the knowledge, then it should be different from this jug), circle (*cakraka*, if this jug is produced by something else produced by this jug, then it should be different from anything produced by something else produced by this jug), vicious infinite (*anavasthā*, e.g., if the class concept "jug" refers to all jugs, it cannot refer to things produced by the jug), contradictory experience (*pramāṇa-bādhitārthaka-prasaṅga*, e.g., if smoke exists where there is no fire, then it could not be produced by fire, or if there was no fire in the hill, there would be no smoke in it)[6].

[1] *tarko na pramāṇa-saṃgṛhīto na pramāṇāntaram;*
pramāṇānām anugrāhakas tattva-jñānāya parikalpyate.
Vātsyāyana-bhāṣya, I. I. I.

[2] *Tarka-bhāṣya*, p. 44.

[3] *vyabhicāra-jñānābhāva-saṃpādakatvena tarkasya vyāpti-grahe upayogaḥ. Bhavānandi* on *Dīdhiti*, quoted in *Nyāya-kośa*, footnote, p. 292.

[4] *Tarka-dīpikā*, p. 88.

[5] *tathā ca dhūmo yadi vahni-vyabhicārī syāt vahni-janyo na syāt ity anena vyabhicāra-śaṅkā-nirāse niraṅkuśena vyāpti-jñānena anumitir iti paramparayā evāsya upayogaḥ. Viśvanātha-vṛtti*, I. I. 40.

[6] Each of the first three has three varieties, according as it refers to knowledge (*jñapti*), production (*utpatti*) and existence (*sthiti*). Thus the threefold example of *ātmāśraya* would be (i) *etad-ghaṭa-jñānaṃ yady etat-ghaṭa-janyaṃ syāt etad-ghaṭa-bhinnaṃ syāt*, (ii) *ghaṭo'yam yady etad-ghaṭa-janakaḥ syāt, etad-ghaṭa-*

Mathurānātha, in explaining the function of *tarka* in the formation of the notion of concomitance (*vyāpti*), says that, even when through noticing the existence of smoke in all known cases of fire and the absence of smoke in all those places where there is no fire, one decides that smoke is produced by fire or not, it is there that *tarka* helps to remove all legitimate doubts. As Gaṅgeśa shows, such a *tarka* would proceed thus: Either smoke is produced by fire or it is not produced there. So, if smoke is produced neither by fire nor by not-fire, it is not produced at all. If, however, there are the doubts whether smoke is from not-fire, or whether it can sometimes be where there is no fire, or whether it is produced without any cause (*ahetuka*), then none of us can have the notion of inseparable existence of fire in all cases of smoke so as to lead us to action (*sarvatva sva-kriyā-vyāghātaḥ*)[1]. A course of thought such as is called *tarka* is helpful to the formation of the notion of concomitance only when a large number of positive and negative cases has been actually perceived and a provisional certainty has been reached. Even when the provisional certainty is reached, so long as the mind is not cleared by the above *tarka* the series of doubts (*saṁśaya-dhārā*) might continue to rise[2]. It cannot be urged, says Gaṅgeśa, that, even when by the above method the notion of concomitance has been formed, there might still arise doubts whether fire might not be the cause of smoke or whether smoke might be without any cause; for, had it been so, you would not always (*niyata*) make fire when you wanted smoke, or eat when you wanted to satisfy your hunger, or use words to carry your ideas to

bhinnaḥ syāt, (iii) *ayaṃ ghaṭo yady etad-ghaṭa-vṛttiḥ syāt, tathātvena upalabhyeta*. Example of *anyonyāśraya* in *jñapti*: *ayaṃ ghaṭo yady etad-ghaṭa-jñāna-janya-jñāna-viṣayaḥ syāt etad-ghaṭa-bhinnaḥ syāt*. Example of *cakraka* in *utpatti*: *ghaṭoyaṃ yady etad-ghaṭa-janya-janya-janyaḥ syāt tadā etad-ghata-janya-janya-bhinnaṃ syāt*. Mādhava, in his *Sarva-darśana-saṃgraha*, speaking of older Nyāya tradition, adds seven others, *vyāghāta* (contradiction), *pratibandhi-kalpanā* (irrelevant thesis), *lāghava* (minimum postulation), *gaurava* (too much postulation), *utsarga* (general rule), *apavāda* (exception), *vaijātya* (class-difference). But Viśvanātha, whose list of these varies somewhat from the above, as he drops *vyāghāta* and has *prathamopasthitatva*, and *vinigamana-viraha* for *pratibandhi-kalpanā*, *apavāda* and *vaijātya*, holds that these are not properly *tarka*, but are so called only because they help as accessories to *pramāṇas* (*pramāṇa-sahakāritva-rūpa-sādharmyāt tathā vyavahāraḥ*). *Viśvanātha-vṛtti*, I. I. 40.

[1] Gaṅgeśa on *tarka* and Mathurānātha's commentary thereon. *Tattva-cintāmaṇi*, Part II, pp. 219–28.

[2] *Ibid.* p. 220; see also Kāmākhyānātha's note, also p. 228.

others. Such regular attempts themselves show that in such cases there are no doubts (*śaṅkā*); for, had there been doubts, these attempts would not be so invariable. It is not possible that you would be in doubt whether fire is the cause of smoke and yet always kindle fire when you try to get smoke. The existence of doubt in such cases would contradict your invariable attempt to kindle fire whenever you wanted smoke; doubts can be admitted only so long as one's actions do not contradict (*sva-kriyā-vyāghāta*) them[1].

Śrīharṣa, however, arguing from the Vedānta point of view, denies the power of *tarka* to dispel doubt. He urges that, if it is said that *tarka* necessarily dispels doubts in all cases and helps the formation of any particular notion of concomitance, then this statement must itself depend on some other notion of concomitance, and so on, leading us to a vicious infinite (*anavasthā*). Moreover, the fact that we know the universal coexistence of fire and smoke, and do not perceive any other element universally abiding in the fire which is equally universally coexistent with fire, does not prove that there is no such element in it which is really the cause of smoke (though apparently fire may appear as its cause). Our perception can certify only the existence or non-existence of all that is visible under the normal conditions of visual perception; it cannot say anything regarding the presence or absence of entities not controlled by these conditions, or we could only say that in the absence of fire there is absence of a specific kind of smoke; we could not say that there would be absence of all kinds of smoke; for it is just possible that there is some other kind of cause producing some special kind of smoke which we have not yet perceived; mere non-perception would not prove that such a special kind of smoke does not exist at all, since perception applies only to entities that are perceptible and is guided by its own conditions, and cannot therefore apply to entities which cannot be brought under those conditions[2]. The *tarka* which is supposed to dispel doubt by the supposition of contradiction of experience and which would thus support conco-

[1] *tad eva hy āśaṅkyate yasminn āśaṅkyamāne sva-kriyā-vyāghāto na bhavatīti; na hi saṃbhavati svayaṃ vahny-ādikaṃ dhumādi-kāryyarthaṃ niyamata upādatte tat-kāraṇaṃ tan netyāśaṅkyate ca. Ibid.* p. 232.

[2] *tad-adarśanasya āpātato hetv-antara-prayojyāvāntara-jāty-adarśanena ayogyatayā avikalpyatvād apy upapatteḥ; yadā tu hetv-antara-prayojyo dhūmasya viśeṣo drakṣyate tadāsau vikalpiṣyate iti saṃbhāvanāyā durnivāratvāt.* Śrīharṣa's *Khaṇḍana-khaṇḍa-khādya*, p. 680.

mitance, not being itself grounded on concomitance, would naturally fail to do its part; for, if such groundless *tarka* could be supposed to establish concomitance, that would itself be contradiction (*vyāghāta*). Udayana had said that, if even when no doubt is present you suppose that doubt might arise in the future, that can only be due to inference, so inference is valid. No doubts need be entertained regarding the concomitance underlying *tarka*, as that would lead to the contradiction of our own actions; for we cannot say that we believe fire to be the cause of smoke and still doubt it. Śrīharṣa had replied to this by saying that, where there is experience of failure of coexistence, that itself makes the supposition of concomitance doubtful; when there is no experience of failure of coexistence, there is no end of indefinite doubts lurking about; for these unknown doubts are only put an end to when a specific failure of coexistence is noticed; so under no circumstances can doubts be dispelled by *tarka*[1]. The main point of the dispute consists in this, that, while Śrīharṣa is afraid to trust *tarka* because of the supposed doubts, Udayana thinks that, if we are so pessimistic, then we should have to stop all our actions. None of them, however, discusses the middle course of probability, which may lead us to action and may yet not be considered as proved valid inference. Vardhamāna, however, in commenting on the above verse of Udayana, refers to Gaṅgeśa as holding that *tarka* does not lead to the formation of the notion of concomitance[2].

Vyāsa-tīrtha, however, in his *Tarka-tāṇḍava*, urges that *tarka* is not an indispensable condition of the notion of concomitance; by faith in trusty persons, or from inherited tendencies, as a result of experiences in past life, or through acquiescence in universally

[1] Udayana's verse ran as follows:

śaṅkā ced anumāsty eva na cec chaṅkā tatastarām
vyāghātāvadhir āśaṅkā tarkaḥ śaṅkāvadhir mataḥ.
Kusumāñjali, III. 7.

Śrīharṣa gave his reply to this by slightly changing Udayana's words as follows:

vyāghāto yadi śaṅkāsti na cec chaṅkā tatastarām
vyāghātāvadhir āśaṅkā tarkaḥ śaṅkāvadhiḥ kutaḥ.
Khaṇḍana-khaṇḍa-khādya, p. 693.

Gaṅgeśa suggests that the word *vyāghāta* in Śrīharṣa means failure of coexistence (*sahānavasthāna-niyama*), while in Udayana it means contradiction of one's own actions (*sva-kriyā-vyāghātaḥ*). But, as Vyāsa-tīrtha shows, the word may be taken in the latter sense even in Śrīharṣa. *Tarka-tāṇḍava* (MS., p. 25).

[2] *atrāsmatpitṛcaraṇāḥ, tarko na vyāpti-grāhakaḥ kintu*
vyabhicāra-jñānābhāva-saharkṛtaṁ sahacāra-darśanam.
Prakāśa, III, p. 26.

accepted views, we may have a notion of concomitance without going through the process of *tarka*. He seems, however, to be largely in agreement with the view of *tarka* as held by Gaṅgeśa according to the above statement of Vardhamāna, in holding that *tarka* does not lead directly to the establishment of concomitance. For he says that *tarka* does not directly lead us to the establishment of concomitance, since concomitance is directly grasped by a wide experience (*bhūyo-darśana*) of coexistence, qualified by a knowledge of absence of failure of coexistence[1]. Vācaspati also holds more or less the same view when he says that it is the sense-organ, aided by the memory of wide experience, that grasps this natural relation of concomitance[2]. Vyāsa-tīrtha says that the determination of absence of vitiating conditions (*upādhi*), which is a function of *tarka*, becomes necessary only in some kinds of inference; it is not always awaited. If it were always necessary, then *tarka* being required for all notions of concomitance and concomitance being the basis of *tarka*, there would be a vicious infinite[3]. If failures of coexistence are not known, then from cases of coexistence the self may immediately form the notion of concomitance[4]. What is necessary therefore is to dispel the doubts as to failure of coexistence (*vyabhicāra-śaṅkā-nivṛtti-dvāra*). But such doubts come only occasionally (*kvacitkaiva*) and not always; and such occasional doubts require to be dispelled by only an occasional recourse to *tarka*. It cannot be argued that the possibility of doubts may remain in all cases and hence in all cases there is necessity for the exercise of the *tarka*; for it may well be asked, do such doubts arise of themselves in our minds or are they raised by others? On the first supposition one may have doubts even as to the perception of one's hands and feet, or one might even have doubts in regard to one's doubts, which would render even the doubts invalid. If it is held that doubts arise only when other possible alternatives are suggested, then it has to be agreed that there will be many cases where no such

[1] *api ca tarko na sākṣād vyāpti-grāhakaḥ bhūyo-darśana-vyabhicārādarśana-sahakṛta-pratyakṣeṇaiva tad-grahaṇāt. Tarka-tāṇḍava* (MS., p. 20).

[2] *bhūyo-darśana-janita-saṃskāra-sahitam indriyam eva svābhāvika-sambandha-grāhi. Tātparya-ṭīkā.*

[3] This has already been pointed out above in dealing with Śrīharṣa's objections.

[4] *adṛṣṭe vyabhicāre tu sādhakaṃ tad ati sphuṭaṃ*
jñāyate sākṣiṇaivāddhā mānavadho na tad bhavet.
Tarka-tāṇḍava (MS., p. 21).

alternatives would be suggested or the probability of one of them might be so strongly suggested that there will be no occasion for doubts. So it must be admitted that in many cases we have a natural belief in certain orders of coexistence, where no doubts arise of themselves (*sva-rasika-viśvāsasyāvaśyakatvān na sarvata śaṅkā*)[1]; no one is seen going through a never-ending series of doubts all his life (*na cāvirala-lagna-śaṅkā-dhārā anubhūyate*). On the second supposition also, no one can suggest that doubts may always arise: in the relation of smoke and fire one cannot suggest that there may still be some other entity, different from fire, which causes smoke; for, if this were a sensible entity, it would have been perceived, and, if it were non-sensible, there would be no proof at all that a non-sensible entity existed or could exist. For, if Śrīharṣa should be so doubtful of all things, it might be suggested that in all the proofs in favour of monism (*advaita*) there may be a thousand faults and in the arguments of the dualists there may be a thousand good points, and so in consequence of these doubts you could not come to any conclusion establishing your doctrine of monism[2]. If a belief in a concomitance arises, the mere indefinite possibility of doubt does not shake one off his natural conviction of the concomitance as valid[3]. If you yourself would eat whenever you had hunger to appease, you cannot say that you have still doubts that eating may not after all be the cause of appeasing of hunger. Moreover, what is gained by urging that possibility of doubts always remains? Is it meant to destroy the validity of all inference or of all notions of concomitance? No one who wishes to admit the usefulness of inference would think of destroying the means—the notion of concomitance—by which it is established. If concomitance is not established, the Vedāntist will find that it is impossible to understand the meanings of those Vedic monistic words by which he wishes to establish monism. Again, if inference is to be valid, that can only be established by inference and not by perception. Without inference the Vedāntist could neither establish anything nor refute any assertions made by his opponents, contradicting his own doctrines. It seems therefore that Śrīharṣa would

[1] *Tarka-tāṇḍava*, pp. 22–3.

[2] *Ibid.* p. 24.

[3] *na hi grāhya-saṃśaya-mātraṃ niścaya-pratibandhakam; na ca utpannasya vyāpti-niścayasya balavad bādhakam asti yena autsargikaṃ prāmāṇyam apodyeta. Ibid.* p. 24.

carry out an inference as if there were no fear of the supposed doubts and yet, merely for the sake of saying it, say that there is a possibility of the existence of doubts in all inferences[1].

The main points that arise from the above discussion are that, while Śrīharṣa would argue that *tarka* cannot remove the doubts threatening the validity of any notion of concomitance and while the Naiyāyikas would hold that *tarka*, on account of its function of removing doubts from notions of concomitance, is a necessary factor of all inferential process, Vyāsa-tīrtha argues that, though the power of *tarka* in removing doubts is admitted, yet, since in many of our inferences no doubts requiring the help of *tarka* would arise, it is not true that *tarka* is a necessary factor in all inferences[2]. From what has been said above it will appear that there is some subtle difference of opinion in the Nyāya school regarding the real function of *tarka*. But the general tendency seems to be to restrict the function of *tarka* to removing doubts and thereby paving the way for the formation of the notion of concomitance; but it does not directly produce the notion of concomitance (*na tu vyāpti-grāhaka*) nor does it verify particular inductions by the application of general principles of uniformity of nature[3].

[1] *Ibid.* pp. 25–31.

[2] It cannot, however, be said that the Nyāya would urge the necessity of *tarka* in all instances of inference. The older Nyāya writers do not say anything explicitly on the subject; but Viśvanātha, in his *Muktāvalī*, states that *tarka* is necessary only in those cases where there are doubts regarding the forming of the notion of concomitance. Where no doubts naturally arise, there is no necessity of *tarka* (*yatra svata eva śaṅkā nāvatarati tatra na tarkāpekṣāpīti*). *Muktāvalī*, 137.

Dinakara, however, in his commentary on the *Muktāvalī* 137, thinks that there are two kinds of *tarka*, clearance of doubts and the formation of concomitance (*tarkaś ca dvividho saṃśaya-pariśodhako vyāpti-grāhakaś ca*). This however is directly opposed to the view of Vardhamāna cited above.

[3] The wording of Dr Seal's brief references to the subject of *tarka* in *A History of Hindu Chemistry* by Dr P. C. Ray (p. 264) is inexact. He says there: "*Tarka* or *Ūha*, then, is the verification and vindication of particular inductions by the application of the general principles of Uniformity of Nature and of Causality, principles which are themselves based on repeated observation (*bhūyo-darśana*) and the ascertainment of innumerable particular inductions of Uniformity or Causality (*bhūyo-darśana-janita-saṃskāra-sahitam indriyam eva svābhāvika-saṃbandha-grāhi* Vācaspati)." Thus *tarka* also helps in dispelling doubt (*saṅdeha*).

On its function in clearing the way to the formation of the notion of concomitance: *mārga-sādhana-dvāreṇa tarkasya tattva-jñānārthatvam iha vivakṣitam. Nyāya-mañjarī*, p. 586. Mathurānātha also points out that the function of *tarka* is to supply such grounds that doubts may not arise, but it is not *vyāpti-grāhaka* (*tarkaḥ śaṅkānutpattau prayojakaḥ*...). Mathurānātha on *Tattva-cintāmaṇi*, Part II, p. 240.

So far Vyāsa-tīrtha has been using the word *tarka* in the accepted Nyāya sense and, using it in that sense, he has been showing that the removal of doubts is not indispensable for the formation of the notion of concomitance. *Tarka* consists according to him, however, in the necessary awakening of the knowledge of absence of the reason owing to absence of the consequence; taken from this point of view, it becomes identical with inference (*anumāna*). Jaya-tīrtha also says in his *Pramāṇa-paddhati* that *tarka* means the necessary assumption of something else (consequence), when a particular character or entity (reason) is perceived or taken for granted (*kasyacid dharmasyāṅgīkare'rthāntarasyāpādanaṃ tarkaḥ*)[1]. Granted that there is no fire in the hill, it must necessarily be admitted that there is no smoke in it; this is *tarka* and this is also inference[2]. *Tarka* is thus the process by which the assumption of one hypothesis naturally forces the conclusion as true. This is therefore a *pramāṇa*, or valid source of knowledge, and should not be considered as either doubt or false knowledge, as some Nyāya writers did, or, as other Nyāya writers considered it to be, different from both doubt and decision (*nirṇaya*). Thus according to Vyāsa-tīrtha *tarka* has a twofold function, one as the dispeller of doubts and a help to other *pramāṇas*, and the other as inference. The main point that Vyāsa-tīrtha urges against Udayana (who holds the function of *tarka* to be merely the removal of undesirable assumptions) and against Vardhamāna (who holds that the function of *tarka* is merely the removal of doubt of the absence of the consequence) is that, if *tarka* does not take account of the material discrepancy or impossibility of facts involved in the assumption of the absence of the consequence (fire) when the smoke is present, then even the doubts or undesirable assumptions will not be removed; and, if it does take account thereof, then it yields new knowledge, is identical with inference, and is a *pramāṇa* itself[3]. *Tarka* may be treated as a negative inference, e.g., "had it been

[1] *Pramāṇa-paddhati*, p. 36*a*. *manmate tu aṅgīkṛtena sādhyābhāvena saha anaṅgīkṛtasya sādhanābhāvasya vyāpakatva-pramā vā sādhyābhāvāṅgīkāra-nimittaka-sādhanābhāvasyāṅgīkartavyatva-pramā vā tarkyate'nena iti vyutpattyā tarkaḥ. Tarka-tāṇḍava* (MS., p. 78).

[2] *parvato nirdhūmatvenāṅgīkartavyaḥ niragnikatvena aṅgīkṛtatvād hradavat ity anumānam eva tarkaḥ. Ibid.* p. 84.

[3] *kiṁ ca para-mate tarkasya kiṃ viṣaya-pariśodhane upayogaḥ kiṃ Udayana-rītyā aniṣṭa-prasañjanatvamātreṇa upayogaḥ, kiṃ vā Varddhamānādi-rītyā sādhyābhāva-sandeha-nivarttanena. Ibid.* p. 92.

without fire, it would have been without smoke; but it is not so". Being such a negative inference, it stands as an independent inference, and, as it may also be used to strengthen a positive inference, it may also be considered in that case an additional support to it (*pramāṇānām anugrāhaka*), just as what is known by perception may again be strengthened by inference[1]. Its function in removing doubts in other cases remains just as it has been shown before; but everywhere the root principle involved in it is necessary supposition rendering other alternatives impossible (*anyathānupapatti*), which is the principle also in inference[2].

Concomitance (Vyāpti).

The word *vyāpti* in Sanskrit is a noun formed from the root *vyāp*, "to pervade". The consequence (e.g., fire) pervades all cases of smoke, i.e., the circle of the consequence is not smaller than the circle of smoke and encloses it; consequence is therefore called the pervader (*vyāpaka*) and the reason (e.g. smoke) as the object of this action of pervading is called the pervaded (*vyāpya*). Thus in the case of smoke and fire there is an unfailing relation (*avyabhicāritā-sambandha*) between them and the former is called *vyāpya* and the latter *vyāpaka*. This unfailing relation may however be of four kinds. First, the two circles might coincide (*samavṛtti*), in which case the reason may be treated as consequence and inferred from the consequence treated as reason and *vice versa*. Thus one may argue both ways: it is sinful because it is prohibited in the Vedas and it is prohibited in the Vedas because it is sinful; here the two circles coincide. Secondly, when one circle is smaller than the other, as in the case of smoke and fire (*nyūnādhika-vṛtti*); the circle of fire is larger than the circle of smoke and so one could infer smoke from fire, but not fire from smoke—*vyāpya* is smaller than the *vyāpaka*. Thirdly, where the two circles are mutually exclusive (*paraspara-parihāreṇaiva vartate*), e.g., the class-concept cow (*gotva*) and the class-concept horse (*aśvatva*); where there is one, there is not the other. There is a relation of exclusion here, but not the relation of a *vyāpya* and *vyāpaka*. Fourthly, where the two are

[1] *sādhanānumānaṃ vinaiva yadi niragnikaḥ syāt tarhi nirdhūmaḥ syāt tathā cāyaṃ nirdhūma iti tarka-rūpānumānenaiva agnisiddheḥ.* *Ibid.* p. 90.

[2] *sākṣād anyathānupapatti-pramāpaka-tarka-viṣaya-kṛta-virodhasya sattvāt.* *Ibid.* p. 89.

sometimes mutually exclusive, yet sometimes found to be coincident; thus cooking is done by women, yet there are men who cook; cook and males are mutually exclusive, though there may be some males who cook (*kvacit samāviṣṭa api kvacit paraspara-parihā-reṇaiva vartate*). The circle of cooking is divided between males and females. Here also there is a relation between cooking and males, but it is not unfailing (*avyabhicāritā*); unfailing relation means that, where there is one, there must be the other also.

When a man observes the coexistence of fire and smoke, he naturally revolves in his mind "is it in this place that fire and smoke are seen together, while in other places and at other times the presence of one excludes the presence of the other, or are they always found together"; then by observing in several instances, he finds that, where there is smoke, there is fire, and that, where there is no fire, there is no smoke, and that in some cases at least there is fire, but no smoke. These observations are followed by a consideration such as this: "since, though in many cases fire coexists with smoke, in some cases at least fire is found where there is no smoke, does smoke, although in all the cases known to me it exists with fire, ever remain without it, or does it always coexist with fire?" Then again the consideration arises that the relation of smoke to fire is determined by the presence of wet wood (*ādrendhana*), which may be called a vitiating condition (*upādhi*), i.e., had this condition not been there, there would have been unqualified coexistence of fire with smoke, and *vice versa*. This vitiating condition (*upādhi*) exists in all cases of smoke, but not in all cases of fire[1]. Where the coexistence is not determined by any such vitiating condition, the coexistence is universally mutual. There are some qualities which are common to both fire and smoke (e.g., both of them are objects of knowledge: *yathā prameyatvam*), and these cannot determine the connection. There are other qualities which do not belong either to smoke or fire, and these also cannot determine the connection. It is only the vitiating condition of the presence of wet wood which by its absence can dissociate fire from smoke, but cannot dissociate smoke from fire. If there were any such condition which was present in all cases of fire, but not in all cases of smoke, then the inference of fire from smoke would have been faulty as the

[1] This vitiating condition will therefore falsify an inference such as "There is smoke in the hill because there is fire."

inference of smoke from fire is faulty. Now, so far as we have observed, there is no such condition which is present in all cases of fire, but not in all cases of smoke; the fear that there may be some vitiating conditions which are too subtle for our senses is illegitimate; for, if it is neither perceived nor known by any other sources of knowledge (*pramāṇāntara-vedya*), the doubt that it may still somehow exist cannot arise. So, when we are satisfied that there are no vitiating conditions, there arises the notion of invariable concomitance (*avinābhāva-pramitiḥ*)[1]. So the invariable concomitance is grasped by perception aided by wide experience, associated with absence of any knowledge of exception to coexistence and ascertainment of absence of vitiating conditions, operating as accessories. When once the mutual invariable relation between smoke and fire is grasped, then, wherever smoke is perceived, fire is inferred[2]. This description of the formation of the notion of concomitance seems to be more or less the same as the Nyāya view; there also the perceiving of coexistence, associated with the knowledge of absence of exception, is said to lead to the formation of the notion of concomitance[3].

[1] Vyāsa-tīrtha remarks here that the ascertainment of the absence of vitiating conditions is necessary in most cases where there are doubts as to their possible existence, but should not be insisted upon as indispensable in all cases; for then, this ascertainment of absence of vitiating conditions being dependent on determination of concomitance and that on previous ascertainment of absence of vitiating conditions, there would be infinite regress (*anavasthā*): *yā tu Paddhatav upādhi-niścayasya sahakāritvoktiḥ sā tu upādhi-śaṅkāsthābhiprāyā na tu sārvatrikābhiprāyā anyathā upādhy-abhāva-niścayasya vyāpti-sāpekṣa-tarkādhīnatvenānavasthāpātāt. Tarka-tāṇḍava* (MS., p. 22).

[2] *Pramāṇa-paddhati*, pp. 31–5.

[3] *vyabhicāra-jñāna-viraha-sahakṛtaṃ sahacāra-darśanaṃ vyāpti-grāhakam. Tattva-cintāmaṇi*, p. 210. Legitimate doubts regarding invariable concomitance may be removed by *tarka*, as has already been described above.

Vyāsa-tīrtha, following the *Nyāya-sudhā*, defines vitiating conditions (*upādhi*) as *sādhya-vyāpakatve sati sādhanāvyāpaka upādhir iti*; and he objects to Udayana's definition of it as *sādhya-sama-vyāptatve sati sādhanāvyāpaka upādhiḥ* and also to Gaṅgeśa's definition of it as *paryavasita-sādhya-vyāpakatve sati sādhanāvyāpaka upādhiḥ*. But the purport aimed at by these various definitions is the same, as has been explained above. The distinctions are more verbal and scholastic than logical or philosophical; it will therefore be an unnecessary digression to enter into these. See the whole discussion on *upādhi* in Vyāsa-tīrtha's *Tarka-tāṇḍava* (MS., pp. 44–61).

Epistemological Process in Inference.

The Nyāya holds that, when a person acquainted with the relation of concomitance existing between smoke and fire sees smoke on a hill, he remembers the relation of concomitance (*vyāpti-smaraṇa*), that this smoke is invariably and unconditionally connected with fire[1]; then the two ideas are connected, namely, that the smoke which has unconditional invariable relations with fire is in the hill. It is this third synthesis of knowledge that leads us to the inference of fire in the hill. Vyāsa-tīrtha, following the *Nyāya-sudhā*, argues that this view may be true in all those cases where a concomitance (*vyāpti*) is remembered on seeing the reason (*hetu*), but, where the concomitance is remembered without seeing the reason, the threefold synthesis cannot be admitted. Prabhākara, however, holds that all inference proceeds from two distinct propositions, and no synthesis is required. The two propositions are "smoke is pervaded by fire" and "the hill is smoky." Prabhākara holds that, since knowledge as formulated in the above two propositions must invariably and unconditionally precede all inference, there is no necessity for believing their synthesis to be the cause of inference, since no such synthesis really happens. Vyāsa-tīrtha, however, argues that such a synthesis is a real psychological state in inference and other mental operations, such as recognition, etc. Moreover, if the identity of the smoke (with which fire was found invariably present) with the smoke now perceived in the hill were not established by the synthesis of the two propositions, it would be a syllogism of four terms and hence invalid[2]. Moreover, the movement of thought involved in inference requires such a synthesis, without which the two propositions would be unrelated and statical (*nirvyāpāka*) and no inference would follow.

Various Considerations regarding Inference.

Inference is of three kinds: (i) of cause from effect (*kāryānumāna*), as the inference of fire from smoke, (ii) of effect from cause (*kāraṇānumāna*), as the inference of rain from gathering

[1] *ayaṃ dhūmo vahni-vyāpya* or *vahni-vyāpya-dhūmavān ayam iti*. Nyāya view.

[2] *evaṃ ca kiṃcit prameyaṃ vahni-vyāpyaṃ paravataś ca prameyavān iti jñāna-dvayam iva kaścid dharmo vahni-vyāpyaḥ parvataś ca dhūmavān iti viśakalitaṃ paraspara-vartanābhijñaṃ jñāna-dvayam api nānumiti-hetuḥ.* *Tarka-tāṇḍava* (MS., p. 68).

clouds, (iii) inference of a different order from cause-effect types (*akārya-kāraṇānumāna*), as the inference of colour from taste (*rase rūpasya*). From another point of view inference is of two kinds: (i) *dṛṣṭa*, where the inferred object is perceivable (*pratyakṣa-yogya*), as of fire from smoke, and (ii) *sāmānyato-dṛṣṭa*, where it is not perceivable (*pratyakṣāyogya*), as of the existence of the sense of vision from the perception of colours. This division of inference into *dṛṣṭa* and *adṛṣṭa* may be made from another point of view. Thus, when an inference is made on the basis of the concomitance directly observed between two entities (e.g., fire and smoke), it is called *dṛṣṭa*; but, when an inference is made on the basis of similarity or analogy, it is called *sāmānyato-dṛṣṭa*, as the inference that, just as ploughing, etc., lead to the production of crops, so sacrifices also produce heavenly enjoyments, since they have this similarity that both are results of effort. Inference may again be considered as being of two kinds: (i) inference of one right knowledge from another right knowledge (*sādhanānumāna*), e.g., of fire from smoke, (ii) the inference of false knowledge (*dūṣaṇānumāna*), e.g., "this cannot prove its conclusion, since it is contradicted by experience." Again, some hold that inference is of three kinds: (i) by absolute agreement in presence (where no case of absence is possible), (ii) by absolute absence (where no outside positive instance is possible), and (iii) by combination of agreement in presence and absence; in accordance with this it is *kevalānvayi* (impossible-negation), *kevala-vyatireki* (impossible-position) and *anvaya-vyatireki* (joint positive-negative). Thus the proposition "all objects of knowledge are expressible" is an example of the first type of inference, since no negative instance is possible of which we could say that this is not an object of knowledge and is not also expressible; the proposition "all living bodies are endowed with souls, since they have lives" is an example of inference of the second type. This can only be proved by an appeal to negative instances such as "all those who are not endowed with souls are not living"; for, since the proposition comprehends all positive instances, no positive instances apart from the proposition under consideration are available. The third type is the ordinary one of inference where concomitance is experienced through both positive and negative instances.

Inference is said again to be of two kinds: first *svārtha*, where the knowledge of the reason with its concomitance rises in one's own mind of itself, and secondly *parārtha*, where such a knowledge is for the instruction of others. As regards the constituent propositions (*avayava*) of inference, Vyāsa-tīrtha discusses the ten-proposition view of older Nyāya writers (*jaran-naiyāyika*), also the five-proposition view of the later Nyāya writers[1], the three-proposition view of the Mīmāṃsā, and also the two-proposition view of example and the application of reason (*udāharaṇopanayaṛ*) of the Buddhists. Vyāsa-tīrtha urges that, since the value of these constituent propositions consists in reminding persons of a particular concomitance or in rousing an enquiry in those who did not know it before, there is necessity only for as many propositions as are necessary for the purpose, in accordance with the circumstances under which the inference is being made or the state of mind of the person who makes it—so that there may be cases where only the enunciating proposition, reason and example are necessary, there may be cases where only the enunciating proposition combined with the reason is necessary (*agni-vyāpta-dhūmavān parvato'gnimān iti hetu-garbha-pratijñā*), or, when in certain cases the discussion presupposes the enunciating proposition, only the reason may be necessary, and so on[2]. So there is no fixed rule as to the number of constituent propositions necessary for inference; it all depends upon the nature of the case whether two, three or more propositions are necessary.

Both Jaya-tīrtha and Vyāsa-tīrtha devote a long discussion to the division of fallacies (*upapatti-doṣa*) and criticize the Nyāya division of the same; but, as these have but little philosophical bearing, I feel inclined to omit them[3].

Testimony.

Madhva and his followers admitted only three kinds of means of knowledge, namely, perception, inference, and the testimony of the Vedas. All other kinds of means of knowledge (*pramāṇa*) admitted in other systems, such as *arthāpatti*, *saṃbhava*, etc., are shown to be but modes of inference[4]. The Vedas are regarded as having by

[1] *jijñāsā-saṃśaya-śakya-prāptiḥ prayojana-saṃśayanirāsāḥ pratijña-hetūdāharaṇopanaya-nigamanāni iti daśāvayavā iti jaran-naiyāyikā āhuh. Tarka-tāṇḍava.*

[2] *vivādenaiva pratijñā-siddhau kutaḥ parvato'gnimān iti praśne agni-vyāpta-dhūmavattvād iti hetu-mātreṇa vā. Tarka-tāṇḍava* (MS., p. 10).

[3] See *Pramāṇa-paddhati*, pp. 48–79; also *Tarka-tāṇḍava* (MS., pp. 114 *et seq.*).

[4] *Pramāṇa-paddhati*, pp. 86–90.

themselves independent force of knowledge. They are uncreated (*apauruṣeya*) and eternal (*nitya*). They are valid means of knowledge, and yet, since their validity is not derived from the speech of any person, they must be regarded as uncreated[1]. No attempt, however, was made to prove that the Vedas were valid means of knowledge; but, as their validity was not questioned by any of the Hindu schools, that was taken as accepted, and then it was argued that, since they were not uttered by anyone, they were uncreated and eternal. It was sought to establish this uncreatedness of the Vedas as against the Nyāya view that they were created by God (Īśvara). Vyāsa-tīrtha argues that it is better to accept the direct validity of the Vedas on the ground of their being uncreated, than to do it in an indirect way through the admission of an omniscient being as their author; for there is no certainty that even such authors would not try to deceive mankind by false statements. Buddha himself is an incarnation of God, and yet he deceived the people by false teachings. Tradition also does not ascribe any author to the Vedas. If they had been created, they would be of the same kind as the holy scriptures of the Buddhists or Jains. If the importance of scriptures were to be judged by the number of people who followed them, then the Mahomedan scriptures would have a superior place. God may be regarded as the great teacher of the Vedas, being the first person who uttered and taught them[2]. He did not create them and He remembers them always; so that there is no chance of the Vedic order of words being destroyed. Ordinarily the claim of facts to validity is prior to that of the words which express them, and the latter depends on the former; but in the case of the Vedas the words and passages have a validity which is prior to facts and independent of them. The Madhva view thus combines the Nyāya and the Mīmāṃsā views of the Vedas without agreeing with either.

[1] *pauruṣeya-śabdāpramāṇakatve sati sapramāṇakatvāt.*
Tarka-tāṇḍava (MS., p. 100).

[2] *īśvaro'pi hy asman-mate.... Veda-saṃpradāya-pravartakatvān mahopādhyāya eva. Ibid.* p. 122.

CHAPTER XXIX

CONTROVERSY BETWEEN THE DUALISTS AND THE MONISTS

Vyāsa-tīrtha, Madhusūdana and Rāmācarya on the Falsity of the World.

THE Vedāntists urge that the world-appearance is false. But before entering into any discussion about the nature of falsehood it is required that the Vedāntists should give a definition of falsehood. Five principal definitions have been adduced by the old Vedāntists; of these the first is that falsehood is that which is the absence of being as well as the absence of non-being (*sattvātyantābhāvattve sati asattvātyantatā-bhāvavattva-rūpaṃ viśiṣṭam*[1]). But Vyāsa-tīrtha urges that, since one of these is the negation of the other, joint assertion of them both will be against the Law of excluded middle and therefore will be self-contradictory; the fact that both being and non-being may be admitted independently is no reason for their joint admission (e.g., the hare and horn both exist separately, but the hare's horn exists nowhere). To this the reply of Madhusūdana is that the Law of excluded middle does not apply to every case of the relation between being and non-being. Thus the false-appearances have being so far as they appear and non-being so far as they are non-existent; exclusion of being does not necessarily lead us to non-being, and *vice versa*. To this the retort given by the author of *Taraṅgiṇī* is that the Śaṅkarites themselves say that, if a thing has no being, it cannot appear, which shows that they themselves admit the Law of excluded middle, the force of which can never be denied, as Logic amply demonstrates in the examination of any and every specific relation of being and non-being.

The second definition of falsehood by the Śaṅkarites is that falsehood is that which can be denied at all times even where it appears to exist (*prati-pannopādhu traikālika-niṣedha-pratiyogitvaṃ*). To this Vyāsa-tīrtha says that, if the denial is true, then this true thing would exist side by side with Brahman and thus the

[1] *Nyāyāmṛta*, p. 22.

theory of extreme monism would break down (*niṣedhasya tattrikatve advaita-hāniḥ*); if the denial is false or true only in a limited manner (*vyāvahārika*), then the world-appearance would become true. Again, what does the denial actually mean? These supposed appearances are said to be produced from a material cause, and they are perceived as existing at the time of perception; and, if it is held that even then they have no existence at all as such, then they must be absolutely without being, like the chimerical hare's horn. If it is held that the difference of the world-appearance from chimerical entities like the hare's horn, etc., is that they are absolutely indescribable, then the reply is that the very term "indescribable" describes their nature. Again, that which is absolutely non-existing cannot in any way appear in knowledge (*asataḥ a-pratītav*), and therefore it is not possible to make reference to it or to relate it in any way to anything else. The Śaṅkarites themselves hold that what is non-existing cannot appear in knowledge (*asac cet na pratīyeta*), and thus they themselves deny the possibility of any being-in-knowledge of that which is non-existing. Again, reality is not the same as mere appearance in knowledge, and consequently, if Brahman remained always uncontradicted in knowledge, its reality could not on that ground be affirmed. Again, it is not true that words denoting absolutely non-existing and chimerical things, such as the hare's horn, produce no knowledge; for they also produce some notion; the difference between ordinary illusions and the chimerical entities is this that, while the ground of the ordinary illusions is right and valid, chimerical entities have no ground at all. Therefore, since chimerical entities can also be made objects of awareness they appear in knowledge as non-existing. The Vedic text "non-being alone existed in the beginning" (*asad eva idam agre āsīt*) also testifies to the fact that "non-being" may appear as existent. Also non-being cannot be defined as that which is different from mere "being" (*sat*) and "the indescribable" (*a-nirvācya*); for the latter can only be understood through the concept of non-being and *vice versa*. Thus non-being may be defined as that which is different from that being which cannot at all times be denied at all places (*sārvatrika-traikālika-niṣedha-pratiyogitva-rūpa-sadanyasyaiva tattvāc ca*). If the indescribable (*a-nirvācya*) is defined as that which can be denied at all times, it is the same as non-being itself. Also non-being cannot be defined as that which is incapable of fulfilling any practical purpose; for even the conch-shell-silver, which is admitted to be false, can serve to rouse an effort to grasp it in the deluded person and thus be considered to have some kind of practical efficiency, and the pure Brahman, which is regarded as ultimately real, is itself unable to serve any practical purpose of any kind. Again, falsehood or non-being cannot be defined as that which has no nature of its own; for, if that were so, then the denial of falsehood could not be said to be directed to its own nature as such; nor could the nature of false-hood be regarded as itself false, since such an interpretation would rest on a mere technical assumption of the meaning of falsehood, and it would not in the least clear the points at issue; for, if the nature of the so-called entity persisted in its own time and place, it would be meaningless to call such a nature false in itself. Such an assumption would also mean that no distinction is made between that which can serve practical efficiency and that which cannot; if that which persists in time and place and can serve a practical purpose could be called false, then there would be no difference between being and non-being, and the absence of the real could be said to be as much a cause of cloth as the thread itself. Thus absolute non-being may be defined as that which can always be denied in all places (*sarvatra traikālika-niṣedha-pratiyogitvaṃ*). Also it cannot be held that "non-being" (*asat*) cannot be the object of an absolute denial simply because it is non-being, as is said in the *Nyāya-makaranda* of Ānandabodha; for, if an absolute denial cannot have any object, then the reason "because it is non-being" as adduced above would have no object itself and would therefore be inapplicable. Moreover, just as positive entities can be denied, so the specific negations referring to positive entities may also be denied and so lead on to their corresponding positive affirmations. Again, it is also agreed that specific positive entities come into being through the negation of their corresponding negations immediately prior to their coming into being (*prāg-abhāva*). This also proves that denial or negation does not necessarily require positive characters or entities for the operation and their function of negation. The whole upshot of this discussion is that, if falsehood means absolute denial of anything where it appears in knowledge, then the implication is that no reality can be affirmed; for what could be affirmed either as false or as true would only apply to entities as they are known, and in that case even the reality of Brahman would be conditional, namely, so far as it is known. Again, absolute negation (*sarvatra traikālika-niṣedha-pratiyogitvaṃ*) cannot be distinguished from what is known as chimerical entities. And, if the world-appearance could be an object of absolute negation, its status would be no better than that of chimerical entities (e.g., the hare's horn).

In reply to the objections of Vyāsa-tīrtha against the definition of falsehood, that, if falsehood be real, then that implies dualism, and that, if falsehood is false, that implies re-affirmation of the world as real, Madhusūdana says that, since the denial is itself identical (so far as its ultimate ground is concerned) with Brahman, the reality of falsehood does not imply dualism; for the reality of the denial does not imply the reality of the phenomenon, denial of which has been denied by the denial of all phenomena. It has only so much reality as is implied in the ground of all phenomena, which is the Brahman. Again, the falsehood of the falsehood does not imply the affirmation of the reality of the world-appearance; for in the case of the conch-shell-silver, though it is known that not only was it false, but, since it is never existent, it never exists, and never will exist, and the attribution of falsity to it is also false, the conch-shell-silver is not for the matter of that re-affirmed as real. It is wrong to suppose that the falsity of the falsity or the denial of the denial is re-affirmation in all cases; it is only when the reality and the denial have the same status and identically the same scope that the denial of the denial means an affirmation; but, when the scope of their meaning varies, the denial of the denial does not imply an affirmation. It may further be pointed out that, when the denial of the denial is intended to re-affirm the positive entity, the denial of the denial leads to affirmation. But, when a denial denies both the positive entity and the denial (which is itself taken as an independent entity), the second denial does not lead to affirmation[1]. The denial of the world-appearance is the denial of the relaity of the very world-appearance as such (*svarūpeṇa*), like the denial of the conch-shell-silver. The fact that the world-appearance is

[1] *Tatra hi niṣedhasya niṣedhe pratijogi-sattvam āyāti, yatra niṣedhasya nisedha-buddhyā pratiyogisattvaṃ vyavasthāpyate, na niṣedha-mātraṃ niṣedhyate, yathā rajate na idaṃ rajatam iti jñānāantaram idam na arajatam iti jñānena rajataṃ vyavasthāpyate. yatra tu prati-yogi-ṅisedhayor ubhayor api niṣedhas tatra na prati-yogi-sattvam.* *Advaita-siddhi*, pp. 105–6.

believed to be a product of *ajñāna* does not in the least imply that its very nature cannot be false; for what is by its very nature false would be so, whether produced or not. The denial of the conch-shell-silver ("this is not silver") means that the conch-shell-silver is other than the real market-silver, i.e., the negation here is that of otherness (*anyo-anya-abhāva*). But, when it is said that "here is no silver," the negation is one of non-existence, and the falsity of the appearance is thereby definitely declared (*sā ca purovartti-rajatasyaiva vyāvahārikam atyanta-abhāvam viṣayīkaroti iti kaṇṭho-ktam eva mithyātvam*), whereas in the former case falsehood is only implied (*idaṃ śābda-nirdiṣṭe purovarti-prātītika-rajate rajata-śabda-nirdiṣṭa-vyāvahārika-rajata-anyonya-abhāva-pratiter ārthi-kaṃ mithyātvam*)[1]. Now, if the world-appearance be denied ("there is no world-appearance here"), then, since there is no world-appearance anywhere else, the denial implies the absolute non-existence of the world-appearance, i.e., world-appearance is as non-existent as any chimerical entity, e.g., the hare's horn. The reply to such an objection, that there is a difference between the absolute negation of the world-experience as indescribable (*anirvācya*) and the absolute negation as chimerical (*tucca*), is that the latter has not even a seeming appearance anywhere, whereas the former appears as really existent until it is contradicted (*kvachid apy upādhau sattvena pratīty-anarhatvam atyanta-asattvaṃ yāvad bādham pratītiyogyatvaṃ prātītika-sattvam*). It must further be noted in this connection that the denial which leads to falsehood must have the same relation and the same extent and scope as the content which is being denied (*yena rūpeṇa yad-adhikaraṇatayā yat pratipannaṃ tena rūpeṇa tan-niṣṭha-atyanta-abhāva-pratiyogitvasya pratipanna-padena sūcitatvāt*; *tac ca rūpaṃ aṃbandha-viśeṣo'vacchedakaviśeṣaś ca*)[2]. The Śaṅkarites, more-over, do not admit negation as a separate category, but consider the negation to be identical with the unqualified nature of the locus where the negation appears. Brahman has no qualities, and this does not therefore mean that it has a negative quality; for, there being more separate negations, the negation of all qualities simply means the pure nature of Brahman. The attribution of so-called positive qualities also as infinitude, etc., means the negation of the opposite qualities of falsehood and limitation, which ultimately

[1] *Advaita-siddhi*, pp. 130–1. [2] *Ibid.* p. 151.

implies a reversion to the pure nature of Brahman, etc. (*adhikaraṇa-atirikta-abhāva-abhyupagamena ukta-mithyātva-abhāva-rūpa-satyatvasya Brahma-svarūpa-virodhāt*)[1].

Ramācārya, in his *Taraṅgiṇī*, refuting the view of Madhusūdana, says that, excepting the case of the negation of the negation-prior-to-becoming (*prāg-abhāva*), the negation of negation means positing and therefore, since no third alternative is possible, the denial of the denial of an entity necessarily posits. Again, the assertion of Madhusūdana, that the illusion consists in the appearance of the illusory silver as the real silver of the market, is groundless; for the material cause that produced the illusory silver is different from the material cause of the silver of the market. The illusory silver ceases to exist only when there is true knowledge removing the ignorance which was the material cause of the illusory silver (*prātibhāsikasya svopādāna-jñāna-nivartaka jñāna-viṣayeṇaiva vā tādātmya-pratīteśca*): where the same material cause produces two different appearances (e.g., the cloth and the whiteness) they may be experienced as identical. But, when the material causes are entirely different, their products can never be experienced as identical[2]. Again, it has been urged by Madhusūdana that the denial that constitutes falsehood must be qualified by the same conditions and relations whereby the positive entities were qualified; but this is unmeaning, for no amount of such conditioning can gainsay the truth that the negation of negations means position, until some definite proof of the existence of a third alternative escaping the sphere of the Law of Excluded Middle can be adduced[3].

Vyāsa-tīrtha says that falsehood moreover cannot be defined as absolute denial of reality; for, unless the meaning of denial is understood, the meaning of reality cannot be comprehended and *vice versa*. The point at issue here is whether conch-silver is denied in its very nature as such or whether its reality is denied. The former alternative is denied on the ground that, if it were accepted, then it would be difficult to account for the awareness of the conch-silver as existing in front of the perceiver; for, if it was absolutely non-existent, it could not be directly perceived. But it may be pointed out with the same force that the second alternative is also unacceptable, because, when the conch-silver was perceived, it was

[1] *Ibid.* p. 156.

[2] *Nyāyāmṛta-taraṅgiṇī*, p. 16(*a*).

[3] *Taraṅgiṇī*, p. 20.

also perceived to be real, and, if that is so, how can that reality be denied? If in reply to this it is suggested that the reality of the conch-shell-silver is only a relative reality and not an absolute reality, then it may be pointed out that, if once a degree of reality be admitted, then infinite regress will follow; for one may as well ask whether the absolute reality is absolutely absolute or relatively absolute and so on. Again, falsehood is defined as that which is liable to be destroyed by knowledge in its function as knowledge. But Vyāsa-tīrtha does not tolerate such a position and says that knowledge of past events and things, even though false, ceases by itself without waiting to be destroyed by the so-called right knowledge; also it is not felt that the silver is destroyed by the knowledge of the conch-shell. It is further urged that right knowledge of the conch-shell also removes the error which, so far as it was an error, was true, and this shows that knowledge removes not only falsehood, but also true things, and on that account the definition in question cannot be a true definition of falsehood. Moreover, when an illusion is removed, the removal is not due to the function of cognition as such, but is by virtue of its perceptual immediacy (*aparokṣa-adhyāsam prati jñānasya-aparokṣatayā nivartakatvena jñānatvena anivartakatvāc ca*)[1]. Again, if a falsehood is defined as that which is destroyed by knowledge which destroys the very material cause of the falsehood (*svopādāna ajñāna-nivartaka jñāna-nivartyatvaṃ*), the objection will be that it does not apply to the beginningless illusion[2]. It may similarly be held that the definition of falsehood as appearance in the place where it does not exist (*svātyanta-abhāva-adhikaraṇe eva pratīyamānatvaṃ*) may also be refuted; for many objections occur, as has already been pointed out, according as we consider the negation to be relatively real or illusory. Again, if falsehood be defined as that which is different both from being and non-being, then, since it has already been pointed out that non-being means absolute denial, the appearances or illusions would be inexplicable. If it be defined as that which is destroyed by knowledge, then that can prove its momentary character, but not its false nature (*dhī-nāśyatve anityatā eva syāt na mṛṣātmatā*)[3].

In reply to the objection of Vyāsa-tīrtha concerning the definition of falsehood as that which is liable to be destroyed by know-

[1] *Nyāyāmṛta*, p. 39(*b*). [2] *Ibid.* p. 40.
[3] *Ibid.* p. 41.

ledge, Madhusūdana says that the real meaning of the definition is that the entity which is destroyed, both in its causal aspect and the aspect as effect, on account of the rise of knowledge is false. The jug though destroyed as effect by the stroke of the club is not destroyed in its causal aspect as the earthy pot. The hare's horn does not exist at all: so its non-existence is not due to knowledge. Again, since the conch-shell-silver appears in consciousness and is destroyed immediately after the rise of true knowledge, its dissolution must be due to knowledge. Also it is not wrong to say that falsehood is negated by knowledge in its function as knowledge; for the later knowledge does not negate the prior knowledge by its function as knowledge, but merely on account of its posteriority; and therefore the definition of falsehood as that which can be negated by knowledge only in its function as knowledge clearly keeps aloof the case of the negation of the prior knowledge by the later, to which it was supposed that the above definition of falsehood could wrongly be extended. It is well, however, to point out that falsehood is negated by knowledge not in an indirect manner, but directly and immediately (*vastutas tu sākṣātkāratvena jñāna-nivartyatvaṃ vivakṣitam*)[1].

To this Rāmācārya replies that it is Madhusūdana who says that the definition of falsehood as that which can be negated by knowledge means the general absence of an entity through the rise of knowledge (*jñāna-prayukta-avasthiti-sāmānya-viraha-pratiyogi-tvaṃ jñāna-nivartyatvaṃ* (see *Advaita-siddhi*, p. 168, and *Taraṅgiṇī*, p. 22)[2]. It may be asked whether the word "generally" (*sāmānya*) or the negation is qualified by the existence (*avasthityā sāmānyaṃ vā viśiṣyate viraho vā*). The first alternative would mean the negation of the cause of an entity through the rise of knowledge; for the word *avasthiti-sāmānya* means cause. But in that case there would be an illicit extension of the definition of falsehood to the negation of the prior knowledge by the posterior knowledge; for the posterior knowledge destroys the cause of the persistence of the prior knowledge, and it would not apply to the beginningless *avidyā*. In the second alternative, i.e., if the word *sāmānya* is

[1] *jñānatva-vyāpya-dharmeṇa jñānanivartyatvam ityapi sādhu, uttarajñānasya pūrva-jñāna-nivartakatvaṃ na jñānatvavyāpyadharmeṇa kintu icchādi-sādhāraṇenodīcyātmaviśeṣaguṇatvena udīcyatvena veti na siddha-sādhanādi.*

Advaita-siddhi, pp. 171–2.

[2] *Ibid.* p. 178.

qualified by the negation, then it may be pointed out that the Śaṅkarite never admits a general negation as distinguished from the negation of any special entity. Moreover, since the conch-shell-silver is denied in its very nature as false, it cannot be said that its general absence (that is, both as cause and effect) was due to the rise of knowledge; for it is not admitted to be existent at any time[1]. Again, as it has been shown by Vyāsa-tīrtha that there ought not to be any difference between the non-existence of the conch-shell-silver and that of the hare's horn, the non-existence of the hare's horn might equally be said to be due to knowledge, if the non-existence of the conch-shell-silver be said to be due to the rise of knowledge.

In supporting the fourth definition of falsehood as "appearance in the locus of its own absence" (*svātyanta-abhāva-adhikaraṇe eva pratīyamānatvaṃ*) or as the "absence in the locus of its own existence" (*svāśraya nisṭha-atyanta-abhāva-pratiyogitvam*), Madhusūdana says that, since an entity may be both present and absent in one identical time, so it may be both present and absent in one identical space. To this Rāmācārya replies that, if this is admitted, then there is no difference between existence and non-existence, and ordinary experience is inexplicable (*tathā sati bhāvābhāvayor ucchinnakathā syāt iti vyāvahārikyapi vyavasthā na syāt*); consequently dualism and its negation, monism, would be the same, and the monistic knowledge would be unable to dispel the dualistic consciousness.

In support of the fifth definition of falsehood as difference from the real (*sad-viviktatvaṃ mithyātvaṃ*) Madhusūdana defines existence of reality as that which is established by knowledge and not invalidated by defects. The definition of existence is further modified by him as that which appears as existent through proofs not invalidated by defects. By this qualification he excludes chimerical entities and Brahman; for chimerical entities do not appear as existent, and Brahman, though it exists in itself, is never an object to any mind to which it appears as existent (*satvā-prakāraka-pratīti-viṣayatābhāvāt*).

The existent is defined as that which is established by proof (*pramāṇa-siddha*), and this is again as that which is uncontradicted.

[1] *śukti-rajatāder-avasthity-aṅgīkāre svarūpeṇa niṣedhokty-ayogaś-ca.* *Taraṅgiṇī*, p. 22.

To this it is objected by Rāmācārya that Brahman is not the object of any proofs, whereas the world, which is established by all proofs, is ultimately contradicted[1].

The question is raised by Vyāsa-tīrtha whether falsehood itself is contradicted or uncontradicted. If it is uncontradicted, then falsehood becomes real, and the doctrine of monism fails. If it is urged in reply that falsehood is identical with the ground of illusion, the Brahman, then the meaning of the phrase "world-appearance is false" (*prapañco mithyā*) is that the world-appearance is identical with Brahman (*mithyā* being identical with Brahman), and this is not disputed by us; for Brahman, being all-pervasive, is in a sense identical with the world-appearance. Moreover, if falsehood be identical with Brahman, the general argument that those things alone are false which are cognizable would be faulty, because falsity, being identical with Brahman, would itself be uncognizable. If falsehood be contradicted, then it is self-false (*bādhya*), and the world would become real. Even if it is again urged that falsehood is not identical with Brahman, but is one with the reality of Brahman as underlying the second denial or the falsehood of the falsehood, to this the reply would be that our very inquiry centres round the question whether the second denial is itself contradicted or uncontradicted, and it is well known that, since the underlying reality is everywhere pure consciousness, the underlying reality of the second falsehood has no separate or independent existence regarding which any affirmation could be made. It is clear that, if in the first case the assertion of falsehood being identical with Brahman be meaningless, the attempt at an extension by making it identical with the pure consciousness underlying the second denial does not in reality lead to any new meaning. If it is again urged that, since the conch-shell-silver is false, the falsehood which is a quality of this conch-shell-silver is necessarily false; if the substance is false, its quality is necessarily false, and therefore the falsehood of this falsehood does not reaffirm the reality of the conch-shell-silver. Since both the falsehoods are based on the falsehood of the substance to which they are attributively associated the negation of negation does not mean a position. The negation of a negation can mean a position only if the substance be real. But this is clearly a confusion; for the absence of qualities follows on the

[1] *Taraṅgiṇī*, p. 23.

absence of the substance only when such qualities are dependent on the nature of the substance; but falsehood is not so, since it is naturally opposed to that to which it refers[1]. Moreover, if the falsehood of the conch-shell-silver becomes false merely because it is associated with the illusory silver, though it is affirmed by an experience of contradiction, then it might equally well be real because of its ultimate association with Brahman, the ground reality of all things; or on the other hand the conch-shell might equally well be false because of its association with the illusory silver, and the non-existent would also be existent because of its association with existence, and *vice versa*[2]. Moreover, the conch-shell-silver is not regarded by the Śaṅkarites as absolutely non-existent, like the chimerical hare's horn, and therefore falsehood cannot be considered to be so on account of its association therewith. Again, the argument that falsehood has not the same status of existence as the world-appearance to which it refers and therefore the assertion of falsehood does not hurt extreme monism, is wrong: for, if falsehood has only a relative existence (*vyāvahā-riktve*), the world of our daily experience, which is opposed to it and which is attested by perception, ought to be regarded as ultimately real. Thus our former objection remains valid, that, if falsehood be uncontradicted, the doctrine of monism fails and, if contradicted, the world would be real[3].

Madhusūdana has the former reply to the above objection that, when the position and negation have a different order of being, the negation of the negation does not imply affirmation. If the negation refers to a relative existence, then such negation does not take away the assertion of a fanciful existence[4]. Thus an entity may be in different senses both true and false. Madhusūdana further says that, when the denial is due to a specific quality, then the negation of negation cannot be an affirmation. Here both the conch-shell and its quality are denied on account of their common

[1] *dharmy-asattve dharmāsattvaṃ tu dharmi-sattvāsāpekṣa-dharma-viṣayam; mithyātvaṃ tu tat-pratikūlam.* *Nyāyāmṛta*, p. 44.

[2] *Ibid.* p. 45.

[3] *mithyātvaṃ yady abādhyaṃ syāt syad advaita-mata-kṣatiḥ*
mithyātvaṃ yadi bādhyaṃ syāt jagat-satyatvam āpatet.
Ibid. p. 47.

[4] *paraspara-viraha-rūpatve'pi viṣama-satvākayor avirodhāt vyāvahārika-mithyātvena vyāvahārika-satyatvāpahāre'pi kālpanika-satyatvānapahārāt.*
Advaita-siddhi, p. 217.

attribute of plausibility. Thus it may be said with impunity that both the horse and the cow may be denied in an elephant[1].

To this Rāmācārya's reply is that existence and non-existence naturally exclude each other, and their denial is therefore not due to any other specific property. That existence and non-existence are mutually exclusive is acknowledged even by the Śaṅkarites when they speak of *māyā* as being different both from existence and non-existence[2].

An important argument establishing the falsity of the world rests upon the fact that the world is cognizable; all that is cognizable is false, like dream experiences. At this point Vyāsa-tīrtha seeks to analyse what may be meant by the word cognizable. Several alternative meanings are offered, of which the first is termed *vṛtti-vyāpyatva*, i.e., that which is a content of a mental state. The Śaṅkarites are thus supposed to say that all that can be a content of a mental state is false. To this Vyāsa-tīrtha's reply is that Brahman and the self must also be the content of at least some kind of mental state, and therefore, if the thesis of the Śaṅkarites be accepted, Brahman also would be false. If it is said that Brahman in its purity can never be the object of any mental state, and it can be so only when it is associated with *ajñāna*, to this the reply is that, if Brahman in its purity cannot manifest itself in awareness, it can never establish itself, and such a theory directly militates against the self-revealing nature of Brahman. Again, it is urged that, though Brahman is self-revealing, yet it cannot be the content of any mental state; for the very expression "Brahman is pure and self-revealing" would make it the content of that verbal cognition; if the expression carries no sense, then there is no meaning in it. Moreover, if Brahman as associated with *ajñāna* be admitted to be the content of a mental state, it would through such an association be a constituent of that mental content and therefore a content in itself. It cannot, moreover, be said that the objection cannot apply to Brahman because Brahman can be a content only in association and not in its nature; for, since the same conditions apply to eternal and transcendental entities of an indeterminate character which

[1] *Advaita-siddhi*, p. 213.

[2] *na tāvat paraspara-viraharūpayor ekaniṣedhyatā-avacchedakāvachinnatvaṃ sambhavati tvayāpi satyatvamithyātvayoḥ paraspara-samuccaye virodhāt bibhyatā sad-asad-vailakṣaṇyasārūpye'ṅgīkārācca. Taraṅgiṇī*, p. 26.

cannot be contents of consciousness in themselves, but only in later associated forms, Brahman would not be false on that account. Again, it is wrong to suppose that, when an object is known, the content of that mental state has the same form as the object of awareness; for we may know a hare's horn through a verbal cognition without assuming that the mental state has the same form as a hare's horn. The assumption therefore that the content of awareness must have the same form as its object is wholly invalid. It is clearly found to be so in the case of Brahma-knowledge; for no awareness can have an infinitude as its content. So to say that an awareness has content as an object simply means that it refers thereto (*tad-viṣayatvam eva tad-ākāratvam*)[1]. Since this is so, the condition of perception that pure consciousness must be reflected in the mental state in superimposition upon the physical object is wholly unnecessary. Thus the objection, that all that is cognizable is on that account false, is invalid.

To this Madhusūdana's reply is that the pure consciousness, which is always self-revealing, is never the content of any awareness. It only appears to be so in association with the *ajñāna* modifications which alone can become the content of knowledge. Thus in all circumstances the pure consciousness is self-revealing and it can never be the content of itself. Madhusūdana would admit all the suggested interpretations of cognizability offered by Vyāsa-tīrtha, excepting the second (*phala-vyāpyatva*)[2]; he, however, admits that a stricter criticism would require the definition to be slightly modified by excluding cognizability through verbal cognition (*vastutas tu śābdājanya-vṛtti-viṣayatvam eva dṛśyatvam*); in this way, though one may be aware of chimerical entities through verbal propositions, they would not on that account be called false; for they are absolutely non-existent entities, which cannot be called either false or true[3]. Madhusūdana further interprets cognizability as that which has a definite formal content (*sva-prakāraka-vṛtti-viṣayatvam eva dṛśyatvaṃ*). By the term "formal" (*sva-prakāraka*)

[1] *Nyāyāmṛta*, p. 57.

[2] The suggested interpretations of cognizability (*dṛśyatva*) as given by Vyāsa-tīrtha are of seven kinds: *kim idaṃ dṛśyatvam; vṛtti-vyāpyatvaṃ vā; phala-vyāpyatvaṃ vā; sādhāraṇaṃ vā; kadācid-kathaṃcid-viṣayatvaṃ vā; sva-vyavahāre svātirikta-saṃvid-antarāpekṣā-niyatir vā; a-sva-prakāśatvaṃ vā. Ibid.* p. 49.

[3] *Advaita-siddhi*, p. 268.

he means any describable characteristic (*sopākhyaḥ kaścid dharmaḥ*) and thereby excludes Brahman, which means purity having no describable characteristic: on the other hand, even the cognition of negations may be described as having the character of negativity. The effect of this interpretation is that cognizability is limited to all that comes within the purview of relative and pragmatic experience. In attempting to clear the meaning of cognizability Madhusūdana defines it as that which is somehow in relation with pure consciousness (*cid-viṣayatva*). This, being identical with self, is devoid of any such two-term relation. In the attempt to classify the meaning further, cognizability of things is defined as dependence for revelation on an alien consciousness (*sva-vyavahāre svātirikta-samvid-apekṣā-niyati-rūpaṃ dṛśyatvaṃ*) or as the character of being other than the self-revealing (*a-sva-prakāśatva-rūpatvaṃ dṛśyatvam*). It is clear therefore that anything other than pure consciousness depends on pure consciousness for revelation.

Rāmācārya, in attempting to refute Madhusūdana, says that merely from the knowledge of the concomitance of impurity (*aśuddhatva*) and dependent revelation (*a-sva-prakāśatva*) one cannot say that pure consciousness is self-revealed; but such a conclusion can be arrived at only when it is known that pure consciousness has no impurity in it. Again, the concomitance of dependent revelation and impurity can be known only when their opposites, "purity" and "self-revealingness," are known to coexist with pure consciousness; thus the knowledge of concomitance of pure consciousness with self-revealingness and that of impure consciousness with dependent revelation are mutually independent. There is therefore no way in which it can be asserted that only pure consciousness is self-revealing[1]. The other reason adduced for falsehood is that the world-appearance is false because it is material. Now what is this materiality? Its character is given as "non-knower" (*ajñātṛtva*), "ignorance" (*ajñānatva*), as "non-self-revealing" (*a-sva-prakāśatva*), or "non-self." If the first meaning of materiality be accepted, then it may be pointed out that according

[1] *na tāvad a-sva-prakāśatvāśuddhatvayor vyāpya-vyāpaka-bhāva-grahamātreṇa śuddhe sva-prakāśatā paryavasyati kintu śuddhe asva-prakāśatva-vyāpakasya aśuddhatvasya vyāvṛttāu jñātāyām eva. tathā ca vyāpaka-vyatireka-grahārtham avaśyaṃ śuddha-jñānam. kiṃcāsva-prakāśatvāśuddhatvayor vyāpya-vyāpaka-bhāva-graho'pi tadubhayavyatirekayoḥ śuddhatva-svaprakāśatvayoḥ śuddhe sahacāra-grahe saty eveti ghaṭṭa-kuṭī-prabhāta-vṛttāntaḥ. Taraṅgiṇī*, p. 31.

to the Śaṅkarites the ego is false, and yet it is the knower; the pure consciousness, which according to the Śaṅkarites is the only reality, is not itself the knower. If it is suggested that pure consciousness may be regarded as the knower through false assumption, then it may well be said that false assumption would validate any false reasoning, and that would be of no avail. Even the body appears as the knower when one says, "I, the white man, know," yet on that account the body cannot be regarded as the knower. The second interpretation, which defines materiality as ignorance (*ajñāna*), cannot be held; for phenomenal knowledge is partly true and partly false. Again, it may in this connection be asked whether the knowledge of the self (*ātman*) has any content or not. If it has, then that content must necessarily be the object of a cognizing activity, and it is impossible that the cognizing activity of the self should direct its activity towards the self. If it is urged in reply that the self has no activity to be directed to itself, but the fact that it is distinguished as self is its cognition of itself, the obvious reply to this is that the cognition of all things is nothing more than the fact that they are distinguished in their specific characters. If again the knowledge of the self has no content, then it is no knowledge at all. If any knowledge be admitted which does not illuminate any object, then even a jug can be called knowledge. Therefore, if materiality be defined as *ajñāna* or ignorance, then even the self would for the above reasons be *ajñāna*. In this connection it may well be remembered that knowledge requires both the object and the knower: there cannot be any experience without the experiencer and the thing experienced. Again, if the self be regarded as mere knowledge, it may well be asked whether that knowledge is right knowledge or illusion. If the former, then, since the modifications of the *avidyā* are known by the self, these would be true. It cannot be the latter, because there is no defect associated with the self. Neither can the self be regarded as bliss: for the phenomenal enjoyment of worldly objects is not admitted as bliss, and there is no way in which the degrees of pleasure or bliss which may lead ultimately to the highest bliss can be admitted; for, once a degree of pleasure is admitted, an extraneous element naturally creeps in. Thus falsity of the world on the ground that it is material is unacceptable in any sense of the term[1].

[1] This argument that the world is false on account of its materiality is adduced *in* the *Tattva-śuddhi*.

To this Madhusūdana's reply is that the second and third interpretations of materiality, i.e., that which is ignorance is material or that which is non-self is material, would be quite suitable. In finding fault with Vyāsa-tīrtha's exposition of knowledge Madhusūdana says that, if knowledge be defined as that which illuminates an object, then even during emancipation objects would be illuminated, which is impossible; the relation of knowledge to objects is extraneous and therefore illusory. If it is objected that, if no objects are revealed during release, then even bliss is not revealed, and in that case no one would care to attain release, the reply is that the emancipated state is itself bliss and there is no separate manifestation of bliss as obtainable therein. The association of an object is perceivable only in sense-knowledge; in the knowledge of the self there is no association with the senses, and it is unreasonable to demand that even then objects should be manifested in knowledge. When it is said that self is of the nature of immediate knowledge, the suggestion that then it must be either valid or erroneous is unacceptable. For the exclusive classification of knowledge as valid or invalid applies to ordinary experienced knowledge. But the self as knowledge is like the indeterminate knowledge that is neither valid nor invalid.

Rāmācārya, however, says that, if the association of knowledge with objects be extraneous, then at the time of the dawn of ultimate knowledge the self should not be regarded as its object. If it is said that this is only so in the case of perceptual knowledge, where pure consciousness is reflected through the *vṛtti* of the form of the object, then the connection of the knowledge with the object would be false; for in that case the necessity of *vṛtti* and the reflection of consciousness through it would have to be admitted at the dawn of the knowledge of the self in the ultimate stage. The relation of the object to knowledge therefore cannot be extraneous and therefore false. In reply to Madhusūdana's statement that, just as according to the Naiyāyikas, though universals and individuals are mutually correlated, yet in the state of ultimate dissolution the universals remain even though there are no individuals, so there may be a state where there is knowledge, but no object; for the sphere of knowledge is wider than that of knowledge with objects. Rāmācārya says that even in the state of *pralaya*, where there is no individual, the knowledge of the universals has the individuals within it as its constituents. Again, the association of objects with knowledge does not mean that the objects produce knowledge, but that knowledge is associated with the objects. Again, if the association with the object be regarded as meaning "necessarily produced by objects," or if it necessarily means "in whichever place or at whichever time this object exists there is knowledge," then the Śaṅkarites would not be able to affirm the unity of the soul. For, since the unity exists in Brahman, it could not be generated by the individual soul. And again, if it is affirmed that, whenever there is unity with Brahman, there is unity with the soul, then, since the Brahman is always one, all individual souls will be emancipated; it will also be impossible to determine the unity of individual souls and the unity of Brahman. So the objects do not generate the determinate knowledge, but are associated with it.

It is argued that whatever is limited and finite is false; now this limitation may be by time or space or by other entities (*paricchinnatvam api deśataḥ kālato vastuto vā*). Now as to this Vyāsa-tīrtha says that time and space cannot be limited by time and space and this is so much the case that even the supreme reality, the Brahman, is often spoken of as existing always and everywhere; time and space are thus universal characteristics and cannot be denied of others or of themselves. Thus the observation of Vācaspati, that whatever does not exist in some places and in some time is on that account absent everywhere and always, and that what is existent must always and everywhere be so (*yat sat tat sadā sarvatra sad eva...tathā ca yat kadācit kutracid asat tat sadā sarvatra asadeva*), is wholly invalid; for, if by non-existence at some particular time existence at any other time can be invalidated, then by existence at that time non-existence at other times may also be invalidated. It is as good logic to say that, because it will not exist then, therefore it does not exist now, as to say that, because it exists now, it must exist then[1]. Again, what is meant by spatial limitation? If it means non-association with all bodies (*sarva-mūrttāsamyogitvam*) or the non-possession of the supreme measure (*parama-mahat-parimāṇānadhikaraṇatvam*), then even Brahman is so; for He is untouchable (*asaṅga*) and He has no measure as His quality; if it means possession of limited measure (*parimāṇa*), then *parimāṇa* or "measure," being a quality, cannot belong to a quality; so qualities would not be limited (*guṇa-karmādau guṇānaṅgīkārāt*). Again,

[1] *Nyāyāmṛta*, p. 79.

temporal limitation cannot be associated with negation as "otherness"; for, if the limitation as otherness be denied at any time, then all things in the world would be one. Now limitation by other entities (which is the third definition of limitation) means "difference" (*bhinnatva*); but such a limitation (according to the Śaṅkarites) is absent in the world of everyday experience; for they deny the reality of difference. Again, difference from falsehood exists also in the self: therefore the argument of Ānandabodha, that whatever things exist divided (*vibhaktatvāt*) are on that account false, is invalid. It is, again, wrong to suppose that the unlimited nature of being consists in the fact that it alone remains universal, whereas everything else changes and must therefore be considered to be imposed upon it, since, when we say "a jug exists," "a jug moves," the jug seems to remain unchanged, while its verb changes, as "exists" and "moves." As "many" is associated with "one," so "one" also is associated with "many"; so nothing can be made of the argument that what remains constant is unlimited and valid and what is changeful is false.

To this Madhusūdana's reply is that, since the Śaṅkarites do not admit universals, it is wrong to suppose that in all cases of the existence of a cow there is something like the cow-universal which persists, and, if that is not so, then the only other explanation is that it is the individuals that come and go and are imposed upon the persistent experience of being, which alone is therefore real. Now, again, it may be argued, the Brahman, as being, is always covered by *ajñāna*; it has no distinguishable form, and so it is wrong to think that Brahman is manifested as being in our experience of the world-objects. To this the reply is that Brahman is itself not covered by *ajñāna* (*sad-ātmanā na brahmaṇo mūlājñānenā-vṛtatvam*): it is only by the limitations of the specific forms of world-objects that its nature is hidden; when the obstacles of these specific forms are broken by the function of the *vṛtti* modification of the mind, the Brahman underlying these objects manifests itself as pure being. It cannot be objected that Brahman, as such a pure being, has no visual characteristics and therefore cannot be perceived by the eye; for Brahman is not perceivable by any of the senses or by any specific sense[1].

[1] *na ca rūpādi-hīnatayā cākṣuṣatvādy-anupapattiḥ bādhikā iti vācyam, prati-niyatendriya-grāhyeṣv eva rūpādy-apekṣā-niyamāt sarvendriya-grāhyaṃ tu sad-rūpaṃ brahma nāto rūpādi-hīnatve'pi cākṣusatvādy anupapattiḥ sattvāyāḥ parair api sarvendriya-grāhyatva-ābhyupagamāt ca.* *Advaita-siddhi*, p. 318.

Rāmācārya in reply says that the universal (as "cow") has to be accepted; for otherwise how can the so-called universal as being be sometimes manifested as cow and at other times as other objects? Again, it is wrong to say that Brahman is not in itself covered by the *avidyā*; for it is said that, even when the being-aspect is revealed, the aspect as bliss may still remain covered; then, since being and bliss must be one (for otherwise the monism would fail), the veil must also be over the being-aspect as well. Again, as Brahman has no form and no characteristic, it cannot be said to be grasped by all the senses (*atyantam avyakta-svabhāvasya brahmanaś cakṣur-ādi-sarvendriyagrāhyatve mānābhāvāt*)[1].

The argument that falsehood consists in the non-existence of the whole in the parts is attacked by Vyāsa-tīrtha. He says that, so far as concerns the view that, because part and whole are identical, therefore the whole cannot be dependent on the part, he has no objection. If the whole is not dependent upon anything else and not on its parts either, then it may not be dependent on anything at all; but it cannot on that account be called false. But it may be pointed out that perception shows that the whole *is* dependent on the parts and rests in them, and therefore on the evidence of perception its non-existence in the parts cannot be admitted. The question arises whether "non-existence" or "negation" is valid or invalid: if it is valid, then monism breaks down, and, if it is invalid, then non-existence is denied, which will be in favour of Vyāsa-tīrtha. Now it cannot be urged that the existence of negation cannot be fatal to monism: for negation includes position as a constituent. Again, Brahman is denoted by the term *advitīya* ("devoid of any second"); this involves a negation, and, if negation is invalid, then its demolition of Brahman will also be invalid. Further, the denial of a second to Brahman may mean a denial not only of positive entities, but of negative entities also; positivity itself means the negative of the negative. Also, if negation is admitted, then, since one of its forms is "otherness," its admission means the admission of otherness and hence of duality. Moreover, it would be difficult for the Śaṅkarites to describe the nature of negation; for, if no positive entities can be described, it goes without saying that it will be still more difficult to describe negative entities. Moreover, not only is the non-existence of the whole in

[1] *Taraṅgiṇī*, p. 52.

the parts contradicted by perceptual experience, but it is opposed to reason also; for, since the whole cannot be subsistent anywhere else, if it is not admitted to be subsistent in the parts, its very nature is inexplicable (*anyāsamavetasyāṃśitvaṃ etat-tantu-samavetatvaṃ vinā na yuktaṃ*)[1].

Again, the view that, since without knowledge nothing is revealed, the so-called things are nothing but knowledge, is wrong; for the things are experienced not as being themselves knowledge, but as those things of which we have knowledge (*ghaṭasya jñānam iti hi dhīḥ na tu ghaṭo jñānam iti*).

In reply to the above Madhusūdana says that, since the experience of cause and effect cannot be explained without assuming some difference between them, such a difference must be admitted for practical purposes, in spite of the fact that they are identical. Discussion regarding the validity or invalidity of negation is brushed aside by Madhusūdana as being out of place. Again, the opposition of perception is no objection; for perception is often illusory. Also, the objection that, if the whole, which is not elsewhere, is also not in the parts, its existence is inexplicable, is invalid; for, though the whole may not exist in the parts as an independent entity, it may still be there as identical with the material cause, the parts; for being materially identical (*etat-samavetatva*) with anything does not necessarily follow from a denial of its negation therein; for, if it were so, then all such qualities as are devoid of negative instances (being on that account present in it) would be materially identical with the thing[2]. But what really determines a thing's material identity with another thing is that the former's negation-prior-to-existence (*prāg-abhāva*) must be in it (*kintu etan-niṣṭha-prāg-abhāva-pratiyogitvād aikyam*). The objection of Vyāsa-tīrtha, that a cloth can have its negation in threads only when such threads are not its constituent parts, is invalid, for the very reason that what determines material identity is the existence of the prior-to-existence negation (*prāg-abhāva-pratiyogitva*) of the whole in the part or of the effect in the cause, and therefore it is not proper to say that a cloth can non-exist only in such threads as are not

[1] *tathā ca aṃśitva-rūpa-hetor etat-tantu-niṣṭhātyantābhāva-pratiyogitva-rūpa-sādhyena virodhaḥ. Nyāyāmṛta-prakāśa*, p. 86.

[2] *etanniṣṭhātyantābhāva-pratiyogitvaṃ hi etatsamavetatve prayojakaṃ na bhavati, paramate kevalānvayi-dharma-mātrasya etatsamavetatvāpatteḥ. Advaita-siddhi*, p. 324.

constituents of it: for the condition of the non-existence of the cloth in the threads is not the fact of the threads not being a constituent of the cloth, but the absence of the prior-to-existence negation of the cloth in the threads.

An objection is urged by Vyāsa-tīrtha that for the self-same reasons on account of which the world is called false Brahman as well may be regarded as false; for Brahman is the substratum of all our experience and therefore may be regarded as false. As to this Madhusūdana says that, so far as Brahman is associated with *ajñāna*, it is false, but, so far as it is beyond our practical experience, it is real. Moreover, if no ground-reality be admitted, then, the whole world-appearance being an illusion, we shall be landed in pure nihilism. Again, the objection that Brahman, being different from non-existent entity, is like the conch-shell-silver, which also, though not real, is different from non-existent entity, cannot be maintained. For difference from non-existent entity is difference from that which cannot appear anywhere as existent, and that alone is different from it which appears somewhere as an existent entity; but this cannot apply to Brahman, since pure Brahman does not appear anywhere as an existent entity.

Vyāsa-tīrtha, after adopting a number of tentative definitions of being, finds fault with them all, and says that, in whatever way being may be defined by the Śaṅkarites, that would be applicable in the same manner to the being of the world. Briefly speaking, the definition of being comes to be "that which at all times and in all places cannot be denied" (*sarva-deśa-kāla-sambandhi-niṣedha-pratiyogitvaṃ sattvaṃ*). It may also be defined as that which, being different from non-being, is not a false imposition, or as that which at some time or other is directly and rightly felt as existing (*astitva-prakāraka-pramāṇam prati kadācid sākṣād-viṣayatvaṃ*).

In reply to the above attempt at a definition of being by Vyāsa-tīrtha, Madhusūdana says that our perceptual experience is absolutely illegitimate in discerning truth as distinguished from falsehood or as opposed to it[1]. Truth and falsehood being mutually related, all attempts at defining them by mutual opposition become circular, and therefore illegitimate; definitions of being which refer in some way or other to the experience of being as such are also

[1] *cakṣurādy-adhyakṣa-yogya-mithyātva-virodhi-satvāanirukteḥ.* *Advaita-siddhi*, pp. 333–4.

false, as they involve the very concept of being which is to be defined. It is also wrong to say that the world has as much reality of the same order as that of Brahman; for falsehood and reality cannot have the same order of being. The being of Brahman is of the nature of one pure luminous consciousness, and it is clear that the material world cannot have that order of being. Now falsehood is defined as non-existence at all times and places (*sarva-deśīya-traikālika-niṣedha-pratiyogitvaṃ*); reality is its opposite. Sense-perception can never bring to us such a negation, and therefore it also cannot bring to us the opposite of negation, i.e., reality. The fact that some things are perceived to exist somewhere at some time is irrelevant; for even a false appearance may have such a temporary perceptual existence. There is a Nyāya view to the effect that there is a special mode of presentation of universals (*sāmānya-pratyāsatti*), by which all the individuals that come under such universals are presented in consciousness, and that it is by this means alone that inductive generalization leading to deductive inference is possible. On this view the contention is that, though all negations of an entity at all times and places may not be visually perceived, they may be presented to consciousness by the above means of presentation, and, if they are thus presented to consciousness, their negation, viz., the reality, may also be perceived.

Madhusūdana's reply to this is, that there is no such special mode of presentation of universals by which all the individuals associated with them are also present in consciousness, i.e., there is no such *sāmānya-pratyāsatti* as is admitted by the Nyāyāyikas. He then indulges in a polemic against such a *sāmānya-pratyāsatti* and tries to show that deductive inferences are possible through the association of the special characteristics of the universals as determining the concomitance[1]; thus, if there is no *sāmānya-pratyāsatti* and if all the negations at all times and places cannot be presented to consciousness, their opposite, reality, cannot be perceived either.

The reply of Rāmācārya is that, though such negations at all times and all places may not be perceived by the senses, yet there

[1] *vyāpti-smṛti-prakāreṇa vā pakṣadharmatā-jñānasya hetutā; mahānasīya eva dhūmo dhūmatvena vyāpti-smṛti-viṣayo bhavati, dhūmatvena parvatīya-dhūma-jñānaṃ cāpi jātam, tac ca sāmānya-lakṣaṇaṃ vinaiva; tāvataiva anumiti-siddheḥ; ...pratiyogitāvacchedaka-prakāraka-jñānād eva tat-sambhavena tad-arthaṃ sakala-pratiyogi-jñāna-janikāyāḥ sāmānya-pratyāsatty anupayogāt.*
Advaita-siddhi, pp. 338, 341.

is no reason why their opposite, reality, cannot be perceived; when one sees a jug, one feels that it is there and nowhere else. One perceives the objects negated and not the negation itself[1]. He further says that, though *sāmānya-pratyāsatti* may not be admitted, yet the unperceived negations may be known by inference, and thus the objection of Madhusūdana that, unless *sāmānya-pratyāsatti* is admitted, such negations cannot be known and their opposite, reality, cannot be perceived either, is doubly invalid[2].

Madhusūdana further says that the testimony of the testifying consciousness (*sākṣī*) in experience reveals only present entities, and in that way the world-objects are relatively real. But the testifying consciousness cannot in any way show whether they will be contradicted in future or not; the testifying consciousness is thus incapable of defying a future denial of world-experience, when the Brahma-knowledge is attained.

Vyāsa-tīrtha had objected to the Vedānta thesis that there is one Being, self-identical with pure consciousness, on which all the so-called forms of object and content of knowledge are imposed, pointing out that the mere fact that one experiences that a jug exists does not prove that the jug is imposed upon the pure being; for pure existence can never be perceived and all the characteristics, including false appearances, may also be considered to have the same existential character as existence itself.

Madhusūdana's simple reply is that instead of admitting a number of individual entities it is much better to admit one constant being on which the various forms of objects are imposed. The assertion of Vyāsa-tīrtha that perceptual evidence is by its very nature stronger than inference, which is slow in establishing itself on account of the various conditions that it has to depend on, is objected to by Madhusūdana, who says that, when perceptual evidence is contradicted by inference and scriptural testimony (e.g., as in the perception of the small dimensions of planetary bodies), it is the former that is negated. So perception has also to depend for its validity on its non-contradiction and other means of proof, and the other means of proof have no more to depend on perception than perception on them. So all these means of proof, being relatively dependent, are of inferior validity to the Vedic testimony, which, not being a man-made document, has naturally an inalien-

[1] *Taraṅgiṇī*, p. 61. [2] *Ibid.* p. 63.

able claim to validity. It is well known that perception through one sense, say the visual, has often to be woven together with perception through other senses, e.g., the tactile, for arriving at valid experience of facts, as in the perception "fire is hot." Thus perceptual evidence has no right of superior validity by reason of being perceptible, though it may be admitted that in certain spheres perception may dispel an ignorance which is not removed by inference[1]. The objection that an inferential evidence, because it establishes itself slowly (on account of its dependence on many facts), is of inferior validity to perception because this comes quicker is invalid; for validity depends upon proper examination and discovery of faultlessness and not on mere quickness. Moreover, since there are many scriptural texts declaring the oneness of all, which cannot be justified except on the assumption of the falsity of the world, and since such an admission would not take away from perception its natural claim to validity in the relative sphere, a compromise may well be effected by allowing perceptual validity to remain uncontrolled in the relative sphere and admitting the scriptural validity of oneness in the absolute sphere.

Again, Vyāsa-tīrtha urges that, since inference and scriptural testimony both depend on visual and auditory perception, it will be wrong to think that the former could invalidate the latter. If perception is not valid in itself, then all inference and scriptural testimony would be invalid, since their data are supplied by perception.

To this Madhusūdana's reply is that the scriptural testimony does not challenge the data supplied by perception, but challenges their ultimate validity, which can never be supplied by perceptual experience[2]. The bare fact that one knowledge springs up because it was preceded by another is no reason why it is to be less valid; the judgement "this is not silver, but conch-shell" is not less valid because it could not have come into being unless there had been a previous error with the perception of conch-shell as silver. It is said that the validity of sense-evidence is determined by a critical examination depending on correspondence. To this Madhusūdana's

[1] *nāpi anumānādy-anivartita-diṅmohanādi-nivartakatvena prābalyam; etāvatā hi vaidharmya-mātraṃ siddhaṃ. Advaita-siddhi*, p.355.

[2] *yat-svarūpam upayujyate tanna bādhyate, bādhyate ca tātvikatvākāraḥ, sa ca nopajīvyate kāraṇatve tasyāpraveśāt. Ibid.* p. 363.

reply is that, so far as concerns the validity of an awareness according to correspondence, the Śaṅkarites have nothing to say against it. What he challenges is that the ultimate validity or ultimate non-contradiction cannot be revealed by any critical examination. It is again argued that, if perception is invalid, the knowledge of concomitance arrived at through it is invalid, and therefore all inference is invalid. This is, however, wrong; for even by a false reasoning a right inference may be possible; from an illusory reflection it is possible to infer the existence of the thing reflected. Moreover, falsity of the evidence (inferential or perceptual) does not imply the falsity of the thing known; so the objection that, if perception is not regarded as valid, then all knowledge becomes invalid, is illegitimate.

Vyāsa-tīrtha urges that, if perceptual testimony can be contradicted in any place by inference, then any and every inference can contradict perception, and fire can be regarded as cold and a hare as having a horn, which is impossible.

To this Madhusūdana's reply is that not any and every inference can be regarded as superior to perception, since it is well known that an illegitimate inference leads to no valid conclusion. The instances which have been adduced by Vyāsa-tīrtha are instances of illegitimate inferences, the fallacy of which is apparent. It is never admitted by anyone that an illegitimate inference is stronger than perception; but it also cannot be denied that there are many instances of illegitimate perception which are rightly denounced by right inferences.

Vyāsa-tīrtha further says that the science of *mīmāṃsā* itself admits in various places the superior validity of perception, and recommends a twisting interpretation of such scriptural passages as are not in harmony with perception. The scriptural text, "That art thou," is directly contradicted in perceptual experience, and therefore should be so interpreted as not to come into conflict therewith.

To this Madhusūdana's reply is that it is indeed true that certain scriptural passages which deal with ordinary mundane affairs are thus brought into harmony with experience and are sometimes interpreted in accordance with perception; but that is no reason why those texts which refer to ultimate experience and which do not refer to the accessory details of sacrifices should also be subordinate to perception.

Vyāsa-tīrtha says that it is wrong to suppose that perception is invalidated by inference or scriptural testimony; what happens in the case of perceptual illusions is that in both cases perception is vitiated by various types of defects, the presence of which is also known by perception.

To this Madhusūdana's simple reply is that the presence of defects cannot be known by perception itself, and that most cases of illusory perception are invalidated by stronger inference. When it is said that the moon is no bigger than a foot the illusory perception is no doubt due to the defect of the long distance, but that this is so can be known only by an inference based upon the observation of the diminution of sizes in trees on distant hill-tops. Thus, though there are cases in which one perception invalidates another, there are also cases in which an inference invalidates a perception.

A question arises whether the present perception of the world-appearance may ultimately be contradicted; but to this Vyāsa-tīrtha says that such a fear of future contradiction may invalidate even that knowledge which contradicts this perception. Ordinarily the waking experience contradicts dream-experience, and, if waking experience be also contradicted, then there would be nothing to contradict dream-experience. In this way it will be difficult to find an instance of false experience. The knowledge that contradicts the illusory perception comprehends within it things which are not known at the time of illusory perception (e.g., the knowledge of the conch-shell which was not present at the time of perception of illusory shell-silver). But it cannot be urged that the knowledge that would contradict world-experience would have the specific nature of not being comprehended within the knowledge of world-appearance. Again, a knowledge that contradicts another knowledge must have a content; contentless knowledge has no opposition to false cognitions, yet Brahma-knowledge is regarded as contentless. Moreover, contradiction is possible only there, where a defect is, and that defect lies with the Śaṅkarites, who give a monistic interpretation of scriptural texts. Again, if the monistic experience is certified by monistic texts, the dualistic experience is also certified by dualistic texts, and a knowledge that would contradict and negate the world-experience would involve a duality by the very fact of such negation. Moreover, the last experience which would contradict the world-experience, being itself an experience, would be equally liable to contradiction; and, if uncontradicted experience be also doubted as being liable to contradiction, then there would be no end to such doubts.

Madhusūdana, in reply to the above objection of Vyāsa-tīrtha, emphasizes the point that it is no essential character of a knowledge that contradicts another that it should have a content; what is essential here is that a right knowledge should be grounded in the realization of the reality and thereby negate the false knowledge. It is also wrong to think that, when Brahma-knowledge negates world-appearance, an affirmation of duality is involved; for the Brahma-knowledge is of the very nature of reality, before which the falsehood, which has only appearance and no existence, naturally dissolves away. He further says that doubts regarding validity can only arise when it is known that there are defects; but, since there can be no defects in Brahma-knowledge, no doubts can arise. The assertion of Vyāsa-tīrtha that, if the world-appearance is false, then it is wrong to speak of the self as being of the nature of pure bliss on the ground that the experience of dreamless sleep reveals such a blissful state, is unwarranted, because the nature of self as blissful is known directly from scriptural testimony, and the experience of dreamless sleep is consistent with it.

Nature of Knowledge.

Vyāsa-tīrtha argues that, if the reasons, cognizability, etc., are supposed to indicate the falsity of the world-appearance and if they are applied to the inferential apparatus, then they also are false; and, if they are not false, then all the world-appearance is false, and the argument for the falsity of the world is fallacious. Vyāsa-tīrtha says further that, if the Śaṅkarite be asked to explain the nature of true reality, he will naturally be liable to confusion. It cannot be regarded as an object of awareness, because chimerical entities are also objects of awareness; it cannot be described as direct awareness, because then it would not belong to any eternal and transcendental entities which are unperceiving, and the world-appearance also, which is directly perceived, would not be false, and the inference, e.g., of fire based upon an illusory perception of the reason (e.g., the water-vapour in a lake), would also be true. Knowledge does not contribute to the existence of things all their properties;

even if fire is not known as fire, it can burn all the same. Thus existence does not depend upon any kind of awareness. It is also wrong to define reality as practical behaviour; for, unless the nature of world-appearance is known, the nature of practical behaviour is not known. The world as such must be either existent or non-existent, and there is no other third way of subsistence; the non-existence of the world cannot be proved by any existent proof, because existence and non-existence are opposed to each other; nor can it be proved by non-existent proofs, simply because they *are* non-existent. There cannot be any being such that it exists in common with non-being and ultimate being[1].

Madusūdana says that the false may be distinguished from the true by exactly the same kind of considerations which lead the opponent to distinguish between the perception of the blueness of the sky and the ordinary objects of experience such as a jug, a rope, etc. The nature of reality that has been conceded to the world-appearance is that it is not contradicted by anything other than Brahma-knowledge.

Vyāsa-tīrtha points out that the contention of the Śaṅkarites that there cannot be any relation between knowledge and its contents is borrowed from the Buddhists, who consider awareness and its objects to be the same. The Śaṅkarites hold that, if the objects are considered to be real, then it is difficult to show how there can be any relation between knowledge and the objects revealed by it; for the two accepted relations of contact and inseparable inherence (*samavāya*) cannot hold between them. The relation of objectivity is also too obscure to be defined; and therefore it must be admitted that the relation between knowledge and the objects is wholly illusory.

To this Vyāsa-tīrtha replies that, though all objects are regarded by the Śaṅkarites as illusorily imposed upon the one supreme perceiver, the Brahman, yet for explanation of specific cognitions of specific individuals, sense-contact, leading to the rise of different perceptions of different individuals, is admitted by them. The Śaṅkarites are not idealists to the same extent as the Buddhists are. Even if it be admitted that pure consciousness may appear different under various conditions, yet there is no reason why the world-

[1] *nāpi sat-trayānugataṃ sat-dvayānugataṃ vā satva-sāmānyaṃ tantraṃ. Nyāyāmṛta*, p. 174.

objects should be considered as impositions upon pure consciousness. Even the admission of the world-objects as illusory impositions does not help us very much; for there cannot be any knowledge of these world-objects without the cognitive function (*vṛtti*) of the mind. Again, if all world-objects are illusory impositions, then it is meaningless to put into the *modus operandi* of the perceptual process a reflection of the pure consciousness through its specific functions, or into the specific cognitive senses the consciousness underlying the objects[1]. The mere fact that neither contact nor inseparable relation can be of any avail does not necessarily imply that perceptual forms are all illusory; for, if there is an actual experience, then relations have naturally to be imagined to explain the situation[2]. Again, if it be admitted for argument's sake that there is no way of proving the validity of the assumption of a relation between knowledge and its object, yet that would not prove the falsity of the objects themselves; what it would do at the utmost would be to deny the validity of relations subsisting between knowledge and its objects. Again, if the Śaṅkarite finds no difficulty in admitting the relation of the pure consciousness to the *vṛtti*, why does he find any difficulty in admitting such a relation to the objects[3]? Even if the world-objects be regarded as indescribable, yet their existence may be regarded as being indescribable in the same way as that of Brahman. The Śaṅkarite has also to admit the existence of the objective world and to offer explanations for the way in which it is perceived. The only difference of this view from that of the realists is that, while the Śaṅkarite considers the objects to be ultimately false, the realist considers them to be real; and the same reason that leads the Śaṅkarites to consider them as having a higher order of reality than the merely illusory leads the realists to consider them as ultimately real[4]. The Brahman itself is in a sense as indescribable as the world-objects[5]. Things, so far as they

[1] *Nyāyāmṛta*, p. 191.

[2] *Ibid.* p. 193: *pramita-vastvanusāreṇa hi prakriyā kalpyā na tu sva-kalpita-prakriyānurodhena pramita-tyāgaḥ.*

[3] *yādṛśaṃ viṣayatvaṃ te vṛttiṃ prati cidātmanaḥ*
tādṛśaṃ viṣayatvaṃ me dṛśyasyāpi dṛśaṃ prati. *Ibid.* p. 205*a*.

[4] *tava sa ākāraḥ sad-vilakṣaṇaḥ mama tu sanniti anirucyamāno'pi sa tava yena mānena aprātibhāsikaḥ tenaiva mama tātviko'stu.* *Ibid.* p. 205.

[5] *kīdṛk tat pratyag iti cet tādṛśī dṛg iti dvayaṃ*
yatra na prasaraty etat pratyag ity-avadhāraya
iti brahmaṇy api durnirūpatvasya uktatvāc ca. *Ibid.* p. 206*a*.

are known and so far as they have certain common characteristics, can well be described, though in their unique nature each of them has such peculiarities that they cannot be properly defined and expressed. Each human face may be well known by the uncontradicted testimony of our senses; but still it cannot be described with its own specific and peculiar characteristics[1]. So it is difficult to describe the specific nature of Brahman as the identity of pure being, bliss and consciousness; yet its reality is not denied. The same is the case with the world-objects, and, though they are indescribable in their specific natures, yet their reality cannot be denied[2].

Madusūdana generally passes over many of the points of objection raised by Vyāsa-tīrtha; one of these points is that relations are grasped directly and that there is no incongruity in thinking that, if relations cannot be mediated, they can yet be grasped directly by the senses. Madhusūdana's contention is that, if relations be described as self-subsistent, then they cannot be explained and must therefore be regarded as false. Vyāsatīrtha now refers to the Śaṅkarite account of perception, and says that in their view the objects are supposed to be there and the veil over them is removed by the mind (*antaḥkaraṇa*) transforming itself into the form of the object; he says also, that, if this is so, then the objects of perception cannot be regarded as mental. If the objects were merely mental, the application of the sense-organs would be unnecessary for their perception; in dreams mental objects are "perceived," but the visual organs are not exercised. The difference between the ordinary practical experience of the world and that of dreams is only that the former is longer in duration, and so, if in dream-experience the mental objects can be perceived without the exercise of the visual organ, there is no reason why the world-objects also cannot be perceived in the same way. Moreover, in the case of non-perceptual cognition (*parokṣa jñāna*) the Śaṅkarites themselves admit that the objects are illuminated without any direct operation of *antaḥkaraṇa*, in association with the senses, involving an actual

[1] *tasmāt pramitasya ittham iti nirvaktum*
aśakyatvaṃ pratipuruṣa-mukhaṃ spaṣṭā-vādhita
-dṛṣṭidṛṣṭam vilakṣaṇa-saṃsthāna-viśeṣasya vā
sattve'py adbhutatvād eva yuktam. *Ibid.* p. 206.

[2] *tasmāt nirvacanāyogyasyāpi viśvasya ikṣukṣīrādi-mādhuryavad brahmavac ca prāmāṇikatvād eva sattva-siddheḥ.* *Ibid.* p. 206.

contact with the objects. There is no reason why the same thing cannot take place in ordinary perception. The difference of the *antaḥkaraṇa* transformation in the two cases might equally well explain the difference between the perceptual (*a-parokṣa*) and non-perceptual (*parokṣa*) cognitions, and for this it is not necessary to assume that in one case the *antaḥkaraṇa* goes out and in another case remains inside. It cannot be held that an immediate intuitive character belongs to the *antaḥkaraṇa*; for the *antaḥkaraṇa* itself being non-intuitive and non-self-illuminating by nature, its modifications also cannot be intuitive or self-illuminating. The mere fact that *antaḥkaraṇa* has fire elements in it does not make it self-illuminating; for then many objects which are supposed to be made up of fire elements would be self-illuminating. Again, it is wrong to suppose that the manifestation of consciousness must be non-transitive by nature; for, though one may speak of the illumination of an object in non-transitive terms, one speaks of knowing in transitive terms. If it is not admitted that the transitive or intransitive character of an action is often of a verbal nature, it would be difficult for a Śaṅkarite to speak of a modification of *antaḥkaraṇa* (which is non-transitive) as equivalent to knowing an object. Moreover, if it is held that it is only the pure consciousness outside the *vṛtti* that is illuminated, then the past, wherein there is no pure consciousness manifesting it, could not reveal itself to us; so it is wholly unwarrantable to conceive of an intermediatory means in order to explain the relation between knowledge and its objects. Even if it be admitted that the *antaḥkaraṇa* goes outside the body, yet it is difficult to conceive of the nature of pure consciousness, which is supposed to illumine the object, either as consciousness reflected in the *vṛtti* of *antaḥkaraṇa* (as stated by Bhāratī-tīrtha), or as the pure consciousness which is the ground of the appearance of objects manifested by the consciousness reflected in the *antaḥkaraṇa-vṛtti* (*vṛtti-pratibimbita-caitanyābhivyaktaṃ viṣayādhiṣṭhānaṃ caitanyam*), as supposed by Sureśvara. The question is whether consciousness as manifested in the *antaḥkaraṇa* illumines the object or whether the ground-consciousness underlying the objects manifests the objects. Neither of these views is tenable. The first view is not possible because, the consciousness reflected in the *antaḥkaraṇa-vṛtti* being false, it is not possible that the world-objects should be imposed on such an illusory entity; the second view is also impossible; for, if the consciousness reflected in the *antaḥkaraṇa-vṛtti* be supposed to remove the veil of the object, it may as well be held to manifest it, and it is, therefore, unnecessary to suppose that the ground-consciousness illumines the object.

Further, it cannot be admitted that the *vṛtti* assumes the form of the gross physical objects; for then it would be as gross and material as the objects are. Moreover, the existence of an object assumes therewith the existence of the negation of other entities; and, if the *antaḥkaraṇa* is supposed to take the form of an object, it must also assume the negative forms; it is, however, difficult to conceive how the *antaḥkaraṇa* can be supposed to assume the positive and the negative forms at one and the same time. Again, following the same supposition in the case of the final intuition, it has to be assumed that the *antaḥkaraṇa-vṛtti* assumes the form of Brahman; this, however, has no form, so that the *antaḥkaraṇa-vṛtti* must be supposed to be here both formless and endowed with form —which is absurd.

Moreover, it is not legitimate to suppose that it is the consciousness underlying the finite self (*jīva-caitanya*) that reveals the object; for, on the supposition that the objects are illusory superpositions on pure consciousness or on the consciousness underlying the objects, the Śaṅkarite theory fails; for in this case the perceiving consciousness, being consciousness underlying the *jīva*, would be different either from pure consciousness or from the consciousness underlying the objects, which is supposed to be the basis of the illusory creations. The *jīva* itself, moreover, cannot be regarded as the basis of the creation; for it is itself an illusory creation. For the same reasons also it cannot be asserted that it is the Brahma-consciousness that illumines the object. Thus the Brahman, being itself as underlying the objects, an illusory creation, cannot be regarded as also illuminating the objects. The pure consciousness underlying the objects, being itself veiled by *ajñāna*, should not also be able to manifest itself; and thus all knowledge of objects would be impossible. If it is argued that, though the pure consciousness is veiled, yet the consciousness limited by the object-form may be manifested by the *vṛtti* of the *antaḥkaraṇa*, that is not correct: for it cannot be admitted that the consciousness limited by the object-forms is itself the basis of those object-forms, since that would amount to an admission that the object-forms are their own basis, which would be a fallacy of self-dependence (*ātmāśraya*), and the original contention of the Śaṅkarites that the objects are illusorily imposed upon pure consciousness fails. Moreover, if the process of knowledge is admitted to be such that the *antaḥkaraṇa-vṛtti* manifests the pure consciousness as limited by objective forms, then the case of final intuition (Brahman-knowledge), where objective characteristics are absent, would be inexplicable. Again, the Śaṅkarites hold that in deep dreamless sleep the *antaḥkaraṇa* is dissolved; and, if that were so, the *jīva*, which is the consciousness limited by a particular *antaḥkaraṇa*, would be renewed after each dreamless sleep, and thus the fruits of the *karma* of one *jīva* ought not to be reaped by the new *jīva*. The view that the pure consciousness is reflected through a *vṛtti* is also inadmissible; for reflections can happen only between two visible objects. The view that consciousness is transformed into a particular state is also inadmissible, since by hypothesis consciousness is unchangeable. Consciousness being entirely unsupported by anything else (*anāśritatvāt*), the analogy of the relation of universal and particular as explaining the conditioning of consciousness is also inadmissible. Moreover, if the consciousness underlying the *jīva* be regarded as manifesting the objects, then, since such a consciousness always exists in an unveiled form, there is no meaning in saying that in effecting its spontaneous manifestation the operation of the *vṛtti* is necessary. Also the pure consciousness cannot be regarded as being limited by the *vṛtti* just as limitless space is supposed to be limited by a jug; for the pure consciousness is all-pervading and, as such, it must also pervade the *vṛtti* and cannot therefore be regarded as being inside it. Neither can the pure consciousness be compared with the ray of light manifesting colour; for the ray of light does so only with the help of accessories, whereas pure consciousness manifests things by itself. Again, if things are manifested spontaneously by the unveiled consciousness (*anāvṛta-cit yadi viṣaya-prakāśikā*), then, since such a consciousness is in touch with objects not only so far as their forms and colours are concerned, but also with their other characteristics such as weight, these also ought to be illuminated along with qualities such as colour, etc. Moreover, the relation of consciousness to the object cannot be of the nature of eternal contact, but must be of the nature of illusory imposition upon it (consciousness); this being so, the relation of consciousness to the object is already there, since all things in the world are imposed upon consciousness. The supposition therefore of a *vṛtti* as an intermediary is quite uncalled for[1]. Again, if the Brahma-consciousness stands in need of the help of a *vṛtti* in order to manifest things, it has no claim to be called by itself omniscient. If it is suggested that Brahman, being the material cause of all, is competent without the help of any conditions to illuminate the world, which is identical with it, then the reply will be that, if Brahman be regarded as transforming itself under the limitation of objective forms, then such a transformation of the limited Brahman does not justify the accepted thesis of the Śaṅkarites that all objects are illusorily imposed on the pure consciousness[2]. It is also not possible to say that it is the pure consciousness, unconditioned by any object-form, that forms the ground cause; for, if that were so, it could not be called omniscient, since omniscience can be affirmed only in relation to object-forms[3].

The supposition that the conception of *vṛtti* is necessary for the removal of the veil is also wrong; for such a veil must attach either to the pure consciousness or to limited consciousness. The former is impossible, since the pure consciousness which forms the basis of all appearances is the intuitive perceiver of all *ajñāna* and its forms, and as such, being self-luminous, cannot have any veil attached to it. The second also is impossible; for without the help of the pure consciousness *ajñāna* itself would be without any *locus standi*, and without the *ajñāna* there would be no limited consciousness and no veil of *ajñāna*. Again, admitting for argument's sake that there is a veil of *ajñāna* over the objects, the conception of its removal by a *vṛtti* is impossible; for, if the *ajñāna* belongs to the individual perceiver, then, if it is destroyed for one individual, it remains the same for another; if it belongs to the object, as is supposed, then, when it is removed by the *vṛtti* of one individual, the

[1] *cito viṣayoparāgas tāvat saṃyogādi-rūpo nāsty eva. tasya dṛśyatvā-prayojakatvāt kintu tatrādhyastatva-rūpa eveti vācyam. sa ca vṛttyapekṣayā pūrvam apy astīti kiṃ cito viṣayoparāgārthayā vṛttyā.*

Śrīnivāsa's *Nyāyāmṛta-prakāśa* on the *Nyāyāmṛta*, p. 226.

[2] *viśiṣṭa-niṣṭhena pariṇāmitva-rūpeṇa sarvopādānatvena viśiṣṭa-brahmaṇaḥ sarvajñatve tasya kalpitatvenādhiṣṭhānatvāyogena tatra jagad-adhyāsāsaṃbhavāt ādhyāsika-saṃbandhena prakāśata iti bhavad-abhimataniyamabhaṅga-prasaṅgaḥ.* *Ibid.* p. 227*a*.

[3] *nāpi śuddha-niṣṭham adhiṣṭhānatvaṃ sārvajñyāder viśiṣṭa-niṣṭhatvāt.* *Ibid.* p. 226*a*.

object should be manifest to other individuals, so that, when a person sees an object, that object should be visible also to other persons at other places. Again, is the *ajñāna* to be accepted as one, according to the author of the *Vivaraṇa*, or as many, according to the author of the *Iṣṭa-siddhi*? In the former case, when by one right knowledge *ajñāna* is removed, there ought to be immediate emancipation. If the *ajñāna* is not removed, then the silver-appearance of conch-shell should not have been contradicted, and the form of conch-shell could not have been manifested. It cannot be said that in the case of the perception of conch-shell through negation of the silver-appearance the *ajñāna* is merely dissolved (just as a jug is reduced to dust by the stroke of a club, but not destroyed), which can only be done through Brahma-knowledge; for *ajñāna* is directly opposed to knowledge, and without destroying ignorance knowledge cannot show itself. If the *ajñāna* were not removed by the knowledge of the conch-shell, then the manifested consciousness would have no relation to the conch-shell, and it could not have been manifested, and in spite of the contradiction the illusion would have remained. Nor can it be suggested that, though *ajñāna* may be removed in some parts, it might continue in others; for *ajñāna* and consciousness are both partless. Nor can it be suggested that, just as by the influence of certain precious stones the burning capacity of fire can be stopped, so by the knowledge of the conch-shell the veiling power of *avidyā* is suspended; for the *antaḥkaraṇa-vṛtti* in the form of the conch-shell, being produced through the agency of the visual organ and other accessories, cannot be in touch with the pure self, which is devoid of all characteristics, and therefore it cannot remove the veiling power. If it is suggested that the *vṛtti* of the form of the conch-shell is in association with the pure consciousness, under the limited form of the conch-shell, and can therefore remove the veil, then the underlying pure consciousness ought to be directly intuited. *Avidyā* cannot have the material objects as its support; for they are themselves the product of *avidyā*. So the veiling power of *avidyā* also can have no reference to the material objects, since a veil can hide only what is luminous; the material objects, not being luminous, cannot be veiled. So there is no meaning in saying that the veil of the objects is removed in perception. If, again, it is said that the veil has reference to the pure self, as modified by the material characteristic, and not to the material characteristic, then with the knowledge of the conch-shell the veil of the conch-shell underlying it might be removed, and this ought to bring immediate emancipation. If it is suggested that the *ajñāna* which forms the substratum of the illusory silver is but a special modified state of a root *ajñāna* which forms the material of the conch-shell, then that virtually amounts to an assumption of many *ajñānas* independent of one another; and, that being so, it would not necessarily follow that the knowledge of the conch-shell could dispel the illusory appearance of silver.

On the view of the author of the *Iṣṭa-siddhi*, if the existence of many *ajñānas* is admitted, then the question is whether by the operation of one *vṛtti* only one *ajñāna* is removed or all the *ajñānas*. In the former view the conch-shell could never remain unmanifested even in the case of illusion, since *vṛtti* manifesting the illusory silver would also manifest silver; and on the second view, there being infinite *ajñānas*, which cannot all be removed, conch-shell would never be manifested. This criticism would apply equally well to the former view that there is only one root *ajñāna* of which there are many states. Again, it is difficult to understand how the conch-shell, which has a beginning in time, can be associated with beginningless *avidyā*. Further, if it is urged in reply that the beginningless *avidyā* limits the beginningless pure consciousness and that later, when other objects are produced, the *ajñāna* appears as the veil of pure consciousness limited by those object-forms, the reply is that, if the veil associated with pure consciousness is the same as the veil associated with consciousness in limited object-forms, then, with the knowledge of any of those objects, the veil of pure consciousness would be removed, and immediate emancipation would result.

Rāmādvaya, the author of the *Vedānta-kaumudī*, suggests that, just as there is an infinite number of negations-precedent-to-production (*prāg-abhāva*), and yet, when anything is produced, only one of them is destroyed, or just as, when there is a thunderbolt falling upon a crowd, only one of them may be killed, while others may only disperse, so with the rise of knowledge only one *ajñāna* may be removed, while others may persist. Vyāsa-tīrtha replies that the analogy is false, since (according to him) negation-precedent-to-knowledge is not a veil but merely the absence of the causes of knowledge. Knowledge, moreover, is not the cause of the cessation of such negation, but behaves as an independent entity, so that one knowledge may produce its effects, while the negation-precedent-to-production of other cognitions of its class may remain. The presence of a cause produces the effect, but it does not involve the condition that for the production of the effect the negations-precedent-to-production of all causes of the same class should be removed. In the case of the Vedāntists, since the *vṛtti* removes the veil of one *ajñāna*, there may still be other *ajñāna*-veils to suspend the operation of cognition. On the view that darkness is absence of light, darkness is not a veil of objects, but merely absence of the conditions of light; nor is light supposed in its operation to destroy darkness, but directly to produce illumination. Darkness, also, should not be regarded as negation of individual light, but as absence of light in general; so that, even if there is one light, there is no darkness. The *ajñānas* also possess no constituent material forms; so the analogy of scattering crowds of men cannot apply to them.

Madhusūdana, in replying to the above criticism of Vyāsa-tīrtha, says that the contention of the latter that whatever is imaginary or mental (*kalpita*) necessarily has no other being than the *percipi* (*pratīti-mātra-śarīratva*), is wrong; for in the instance under discussion, when logic shows that the relation between the perceiver and the perceived is so absurd that the perceived entities cannot be anything more than illusory, perception shows that the perceived entities do persist even when they are not perceived. The persistence of the perceived entities is well attested by experience and cannot be regarded as imaginary, like the illusory perception of silver.

But yet it may be objected that, just as in mediate knowledge (*parokṣa*) no necessity is felt for admitting a *vṛtti*, so in immediate perception also there may be an illumination of the object without it. The reply to this is that in mediate knowledge also a mediate (*parokṣa*) *vṛtti* is admitted; for there also the illumination takes place by the manifestation of consciousness through a mediate *vṛtti*[1]. It is wrong to contend that, since the pure consciousness is the principle of manifestation in both cases, mediate cognition

[1] *parokṣasthale'pi parokṣa-vṛtty-uparakta-caitanyasya iva prakāśakatvāt. Advaita-siddhi*, p. 480.

should, on our theory, be expected to behave as immediate; for in the case of immediate perception there is a direct identity of consciousness and the object through the *vṛtti*, and therefore the object behaves as the object of cognition in that specific direct relation. The mediacy or immediacy of cognition depends on the specific nature of the object, and not on the specific modifications of the *vṛtti* in the two cases, nor can the two be regarded as two different classes of cognition; for on such a supposition such cognition or recognition as "this is the man I knew," where there seems to be a mixture of mediate and immediate cognition, will involve a joint operation of two distinct classes of cognition in the same knowledge; which is obviously absurd.

It must be borne in mind that the *vṛtti* by itself is merely an operation which cannot constitute conscious illumination; the *vṛtti* can lead to an illumination only through its association with pure consciousness, and not by itself alone. It is wrong to suppose that there is no difference between a transitive (as when one says "I know a jug") and an intransitive (as when one says "the jug has come into consciousness") operation; for the distinction is well attested in experience as involving a direct and an indirect method. The same *vṛtti* (operation), however, cannot be regarded as both transitive and intransitive at the same time, though with different and indifferent circumstances an operation may be both transitive and intransitive. Such instances of experience as "the past is revealed" are to be explained on the supposition that the pure consciousness is revealed through a particular modification of the *vṛtti* as past.

Again, it is contended by the opponents that, though it may be admitted that pure consciousness manifests the object, yet there is no necessity why the *antaḥkaraṇa* should be supposed to go out of the body and be in contact with the object of perception. The difference between mediate and immediate knowledge may well be accounted for on the supposition of different kinds of mediate or immediate operation through which the consciousness is revealed in each case[1]: for, just as in mediate knowledge there is no actual contact of the *antaḥkaraṇa-vṛtti* with the object, but yet the cognition is possible through the presence of adequate causes which

[1] *parokṣa-vailakṣaṇyāya viṣayasyābhivyaktāparokṣa-cid-uparāga eva vaktavyaḥ. Ibid.* p. 482.

generate such cognition, the same explanation may be adduced in explaining immediate cognition of objects. To this the reply is that the Śaṅkarites do not consider that the *antaḥkaraṇa-vṛtti* must assume the form of the object, but they certainly do consider it to be indispensable. There should be in immediate cognition an actual contact between the object and the *vṛtti*. If the *vṛtti* so acts in any particular case, that does not constitute its essential function in conditioning the awareness. Thus the function of the ray of light in illumination is that it dispels darkness; that it also spreads over the object is only an accidental fact[1]. The mere fact that a *vṛtti* may be in contact with an object does not necessarily mean that it assumes its form; thus, though the *antaḥkaraṇa-vṛtti* may travel up to the pole star or be in contact with objects having an atomic structure, that does not imply that all objects in the space intermediate between the eye and the star or the atoms should be perceived; such perceptions are baffled through the absence of such accessory causes as might have caused the *vṛtti* to assume their form. In the case of tactile perception the *antaḥkaraṇa-vṛtti* comes into contact with the object through the tactile organ; there is no restriction such that the *antaḥkaraṇa* should come out only through the eye and not through other organs[2]. The contention that in the case of other mental operations, such as desire or aversion, there is no assumption of the migration of *antaḥkaraṇa* outside is pointless; for in these cases there is not a removal of a veil as in the case of cognition.

Madhusūdana urges that the basis or the ground-consciousness (*adhiṣṭhāna-caitanya*) which illumines everything is directly connected with the objects through illusory imposition. This self-illuminating entity can, indeed, manifest all that is associated with it; but, as it is, it is in an unmanifested state, like a veiled lamp, and the operation of the *vṛtti* is regarded as necessary for its manifestation. In the case of mediate knowledge this unmanifested consciousness manifests itself in the form of the *vṛtti*; and in the case of immediate perception through the contact of the *vṛtti* the veil of *ajñāna* is removed, since the *vṛtti* extends so as to reach the objects.

[1] *viṣayeṣu abhivyakta-cid-uparāge na tad-ākāratva-mātraṃ tantram. Advaita-siddhi*, p. 482.

[2] *na ca spārśana-pratyakṣe cakṣurādivat niyata-golakadvārā-bhāvena antaḥkaraṇa-nirgaty-ayogād āvaraṇābhibhavānupapattir iti vācyam. sarvatra tat-tad-indriyādhiṣṭhānasyaiva dvāratva-saṃbhavāt. Ibid.* p. 482.

So in the case of mediate cognition the knowledge is of a mental state, and not of an object, whereas in immediate perception the illumination is of the object through the association of the *vṛtti*. In the case of mediate cognition there is no way by which the *antaḥkaraṇa* could go out.

To the objection of Vyāsa-tīrtha that it is absurd to think of the *antaḥkaraṇa* as taking the shape of gross physical objects, Madhusūdana's reply is that "taking the shape of an object" only means the capacity of the *vṛtti* to remove the veil of *ajñāna* which had stood in the way of the affirmation of the existence of the object[1]; thus the functioning of the *vṛtti* consists only in the removal of the veil of *ajñāna*.

To the objection that, if the pure consciousness is veiled by *ajñāna*, no cognition is possible, Madhusūdana's reply is that, though *ajñāna* in its extensive entirety may remain intact, yet a part of it may be removed by coming into association with the *vṛtti*, and thus the object may be revealed.

To the objection of Vyāsa-tīrtha that in the last emancipatory intuition one would expect that the *antaḥkaraṇa* should have the form of Brahman as object (which is absurd, Brahman being formless), the reply of Madhusūdana is that the Brahman which forms the object of the last immediate intuition, being absolutely unconditioned, does not shine as associated with any particular form. The manifestation of objects in worldly experience is always with specific condition, whereas, the object of this last manifestation being without any condition, the absence of any form is no objection to it; its cognition results in the absolute cessation of all *ajñāna* and thus produces emancipation. Again, the objection that, if during dreamless sleep the *antaḥkaraṇa* is dissolved, then on reawakening there will be new *antaḥkaraṇa*, and thus the deeds associated with the former *antaḥkaraṇa* will have no continuity with the new *antaḥkaraṇa*, is invalid; for even in deep sleep the causal *antaḥkaraṇa* remains, what is dissolved being the manifested state of the *antaḥkaraṇa*.

Again, the objection that there cannot be any reflection in the *antaḥkaraṇa* because it has neither manifest colour (*udbhūtā-rūpatvāt*) nor visibility, is invalid; for what may be regarded as the

[1] *astitvādi tad-viṣayaka-vyavahāra-pratibandhaka-jñāna-nivartana-yogyatvasya tad-ākāratva-rūpatvāt. Ibid.* p. 483.

necessary qualification for reflection is not visibility or the possession of colour, but transparence, and such transparency is admitted to belong to *antaḥkaraṇa* or its *vṛtti*. The *ajñāna*, which is regarded as constituted of the three *guṇas*, is also considered to be capable of reflection by virtue of the fact that it contains *sattva* as one of its elements.

The objection that, as a ray of light illuminates not only colours, but also other entities, so the pure consciousness also should illuminate not only the colour of the object, but also its other properties, such as weight, is invalid; for the pure consciousness is not in touch with any quality or characteristic, and therefore can illuminate only those characters which are presented to it through the transparent *vṛtti*; this is why, in the case of the illusion "this is silver," the *vṛtti* implied in the cognition "this" does not manifest the illusory silver, for the manifestation of which a separate *vṛtti* of *avidyā* has to be admitted. The *antaḥkaraṇa-vṛtti*, however, can directly receive the reflection of the pure consciousness and therefore does not require for such a reflection a further *vṛtti*, and there is accordingly no vicious infinite. The function of the *vṛtti* is to manifest the identity of the *jīva*-consciousness and the consciousness underlying the object, without which the relation between the knower and the known as "this is known by me" could not be manifested[1].

Though Brahman is absolutely untouched by anything, yet, since all things are illusorily imposed upon it, it can manifest them all without the aid of *māyā*; this justifies the omniscience of Brahman, and the criticism that the pure Brahman cannot be omniscient is invalid.

Regarding the destruction of the veil of *ajñāna* it may be pointed out that the veiling power of the *ajñāna* pertaining to one individual is destroyed by the functioning of his *vṛtti*, so that he alone can perceive, and not any other individual in whose case the veiling power has not been destroyed. The difference between the veiling power and darkness is this: the veiling power has relation both to the object and to the perceiver, whereas darkness relates only to the object; so that, when darkness is destroyed, all can see, but not so in the case of the veiling power. This refutes the criticism that, if

[1] *jīvacaitanyasyādhiṣṭhāna-caitanyasya vābhedābhivyaktārthatvād vṛtteḥ. anyathā mayedaṃ viditam iti saṃbandhāvabhāso na syāt. Advaita-siddhi*, p. 485.

there is one *ajñāna*, the perception of one object ought to lead to immediate emancipation.

The criticism that, since knowledge must necessarily dispel ignorance, the illusion of silver cannot be destroyed, is invalid; for knowledge destroys ignorance only in the last instance, i.e., only before emancipation. The knowledge of the conch-shell cannot destroy the supreme veiling power of the root *ajñāna* covering the unlimited consciousness, but can only remove the relative *ajñāna* covering the limited consciousness, thereby opening up the consciousness underlying the limited object-forms, and so producing the contradiction of the illusory silver and the intuition of the conch-shell.

The objection that *ajñāna* cannot veil the material objects, because they are not luminous, is quite beside the point; for the Śaṅkarite theory does not assume that the *ajñāna* veils the material objects. Their view is that the veiling relates to the pure consciousness on which all material objects are illusorily imposed. The *ajñāna* veiling the underlying consciousness veils also the material objects the existence of which depends on it, being an imposition upon it. When by the *vṛtti* the ground-consciousness of an object is manifested, the result is not the manifestation of the pure consciousness as such, but of the limited consciousness only so far as concerns its limited form with which the *vṛtti* is in contact. Thus the objection that either the removal of the veil is unnecessary or that in any particular cognition it necessarily implies emancipation is invalid.

Again, the states of the ignorance must be regarded as being identical with it, and the knowledge that is opposed to ignorance is also opposed to them; so the states of *ajñāna* can very well be directly removed by knowledge. The objection that there are many *ajñānas*, and that even if one *ajñāna* is removed there would be others obstructing the manifestation of cognition, is invalid; for, when one *ajñāna* is removed, its very removal is an obstruction to the spread of other *ajñānas* to veil the manifestation, so that, so long as the first *ajñāna* remains removed, the manifestation of the object continues.

An objection is put forward that, the consciousness being itself partless, there cannot be any manifestation of it in part, with reference to certain object-forms only. If it is held that such conditioned manifestation is possible with reference to the conditioning fact of object-forms, then even previous to the existence of definite object-forms there cannot be any *ajñāna*, or, in other words, *ajñāna* cannot exist as a pre-condition, it being only coterminous with definite object-forms. To this Madhusūdana's reply is that the object-forms, being imposition upon pure consciousness and the latter being their ground, the manifestation of consciousness with reference to any object-form depends upon the removal of *ajñāna* with reference to the illusory creation of that object-form imposed upon the ground-consciousness. The *ajñāna* itself does not constitute the object-form; therefore the removal of *ajñāna* has reference not to object-forms as separate and independent entities, but only to the creation of such object-forms imposed upon the ground-consciousness. Thus there is no objection; the existence of *ajñāna* as a pre-condition is such that, when along with itself object-forms are created, the veil on these is removed by the *vṛtti* contact leading to their cognition. The position is that, though the ground-consciousness reveals the object-forms imposed upon it, yet such a revelation takes place only with reference to that perceiver whose *vṛtti* comes into contact with the object, and not with reference to others. The condition of the revelation is that the consciousness underlying the perceiver, the *vṛtti* and the object-form becomes identical, as it were, through the imposition of the *vṛtti* upon the object. This tripartite union being a condition of the manifestation of an object to a particular perceiver, the object, revealed by the ground-consciousness underlying it, is not manifested to other perceivers.

The World as Illusion.

Vyāsa-tīrtha tried to refute the Śaṅkarite theory that the world is an illusory imposition. He contends that, if the world is an illusory creation, it must have a basis (*adhiṣṭhāna*) which in a general manner must be known, and must yet be unknown so far as its special features are concerned. Brahman, however, has no general characteristic, and, since it is devoid of any specific peculiarities, any affirmation that it stands as the entity of which the specific peculiarities are not known would be inadmissible[1]. To this

[1] *adhiṣṭhānatva-sāmānyatve jñāte saty ajñāta-viśeṣavattvasya prayojakatvāt. brahmaṇaḥ sāmānya-dharmopetatvādinā tāvat jñātatvaṃ na saṃbhavati. nissāmānyatvāt. ajñāta-viśeṣavattvaṃ ca na saṃbhavati nirviśeṣatvāṅgīkārāt.* Śrīnivāsa's *Nyāyāmṛta-prakāśa,* on the *Nyāyāmṛta,* p. 234.

Madhusūdana's reply is that a knowledge of the general characteristic of the locus of illusion is by no means indispensable; what is necessary is that the true nature of the object should be known without any of its specific details. In the case of Brahman the nature is self-luminous bliss, but the specific characters of such bliss, as greater or less, and any variation in its quality, are not known; so there is no impropriety in considering Brahman as the locus of illusion. But the defence may be made in another way; for Madhusūdana says that an imaginary general characteristic and special features may well be conceived of Brahman without involving the fallacy of the circle (*anyonyāśraya*), if we assume the beginningless character of all such imaginary qualities. The characters of Brahman as being and bliss may be regarded as generic, and the fullness of the bliss may be regarded as specific. So the quality of existence or being that is found in all things may be regarded as a generic quality of Brahman, on the basis of which the illusions take place in the absence of the specific quality of Brahman as fullness of bliss. The inadequacy of the reply is obvious; for the objection was made on the ground that all illusions are psychological in their nature and are possible only through confusion of individual things, which have both universal and specific qualities, whereas the Brahman, being the absolute, is devoid of all characters on the basis of which any illusion is possible.

Vyāsa-tīrtha in this connection further points out that, if it is suggested that an illusion can remain when there is no cognition antagonistic to illusory perception and that the *ajñāna* in itself is opposed not to the illusion of world-appearance, but to its form as *vṛtti*, the reply is that, since the definition of *ajñāna* is "that which is opposed to consciousness," the above view, which considers that the *ajñāna* is not opposed to consciousness, would hardly justify us in speaking of *ajñāna* as *ajñāna*; for, if it is not opposed to knowledge, it has no right to be so called. Moreover, the self and the not-self, the perceiver and the perceived, are so different from each other, that there is no scope for illusion between them. Thus Vedāntists themselves assert that, among entities that are spatially separated or whose essences are entirely different, the speaker and the person spoken to, there cannot be any possibility of doubt about their identity. Moreover, unless the nature of the locus of illusion is hidden from view, there cannot be an illusion, and the pure consciousness, being always self-manifested, is such that its nature can never be hidden; and so it is difficult to conceive how there can be an illusion. Again, the "self," which is the nature of Brahman, is never associated with the objects of world-appearance, which are always apparent to us as non-self, and, this being so, how can these objects be regarded as an imposition upon the self, as in the case of the illusion of silver, which is always associated with "this" as its locus? The position cannot be justified by saying that all objects of world-appearance are associated with "being," which is the nature of Brahman; for this does not imply that these objects are not imposed upon being as its locus, since in these instances existence appears as a quality of the objects, like colour, but the objects do not appear as illusory qualities imposed upon existence, which should have been the case, if the former are to be regarded as an illusory imposition upon the latter. Nor can it be asserted that the "being" is a self-luminous entity underlying the world-objects; for, if it were so, then these world-objects should have manifested themselves directly through their association with that pure consciousness, and the acceptance of a *vṛtti* would be wholly unnecessary. It is also wrong to say that the manifestation of an object implies that the object is an imposition upon the fact of manifestation; for the latter appears as being only qualitative in relation to the object[1]. It is sometimes suggested that the knowledge of the true basis is not essential for explanation, because even an illusory notion of such a basis is sufficient to explain illusion, and therefore, even if the true basis (Brahman) is not apparent in perception, it is no valid objection to the possibility of illusion. But the reply to such a view is that the infinite occurrences of previous illusion would then be competent to explain present illusion, and there would be no point in admitting the existence of the true Brahman as being the foundation-truth of all illusory appearance; which would land us in Buddhist nihilism[2].

If the world-appearance, which is supposed to be false, is able to exert causal efficiency and behave as real, a thing well attested by scriptural texts affirming the production of sky from the self,

[1] *ghaṭaḥ sphurati tasya ca sphuraṇānubhavatvena ghaṭānubhavatvāyogāt. Nyāyāmṛta*, p. 236.

[2] *Ibid.* p. 237*a*.

then it is clearly different from ordinary illusions, which have no such causal efficiency (*artha-kriyā-kāritva*). Moreover, following the analogy of the conch-shell-silver, which is regarded as false in relation to the silver of the silversmith, one may likewise expect that the world-appearance should be false only in relation to some other real world-appearance; but no such real entities are known.

Again, it is suggested in the *Vivaraṇa* that, though there is no real similarity between Brahman and illusion, yet there is no difficulty in admitting that even without any real similarity there is the world-illusion based upon Brahman through some imaginary similarity. But in reply to these it may be pointed out that such an imaginary similarity can only be supposed to be due to *avidyā*; but *avidyā* itself, being imaginary, will itself depend on some other illusion, and such an illusion would demand another similarity, and thus there would be a vicious circle. It is suggested that illusions are possible even without similarity, as in the case of red crystal; but in reply it may be said, first, that red crystal is a case of a reflection of the red in the crystal and may hence not stand in need of any similarity as the cause of the illusion, whereas in all other cases which are not of this nature an illusion would naturally require some kind of similarity as pre-condition; secondly, here also it may be admitted that the red substance and the crystal substance have this similarity between them, that they are both made up of the same substance, and such a similarity is not admissible between Brahman and the world. Again, it is well known that without the agency of extraneous defect there can be no false knowledge, since otherwise all knowledges may be invalid by themselves. So also there cannot be any illusion without a perceiver able to have both the false knowledge and the right knowledge to contradict it; and for this the presence of the body and the senses are indispensable. In the state of dissolution, though there may be *ajñāna*, yet, there being no body, there cannot be either illusion or right knowledge.

It cannot be suggested that, just as in ordinary illusions of conch-shell-silver, ordinary defects of observation having relative existence are to be admitted, so the world-illusion also is to be explained on the supposition of the existence of such relative defects. The reply to such a suggestion is, that, unless the status of world-illusion is determined, no meaning can be attached to the status of the defects producing the world-appearance, which has a relative existence. The tables cannot be turned on the dualists by supposing that on their side also the reality of the defects, body and senses, can be affirmed only when the non-illusory nature of the world is known, and that the knowledge of the latter is dependent upon that of the former; for knowledge of the reality of the world is to be obtained directly from experience, and not through such a logical quibble. It may also be pointed out that, if the analogy of the conch-shell-silver be pursued, then, since the defects there have the same status as the locus of the illusion, viz., the "this" of the conch-shell, so in the world-illusion also the defects should have the same status as the locus.

Again, if the defects are not regarded as ultimately real, but only as illusory, then it must be admitted that there are in the world no real defects, which would imply that our world-knowledge is valid. The assumption that defect, the body, the senses, etc., are all illusory demands that this be due to the presence of other defects; these in turn must depend on some other defects, and thus we may have a vicious infinite. If the defects are spontaneously imagined in the mind, then the self-validity of knowledge must be sacrificed. If it is urged that the *avidyā* is either beginningless or self-sustained and immediate (like the concept of difference), there is no vicious infinite, the reply is that, if *avidyā* is self-sustained and beginningless, it ought not to depend upon any locus or ground of world-illusion, Brahman, as its *adhiṣṭhāna*. Again, if the experience of *avidyā* be not regarded as due to some defects, it could not be regarded as invalid. But it would be difficult to imagine how *avidyā* could be due to some defect; for then it would have to exist before itself in order to produce itself. Again, the conception that the world is an illusion because it is contradicted is false, because the contradiction itself is again contradicted; this may lead to a vicious infinite, since it cannot be admitted that the knowledge that contradicts is itself contradicted.

Just as in the silver illusion the locus of the illusion has the same kind of existence as the defect, so in the world-illusion also the locus of the illusion might have the same kind of relative existence as the defects; which would mean that Brahman also is relative. Moreover, it is wrong to say that the knowledge of the locus (*adhiṣṭhāna*) of the world-illusion is ultimately real, while the defects have only a relative existence; for such a different treatment would be unjustifiable, unless the defects should be found to be contradicted, whereas it has been shown above that the very concept of contradiction is illegitimate. It cannot be said that the falsehood of the defects constitutes their contradiction; for the concept of defect is unintelligible without the comprehension of falsehood; moreover, in all illusions the knowledge of the locus seems to have no antagonism to the defects which cause the illusion. Therefore there is no reason why, even if the world-appearance be regarded as illusion, the knowledge of the Brahman as the locus of the illusion should be able to dispel the defect which has produced it. Therefore, just as the Brahman is real, so the defects are also real. If bondage were absolutely false, no one would have tried to be liberated from it; for that which is non-existent cannot come into being. Again, if the bondage itself were an illusory imposition upon Brahma, it could not be expected that the intuitional knowledge of Brahman should be able to dispel it. Moreover, the supposition that the world-appearance is illusion is directly contradicted in most of the *sūtras* of the *Brahma-sūtra*, e.g., the definition of Brahman as "that which causes the birth, sustenance and dissolution of the world." So, from whichever way we can look at it, the supposition that the world-process is illusory is found to be wholly illogical.

Madhusūdana's contention that the position that an illusion is possible only when the locus is hidden only so far as its special features are concerned holds good in the case of world-illusion also; for, though Brahman is manifest so far as its nature as pure being is concerned, it is hidden in regard to its nature as fullness of bliss. The condition that illusion is only possible when there is no knowledge contradicting the illusion holds good in the case of world-illusion; for the knowledge that contradicts the *ajñāna* constituting the world illusion must be of the nature of a *vṛtti* cognition. Thus, so long as there is no *vṛtti* cognition of the pure nature of Brahman, there is no cognition contradicting the world-cognition; for the pure consciousness in its own nature is not opposed to *ajñāna*. The objection that the distinction between the perceiver and the perceived, the self and the non-self, is so obvious that one cannot be mistaken for the other, is met by Madhusūdana with the supposition that in the case of the silver-illusion also the difference between the presented "this" and the unpresented "that" (silver) is known and yet there is an illusion. Moreover, the difference conceived in a particular manner cannot thwart the imposition of identification of any two entities in other forms; thus, though the opposition between the perceiver and the perceived, self and the not-self, is quite obvious in this particular form, yet the distinction between "being" and "jug" is not at all apparent; for the notion of the jug is permeated through and through by the notion of being, so that there is no difficulty in conceiving the possibility of false identification between the being and the jug[1]. Moreover, nature as being is an object of all cognition, so that, though formless like time, it can well be conceived to be an object of visual perception, like time[2].

The world-illusions occur in a successive series, the later ones being similar to the previous ones. This is all the condition that is needed; it is not at all necessary that the illusory forms that are imposed should also be real. It is sufficient that there should be a cognition of certain forms giving place to certain other forms. What is necessary for a silver-illusion is that there should be a knowledge of silver; that the silver should also be real is quite unimportant and accidental. So the reality of the world-appearance as an entity is never the condition of such an illusion. The objection that, following the same analogy, it may also be contended that the reality of the locus of illusion is quite uncalled-for and that an awareness of such a locus is all that is needed in explaining an illusion, is invalid; for the locus of illusion is not the cause of illusion through awareness of it, but through ignorance of it. Moreover, if the reality of the locus of reality is not demanded as a pre-condition of illusion, contradiction of illusion will be meaningless; for the latter dispels only the illusory notion regarding a real entity.

The objection that, if the world-illusion is capable of practical efficiency and behaviour, it cannot be regarded as invalid, is untenable; for dreams also have some kind of practical efficiency. The story in the scriptural texts of the creation of the sky from the self need not lead us to think of the reality of such scriptural texts; for the scriptures speak of the dream-creations also. The objection

[1] *na hi rūpāntareṇa bheda-graho rūpāntareṇādhyāsa-virodhī. san-ghaṭa ityādi-pratyaye ca sad-rūpasyātmano ghaṭādy-anuvidhāyatayā bhānān na tasya ghaṭādy-adhyāsādhiṣṭhānā-nupapattiḥ. Advaita-siddhi,* p. 495.

[2] *sad-rūpeṇa ca sarva-jñāna-viṣayatopapatter na rūpādi-hīnasyāpy ātmanaḥ kālasyeva cākṣusatvādy anupapattiḥ. Ibid.* p. 495.

that, if the root-impression of illusion at the beginning of creation be due to those of other cycles, then the root-impressions of previous birth ought to manifest themselves in each and every experience of this life, is invalid; for not all root-impressions of previous birth are manifested in this life, and the agency of such root-impressions in influencing the experiences of this life, as in the case of the instinctive desire of the baby to suck its mother's breasts, is to be accepted in those cases where they do in fact occur. So also the objection that illusion cannot be due to the root-impressions of one's own wrong imagination, because before the erroneous perception takes place there cannot be root-impressions of illusory perceptions, and therefore the existence of the illusory world existent as a prior fact and a pre-condition of one's illusory perceptions, cannot be regarded as valid; for it is just the nature of things that is responsible for two kinds of illusions such that, though bangles can be made out of the illusory silver in the silversmith's shop, nothing can be done with the illusory silver in the conch-shell. So the root-impressions of one's own illusion may act as constituent stuff of the illusion of the world-appearance, and even before the occurrence of such illusory experience of the world-appearance the stuff of the world-appearance, derived from the root-impression of one's own illusion, may already be objectively there as a pre-condition of the illusory perception. The objection that, since illusory perceptions must have as their pre-condition a similarity between the entities falsely identified, and since also no such similarity can be traced between Brahman and the world-appearance, there cannot be any false identification between them, is invalid; first, because *avidyā*, being beginningless, does not stand in need of any similarity. Secondly, the supposition that similarity is an essential pre-condition of illusion is likewise false; for even in those cases where similarity seems to induce illusion it does so by generating a mental state congenial to production of illusion, and, if such a mental state is produced in other ways, say as a fruit of one's own *karma* and *adṛṣṭa*, the necessity that the similarity should behave as a pre-condition vanishes, and so the indispensable character of similarity as a pre-condition to illusion cannot be admitted. Invalid also is the objection that, if there may be an illusion without defect, then that means that all cognitions are by themselves invalid and that, if illusions be regarded as due to defects, then defects also are results of illusory impositions, and thus there will be a vicious infinite; for illusion through beginningless *avidyā* does not belong to defects, and, though illusions which have a temporal beginning are due to the beginningless *avidyā*-defect, this does not render all cognitions invalid, since only illusions which have a temporal beginning are due to the defect of *avidyā*, and, since *avidyā* itself is beginningless, it cannot stand in need of any defects, and so there cannot be any vicious infinite. It must be borne in mind that, though illusion in time is due to defects, or *doṣa*, the beginningless defect of *avidyā*, it is not necessarily due to any such defect, and therefore stands directly and spontaneously as an illusory creative agent; and is called illusion, not because it is produced by defects, but because it is contradicted by Brahma-knowledge. Thus the objection that *avidyā* is due to defect, and defect is due to *avidyā*, is invalid; that which is a product of defects is bound to be contradicted; but the converse of this is not necessarily true.

It cannot be urged that, if *avidyā* is independent of *doṣa*, the world-illusion may be regarded as independent of the locus or basis of illusion, viz., the Brahman; for, though the basis of illusion may not be regarded as producing illusion, it has to be regarded as the support and ground thereof and also as its illuminator[1].

Again, the objection that illusion must depend on sense-functioning, on the existence of the body, is invalid; for these are necessary only for intuitive perception. But in the cases of illusion, of the imposition of the *avidyā* upon the pure consciousness, the latter is the spontaneous reflector of the *avidyā* creations, and so for the purpose there is no necessity of the sense-functioning.

Again, it is urged that, since the defects are imaginary impositions, the negation of defects becomes real, and therefore the defects, being unreal, cannot render the knowledge of world-appearance unreal; and, if this is so, the world-appearance being real, this would be our admission of reality (as an illustration of this, it is urged that the criticism of the Buddhists against the Vedas, being invalid and illusory, cannot stultify the validity of the Vedas). To this the reply is that the criticism of the defects pointed out against the Vedas by the Buddhists is illusory, because the defects are only imagined by them; the Vedas are not affected

[1] *Advaita-siddhi*, p. 498.

by this, because their truth is affirmed by our practical experience. The defects imagined are not therefore coterminous with the reality of the Vedas; the defect of *avidyā* and the manifold world-appearance have the same kind of existence—one is the effect of the other; and thus, if the defects are illusory, their product (the world) also becomes illusory, and so the illusory nature of defects does not prove the reality of the world. The world-appearance is called relatively true only because it is not contradicted by anything else except the Brahma-knowledge. Its relative character therefore does not depend upon the determination of the nature of falsehood, which in its turn might be conceived to be determinable by the nature of the world as relative, thus involving a vicious nature of dependence[1]. It is urged that the reality of the defects is directly grasped by the senses, and that therefore they can behave as the cause of error only if they are ultimately real; to this the reply is that the existence of the defects can be grasped only by the senses, but that they will never be contradicted at any time (*traikālikā-bādhyatva*) can never be ascertained on any intuitive basis, and so the reality of the defects can never be affirmed. It must always be borne in mind that the defects have never the same status as pure consciousness, upon which illusory conch-shell is imposed. Nor can it be said that the knowledge which contradicts the world-appearance is real on the ground that, if it were not real, it would require some other knowledge to contradict it and this would land us in a vicious infinite; for this final contradiction of world-appearance may well be regarded as contradicting itself also, for the very simple reason that the content of this contradiction applies to the whole range of the knowable, and this final contradiction, being itself within the field of the knowable, is included within the contradiction. It is urged that, if bondage is false in the sense that it is at all times non-existent, there is no reason why anyone should be anxious to remove that which is already non-existent; to this the reply is that the true (Brahman) can never cease to exist—the falsity of the bondage means that it is an entity which is liable to cease immediately on the direct intuition of the basic truth. It is like the case of a man who has forgotten that he has his necklace round his neck and is anxiously searching for it, and who the instant he is reminded of it gives up his search. It is wrong to suppose that,

[1] *Ibid.* p. 499.

because no effort could be directed towards the chimerical, which is non-existent at all times, therefore no effort could be made for the removal of the illusory; for, though the illusory and the chimerical may be in agreement so far as their non-existence at all times is concerned, there is no reason why these two should agree in other respects also. The concept of the cessation of the bondage may not have any other content than the intuition of the real, or it may be regarded as indefinable or of an entirely unique nature. The illusory bondage and the world-appearance can cease only when the basic truth, the Brahman, is intuited, just as the silver illusion ceases with the knowledge of the conch-shell on which it is imposed. The objection that some of the *sūtras* of Bādarāyaṇa imply the existence of a realistic world is invalid, if it is remembered that the import of those *sūtras* merely points to the existence of a relative order of things which ceases entirely as soon as the basic truth on which they are imposed is known.

The *dṛṣṭi-sṛṣṭi* view is the supposition that the existence of all things consists in their being perceived. Vyāsatīrtha says that, if things existed only so long as they are perceived, then they would be only momentary; and so all the objections against Buddhist momentariness, to the effect that they do not admit the permanence of things as attested by recognition, might equally well be levelled against the Śaṅkarites themselves. To this Madhusūdana's reply is that, though the existence of objects as realities is not admitted, yet their existence in the causal state, as *ajñāna*, is on this view not denied; this would be its difference from the Buddhist position, which does not admit any such causal existence of things.

If the world-objects have no existence outside their perception, then they are plainly independent of definite causes, and, if that is so, then the definite cause-and-effect relation between sacrifices and their fruits, and the import of all the Vedāntic texts regarding definite cause and effect, are meaningless. To this Madhusūdana's reply is that the specification of cause-and-effect relation in the scriptures and the experience of them in mundane life is like cause and effect in dreams; these dream-causes and their effects also have a certain order among themselves, known by contradiction in experiences.

It is objected that on the *dṛṣṭi-sṛṣṭi* view (that the objects do not exist prior to perception) world-experience is inexplicable. It would be difficult also to explain how, if the "this" which forms a basis of illusion is not already there outside us, there can be any sense-relation to it and to the foundation of the illusory image. To this Madhusūdana's reply is that the ordinary explanation of illusion depending upon sense-relation and other conditions is only an explanation for people of the lower order. For people of the higher order the definition of illusion would be "the manifestation of a true entity in association with a false one," and such a definition would hold good even on the *dṛṣṭi-sṛṣṭi* view. The consciousness underlying the "this" is a substance, and the false silver is manifested in association with it.

It is further objected that at the time of the illusory perception ("this is silver"), if there is no conch-shell as an objective fact, then the illusion cannot be explained, as is generally done, as effect of ignorance about the conch-shell. The reply is that, even if the conch-shell is absent, the *ajñāna* that forms its stuff is there. To the objection that the two perceptions "this is silver" and "this is not silver" are directed to two different perceptions and do not refer to one common objective fact, and that therefore neither of them can be regarded as the contradiction of the other, since such a contradiction is only possible when two affirmations refer to one and the same objective fact—the reply is that on the analogy of dream-experiences the contradiction is possible here also. Vyāsatīrtha further says that, since the contradiction of an illusion is not an objective fact, but a mere perception, it has no better status than the illusory perception and therefore cannot be regarded as necessarily truer than the illusion which it is supposed to contradict. He further says that in dreamless sleep and in dissolution, since there is no differential perception as between Brahman and the *jīva*, such a difference between Brahman and the *jīva* ceases in each dreamless sleep and in each cyclic dissolution. Thus in the absence of difference between Brahman and the *jīva* there cannot be at the end of each dreamless sleep and dissolution any return to world-experience. In the case of a person who is sleeping and whose root-impressions on that account are not perceivable (and are therefore non-existent), there is no explanation how the world-experience may again be started. Emancipation also, being only a perception, cannot have a better status of existence than the world-experience; moreover, if the pure consciousness appeared as all the world-objects, then there could not have been any time when such objects could remain unmanifested.

To this Madhusūdana's reply is that the relation of *jīva* and Brahman, being beginningless, does not depend upon perception; in dreamless sleep, though the root-impressions vanish as effect, they still remain in their causal character; emancipation also, being of the nature of Brahman, has the pure intuitive character of perception.

An objection is urged that, if pure consciousness is the intuition of objects, then they should always be manifested. To this the reply is that perception here means the manifestation of consciousness through a *vṛtti* which does not stand in need of further *vṛtti* for its relation to consciousness; the possibility of illusion without bodies can well be explained by analogy with dreams. Again, the objection that, since the perception is as much an illusory intuition as the object of which it is conceived to be the essence, the object in itself ceases to have its essence as mere intuition, is invalid; because, though the perception has no other existence than the intuition itself, that is no bar to the conception of the object as having no essence but perception. An objection may again be raised that recognition shows permanent existence of objects; but reply to it may easily be found in the illustration of dream-experiences, and also in the possibility of accidental agreement between the mis-perception of different perceivers. The objection that the notion of identity of Brahman and *jīva*, being itself mental, cannot contradict duality is invalid; for the notion of such identity is identical with the self and therefore cannot be called mental. Again, the intuition of the ultimate truth cannot itself be called invalid because it is mental; for its validity depends upon the fact that it is never contradicted.

CHAPTER XXX

CONTROVERSY BETWEEN THE DUALISTS AND THE MONISTS (CONTINUED)

A Refutation of the definition of Avidyā (nescience).

Avidyā is defined as that beginningless positive entity which is removable by knowledge. The objection to this, as given by Vyāsa-tīrtha, is, first, that, the objects of the world being in time, the ignorance that limits the consciousness underlying it cannot be beginningless. Moreover, since according to the Vedāntist negation has no constituent material stuff as its material cause, *ajñāna* cannot be regarded as its cause. Even on the assumption of illusory negation *ajñāna*, which is regarded as being in its nature positive, cannot be regarded as its cause; for, if negation has for its cause a positive entity, then the unreal may have the real as its cause. Again, if *ajñāna* is not the cause of the negation, then knowledge ought not to be able to dispel it, and the negation of a jug should not be liable to cease on its negation. Again, on the Śaṅkarite view the *ajñāna* is supposed to veil the object; we cannot have any cognition of Brahman, because it is hidden by *ajñāna*. They also hold that the *vṛtti* knowledge cannot intuit Brahman. If that is so, then in the last emancipatory knowledge through *vṛtti* there is no intuition of Brahman; without this the *ajñāna* concealing Brahman cannot be removed, and hence emancipation is impossible. Again, if it is supposed that the *ajñāna* is removed, then in the *jīvan-mukti* state the saint ought to have no experience of worldly things.

Again, it must be admitted that knowledge removes *ajñāna* directly and spontaneously, without waiting for the assistance of any accessory cause; for otherwise, when a thing is known, its ignorance would not have vanished spontaneously with it. But, if that were so, then in cases where an *ajñāna* is associated with certain conditions, the removal of the *ajñāna* would not stand in need of the removal of the conditions also together with it. What is to be expected is that the *ajñāna* should be removed irrespective of the removal of the conditions, and this is not admitted. Again, if it is held that the removal of the conditions is awaited, then pure consciousness cannot be regarded as capable of removing *avidyā* directly. Again, if knowledge can directly and spontaneously remove *ajñāna*, then it is useless to restrict the scope by saying that it removes only the beginningless *ajñāna*. The restriction is imposed in order to distinguish the cosmic *avidyā* from the phenomenal *avidyā* of silver-illusion, and if the spontaneous removal of *ajñāna* serves in both places, there is no utility in restricting the scope. It cannot be said that the epithet "beginningless" is given to *ajñāna* because it is the product of beginningless illusory imposition through defects; for it has already been pointed out that such a view would lead to a vicious infinite, because there can be no defect without *avidyā*. Again, *ajñāna* cannot be beginningless, because whatever is different from knowledge and also from negation cannot be beginningless like the illusory silver. Again, it is wrong to define *ajñāna* as positive; for on the Śaṅkarite view *ajñāna* is different from both positive and negative, and therefore cannot be negative. If an entity is not positive, it must be negative; for, being different from positive, it cannot also be different from negative. Again, if there is an entity which is not a negation and has no beginning, it is not capable of being negated, but has an unnegatived existence like the self. The self also cannot be designated by any predicate explaining its positiveness, except that it is not negated. It has been pointed out in the *Vivaraṇa* that it is immaterial whether an entity is beginningless or has a beginning; for in either case it may be destructible, provided that there is sufficient cause for its destruction. The general inference that a beginningless positive entity cannot cease has its exception in the special case of *ajñāna*, which would cease to exist with the dawn of *jñāna*. If it is urged that, since *ajñāna* is both beginningless and different from negation, it ought to persist eternally, like the self, it may also be urged on the opposite side that, since *ajñāna* is different also from "positive," it ought to be liable to destruction, like negation-precedent-to-production. To this the reply is that the inference is that no beginningless positive entity is confronted with anything which can oppose or destroy it. Any refutation of this argument must take the form of citing an instance where the concomitance fails, and not of any mere opposite assertion. No instance can be adduced to illustrate the assertion that the beginningless *ajñāna* can be removed by *jñāna*; for the removal of ignorance by knowledge is always with reference to such ignorance as has a beginning in time, as in the case of silver-illusion. So all that could be said would be that whatever opposes ignorance destroys it, and such a general statement has no special application to the case of the supposed beginningless *ajñāna*. Again, if *ajñāna* is regarded as different from positive entity, then it is like negation, and its cessation would mean position once more. Again, *ajñāna* (or ignorance) cannot have any existence apart from its perception, and, since *ajñāna* has always as its basis the pure consciousness, its perception can never be negative, so that it can never cease to exist[1]. Moreover, if *ajñāna* is false in the sense that it is non-existent in the locus in which it appears, it cannot be destroyed by knowledge. No one thinks that the illusory silver is destroyed by the perception of the conch-shell.

The second alternative definition of *ajñāna* is that it is the material cause of illusion. But according to the Śaṅkarite theory that there are different *ajñānas* corresponding to the different *jñānas*, the knowledge of the conch-shell would remove ignorance of it, and the knowledge of a negation would remove ignorance of it; but in neither of these cases can ignorance be defined as a constituent of illusion. Negation, in itself, has no constituent material cause, and thus it cannot have *ajñāna* as a constituent.

There is a Śaṅkarite view that *māyā* is the material cause of the world and Brahman is its locus. On such a view, *māyā* or *ajñāna* being the material cause of the world, and illusion (*bhrama*) being a part of the world, *ajñāna* becomes a constituent cause of *bhrama*, and not *vice versa*. On the other view, that both Brahma and *māyā* are causes of the world-appearance, *māyā* cannot by itself become the cause of illusion. Moreover, an illusion, being itself different from a positive entity, is more like negation and cannot have any constituent material of its own, and so it cannot itself be the constituent material of *ajñāna*. Moreover, on the Śaṅkarite view, the illusory object, "having no being" (*sad-vilakṣaṇatvena*), has no constituent, and so the illusory cannot be a constituent of *ajñāna*. If anything is to be a constituent of anything, it must be positively existing, and not merely different from non-existents. Again, whenever anything is a material stuff of other things, the former appears as a constant factor of the latter; but neither the illusory

[1] *pratīti-mātra-śarīrasya ajñānasya yāvat sva-viṣaya-dhī-rūpa-sākṣi-sattvam anuvṛtti-niyamena nivṛtty-ayogāc ca. Nyāyāmṛta*, p. 304.

silver nor its knowledge appears as *ajñāna*. Thus the two definitions of *ajñāna* fail.

In reply to this Madhusūdana says that the *ajñāna* which forms the stuff of the illusory silver is the beginningless *ajñāna*. The *ajñāna* is called positive in the sense that it is different from the negative. It is for this reason that the *ajñāna* which is regarded as the material stuff of the illusory negation can be regarded as different from negation, and therefore it can be regarded as constituent of the illusory negation. It is by no means true that the effect must be of exactly the same stuff as the cause. Things which are absolutely similar in nature or absolutely dissimilar cannot be related to each other as cause and effect; it is for this reason that truth cannot be the material stuff of untruth. For in that case, since truth never ceases to manifest itself, and never suffers change, untruth also would never cease to manifest itself. The truth, however, can behave as the cause of untruth in the sense that it remains as the basis of the illusory changes of the untruth. It is wrong also to suppose that, since the *ajñāna* of Brahman cannot be removed through a *vṛtti*, which itself is a manifestation of *ajñāna*, Brahma-knowledge itself becomes impossible; for, so far as Brahman is a content, this *ajñāna* (as content) can be removed by a *vṛtti*. In the case of *jīvan-mukti*, though the ultimate cessation may be delayed through absence of the obstructive factors of the right *karmas* of the past and other conditions, these may well be regarded as liable to cessation through knowledge. Certain causes may produce certain effects; but that such production may be delayed for some reason does not invalidate the causal character of the cause. It is well admitted by the Śaṅkarites that knowledge directly removes *ajñāna*, the removal being itself a part of *ajñāna*.

It is wrong to suppose that whatever is imaginary must necessarily be an idea due to defects or must have a temporal beginning; but it must be a product which is simultaneous with the imagination that produces it[1].

It is also wrong to suppose that, if any entity is not positive, it must be negative or that, if it is not negative, it must be positive; for there is always scope for a third alternative, viz., that which is neither positive nor negative. According to the Śaṅkarites the

[1] *kalpitatva-mātraṃ hi na doṣa-janya-dhī-mātra-śarīratve sāditve vā tantram. kiṃtu prātibhāsa-kalpaka-samānakālīna-kalpakattvaṃ. Advaita-siddhi*, p. 544.

principle of the excluded middle is a false premiss of logic, and thus they admit the possibility of an extra-logical category, that which is neither positive nor negative. The supposed inference that beginningless positive entity must necessarily be permanent, like the self, is false; for it is only in the case of self that beginningless positive entity is found eternally to persist.

It is also wrong to suppose that, since *ajñāna* is always manifested through pure consciousness, it can never cease to exist; for there is no law that whatever is manifested by the *sākṣi*-consciousness must remain during the whole period while the *sākṣi* persists; so there is no incongruity in supposing that the *ajñāna* ceases, while the *sākṣi*-consciousness persists. Moreover, the *avidyā* that becomes manifested is so only through the *sākṣi*-consciousness as modified or limited by it; such a limited consciousness may cease to exist with the cessation of the *avidyā*. It is also wrong to suppose that through the operation of the *vṛtti* the *avidyā* ceases to exist; for even in such cases it persists in its subtle causal form.

When *avidyā* is defined as being constituted of the stuff of illusion (*bhramopādāna*), what is meant is that it is changing and material. It is not necessary to suppose also that a cause and effect must necessarily be positive; for the self, which is a positive entity, is neither a cause nor an effect. What constitutes the defining characteristic of a material cause is that it is continuous with all its effects (*anvayi-kāraṇatvam upādānatve tantram*); and what is an effect must necessarily have a beginning in time. A negation-precedent-to-production of knowledge cannot be regarded as the material cause of illusion; for such negation can only produce the correlative positive entity with which it is connected. It cannot therefore be the cause of production of illusion; so there is no incongruity in supposing that *ajñāna* or illusion, neither of which is real, are related to each other as cause and effect. It is also not correct to contend that a material cause should always be found to persist as a perceivable continuous constituent of all its effects; the colour of the material cause of a jug is not found in the jug. The fact that, when the *ajñāna* is removed with the knowledge of the conch-shell, no illusion is experienced, is no proof that *ajñāna* is not a constituent of illusion. Not all things that are related as cause and effect are always experienced as such. Thus the definitions of *ajñāna* as *anādi-bhāva-rūpatve sati jñāna-nivartyatvam* or as *bhramopādānatvam* are valid.

Perception of ajñāna (ignorance).

The Śaṅkarites urge that *ajñāna* can be directly intuited by perception and that therefore its existence is attested by perception. In regard to this Vyāsa-tīrtha says that what is regarded as perception of ignorance as a positive entity is nothing more than negation of knowledge. Thus the substratum of the ego (*aham-artha*) is not admitted to be a support of the positive entity of ignorance. The apperception "I am ignorant" is to be explained therefore as being the experience of absence of knowledge and not of a positive ignorance (*ajñāna*). Again, since neither pleasure, pain, nor the illusory entities cognized in illusion are directly manifested by the *sākṣi*-consciousness, absence of such knowledge (e.g., "I do not know pleasure," "I do not know pain," "I do not know conch-shell-silver") is to be explained as negation of knowledge and not as due to an experience of positive ignorance. So also, when one says "I do not know what you say," there is only an experience of negation of knowledge and not of positive ignorance. In mediate knowledge also, since the illumination does not proceed by direct removal of the veil of *ajñāna* from the face of the object, the theory that all knowledge which does not involve the removal of *ajñāna* involves an intuition of positive ignorance would land us into the position that, when something is known in mediate knowledge, one should feel as if he did not know it, since no *ajñāna* is directly removed here.

On the Śaṅkarite view it is not admitted that there is any veil covering material objects; consequently the explanation of the experience of ignorance in such cases as "I do not know what you say" is to be found in the supposition, not of a positive ignorance, but of absence of knowledge. It may be contended that, though there may not be any *ajñāna* veiling the objects, yet these very material creations represent the creative (*vikṣepa*) part of *ajñāna* and so the experience of the unknown objects represents an experience of positive *ajñāna*, since *ajñāna* creations do not always arrest knowledge. Thus, for instance, when a jug is known as a jug, if someone says that it is a cloth and not a jug, that does not produce a confusion in the perceiver of the jug, though the delusive words of the speaker must be supposed to produce a false impression—a *vikṣepa* of *ajñāna*. It will be shown later that the experience "I do not know" with reference to a material object does not refer to pure consciousness as limited by material qualities[1]. On the view which admits the *vṛtti* in order to explain the reflection of pure consciousness no *ajñāna* can be admitted as veiling the consciousness under material limitations. Moreover, if the experience "I am ignorant" (*aham ajñaḥ*) is explained as being a direct intuition of *ajñāna* and, as such, different from the experience "there is no knowledge in me" (*mayi jñānaṃ nāsti*), then the two propositions "the ground without the jug" and "there is no jug in the ground" are different in meaning, which is absurd; for certainly the two propositions do not differ in meaning, any more than any other two propositions, e.g., "I have a desire" and "I have no antipathy." There is no difference between the two concepts of absence of knowledge and ignorance. Again, when one is engaged in Vedāntic discipline for the attainment of Brahma-knowledge, there is at that time the negation-precedent-to-the-production of Brahma-knowledge; for, if it were not so, then there would be the Brahma-knowledge and there would be no necessity for Vedāntic discipline. Now a negation-precedent-to-production cannot be known without the knowledge of the entity to which it refers. If this is admitted, then without the knowledge of Brahman there cannot be any knowledge of its negation-precedent-to-production; and, if there is knowledge, then Brahman becomes known, and, if it is considered that such a negation of Brahma-knowledge is known as a positive entity by direct intuition (as it would be on the theory of the direct intuition of *ajñāna*), then Brahman also would be known directly at the stage of the negation precedent to it, which is self-contradictory.

Moreover, the concept of *ajñāna* is clearly that of negation of knowledge, as in the sentence "I do not know." Even in cases when one says "I am ignorant" the sense of negation is apparent, though there is no negative particle. The *Vivaraṇa* also admits the opposition of *ajñāna* to knowledge; and, if this were admitted, then with the knowledge of such opposition there would not be knowledge of ignorance as a positive entity, and without such knowledge of opposition there will be no knowledge of *ajñāna*, that being the

[1] *jaḍe na jānāmīty anubhavasya jaḍāvacchinnaṃ caitanyaṃ viṣaya iti cen na, nirasiṣyamāṇatvāt. Nyāyāmṛta*, p. 309(*c*).

essential concept of *ajñāna*. Even a negation of knowledge which has a reference to the object of which there is the negation may also have no such reference when it is taken up as being itself an object of the enquiry of knowledge. Thus there is no way in which *ajñāna* can be regarded as anything but a negation of knowledge; and the supposition that *ajñāna*, though in its analytical concept it involves two constituents—knowledge and its negation—yet is only a name for a positive concept which does not involve these constituents, is wrong[1]. If *ajñāna* can be removed by *vṛtti* knowledge, it is unnecessary to suppose that it has any other meaning different from that involved in its constituent negative particle qualifying knowledge. Experience also shows that *ajñāna* has no other meaning than the negation of knowledge; so, unless the entity which is the defining reference of *ajñāna* is known, there cannot be any knowledge of *ajñāna*. But such a defining reference being Brahma-knowledge which has no *ajñāna* associated with it, the inclusion of the defining reference would make the concept impossible: hence there cannot be any knowledge of *ajñāna*[2].

The reply made by the Śaṅkarites is that the defining reference of *ajñāna* is Brahma-knowledge and this Brahma-knowledge as *sākṣi*-consciousness, being the manifester of *ajñāna*, is not opposed to it; for it is only the *vṛtti* shade mind that is opposed to *ajñāna*. So, there being no opposition between the Brahma-knowledge as *sākṣi*-consciousness and the *ajñāna*, it is quite possible to have a knowledge of *ajñāna* in spite of the fact that Brahma-knowledge becomes in a sense its constituent as a defining reference. But it may be pointed out in reply that the awareness of Brahma-knowledge is the *sākṣi*-consciousness; the experience "I do not know" is a negation of *vṛtti* knowledge and, as such, it may be referred to the *sākṣi*-consciousness even when there is no *vṛtti* knowledge. Thus the solution in the theory that *ajñāna* is nothing but negation of knowledge would be just the same as in the theory of *ajñāna* as positive entity. If it is contended that, though denial of knowledge may be related to the defining reference in a general manner, yet it may, in its specific form, appear as a mere positive ignorance

[1] *jñānābhāvo'pi hi prameyatvādinājñāne pratiyogy-ādi-jñānānapekṣa etena nipuṇe kuśalādi-śabdavat bhāva-rūpa-jñāne ajñānaśabdo rūḍha iti nirastam. Nyāyāmṛta*, p. 312.

[2] *api ca bhāva-rūpājñānāvacchedaka-viṣayasyājñāne ajñāna-jñānāyogāt jñāne ca ajñānasaivābhāvāt kathaṃ bhāva-rūpājñānajñānaṃ. Ibid.* p. 313.

without involving such an explicit relation to the defining reference —to this the reply is that, even if this contention is admitted, it does not lend any support to the admission of a positive ignorance; for even in the case of a negation of knowledge one may well admit that, though it may be generally related to a defining reference, yet in any specific case it may not always involve such a reference. It is further urged by some that an entity may be known directly and that such knowledge may not involve always the specific defining relations of that entity; it is only the latter type of knowledge which makes doubt impossible. But the fact that there may be doubt regarding an object that is known shows clearly that an object may be known without its specific and negative relations being manifested at the same time.

Moreover, if *ajñāna* cannot be grasped by the *vṛtti* knowledge, then there also cannot be any possibility of inference regarding *ajñāna*. When one says "you do not know the secret," the hearer to whom the secret is presented through a mediate cognitional state would not be able to have the awareness of the *ajñāna*, if the *ajñāna* could not be presented through a *vṛtti* cognition. It cannot be said that the mediate cognitional state is not opposed to *ajñāna*; for, if that were so, then even when an entity was known through a mediate cognition he might have had the experience that he did not know it. It is admitted by the Śaṅkarites that the *vṛtti* of direct intuition through perception is opposed to *ajñāna*; and, if *vṛtti* of mediate cognition also is opposed to *ajñāna*, then there is no mental state through which *ajñāna* can be known.

The experience in deep dreamless sleep, "I did not know anything so long," also refers to absence of knowledge, and not to any positive ignorance. It cannot be said that, since at that time all other knowledge has ceased (there being no awareness of the perceiver or of any other content), there cannot be any awareness regarding the absence of knowledge; for the objection would be the same with regard to the experience of positive ignorance. If it is urged that in that state *ajñāna* is experienced directly as a positive entity, but its relationing with regard to its special defining reference becomes apparent in the waking state, the same explanation may equally well be given if the experience in the dreamless sleep be regarded as being that of absence of knowledge; for negation of knowledge may also be experienced as a knowable entity without any relation to its defining reference; or the so-called experience of ignorance may be explained as an inference of the absence of knowledge, in the dreamless state, made from physical and physiological conditions in the waking state. In the Śaṅkarite view also, since the ego cannot be experienced in that state, the experience "I did not know anything" must be regarded as being in some sense illusory. If it is urged that in the dreamless state *ajñāna*, being reflected through a state of *avidyā* (*avidyā-vṛtti*), is intuited by the *sākṣi*-consciousness, then it might equally well be intuited in the same manner in the waking state also. If it is regarded as being intuited directly by the *sākṣi*-consciousness, then, being an eternal cognition, it would have no root-impression (*saṃskāra*) and could not be remembered. Moreover, if it is not agreed that the absence of knowledge in the dreamless state is a matter of inference from conditions in the waking state, then the absence of knowledge in the dreamless state cannot in any other way be proved; for it cannot be inferred from a positive *ajñāna*, since the negation of knowledge, being material (*jaḍa*), has no *ajñāna* associated with it as a veiling factor. Moreover, if from *ajñāna*, a positive entity, the negation of knowledge can always be inferred, then from the negation of attachment in the dreamless state positive antipathy will have to be inferred. Thus the *ajñāna* can never be regarded as being susceptible of direct intuition.

Madhusūdana's reply is that, though the ego perceived cannot be a support of the *ajñāna*, yet, since the *antaḥkaraṇa* in its causal form is falsely identified with the pure consciousness which is the support of the *ajñāna*, the *ajñāna* appears to be associated with the ego perceived. This explains the experience in the dreamless sleep, "I did not know anything." In the case of the experience "I do not know the jug" also, though there cannot be any veil on the jug, yet, since *ajñāna* has for its support consciousness limited by the jug-form, there is the appearance that the jug-form itself is the object of the veil of *ajñāna*. The objection that in the mediated cognition, there being the veil of *ajñāna* on the object, there ought to be the negation of awareness is also invalid; for, when the *ajñāna* is removed from the knower, the enlightenment of knowledge cannot be obstructed by the presence of the *ajñāna* in the object.

The objection of Vyāsa-tīrtha that *ajñāna* is only a negation of knowledge and that therefore, instead of admitting *ajñāna* as existing as a positive entity in the perceiver, it is better to admit the negation of knowledge only, is invalid; for the experience of negation of knowledge is invalid in this form, because negation implies the defining reference as a constituent. In order to know that "there is no knowledge in me" there must be a knowledge of knowledge in me, which is self-contradictory. The experience of negation of knowledge in the perceiver without involving any relation to a defining reference can only be valid in the case of positive *ajñāna*. A specific negation can never appear as a universal negation; for, if this were admitted, then even when there is a particular book on the table there may be an experience of there being no book on the table; since according to the proposed theory of the opponent a specific negation of this or that book is to appear as universal negation. Madhusūdana urges that what constitutes the difference between negations is not a difference between negations *per se*, but is due to the difference among the defining references which are a constituent in them. It is thus impossible that the experience of one's ignorance could be explained on the supposition that such an experience referred to experience of negation; for it has already been shown that such negation can be neither specific nor universal. So the experience of ignorance is to be regarded as the experience of a positive entity.

It may however be contended that the concept of *ajñāna* also involves a reference by way of opposition to knowledge and thus implies knowledge as its constituent, so that all the objections raised against the concept of negation apply equally well to the concept of *ajñāna*. The reply is that on the Śaṅkarite view the pure *sākṣi*-consciousness grasps at the same time both *ajñāna* and the object as veiled by it without consequent destruction or contraction of either of them. Thus there is no chance of any self-contradiction; for the awareness of *ajñāna* does not involve any process which negates it[1]. If it is contended by the opponent that in the case of the awareness of negation also a similar reply is possible (on the assumption that the object of negation is directly known by the *sākṣi*-consciousness), Madhusūdana's reply is that, since *ajñāna* can be known by *sākṣi*-consciousness, its defining reference is also

[1] *pramāṇa-vṛtti-nivartyasyāpi bhāva-rūpājñānasya sākṣi-vedyasya virodhi-nirūpaka-jñāna-tad-vyāvartaka-viṣaya-grāhakeṇa sākṣiṇā tat-sādhakena tad-anāśād vyāhaty-anupapatteḥ. Advaita-siddhi*, p. 550.

intuited thereby—in the same manner; but, since negations are not intuited directly by the *sākṣi*-consciousness, but only through the *pramāṇa* of non-perception, the defining reference of *ajñāna* also cannot be intuited by the *sākṣi*. It cannot be contended that negation no less than knowledge may be manifested by the *sākṣi*-consciousness; for knowledge implies the non-existence of negation, and so the two cannot be manifested by *sākṣi*-consciousness at the same time; but unproduced knowledge may appear in a qualitative relation to *ajñāna*, since, the relation being qualitative, there is no contradiction between the two, and this explains the possibility of the knowledge of *ajñāna*. The Śaṅkarites do not admit that the knowledge of a qualified entity presupposes the knowledge of the quality; and so the objection that, the entity which forms the defining relation of *ajñāna* not being previously known, *ajñāna* cannot have such defining reference as its adjectival constituent is invalid[1].

An objection may be raised to the effect that, since Brahma-knowledge is to be attained by a definite course of discipline, so long as that is not passed through there is a negation-precedent-to-Brahma-knowledge; and admission of such a negation exposes the Śaṅkarites to all the criticisms which they wished to avoid. The reply is to be found in the view that instead of admitting a negation-precedent here the Śaṅkarites assume that there may either be knowledge of Brahman or *ajñāna* relating to it, i.e., instead of admitting a negation-precedent-to-Brahma-knowledge, they admit a positive ignorance regarding Brahma-knowledge; and thus there is no contradiction.

Vyāsa-tīrtha's contention is that negation of an entity does not necessarily imply the knowledge of any particular entity in its specific relations as a constituent of the knowledge of it, and such knowledge may arise without any specific reference to the particularities of the defining reference. In such experience as "I do not know" no specific defining reference is present to the mind and there is only a reference to entities in general. On such a view, since the knowledge of the defining reference is not a constituent of the knowledge of negation, there is no contradiction on the ground

[1] *na ca avacchedakasya viṣayādeḥ prāgajñāne katham tad-viśiṣṭājñāna-jñānaṃ. viśeṣaṇa-jñānādhīnatvād viśiṣṭa-jñānasyeti vācyaṃ viśeṣaṇa-jñānasya viśiṣṭa-jñāna-jñanatve mānābhāvāt. Advaita-siddhi*, p. 550.

that, since negation is affirmed with regard to the defining reference, its presence as a constituent is impossible. To this Madhusūdana's reply is that no negation of any particular entity can appear merely in a general reference without regard to the specific relations of that particular entity. If it is urged that no negation-precedent can appear in association with the specific particularities of the defining reference as a constituent and that all negations-precedent can appear only in a general reference, the criticism is answered by Madhusūdana to the effect that such negations-precedent as are associated only with the general reference to their defining character are impossible[1]. The opponent of Madhusūdana is supposed to argue that the nature of the defining reference in a negation involves only that particular content which is a character inherent in the thing or things negated. Such characters, forming the content of the knowledge of negation, may indeed constitute the defining limit as such of a thing or things negated; but such an objective reference is wholly irrelevant for the knowledge of any negation. What is essential in the knowledge of the negation is the content, which, indeed, involves the character associated with the things negated, and so the defining reference involved in the knowledge of negation has reference only to such characters as are psychologically patent in experience and do not imply that they are objectively the defining characters of the things negated. Thus, since on such a view the knowledge of negation does not involve as a constituent the things negated, there is no such contradiction as is urged by the Śaṅkarites. As to this Madhusūdana says that such a reply does not provide any escape from the strictures already made by him; for the opponents seem to think that it is sufficient if the defining reference involved in a negation is regarded as a defining character of the knowledge of negation and does not involve the supposition that at the same time it is also the defining character of the objects negated, and they hold that in a knowledge of negation the particular entity that is negated does not appear in its specific character, but only generically, and, if this were so, then, even when an object is present in a spot as a particular, there may be an experience of negation of it in a general manner, since according to the opponents' supposition particular negations always appear

[1] *pratiyogitāvacchedaka-prakāraka-jñānābhāvena prāg-abhāva-pratītir asiddhaiva. Ibid.* p. 552.

only generically. Thus, when one says "I have no knowledge," if knowledge here has only a generic reference, the proposition is absurd, since the knowledge of not having knowledge is itself a knowledge, and in the proposition the negation of knowledge, having a general reference, contradicts the very supposition of not having knowledge.

It may be urged that, if the above criticisms against the knowledge of negation be valid, then the same would apply to negation-precedent also. To this Madhusūdana's reply is that there is no necessity to admit "negation-precedent"; for the real meaning of the so-called negation-precedent is future production, which, again, means nothing more than that time-entity which is not qualified by any object or its destruction—such object being that which is supposed to be the defining reference of the so-called negation-precedent. This is also the meaning of futurity[1]. It must be noted in this connection that production must be defined as a specific relation which stands by itself; for it cannot be defined in terms of negation-precedent, since the negation-precedent can be defined only in terms of production, and thus, if negation-precedent is made a constituent of the definition of production, this entails a vicious circle. So, even if negation-precedent be admitted, it would be difficult to show how it could be intuited; and, on the other hand, one loses nothing by not admitting negation-precedent as a separate category. The negation involved in a negation-precedent is equivalent, so far as merely the negation is concerned, to the absence of the negated object at a particular point of time, which, again, has for its content a specific negation limited by a particular time, where the specific object appears only in a generic relation. An analysis of this shows that in negation-precedent (*prāg-abhāva*) there is negation of a specific object as limited by the present, yet that specific object does not appear in its character as specific and particular, but only in a generic manner[2]. The dilemma here is that negation of a specific object (*viśeṣābhāva*) cannot have for the content of its defining reference merely the generic character of the thing negated, without involving any of its particularities; and, if

[1] *bhaviṣyatvaṃ ca pratiyogi-tad-dhvaṃsānādhāra-kāla-saṃbandhitvam. Advaita-siddhi*, p. 552.

[2] *ihedānīṃ ghaṭo nāstīti pratītis tu sāmānya-dharmāvacchinna-pratiyogitāka-tat-kālāvacchinna-yāvad-viśeṣābhāva-viṣayā. Ibid.* p. 553.

this is so, then there cannot be any negation-precedent involving this condition. Again, if the possibility of such a contingency be admitted, then general negation (*sāmānyābhāva*) is impossible; for no negation limited by any kind of particularity either of time or of object would be entitled to be called a general negation. Thus both the negation-precedent and the general negation appear to be interdependent in their conception, and so thwart each other that neither of them can be admitted. The main contention of Madhusūdana in all these cases is that no specific object can as defining reference in any negation appear only in a generic nature devoid of relation to particularity. Thus, when one says "I do not know," the experience involved in such a proposition is not that of the negation of a particular object appearing only in a generic aspect. If this contention is admitted, then the experience involved in "I do not know" cannot be interpreted as being one of general negation.

Again, it is a matter of common experience that the mere locus of the negation can itself furnish the awareness of negation; thus the bare spot is also the negation of the jug on it. Looked at from this point of view, even positive entities may yield a comprehension of negation. It is wrong to suggest that the nature of the defining reference defines the nature of the negation; for, if this were so, then it would have been impossible that the different negations, such as negation-precedent, destruction, etc., should be classed as different, since they all have the same defining reference. According to the view of Madhusūdana the differences of negation are due to illusory impositions no less than are differences in positive entities.

Even if it is held that there is only one negation, which under different conditions appears as diverse, the Śankarites will have nothing to object to; for according to them both negation and position are but illusory impositions. But Madhusūdana points out that, since the experience "I am ignorant" does not (even under the trenchant analysis undergone above) disclose as its origin any negation, it must be admitted that it is due to the experience of the positive entity of *ajñāna*.

So Madhusūdana further urges that the apperception in the waking state of the experience of the dreamless sleep, viz., "I did not know anything so long," refers to a positive *ajñāna*. Now, if this apperception be an inference, the opponent points out that it may be an inference of negation of knowledge and not of positive ignorance. For one may well infer that, since he existed and during the interval between the two waking stages had a state of mind, that state must have been a state of absence of knowledge. The apperception cannot be said to be mere memory; for memory can only be through root-impressions. The intuition of the *sākṣi*-consciousness being eternal, no root-impression can be produced by such knowledge; for the mechanism of root-impressions is only a psychological device for producing memory by such cognitions as are transitory. To this Madhusūdana's reply is that the apperception under discussion cannot be called an inference; for the inference is based on the ground that the sleeper had a mental state during the dreamless condition. But, if he had no knowledge at the time, it is impossible for him to say that he was at that time endowed with any specific mental state. It also cannot be said that negation of knowledge during dreamless sleep can be inferred from the fact that at that time there was no cause for the production of knowledge; for the absence of such cause can be known only from the absence of knowledge (and *vice versa*), and this involves a vicious circle. Nor can it be said that absence of cause of knowledge can be inferred from the blissful condition of the senses, which could happen only as a consequence of the cessation of their operation; for there is no evidence that the cessation of the operation of the senses would produce the blissful condition. It must be noted in this connection that intuition of *ajñāna* is always associated with absence of knowledge; so that in every case where there is an intuition of *ajñāna* the inference of absence of knowledge would be valid. The so-called non-perception is really an inference from positive *ajñāna*; thus, when one has perceived in the morning an empty yard, he can infer from the absence of the knowledge of an elephant in it the fact of his positive ignorance of an elephant there. Thus the apperception of absence of knowledge can be explained as inference. It can also be explained as a case of memory. The objection that the intuition of *ajñāna* cannot have any root-impression is also invalid; for the *ajñāna* which is the object of the *sākṣi*-consciousness during dreamless sleep is itself a reflection through a *vṛtti* of *ajñāna*, since it is only under such conditions that *ajñāna* can be an object of *sākṣi*-consciousness. Since a *vṛtti* is admitted in the intuition of *ajñāna*, with the cessation of the *vṛtti* there must be a root-impression and through that there can be memory of the *vṛtti*, as in the case of the memory of any other cognition[1]. It cannot be contended that, if *ajñāna* requires for its cognition a *vṛtti* state, then, if there is no such *vṛtti*, there may be doubt regarding *ajñāna*; for there cannot be any *ajñāna* regarding *ajñāna*, and doubt itself, being a modification of *ajñāna*, has the same scope as *ajñāna*. It cannot be urged that, like *ajñāna*, negation may also be perceived by the *sākṣi*-consciousness; for, since negation is always associated with its defining reference, it cannot be intuitively perceived by the indeterminate intuitive *sākṣi*-consciousness. Though *ajñāna* involves an opposition to knowledge, yet the opposition is not as such intuited in the dreamless state. Madhusūdana says that it is contended that, since there is a continuous succession of *ajñāna* states, from the dreamless condition to the waking stage (for in the waking state also all cognitions take place by reflection through *ajñāna* states), there is no occasion for a memory of the dreamless intuition of *ajñāna*; for through *saṃskāras* memory is possible on the destruction of a *vṛtti* state of cognition. To this the reply is that the *ajñāna* state of dreamless condition is of a specific nature of darkness (*tamasī*) which ceases with sleep, and hence there is no continuity of succession between this and the ordinary cognitive states in the waking condition. From one point of view, however, the contention is right; for it may well be maintained that in the dreamless state *ajñāna* exists in its causal aspect, and thus, since the *ajñāna* is the material for experience of both dreamless sleep and waking state, there is in reality continuity of succession of *ajñāna*, and thus there cannot be any memory of dreamless experience of *ajñāna*. It is for this reason that Sureśvara has discarded this view. The view taken by the author of the *Vivaraṇa* follows the conception of sleep in the *Yoga-sūtras*, where a separate *vṛtti* in the dreamless state is admitted. Thus the experience of the dreamless state may well be described as relating to experience of positive *ajñāna*.

[1] *ajñānasyājñāna-vṛtti-prativiṃbita-sākṣi-bhāsyatvena vṛtti-nāśād eva saṃskāropapatteḥ. Advaita-siddhi*, p. 557.

Inference of ajñāna.

It is held by Prakāśānanda in his *Vivaraṇa* that *ajñāna* can be inferred; the form of the inference that he suggests is: "A valid cognition is associated with a positive veil upon its object, which veil is removable by the cognition itself, and such a veil is different from the negation-precedent of its self."[1] Vyāsa-tīrtha, in refuting this inference, starts by criticizing the concept of the minor term (*pakṣa*, i.e., *pramāṇa-jñāna*). He says that according to the above form of inference consciousness of pleasure, which is a valid cognition, should also appear after removing the veil on itself, but the pleasure-consciousness, being of the nature of *sākṣi*-consciousness, is unable (according to the theory of the Śaṅkarites themselves) to remove *ajñāna*. If the concept of the minor term is narrowed to *vṛtti-jñāna*, or cognitive states in general, then also it is not possible; for, if a mediate cognitive state be supposed to remove the veil upon its object, that would mean that there is a direct revelation of intuitive consciousness through the object, which would be the same as saying that mediate cognition is perception. If the concept of the minor be narrowed down to immediate perception, then the above definition would not apply to mediate cognition, which is a valid cognition. Even in the case of the immediate cognition of error there is an element of the intuition of "being" to which also the above definition would apply; for certainly that does not manifest itself after removing a veil of non-being, since the intuition of being is universal. Moreover, if that could remove the *ajñāna*, then *ajñāna* would have no being and so could not be the material cause of illusion. The *ajñāna* which has "being" for its support is regarded as the material cause of illusion, but is never the object of illusion itself. If the concept of the minor is further narrowed, so as to mean merely the cognitive states, excluding the underlying "being," then in the case of successive awareness of the same entity the awareness at the second and third moments cannot be supposed to remove the veil itself, since that was removed by the first awareness. If the concept of the

[1] *vivāda-gocarāpannaṃ pramāṇa-jñānaṃ sva-prāg-abhāva-vyatirikta-sva-viṣayāvaraṇa-sva-nivartya-sva-deśa-gata-vastv-antara-pūrvakaṃ bhavitum arhati aprakāśitārtha-prakāśakatvād andhakāre prathamotpanna-pradīpa-prabhāvad iti. Pañca-pādikā-vivaraṇa*, p. 13.

minor term is further narrowed, so as to mean merely the direct cognition of the material object, then also, since the Śaṅkarites do not admit that there are veils on the object, the object-cognition cannot be regarded as having removed such a veil. If in answer to this it is held that the mental state, e.g., the cognition of jug, involves a limitation of the pure consciousness by the jug-form and, since the *ajñāna* has the same scope as the above limitation, the removal of the veil on the jug-form limitation means also the removal of the veil of *ajñāna* to that extent, the reply is, first, that on the view that there is only one *ajñāna* the above explanation does not hold; secondly, since the pure consciousness, limited in any form, is not self-luminous, it cannot, according to the Śaṅkarites, be associated with a veil, which can only be associated with the pure self-luminous consciousness. Moreover, if the removal of the veil is spoken of as having reference only to material objects, then, since the verbal proposition "this is a jug" has the same content as the jug itself, the removal of the veil with reference to the material object—the jug—which has the same content as the mediate verbal proposition, ought not to take place.

Again, since on the Śaṅkarite view the *vṛtti*-knowledge is itself false, there cannot be any possibility that illusory objects should be imposed upon it. On the other hand, if the pure consciousness, as manifested by the *vṛtti*, be synonymous with knowledge, then, since such a consciousness is the support of *ajñāna*, it cannot be regarded as removing *ajñāna*. Thus the requirement of the inference that knowledge establishes itself by removing *ajñāna* fails; further, the requirement of the definition that the veil that is removed has the same location as the knowledge fails, since the *ajñāna* is located in pure consciousness, whereas the cognition is always of the conditioned consciousness.

The inference supposes that there is a removal of the veil because there is a manifestation of the unmanifested; but this cannot hold good, since the Brahma-knowledge cannot be manifested by any thing other than pure consciousness, and the self-luminous, which is the basis of all illusions, is ever self-manifested, and thus there is no possibility here of the unmanifested being manifested. Moreover, if the *ajñāna* be a positive entity existing from beginningless time, then it would be impossible that it should be removed. It is also impossible that that which is a veil should be beginningless. So it is possible to have such counter-arguments as that beginninglessness can never be associated with veils, since it exists only as beginningless, like the negation-precedent; or that a valid knowledge can never remove anything else than negation, because it is knowledge. The manifestation of the unmanifested does not imply any positive fact of unmanifestation, but may signify only an absence of manifestation. Moreover, the light manifests the jug, etc., by removing darkness, because light is opposed to darkness, but the manifestation of knowledge cannot be opposed to *ajñāna*; for pure consciousness underlying the objects is not opposed to *ajñāna*. The opposition of *vṛtti* to *ajñāna* is irrelevant; for *vṛtti* is not knowledge. What may be said concerning the rise of a new cognition is that it removes the beginningless negation of the knowledge of an object of any particular person.

Madhusūdana in reply says that the term "valid knowledge," which is the minor term, has to be so far restricted in meaning that it applies only to the *vṛtti*-knowledge and not to the *sākṣi*-consciousness which reveals pleasure or bliss; the *vṛtti*-knowledge also has to be further narrowed down in its meaning so as to exclude the substantive part (*dharmy-aṃśa*) of all cognitions, the "this" or the "being" which is qualified by all cognitive characters. *Pramāṇa-jñāna*, or valid knowledge, which is inferred as removing a veil, means therefore only the cognitive characters revealed in the *vṛtti*. Even in the case of *parokṣa* (mediate knowledge) there is the removal of its veil, consisting in the fact of its non-existence to the knower; which veil being removed, the object of the mediate cognition is revealed to the knower. Thus the valid cognition includes the cognitive characters as appearing both in mediate and in immediate *vṛttis*. The reason for the exclusion of the substantive part, or the "this," from the concept of valid knowledge under discussion is apparent from the fact that there is no error or illusion regarding the "this"; all errors or doubts can happen only with regard to the cognitive characters. The "this" is as self-existent as the experience of pleasure. There cannot, therefore, be any such objection as that in their case also there is a revelation of the unknown and therefore a removal of the veil. If, however, it is urged that, though there may not be any error or doubt regarding the "this," yet, since there remains the fact that it was first unknown, and then known, and therefore it involves the removal of a veil, there would be objection on the part of the Śaṅkarites to admitting such a removal, which may well be effected by the cognitive state or the *pramāṇa-vṛtti*. In such a case, however, the removal of the veil is not of the ordinary nature; for this *ajñāna*, which consists only in the fact that the entity is unknown, is different from the *ajñāna* the extent and limit of which can be regarded as a positive ignorance having the same defining reference as the object of cognition. In this view, therefore, the *ajñāna* is to be defined as that which has the capacity of producing errors, since there cannot be any error with regard to the substantive part, the "this." The fact that it remains unknown until cognized involves no *ajñāna* according to our definition. Thus it may well be supposed that in the case of the cognition of the "this" there is, according to the definition contemplated in the scheme of the inference of *ajñāna* under discussion, no removal of *ajñāna*.

In the case of continuous perception, though the object may remain the same, yet a new time-element would be involved in each of the succeeding moments, and the removal of the veil may be regarded as having a reference to this new factor. It is well known that according to the Śaṅkarites time can be perceived by all the *pramāṇas*. Again, the objection that, since material objects can have no veil and since the *ajñāna* cannot be said to hide pure consciousness which is its support, it is difficult to say which of these is veiled by *ajñāna*, is not valid; for, though the pure consciousness exists in its self-shining character, yet for its limited appearance, as "it exists," "it shines," *ajñāna* may be admitted to enforce a limitation or veiling and to that extent it may be regarded as a veil upon that pure consciousness. Madhusūdana further adds arguments in favour of the view that *ajñāna* can be inferred; these are of a formal nature and are, therefore, omitted here.

The theory of Avidyā refuted.

Vyāsa-tīrtha says that it cannot be assumed that an entity such as the *avidyā* must exist as a substratum of illusion, since otherwise illusions would be impossible; for it has been shown before that the definition of *avidyā* as the material cause of illusion is untenable. Moreover, if it is held that illusions such as the conch-shell-silver are made out of a stuff, then there must also be a producer who works on the stuff to manufacture the illusions. Neither God nor the individual can be regarded as being such a producer; nor can the changeless Brahman be considered to be so. Again, *avidyā*, being beginningless, ought to be as changeless as Brahman. Moreover, if Brahman be regarded as the material cause of the world, there is no necessity for admitting the existence of *avidyā*; for under the Śaṅkarite supposition Brahman, though not changing, may nevertheless well be the basis of the illusions imposed upon it. If that were not so, then *avidyā*, which needs a support, would require for the purpose some entity other than Brahman. It may be suggested that the supposition of *avidyā* is necessary for the purpose of explaining the changing substratum of illusion; for Brahman, being absolutely true, cannot be regarded as the material cause of the false illusion, since an effect must have for its cause an entity similar to it. But, if that is so, then Brahman cannot be regarded as the cause of the sky or other physical elements which are unreal in comparison with Brahman. It cannot be urged that, since the individual and the Brahman are identical in essence, without the assumption of *avidyā* the limited manifestation of bliss in the individual would be inexplicable; for the very supposition that Brahman and the individual are identical is illegitimate, and so there is no difficulty in explaining the unlimited and limited manifestation of bliss, in Brahman and the individual, because they are different.

Madhusūdana in reply to the above says that *antaḥkaraṇa* (or mind) cannot be regarded as the material cause of illusion; first, because the *antaḥkaraṇa* is an entity in time, whereas illusions continue in a series and have no beginning in time; secondly, the *antaḥkaraṇa* is in its processes always associated with real objects of the world, and would, as such, be inoperative in regard to fictitious conch-shell-silver—and, if this is so, then without the supposition of *avidyā* there would be no substratum as the material cause of *avidyā*. Brahman also, being unchangeable, cannot be the cause of such illusion. It cannot be suggested that Brahman is the cause of illusion in its status as basis or locus of illusion; for, unless the cause which transforms itself into the effect be admitted, the unchanging cause to which such effects are attributed itself cannot be established[1], since it is only when certain transformations have

[1] *na ca vivartādhisṭhānatvena śukty-āder ivopādānatvam avidyām antareṇā-tāttvikānyathā-bhāva-lakṣaṇasya vivartasysaṃbhavāt. Advaita-siddhi*, p. 573.

been effected that they are referred to a certain ground or basis as belonging to it.

Again, if *ajñāna* be itself invalid, as the Śaṅkarites say, it is impossible that it should be amenable to the different valid means of proof. If it is contended that *ajñāna* has only an empirical existence (*vyāvahārika*), then it could not be the stuff of the ordinary illusory experience; for the stuff of the empirical cannot be the cause of the illusory, and there is no evidence that the *avidyā* is illusory. If it is contended that the valid means of proof serve only for negating the non-existence of *avidyā*, then the reply is that, since the *ajñāna* is grasped by the faultless *sākṣi*-consciousness, it must be admitted to be valid. It is wrong also to suppose that the means of proof negate only the non-existence of *ajñāna*; for, unless the nature of *ajñāna* could be known by inference, the negation of its non-existence could also not be known. It must also be noted that, when the valid means of proof reveal the *ajñāna*, they do so as if it were not an illusory conch-shell-silver known by the *sākṣi*-consciousness, but a valid object of knowledge, and they also do not reveal the non-existence of *ajñāna* in the locus of its appearance. Thus the valid means of proof by which *ajñāna* is supposed to be made known indicate its existence as a valid object of knowledge. The *avidyā*, therefore, may be regarded as non-eternal (being removable by knowledge), but not false or invalid. The statement of the Śankarites, therefore, that *avidyā* is invalid by itself and yet is known by valid means of proof, is invalid.

If *avidyā* is apprehended by the pure faultless consciousness, it should be ultimately true, and it ought to persist after emancipation. It cannot be said that it may not persist after emancipation, since, its *esse* being its *percipi*, so long as its perception exists (as it must, being apprehended by the eternal pure consciousness) it also must exist. If it is held that *avidyā* is known through a *vṛtti*, then the obvious difficulty is that the two conditions which can generate a *vṛtti* are that of valid cognitive state (*pramāṇa*) or defects (*doṣa*), and in the case of the apprehension of *avidyā* neither of these can be said to induce the suitable *vṛtti*. There being thus no possibility of a *vṛtti*, there would be no apprehension of *avidyā* through the reflection of consciousness through it. Again, the *vṛtti*, being itself an *avidyā* state, would itself require for its comprehension the help of pure consciousness reflected through another *vṛtti*, and that another, and so on; and, if it is urged that the comprehension of the *vṛtti* does not stand in need of reflection through another *vṛtti*, but is directly revealed by *sākṣi*-consciousness, then such a *vṛtti* would be experienced even after emancipation. Moreover, it is difficult to conceive how an entity like *avidyā*, whose *esse* is *percipi*, can be regarded as capable of conditioning a *vṛtti* by the reflection of the consciousness through which it can be known. For there is no *esse* of the thing before it is perceived, and according to the supposition it cannot be perceived unless it has a previous *esse*.

The reply of Madhusūdana is that the above objections are invalid, since the *ajñāna*, being perceived by the *sākṣi*-consciousness, which is always associated with the perceiver, has no such ontological appearance or revelation. In reply to some of the other criticisms Madhusūdana points out that, *avidyā* being a defect and being itself a condition of its own *vṛtti*, the objections on these grounds lose much of their force.

Vyāsa-tīrtha says that the Śaṅkarites think that, since everything else but the pure consciousness is an imaginary creation of *avidyā*, the *avidyā* can have for its support only Bṛahman and nothing else. He points out that it is impossible that ignorance, which is entirely opposed to knowledge, should have the latter as its support. It may well be remembered that ignorance is defined as that which is removable by knowledge. It cannot be said that the opposition is between the *vṛtti*-knowledge and *ajñāna*; for, if that were so, then *ajñāna* should be defined as that which is opposed to knowledge in a restricted sense, since *vṛtti*-knowledge is knowledge only in a restricted sense (the real knowledge being the light of pure consciousness). If consciousness were not opposed to ignorance, there could not be any illumination of objects. The opposition of ignorance to knowledge is felt, even according to the Śaṅkarites, in the experience "I do not know." It is also well known that there is no ignorance with regard to pleasure or pain, which are directly perceived by the *sākṣi*. This is certainly due to the fact that pure consciousness annuls *ajñāna*, so that whatever is directly revealed by it has no *ajñāna* in it. It is contended that there are instances where one of the things that are entirely opposed to each other may have the other as its basis. Persons suffering from photophobia may ascribe darkness to sunshine, in which case darkness is seen to be based on sunshine; similarly, though knowledge and ignorance are so much opposed, yet the latter may be supposed to be based on the former. To this the reply is that, following the analogy where a false darkness is ascribed to sunlight, one may be justified in thinking that a false *ajñāna* different from the *ajñāna* under discussion may be based on the pure consciousness. Moreover, the experience "I am ignorant" shows that the ignorance (*avidyā*) is associated with the ego and not with pure consciousness. It cannot be suggested that, both the ego and the ignorance being at the same time illusorily imposed on the pure consciousness, they appear as associated with each other, which explains the experience "I am ignorant"; for without first proving that the *ajñāna* exists in the pure consciousness the illusory experience cannot be explained, and without having the illusory experience first the association of *ajñāna* with pure consciousness cannot be established, and thus there would be a vicious circle. It is also wrong to suppose that the experience "I am ignorant" is illusory. Moreover, the very experience "I am ignorant" contradicts the theory that *ajñāna* is associated with pure consciousness, and there is no means by which this contradiction can be further contradicted and the theory that *ajñāna* rests on pure consciousness be supported. The notions of an agent, knower, or enjoyer are always associated with cognitive states and therefore belong to pure consciousness. If these notions were imposed upon the pure consciousness, the *ajñāna* would belong to it (which, being a false knower, is the same as the individual self or *jīva*), and, so would belong to *jīva*; this would be to surrender the old thesis that *ajñāna* belongs to pure consciousness. It is also not right to say that the *ajñāna* of the conch-shell belongs to the consciousness limited by it; it is always experienced that knowledge and ignorance both belong to the knower. If it is contended that what exists in the substratum may also show itself when that substratum is qualified in any particular manner, and that therefore the *ajñāna* in the pure consciousness may also show itself in the self or *jīva*, which is a qualified appearance of pure consciousness, to this the reply is that, if this contention is admitted, then even the pure consciousness may be supposed to undergo through its association with *ajñāna* the world-cycles of misery and rebirth.

The supposition that the *jīva* is a reflection and the impurities are associated with it as a reflected image and not with the Brahman, the reflector, is wrong; for, if the *ajñāna* is associated with pure consciousness, it is improper to think that its effects should affect the reflected image and not Brahman. Moreover, the analogy of reflection can hold good only with reference to rays of light, and not with reference to consciousness. Again, if the *jīvas* be regarded as a product of reflection, this will necessarily have a beginning in time. Moreover, the reflection can occur only when that through which anything is reflected has the same kind of existence as the former. A ray of light can be reflected in the surface of water and not in mirage, because water has the same status of existence as the ray of light; but, if Brahman and *ajñāna* have not the same kind of existence, the former cannot be reflected in the latter. Moreover, *ajñāna*, which has no transparency, cannot be supposed to reflect Brahman. Again, there is no reason to suppose that the *ajñāna* should be predisposed to reflect the Brahman, and, if the *ajñāna* is transformed into the form of *ākāśa*, etc., it cannot also at the same time behave as a reflector. Moreover, just as apart from the face and its image through reflection there is no other separate face, so there is also no separate pure consciousness, apart from Brahman and the *jīva*, which could be regarded as the basis of *ajñāna*. Also it cannot be suggested that pure consciousness as limited by the *jīva*-form is the basis of the *ajñāna*; for without the reflection through *ajñāna* there cannot be any *jīva*, and without the *jīva* there cannot be any *ajñāna*, since on the present supposition the *ajñāna* has for its support the consciousness limited by *jīva*, and this involves a vicious circle. Again, on this view, since Brahman is not the basis of *ajñāna*, though it is of the nature of pure consciousness, it may well be contended that pure consciousness as such is not the basis of *ajñāna*, and that, just as the *jīva*, through association with *ajñāna*, undergoes the cycles of birth, so Brahman also may, with equal reason, be associated with *ajñāna*, and undergo the painful necessities of such an association.

The analogy of the mirror and the image is also inappropriate on many grounds. The impurities of the mirror are supposed to vitiate the image; but in the present case no impurities are directly known or perceived to exist in the *ajñāna*, which stands for the mirror; even though they may be there, being of the nature of root-impressions, they are beyond the scope of the senses. Thus, the view that the conditions which are perceived in the mirror are also reflected in the image is invalid.

It cannot be held that, just as in the Nyāya view the soul is associated with pain only through the intermediacy of body, so the pure consciousness may be regarded as associated with *ajñāna* in association with its limited form as *jīva*; for, since pure consciousness is itself associated with the mischievous element, the *ajñāna*, the attainment of Brahmanhood cannot be regarded as a desirable state.

Madhusūdana in reply says that pure consciousness, in itself not opposed to *ajñāna*, can destroy *ajñāna* only when reflected through modification of *ajñāna* as *vṛtti*, just as the rays of the sun, which illuminate little bits of paper or cotton, may burn them when reflected through a lens. It is wrong also to suppose that the ignorance has its basis in the ego; for the ego-notion, being itself a product of *ajñāna*, cannot be its support. It must, therefore, have as its basis the underlying pure consciousness. The experience "I am ignorant" is, therefore, to be explained on the supposition that the notion of ego and ignorance both have their support in the pure consciousness and are illusorily made into a complex. The ego, being itself an object of knowledge and removable by ultimate true knowledge, must be admitted to be illusory. If *ajñāna* were not ultimately based on pure consciousness, then it could not be removable by the ultimate and final knowledge which has the pure consciousness as its content. It is also wrong to suppose that the *ajñāna* qualifies the phenomenal knower; for the real knower is the pure consciousness, and to it as such the *ajñāna* belongs, and it is through it that all kinds of knowledge, illusory or relatively real, belong to it. The criticism that, there being *ajñāna*, there is the phenomenal knower, and, there being the phenomenal knower, there is *ajñāna*, is also wrong; for *ajñāna* does not depend for its existence upon the phenomenal knower. Their mutual association is due not to the fact that *avidyā* has the knower as its support, but that ignorance and the ego-notion are expressed together in one structure of awareness, and this explains their awareness. The unity of the phenomenal knower and the pure consciousness subsists only in so far as the consciousness underlying the phenomenal knower is one with pure consciousness. It is well known that, though a face may stand before a mirror, the impurities of the mirror affect the reflected mirror and not the face. The reflected image, again, is nothing different from the face itself; so, though the pure consciousness may be reflected through impure *ajñāna*, impurities affect not the pure consciousness, but the *jīva*, which, again, is identical in its essence with the consciousness. It must be noted in this connection that there are two *ajñānas*, one veiling the knower and the other the object, and it is quite possible that in some cases (e.g., in mediate knowledge) the veil of the object may remain undisturbed as also the veil of the subject.

It is wrong to suppose that reflection can only be of visible objects; for invisible objects also may have reflection, as in the case of *ākāśa*, which, though invisible, has its blueness reflected in it from other sources. Moreover, that Brahman is reflected through *ajñāna* is to be accepted on the testimony of scripture. It is also wrong to contend that that which is reflected and that in which the reflection takes place have the same kind of existence; for a red image from a red flower, though itself illusory and having therefore a different status of existence from the reflecting surface of the mirror, may nevertheless be further reflected in other things. Moreover, it is wrong to suppose that *ajñāna* cannot be predisposed to reflect pure consciousness; for *ajñāna*, on the view that it is infinite, may be supposed to be able to reflect pure consciousness in its entirety; on the view that it is more finite than pure consciousness there is no objection that a thing of smaller dimensions could not reflect an entity of larger dimensions; the sun may be reflected in water on a plate. Moreover, it is not a valid objection that, if *ajñāna* has transformation into particular forms, it is exhausted, and therefore cannot reflect pure consciousness; for that fraction of *ajñāna* which takes part in transformation does not take part in reflection, which is due to a different part of *ajñāna*. Again, the criticism that, in contradistinction to the case of reflection of a neutral face appearing as many images, there is no neutral consciousness, apart from the *jīva* and Brahman, is ineffective; for the neutral face is so called only because the differences are not taken into account, so that the pure consciousness also may be said to be neutral when looked at apart from the peculiarities of its special manifestation through reflection.

It must be noted that the function of reflection consists in largely attributing the conditions (such as impurities, etc.) of the reflector to the images. This is what is meant by the phrase *upādheḥ pratibimba-pakṣapātitvam* (i.e., the conditions show themselves in the images). It is for this reason that the impurities of *ajñāna* may show themselves in the reflected *jīvas* without affecting the nature of pure consciousness.

Also it cannot be said that *māyā* is associated with Brahman; for, if this *māyā* be *ajñāna*, then the possibility of its association with Brahman has already been refuted. *Māyā*, being *ajñāna*, also cannot be regarded as a magical power whereby it is possible to show things which are non-existent (*aindrajālikasyeva avidyamāna-pradarśana-śaktiḥ*); for, since *ajñāna* in general has been refuted, a specific appearance of it, as magic, cannot be admitted; also it is never seen that a magician demonstrates his magical feats through *ajñāna*. If *māyā* be regarded as a special power of Brahman by which He creates the diverse real objects of the world, then we have no objection to such a view and are quite prepared to accept it. If it is held that *māyā* is a power of deluding other beings, then, since before its application there are no beings, the existence of *māyā* is unjustifiable. Again, if such a power should be regarded as having a real existence, then it would break monism. If it be regarded as due to the false imagination of the *jīvas*, then it cannot be regarded as deluding these. If it be regarded as due to the false imagination of Brahman, then it must be admitted that Brahman has *ajñāna*, since without *ajñāna* there cannot be any false imagination.

The view of Vācaspati that *avidyā* resides in the *jīva* is also wrong—for, if *jīva* means pure consciousness, then the old objection holds good; if *jīva* means pure consciousness as limited by reflection from *ajñāna* or the *ajñāna*-product, the *buddhi*, then this involves a vicious circle; for without first explaining *avidyā* it is not possible to talk about its limitation. If it is said that *avidyā*, standing by itself without any basis, produces the *jīvas* through its reference to pure consciousness, and then, when the *jīva* is produced, resides in it, then it will be wrong to suppose that *avidyā* resides in the *jīva*; even the production of the *jīva* will be inexplicable, and the old objection of the vicious circle will still be the same. Nor can it be held that, the *jīva* and the *avidyā* being related to each other in a beginningless relation, the criticism of the vicious circle through mutual dependence is unavailing is not correct; for, if they do not depend on each other, they also cannot determine each other. If the *ajñāna* and the *jīva* are not found to be related to each other in any of their operations, they also cannot depend upon each other; that which is entirely unrelated to any entity cannot be said to depend on it. It is held that the difference between *jīva* and Brahman consists in the fact of the former being a product of *avidyā*, and it is also held that the *avidyā* has the *jīva* as its basis, so that without the knowledge of *jīva* there cannot be *avidyā*, and without the knowledge of *avidyā* there cannot be any *jīva*.

To this Madhusūdana's reply is that the so-called vicious circle of mutual dependence is quite inapplicable to the case under discussion, since such mutual dependence does not vitiate the production, because such production is in a beginningless series. There is not also a mutual agency of making each other comprehensible; for, though the *ajñāna* is made comprehensible by pure consciousness, yet the latter is not manifested by the former. There is, further, no mutual dependence in existence; for, though the *ajñāna* depends upon pure consciousness for its existence, yet the latter does not depend upon the former. Madhusūdana further points out that according to Vācaspati it is the *ajñāna* of the *jīva* that creates both the *īśvara* and the *jīva*.

The *ajñāna* is supposed to veil the pure consciousness; but the pure consciousness is again supposed to be always self-luminous, and, if this is so, how can it be veiled? The veil cannot be of the *jīva*, since the *jīva* is a product of *ajñāna*; it cannot be of the material objects, since they are themselves non-luminous, so that no veil is necessary to hide them. The veiling of the pure consciousness cannot be regarded as annihilation of the luminosity of the self-luminous (*siddha-prakāśa-lopaḥ*); nor can it be regarded as obstruction to the production of what after it had come into existence would have proved itself to be self-luminous; for that whose essence is self-luminous can never cease at any time to be so. Moreover, since the self-luminosity is ever-existent, there cannot be any question regarding production of it which the *ajñāna* may be supposed to veil. Again, since it is the nature of knowledge to express itself as related to objects, it cannot stand in need of anything else in order to establish its relationing to the objects, and there cannot be any time when the knowledge will exist without relationing itself to the objects. Moreover, on the Śaṅkarite view the pure consciousness, being homogeneous in its self-luminosity, does not stand in need of any relationing to objects which could be obstructed by the veil. Nor can it be said that the veil acts as an obstruction to the character of objects as known (*prākaṭya-pratibandha*); even according to the Śaṅkarites the *prākaṭya*, or the character of objects as known, is nothing but pure consciousness. It cannot be said that such awareness as "this exists," "it does not shine" cannot be said to appertain to pure consciousness; for even in denying the existence of consciousness we have the manifestation of consciousness. Even erroneous conceptions of the above forms cannot be said to be the veil of *ajñāna*; for error arises only as a result of the veiling of the locus (e.g., it is only when the nature of the conch-shell is hidden that there can appear an illusory notion of silver) and cannot therefore be identified with the veil itself. Citsukha defines self-luminosity as that which, not being an object of awareness, has a fitness for being regarded as immediate (*avedyatve sati aparokṣa-vyavahāra-yogyatvam*). The view that the self-luminosity is the fitness for not being immediate or self-shining as an explanation of the veil of *ajñāna* that exists in it, is wrong, for that is self-contradictory, since by definition it has fitness for being regarded as immediate.

Again, a veil is that which obstructs the manifestation of that which is covered by it; but, if a self-luminous principle can manifest itself through *ajñāna*, it is improper to call this a veil.

Again, if a veil covers any light, that veil does not obstruct the illumination itself, but prevents the light from reaching objects beyond the veil. Thus a light inside a jug illuminates the inside of the jug, and the cover of the jug only prevents the light from illuminating objects outside the jug. In the case of the supposed obstruction of the illumination of the pure consciousness the same question may arise, and it may well be asked "To whom does the veil obstruct the illumination of the pure consciousness?" It cannot be with reference to diverse *jīvas*; for the diversity of *jīvas* is supposed to be a product of the action of the veil, and they are not already existent, so that it may be said that the pure consciousness becomes obstructed from the *jīvas* by the action of the veil. It is also wrong to suppose that the illumination of the Brahman so far differs from that of ordinary light that it does not manifest itself to itself; for, if that were so, it might equally remain unmanifested even during emancipation and there would be no meaning in introducing *ajñāna* as the fact of veiling. It is held that even while the *sākṣi*-consciousness is manifesting itself the *ajñāna* may still be there, since the *sākṣi*-consciousness manifests the *ajñāna* itself. It is further held that in such experiences as "I do not know what you said" the *ajñāna*, though it may not veil anything, may yet be manifested in pure consciousness, as may be directly intuited by experience. To this the reply is that the conception of the *ajñāna* aims at explaining the non-manifestation of the unlimited bliss of Brahman, and, if that is so, how can it be admitted that *ajñāna* may appear without any veiling operation in the manifested consciousness? Though in the case of such an experience as "I do not know what you said" the *ajñāna* may be an object of knowledge, in the case of manifestation of pleasure and pain there cannot be any experience of the absence of manifestation of these, and so no *ajñāna* can appear in consciousness with reference to these. Moreover, even when one says "I do not know what you say" there is no appearance of *ajñāna* in consciousness; the statement merely indicates that the content of the speaker's words is known only in a general way, excluding its specific details. So far, therefore, there is thus a manifestation of the general outline of the content of the speaker's words, which might lead, in future, to an understanding of the specific details. Anyway, the above experience does not mean the direct experience of *ajñāna*. Just as God, though not subject like ourselves to illusions, is yet aware that we commit errors, or just as we, though we do not know all things that are known by God, yet know of the omniscience of God, so without knowing the specific particularities of *ajñāna* we may know *ajñāna* in a general manner. If the above view is not accepted, and if it is held that there is a specific cognitive form of *ajñāna*, then this cognitive form would not be opposed to *ajñāna*, and this would virtually amount to saying that even the cessation of *ajñāna* is not opposed to *jñāna*, which is absurd. Moreover, if *ajñāna* were an object of knowledge, then the awareness of it would be possible only by the removal of another *ajñāna* veil covering it.

Again, if it is said that *ajñāna* exists wheresoever there is a negation of the *vṛtti-jñāna*, which alone is contradictory to it, then it should exist also in emancipation. But, again, when one says "I do not know," the opposition felt is not with reference to *vṛtti*-

knowledge specifically, but with reference to knowledge in general. Moreover, if *caitanya* (pure consciousness) and *ajñāna* were not opposed to each other, it would be wrong to designate the one as the negation of the other, i.e., as knowledge (*jñāna*) and ignorance (*ajñāna*). Moreover, if cognitions are only possible and ignorances can only be removed through the manifestation of the self-shining pure consciousness, it stands to reason that it is the pure consciousness that should be opposed to *ajñāna*. It is also unreasonable to suppose that the self could have *ajñāna* associated with it and yet be self-luminous. There ought to be no specific point of difference between the *vṛtti* and the *sākṣi*-consciousness in their relation to *ajñāna*; for they may both be regarded as opposed to *ajñāna*. If the *sākṣi*-consciousness were not opposed to *ajñāna*, then it could not remove ignorance regarding pleasure, pain, etc. There is no reason to suppose that no *ajñāna* can be associated with whatever is manifested by *sākṣi*-consciousness. It is indeed true that there is no *ajñāna* in the knower, and the knower does not stand in need of the removal of any ignorance regarding itself. The self is like a lamp ever self-luminous; no darkness can be associated with it. It is for this reason that, though ordinary objects stand in need of light for their illumination, the self, the knower, does not stand in need of any illumination. It is also wrong to suppose that the pure consciousness is opposed to *ajñāna* only when it is reflected through a *vṛtti* state, and that in the case of the experience of pleasure the *sākṣi*-consciousness is reflected through a *vṛtti* of the pleasure-form; for, if this is admitted, then it must also be admitted that the pleasure had a material existence before it was felt, and thus, as in the case of other objects, there may be doubts about pleasure and pain also; and so the accepted view that the perception of pleasure is also its existence must be sacrificed. Thus it has to be admitted that pure consciousness is opposed to ignorance regarding pleasure, pain, etc. There is, therefore, as regards opposition to knowledge no difference between pure consciousness and pure consciousness manifested through a *vṛtti*. Nor can it be said that pleasure, pain, etc., are perceived by the pure consciousness as reflected through the *vṛtti* of the *antaḥkaraṇa;* for the *vṛtti* of the *antaḥkaraṇa* can arise only through sense-functioning, and in the intuition of internal pleasure there cannot be any such sense-function. Nor can it be a reflection through the *vṛtti* of *avidyā;* for that is possible only in the presence of a defect or defects. If, like things immersed in darkness, like absence of knowledge, *ajñāna* be utter unmanifestation, then it cannot be manifested by the *sākṣi*-consciousness. Again, if it is held that *vṛtti* is opposed to *ajñāna*, then, since there exists the ego-*vṛtti* forming the *jīva* and the object-formed *vṛtti* representing the knowledge of the material objects, it might well be expected that these *vṛttis* would oppose the existence of *ajñāna* and that there would be immediate emancipation.

To this Madhusūdana's reply is that the *ajñāna* is called a veil in the sense that it has a fitness (*yogyatā*) by virtue of which it is capable of making things appear as non-existent or unmanifested, though it may not always exert its capacity, with the result that in dreamless sleep the operation of the veil exists, while in emancipation it is suspended. Generally speaking, the veil continues until the attainment of Brahma-knowledge. It may be objected that the concept of a veil, being different from that of pure consciousness, is itself a product of false imagination (*kalpita*), and therefore involves a vicious circle; to this the reply would be that *avidyā* is beginningless, and hence, even if a false imagination at any particular stage be the result of a preceding stage and that of a still further preceding stage, there cannot be any difficulty. Moreover, the manifestation of the *āvaraṇa* does not depend on the completion of the infinite series, but is directly produced by pure consciousness. It must be remembered that, though the pure consciousness in its fulness is without any veil (as during emancipation), yet on other occasions it may through the operation of the veil have a limited manifestation. Against the objection of Vyāsa-tīrtha that pure consciousness, being homogeneous, is incapable of having any association with a veil, Madhusūdana ends by reiterating the assertion that veiling is possible—for which, however, no new reason is given. To the objection that the veil, like the jug, cannot avert the illumination of the lamp inside, and can obstruct only with reference to the things outside the jug, but that in the case of the obstruction of pure consciousness no such external entity is perceivable, Madhusūdana's reply is that the obstruction of the pure consciousness is with reference to the *jīva*. The veiling and the *jīva* being both related to each other in a beginningless series, the question regarding their priority is illegitimate. Madhusūdana points out that, just as in the experience "I do not know what you say" the ignorance is associated with knowledge, so also, in the manifestation of pleasure, pleasure is manifested in a limited aspect with reference to a particular object, and such limitation may be considered to be due to the association with *ajñāna* which restricted its manifestation. Madhusūdana contends that in such experiences as "I do not know what you say" the explanation that there is a general knowledge of the intention of the speaker, but that the specific knowledge of the details has not yet developed, is wrong; for the experience of *ajñāna* may here be regarded from one point of view as having reference to particular details. If the specific details are not known, there cannot be any ignorance with reference to them. But, just as, even when there is the knowledge of a thing in a general manner, there may be doubt regarding its specific nature, so there may be knowledge in a general manner and ignorance regarding the details. It may also be said that ignorance is directly known in a general manner without reference to its specific details. Vyāsa-tīrtha had contended that the knowledge of ignorance could only be when the particulars could not be known; thus God has no illusion, but has a knowledge of illusion in general. Against this Madhusūdana contends that in all the examples that could be cited by the opponents ignorance in a general manner can subsist along with a knowledge of the constituent particulars. Again, it is argued that, since *ajñāna* is an object of knowledge, it would be necessary that the veil of *ajñāna* should be removed; this is self-contradictory. To this Madhusūdana's reply is that, just as in the case of the knowledge of specific space-relations the presence of an object is necessary, but yet but for the knowledge of its negation presence of the object would be impossible, so also in the case of the knowledge of *ajñāna* the removal of a further veil is unnecessary, as this would be self-contradictory.

It may be urged that *ajñāna* is known only when the object with reference to which the ignorance exists is not known; later on, when such an object is known, the knower remembers that he had ignorance regarding the object; and the difference between such an *ajñāna* and negation of *jñāna* (*jñānābhāva*) lies in the fact that negation cannot be known without involving a relationing to its defining reference, whereas *ajñāna* does not stand in need of any such defining reference. To this supposed explanation of *ajñāna* by Vyāsa-tīrtha Madhusūdana's reply is that the Śaṅkarites virtually admit the difference between *ajñāna* and *abhāva*, against which they have been contending so long. Moreover, when one says "I do not know what you say," the *ajñāna* with reference to the speech of the speaker is directly known at the present time, and this would be inexplicable if the cognition of *ajñāna* did not involve a cognition of the defining reference. So, since *ajñāna* is cognized along with its object, there is no discrepancy in the object being manifested in its aspect as under the grasp of *ajñāna* as intuited by the *sākṣi*-consciousness. Madhusūdana urges that the pure consciousness can remove *ajñāna* only by being reflected through the *pramāṇa-vṛtti* and not through its character as self-luminous or through the fact of its being of a class naturally opposed to *ajñāna*[1]. The difference between the *vṛtti* and the *sākṣi*-consciousness in relation to *ajñāna* consists in the fact that the former is opposed to *ajñāna*, while the latter has no touch of *ajñāna*. The latter, i.e., the *sākṣi*-consciousness, directly manifests pleasures, pains, etc., not by removing any *ajñāna* that was veiling them, but spontaneously, because the veil of *ajñāna* was not operating on the objects that were being directly manifested by it[2].

Ajñāna and Ego-hood (ahaṃkāra).

The Śaṅkarites hold that, though during dreamless sleep the self-luminous self is present, yet, there being at the time no non-luminous ego, the memory in the waking stage does not refer the experience of the dreamless state to the ego as the self; and the scriptural texts also often speak against the identification of the self with the ego. In the dreamless stage the ego is not manifested; for, had it been manifested, it would have been so remembered.

To this Vyāsa-tīrtha's reply is that it cannot be asserted that in dreamless sleep the self is manifested, whereas the ego is not; for the opponents have not been able to prove that the ego is something different from the self-luminous self. It is also wrong to say that the later memory of sleeping does not refer to the ego; for all memory refers to the self as the ego, and nothing else. Even when

[1] *pramāṇa-vṛtty-upārūḍha-prakāśatvena nivartakatvaṃ brūmaḥ, na tu jāti-viśeṣeṇa, prakāśatva-mātreṇa vā. Advaita-siddhi*, p. 590.

[2] *sākṣiṇi yad ajñāna-virodhitvam anubhūyate tan nājñāna-nivartakatva-nibandhanaṃ, kintu sva-viṣayecchādau yāvatsattvam prakāśād ajñānāprasakti-nibandhanam. Ibid.* p. 590.

one says "I slept," he uses the "I," the ego with which his self is associated. The *Vivaraṇa* also says that recognition is attributed to the self as associated with the *antaḥkaraṇa*. If the ego were not experienced as the experiencer of the dreamless state, then one might equally well have entertained doubts regarding it. It is wrong also to suppose that the entity found in all perceivers is the self, and not the ego; for, howsoever it may be conceived, it is the ego that is the object of all such reference, and even the *Vivaraṇa* says that the self, being one in all its experiences in separate individuals, is distinct only through its association with the ego. It cannot be said that reference to the ego is not to the ego-part, but to the self-luminous entity underlying it; for, if this be admitted, then even ignorance would have to be associated with that entity. The *ajñāna* also appears in experiences as associated with the ego, and the ego appears not as the sleeper, but as the experiencer of the waking state, and it recognizes itself as the sleeper. Nor can it be denied that in the waking state one remembers that the ego during the sleep has experienced pleasure; so it must be admitted that in dreamless sleep it is the ego that experiences the sleep. The fact that one remembers his dream-experience as belonging to the same person who did some action before and who is now remembering shows that the action before the dream-experience and the present act of remembering belong to the same identical ego, the experiencer; even if the underlying experiencer be regarded as pure consciousness, yet so far as concerns the phenomenal experiencer and the person that remembers it is the ego to which all experience may be said to belong. Moreover, if the ego is supposed to be dissolved in the dreamless sleep, then even the bio-motor functions of the body, which are supposed to belong to the ego, would be impossible. Moreover, since our self-love and our emotion for self-preservation are always directed towards the self as the ego, it must be admitted that the experiences of the permanent self refer to the ego-substratum. It cannot be urged that this is possible by an illusory imposition of the ego on the pure self; for this would involve a vicious circle, since, unless the pure self is known as the supreme object of love, there cannot be any imposition upon it and, unless there is an imposition of the ego upon it, the self cannot be known as the supreme object of love. Moreover, there is no experience of a self-love which could be supposed to be directed to pure consciousness and not to the phenomenal self. Similar criticisms may also be made in the case of the explanation of such experience as "I shall attain the ultimate bliss," as based on the imposition of the ego upon the pure self[1]. Moreover, if the notion of the ego has as a constituent the mind, then such experience as "my mind," where the mind and the ego appear as different, would be impossible, and the experience of mind and ego would be the same. Moreover, all illusions have two constituents—the basis and the appearance; but in the ego no such two parts are experienced. It is also wrong to suppose that in such experiences as "I appear to myself" (*ahaṃ sphurāmi*) the appearance in consciousness is the basis and "appear to myself" is the illusory appearance[2]. For, the appearance (*sphuraṇa*) of the ego being different from the ego-substance (*aham-artha*), there is no appearance of identity between them such that the former may be regarded as the basis of the latter. The ego is, thus, directly perceived by intuitive experience as the self, and inference also points to the same; for, if the ego is enjoined to go through the ethical and other purificatory duties, and if it is the same that is spoken of as being liberated, it stands to reason that it is the ego substance that is the self. Vyāsa-tīrtha further adduces a number of scriptural texts in confirmation of this view.

To this Madhusūdana's reply is that, if the ego-substance had been present in sleep, then its qualities, such as desire, wish, etc., would have been perceived. A substance which has qualities can be known only through such qualities: otherwise a jug with qualities would not require to be known through the latter. It is true, no doubt, that we affirm the existence of the jug in the interval between the destruction of its qualities of one order and the production of qualities of another order. But this does not go against the main thesis; for though a qualified thing requires to be known through its qualities, it does not follow that a qualityless thing should not be knowable. So it must be admitted that, since no qualities are apprehended during deep sleep, it is the qualityless self that is known in deep sleep; if it had not been perceived, there would have been no memory of it in the waking state. Moreover,

[1] *Nyāyāmṛta*, p. 283(*a*).

[2] *iha tu sphuraṇamātram adhiṣṭhānamiti sphurāmīty eva dhīr iti cen na. Ibid.* p. 38(*a*).

during dreamless sleep the self is perceived as supporting ignorance (as is testified by the experience "I did not know anything in deep sleep"), and hence it is different from the ego. The memory refers to pure consciousness as supporting *ajñāna*, and not to the ego. It is true that the *Vivaraṇa* holds that recognition (*pratyabhijñā*) can be possible only of pure consciousness as associated with the *antaḥkaraṇa;* but, though this is so, it does not follow that the apprehension (*abhijñā*) of the pure consciousness should also be associated with the *antaḥkaraṇa*. In the dreamless state, therefore, we have no recognition of pure consciousness, but an intuition of it. In the waking stage we have recognition not of the pure consciousness, but of the consciousness as associated with *ajñāna*. The emphasis of the statement of the *Vivaraṇa* is not on the fact that for recognition it is indispensable that the pure consciousness should be associated with the *antaḥkaraṇa*, but on the fact that it should not be absolutely devoid of the association of any conditioning factor; and such a factor is found in its association with *ajñāna*, whereby recognition is possible. The memory of the ego as the experiencer during dreams takes place through the intuition of the self during dreamless sleep and the imposition of the identity of the ego therewith. It is the memory of such an illusory imposition that is responsible for the apparent experience of the ego during dreamless sleep. It is wrong to suggest that there is a vicious circle; for it is only when the ego-substratum is known to be different from the self that there can be illusory identity and it is only when there is illusory identity that, as the ego does not appear during dreamless state, the belief that it is different is enforced. For it is only when the self is known to be different from the ego that there can be a negation of the possibility of the memory of the self as the ego. Vyāsa-tīrtha says that, the ego-substratum (*aham-artha*) and the ego-sense (*ahaṃ-kāra*) being two different entities, the manifestation of the former does not involve as a necessary consequence the manifestation of the latter, and this explains how in the dreamless state, though the ego-substratum is manifested, yet the ego-sense is absent. To this Madhusūdana's reply is that the ego-substratum and the ego-sense are co-existent and thus, wherever the ego-substratum is present, there ought also to be the ego-sense, and, if during the dreamless state the ego-substratum was manifested, then the ego-sense should also have been manifested with it. He adds that the same objection cannot be made in regard to the manifestation of the self during the dreamless state; for the self is not associated with the ego-sense. Vyāsa-tīrtha has said that, just as the Śaṅkarites explain the manifestation of *ajñāna* in the dreamless state as having reference to objective entities only, and not to the pure *sākṣi*-consciousness (as it could not without contradiction be manifested and be at the same time the object of *ajñāna*), so the manifestation of the ego-substratum is not contradicted by the association with *ajñāna*, but may be regarded as having reference to extraneous objective entities. To this Madusūdana's reply is that there is no contradiction in the appearance of *ajñāna* in the *sākṣi*-consciousness, as it may be in the case of its association with the ego-substratum, and so the explanation of Vyāsa-tīrtha is quite uncalled-for.

Madhusūdana says that the ego-substratum may be inferred to be something different from the self, because, like the body, it is contemplated by our ego-perception or our perception as "I." If it is held that even the self is contemplated by the ego-perception, the reply is that the self, in the sense in which it is contemplated by the ego-perception, is really a non-self. In its essential nature the self underlying the ego-perception cannot be contemplated by the ego-perception. Again, the view of Vyāsa-tīrtha, that the fact of our feeling ourselves to be the supreme end of happiness shows that supreme happiness belongs to the ego-substratum, is criticized by the Śaṅkarites to the effect that the supreme happiness, really belonging to the self, is illusorily through a mistaken identity imposed upon the ego-substratum. This criticism, again, is criticized by the Madhvas on the ground that such an explanation involves a vicious circle, because only when the supremely happy nature of the ego-substratum is known does the illusory notion of identity present itself; and that only when the illusory notion of identity is present is there awareness of that supremely happy nature. To this, again, the reply of Madhusūdana is that the experiencing of the dreamless stage manifests the self as pure consciousness, while the ego-substratum is unmanifest; thus through the testimony of deep sleep the ego-substratum is known to be different from the self. The ego-substratum is by itself unmanifested, and its manifestation is always through the illusory imposition of identity with the pure self. What Madhusūdana wishes to assert is that the supremely happy experience during deep sleep is a manifestation of the pure self and not of the ego-substratum; the ego is felt to be happy only through identification with the pure self, to which alone belongs the happiness in deep sleep.

The objection of Vyāsa-tīrtha is that in emancipation the self is not felt as the supreme end of happiness, because there is no duality there, but, if such an experience be the nature of the self, then with its destruction there will be destruction of the self in emancipation. To this Madhusūdana's reply is that the experience of the self as the end of supreme happiness is only a conditional manifestation, and therefore the removal of this condition in emancipation cannot threaten the self with destruction.

It is urged by the Śaṅkarites that the agency (*kartṛtva*) belonging to the mind is illusorily imposed upon the self, whereby it illusorily appears as agent, though its real changeless nature is perceived in deep sleep. Vyāsa-tīrtha replies that there are two specific illustrations of illusion, viz., (i) where the red-colour of the *japā*-flower is reflected on a crystal, whereby the white crystal appears as red, and (ii) where a rope appears as a dreadful snake. Now, following the analogy of the first case, one would expect that the mind would separately be known as an agent, just as the *japā*-flower is known to be red, and the pure consciousness also should appear as agent, just as the crystal appears as red. If the reply is that the illusion is not of the first type, since it is not the quality of the mind that is reflected, but the mind with its qualities is itself imposed, there it would be of the second type. But even then the snake itself appears as dreadful, following which analogy one would expect that the mind should appear independently as agent and the pure consciousness also should appear so.

Madhusūdana in reply says that he accepts the second type of illusion, and admits that agency parallel to the agency of the mind appears in the pure consciousness and then these two numerically different entities are falsely identified through the identification of the mind with the pure consciousness. As a matter of fact, however, the illusion of the agency of the mind in the pure consciousness may be regarded as being of both the above two types. The latter type, as *nirupādhika*, in which that which is imposed (*adhyasyamāna*, e.g., the dreadful snake), being of the *Vyāvahārika* type of existence, has a greater reality than the illusory knowledge (the rope-snake which has only a *prātibhāsika* existence), as has been shown above. It may also be interpreted as being a *sopādhika* illusion of the first type, since both that which is imposed (the agency of the mind) and that which is the illusory appearance (the agency of the pure consciousness) have the same order of existence, viz., *Vyāvahārika*, which we know to be the condition of a *sopādhika* illusion as between *japā*-flower and crystal.

Madhusūdana points out that ego-hood (*ahaṃ-kāra*) is made up of two constituents, (i) the underlying pure consciousness, and (ii) the material part as the agent. The second part really belongs to the mind, and it is only through a false identification of it with the pure consciousness that the experience "I am the doer, the agent" is possible: so the experience of agency takes place only through such an illusion. So the objection that, if the agency interest in the mind is transferred to the ego-substratum, then the self cannot be regarded as being subject to bondage and liberation, is invalid; for the so-called ego-substratum is itself the result of the false identification of the mind and its associated agency with the pure consciousness. Vyāsa-tīrtha had pointed out that in arguing with Sāṃkhyists the Śaṅkarites had repudiated (*Brahma-sūtra*, II. 3. 33) the agency of the *buddhi*. To this Madhusūdana's reply is that what the Śaṅkarites asserted was that the consciousness was both the agent and the enjoyer of experiences, and not the latter alone, as the Sāṃkhyists had declared; they had neither repudiated the agency of *buddhi* nor asserted the agency of pure consciousness.

Vyāsa-tīrtha says that in such experience as "I am a Brahmin" the identification is of the Brahmin body with the "I" and this "I" according to the Śaṅkarites is different from the self; if that were so, it would be wrong to suppose that the above experience is due to a false identification of the body with the "self"; for the "I" is not admitted by the Śaṅkarites to be the self. Again, if the identity of the body and the self be directly perceived, and if there is no valid inference to contradict it, it is difficult to assert that they are different. Moreover, the body and the senses are known to be different from one another and cannot both be regarded as identical with the self. Again, if all difference is illusion, the notion of identity, which is the opposite of "difference," will necessarily be true. Moreover, as a matter of fact, no such illusory identification of the body and the self ever takes place; for, not to speak of men, even animals know that they are different from their bodies and that, though their bodies change from birth to birth, they themselves remain the same all through.

Madhusūdana says in reply that the false identification of the body and the ego is possible because ego has for a constituent the pure consciousness, and thus the false identification with it means identification with consciousness. Moreover, it is wrong to say that, if perception reveals the identity between the body and self, then it is not possible through inference to establish their difference. For it is well known (e.g., in the case of the apparent size of the moon in perception) that the results of perception are often revised by well-established inference and authority. Again, the objection that, all difference being illusory, the opposite of difference, viz., false identification, must be true, is wrong; for in the discussion on the nature of falsehood it has been shown that both the positive and the negative may at the same time be illusory. Moreover, the false identification of the body with the self can be dispelled in our ordinary life by inference and the testimony of scriptural texts, whereas the illusion of all difference can be dispelled only by the last cognitive state preceding emancipation. Madhusūdana holds that all explanation in regard to the connection of the body with the self is unavailing, and the only explanation that seems to be cogent is that the body is an illusory imposition upon the self.

Indefinability of World-appearance.

It is urged by Vyāsa-tīrtha that it is difficult for the Śaṅkarites to prove that the world-appearance is indefinable (*anirvacya*), whatever may be the meaning of such a term. Thus, since it is called indefinable, that is in itself a sufficient description of its nature; nor can it be said that there is an absence of the knowledge or the object which might have led to a definition or description; for in their absence no reference to description would be at all possible. Nor can it be said that indefinability means that it is different from both being and non-being; for, being different from them, it could be the combination of them. To this Madhusūdana's reply is that the indefinability consists in the fact that the world-appearance is neither being nor non-being nor being-and-non-being. Indefinability may also be said to consist in the fact that the world-appearance is liable to contradiction in the context wherein it appears. It cannot be said that the above position does not carry us to a new point, since one existent entity may be known to be different from any other existent entity; for the negation here is not of any particular existence, but of existence as such. If it is possible to assert that there may be an entity which is neither existence nor non-existence, then that certainly would be a new proposition. Madhusūdana further points out that "existence" and "non-existence" are used in their accepted senses and, both of them being unreal, the negation of either of them does not involve the affirmation of the other, and therefore the law of excluded middle is not applicable. When it is said that the indefinability consists in the fact that a thing is neither being nor non-being, that means simply that, all that can be affirmed or denied being unreal, neither of them can be affirmed; for what is in itself indescribable cannot be affirmed in any concrete or particularized form[1].

Vyāsa-tīrtha contends that the inscrutable nature of existence and non-existence should not be a ground for calling them indefinable; for, if that were so, then even the cessation of *avidyā*, which is regarded as being neither existent nor non-existent nor existent-non-existent nor indefinable, should also have been called indefinable. The reply of Madhusūdana to this is that the cessation of *avidyā* is called unique, because it does not exist during emancipation; he further urges that there is no incongruity in supposing that an entity as well as its negation (provided they are both unreal) may be absent in any other entity—this is impossible only when the positive and the negative are both real. Madhusūdana further says that being and non-being are not mutual negations, but exist in mutually negated areas. Being in this sense may be defined as the character of non-being contradicted, and non-being as incapability of appearing as being. It may be argued that in this sense the world-appearance cannot be regarded as different from both being and non-being. To this the reply is that by holding the view that being and non-being are not in their nature exclusive, in such a way that absence of being is called non-being and *vice versa*, but that the absence of one is marked by the presence of another, a possibility

[1] *na ca tarhi sad-ādi-vailakṣaṇyoktiḥ kathaṃ tat-tat-pratiyogi-durnirūpatā-mātre prakaṭanāya, na hi svarūpato durnirūpasya kiṃcid api rūpaṃ vāstavaṃ sambhavati. Advaita-siddhi*, p. 621.

is kept open whereby both may be absent at one and the same time. Thus, if eternity and non-eternity be defined as being-associated-with-destruction and being-unassociated-with-destruction, then they may be both absent in generality, which has no being; and, again, if eternity be defined as absence of a limit in the future, and non-eternity be defined as liability to cessation on the part of entities other than being, then negation-precedent-to-production (*prāg-abhāva*) may be defined as an entity in which there is neither entity nor non-entity; for a negation-precedent-to-destruction has a future and at the same time cannot be made to cease by any other thing than a positive entity, and so it has neither eternity nor non-eternity in the above senses. So the false silver, being unreal, cannot be liable to contradiction or be regarded as uncontradicted. The opponent, however, contends that the illustration is quite out of place, since generality (*sāmānya*) has no destruction and is, therefore, non-eternal, and negation-precedent-to-production is non-eternal, because it is destroyed. To this Madhusūdana's reply is that the Śaṅkarites do not attempt to prove their case simply by this illustration, but adduce the illustration simply as a supplement to other proofs in support of their thesis. The reason why the qualities of being and non-being may be found in the world-appearance without contradiction is that, being qualities of imaginary entities (being and non-being), they do not contradict each other[1]. If an entity is not regarded as non-eternal in a real sense, there is no contradiction in supposing it to be non-eternal only so long as that entity persists. Madhusūdana puts forward the above arguments to the effect that there is no contradiction in affirming the negation of any real qualities on the ground that those qualities are imaginary[2], against the criticism of Vyāsa-tīrtha that, if the world-appearance is pronounced by any person for whatever reasons to be indefinable, then that itself is an affirmation, and hence there is a contradiction. To be indefinable both as being and as non-being means that both these are found to be contradicted in the entity under consideration. When it is said that the imaginary world-appearance ought not to be liable to being visible, invisible,

[1] *dharmiṇa eva kalpitatvena viruddhayor api dharmayor abhāvāt. Ibid.* p. 622.

[2] *atāttvika-hetu-sad-bhāvena tāttvika-dharmābhāvasya sādhanena vyāghātā-bhāvāt. Ibid.* p. 623.

contradicted or uncontradicted, there is a misunderstanding; for it is certainly outside such affirmations in any real sense, but there is no incongruity in the affirmation of these qualities as imaginary appearances, since they are presented in those forms to all experience. The whole point is that, when qualities that are contradictory are in themselves imaginary, there is no incongruity in their mutual negation with reference to a particular entity; if the mutual negation is unreal, their mutual affirmation is equally unreal. Vyāsa-tīrtha argues that indefinability of the world-appearance (*anirvācytva*) cannot mean that it is not the locus of either being or non-being; for both non-being and Brahman, being qualityless, would satisfy the same conditions, and be entitled to be called indefinable. It cannot be said that Brahman may be regarded as the locus of imaginary being, for the reply is that the same may be the case with world-appearance. Again, since Brahman is qualityless, if being is denied of it, absence of being also cannot be denied; so, if both being and absence of being be denied of Brahman, Brahman itself becomes indefinable. The reply of Madhusūdana is that the denial of both being and non-being in the world-appearance is indefinable or unspeakable only in the sense that such a denial applies to the world appearance only so long as it is there, whereas in the Brahman it is absolute. Whereas the main emphasis of the argument of Vyāsa-tīrtha is on the fact that both being and non-being cannot be denied at the same time, Madhusūdana contends that, since the denial of being and the affirmation of it are not of the same order (the latter being of the *Vyāvahārika* type), there is no contradiction in their being affirmed at the same time. In the same way Madhusūdana contends that the denial of quality in Brahman (*nirviśeṣatva*) should not be regarded as a quality in itself; for the quality that is denied is of imaginary type and hence its denial does not itself constitute a quality. Vyāsa-tīrtha further urges that, following the trend of the argument of the Śaṅkarites, one might as well say that there cannot be any contradiction of the illusory conch-shell-silver by the experiential conch-shell, the two being of two different orders of existence: to this Madhusūdana's reply is that both the illusory and the experiential entities are grasped by the *sākṣi*-consciousness, and this constitutes their sameness and the contradiction of one by the other; there is no direct contradiction of the illusory by the experiential, and therefore the criticism of Vyāsa-tīrtha fails.

Nature of Brahman.

Vyāsa-tīrtha, in describing the nature of illusion, says that, when the subconscious impression of silver is roused, the senses, being associated with specific defects, take the "thisness" of conch-shell as associated with silver. There is, therefore, no production of any imaginary silver such as the Śaṅkarites allege; the silver not being there, later perception directly shows that it was only a false silver that appeared. Inference also is very pertinent here; for whatever is false knowledge refers to non-existent entities simply because they are not existent. Vyāsa-tīrtha further points out that his view of illusion (*anyathā-khyāti*) is different from the Buddhist view of illusion (*a-sat-khyāti*) in this, that in the Buddhist view the appearance "this is silver" is wholly false, whereas in Vyāsa-tīrtha's view the "this" is true, though its association with silver is false.

Vyāsa-tīrtha further points out that, if the illusory silver be regarded as a product of *ajñāna*, then it will be wrong to suppose that it is liable to negation in the past, present and future; for, if it was a product of *ajñāna*, it was existing then and was not liable to negation. It is also wrong to say that the negation of the illusory appearance is in respect of its reality; for, in order that the appearance may be false, the negation ought to deny it as illusory appearance and not as reality, since the denial of its reality would be of a different order and would not render the entity false.

Vyāsa-tīrtha had contended that, since Brahman is the subject of discussion and since there are doubts regarding His nature, a resolution of such doubts necessarily implies the affirmation of some positive character. Moreover, propositions are composed of words, and, even if any of the constituent words is supposed to indicate Brahman in a secondary sense, such secondary meaning is to be associated with a primary meaning; for as a rule secondary meanings can be obtained only through association with a primary meaning, when the primary meaning as such is baffled by the context. In reply to the second objection Madhusūdana says that a word can give secondary meaning directly, and does not necessarily involve a baffling of the primary meaning. As regards the first objection the reply of Madhusūdana is that the undifferentiated character of Brahman can be known not necessarily through any affirmative character, but through the negation of all opposite concepts. If it is objected that the negation of such opposing concepts would necessarily imply that those concepts are constituents of Brahma-knowledge, the reply of Madhusūdana is that, such negation of opposing concepts being of the very nature of Brahman, it is manifested and intuited directly, without waiting for the manifestation of any particular entity. The function of ordinary propositions involving association of particular meanings is to be interpreted as leading to the manifestation of an undivided and unparticularized whole, beyond the constituents of the proposition which deal with the association of particular meanings.

Vyāsa-tīrtha contends that, if Brahman is regarded as differenceless, then He cannot be regarded as identical with knowledge or with pure bliss, or as the one and eternal, or as the *sākṣi*-consciousness. Brahman cannot be pure consciousness; for consciousness cannot mean the manifestation of objects, since in emancipation there are no objects to be manifested. To this Madhusūdana's reply is that, though in emancipation there are no objects, yet that does not detract from its nature as illuminating. To Vyāsa-tīrtha's suggestion that Brahman cannot be regarded as pure bliss interpreted as agreeable consciousness (*anukūla-vedanatva*) or mere agreeableness (*anukūlatva*), since this would involve the criticism that such agreeableness is due to some extraneous condition, Madhusūdana's reply is that Brahman is regarded as pure bliss conceived as unconditional desirability (*nirupādhikeṣṭarūpatvāt*). Madhusūdana urges that this cannot mean negation of pain; for negation of pain is an entity different from bliss and in order that the definition may have any application it is necessary that the negation of pain should lead to the establishment of bliss. Vyāsa-tīrtha further argues that, if this unconditional desirability cannot itself be conditional, then the blissful nature of Brahman must be due to certain conditions. Moreover, if Brahman's nature as pure bliss be different from its nature as pure knowledge, then both the views are partial; and, if they are identical, it is useless to designate Brahman as both pure knowledge and pure bliss. To this Madhusūdana's reply is that, though knowledge and bliss are identical, yet through imaginary verbal usage they are spoken of as different. He further urges that objectless pure knowledge is defined as pure bliss[1]; pure bliss is nothing but pure perceiver (*dṛg-anatirekāt*). On this view again there is no difference between bliss and its consciousness. Vyāsa-tīrtha contends that, if Brahman is regarded as non-dual, then that involves the negation of duality. If such a negation is false, then Brahman becomes dual; and, if such a negation is affirmed, then also Brahman becomes dual, for it involves the affirmation of negation. To this Madhusūdana's reply is that the reality of negation is nothing more than the locus in which the negation is affirmed; the negation would then mean nothing else than Brahman, and hence the criticism that the admission of negation would involve duality is invalid.

Regarding the *sākṣi*-consciousness Vyāsa-tīrtha contends that the definition of *sākṣi* as pure being is unacceptable in the technical sense of the word as defined by Pāṇini. To this Madhusūdana's reply is that *sākṣi* may be defined as the pure consciousness reflected either in *avidyā* or a modification of it; and thus even the pure being may, through its reflection, be regarded as the *draṣṭā*. The objection of circular reasoning, on the ground that there is interdependence between the conditions of reflection and the seeing capacity of the seer, is unavailing; for such interdependence is beginningless. The *sākṣi*-consciousness, according to Madhusūdana, is neither pure Brahman nor Brahman as conditioned by *buddhi*, but is the consciousness reflected in *avidyā* or a modification of it; the *sākṣi*-consciousness, though one in all perceivers, yet behaves as identified with each particular perceiver, and thus the experiences of one particular perceiver are perceived by the *sākṣi*-consciousness as identified with that particular perceiver, and so there is no chance of any confusion of the experience of different individuals on the ground that the *sākṣi*-consciousness is itself universal[2].

[1] *etena viṣayānullekhi-jñānam evānandam ity api yuktam. Advaita-siddhi*, p. 751.

[2] *sarva-jīva-sādhāraṇyepi tat-taj-jīva-caitanyābhedenābhivyaktasya tat-tad-duḥkhādi-bhāsakatayā atiprasaṅgābhāvāt. Ibid.* p. 754.

Refutation of Brahman as material and instrumental cause.

Vyāsa-tīrtha says that a material cause always undergoes transformation in the production of the effect; but Brahman is supposed to be changeless, and, as such, cannot be the material cause. There are, however, three views: viz., that Brahman and *māyā* are jointly the cause of the world, just as two threads make a string, or that Brahman with *māyā* as its power is the cause, or that Brahman as the support of *māyā* is the cause. The reconciliation is that the Brahman is called changeless so far as it is unassociated with *māyā* either as joint cause or as power or as instrument. To this Vyāsatīrtha says that, if the permanently real Brahman is the material cause of the world, the world also would be expected to be so. If it is said that the characteristics of the material cause do not inhere in the effect, but only a knowledge of it is somehow associated with it, then the world-appearance also cannot be characterized as indefinable (or *anirvācya*) by reason of the fact that it is constituted of *māyā*. Since only Brahman as unassociated with *māyā* can be called changeless, the Brahman associated with *māyā* cannot be regarded as the material cause of the world, if by such material cause the changeless aspect is to be understood. If it is urged that the changes are of the character (*māyā*), then, since such a character is included within or inseparably associated with the characterized, changes of character involve a change in the characterized, and hence the *vivarta* view fails. If the underlying substratum, the Brahman, be regarded as devoid of any real change, then it is unreasonable to suppose that such a substratum, in association with its power or character, will be liable to real change; if it is urged that the material cause may be defined as that which is the locus of an illusion, then it may be pointed out that earth is never regarded as the locus of an illusion, nor can the conch-shell be regarded as the material cause of the shell-silver.

The reply of Madhusūdana is that Brahman remains as the ground which makes the transformations of *māyā* possible. The Brahman has a wider existence than *māyā* and so cannot participate in the changes of *māyā*. Further, the objection that, if the Brahman is real, then the world which is its effect should also be real is not valid; for only the qualities of the transforming cause (as earth or of gold) are found to pass over to the effect, whereas, Brahman being the ground-cause, we have no analogy which should lead us to expect that it should pass on to the effect.

Vyāsa-tīrtha further says that, just as one speaks of the being of jugs, so one may speak of the non-being of chimerical entities, but that does not presuppose the assertion that chimerical entities have non-being as their material cause. Again, if the world had Brahman for its material cause, then, since Brahman was pure bliss, the world should also be expected to be of the nature of bliss, which it is not. Again, on the *vivarta* view of causation there is no meaning in talking of a material cause. Moreover, if Brahman be the material cause, then the *antaḥkaraṇa* cannot be spoken of as being the material and transforming cause of suffering and other worldly experiences.

Vyāsa-tīrtha, in examining the contention of the Śaṅkarites that Brahman is self-luminous, says that the meaning of the term "self-luminous" (*svaprakāśa*) must first be cleared. If it is meant that Brahman cannot be the object of any mental state, then there cannot be any dissension between the teacher and the taught regarding the nature of Brahman; for discussions can take place only if Brahman be the object of a mental state. If it is urged that Brahman is self-luminous in the sense that, though not an object of cognition, it is always immediately intuited, then it may be pointed out that the definition fails, since in dreamless sleep and in dissolution there is no such immediate intuition of Brahman. It cannot be said that, though in dreamless sleep the Brahman cannot be immediately intuited, yet it has the status or capacity (*yogyatā*) of being so intuited; for in emancipation, there being no characters or qualities, it is impossible that such capacities should thus exist.

Even if such capacity be negatively defined, the negation, being a category of world-appearance, cannot be supposed to exist in Brahman. Moreover, if Brahman can in no way be regarded as the result of cognitive action, then the fact that it shines forth at the culmination of the final knowledge leading to Brahmahood would be inexplicable. Nor can it be argued that pure consciousness is self-luminous, i.e., non-cognizable, because of the very fact that it is pure consciousness, since whatever is not pure consciousness is not self-luminous; for non-cognizability, being a quality, must exist somewhere, and, if it is absent everywhere else, it must by reduction be present at least in pure consciousness. But it may be urged that, even if pure consciousness be self-luminous, that does not prove the self-luminosity of the self. The obvious reply is that the self is identical with pure consciousness. To this Vyāsa-tīrtha's objection is that, since there cannot be any kind of quality in the self, it cannot be argued that self-luminosity exists in it, whether as a positive quality, or as a negation of its negation, or as capacity. For all capacity as such, being outside Brahman, is false, and that which is false cannot be associated with Brahman. If non-cognizability is defined as that which is not a product of the activity of a mental state (*phala-vyāpyatvaṃ*), and if such non-cognizability be regarded as a sufficient description of Brahman, then, since even the perception of a jug or of the illusory silver or of pleasure and pain satisfies the above condition, the description is too wide, and, since the shining of Brahman itself is the product of the activity of the destruction of the last mental state, the definition is too narrow[1]. It cannot be said that *phala-vyāpyatva* means the accruing of a speciality produced by the consciousness reflected through a mental state, and that such speciality is the relationing without consciousness on the occasion of the breaking of a veil, and that such a *phala-vyāpyatva* exists in the jug and not in the self. Nor can it be said that *phala-vyāpyatva* means the being of the object of consciousness of the ground manifested through consciousness reflected through a mental state. For the Śaṅkarites do not think that a jug is an object of pure consciousness as reflected through a *vṛtti* or mental state, but hold that it is directly the object of a mental state. It is therefore wrong to suggest that the definition of *phala-vyāpyatva* is such that it applies to jug, etc., and not to Brahman. By Citsukha pure self-shiningness of consciousness is regarded as an objectivity of consciousness, and, if that is so, Brahman must always be an object of consciousness, and the description of it as non-objectivity to consciousness, or non-cognizability, would be impossible. Citsukha, however, says that Brahman is an object of consciousness (*cid-viṣaya*), but not an object

[1] *nāpi phalāvyāpyatvaṃ dṛśyatva-bhaṅge ukta-rītyā prātibhāsike rūpyādau vyāvahārike avidyāntaḥkaraṇa-tad-dharma-sukhādau ghaṭādau ca lakṣaṇasyātivyāpteḥ. tatroktarītyaiva brahmaṇo'pi carama-vṛtti-pratibimbita-cid-rūpa-phala-vyāpyatvenāsambhavāc ca.* *Nyāyāmṛta*, p. 507(*b*).

of cognizing activity (*cid-akarmatva*). If, following Citsukha, *avedyatva* (or non-cognizability) be regarded as the status of that which is not the object of a cognitive operation, and if by cognitive operation one expresses that consciousness is manifested through a particular objective form, as in the case of a jug, then, since Brahman also in the final stage is manifested through a corresponding mental state, Brahman also must be admitted to be an object of cognitive operation; otherwise even a jug cannot be regarded as an object of cognitive operation, there being no difference in the case of the apprehension of a jug and that of Brahman. If it is urged that object of cognizability means the accruing of some special changes due to the operation of cognizing, then also Brahman would be as much an object as the jug; for, just as in the case of the cognition of a jug the cognizing activity results in the removal of the veil which was obstructing the manifestation of the jug, so final Brahma-knowledge, which is an intellectual operation, results in the removal of the obstruction to the manifestation of Brahman. The objectivity involved in cognizing cannot be regarded as the accruing of certain results in the object of cognition through the activity involved in cognizing operation; for, the pure consciousness not being an activity, no such accruing of any result due to the activity of the cognizing operation is possible even in objects (as jug, etc.) which are universally admitted to be objects of cognition. If reflection through a mental state be regarded as the cognizing activity, then that applies to Brahman also; for Brahman also is the object of such a reflection through a mental state or idea representing Brahman in the final state.

Citsukha defines self-luminosity as *aparokṣa-vyavahāra-yogyatva*, i.e., capability of being regarded as immediate. A dispute may now arise regarding the meaning of this. If it signifies "that which is produced by immediate knowledge," then virtue and vice, which can be immediately intuited by supernatural knowledge of Yogins and Gods, has also to be regarded as immediate; and, when one infers that he has virtue or vice and finally has an immediate apprehension of that inferential knowledge, or when one has an immediate knowledge of virtue or vice as terms in inductive proposition (e.g., whatever is knowable is definable, such a proposition including virtue and vice as involved under the term "knowable"), one would be justified in saying that virtue and vice are also immediate, and thus immediacy of apprehension would be too wide for a sufficient description of Brahman. Thus, though virtue and vice are not cognizable in their nature, it is yet possible in the case of Yogins and of God to have immediate apprehension of them, and so also in our case, so far as concerns the direct apprehension of inference of them.

If immediacy signifies "that which may be the object of immediate knowledge," and if the self be regarded as immediate in this sense, then it is to be admitted that the self is an object of immediate cognition, like the jug[1]. Nor can it be urged that the immediacy of an object depends upon the immediacy of the knowledge of it; for the immediacy of knowledge also must depend upon the immediacy of the object. Again, Vyāsa-tīrtha contends that immediacy cannot signify that the content is of the form of immediacy (*aparokṣa-ity-ākāra*); for it is admitted to be pure and formless and produced by the non-relational intuition of the Vedāntic instructions.

Vyāsa-tīrtha, in his *Nyāyāmṛta*, tries to prove that Brahman is possessed of qualities, and not devoid of them, as the Śaṅkarites argue; he contends that most of the scriptural texts speak of Brahman as being endowed with qualities. God (Īśvara) is endowed with all good qualities, for He desires to have them and is capable of having them; and He is devoid of all bad qualities, because He does not want them and is capable of divesting Himself of them. It is useless to contend that the mention of Brahman as endowed with qualities refers only to an inferior Brahman; for, Vyāsa-tīrtha urges, the scriptural texts do not speak of any other kind of Brahman than the qualified one. If the Brahman were actually devoid of all qualities, it would be mere vacuity or *śūnya*, a negation; for all substances that exist must have some qualities. Vyāsa-tīrtha further contends that, since Brahman is the creator and protector of the world and the authorizer of the Vedas, He must have a body and organs of action, though that body is not an ordinary material body (*prākṛtāvayavādi-niṣedha-paratvāt*); and it is because His body is spiritual and not material that in spite of the possession of a body He is both infinite and eternal and His abode is also spiritual and eternal[2].

[1] *vastuna āparokṣyam aparokṣa-jñāna-viṣayatvaṃ ced ātmāpi ghaṭādivad vedyaḥ syāt. Nyāyāmṛta*, p. 511 (*a*).

[2] *Ibid.* pp. 496–8.

Again, it is also wrong to say that Brahman is both the material cause and the instrumental cause of the world, as the substance-stuff of the world and as the creator or modeller of the world; for the material cause undergoes modifications and changes, whereas the Brahman is unchangeable. Brahman, again, is always the master, and the individual selves or souls are always His servants: so God alone is always free (*nitya-mukta*), whereas individual souls are always related and bound to Him[1]. The *guṇas* belong to *prakṛti* or *māyā* and not to the individual souls; and therefore, since the *guṇas* of *prakṛti* are not in the individual souls, there cannot be any question of the bondage of individual souls by them or of liberation from them. Whatever bondage, therefore, there is by which the *guṇas* tie the individual souls is due to ignorance (*avidyā*). The *guṇas*, again, cannot affect God; for they are dependent (*adhīna*) on Him. It is only out of a part of God that all individual souls have come into being, and that part is so far different from God that, though through ignorance the individual souls, which have sprung forth from this part, may be suffering bondage, God Himself remains ever free from all such ignorance and bondage[2]. The *māyā* or *prakṛti* which forms the material cause of the world is a fine dusty stuff or like fine cotton fibres (*sūkṣma-reṇumayī sā ca tantu-vāyasya tantuvat*), and God fashions the world out of this stuff[3]. This

[1] *muktāv api svāmi-bhṛtya-bhāva-sadbhāvena bhakty-ādi-bandha-sadbhāvāt nitya-baddhatvaṃ jīvasya kṛṣṇasya tu nitya-muktatvam eva.* *Bhāva-vilāsinī* (p. 179) on *Yukti-mallikā*.

[2] *ekasyaiva mamāṃśasya jīvasyaivaṃ mahāmate*
bandhasyāvidyayānādi vidyayā ca tathetaraḥ
sva-bhinnāṃśasya jīvākhyā ajasyaikasya kevalam
bandhaś ca bandhān mokṣaś ca na svasyety āha sa prabhuḥ.
Yukti-mallikā, p. 179.

The *Bhāva-vilāsinī* (p. 185) also points out that, though God has His wives and body and His heavenly abode in *Vaikuṇṭha*, yet He has nothing to tie Himself with these; for these are not of *prakṛti*-stuff, and, as He has no trace of the *guṇas* of *prakṛti*, He is absolutely free; only a tie of *prakṛti*-stuff can be a tie or bondage. But *prakṛti* cannot affect Him; for He is her master—*mama guṇā vastūni ca śruti-smṛtiṣu aprākṛtatayā prasiddhāḥ*. It may be noted in this connection that the Madhva system applies the term *māyā* in three distinct senses: (i) as God's will (*harer icchā*); (ii) as the material *prakṛti* (*māyākhyā prakṛtir jaḍā*); and (iii) *māyā* or *mahā-māyā* or *avidyā*, as the cause of illusions and mistakes (*bhrama-hetuś ca māyaikā māyeyaṃ trividhā matā*). *Yukti-mallikā*, p. 188. There is another view which supposes *māyā* to be of five kinds; it adds God's power (*śakti*) and influence (*tejas*).

[3] This stuff is said to be infinitely more powdery than the atoms of the Naiyāyikas (*tārkikābhimata-paramāṇuto'py ananta-guṇita-sūkṣma-reṇumayī*). *Bhāva-vilāsinī*, p. 189. The *Srīmad-bhāgavata*, which is considered by Madhva

prakṛti is eightfold, inasmuch as it has five modifications as the five elements, and three as *manas*, *buddhi* and *ahaṃkāra*. The *māyā*, by the help of which God creates the world, is like the mother of the world and is called, in the theological terminology of the Madhva school, *Lakṣmī*. The creative *māyā*, or the will of God, is also called the *svarūpa-māyā*, because she always abides with the Lord. The *māyā* as *prakṛti*, or as her guiding power (*mayāśrayin*), is outside of God, but completely under His control[1].

God is referred to in the *Gītā* and other sacred texts as possessing a universal all-pervading body, but this body is, as we have already said, a spiritual body, a body of consciousness and bliss (*jñānānandātmako hy asau*). This His universal body transcends the bounds of all the *guṇas*, the *māyā* and their effects. All throughout this universal all-transcending spiritual body of the Lord is full of bliss, consciousness and playful activity[2]. There is no room for pantheism in true philosophy, and therefore Vedic passages which seem to imply the identity of the world and God are to be explained as attributing to God the absolute controlling power[3]. Again, when it is said that the individual souls are parts of God, it does not mean that they are parts in any spatial sense, or in the sense of any actual division such as may be made of material objects. It simply means that the individual souls are similar to God in certain respects and are at the same time much inferior to Him[4].

and his followers to be authoritative, speaks of the four wives of Vāsudeva, Saṅkarṣaṇa, Pradyumna and Aniruddha, as Māyā, Jayā, Kṛti and Śānti, which are but the four forms of the goddess Śrī, corresponding to the four forms of Hari as Vāmadeva, Saṅkarṣaṇa, Pradyumna and Aniruddha. *Yukti-mallikā*, p. 191.

[1] It is curious to note that the *māyā* which produces illusion and which affects only the individual souls, counted in one place referred to above as the third *māyā*, is counted again as the fourth *māyā*, and *prakṛti* (or *jaḍa-māyā* and *māyā-śrī*) as the second and the third *māyās*. *Yukti-mallikā*, p. 192 *a*, *b*.

[2] The *Bhāva-vilāsinī* (p. 198), giving the meaning of the word *śarīra* (which ordinarily means "body," from a root which means "to decay") with reference to God, assigns a fanciful etymological meaning; it says that the first syllable *śa* means bliss, *ra* means "play," and *īra* means "consciousness." In another place Varadarāja speaks of the Lord as being of the nature of the pure bliss of realization and the superintendent of all intelligence: *vidito'si bhavān sākṣāt puruṣaḥ prakṛteḥ paraḥ kevalānubhavānandasvarūpas sarva-buddhi-dṛk*. *Yukti-mallikā*, p. 201.

[3] *ataḥ puruṣa eveti prathamā pañcamī yadā*
sadā sarva-nimittatva-mahimā puṃsi varṇyate.
yadā tu saptamī sarvādhāratvaṃ varṇayet tadā
sūktasyaikārthatā caivaṃ satyeva syān na cānyathā. *Ibid.* p. 211.

[4] *tat-sadṛśatve sati tato nyūnatvaṃ jīvasya aṃśatvaṃ na tu ekadeśatvaṃ.* *Nyāyāmṛta*, p. 606.

It may be pointed out in this connection that as God is all-pervasive, so the individual souls are by nature atomic, though by their possession of the quality of consciousness, which is all-pervasive, they can always feel the touch of any part of their body just as a lamp, which, remaining at one place, may have its rays illuminating all places around it[1].

At the end of *pralaya* God wishes to create, and by His wish disturbs the equilibrium of *prakṛti* and separates its three *guṇas*, and then creates the different categories of *mahat*, *buddhi*, *manas* and the five elements and also their presiding deities; and then He permeates the whole world, including the living and the non-living[2]. In all the different states of existence (e.g., the waking, dream, deep sleep, swoon and liberation) it is God who by His various forms of manifestation controls all individual souls, and by bringing about these states maintains the existence of the world[3]. The destruction or *pralaya* also of the world is effected by His will[4]. Moreover, all knowledge that arises in all individual souls either for mundane experience or for liberation, and whatever may be the instruments employed for the production of such knowledge, have God as their one common ultimate cause[5].

Liberation (mokṣa).

Bondage is due to attachment to worldly objects, and liberation is produced through the direct realization of God (*aparokṣa-jñānaṃ Viṣṇoḥ*). This is produced in various ways, viz.: Experience of the sorrows of worldly existence, association with good men, renunciation of all desires of enjoyment of pleasures, whether in this world

[1] *Nyāyāmṛta*, p. 612. The view that the atomic soul touches different parts of the body at different successive moments for different touch-experiences is definitely objected to.

[2] *Padārtha-saṃgraha-vyākhyāna*, pp. 106–8.

[3] The five manifestations of God, controlling the five states above mentioned (waking, dream, etc.), are called *Prājña*, *Viśva*, *Taijasa*, *Bhagavān* and *Turīya Bhagavān* respectively.

[4] There are two kinds of destruction or *pralaya* in this system: (*a*) the *mahā-pralaya*, in which everything but *prakṛti* is destroyed, only absolute darkness remains, and *prakṛti* stops all her creative work, except the production of time as successive moments; (*b*) the secondary destruction, called *avāntara pralaya*, which is of two kinds, one in which along with our world the two imaginary worlds are also destroyed, and one in which only the living beings of this world are destroyed. *Ibid.* pp. 117–19.

[5] *Ibid.* p. 119.

or in some heavenly world, self-control and self-discipline, study, association with a good teacher, and study of the scriptures according to his instructions, realization of the truth of those scriptures, discussions on the proper meaning for strengthening one's convictions, proper respectful attachment to the teacher, respectful attachment to God (*paramātma-bhakti*), kindness to one's inferiors, love for one's equals, respectful attachment to superiors, cessation from works that are likely to bring pleasure or pain, cessation from doing prohibited actions, complete resignation to God, realization of the five differences (between God and soul, soul and soul, soul and the world, God and the world and between one object of the world and another), realization of the difference between *prakṛti* and *puruṣa*, appreciation of the difference of stages of advancement among the various kinds of men and other higher and lower living beings, and proper worship (*upāsanā*). As regards the teachers here referred to, from whom instructions should be taken, two distinct types of them are mentioned: there are some who are permanent teachers (*niyata guru*) and others who are only occasional teachers (*aniyata guru*). The former are those who can understand the nature and needs of their pupils and give such suitable instructions to them as may enable them to realize that particular manifestation of Viṣṇu which they are fit to realize; the occasional teachers are those who merely instruct us concerning God. In another sense all those who are superior to us in knowledge and religious discipline are our teachers. As regards worship, it is said that worship (*upāsanā*) is of two kinds: worship as religious and philosophical study, and worship as meditation (*dhyāna*)[1]; for there are some who cannot by proper study of the scriptures attain a true and direct realization of the Lord, and there are others who attain it by meditation. Meditation or *dhyāna* means continual thinking of God, leaving all other things aside[2], and such a meditation on God as the spirit, as the existent, and as the possessor of pure consciousness and bliss is only possible when a thorough conviction has been generated by scriptural studies and rational thinking and discussions, so that all false ideas have been removed and all doubts have been dispelled.

[1] *upāsanā ca dvividhā, satataṃ śāstrābhyāsa-rūpā dhyāna-rūpā ca. Madhva-siddhānta-sara*, p. 500.

[2] *dhyānaṃ ca itara-tiraskāra-pūrvaka-bhagavad-viṣayakākhaṇḍa-smṛtiḥ. Ibid.* p. 502. This *dhyāna* is the same as *nididhyāsana*.

God alone is the cause of all bondage, as well as of all liberation[1]. When one directly realizes the nature of God, there arises in him devotion (*bhakti*) to the Lord; for without personal, direct and immediate knowledge of Him there cannot be any devotion. Devotion (*bhakti*) consists of a continual flow of love for the Lord, which cannot be impaired or affected by thousands of obstacles, which is many times greater than love for one's own self or love for what is generally regarded as one's own, and which is preceded by a knowledge of the Lord as the possessor of an infinite number of good and benign qualities[2]. And when such a *bhakti* arises, the Lord is highly pleased (*atyartha-prasāda*), and it is when God is so pleased with us that we can attain salvation.

Though individual souls are self-luminous in themselves, yet through God's will their self-luminous intelligence becomes veiled by ignorance (*avidyā*). When, as a modification of the mind or inner organ (*antaḥkaraṇa*), direct knowledge of God arises, such a modification serves to dispel the ignorance or *avidyā*; for, though *avidyā* is not directly associated with the mind, yet such a mental advancement can affect it, since they are both severally connected with the individual self. Ordinarily the rise of knowledge destroys only the deeds of unappointed fruition, whereas the deeds of appointed fruition (*prārabdha-karma*) remain and cause pleasure and pain, cognition and want of cognition. So ordinarily the realization of God serves to destroy the association of *prakṛti* and the *guṇas* with an individual, as also his *karmas* and subtle body (*liṅga-deha*),

[1] God maintains or keeps in existence all other entities, which are all wholly dependent on Him. He creates and destroys only the non-eternal and eternal-non-eternal entities. Again, with reference to all beings except Lakṣmī, it is He who holds up the veil of positive ignorance (*bhāva-rūpā avidyā*) of *prakṛti*, either as the first *avidyā*, the *guṇas* of *sattva*, *rajas* and *tamas*, or as the second *avidyā* of desire (*kāma*), or as the third *avidyā* of actions of appointed fruition (*prārabdha-karma*), or as the subtle body, or finally as His own will. It is the last, the power of Hari, which forms the real stuff of all ignorance; the *avidyā* is only an indirect agent (*parameśvara-śaktir eva svarūpāvaraṇā mukhyā, avidyā tu nimitta-mātram*); for, even if *avidyā* is destroyed, there will not arise supreme bliss, unless God so desires it. It is again He who gives knowledge to the conscious entities, happiness to all except those demons who are by nature unfit for attaining it, and sorrow also to all except Lakṣmī, who is by nature without any touch of sorrow. *Tattva-saṃkhyāna-vivaraṇa* and *Tattva-saṃkhyāna-ṭippaṇa*, pp. 43–7.

[2] *parameśvara-bhaktir nāma niravadhikānantānavadya-kalyāṇa-guṇatvā-jñānapūrvakaḥ svātmātmīya-samasta-vastubhyaḥ aneka-guṇādhikaḥ antarāya-sahasreṇāpi apratibaddhaḥ nirantara-prema-pravāhaḥ*. *Nyāya-sudhā* on *Anuvyākhyāna*.

consisting of the senses, five *prāṇas* and *manas*, until the deeds of appointed fruition are exhausted by suffering or enjoyment[1]. During *pralaya* the liberated souls enter the womb of God and cannot have any enjoyment; but again after creation they begin to enjoy. The enjoyment of liberated souls is of four kinds: *sālokya*, *sāmīpya*, *sārūpya* and *sāyujya* (*sārṣṭi* being counted as a species of *sāyujya* and not a fifth kind of liberation). *Sāyujya* means the entrance of individual souls into the body of God and their identification of themselves with the enjoyment of God in His own body; *sārṣṭi-mokṣa*, which is a species of *sāyujya-mokṣa*, means the enjoyment of the same powers that God possesses, which can only be done by entering into the body of God and by identifying oneself with the particular powers of God. Only deities or Gods deserve to have this kind of liberation; they can, of course, at their will come out of God as well and remain separate from Him; *sālokya-mokṣa* means residence in heaven and being there with God to experience satisfaction and enjoyment by the continual sight of Him. *Sāmīpya-mokṣa* means continuous residence near God, such as is enjoyed by the sages. *Sārūpya-mokṣa* is enjoyed by God's attendants, who have outward forms similar to that which God possesses[2]. The acceptance of difference amongst the liberated souls in the states of enjoyment and other privileges forms one of the cardinal doctrines of Madhva's system; for, if it is not acknowledged, then the cardinal dualistic doctrine that all individual souls are always different from one another would fail[3]. It has already been said that liberation can be attained only by *bhakti*, involving continuous pure love (*sneha*)[4]. Only gods and superior men deserve it, whereas ordinary men deserve only to undergo rebirth, and the lowest men and the demons always suffer in hell. The Gods cannot go to hell, nor can the demons ever attain liberation, and ordinary persons neither obtain liberation nor go to hell[5].

[1] *Bhāgavata-tātparya*, I. 13, where a reference is made also to *Brahma-tarka*.

[2] Jaya and Vijaya, the two porters of God, are said to enjoy *Sārūpya-mokṣa*.

[3] *muktānāṃ ca na hīyante tāratamyaṃ ca sarvadā. Mahābhārata-tātparya-nirṇaya*, p. 4. See also *Nyāyāmṛta*.

[4] *acchidra-sevā* (faultless attendance) and *niṣkāmatva* (desirelessness) are also mentioned as defining the characteristic *bhakti*. Gifts, pilgrimage, *tapas*, etc., also are regarded as secondary accessories of attendance on, or *sevā* of, God. *Ibid.* p. 5.

[5] *Ibid.* p. 5.

As the imperative duties of all men upwards of eight years and up to eighty years of age, Madhva most strongly urges the fasting on the *Ekādaśī* (eleventh day of the moon), marking the forehead with the black vertical line characteristic of his followers even to the present day. One should constantly worship Lord Kṛṣṇa with great devotion (*bhakti*) and pray to Him to be saved from the sorrows of the world. One should think of the miseries of hell and try to keep oneself away from sins, and should always sing the name of Hari, the Lord, and make over to Him all the deeds that one performs, having no desire of fruits for them[1].

[1] *Kṛṣṇāmṛta-mahārṇava.*

CHAPTER XXXI

THE PHILOSOPHY OF VALLABHA

Vallabha's Interpretation of the Brahma-sūtra.

MOST systems of Vedānta are based upon an inquiry regarding the ultimate purport of the instruction of the text of the Upaniṣads which form the final part of the Vedas. The science of *mīmāṃsā* is devoted to the enquiry into the nature of Vedic texts, on the presumption that all Vedic texts have to be interpreted as enjoining people to perform certain courses of action or to refrain from doing others; it also presumes that obedience to these injunctions produces *dharma* and disobedience *adharma*. Even the study of the Vedas has to be done in obedience to the injunction that Vedas must be studied, or that the teacher should instruct in the Vedas or that one should accept a teacher for initiating him to the holy thread who will teach him the Vedas in detail. All interpreters of Mīmāṃsā and Vedānta agree on the point that the study of the Vedas implies the understanding of the meaning by the student, though there are divergences of opinion as to the exact nature of injunction and the exact manner in which such an implication follows. If the Brahmacārin has to study the Vedas and understand their meaning from the instruction of the teacher at his house, it may generally be argued that there is no scope for a further discussion regarding the texts of the Upaniṣads; and if this is admitted, the whole of the *Brahma-sūtra*, whose purpose is to enter into such a discussion, becomes meaningless. It may be argued that the Upaniṣad texts are pregnant with mystic lore which cannot be unravelled by a comprehension of the textual meaning of words. But, if this mystic lore cannot be unravelled by the textual meaning of the word, it is not reasonable to suppose that one can comprehend the deep and mystic truths which they profess to instruct by mere intellectual discussions. The Upaniṣads themselves say that one can comprehend the true meaning of the Upaniṣads through *tapas* and the grace of God[1].

[1] *a-laukiko hi vedārtho na yuktyā pratipadyate tapasā*
veda-yuktyā tu prasādāt paramātmanaḥ.
Vallabha's *Bhāṣya* on *Brahma-sūtra* (Chowkhamba edition, p. 13).

To this Vallabha's reply is that, since there are diverse kinds of *śāstras* offering diverse kinds of instructions, and since Vedic texts are themselves so complicated that it is not easy to understand their proper emphasis, an ordinary person may have legitimate doubt as to their proper meaning, unless there is a *śāstra* which itself discusses these difficulties and attempts to solve them by textual comparisons and contrasts; it cannot be denied that there is a real necessity for such a discussion as was undertaken by Vyāsa himself in the *Brahma-sūtra*[1].

According to Rāmānuja the *Brahma-sūtra* is a continuation of the *Mīmāṃsā-sūtra*; though the two works deal with different subjects, they have the same continuity of purpose. The study of the *Brahma-sūtra* must therefore be preceded by the study of the *Mīmāṃsā-sūtra*. According to Bhāskara the application of the *Mīmāṃsā-sūtra* is universal; all double-born people must study the *Mīmāṃsā* and the nature of *dharma* for their daily duties. The knowledge of Brahman is only for some; a discussion regarding the nature of Brahman can therefore be only for those who seek emancipation in the fourth stage of their lives. Even those who seek emancipation must perform the daily works of *dharma*; the nature of such *dharma* can only be known by a study of the *Mīmāṃsā*. The enquiry regarding Brahman must therefore be preceded by a study of the *Mīmāṃsā*. It is also said by some that it is by a long course of meditation in the manner prescribed by the Upaniṣads that the Brahman can be known. A knowledge of such meditation can only be attained by a knowledge of the due nature of sacrifices. It is said also in the *smṛtis* that it is by sacrifices that the holy body of Brahman can be built (*mahā-yajñaiś ca yajñaiś ca brāhmīyaṃ kriyate tanuḥ*)[2]; so it is when the forty-eight *saṃskāras* are performed that one becomes fit for the study or meditation on the nature of the Brahman. It is also said in the *smṛtis* that it is only after discharging the three debts—study, marriage, and performance of sacrifices—that one has the right to fix his mind on Brahman for emancipation. According to most

1 *sandeha-vārakaṃ śāstraṃ buddhi-doṣāt tad-udbhavaḥ*
viruddha-śāstra-saṃbhedād aṅgaiś cāśakya-niścayaḥ
tasmāt sūtrānusāreṇa kartavyaḥ sarva-nirṇayaḥ
anyathā bhraśyate svārthān madhyamaś ca tathāvidhaḥ.
Ibid. p. 20.

2 Manu, II. 28.

people the sacrificial duties are useful for the knowledge of Brahman; so it may be held that enquiry about the nature of Brahman must follow an enquiry about the nature of *dharma*[1].

But, even if the theory of the joint-performance of sacrifice and meditation on Brahman be admitted, it does not follow that an enquiry into the nature of Brahman must follow an enquiry about the nature of *dharma*. It can only mean that the nature of the knowledge of Brahman may be held to be associated with the nature of *dharma*, as it is properly known from the *Mīmāṃsā-śāstra*. On such a supposition the knowledge of the nature of the self is to be known from the study of the *Brahma-sūtra;* but since the knowledge of the self is essential even for the performance of sacrificial actions, it may well be argued that the enquiry into the nature of *dharma* must be preceded by an enquiry about the nature of the self from the *Brahma-sūtra*[2]. Nor can it be said that from such texts as require a person to be self-controlled (*śānto dānto*, etc.) it may be argued that enquiry into the nature of *dharma* must precede that about Brahman: the requirement of self-control does not necessarily mean that enquiry about the nature of *dharma* should be given precedence, for a man may be self-controlled even without studying the *Mīmāṃsā*.

Nor can it be said, as Śaṅkara does, that enquiry into the nature of Brahman must be preceded by a disinclination from earthly and heavenly joys, by mind-control, self-control, etc. On this point Bhāskara argues against the Vallabha views, and his reason for their rejection is that such attainments are extremely rare; even great sages like Durvāsas and others failed to attain them. Even without self-knowledge one may feel disinclined to things through sorrows, and one may exercise mind-control and self-control even for earthly ends. There is moreover no logical relation between the attainment of such qualities and enquiry about the nature of Brahman. Nor can it be argued that, if enquiry into the nature of Brahman is preceded by an enquiry into the *Mīmāṃsā*, we can attain all these qualities. Moreover, an enquiry about the nature of Brahman can only come through a conviction of the importance of

[1] Puruṣottama's commentary on Vallabhācārya's *Anubhāṣya*, pp. 25–6.

[2] *pūrvaṃ vedānta-vicāreṇa tad avagantavyaṃ nānā-balair ātma-svarūpe vipratipanna-vaidikānāṃ veda-vākyair eva tan nirāsasyāvaśyakatvāt jñāte tayoḥ sva-rūpe karmaṇi sukhena pravṛtti-darśanaṃ. Ibid.* p. 27.

the knowledge alone, and for the comprehension of such importance the enquiry about Brahman is necessary: there is thus an argument in a circle. If it is held that, when knowledge of the Vedāntic texts is properly acquired by listening to instruction on the Vedas, one may then turn to an enquiry into the nature of Brahman, that also is objectionable; for, if the meaning of the Vedāntic texts has been properly comprehended, there is no further need for an enquiry about the nature of Brahman. If it is held that the knowledge of Brahman can come only through the scriptural testimony of such texts as "that art thou" or "thou art the truth," that too is objectionable: for no realization of the nature of Brahman can come by scriptural testimony to an ignorant person who may interpret it as referring to an identity of the self and the body. If by the scriptural texts it is possible to have a direct realization of Brahman, it is unnecessary to enjoin the duty of reflection and mediation. It is therefore wrong to suppose that an enquiry into the nature of Brahman must be preceded either by *dharmavicāra* or by the attainment of such extremely rare qualities as have been referred to by Śaṅkara. Again, it is said in the scriptures that those who have realized the true meaning of the Vedānta should renounce the world; so renunciation must take place after the Vedāntic texts have been well comprehended and not before. Again, without an enquiry into the nature of Brahman one cannot know that Brahman is the highest object of attainment; without a knowledge of the latter one would not have the desired and other attainments of the mind and so be led to a discussion about Brahman. Again, if a person with the desired attainments listens to the Vedāntic texts, he would immediately attain emancipation and there would be no one to instruct him.

The enquiry about the nature of Brahman does not require any preceding condition; anyone of the double-born caste is entitled to do it. The Mīmāṃsakas say that all the Vedāntic texts insisting upon the knowledge of Brahman should be interpreted as injunctions by whose performance *dharma* is produced. But this interpretation is wrong; though any kind of prescribed meditation (*upāsanā*) may produce *dharma*, Brahman itself is not of the nature of *dharma*. All *dharmas* are of the nature of actions (*dharmāśya ca kriyā-rūpatvāt*); but Brahman cannot be produced, and is therefore not of the nature of action. The seeming injunction for meditation on Brahman is intended to show the greatness of Brahma-knowledge; such meditations are merely mental operations akin to knowledge and are not any kind of action. This Brahma-knowledge is also helpful for the proper discharge of one's duties; for this reason people like Janaka had it and so were able to discharge their duties in the proper manner. It is wrong to suppose that those who do not have the illusory notion of the self as the body are incapable of performing *karma;* for the *Gītā* says that the true philosopher knows that he does not work and yet is always associated with work; he abnegates all his *karmas* in Brahman and acts without any attachment, just as a lotus leaf never gets wet by water. The conclusion is therefore that only he who knows Brahman can by his work produce the desired results; so those who are engaged in discussing the nature of *dharma* should also discuss the nature of Brahman. The man who knows Brahman and works has no desire for the fruits of his *karma*, for he has resigned all his works to Brahman. It is therefore wrong to say that only those who are desirous of the fruits of *karma* are eligible for their performance; the highest and the most desired end of *karma* is the abnegation of its fruits[1]. It is the intention of Vallabha that both the *Pūrva-mīmāṃsā* and the *Uttara-mīmāṃsā* (or the *Brahma-sūtra*) are but two different ways of propounding the nature of Brahman; the two together form one science. This in a way is the view of all the Vedāntic interpreters except Śaṅkara, though they differ in certain details of mode of approach[2]. Thus according to Rāmānuja the two *Mīmāṃsās* form one science and the performance of sacrifices can be done conjointly with continual remembering of Brahman, which (with him) is devotion, meditation and realization of Brahman. According to Bhāskara, though the subject of the *Pūrva-mīmāṃsā* is different from that of the *Uttara-mīmāṃsā*, yet they have one end in view and form one science, and the ultimate purport of them both is the realization of the nature of Brahman. According to Bhikṣu the purpose of the *Brahma-sūtra* is to reconcile the apparently contradictory portions of the Vedāntic texts which have

[1] *phala-kāmādy-anupayogāt anenaiva tat-samarpaṇāt nityatvād apy artha-jñānasya na phala-prepsur adhikārī.* Puruṣottama's commentary on Vallabhācārya's *Anubhāṣya*, p. 43.

[2] *prakāra-bhedenāpi kāṇḍa-dvayasyāpi brahma-pratipādakatayaikavākyatva-samarthanan mīmāṃśā-dvayasyaika-śāstrasya sūcanena vṛttikāra-virodhato'pi bodhitaḥ. Ibid.* p. 46.

not been taken by *Pūrva-mīmāṃsā*. The purpose of the *Brahma-sūtra* is the same as that of the *Pūrva-mīmāṃsā*, because enquiry into the nature of the Brahman is also due to the injunction that Brahman should be known, and the highest *dharma* is produced thereby. The *Uttara-mīmāṃsā* is a supplement of the *Pūrva-mīmāṃsā*. According to Madhva it is those who have devotion who are eligible for enquiry into the nature of Brahman.

Vallabha combines the second and the third *sūtra* of *Adhyāya* I, *Pāda* I, of the *Brahma-sūtra* and reads them as *Janmādyasya yataḥ, śāstrayonitvāt*. The commentator says that this is the proper order, because all topics (*adhikaraṇas*) show the objections, conclusions and the reasons; the reasons would be missing if the third *sūtra* (*śāstrayonitvāt*) were not included in the second, forming one *adhikaraṇa*. Brahman is the cause of the appearance and disappearance of the world, and this can be known only on the evidence of the scriptures. Brahman is thus the final and the ultimate agent; but, though production and maintenance, derangement and destruction are all possible through the agency of Brahman, yet they are not associated with Him as His qualities. The *sūtra* may also be supposed to mean that that is Brahman from which the first (i.e., *ākāśa*) has been produced[1].

The view of Śaṅkara that Brahman is the producer of the Vedas and that by virtue of this He must be regarded as omniscient is rejected to-day by Puruṣottama. To say the Vedas had been produced by God by His deliberate desire would be to accept the views of the Nyāya and Vaiśeṣikas; the eternity of the Vedas must then be given up. If the Vedas had come out of Brahman like the breath of a man, then, since all breathing is involuntary, the production of the Vedas would not show the omniscience of God (*niḥśvāsātmaka-vedopādānatvena abuddhi-pūrvaka-niḥśvāsopādāna-puruṣadṛṣṭānta-sanāthena pratisādhanena apāstam*)[2]. Moreover, if Brahman had produced the Vedas in the same order in which they existed in the previous *kalpa*, He must in doing so have submitted Himself to some necessity or law, and therefore was not independent[3]. Again, the view of Śaṅkara that the Brahman associated

[1] *Janma ādyasya ākāśasya yataḥ. Anubhāṣya*, p. 61.

[2] Commentary on *Anubhāṣya*, p. 64.

[3] *tādṛśānupūrvī-racanayā asvātantrye rājājñānuvādaka-rāja-dūtavadānupūrvī-racanā-mātreṇeśvara-sārvajñāsiddhyā vyākhyeya-grantha-virodhāc ca. Ibid.* p. 64.

with *ajñāna* is to be regarded as the omniscient Īśvara can be accepted on his authority alone.

It is no doubt true that the nature of Brahman is shown principally in the Upaniṣads, and from that point of view the word *śāstra-yoni*, "he who is known by the Upaniṣads," may well be applied to Brahman; yet there may be a legitimate objection that other parts of the Vedas have no relevant connection with Brahman. The reply is that it is by actions in accordance with other parts of the Vedas that the mind may be purified, and thus God may be induced to exercise His grace for a revelation of His nature. So in a remote manner other parts of the Vedas may be connected with the Vedas. So the knowledge of the Vedānta helps the due performance of the scriptural injunctions of other parts of the Vedas. The *karma-kāṇḍa* and the *jñāna-kāṇḍa* are virtually complementary to each other and both have a utility for self-knowledge, though the importance of the Upaniṣads must be superior.

We know already that Rāmānuja repudiated the idea of inferring the existence of God as omniscient and omnipotent from the production of the world, and established the thesis that God cannot be known through any means of proof, such as perception, inference and the like, but only through the testimony of the scriptural texts.

The tendency of the Nyāya system has been to prove the existence of God by inference; thus Udayana gives nine arguments in favour of the existence of God. The first of these is that the word, being of the nature of effect, must have some cause which has produced it (*kāryānumāna*). The second is that there must be some one who in the beginning of the creation set the atoms in motion for the formation of molecules (*āyojanānumāna*). The third is that the earth could not have remained hanging in space if it were not held by God (*dhṛtyanumāna*). The fourth is that the destruction of the world also requires an agent and that must be God (*vināśānumāna*). The fifth is that meanings ascribed to words must have been due to the will of God (*padānumāna*). The sixth is that merit and demerit, as can be known from the prescription of the Vedas, must presume an original acquaintance of the person who composed the Vedas (*pratyanumāna*). The seventh is that the scriptures testify to the existence of God. The eighth (*vākyānumāna*) is the same as the seventh. The ninth is as follows: the accretion of the mass of atoms depends upon their number, as they are partless; the numerical conception is dependent upon relative mental comparison on the part of the perceiver; at the time of creation there must have been some one by whose numerical conception the accretion of mass is possible. This is the ninth *anumāna* (*saṃkhyā-numāna*). Though God is regarded as the cause of the world, yet He need not have a body; for cause as producer does not necessarily involve the possession of a body; there are others, however, who think that God produces special bodies, the *avatāra* of Rāma, Kṛṣṇa, etc., by which He acts in special ways.

Vijñāna-bhikṣu, however, thinks that the Sāṃkhya categories of *buddhi*, etc., being products, presume the existence of their previous causes, about which there must be some intuitive knowledge, and whose purpose is served by it; such a person is Īśvara. The procedure consists in inferring first an original cause (the *prakṛti*) of the categories, and God is He who has direct knowledge of the *prakṛti* by virtue of which He modifies it to produce the categories, and thus employs it for His own purpose.

There are some who hold that even in the Upaniṣadic texts there are instances of inferring the nature of Brahman, and though Bādarāyaṇa does not indulge in any inferences himself, he deals with such texts as form their basis. The point of view of the syllogists has been that the inferences are valid inasmuch as they are in consonance with the Upaniṣad texts. But Vallabha agrees with Rāmānuja and Bhāskara that no inference is possible about the existence of God, and that His nature can only be known through the testimony of the Upaniṣadic texts[1].

The nature of Brahman.

Brahman is both the material and instrumental cause of the world. There is no diversity of opinion regarding the Brahman as the instrumental (*nimitta*) cause of the world, but there is difference of opinion whether Brahman is its creator or whether He is its material cause, since the Vedānta does not admit the relation of *samavāya*, the view that Brahman is the inherent (*samavāyi*) cause of the world. The objection against Brahman being the *samavāyi*

[1] The commentator Puruṣottama offers a criticism of the theistic arguments after the manner of Rāmānuja. Commentary on *Anubhāṣya*, pp. 74–8.

kāraṇa is further enhanced by the supposition that, if He were so He must be liable to change (*samavāyitve vikṛtatvasyāpatteḥ*). Vallabha holds that the *sūtra* "*tat tu samanvayāt*" establishes the view that Brahman is the inherent cause (*samavāyikāraṇa*), because it exists everywhere in His tripartite nature, as being, thought and bliss. The world as such (the *prapañca*) consists of names, forms and actions, and Brahman is the cause of them all, as He exists everywhere in His tripartite forms. The Sāṃkhyists hold that it is the *sattva*, *rajas* and *tamas* which pervade all things, and all things manifest these qualities; a cause must be of the nature of the effects, since all effects are of the nature of *sattva*, *rajas* and *tamas*. So the reply is that there is a more serious objection, because the *prakṛti* (consisting of *sattva*, *rajas* and *tamas*) is itself a part of Brahman (*prakṛter api svamate tadaṃśatvāt*)[2]. But yet the Sāṃkhya method of approach cannot be accepted. The pleasure of *prakṛti* is of the nature of ignorance, and is limited by time and space; things are pleasant to some and unpleasant to others; they are pleasant at one time and not pleasant at another; they are pleasant in some places and unpleasant in other places. But the bliss of Brahman is unlimited by conditions; the relation of bliss and the self as associated with knowledge is thus different from the pleasure of *prakṛti* (*ātmānandajñānena prākṛtikapriyatvādau bādhadarśanāt*)[3]. The Brahman therefore pervades the world in His own true nature as knowledge and bliss. It is by His will that He manifests Himself as many and also manifests His three characters—thought, being and bliss—in different proportions in the material world of *antaryāmins*. This pervasion of Brahman as many and all is to be distinguished from the Śaṅkarite exposition of it. According to Śaṅkara and his followers the phenomenal world of objects has the Brahman as its basis of reality; the concrete appearances are only impositions on this unchanging reality. According to this view the concrete appearances cannot be regarded as the effects of Brahman, or, in other words, Brahman cannot be regarded as the *upādāna* or the material cause of the stuff of the concrete objects. We know that among the Śaṅkarites also there are diverse opinions regarding the material cause of the world. Thus the author of the *Padārtha-nirṇaya* thinks that Brahman and *māyā* are jointly the

[1] Vallabha's *Anubhāṣya*, p. 85.
[2] Puruṣottama's commentary, p. 86.

cause of the world, Brahman being the unchanging cause and *māyā* being the transforming cause. Sarvajñātmamuni, the author of the *Saṃkṣepa-śārīraka*, thinks that Brahman is the material cause through the instrumentality of *māyā*. Vācaspati Miśra thinks that the *māyā* resting in *jīva* as associated with Brahman jointly produces the world; *māyā* here is regarded as the accessory cause (*sahakāri*). The author of the *Siddhānta-muktāvalī* thinks that the *māyā-śakti* is the real material cause and not the Brahman; Brahman is beyond cause and effect[1].

Vallabha, however, disagrees with this view for the reason that according to this the causality of Brahman is only indirect, and as regards the appearances which are illusory impositions according to Śaṅkara no cause is really ascribed; he therefore holds that Brahman by His own will has manifested Himself with preponderance of the elements of being, consciousness, and bliss in His three forms as matter, soul and the Brahman. Brahman is therefore regarded as the *samavāyikāraṇa* of the world[2].

Bhāskara also holds that Brahman is at once one with the world and different from it, just as the sea is in one sense one with the waves and in another sense different from them. The suggestion that a thing cannot be its opposite is meaningless, because it is so experienced. All things as objects may be regarded as one, but this does not preclude their specific characters and existence; in reality there is no opposition or contradiction, like heat and cold or as between fire and sparks, between Brahman and the world, for the world has sprung out of Him, is maintained in Him and is merged in Him. In the case of ordinary contradiction this is not the case; when the jug is produced out of the earth, though the earth and the jug may seem to be different, yet the jug has no existence without the earth—the former is being maintained by the latter. So, as effect, the world is many; as cause, it is one with Brahman[3].

Vallabha's point of view is very close to that of Bhāskara, though not identical; he holds that it is the same Brahman who is present in all His fullness in all objects of the world and in the selves. He only manifested some qualities in their preponderating

[1] See *Siddhāntaleśa* (ed. Lazaras, 1890), pp. 12–13.

[2] *anāropitānāgantuka-rūpeṇa anuvṛttir eva samavāya iti idam eva ca tādātmyam.* Puruṣottama's commentary on *Anubhāṣya*, p. 90.

[3] *kāryarūpeṇa nānātvam, abhedaḥ kāraṇātmanā hemātmanā yathā'bhedaḥ kuṇḍalādyātmanā bhedaḥ.* *Bhāskara-bhāṣya*, p. 18.

manner in the different forms; multiplicity therefore does not involve any change. It is for this reason that he prefers the term *samavāyikāraṇa* to *upādānakāraṇa*; according to him the concept of *samavāyikāraṇa* consists in universal and unconditional pervasion. The concept of *upādāna* involves a concept of change, though the effects caused by the change are maintained by the *upādāna* (or the material cause) and though it ultimately merges into it[1]. So far as the Brahman may be regarded as being one with all the multiplicity, Vallabha is in agreement with Bhāskara.

Vallabha again denies the relation of *samavāya*, like other Vedāntic thinkers, though he regards Brahman as the *samavāyikāraṇa* of the world. His refutation of *samavāya* follows the same line as that of the other Vedāntic interpreters, Śaṅkara and Rāmānuja, and need not be repeated here. *Samavāya*, according to Vallabha, is not a relation of inherence such as is admitted by the Nyāya writers; with him it means identity (*tādātmya*). According to the Nyaiyāyikas *samavāya* is the relation of inherence which exists between cause and effect, between qualities and substance, between universals and substance; but Vallabha says that there is no separate relation of inherence here to combine these pairs; it is the substance itself that appears in action, qualities and as cause and effect. It is thus merely a manifestation of identity in varying forms that gives us the notion of diversity in contraries; in reality there is no difference between the varying forms which are supposed to be associated together by a relation of inherence[2].

Puruṣottama, in his *Prasthāna-ratnākara*, says that *māyā* is a power of Brahman, and is thus identical with Him (*māyāyā api bhagavac-chaktitvena śaktimad-abhinnatvāt*)[3]; *māyā* and *avidyā* are the same. It is by this *māyā* that God manifests Himself as many. This manifestation is neither an error nor a confusion; it is a real manifestation of God in diverse forms without implying the notion of change or transformation. The world is thus real, being a real manifestation of God. Brahman Himself, being of the nature of

[1] *nanv atropādāna-padaṃ parityajya samavāyi-padena kuto vyavahāra iti ced ucyate. loke upādāna-padena kartṛ-kriyayā vyāptasya paricchinnasyaivābhidhāna-darśanāt prakṛtir hy asyopādānam iti.* Puruṣottama's commentary, p. 118.

[2] *nanu dūṣite samavāye ayuta-siddhayoḥ kaḥ sambandho'ṅgīkartavyaḥ iti cet tādātmyam eva iti brūmaḥ. katham iti cet itthaṃ pratyakṣād yad-dravyaṃ yad-dravya-samavetaṃ tad tadātmakamiti vyāpteḥ...kāraṇa-kārya-tādātmyaṃ dravyayor nirvivādam. Ibid.* p. 627.

[3] *Prasthāna-ratnākara*, p. 159.

sat, *cit* and *ānanda*, can manifest Himself in His partial aspects in the world without the help of any instrument. It is possible to conceive Brahman in His aspects or characters as knowledge, bliss, activity, time, will, *māya*, and *prakṛti*. The *kāla* represents the *kriyā-śakti* or power of action. The determination of the creation or dissolution through time (*kāla*) means the limitation of His power of action; determined by this power of action His other parts act consonantly with it. By His will He conceives His selves as different from Him and through different forms thus conceived He manifests Himself; in this way the diverse characters of Brahman manifesting Himself in diverse forms manifest Himself also as differing in diverse ways. Thus, though He is identical with knowledge and bliss, He appears as the possessor of these. The power of God consists in manifesting His nature as pure being, as action and as producing confusion in His nature as pure intelligence. This confusion, manifesting itself as experiential ignorance (which shows itself as egotism), is a part of the *māyā* which creates the world, and which is instrument of God as pure bliss in His manifestation as the world. This *māyā* thus appears as a secondary cause beyond the original cause, and may sometimes modify it and thereby act as a cause of God's will. It must, however, be understood that *māyā* thus conceived cannot be regarded as the original cause; it serves in the first instance to give full play to the original desire of God to become many; in the second place it serves to create the diversity of the grades of existence as superior and inferior. It is in relation to such manifestation of God's knowledge and action that God may be regarded as the possessor of knowledge and action. The aspect of *māyā* as creating confusion is regarded as *avidyā*. This confused apperception is also of the nature of understanding such as we possess it; through this confused understanding there comes a desire for association with the nature of bliss conceived as having a separate existence and through it come the various efforts constituting the life in the living. It is by virtue of this living that the individual is called *jīva*. The nature as being when posited or a product of the action appears as inanimate objects, and is later on associated again with action and goes to manifest itself as the bodies of the living. So from His twofold will there spring forth from His nature as pure being the material *prāṇas*, which serve as elements of bondage for the *jīvas* and are but manifestations of His nature as being: there also spring forth from His nature as pure intelligence the *jīvas* which are the subject of bondage; and there spring forth like sparks from His nature as pure bliss the *antaryāmins* which control the *jīvas*[1]. So among the *jīvas* who are bound there may be some with whom God may be pleased and to whom He may grant the complete power of knowledge; the confusing *māyā* leaves its hold upon such persons; they thus remain in a free state in their nature as pure intelligence, but they have not the power to control the affairs of the Universe.

Brahman may be described in another way from the essential point of view (*svarūpa*) and the causal point of view (*kāraṇa*). From the essential point of view God may be viewed in three aspects, as action, knowledge, and knowledge and action. The causes prescribed in the sacrificial sphere of the Vedas represent His nature in the second aspect. The third aspect is represented in the course of *bhakti* in which God is represented as the possessor of knowledge, action and bliss. In the aspect as cause we have the concept of the *antaryāmins*, which, though they are in reality of the essential nature of Brahman, are regarded as helping the *jīvas* in their works by presiding over them[2]; the *antaryāmins* are thus as infinite in number as the *jīvas*. But apart from these *antaryāmins*, God is also regarded as one *antaryāmin* and has been so described in the *Antaryāmi-brahman*.

The Categories.

Time is also regarded as a form of God. Activity and nature (*karma-svabhāvam*) are involved in the concept of time or *kāla*. Time in its inner essence consists of being, intelligence, and bliss, though in its phenomenal appearance it is manifest only with a slight tinge of being[3]. It is supra-sensible and can be inferred only from the nature of effects (*kāryānumeya*). It may also be defined

[1] *evaṃ ca ubhābhyām icchābhyāṃ sac-cid-ānandarūpebhyo yathā-yathaṃ prāṇādyā jaḍāś cid-aṃśa-jīva-bandhana-parikara-bhūtāḥ sadaṃśāḥ jīvāś cidaṃśā bandhanīyā ānandāṃśās tan-niyāmakā antar-yāmiṇaś ca visphuliṅga-nyāyena vyuccaranti.* Commentary on *Anubhāṣya*, pp. 161–2.

[2] *antaryāmiṇāṃ sva-rūpa-bhūtatve'pi jīvena saha kārye praveśāt tad-bhedānām ānantye'pi kāranī-bhūta-vakṣyamāṇa-tattva-śarīre praviśya tat-sahāya-karaṇāt kāraṇa-koṭāv eva niveśo na tu sva-rūpa-koṭau.* *Ibid.* pp. 164–5.

[3] *etasyaiva rūpāntaraṃ kāla-karma-svabhāvāḥ kālasyāṃśa-bhūtau karma-svabhāvau tatra antaḥ-sac-ci-dānando vyavahāre īṣat-sattvāṃśena prakaṭaḥ kāla iti kālasya svarūpa-lakṣanaṃ.* *Ibid.* p. 165.

as eternally pervasive and the cause and support of all things. Time is the first cause that disturbs the equilibrium of the *guṇas*. The sun, the moon, etc., are its *ādhibhautika* forms, the atoms are its *ādhyatmika* form, and God is its *ādhidaivika* form. The time that the sun takes in passing an atom is the time-atom; being thus too small it cannot be any further divided. It is only by the conglomeration of the smallest time-units that long spans of time are produced; for time is not one whole of an all-pervasive character of which the smaller units of time are parts.

Karma or action of all descriptions is regarded as universal; it only manifests itself in diverse forms and specific conditions as specific actions of this or that individual. Since it is this universal *karma* that manifests itself as different actions of diverse men, it is unnecessary to admit *adṛṣta* as a separate category belonging to self, which remains after the destruction of a *karma* and gives its fruit after a remote time; it is also unnecessary to admit *dharma* and *adharma* as important categories; for they are all included in the concept of this universal *karma*, which manifests itself in diverse forms under diverse conditions. The application of the terms *dharma* and *adharma* is thus only the method of logical interest; it thus explains how the specific can produce *svarga* without the intermediary of *adṛṣta*, or how the *karma* of one person (*putreṣṭi*, "sacrifice") can produce fruit in another, i.e., the son. How a *karma* should manifest itself in its fruits or with reference to the performer and other persons is determined by the conditions and as explained in the scriptures; the production of a fruit in specific forms in specific centres does not mean its destruction but its disappearance[1].

Svabhāva ("nature") is admitted as a separate category. It also is identified with God; its function consists in the inducement of God's will. It is therefore defined as that which produces change (*pariṇāma-hetutvaṃ tal-lakṣaṇam*); it is universal and reveals itself by itself before all other things. There may, however, be subtle changes which are not at first noticeable; but, when they become manifest, they presume the function of *svabhāva*, without which they could not have come about. It is from this that the twenty-

[1] *tal-lakṣaṇaṃ ca vidhi-niṣedha-prakāreṇa laukika-kriyābḥiḥ pradeśato'-bhivyañjana-yogyā vyāpikā kriyeti...etenaivādṛṣtasyāpyātma-guṇatvaṃ nirākṛtaṃ veditavyam. evaṃcāpurvādṛṣṭadharmādharmādipadairapīdamevocyate. ataḥ sādhāranye'pi phala-vyavasthopapatter na karma-nānātvamity api. dāna-hiṃsādau tu dharmādharmādi-prayogo' bhivyañjakatvopādhinā bhāktaḥ. Ibid.* pp. 168–9.

eight categories have evolved: they are called *tattva*, because they are of the nature of "that," i.e., God; all *tattvas* are thus the unfolding of God. The causality involved in the manifestation of *svabhāva* is a specific causality following a definite cause, and is giving rise to the evolutionary series of the *tattvas*; in this sense it is different from the causality of God's will, and is only a cause in the general manner. Of these categories *sattva* may be counted first. *Sattva* is that which, being of the nature of pleasure and luminosity of knowledge and non-obstructive to the manifestation of pleasure, behaves as the cause of attachment to pleasure and knowledge in individuals[1]. *Rajas* is that which, being of the nature of attachment, produces clinging or desire for actions in individuals. *Tamas* is that which produces in individuals a tendency to errors, laziness, sleep, etc. There is a difference between the Sāṃkhya conception of these *guṇas* and Vallabha's characterization of them (which is supposed to follow the *Pañcarātra*, *Gītā* and *Bhāgavata*). Thus, according to the Sāṃkhya, the *guṇas* operate by themselves; but this is untenable, as it would lead to the theory of natural necessity and atheism. Nor can *rajas* be defined as being of the nature of sorrow; for the authoritative scriptures speak of its being of the nature of attachment. When these qualities are conceived as being produced from God, they are regarded as being of the nature of *māyā* as the power of intelligence and bliss of God[2]. These (*sattva*, *rajas* and *tamas*) should be regarded as identical with *māyā* and products of *māyā*. Nor are these *guṇas* for the sake of others (*parārtha*), as is conceived by the Sāṃkhya; nor are they inextricably mixed up with another, but their co-operation is only for building the *puruṣa*. God thus manifests Himself as the form of the *māyā*, just as cotton spreads itself as threads. God, as unqualified, produces all His qualities by Himself; in His nature as pure being He produces *sattva*, in His nature as bliss He produces *tamas*, in His nature as intelligence He produces *rajas*[3].

Puruṣa or *ātman* may be defined from three points of view: it may be defined as beginningless, qualityless, the controller of

[1] *sukhānāvarakatve prakāśakatve sukhātmakatve ca sati sukhāsktyā jñānāsaktyā ca dehino dehādy-āsakti-janakaṃ sattvam.* Commentary on *Anubhāṣya*, p. 170.

[2] *ete ca guṇā yadā bhagavataḥ sakāśād eva utpadyante tadā māyā cic-chakti-rūpā ānanda-rūpā vijñeyā. Ibid.* p. 171.

[3] *sad-aṃśāt sattvam, ānandāṃśāt tamaḥ, cidaṃśāt rajas. Ibid.* p. 172.

prakṛti, and apperceivable as the object of the notion of "I"; it may also be defined as purely self-luminous; and, again, as that which, though not in reality affected by the qualities or defects of the universe, is yet associated with them. In the self-being of a self-luminous and blissful nature there is some kind of consciousness and bliss in the absence of all kinds of objects, as in deep dreamless sleep. It is thus consciousness which represents the true nature of the self, which, in our ordinary experience, becomes associated with diverse kinds of ignorance and limits itself by the objects of knowledge. The *puruṣa* is one, though it appears as many through the confusing power of *māyā* due to the will of God. The notion of the doer and the enjoyer of experiences is thus due to misconception. It is for this reason that emancipation is possible; for, had not the self been naturally free and emancipated, it would not be possible to liberate it by any means. It is because the self is naturally free that, when once it is liberated, it cannot have any further bondage. If the bondage were of the nature of association of external impurities, then even in emancipation there would be a further chance of association with impurities at any time; it is because all bondage and impurities are due to a misconception that, when once this is broken, there is no further chance of any bondage[1]. *Prakṛti*, however, is of two kinds: (*a*) as associated with ignorance, causing the evolutionary series, and (*b*) as abiding in God and holding all things in God—the Brahman. Jīva, the phenomenal individual, is regarded as a part of the *puruṣa*. It may be remembered that the concept of *puruṣa* is identical with the concept of Brahman; for this reason the *jīva* may on the one hand be regarded as a part of the *puruṣa* and on the other as part of the Brahman, the unchangeable. The various kinds of experiences of the *jīva*, though apparently due to *karma*, are in reality due to God's will; for whomsoever God wishes to raise, He causes to do good works, and, whomsoever He wishes to throw down, He causes to perform bad works. *Prakṛti* is in its primary sense identical with Brahman; it is a nature of Brahman by which He creates the world. As Brahman is on the one hand identical with the qualities of being, intelligence and bliss, and on

[1] *evaṃ tasya kevalatve siddhe yas tasmin kartṛtvādinā saguṇatvapratyayaḥ sa sṛṣty-anukūla-bhagavad-icchayā prakṛty-ādy-aviveka-kṛtaḥ...ata eva ca mukti-yogyatvam. anyathā bandhasya svābhāvikatvāpattau mokṣa-sāṣtra-vaiyarthyā-patteḥ svābhāvikasya nāśāyogāt pravṛtti-vidhau tu anuṣthāna-lakṣaṇāprāmāṇyā-patteś ca...so'yaṃ na nānā, kintv-eka eva sarvatra. Ibid.* pp. 175–6.

the other hand regarded as associated with them, so also the *prakṛti* may be regarded as the identity of the *guṇas* and also as their possessor. This is the distinction of Vallabha's conception of *prakṛti* from the Saṃkhya view of it. The other categories of *mahat*, etc., are also supposed to evolve from the *prakṛti* more or less in the Saṃkhya fashion: *manas*, however, is not regarded as an *indriya*.

The Pramāṇas.

Puruṣottama says that knowledge (*jñāna*) is of many kinds. Of these, eternal knowledge (*nitya-jñāna*) is of four kinds: the essential nature of God, in which He is one with all beings and the very essence of emancipation (*mokṣa*); the manifestation of His great and noble qualities; His manifestation as the Vedas in the beginning of the creation; His manifestation as verbal knowledge in all knowable forms of the deity. His form as verbal knowledge manifests itself in the individuals; it is for this reason that there can be no knowledge without the association of words—even in the case of the dumb, who have no speech, there are gestures which take the place of language .This is the fifth kind of knowledge. Then there are one kind of sense-knowledge and four kinds of mental knowledge. Of mental knowledge, that which is produced by *manas* is called doubt (*saṃśaya*); the function of *manas* is synthesis (*saṃkalpa*) and analysis (*vikalpa*). The function of *buddhi* is to produce knowledge as decision, superseding doubt, which is of an oscillatory nature. The knowledge of dreams is from *ahaṃkāra* (egoism) as associated with knowledge. *Citta* perceives the self in the state of deep dreamless sleep. There is thus the fourfold knowledge of the *antaḥkaraṇa*; this and sense-knowledge and the previous five kinds of knowledge form the ten kinds of knowledge. From another point of view will (*kāma*), conceiving (*saṃkalpa*), doubt (*vicikitsā*), faith (*śraddhā*), absence of faith (*aśraddhā*), patience (*dhṛti*), absence of patience (*adhṛti*), shame (*hrī*), understanding (*dhī*), fear (*bhī*), are all *manas*. Pleasure and pain also belong to it, because they are not associated with the senses. Knowledge does not stay only for three moments, but stays on until it is superseded by other objects of knowledge, and even then it remains as impression or *saṃskāra*. This is proved by the fact that *manas* can discover it in memory when it directs its attention towards it; it is because the *manas* is busy with other objects and it ceases to be discovered. Memory can be strengthened by proper exercise, and things can be forgotten or wrongly remembered through diverse kinds of defects; in these cases also knowledge is not destroyed, but only remains hidden through the effect of *māyā*.

The knowledge that is associated with the *pramāṇas* is the *sāttvika* knowledge; the *sattva* is associated with *pramā* (or right knowledge), and when it disappears there is error. *Pramā* is defined as uncontradicted knowledge or knowledge that is not liable to contradiction[1]. The increase of the *sattva* by which knowledge is produced may be due to various causes, e.g., scriptures, objects, people, country, time, birth, *karma*, meditation, *mantras*, purifications, *saṃskāras*. The knowledge which is primarily predominant in *sattva* is the notion that one universal essence is present everywhere; this knowledge alone is absolutely valid. The knowledge which is associated with *rajas* is not absolutely valid; it is that which we find in all our ordinary or perceptual scientific knowledge, which is liable to errors and correction. This *rajas* knowledge at the time of its first manifestation is indeterminate in its nature, conveying to us only the being of things. At this stage, however, we have the first application of the senses to the objects which rouse the *sattva* quality, and there is no association with *rajas*; as such this indeterminable knowledge, though it forms the beginning of *rajas* knowledge, may be regarded as *sāttvika*. Later on, when the *manas* functions with the senses, we have the *saṃkalpa* knowledge, and regard it as *rajas*. The pure sensory knowledge or sensation is not regarded as inherent in the senses. The sense-operation in the first instance rouses the *sattva*, and therefore the knowledge produced by the application of the senses in the first instance does not convey with it any of the special qualities of the senses, visual, auditory and the like, but merely the being, which is not the specific quality of any sense, but only a revelation of the nature of *sattva*; such knowledge, though roused by the senses, does not belong to them. It is by the function of the *vikalpa* of the *manas* that this knowledge as pure being assumes distinct forms in association with sense-characteristics. The application of this function is too rapid to be easily apprehended by us, and for this

[1] *a-bādhita-jñānatvaṃ bādha-yogya-vyatiriktatvaṃ vā tal-lakṣaṇam.*
Prasthānaratnākara, p. 6.

reason we often fail to detect the prior existence of the *nirvikalpa* knowledge.

In the case of determinate knowledge, whether it be simple as of a jug, or complex as of a jug on the ground, we have the same procedure of having first through the senses the indeterminate perception of the being, which by a later influence of *rajas* becomes associated with names and forms; it is the being given by the senses, which appears in names and forms through the influence of the *antaḥkaraṇa* as moved by the *rajas* in association with the senses. The principle followed in perception is analogous to the cosmic appearance of Brahman as manifold, in which the pure Brahman by His will and thought shows Himself as the many, though He remains one in Himself all the time; in the case of perception the senses by their first application cause an influx of *sattva*, resulting in the apperception of pure being, which later on becomes associated with diverse names and forms through the *rajas* element of the *antaḥkaraṇa* operating with the senses. The determinate knowledge is of two kinds: *viśiṣṭa-buddhi* and *samūhālambana-buddhi*; the former means associated knowledge ("a man with a stick"), and the latter means knowledge as conglomeration of entities ("a stick and a book"). The knowledge of simple objects (such as a jug) is regarded as an associated knowledge. All these varied types of determinate cognitions are in reality of one type, because they all consist of the simple process of a revelation of being by the senses and an attribution of names and forms by the *antaḥkaraṇa*.

From another point of view the determinate knowledge can be of five kinds: (i) *saṃśaya* (doubt), (ii) *viparyāsa* (error), (iii) *niścaya* (right knowledge), (iv) *smṛti* (memory), (v) *svapna* (dream).

Doubt is defined as the apprehension of two or more opposite attributes or characters in the same object (*ekasmin dharmiṇi viruddha-nānā-koṭy-avagāhi jñānaṃ saṃśayam*). Error is defined as the apprehension of external objects other than those with which the senses are in contact. *Niścaya* means right apprehension of objects; such an apprehension must be distinguished from memory, because apprehension (*anubhava*) always means the intuition of an object, while memory is purely internal though produced by a previous apprehension. Such a right knowledge can be perception, inference, verbal knowledge, and analogy (*upamiti*, which arises through the senses associated with a knowledge of similarity: *sādṛśyādi-sahakṛtendriyārtha-saṃsargajanya*).

This right knowledge can be of two kinds: perception (*pratyakṣa*) and that which is not perception (*parokṣa*). Perception arises from a real contact of the sense and its objects (*indriyārtha-sat-samprayoga-janyaṃ jñānam*)[1]. Memory (*smṛti*) is defined as knowledge which is produced neither by sleep nor by external objects, but by past impressions, which consist of the subtle existence of previous apprehensions. Dream-experiences are special creations, and should therefore be distinguished from the world of things of ordinary experience; they are out of and through *māyā* by God. This is indeed different from the view of Madhva; for according to him the dream-appearances are without any stuff and should not be regarded as creations; they are mere illusions produced by thought. The dream-appearances being creations according to Vallabha, their knowledge is also to be regarded as real. Dreamless sleep is a special class of dream-experience in which the self manifests itself (*tatra ātma-sphuraṇaṃtu svata eva*). Reflection (as synthesis or analysis, or by the methods of agreement and difference, or as mental doubt, or meditation) is included within memory. Shame, fear (*hrī, bhī*), etc., are the functions of egoism and not cognitive states. Recognition is regarded as right knowledge (*niścaya*). In the case of firm knowledge growing out of habit the impressions of past knowledge act as a determinant (*sahakārī*), and in the case of recognition memory acts as a determinant[2]. Recognition is thus regarded as due to memory rather than past impressions. The reason for this preference is that, even though there may be an operation of past impressions, the function of memory is a direct aid to it. Recognition is distinguished from memory in this, that, while the latter is produced directly from past impressions, the former is produced in association with the present perception, directly through the operation of memory, and indirectly through the operation of past impressions.

[1] *Prasthānaratnākara*, p. 20.

[2] *abhyāsa-janye dṛḍha-pratīti-rūpe jñāne yathā pūrvānubhava-saṃskāraḥ sahakārī tathā pratyabhijñāyāṃ smṛtiḥ sahakāriṇī, viśeṣaṇatāvacchedaka-prakāraka-niścayārthaṃ tasyā avaśyam apekṣaṇāt. ato yatha'nugrāhakāntara-praveśe'pi yathārthānubhavatvānapāyād abhyāsajñānaṃ niścaya-rūpaṃ tathā smṛtyā viṣayeṇa ca pūrva-sthita-jñānasyoddīpanāt pratyabhijñā'pi iti jñeyam. Ibid.* p. 25.

The distinction between right knowledge and error consists in the fact that the latter contains somewhat more than the former; thus, in the case of conch-shell-silver, right knowledge consists in the perception of conch-shell, but false knowledge consists in the further attribution of silver to it; this additional element constitutes error[1]. There may be cases which are partly correct and partly false and in these knowledge may be called right or false according as there is or is not a preponderance of right knowledge. Upon this criterion of Puruṣottama painting, art creations and impersonations in dramatic perceptions have a preponderance of right knowledge, as they produce through imitation such pleasures as would have been produced by the actual objects which they have imitated.

Puruṣottama makes a distinction between *karaṇa* (the instrumental) and *kāraṇa* (the cause). *Karaṇa* is a unique agent, associated with a dynamic agent with reference to the effects that are to be produced (*vyāpāravad asādhāraṇam*); *kāraṇa* is that seat of power which may produce appearance and disappearance of forms (*āvirbhāva-śaktyādhāratvaṃ kāraṇatvam*). That which produces particular forms, or works for the disappearance of certain forms, is regarded as corresponding causes; hence the power which can make the effects of a material cause manifest for our operation is regarded as the *āvirbhāva-kāraṇa* of that effect. *Āvirbhāva*, "manifestation of appearances," is that aspect of things by which or in terms of which they may be experienced or may be operated upon, and its negation is "disappearance" (*tirobhāva*)[2]. These powers of manifestation and disappearance belong primarily to God, and secondarily to objects with which He has associated them in specific ways. The Naiyāyika definition of cause as invariable unconditional antecedent of the effect is regarded as invalid, inasmuch as it involves a mutual dependence. Invariable antecedence to an effect involves the notion of causality and the notion of causality involves invariable antecedence; so unconditionality involves the notion of causality and causality involves unconditionality.

Cause is of two kinds: identity (*tādātmya*, also called *samavāyi*), and instrument. This identity however involves the notion of

[1] *bhrama-pramā-samūhālambanaṃ tu, eka-deśa-vikṛtam ananyavad bhavatīti nyāyena bhramādhikye viparyāsa eva. pramādhikye ca niścayaḥ. Prasthānaratnākara*, pp. 25–6.

[2] *upādānasya kāryaṃ yā vyavahāra-gocaraṃ karoti sā śaktir āvirbhāvikā. āvirbhāvaśca vyavahāra-yogyatvam. tirobhāvaśca tadayogyatvam. Ibid.* p. 26.

identity-in-difference, in which difference appears as a mode of the identity which is to be regarded as the essence of causality. Puruṣottama discards the notion of substance and quality, which is explained on the basis of the relation of *samavāya*, and in which substance is regarded as the cause of quality; a quality is only an appearance simultaneous with the substance, and the latter cannot be regarded as the cause of the former. The concept of material cause (*upādāna-kāraṇa*) is of two kinds: unchanging (e.g., the earth unchanging, in jugs, etc.), and changing (e.g., knowledge appearing as a function of the mind, the instrumental cause). The contact of parts or movement involved in the material cause is *not* regarded as a separate cause, as it is by the Naiyāyika, but is regarded as a part of the material cause.

The nature of concomitance that determines the nature of a *hetu* is of two kinds: *anvaya* and *vyatireka*. *Anvaya* means agreement in presence of an element such that to its sole presence (in the midst of many irrelevant elements or conditions present with it) the effect is due[1]. *Vyatireka* means the negation of that element which involves the negation of the effect, i.e., that element which does not exist if the effect is absent (*kāryātirekeṇānavasthānam*). The causal movement (*vyāpāra*) is that which exists as a link between the cause and the effect; thus sense-object contact has for its dynamic cause the movement of the senses. In the case of God's will no dynamic movement is regarded necessary for the production of the world.

The *pratyakṣa pramāṇa*, the means of perceptual experience, is defined as the sense-faculties corresponding to the different kinds of perception. There are thus six *pramāṇas*, viz., visual, tactual, gustatory, auditory, olfactory and mental; as opposed to the monistic Vedāntic view of Śaṅkara, *manas* is regarded here as a sense-faculty. All faculties are regarded as being atomic in their nature. The visual organ can perceive colours only when there is a "manifested colour" (*udbhūta-rūpavattva*); the atoms of ghosts are not visible because they have no manifested colour. So for perception of all sense-qualities by the corresponding senses we have to admit that the sense-qualities, of touch, of smell, etc., must be manifested in order to be perceived.

[1] *Tatra sva-sva-vyāpyetara-yāvat-kāraṇa-sattve yat-sattve avaśyaṃ yat-sattvam anvayaḥ. Ibid.* p. 32.

In agreement with the monistic Vedānta of Śaṅkara *tamas* (darkness) is regarded here as a separate category and not as the mere negation of light. Negation itself is regarded as the positive existence of the locus in which the negation appears with specific reference to the appearance or disappearance of the negated object. Thus in the case of negation-precedent-to-production (*prāg-abhāva*) of a jug, the simple material cause which will be helpful to the production or the appearance of the jug is regarded as the negative-precedent-to-production of the jug. In the case of negation of destruction (*dhvaṃsābhāva*) the cause is helpful to the disappearance of the jug, and is thus associated with the special quality that is regarded as the negation of destruction. The concept of negation is thus included in the conception of the cause; negation is thus a specific mode of *samavāyi kāraṇa* and therefore identical with it.

Regarding the manner in which visual cognitions of things are possible, the Sāṃkhya and Vedānta uphold the subsistence of a *vṛtti* (*vṛtti* means mental state). When after looking at a thing we shut our eyes, there is an after-image of the object. This after-image cannot belong to the object itself, because our eyes are shut; it must itself belong to the *ahaṃkāra* or the *buddhi*. It is supposed by the Sāṃkhya and the Vedānta that this *vṛtti* goes to external objects near and far and thereby produces a relation between the *buddhi* and the object. It may naturally be objected that this *vṛtti* is not a substance and therefore cannot travel far and wide. The Sāṃkhya and the Vedānta reply again that, since such travelling is proved by the facts of perception, we have to admit it; there is no rule that only existing substances should be able to travel and that in the absence of substance there should be no travelling. The Naiyāyikas, however, think that certain rays emanate from the eye and go to the object, sense-contact is thereby produced in association with the *manas* and *ātman*, and the result is sense-cognition; they therefore do not admit the existence of a separate *vṛtti*. Puruṣottama, however, admits the *vṛtti*, but not in the same way as the Vedāntists and the Sāṃkhya; according to him this *vṛtti* is a state of the *buddhi* which has been roused through the category of time and has manifested a preponderance of *sattva* quality. Time is hereby admitted as a category existing in the *buddhi* and not in the senses as it is in the Vedānta of Śaṅkara (explained by Dharmarājā-dhvarīndra in the *Vedānta-paribhāṣā*). According to him time does not possess any colour, but can yet be perceived by the visual organs. But according to Puruṣottama time is a determinant of the *buddhi* and is the agent responsible, along with other accessories, for mental illumination; he says further that rays from the object penetrate the eye-ball and produce there certain impressions which remain even when the rays are cut off by the shutting of the eye. These retinal impressions are accessory to the production of illumination in the *buddhi* as the manifestation of *sattva-guṇa*[1]. *Vṛtti* is thus a condition of *buddhi*.

In the illusory perception of conch-shell-silver it is supposed that by the power of *rajas* the impressions of silver experienced before are projected on to the object of perception, and by *tamas* the nature of conch-shell as such is obscured; in this manner a conch-shell is perceived as silver.

The indeterminate knowledge arises at that stage in which the *buddhi* functions at the first moment of sense-operation; and it becomes determinate when in association with the sense-faculty there is modification in the *buddhi* as *vṛtti*. Though with the rise of one *vṛtti* a previous one disappears, it still persists in the form of impression (*saṃskāra*); when these *saṃskāras* are later roused by specific causes or conditions, we have memory.

The intuition of God is not, however, produced by the ordinary method of perception only by God's grace, which is the seed of *bhakti* in all, can His nature be intuited; in the individual this grace manifests itself as devotion[2].

[1] *ukta-sannikarṣa-janyam api savikalpakaṃ jñānaṃ cākṣuṣādi-bhedena buddhi-vṛttyā janyata iti vṛttir vicāryate. tatra netra-nimīlane kṛte bahir-dṛṣṭa-padārthasyeva kaścidākāro netrāntarbhāsate. sa ākāro na bāhya-vastunaḥ. āśrayam atihāya tatra tasyāśakya-vacanatvāt. ataḥ sa āntarasyaiva kasyacana bhavitum arhatīti....*

yā buddhi-vṛttiḥ saṃskārādhānādyarthaṃ janyata ity ucyate sā vṛttir buddher na tattvāntaraṃ nāpy antaḥkaraṇa-pariṇāmāntaram. kintu buddhi-tattvasya kāla-kṣubdha-sattvādi-guṇa-kṛto'vasthā-viśeṣa eva. na ca tasyāvasthā-viśeṣatve nirgamābhāvena viṣayāsaṃsargāt tad-ākārakatvaṃ vṛtter durghaṭatvam iti śaṅkyam. māyā-guṇasya rajasaścañcalatvena vikṣepakatvena ca darpaṇe mukhasyeva netra-golake'pi bāhya-viṣayākāra-samarpaṇa-tad-ākārasya sughaṭatvāt. sa evaṃ māyika ākāro nayana-kiraṇeṣu netra-mudraṇe pratyāvṛtteṣu golakāntar anubhūyate. Prasthānaratnākara, pp. 123–5.

[2] *varaṇaṃ cānugrahaḥ. sa ca dharmāntaram eva, na tu phalāditsā. yasyānugraham icchāmītivākyāt. sa ca bhakti-bīja-bhūtaḥ. ato bhaktyā mām abhijānāti, bhaktyā tvananyayā śakyaḥ bhaktyā'ham ekayā grāhya ity ādiṣu na virodhaḥ. Ibid.* p. 137.

Inference (*anumāna*) as a *pramāṇa* is defined as instrument by which influential knowledge is attained; in other words, inference is the knowledge which is derived through the mediation of other knowledge, a process which is, of course, affected by the knowledge of concomitance (*vyāpti-jñāna*). *Vyāpti* means the unconditioned existence of *hetu* in the *sādhya*, i.e., where there is a *hetu*, there is a *sādhya*, and wherever there is absence of *sādhya*, there is absence of *hetu*; *hetu* is that by which one proceeds to carry on an inference, and *sādhya* is affirmation or denial. Following the *Sāṃkhya-pravacana-sūtra* Puruṣottama says that, when there is an unconditional existence of one quality or character in another, there may be either a mutual or a one-sided concomitance between them; when the circle of the *hetu* coincides with the circle of the *sādhya*, we have *samavyāpti*, and when the circle of the *hetu* falls within the circle of the *sādhya*, there is *viṣama-vyāpti*[1].

Puruṣottama does not admit the *kevalānvayi* form of inference; for in the Brahman there is the absence of the *sādhya*. The objection that such a definition will not hold good in the case of inference (where no negative existences are available), namely, that it is knowledge because it is definable, is invalid; for the Brahman is neither knowable nor definable. Even when an object is knowable in one form, it may be not knowable in another form. So even in the aforesaid inference negative instances are available; therefore the *kevalānvayi* form of inference, where it is supposed that concomitance is to be determined only by agreement, cannot be accepted[2].

When the co-existence of the *hetu* with the *sādhya* is seen in one instance or in many, it rouses the part-impressions and though in the memory of them necessary co-existence, and, following that, the *hetu* determines the *sādhya*. When we see in the kitchen the co-existence of fire and smoke, the necessary co-existence of the smoke with the fire is known; then later on, when smoke is seen in the hill and the co-existence of the smoke with the fire is remembered, the smoke determines the existence of the fire: this right knowledge is called *anumiti*. It is the *liṅga* that is the cause of the *anumiti*. Two

[1] *niyata-dharma-sāhitye ubhayor ekatarasya vā vyāptir iti. ubhayoḥ sama-vyāptikayoḥ kṛtakatvānityatvādi-rūpayorekatarasya viṣama-vyāptikasya dhūmāder niyata-dharma-sāhitye a-vyabhicarita-dharma-rūpe sāmānādhikaraṇye vyāptiḥ. Prasthānaratnākara*, pp. 139–40.

[2] *sarvatrāpi kenacid rūpeṇa jñeyatvādi-sattve'pi rūpāntareṇa tad-abhāvasya sarvajanīnatvāc ca kevalānvayi-sādhyakānumānasyaivābhāvāt. Ibid.* p. 141.

kinds of *anumāna* are admitted by Puruṣottama, viz., *kevala-vyatireki*, where positive instances are not available and the concomitance is only through negation, and *anvaya-vyatireki*, where the concomitance is known through the joint method of agreement and difference.

Five propositions are generally admitted for convincing others by inference; these are *pratijñā, hetu, udāharaṇa, upanaya*, and *nigamana*. Thus "the hill is fiery" is the *pratijñā*, "because it is smoky" is the *hetu*, "as in the case in the kitchen" is the *udāharaṇa*, "whatever is smoky is fiery and whatever is not so is not so" is the *upanaya*, "therefore the smoke now visible is also associated with fire" is *nigamana*. But these need not be regarded as separate propositions; they are parts of one synthetic proposition[1]. But Puruṣottama in reality prefers these three, viz., *pratijñā, hetu* and *dṛṣṭānta*.

Puruṣottama does not admit either *upamāna* or *anupalabdhi* as separate *pramāṇas*. *Upamāṇa* is the *pramāṇa* by which a previous knowledge of similarity between two objects of which one is known enables one to know the other when one sees it; thus a man who does not know a buffalo, but is told that it is similar in appearance to the cow, sees the buffalo in the forest and knows it to be a buffalo. The sight of it makes him remember that a buffalo is an animal which is similar in appearance to the cow, and thus he knows it is a buffalo. Here perception as helped by memory of similarity is the cause of the new apprehension of the animal as a buffalo; what is called *upamāna* thus falls within perception.

Puruṣottama also admits *arthāpatti*, or implication, as separate *pramāṇa*, in the manner of Pārthasārathimiśra. This *arthāpatti* is to be distinguished from inference. A specific case of it may be illustrated by the example in which one assumes the existence of someone outside the house when he is not found inside; the knowledge of the absence of a living person from the house is not connected with the knowledge of the same man's presence outside the house as cause and effect, and yet they are simultaneous. It is by the assumption of the living individual outside the house that his non-existence in the house can be understood; the complex notion of life and non-existence in the house induces the notion of his existence outside the house. It is the inherent contradiction that

[1] *Ibid.* p. 143.

leads us from the known fact to the unknown, and as such it is regarded as a separate *pramāṇa*.

Puruṣottama thinks that in some cases where knowledge is due to the accessory influence of memory its validity is not spontaneous, but is to be derived only through corroborative sources, whereas there may be other cases where knowledge may be self-valid.

Concept of bhakti.

Madhva, Vallabha and Jīva Gosvāmī were all indebted to the *Bhāgavata-puraṇa*, and held it in high reverence; Madhva wrote *Bhāgavata-tātparya*, Jīva Gosvāmī *Ṣaṭ-sandarbha*, and Vallabha wrote not only a commentary on the *Bhāgavata* (the *Subodhinī*) but also a commentary (*Prakāśa*) on his own *kārikās*, the *Tattvadīpa*, based on the teachings of the *Bhāgavata*. The *Tattvadīpa* consists of four books: the *Śāstrārthanirūpaṇa*, the *Sarvanirṇaya* of four chapters, *Pramāṇa*, *Prameya-phala*, and the *Sādhanā*, of which the first contains 83 verses, the second 100 verses, the third 110 and the fourth 35. The third book, of 1837 verses, contains observations on the twelve *skandhas* of the *Bhāgavata-puraṇa*. The fourth book, which dealt with *bhakti*, is found only in a fragmentary condition. This last has two commentaries on it, the *Nibandha-ṭippaṇa*, by Kalyāṇarāja, and one by Gotthulal (otherwise called Bālakṛṣna). The *Prakāśa* commentary on the *kārikās* was commented upon by Puruṣottama in the *Āvaraṇa-bhaṅga*, but the entire work has not been available to the present writer. According to the *Tattvadīpa* the only *śāstra* is the *Gītā*, which is sung by the Lord Himself, the only God is Kṛṣṇa the son of Devakī, the *mantras* are only His name and the only work is the service of God, the Vedas, the words of Kṛṣṇa (forming the *smṛtis*), the *sūtras* of Vyāsa and their explanations by Vyāsa (forming the *Bhāgavata*) are their four *pramāṇas*. If there are any doubts regarding the Vedas, they are solved by the words of Kṛṣṇa; any doubts regarding the latter are explained by reference to the *sūtras*, and difficulties about the *Vyāsa-sūtras* are to be explained by the *Bhāgavata*. So far as the other *smṛtis* are concerned, such as that of Manu and others, only so much of them is valid as is in consonance with these; but, if they are found contradictory in any part, they are to be treated as invalid. The true object of the *śāstras* is devotion to Hari, and the wise man who takes to devotion is best of all; yet there have been many systems of thought which produce delusion by preaching creeds other than that of *bhakti*. There is no greater delusion than devoting oneself to *śāstras* and not to God; such devotees are always under bondage and suffer birth and rebirth. The culmination of one's knowledge is omniscience, the culmination of *dharma* is the contentment of one's mind, the culmination of *bhakti* is when God is pleased. With *mukti* there is destruction of birth and rebirth; but the world, being a manifestation of Brahman, is never destroyed except when Kṛṣṇa wishes to take it back within Himself. Wisdom and ignorance are both constituents of *māyā*.

Bhakti consists in firm and overwhelming affection for God with a full sense of His greatness; through this alone can there be emancipation[1]. Though *bhakti* is the *sādhanā* and *mokṣa* is the goal, yet it is the *sādhanā* stage that is the best. Those who enter into the bliss of Brahman have the experience of that bliss in their selves; but those devotees who do not enter into this state nor into the state of *jīvan-mukti*, but enjoy God with all their senses and the *antaḥkaraṇa*, are better than the *jīvan-muktas*, though they may be ordinary householders[2].

The *jīva* is atomic in nature, but yet, since the bliss of God is manifested in it, it may be regarded as all-pervasive. Its nature as pure intelligence cannot be perceived by the ordinary senses, but only by *yoga*, or knowledge through that special vision by which one sees God. The views of the monistic Vedānta that the *jīvas* are due to *avidyā* is repudiated on the ground that, if *avidyā* was destroyed by right knowledge, the bodily structure of the individual formed through the illusion of *avidyā* would immediately be destroyed and as *jīvan-mukti* would be possible.

Brahman is described here as *saccidānanda*—all-pervasive, independent, omniscient. He is devoid of any reduplication, either of this class or of a different class or as existing in Him—i.e., *jīvas*,

1 *māhātmya-jñāna-pūrvas tu sudṛḍhaḥ sarvato'dhikaḥ,*
sneho bhaktir iti proktas tayā muktir na cānyathā.
Tattvārthadīpa, p. 65.

2 *sva-tantra-bhaktānāṃ tu gopikādi-tulyānāṃ sarvendriyais tathā'ntaḥkaraṇaiḥ sva-rūpeṇa cā'nandānubhavaḥ. ato bhaktānāṃ jīvan-muktyapekṣayā bhagavat-kṛpā-sahita-gṛhāśrama eva viśiṣyate.* Vallabha's commentary on *Tattvadīpana*, p. 77.

the material world and the *antaryāmi*: these are the three forms of God, they are not different from Him[1]. He is also associated with a thousand other noble qualities, purity, nobility, kindness, etc.; He is the upholder of the universe, controller of *māyā*. God is on the one hand the *samavāya* and the *nimittakāraṇa* of the world, delights in His creation, and sometimes takes delight in withdrawing it within Himself; He is the repository of all contradictory qualities and causes delusion in various forms and appearances and disappearances of worldly manifestation. He is the changeable as well as the unchangeable[2]. Since the creation is a manifestation of Himself, the diversity of existence and the diversity in the distribution of pleasure and pain cannot make Him liable to the charge of cruelty or partiality. The attempt to explain diversity as due to *karma* leads to the further difficulty that God is dependent on *karma* and is not independent; it also leaves unexplained why different persons should perform different *karmas*. If God as *antaryāmin* Himself makes us perform good or bad actions, He cannot also make us responsible for the same and distribute happiness to some and displeasure to others: but on the view that the whole creation is self-creative and that self-manifestation and the *jīvas* are nothing but God all these difficulties are removed[3]. God is the creator of the world, yet He is not *saguṇa*, possessed of qualities; for the simple reason that the elements that constitute His qualities cannot stand against Him and deprive Him of His independence. Since He is the controller of the qualities, their existence and non-existence depend on Him. The conception of the freedom of God thus necessarily leads to the concept of His being both *saguṇa* and *nirguṇa*. The view of Śaṅkara that Brahman appears as the world through the bondage of *avidyā* is a delusive teaching (*pratāraṇā-śāstra*), because it lowers the dignity of God, and it should be rejected by all devotees.

[1] *sa-jātīya-vijātīya-sva-gata-dvaita-varjitam. . . . sa-jātīyā jīvā, vijātīyā jaḍāḥ, sva-gatā antar-yāmiṇaḥ. triṣv api bhagavān anusyūtas trirūpaś ca bhavatīti tair nirūpitaṃ dvaitaṃ bhedas tad varjitam. Tattvārthadīpa* and the commentary on it, p. 106.

[2] *sarva-vādānavasaraṃ nānā-vādānurodhi tat.*
ananta-mūrti tad brahma kūṭasthaṃ calam eva ca.
virūddha-sarva-dharmāṇamāśrayaṃ yukty-agocaram.
āvirbhāva-tirobhāvair mohanaṃ bahu-rūpatah. Ibid. p. 115.

[3] *ātma-sṛṣṭer na vaiṣamyaṃ nairghṛṇyaṃ cāpi vidyate.*
pakṣāntare'pi karma syān niyataṃ tat punar bṛhat.
Ibid. pp. 129–30.

He who thinks of God as all and of himself as emanating from Him, and who serves Him with love, is a devotee. In the absence of either knowledge or love we have only a lower kind of devotee; but in the absence of both one cannot be a devotee, though by listening to the scriptures one may remove one's sins. The highest devotee leaves everything; his mind is filled with Kṛṣṇa alone; for him there is no wife, no home, no sons, no friends, no riches, but he is wholly absorbed in the love of God. No one, however, can take the path of *bhakti* except through the grace of God. *Karma* itself, being of the nature of God's will, manifests itself as His mercy or anger to the devotee; He approaches with His mercy and relieves him even if he be in a low state, and those who do not obey His commands or proceed in the wrong path He approaches with anger and causes to suffer. It is said that the law of *karma* is mysterious; the reason is that we do not know the manner in which God's will manifests itself; sometimes by His grace He may even save a sinner, who may not have to take the punishment due to him.

In the *Śāṇḍilya-sūtra bhakti* is defined as the highest attachment (*parānurakti*) to God. *Anurakti* is the same as *rāga*; so the *sūtra* "*parānuraktir īśvare*" means highest attachment to the object of worship (*ārādhya-viṣayaka-rāgatvam*)[1]. This attachment is associated with pleasure (*sukha-niyato rāga*). We remember that in the *Viṣṇu-purāṇa* Prahlāda expresses the wish that he may have that attachment to God that is experienced with regard to sense-objects[2]. Onc must find supreme pleasure in God; it is this natural and spontaneous attachment to God that is called *bhakti*[3]. Even if there is no notion of worship, but merely love, there also we can apply the term *bhakti*, as in the case of *gopīs* towards Kṛṣṇa. But ordinarily it arises from the notion of the greatness of God. This devotion, being of thc naturc of attachment, is associated with will and not with action; just as in the case of knowledge no action is necessary, but the only result is enlightenment, so the will that tends

[1] *Śāṇḍilya-sūtra*, I. 2. (commentary by Svapneśvara).

[2] *yā prītir a-vivekānāṃ viṣayeṣv anapāyinī,*
tām 'anusmarataḥ sā me hṛdayān māpasarpatu.
Viṣṇu-purāṇa, I. 20. 19.

[3] Compare *Gītā*, X. 9:
mac-cittā mad-gata-prāṇā bodhayantaḥ paras-param
kathayantaś ca māṃ nityam tuṣyantica ramanti ca....

to God is satisfied with devotion or attachment[1]. *Bhakti* cannot also be regarded as knowledge: *jñāna* and *bhajana* are two different concepts. Knowledge may be only indirectly necessary for attachment, but attachment does not lead to knowledge. A young woman may love a young man; this love does not lead to any new knowledge, but finds its fulfilment in the love itself. In the *Viṣṇu-purāṇa* we hear of the *gopīs*' attachment of emancipation through excess of love; so attachment may lead to emancipation without any knowledge[2]. *Yoga*, however, is accessory both to knowledge and to *bhakti*. *Bhakti* is different also from *śraddhā* (or faith), which may be an accessory even to *karma*. According to Kasya *bhakti* with the notion of the majesty of God leads to emancipation. According to Bādarāyaṇa this emancipation consists in the nature of self as pure intelligence. According to Śāṇḍilya emancipation is associated with the notion of transcendence, immanence in the self. Through an excess of devotion understanding of the *buddhi* is dissolved in the bliss of God; it is this *buddhi* which is the *upādhi* or condition through which God manifests Himself as the *jīva*.

Gopeśvarajī Mahārāja, in his *Bhakti-mārtaṇḍa*, follows the interpretation of *bhakti* in the *Śāṇḍilya-sūtra* and enters into a long discussion regarding its exact connotation. He denies that *bhakti* is a kind of knowledge or a kind of *śraddhā* (or faith); nor is *bhakti* a kind of action or worship. Rāmānuja defines *bhakti* as *dhruvām smṛti*, and regards it as only a kind of knowledge. Various forms of worship or prescribed ritual connected therewith lead to *bhakti*, but they cannot themselves be regarded as *bhakti*. In the *Bhakti-cintāmaṇi*, *bhakti* has been defined as *yoge viyogavṛttiprema*, i.e., it is that form of love in which even when the two are together they are afraid of being dissociated and when they are not together they have a painful desire for union[3]. Śāṇḍilya, Haridāsa and Guptācārya also follow the same view. Govinda Chakravarti, however, defines

[1] *na kriyākṛty-apekṣaṇā jñānavat. Śāṇḍilya-sūtra*, I. I. 7. *sā bhaktir na kriyātmikā bhavitum arhati prayatnānuvedhābhāvāt.* Commentary on Svapneśvara.

[2] *tathāpi brahma-viṣayiṇyāḥ rater brahma-viṣaya-jñānopakārakatvaṃ na pratyakṣa-gamyam. kintu tarūṇyādeḥ ratau tathādarśanena brahmagocarāyām apy anumātavyam.* Svapneśvara's commentary on—I. 2. 15, *ibid.*

[3] *A-dṛṣṭe darśanotkaṇṭhā dṛṣṭe viśleṣa-bhīrutā*
nādṛṣṭena na dṛṣṭena bhavatā labhyate sukhaṃ.
Bhakti-mārtaṇḍa, p. 75.

this love as the yearning which never ceases even in spite of many difficulties and dangers[1], and Paramārtha Ṭhakkuna, in his *Premalakṣaṇa-candrikā*[2], as an unspeakable yearning referring to an object. Viśvanātha, in his *Premarasāyina*, defines it as a loving yearning or desire. Guṇakara supplements the view of the *Bhakti-cintāmaṇi* and defines it as that which culminates in intense enjoyment[3].

Gopeśvarajī Mahārāja differs from all these definitions of *bhakti* that regard yearning and desire as its principal element. No desire can be an object of desire (*puruṣārtha*); in the love of a son or any other dear relation we do not find any kind of desire playing a part; moreover desire refers to an unattained object, while *bhakti*, attachment, is not so.

Some say that *bhakti* is the cause of the melting of the mind; that is not acceptable either, for it has no reference to the object. There are others who define it as the object or condition with reference to which the amorous sentiment called love flows[4]. This definition is too wide, because all *bhakti* must have a reference to God, and according to it *bhakti* becomes a part of sex-sentiment. Gopeśvarajī, however, refers to the *Tattvadīpa-prakāśa* of Vallabha and accepts the view there adopted, according to which *bhakti* is composed of the root *bhaj* and suffix *kti*; the suffix means "love" and the root "service." It is the general rule that root and suffix together form a complete meaning in which the meaning of the suffix is dominant; *bhakti* thus means the action of *bhaj*, i.e., service (*sevā*). *Sevā* (service) is a bodily affair (e.g., *strīsevā*, *auṣadhasevā*). Service, in order that it may be complete, implies love, and without love the service would be troublesome, but not desirable; love also for its completion requires service. This view has been objected to by Puruṣottama in his *Bhakti-haṃsa-vivṛti*.

Referring to the *Tattva-dīpa-prakāśa* Gopeśvarajī Mahārāja thinks that according to Vallabha *bhakti* means *sneha* or affection, but, if we take the word analytically, it means *sevā* or service; he thinks that both *prema* and *sevā* form the connotative meaning of

[1] *gāḍha-vyasana-sāhasra-sampāte'pi nir-antaraṃ na hīyate yadīheti svādu tat prema-lakṣaṇam.* *Ibid.*

[2] *vastu-mātra-viṣayiṇī vacanānarhā samīhā prema.* *Ibid.*

[3] *yathā yoge viyoga-vṛttiḥ prema tathā viyoge yoga-vṛttir api prema.* *Ibid.*

[4] *yam upādhiṃ samāśritya rasa ādyo nigadyate tam*
upādhiṃ budhottaṃsāḥ premeti paricakṣata. *Ibid.* p. 76.

bhakti[1]. He, however, develops further the concept of *bhakti*, and says that the idea of *sevā* forming the connotation of *bhakti* means the state of mind which slowly lowers down and merges itself into God[2].

One of the results of *bhakti* or rather one of its characteristics has been described as the oneness of all with the self (*sarvātma-bhāva*). Through the deep notion of love one sees everywhere one's beloved, and even in separation one always perceives one's beloved round one; but, God being all, it is natural that through intense attachment to Him one should perceive Him in all things; for these are all manifestations of God[3]. This identity of the self with all cannot be regarded as an illustration of Vedāntic monism, as is explained by the followers of *maryādā-marga*; it is associated with intense love. This view of the *puṣṭi-mārga* (Vallabha school) is also shared by Haricaraṇa, who is quoted by Gopeśvara in support of his own view[4].

Bhakti is regarded as parallel to the other *rasas* described in the *alaṁkāra-śāstra*; as such, it affects the *manas* and the body with intense delight, coalescing with God, as it were[5]; affection is thus the dominant phase (*sthāyī-bhāvā*) of the *bhakti-rasa*. Some have defined it as a reflection of God in the melted heart; this has been objected to both by Puruṣottama in his *Pratibimba-vāda* and by Gopeśvara on the ground that formless God cannot have His reflection, and also on the ground that this would

[1] *prema-pūrvakaṃ kāyika-vyāpāratvaṃ bhaktitvam... athavā śrī-kṛṣṇa-viṣayaka-prema-pūrvaka-kāyika-vyāpāratvaṃ. Bhakti-mārtaṇḍa*, p. 79.

[2] *tasmin kṛṣṇe pūrvaṃ āvarjitaṃ tata āyattaṃ tadadhīnaṃ tataḥ krameṇa bhagavad-ekatānam....gambhīratāṃ prāptaṃ yac cetas tad eva sevārūpam. samādhāv iva bhagavati layaṃ prāptam iti yāvat. Ibid.* p. 82.

He further quotes a passage from Vallabha's *Bhakti-vardhinī* in support of his statement:

tataḥ prema tathā śaktir vyasanañca yadā bhaved iti,
yadā syād vyasanaṃ kṛṣṇe kṛtārthaḥ syāt tadaivahi. *Ibid.* p. 82.

[3] *vigāḍha-bhāvena sarvatra tathānubhava-rūpaṃ yat kāryaṃ tādṛśapriya-tvānubhavaḥ, iti sarvātma-bhāvo lakṣitaḥ. Bhāsya-prakāśa* on *Brahma-sūtra*, quoted in *Bhakti-mārtaṇḍa*, p. 85.

[4] *ataḥ sarvātma-bhāvo hi tyāgātmāpekṣayā yutaḥ bhāva-*
svarūpaphalakaḥ sva-sambandha-prakāśakaḥ.
dehādi-sphūrti-rahito viṣaya-tyāga-pūrvakaḥ
bhāvātma-kāma-sambandhi-ramaṇādi-kriyāḥ.
sva-tantra-bhakti-śabdākhyaḥ phalātmā jñāyatāṃ janaiḥ.
Ibid. p. 86.

[5] *yatra manaḥsarvendriyāṇām ānanda-mātra-kara-pāda-mukhodarādi-bhagavad-rūpatā tatra bhakti-rasa eva. Ibid.* p. 102.

make *bhakti* identical with God, and it is difficult to identify affection with the melting of the heart[1]. If *ātmānubhava* be understood merely as the comprehension of identity with the self, in the fashion of Śaṅkara monism, then there would be no pleasure in the attachment of God[2].

The assertion of the philosophic identity of the self and the Brahman is only for the purpose of strengthening the nature of *bhakti*; it merely shows that the oneness that is felt through attachment can also be philosophically supported. In the intensity of love there is revealed a feeling of oneness with Kṛṣṇa which is to be regarded as one of the transitory phases (*vyābhicāri bhāva*) of the emotion of *bhakti*, of which affection is the dominant phase (*sthāyi bhāva*); the feeling of oneness is thus not the culminating result, but only a transitory phase. Thus *bhakti* does not result finally in knowledge; knowledge is an *aṅga* of *bhakti*[3]. As God is spiritual, so also is *bhakti* spiritual; as by the measures of fire objects become more or less heated, so relative proximity to God gives an experience of greater or less intensity of *bhakti*[4].

Bhakti may be classified as *phala-rūpa* ("fruit"), as *sādhana-rūpa* ("means"), and as *saguṇa*. The *saguṇa-bhakti* is of three kinds, as forming part of different kinds of meditation, as part of knowledge, and as part of *karma*. These again may be of eighty-one kinds, as associated with different kinds of quality. *Bhakti* as a *phala* is of one kind, and as *sādhanā* ("means") is of two kinds, viz., as part of knowledge (*jñānāṅgabhūta*), and as directly leading to emancipation (*bhaktiḥ svātantryena muktidātrī*). The *jñānāṅgabhūta-bhakti* is itself of two kinds, as *saguṇa* and *nirguṇa*, of which the former is of three kinds, *jñāna-miśra*, *vairāgya-miśra* and *karma-*

[1] It is interesting to refer here to the definition of *bhakti* as given by *jīva* in the *Ṣaṭ-sandarbha* (p. 274), where *bhakti* is described as a dual existence in God, and, the *bhakta* being itself of the nature of blissful experience, *sva-rūpaśakteḥ sārabhūtā hlādinī nāma yā vṛttis tasyā eva sārabhūta-vṛttiviśeṣo bhaktiḥ sā ca ratyaparaparyāyā. bhaktir bhavati bhakteṣu ca nikṣipta-nijābhayakoṭiḥ sarvadā tiṣṭhati. uta evoktaṃ bhagavān bhakto bhaktimān.*

[2] *kena kaṃ paśyet iti śruteḥ bheda-vilopakatvena bhajanānandāntarāya-bhūtaṃ yadi svātmatvena jñānaṃ sampādayed bhajanāṇdaṃ nādadyāt.*

Bhakti-mārtaṇḍa, p. 136.

[3] *ati-gāḍha-bhāvo' bhedasphūrtir api ek ovyābhicāribhāvaḥ. na tu sārvadika-stadā svātmānaṃ tattvena viśiṃṣanti. Ibid.* p. 139.

[4] *yathā bhagavān mānasīyas tadvad bhagavatsambandha-naikaṭyāt mana-syāvirbhavantī bhaktir api mano-dharmatvena vyavahriyate. yathā vahni-naikaṭya-tāratamyena bhaktyanubhava-tāratamyam. Ibid.* p. 142.

miśra. The *jñāna-miśra* ("mixed with knowledge") may be of three kinds, high, middling and lower. The *vairāgya-miśra* ("mixed with detachment") is only of one kind. The *karma-miśra* ("mixed with action") is of three kinds.

The principal means by which *bhakti* is attained through the grace of God is purity of heart. There are sixteen means prescribed for attaining purity of heart, of which some are external and some internal. The three externals are ablutions, sacrifices and image-worship. The practice of meditation of God in all things is the fourth. The development of the *sattva* character of the mind is the fifth. Abnegation of all *karmas* and cessation of attachment is the sixth; showing reverence to the revered is the seventh. Kindness to the poor is the eighth. To regard all beings as one's equals and friends is the ninth. *Yamas* and *niyamas* are the tenth and eleventh respectively. Listening to the scriptures from teachers is the twelfth, and listening to and chanting of God's name is the thirteenth. Universal sincerity is the fourteenth. Good association is the fifteenth. Absence of egoism is the sixteenth.

There is however a difference of view between two important schools of the *bhakti*-path. Those who follow the *maryādā-bhakti* think that *bhakti* is attainable by one's own efforts in following specific courses of duties and practices; the followers of the *puṣṭi-bhakti* think that even without any effort *bhakti* can be attained by the grace of God alone[1].

The Vallabhas belong to the *puṣṭi-bhakti* school and therefore do not admit the absolute necessity of personal effort. The followers of the *maryādā* school also agree that the *sādhanas* are to be followed only so long as affection does not show itself; when once that has manifested itself, the *sādhanas* can no longer be regarded as determining it, for it manifests itself spontaneously. For the followers of the *puṣṭi* school the *sādhanas* can at no stage determine the *bhakti*; for it is generated through the grace of God (*puṣṭimārge varaṇam eva sādhanam*). According to the *maryādā* school sins are destroyed by the practice of the *sādhanas* and emancipation attained through the rise of affection. To the followers of the *puṣṭi* school the grace of God is sufficient to destroy obstructions of sins, and there is no definite order about the practices following affection or

[1] *kṛti-sādhya-sādhana-sādhya-bhaktir maryādā-bhaktiḥ tadrahitānāṃ bhagavad-anugrahaika-prāpya-puṣṭi-bhaktiḥ. Bhakti-mārtaṇḍa*, p. 151.

affection following the practices[1]. In the *Pañcarātra bhakti* is defined as affection associated with the majesty of God; but the association of the majesty of God is not a necessary part of *bhakti*. Puruṣottama defines *bhakti* as attachment to God with detachment from all fruits. Purity of mind can be attained both by knowledge and *bhakti* as produced by *puṣṭi* or the grace of God; so the only condition that can be attached to the rise of affection is the grace of God.

It is impossible to say for what reason God is pleased to extend His grace; it cannot be for the relief of suffering, since there are many sufferers to whom God does not do so. It is a special character of God, by which He adapts certain people for manifesting His grace through them.

As regards the fruit of *bhakti*, there are diverse opinions. Vallabha has said in his *Sevāphala-vivṛti* that as a result of it one may attain a great power of experiencing the nature of God (*a-laukika-sāmarthya*), or may also have the experience of continual contact with God (*sājujya*), and also may have a body befitting the service of God (*sevopayogi deha*). This is his description of the *puṣṭi-mārga*. He has also described two other *mārgas*, the *pravāha* and the *maryādā*, in his *Puṣṭi-pravāha-maryādā*. The *pravāha-mārga* consists of the Vedic duties which carry on the processes of birth and rebirth. Those however who do not transgress the Vedic laws are said to belong to the *maryādā-mārga*. The *puṣṭi-mārga* differs from the other two *mārgas* in this, that it depends upon the grace of God and not on Vedic deeds[2]; its fruits are therefore superior to those of other *mārgas*[3].

Vallabha, in his *Bhakti-vardhinī*, says that the seed of *bhakti* exists as *prema* or affection due to the grace of God, and, when it is firm, it increases by renunciation, by listening to the *bhakti-śāstra*, and by chanting God's name. The seed becomes strong when in

[1] *maryādāyāṃ hi śravaṇādibhiḥ pāpakṣaye premotpattis tato muktiḥ. puṣṭi-mārgāṅgīkṛtes tu atyanugraha-sādhyatvena tatra pāpāder aprati-bandhakatvāc chravaṇādirūpā premarūpā ca yugapat paurvāparyeṇa vā vaiparītyena vā bhavati. Ibid.* p. 152.

[2] *ato vedoktatve'pi veda-tātparya-gocaratve'pi jīva-kṛtavaidha-sādhaneṣva-praveśāt tad-asādhya-sādhanāt phala-vailakṣanyāc ca sva-rūpataḥ kāryataḥ phalataś cotkarṣāc ca vedokta-sādhanebhyo'pi bhinnaiva tat tadākārikā puṣṭir-astītyato hetoḥ siddhaṃ iti mārga-trayo'tra na sandeha ityarthaḥ.*

Commentary on *Puṣṭi-pravāha-maryādā-bhedaḥ*, p. 8.

[3] *yeṣu sādhana-dvārā bhaktyabhivyaktiḥ teṣu sā anudbhūtā bhāva-rūpeṇa manasi tiṣṭhati, tataḥ pūjādiṣu sādhaneṣ vanuṣṭhīyamāneṣu premādi-rūpeṇa kramād udbhūtā bhavati. Bhakti-vardhinī-vivṛti* (by Puruṣottama), *śloka* 5.

the householder's state one worships Kṛṣṇa, following one's caste-duties with a complete absorption of mind. Even when engaged in duties one should always fix one's mind on God; in this way there grows the love which develops into attachment or passion. The firm seed of *bhakti* can never be destroyed; it is through affection for God that other attachments are destroyed, and by the development of this affection that one renounces the home. It is only when this affection for God grows into a passion (*vyasana*) that one attains one's end easily. The *bhakti* rises sometimes spontaneously, sometimes in association with other devotees, and sometimes through following favourable practices[1]. Gradual development of *bhakti* is described through seven stages in an ascending order; these are *bhāva*, *prema*, *praṇaya*, *sneha*, *rāga*, *anurāga*, and *vyasana*. The passion or *vyasana* for God, which is the deepest manifestation of affection, is the inability to remain without God (*tadvināṇa sthātum aśaktiḥ*); it is not possible for a man with such an attachment to stay at home and to carry on his ordinary duties. In the previous stages, though one may try to remain at home like a guest in the house, yet he always feels various obstructions in the proper manifestation of his emotion; worldly attachments are always obstacles to the divine attachment of worldly ties which helps the development of *bhakti*[2].

Vallabha, however, is opposed to renunciation after the manner of monistic *sannyāsa*, for this can only bring repentance, as being inefficacious[3]. The path of knowledge can bring its fruit in hundreds of births and it depends upon various other practices; the path of *bhakti* therefore should be taken up instead of the path of knowledge[4]. Renunciation in the *bhakti-mārga* proceeds only out of the necessity of the *bhakti* and for its proper maintenance, and not as a matter of duty.

The fruits of *bhakti* have already been described as *a-laukika-sāmarthya*, *sāyujya* and *sevopayogī-deha*, and are further discussed

[1] See note 3, p. 355.

[2] *snehāśakti-vyasanānāṃ vināśanaṃ. tathā sati kṛtam-api sarvaṃ vyarthaṃ syāt. tena tat-tyāgaṃ kṛtvā yateta.* Bālakṛṣṇa's commentary on *Bhakti-vardhinī*, *śloka* 6.

[3] *ataḥ kalau sa san-nyāsaḥ pascāt tāpāya nānyathā. pāṣaṇḍitvaṃ bhavet cāpi tasmāt jñāne na saṃ-nyaset.*

Vallabha's *San-nyāsa-nirṇaya*, *śloka* 16.

[4] *jñānārtham uttaraṅgaṃ ca siddhir janmaśataiḥ, jñānaṃ ca sādhanāpekṣaṃ yajñādi-śravaṇān matam param.* *San-nyāsa-nirṇaya* of Vallabha, with Gokulanātha's *Vivaraṇa*, *śloka* 15.

in Vallabha's *Sevāphala*, upon which various commentators have written with their several differences. Thus Devakīnandana and Puruṣottama think that *a-laukika-sāmarthya* means that God has a special *āveśa* or that He favours the devotee with a special inspiration, enabling him to experience the nature of the full bliss of God. Harirāja, however, thinks that it means the capacity for experiencing the separation of God; Kalyāṇarāja thinks that it means participation in divine music in heaven with God. Gopīśa thinks that it means special fitness (*svarūpa-yogyatā*) for experiencing the supernatural joy of worshipping God[1]. The second fruit of *bhakti* (*sāyujya*) is considered by Puruṣottama, Baca Gopīśa, and Devakīnandana to be the merging of the devotee in the nature of God; Harirāja, however, regards it as a capacity for continual association with God.

The obstacles to *bhakti* are regarded as *udvega*, *pratibandha*, and *bhoga*. *Udvega* means fear caused by evil persons or unsteadiness of mind through sins; *pratibandha* means obstacles of a general nature, and *bhoga* means ordinary experiences of pleasures and pains of body and mind. These obstacles can be removed by comprehending the false nature of causes that give rise to them; but if on account of the transgressions of the devotee God is angry and does not extend His mercy, then the obstacles cannot be removed[2]. The true knowledge, by which the false comprehension giving rise to the obstacles can be removed, consists in the conviction that everything is given by God, everything is Brahman, that there is no *sādhanā*, no *phala* and no enjoyer[3]. He who tries to enjoy the blessed nature of God easily removes the obstacles. The experiencing of God's nature as a devotee is better than the bliss of Brahman itself and the pleasure of sense-objects (*viṣayānandabrahmānandāpekṣayā bhajanānandasya māhāttvāt*). Mental unsteadiness as a result of

[1] *tatra alaukika-sāmarthyaṃ nāma para-prāpti-vivaraṇa-śrutyukta-bhagavat-sva-rūpānubhave pradīpavadāveśa iti sūtrokta-rītika-bhagavadāveśajā yogyatā yayā rasātmakasya bhagavataḥ pūrṇa-sva-rūpānandānubhavaḥ. śrī-devakī-nandanādāvapyevam āhuḥ. śrī-hari-rāyās tu bhagavad-virahānubhava-sāmarthyam ity āhuḥ. śrī-kalyāṇa-rāyās tu bhagavatā saha gānādi-sāmarthyaṃ mukhyānām evetyāhuḥ. tathā gopīnāntvalaukika-bhajanānandānubhave sva-rūpa-yogyatā ityahuḥ.* Puruṣottama's commentary on *Sevāphala*, *śloka* 1.

[2] *kadācit duḥsaṅgādinā ati-pakṣapāti-prabhu-priya-pradveṣeṇa taddrohe prabhor atikrodhena prārthanayāpi kṣamā-saṃ-bhāvanā-rahitena tasmin prabhuḥ phala-pratibandhaṃ karotīti sa bhagatat-kṛta-pratibandhaḥ.*

Harirāja's commentary on *Sevāphala*, *śloka* 3.

[3] *vivekas tu mamaitad eva prabhunā krtaṃ sarvaṃ brahmātmakaṃ ko'haṃ kiñca sādhanaṃ kiṃ phalaṃ ko dātā ko bhoktā ityādi-rūpaḥ. Ibid.*

attachment to worldly things stands in the way of extension of God's grace; it can be removed by abnegating the fruits of *karma*. The emancipation that has been spoken of before as a result of *bhakti* is to be interpreted as the three-fold *Sevāphala*, superior, middling and inferior, viz., *a-laukika-sāmarthya* (*uttama-sevā-phala*), *sāyujya* (*madhyama-sevāphala*) and *bhajanopayogi deha* (*adhama-sevā-phala*)[1].

Topics of Vallabha Vedānta as explained by Vallabha's followers.

A number of papers, which deserve some notice, were written by the followers of Vallabha on the various topics of the Vedānta. According to the *Bhāgavata-purāṇa* (III. 7, 10–11), as interpreted by Vallabha in his *Subodhinī*, error is regarded as wrong attribution of a quality or character to an entity to which it does not belong[2]. Taking his cue from Vallabha, Bālakṛṣṇa Bhaṭṭa (otherwise called Dallū Bhaṭṭa) tries to evolve a philosophic theory of illusion according to the Vallabha school. He says that in the first instance there is a contact of the eye (as associated with the *manas*) with the conch-shell, and thereby there arises an indeterminate knowledge (*sāmānyajñāna*), which is prior to doubt and other specific cognitions; this indeterminate cognition rouses the *sattvaguṇa* of the *buddhi* and thereby produces right knowledge. It is therefore said in the *Sarvanirṇaya* that *buddhi* as associated with *sattva* is to be regarded as *pramāṇa*. In the *Bhāgavata* (III. 26. 30) doubt, error, definite knowledge, memory and dream are regarded as states of *buddhi*; so the defining character of cognition is to be regarded as a function of *buddhi*. Thus it is the *manas* and the senses that produce indeterminate knowledge, which later on becomes differentiated through the function of *buddhi*. When through the *tamas* quality of *māyā* the *buddhi* is obscured, the conch-shell with which the senses are in contact is not perceived; the *buddhi*, thus obscured, produces the notion of silver by its past impression of silver, roused by the shining characteristic of the conch-shell, which is similar to

[1] *bhakti-mārge sevāyā uttama-madhyama-sādhāraṇādhikārakrameṇa etat phala-trayam eva, no mokṣādiḥ.* Hariraja's commentary on *Sevāphala*, *śloka* 6.

[2] *yathā jale candramasaḥ pratibiṃbitasya tena jalena kṛto guṇaḥ kampādi-dharmaḥ āsanno vidyamāno mithyaiva dṛśyate na vastutaścandrasya evam anātmano dehader dharmo janma-bandha-duḥkhādirūpo draṣṭur ātmano jīvasya na īśvarasya. Subodhinī*, III. 7. 11.

silver. In the Śaṅkara school of interpretation the false silver is created on the conch-shell, which is obscured by *avidyā*. The silver of the conch-shell-silver is thus an objective creation, and as such a relatively real object with which the visual sense comes in contact. According to Vallabha the conch-shell-silver is a mental creation of the *buddhi*[1]. The indefinite knowledge first produced by the contact of the senses of the *manas* is thus of the conch-shell, conch-shell-silver being a product of the *buddhi*; in right knowledge the *buddhi* takes in that which is grasped by the senses. This view of illusion is called *anyakhyāti*, i.e., the apprehension of something other than that with which the sense was in contact. The Śaṅkara interpretation of illusion is false; for, if there was a conch-shell-silver created by the *māyā*, it is impossible to explain the notion of conch-shell; for there is nothing to destroy the conch-shell-silver which would have been created. The conch-shell-silver having obscured the conch-shell and the notion of conch-shell-silver not being destructible except without the notion of the conch-shell, nothing can explain how the conch-shell-silver may be destroyed. If it is suggested that the conch-shell-silver is produced by *māyā* and destroyed by *māyā*, then the notion of world-appearances produced by *māyā* may be regarded as destructible by *māyā*, and no effort can be made for the attainment of right knowledge. According to Vallabha the world is never false; it is our *buddhi* which creates false notions, which may be regarded as intermediate creation (*antarālikī*). In the case of transcendental illusion—when the Brahman is perceived as the manifold world—there is an apprehension of Him as being, which is of an indefinite nature. It is this being which is associated with characters and appearances, e.g., the jug and the pot, which are false notions created by *buddhi*. These false notions are removed when the defects are removed, and not by the intuition of the locus of the illusion; the intellectual creation of a jug and a pot may thus be false, though this does not involve the denial of a jug or a pot in the actual world[2]. So the notion of world-creation and world-destruction are false notions created by us. The *jīva*, being a part of God, is true; it is false only

[1] *iad idaṃ bauddham eva rajataṃ buddhyā viṣayī-kriyate. na tu sāmānya-jñāne cakṣur-viṣayī-bhūtam iti vivekaḥ. Vādāvali*, p. 3.

[2] *atrāpi bauddha eva ghaṭo mithyā, na tu prapañcāntar-vartīti niṣkarṣaḥ. Ibid.* p. 6.

in so far as it is regarded as the subject of the cycle of birth and rebirth. The falsity of the reality of the world thus depends on the manner in which it is perceived[1]; so, when one perceives the world and knows it as Brahman, his intellectual notion of the real diversity of the world vanishes, though the actually perceived world may remain as it is[2]. The creation of *māyā* is thus not external, but internal. The visible world, therefore, as such is not false; only the notion of it as an independent reality, apart from God, is false. The word *māyā* is used in two senses, as the power of God to become all, and as the power of delusion; and the latter is a part of the former.

Puruṣottama, however, gives a different interpretation in his *Khyātivāda*. He says that the illusion of conch-shell-silver is produced by the objective and the external projection of knowledge as a mental state through the instrumentality of *māyā*; the mental state thus projected is intuited as an object[3]. This external projection is associated with the rising of older impressions. It is wrong to suppose that it is the self which is the basis of illusion; for the self is the basis of self-consciousness and in the perception of the conch-shell-silver no one has the notion "I am silver."

Speaking against the doctrine of the falsity of the world, Giridhara Gosvāmī says in his *Prapañcavāda* that the illusoriness of the world cannot be maintained. If the falsity of the perceived world is regarded as its negation in past, present and future, then it could not have been perceived at all; if this negation be of the nature of *atyantābhāva*, then, since that concept is dependent on the existence of the thing to be negated and since that thing also does not exist, the negation as *atyantābhāva* does not exist either. If the negation of the world means that it is a fabrication of illusion, then again there are serious objections; an illusion is an illusion only in comparison with a previous right knowledge; when no comparison with a previous right knowledge is possible, the world cannot be an illusion.

[1] *tathā ca siddhaṃ viṣayatā-vaiśiṣṭyena prapañcasya satyatvaṃ mithyātvañ-ca. evaṃ svamate prapañcasya pāramārthika-vicāre brahmātmakatvena satyatvam. Vādāvali*, p. 8.

[2] *tathātra cakṣuḥ-saṃyukta-prapañca-viṣayake brahmatva-jñāne utpanne bauddha eva prapañco naśyati. na tu cakṣur-gṛhīto'yam ity arthaḥ. Ibid.* p. 8.

[3] *ataḥ śukti-rajatādi-sthale māyayā bahiḥ-kṣipta-buddhi-vṛtti-rūpaṃ jñānam eva arthākāreṇa khyāyata iti mantavyam. Ibid.* p. 121.

If the nature of the world be regarded as due to *avidyā*, one may naturally think, to whom does the *avidyā* belong? Brahman (according to the Śaṅkarites) being qualityless, *avidyā* cannot be a quality of Brahman. Brahman Himself cannot be *avidyā*, because *avidyā* is the cause of it. If *avidyā* is regarded as obscuring the right knowledge of anything, then the object of which the right knowledge is obscured must be demonstrated. Again, the Śaṅkarites hold that the *jīva* is a reflection of Brahman on *avidyā*. If that is so, then the qualities of the *jīva* are due to *avidyā* as the impurities of a reflection are due to the impurity of the mirror. If that is so, the *jīva* being a product of the *avidyā*, the latter cannot belong to the former. In the Vallabha view the illusion of the individual is due to the will of God.

Again, the *avidyā* of the Śaṅkarites is defined as different from being and non-being; but no such category is known to anybody, because it involves self-contradiction. Now the Śaṅkarites say that the falsity of the world consists in its indefinableness; in reality this is not falsity—if it were so, Brahman Himself would have been false. The *śruti* texts say that He cannot be described by speech, thought or mind. It cannot be said that Brahman can be defined as being; for it is said in the text that He is neither being nor non-being (*na sat tan nāsad ity ucyate*). Again, the world cannot be regarded as transformation (*vikāra*); for, if it is a *vikāra*, one must point out that of which it is a *vikāra*; it cannot be of Brahman, because Brahman is changeless; it cannot be of anything else, since everything except Brahman is changeable.

In the Vallabha view the world is not false, and God is regarded as the *samavāyi* and *nimitta-kāraṇa* of it, as has been described above. *Samavāyi-kāraṇa* is conceived as pervading all kinds of existence, just as earth pervades the jug; but, unlike the jug, there is no transformation or change (*vikāra*) of God, because, unlike the earth, God has will. The apparent contradiction, that the world possessed of quality and characters cannot be identified with Brahman, is invalid, because the nature of Brahman can only be determined from the scriptural texts, and they unquestionably declare that Brahman has the power of becoming everything.

In the *Bhedābheda-svarūpa-nirṇaya* Puruṣottama says that according to the *satkāryavāda* view of the Vedānta all things are existent in the Brahman from the beginning. The *jīvas* also, being the parts of God, exist in Him. The difference between the causal and the effect state is that in the latter certain qualities or characters become manifest. The duality that we perceive in the world does not contradict monism; for the apparent forms and characters which are mutually different cannot contradict their metaphysical character of identity with God[1]. So Brahman from one point of view may be regarded as partless, and from another point of view as having parts.

There is a difference, however, between the *prapañca* and the manifold world and *saṃsāra*, the cycle of births and rebirths. By the concept of *saṃsāra* we understand that God has rendered Himself into effects and the *jīvas* and the notion of their specific individuality as performers of actions and enjoyers of experience. Such a notion is false; there is in reality no cause and effect, no bondage and salvation, everything being of the nature of God. This idea has been explained in Vallabha Gosvāmī's *Prapañca-saṃsāra-bheda*. Just as the sun and its rays are one and the same, so the qualities of God are dependent upon Him and identical with Him; the apparent contradiction is removed by the testimony of the scriptural texts[2].

Regarding the process of creation Puruṣottama, after refuting the various views of creation, says that Brahman as the identity of *sat*, *cit*, and *ānanda* manifests Himself as these qualities and thereby differentiates Himself as the power of being, intelligence and action, and He is the delusive *māyā*. These differentiated qualities show themselves as different; they produce also the notion of difference in the entities with which they are associated and express themselves in definite forms. Though they thus appear as different, they are united by God's will. The part, as being associated with the power of action, manifests itself as matter. When the power of intelligence appears as confused it is the *jīva*[3]. From the point of view of the world the Brahman is the *vivartakāraṇa*; from the point of view of the self-creation of God, it is *pariṇāma*[4].

[1] *sṛṣṭi-daśāyāṃ jagad-brahmaṇoḥ kārya-kāraṇa-bhāvāj jagajjīvayor aṃṣāṃśi-bhāvāc ca upacāriko bhavan nāpi na vāstavābhedaṃ nihanti. tenedānīm api bheda-sahiṣṇur evā'bhedaḥ. Vādāvali*, p. 20.

[2] *vādakathā* of Gopeśvarasvāmī in *Vādāvali*, p. 31.

[3] See Puruṣottama's *Sṛṣṭibhedavāda*, p. 115.

[4] *evaṃ ca antarā-sṛṣṭiṃ prati vivartopādānatvam ātma-sṛṣṭiṃ prati pariṇā-myupādānatvaṃ brahmaṇaḥ. Ibid.* p. 113.

Viṭṭhala's Interpretation of Vallabha's Ideas.

Viṭṭhala, the son of Vallabha, wrote an important treatise called *Vidvanmaṇḍana* upon which there is a commentary, the *Suvarṇa-sūtra*, by Puruṣottama. The central ideas of this work may now be detailed.

There are many Upaniṣadic texts which declare that Brahman is without any determinate qualities (*nirviśeṣa*) and there are others which say that He is associated with determinate qualities, i.e., He is *saviśeṣa*. The upholders of the former view say that the *guṇas* or *dharmas* which are attributed by the other party must be admitted by them as having a basis of existence somewhere. This basis must be devoid of qualities, and this qualityless being cannot be repudiated by texts which declare the Brahman to be endowed with qualities; for the latter can only be possible on the assumption of the former, or in other words the former is the *upajīvya* of the latter. It may, however, be argued that the *śruti* texts which declare that the Brahman is qualityless do so by denying the qualities; the qualities then may be regarded as primary, as the ascertainment of the qualityless is only possible through the denial of the qualities. The reply is that, since the *śruti* texts emphasize the qualityless, the attempt to apprehend the qualityless through qualities implies contradiction; such a contradiction would imply the negation of both quality and qualityless and lead us to nihilism (*śūnya-vāda*). If, again, it is argued that the denial of qualities refers only to ordinary mundane qualities and not to those qualities which are approved by the Vedas, then there is also a pertinent objection; for the *śruti* texts definitely declare that the Brahman is absolutely unspeakable, indefinable. But it may further be argued that, if Brahman be regarded as the seat of certain qualities which are denied of it, then also such denial would be temporarily qualified and not maintained absolutely. A jug is black before being burnt and, when it is burnt, it is no longer black, but brown. The reply proposed is that the qualities are affirmed of Brahman as conditioned and denied of Brahman as unconditioned. When one's heart becomes pure by the worship of the Brahman as conditioned he understands the nature of Brahman as unconditioned. It is for the purpose of declaring the nature of such a Brahman that the texts declare Him to be qualityless: they declare Him to be endowed with qualities when He is conditioned by *avidyā*. To this Viṭṭhala says that, if Brahman is regarded as the Lord of the world, He cannot be affirmed as qualityless. It cannot be argued that these qualities are affirmed of Brahman as conditioned by *avidyā*; for, since both Brahman and *avidyā* are beginningless, there would be a continuity of creation; the creation, being once started by *avidyā*, would have nothing else to stop it. In the Vedāntic text it is the Brahman associated with will that is regarded as the cause of the world; other qualities of Brahman may be regarded as proceeding from His will. In the Śaṅkarite view, according to which the will proceeds from the conditioned Brahman, it is not possible to state any reason for the different kinds of the will. If it is said that the appearance of the different kinds of will and qualities is the very nature of the qualities of the conditioned, then there is no need to admit a separate Brahman. It is therefore wrong to suppose that Brahman exists separately from the *guṇas* of which He is the seat through the conditions. In the *Brahma-sūtra* also, immediately after launching into an enquiry about Brahman, Bādarāyaṇa defines His nature as that from which the creation and destruction of the world has proceeded; the *Brahma-sūtra*, however, states that such creative functions refer only to a conditioned Brahman. It is wrong to say that, because it is difficult to explain the nature of pure Brahman, the *Brahma-sūtra* first speaks of the creation of the world and then denies it; for the world as such is perceived by all, and there is no meaning in speaking of its creation and then denying it—it is as if one said "My mother is barren". If the world did not exist, it would not have appeared as such. It cannot be due to *vāsanā*; for, if the world never existed, there would be no experience of it and no *vāsanā*. *Vāsanā* also requires other instruments to rouse it, and there is no such instrument here.

It cannot be said that the *avidyā* belongs to the *jīvas*, because the *jīvas* are said to be identical with Brahman and the observed difference to be due to false knowledge. If knowledge destroys *avidyā*, then the *avidyā* of the *jīva* ought to be destroyed by the *avidyā* underlying it. Again, if the world is non-existent, then its cause, the *avidyā*, ought also to be non-existent. What is *jīva*? It cannot be regarded as a reflection of Brahman; for only that which has colour can have reflection; it is not the formless sky that is reflected in the sky, but the rays of the sun hovering above.

Moreover, *avidyā* is all-pervasive as Brahman: how can there be reflection? Again such a theory of reflection would render all our moral efforts false, and emancipation, which is their result, must also be false; for the means by which it is attained is very false. Moreover, if the Vedas themselves are false, as mere effects of *avidyā*, it is wrong to suppose that the nature of Brahman as described by them is true. Again, in the case of reflections there are true perceivers who perceive the reflection; the reflected images cannot perceive themselves. But in the case under discussion there are no such perceivers. If the Paramātman be not associated with *avidyā*, He cannot perceive the *jīvas*, and if He is associated with *avidyā*, He has the same status as the *jīvas*. Again, there is no one who thinks that *jīva* is a reflection of the Brahman on the *antaḥkaraṇa;* upon such a view, since the *jīvanmukta* has an *antaḥkaraṇa*, he cannot be a *jīvanmukta*. If the *jīva* is a reflection on *avidyā*, then the *jīvanmukta* whose *avidyā* has been destroyed can no longer have a body. Since everything is destroyed by knowledge, why should there be a distinction in the case of the *prārabdha karma*? Even if by the *prārabdha karma* the body may continue to exist, there ought not to be any experience. When one sees a snake his body shakes even when the snake is removed; this shaking is due to previous impressions, but *prārabdha karma* has no such past impressions, and so it ought to be destroyed by knowledge; the analogy is false. It is therefore proved that the theory of the *jīva* as reflection is false.

There is another interpretation of the Śaṅkara Vedānta, in which it is held that the appearance of the *jīva* as existing separate from Brahman is a false notion; impelled by this false notion people are engaged in various efforts for self-improvement[1]. On this explanation too it is difficult to explain how the erroneous apprehension arises and to whom it belongs. The *jīva* himself, being a part of the illusion, cannot be a perceiver of it, nor can the nature of the relation of the *avidyā* and the Brahman be explained; it cannot be contact, because both *avidyā* and Brahman are self-pervasive; it cannot be illusory, since there is no illusion prior to illusion; it cannot

[1] *asmin pakṣe jīvasya vastuto brahmatve bheda-bhānasya jīva-padavācyatāyāś ca duṣṭatvaṃ na tu svarūpātirekatvaṃ na vā mokṣasya apuruṣārthatvaṃ na vā pāralaukika-prayatna-pratirodhaḥ.* Puruṣottama's *Suvarṇa-sūtra* on *Vidvanmaṇḍana*, p. 37.

be unique, since in that case even an emancipated person may have an error. Again, if *avidyā* and its relation are both beginningless and *jīva* be also beginningless, then it is difficult to determine whether *avidyā* created *jīva* or *jīva* created *avidyā*.

It must therefore be assumed that the bondage of the *jīvas* or their existence as such is not beginningless. Their bondage is produced by *avidyā*, which is a power of God, and which operates only with reference to those *jīvas* whom God wishes to bind. For this reason we have to admit a number of beings, like snakes and others, who were never brought under the binding power of *avidyā*[1]. All things appear and disappear by the grace of God as manifesting (*āvirbhāva*) and hiding (*tirobhāva*). The power of manifesting is the power by which things are brought within the sphere of experience (*anubhava-viṣayatva-yogyatāvirbhāvaḥ*), and the power of hiding is the power by which things are so obscured that they cannot be experienced (*tad-aviṣaya-yogya tātirobhāvaḥ*). Things therefore exist even when they are not perceived; in the ordinary sense existence is defined as the capacity of being perceived, but in a transcendental sense things exist in God even when they are not perceived. According to this view all things that happened in the past and all that may happen in the future—all these exist in God and are perceived or not perceived according to His will[2].

The *jīva* is regarded as a part of God; this nature of *jīva* can be realized only on the testimony of the scriptures. Being a part of God, it has not the fullness of God and therefore cannot be as omniscient as He. The various defects of the *jīva* are due to God's will: thus, in order that the *jīva* may have a diversity of experience, God has obscured His almighty power in him and for securing his moral efforts He has associated him with bondage and rendered him independent. It is by obscuring His nature as pure bliss that the part of God appears as the *jīva*. We know that the followers of Madhva also regard the *jīvas* as parts of God; but according to them they are distinct from Him, and the identity of the Brahman and the *jīva* is only in a remote sense. According to the Nimbārkas

[1] *yad-bandhane tad-icchā tam eva sa badhnāti.* Puruṣottama's *Suvarṇa-sūtra*, p. 35.

[2] *asmin kāle asmin deśe idaṃ kāryam idaṃ bhavatu iti icchā-viṣayatvam āvir-bhāvaḥ tadā tatra tat mā bhavatu iti icchā-viṣayatvaṃ tirobhāvaḥ. Ibid.* p. 56.

jīvas are different from God, and are yet similar to Him: they too regard *jīvas* as God's parts, but emphasize the distinctness of the *jīvas* as well as their similarity to Him. According to Rāmānuja God holds the *jīvas* within Himself and by His will dominates all their functions, by expanding or contracting the nature of the *jīva's* knowledge. According to Bhāskara *jīva* is naturally identical with God, and it is only through the limiting conditions that he appears as different from Him. According to Vijñāna-bhikṣu, though the *jīvas* are eternally different from God, because they share His nature they are indistinguishable from Him[1].

But the Vallabhas hold that the *jīvas*, being parts of God, are one with Him; they appear as *jīvas* through His function as *āvirbhāva* and *tirobhāva*, by which certain powers and qualities that exist in God are obscured in the *jīva* and certain other powers are manifested. The manifestation of matter also is by the same process; in it the nature of God as intelligence is obscured and only His nature as being is manifested. God's will is thus the fundamental determinant of both *jīva* and matter. This also explains the diversity of power and character in different individuals, which is all due to the will of God. But in such a view there is a serious objection; for good and bad *karmas* would thus be futile. The reply is that God, having endowed the individual with diverse capacities and powers for his own self-enjoyment, holds within His mind such a scheme of actions and their fruits that whoever will do such actions will be given such fruits. He does so only for His own self-enjoyment in diverse ways. The law of *karma* is thus dependent on God and is dominated by Him[2]. Vallabha, however, says that God has explained the goodness and badness of actions in the scriptures. Having done so, He makes whoever is bent upon following a particular course of conduct do those actions. *Jīva's* will is the cause of the *karma* that he does; the will of the person is determined by his past actions; but in and through them all God's will is the ultimate dispenser. It is here that one distinguishes the differences between the *maryādā-mārga* and the *puṣṭi-mārga*: the *maryādā-*

[1] *jīvānāṃ nitya-bhinnatvam aṅgīkṛtya avibhāga-lakṣaṇam aṅgīkṛtya sajātīyatve sati avibhāga-pratiyogitvam aṃśatvaṃ tad-anuyogitvaṃ ca aṃśitvam. Suvarṇa-sūtra*, p. 85.

[2] *krīḍaiva muktyā anyat sarvam upasarjanībhūtaṃ tathā ca tadapekṣyā bhagavān vicitra-rasānubhavārtham evaṃ yaḥ kariṣyati tam evaṃ kariṣyāmīti svayam eva kāryādau cakāra. Vidvan-maṇḍana*, p. 91.

mārga is satisfied that in the original dispensation certain *karmas* should be associated with certain fruits, and leaves the individual to act as he pleases; but the *puṣṭi-mārga* makes the playful activity of God the cause of the individual's efforts and also of the law of *karma*[1].

The Upaniṣad says that, just as sparks emanate from fire, so the *jīvas* have emanated from Brahman. This illustration shows that the *jīvas* are parts of God, atomic in nature, that they have emanated from Him and may again merge in Him. This merging in God (*Brahma-bhāva*) means that, when God is pleased, He manifests His blissful nature as well as His powers in the *jīva*[2]. At the time of emancipation the devotees merge in God, become one with Him, and do not retain any separate existence from Him. At the time of the incarnation of God at His own sweet will He may incarnate those parts of Him which existed as emancipated beings merged in Him. It is from this point of view that the emancipated beings may again have birth[3].

It is objected that the *jīvas* cannot be regarded as atomic in nature, because the Upaniṣads describe them as all-pervasive. Moreover, if the *jīvas* are atomic in natūre, they would not be conscious in all parts of the body. The analogy of the sandal-paste, which remaining in one place makes the surrounding air fragrant, does not hold good; for the surrounding fragrance is due to the presence of minute particles. This cannot be so with the souls; consciousness, being a quality of the soul, cannot operate unless the soul-substance is present there. The analogy of the lamp and its rays is also useless; the lamp has no pervasive character; for the

[1] *ācāryas tu yathā putraṃ yatamāna-valaṃ vā padārtha-guṇa-doṣau varṇayan api yat-prayatnābhiniveśaṃ paśyati tathaiva kārayati. phala-dānārthaṃ śrutau karmāpekṣā-kathanāt phaladāne karmāpekṣaḥ karma-karaṇe jīva-kṛta-prayatnāpekṣaḥ, prayatne tat-karmāpekṣaḥ, svargādi-kāme ca lokapravāhāpekṣaḥ kārayatīti na brahmaṇo doṣagandho'pi, na caivam anīśvaratvam. ṃaryādāmārgasya tathaiva nirmāṇāt. yatra tvanyathā tatra puṣṭi-mārgāṅgīkāra ityāhuḥ. ayamapi pakṣaḥ svakṛtamaryādayā eva hetutvena kathanān maryādākaraṇe ca krīḍeccham ṛte hetvantarasya sambhavād asmaduktānnātiricyate. Vidvan-maṇḍana*, p. 92.

[2] *brahma-bhāvaśca bhagavad-ukta-sādhanakaraṇena santuṣṭāt bhagavata ānanda-prākaṭyāt svaguṇa-svarūpaiśvaryādi-prākaṭyāc ceti jñeyam.... Ibid.* p. 96.

[3] *mokṣe jīva-brahmaṇor abhinnatvād abhinnasvabhāvenaiva nirūpaṇād ityarthaḥ. tenādi-madhyāvasāneṣu śuddha-brahmaṇa evopādānatvāt....svāvatārasamaye krīḍārthaṃ sākṣād yogyās ta eva bhavantīti tāṇapyavatārayatīti punar nirgama-yogyatvam, idameva, muktānupasṛpya vyapadeśāditisūtreṇoktam.... muktā api līlā-vigrahaṃ kṛtvā bhajanti iti. Ibid.* p. 97.

illumination is due to the presence of minute light-particles. To this Viṭṭhala replies that Bādarāyaṇa himself describes the nature of the *jīvas* as atomic. The objection that qualities cannot operate in the absence of the substance is not valid either. Even the Naiyāyikas admit that the relation of *samavāya* may exist without the relata. The objection that the fragrance of a substance is due to the presence of minute particles of it is not valid; for a piece of musk enclosed in a box throws its fragrance around it, and in such cases there is no possibility for the minute particles of the musk to come out of the box; even when one touches garlic, the smell is not removed even by the washing of the hand. It must therefore be admitted that the smell of a substance may occupy a space larger than the substance itself. There are others who think that the soul is like fire, which is associated with heat and light, the heat and light being comparable to consciousness; they argue that, being of the nature of consciousness, the soul cannot be atomic. This is also invalid; for the Upaniṣad texts declare that knowledge is a quality of the soul, and it is not identical with it. Even heat and light are not identical with fire; through the power of certain gems and *mantras* the heat of the fire may not be felt; warm water possesses heat, though it has no illumination. Moreover, the Upaniṣad texts definitely declare the passage of the soul into the body, and this can only be possible if the soul is atomic. The objection that these texts declare the identity of souls with Brahman cannot be regarded as repudiating the atomic nature of the *jīvas*; because this identification is based on the fact that the qualities of knowledge or intuition that belong to the *jīvas* are really the qualities of God. The *jīvas* come out of Brahman in their atomic nature and Brahman manifests His qualities in them, so that they may serve Him. The service of God is thus the religion of man; being pleased with it God sometimes takes man within Himself, or at other times, when He extends His highest grace, He keeps him near Himself to enjoy the sweet emotion of his service[1].

The Śaṅkarites think that Brahman is indeterminate (*nirviśeṣa*) and that all determination is due to *avidyā*. This view is erroneous;

[1] *ata eva sahaja-hari-dāsya-tadaṃśatvena brahma-svarūpasya ca nijanisarga-prabhu-śrīgokula-nātha-caraṇa-kamala-dāsyam eva sva-dharmaḥ. tena cātisaṃtuṣṭaḥ svayaṃ prakaṭībhūya nija-gunāṃs tasmai dattā svasmin praveśayati svarūpānandānubhavārtham. athavā'tyanugrahe nikate sthāpayati tato'dhika-rasa-dāsya-karaṇārtham iti.* *Ibid.* p. 110

for the supposed *avidyā* cannot belong to the *jīvas*; if it did, it could not affect the nature of Brahman. Nor can it belong to Brahman, because Brahman, being pure knowledge, is destructive of all *avidyā*; again, if the *avidyā* belonged to the Brahman from beginningless time, there would be no *nirviśeṣa* Brahman. It must therefore be admitted that Brahman possesses the power of knowledge and action and that these powers are natural to and identical with Him. Thus God, in association with His powers, is to be regarded as both determinate and indeterminate; the determinate forms of Brahman are, however, not to be regarded as different from Brahman or as characters of Him; they are identical with Brahman Himself[1].

If *māyā* is regarded as the power of Brahman, then Vallabha is prepared to admit it; but, if *māyā* is regarded as something unreal, then he repudiates the existence of such a category. All knowledge and all delusion come from Brahman, and He is identical with so-called contradictory qualities. If a separate *māyā* is admitted, one may naturally enquire about its status. Being unintelligent (*jaḍā*), it cannot of itself be regarded as the agent (*kartṛ*); if it is dependent on God, it can be conceived only as an instrument—but, if God is naturally possessed of infinite powers, He cannot require any such inanimate instrument. Moreover, the Upaniṣads declare that Brahman is pure being. If we follow the same texts, Brahman cannot be regarded as associated with qualities in so far as these *guṇas* can be considered as modifications of the qualities of *sattva*, *rajas* and *tamas*. It is therefore to be supposed that the *māyā* determines or modifies the nature of Brahman into His determinate qualities. To say that the manifestation of *māyā* is effected by the will of God is objectionable too; for, if God's will is powerful in itself, it need not require any *upādhi* or condition for effecting its purpose. In reality it is not possible to speak of any difference or distinction between God and His qualities.

[1] *brahmaṇyapi mūrtāmūrtarūpe sarvataḥ veditavye evaṃ tvanena prakāreṇa veditavye brahmaṇa ete rūpe iti; kintu brahmaiva iti veditavye. Vidvanmaṇḍana*, p. 138.

Life of Vallabha (1481–1533).

Vallabha was born in the lineage of Yajñanārāyaṇa Bhaṭṭa; his great-grandfather was Gaṅgādhara Bhaṭṭa, his grandfather Gaṇapati Bhaṭṭa, and his father Lakṣmaṇa Bhaṭṭa. It is said that among themselves they performed one hundred *somayāgas* (soma sacrifices). The family was one of Telugu Brahmins of South India, and the village to which they belonged was known as Kamkar Khamlh; his mother's name was Jllamagaru. Glasenapp, following N. G. Ghosh's sketch of Vallabhācārya, gives the date of his birth as A.D. 1479; but all the traditional accounts agree in holding that he was born in Pampāraṇya, near Benares, in *Samvat* 1535 (A.D. 1481), in the month of *Vaiśākha*, on the eleventh lunar day of the dark fortnight. About the time of his birth there is some discrepancy of opinion; but it seems very probable that it was the early part of the night, when the Scorpion was on the eastern horizon. He was delivered from the womb in the seventh month underneath a tree, when Lakṣmaṇa Bhaṭṭa was fleeing from Benares on hearing of the invasion of that city by the Moslems; he received initiation from his father in his eighth year, and was handed over to Viṣṇucitta, with whom he began his early studies. His studies of the Vedas were carried on under several teachers, among were them Trirammalaya, Andhanārāyaṇadīkṣita and Mādhavayatīndra. All these teachers belonged to the Madhva sect. After his father's death he went out on pilgrimage and began to have many disciples, Dāmodara, Śambhū, Svabhū, Svayambhū and others. Hearing of a disputation in the court of the king of Vidyānagara in the south, he started for the place with his disciples, carrying the *Bhāgavata-purāṇa* and the symbolic stone (*śālagrāma śilā*) of God with him. The discussion was on the problem of the determinate nature of Brahman; Vallabha, being of the Viṣṇusvāmī school, argued on behalf of the determinate nature of Brahman, and won after a protracted discussion which lasted for many days. He met here Vyāsa-tīrtha, the great Madhva teacher. From Vidyānagara he moved towards Pampā and from there to the Ṛṣyamukha hill, from there to Kāmākāṣnī, from there to Kāncī, from there to Cidambaram and from there to Rāmeśvaram. Thence he turned northwards and, after passing through many places, came to Mahiṣapurī and was well received by the king of that place; from there he came to Molulakota (otherwise called Yādavādri). From there he went to Udipi, and thence to Gokarṇa, from where he again came near Vidyānagara (Vijayanagara) and was well received by the king. Then he proceeded to Pāṇḍuraṅga, from there to Nāsik, then by the banks of the Revā to Mahiṣmatī, from there to Visāla, to a city on the river Vetravati to Dhalalāgiri, and from there to Mathurā. Thence he went to Vṛndāvana, to Siddhapura, to the Arhatpattana of the Jains, to Vṛddhanagara, from there to Viśvanagara. From Viśvanagara he went to Guzerāt and thence to the mouth of the river Sindh through Bhāruch. From there he proceeded to Bhamkṣetra, Kapilakṣetra, then to Prabhāsa and Raivata, and then to Dvārakā. From there he proceeded to the Punjab by the banks of the river Sindh. Here he came to Kurukṣetra, from there to Hardwar and to Hṛṣīkeśa, to Gaṅgottri and Yamunottri. After returning to Hardwar he went to Kedāra and Badarikāśrama. He then came down to Kanauj, then to the banks of the Ganges, to Ayodhyā and Allāhābad, thence to Benares. From there he came to Gayā and Vaidyanātha, thence to the confluence of the Ganges and the sea. He then came to Purī. From there he went to Godāvarī, proceeded southwards and came again to Vidyānagara. Then he proceeded again to Dvārakā through the Kathiāwād country; from there he came to Puṣkara, thence again to Bṛndāvana and again to Badarikāśrama. He then came again to Benares; after coming again to the confluence of the Ganges he returned to Benares, where he married Mahā-lakṣmī, the daughter of Devaṇṇa Bhaṭṭa. After marriage he started again for Vaidyanātha and from there he again proceeded to Dvārakā, thence again to Badarikāśrama; from there he came to Bṛndāvana. He again returned to Benares. He then came to Bṛndāvana. From there he came to Benares, where he performed a great *somayāga*. His son Viṭṭhalanātha was born in 1518 when he was in his thirty-seventh year. For his later life he renounced the world and became a *sannyāsiṇ*. He died in 1533. He is said to have written eighty-four works and had eighty-four principal disciples.

Works of Vallabha and his Disciples.

Of the eighty-four books (including small tracts) that Vallabha is said to have written we know only the following; *Antaḥkaraṇa-prabodha* and commentary, *Ācārya-kārikā*, *Ānandādhikaraṇa*, *Āryā*, *Ekānta-rahasya*, *Kṛṣṇāśraya*, *Catuḥślokibhāgavata-ṭīkā*, *Jalabheda*, *Jaiminisūtra-bhāṣya-mīmāṃsā*, *Tattvadīpa* (or more accurately *Tattvārthadīpa* and commentary), *Trividhalīlānāmāvalī*, *Navaratna* and commentary, *Nibandha*, *Nirodha-lakṣaṇa* and *Vivṛti*, *Patrāvalambana*, *Padya*, *Parityāga*, *Parivṛddhāṣṭaka*, *Puruṣottamasahasranāma*, *Puṣṭi-pravāha-maryādābheda* and commentary, *Pūrva-mīmāṃsā-kārikā*, *Premāmṛta* and commentary, *Prauḍhacaritanāma*, *Bālacaritanāman*, *Bālabodha*, *Brahma-sūtrāṇubhāṣya*, *Bhakti-vardhinī* and commentary, *Bhakti-siddhānta*, *Bhagavad-gītā-bhāṣya*, *Bhāgavata-tattvadīpa* and commentary, *Bhāgavata-purāṇa-ṭīkā Subodhinī*, *Bhāgavata-purāṇa-daśamaskandhānukramaṇikā*, *Bhāgavata-purāṇa-pañcamaskandha-ṭīkā*, *Bhāgavata-purāṇa-ikādaśaskandhārthanirūpaṇa-kārikā*, *Bhāgavatasāra-samuccaya*, *Maṅgalavāda*, *Mathurā-māhātmya*, *Madhurāṣṭaka*, *Yamunāṣṭaka*, *Rājalīlānāma*, *Vivekadhairyāśraya*, *Vedastutikārikā*, *Śraddhāprakaraṇa*, *Śrutisāra*, *Sannyāsanirṇaya* and commentary, *Sarvottamastotra-ṭippana* and commentary, *Sākṣātpuruṣottamavākya*, *Siddhānta-muktāvalī*, *Siddhānta-rahasya*, *Sevāphala-stotra* and commentary, *Svāminyaṣṭaka*[1].

The most important of Vallabha's works are his commentary on the *Bhāgavata-purāṇa* (the *Subodhinī*), his commentary on the *Brahma-sūtra*, and his commentary *Prakāśa* on his own *Tattvadīpa*. The *Subodhinī* had another commentary on it called the *Subodhinī-lekha* and the *Subodhinī-yojana-nibandha-yojana*; the commentary on the *Rasapañcādhyāya* was commented upon by Pītāmbara in the *Rasapañcādhyāyī-prakāśa*. Vallabha's commentary on the *Brahma-sūtra*, the *Aṇubhāṣya*, had a commentary on it by Puruṣottama (the *Bhāṣya-prakāśa*), another by Giridhara (*Vivaraṇa*), another by Icchārama (the *Brahma-sūtrāṇubhāṣya-pradīpa*), and another, the *Balaprabodhinī*, by Śrīdhara Śarma. There was also another commentary on it, the *Aṇubhāṣya-nigūḍhārtha-dīpikā* by Lalu Bhaṭṭa, of the seventeenth century; another by Muralīdhara, the pupil of Viṭṭhala (the *Aṇubhāṣya-vyākhyā*), and the *Vedānta-candrikā* by an

[1] See Aufrecht's *Catalogus Catalogorum.*

anonymous writer. Vallabha's own commentary *Prakāśa* on the *kārikās* he had written had a commentary on the first part of it, the *Āvaraṇa-bhaṅga* by Pītāmbaraji Mahārāja. The *Tattvārthadīpa* is divided into three sections, of which the first, the *Śāstrārtha-prakaraṇa*, contains 105 *kārikās* of a philosophical nature; the second section, the *Sarvanirṇaya-prakaraṇa*, deals with eschatology and matters relating to duties; the third, the *Bhāgavatārtha-prakaraṇa*, containing a summary of the twelve chapters of the *Bhāgavata-purāṇa*, had a commentary on it, also called the *Āvaraṇa-bhaṅga*, by Puruṣottamaji Mahārāja. There was also another commentary on it by Kalyāṇarāja, which was published in Bombay as early as 1888.

Coming to the small tracts of Vallabha, we may speak first of his *Sannyāsa-nirṇaya*, which consists of twenty-two verses in which he discusses the three kinds of renunciation: the *sannyāsa* of *karma-mārga*, the *sannyāsa* of *jñāna-mārga* and the *sannyāsa* of *bhakti-mārga*. There are at least seven commentaries on it, by Gokulanātha, Raghunātha, Gokulotsava, the two Gopeśvaras, Puruṣottama and a later Vallabha. Of these Gokulanātha (1554–1643) was the fourth son of Viṭṭhalanātha; he also wrote commentaries on *Śrī Sarvottama-stotra*, *Vallabhāṣṭaka*, *Siddhānta-muktāvalī*, *Puṣṭi-pravāha-maryādā*, *Siddhānta-rahasya*, *Catuḥśloki*, *Dhairyyāśraya*, *Bhakti-vardhinī* and *Sevāphala*. He was a great traveller and preacher of Vallabha's views in Guzerat, and did a great deal to make the *Subodhinī* commentary of Vallabha popular. Raghunātha, the fifth son of Viṭṭhalanātha, was born in 1557; he wrote commentaries on Vallabha's *Ṣoḍaśa-grantha* and also on *Vallabhāṣṭaka*, *Madhurāṣṭaka*, *Bhakti-haṃsa* and *Bhakti-hetu*; also a commentary on *Puruṣottama-nāma-sahasra*, the *Nāma-candrikā*. Gokulotsava, the younger brother of Kalyāṇarāja and uncle of Harirāja, was born in 1580; he also wrote a commentary on the *Ṣoḍaśa-grantha*. Gopeśvara, the son of Ghanaśyāma, was born in 1598; the other Gopeśvara was the son of Kalyāṇarāja and the younger brother of Harirāja. Puruṣottama, also a commentator, was born in 1660. Vallabha, son of Viṭṭhalarāja, the other commentator, great-great-grandson of Raghunātha (the fifth son of Vallabhācārya) was born in 1575, and wrote a commentary on the *Aṇubhāṣya* of Vallabhā-cārya. He should be distinguished from the earlier Vallabha, the son of Viṭṭhaleśvara.

The *Sevāphala* of Vallabha is a small tract of eight verses which discusses the obstacles to the worship of God and its fruits; it was commented upon by Kalyāṇarāja. He was the son of Govindarāja, the second son of Viṭṭhalanātha, and was born in 1571; he was the father of Harirāja, and wrote commentaries on the *Ṣoḍaśa-grantha* and also on the rituals of worship. This work was also commented on by Devakīnandana, who was undoubtedly prior to Puruṣottama. One Devakīnandana, the son of Raghunātha (the fifth son of Viṭṭhalanātha), was born in 1570; a grandson of the same name was born in 1631. There was also a commentary on it by Haridhana, otherwise called Harirāja, who was born in 1593; he wrote many small tracts. There was another commentary on it by Vallabha, the son of Viṭṭhala. There were two other Vallabhas—one the grandson of Devakīnandana, born in 1619, and the other the son of Viṭṭhalarāja, born in 1675; it is probable that the author of the commentary of the *Sevāphala* is the same Vallabha who wrote the *Subodhinī-lekha*. There are other commentaries by Puruṣottama, Gopeśa, and Lālu Bhaṭṭa, a Telugu Brāhmin; his other name was Bālakṛṣṇa Dīkṣita. He probably lived in the middle of the seventeenth century; he wrote *Aṇubhāṣya-nigūḍhārtha-prakāśikā* on the *Aṇubhāṣya* of Vallabha and a commentary on the *Subodhinī* (the *Subodhinī-yojana-nibandha-yojana Sevākaumudī*), *Nirṇayārṇava*, *Prmeya-ratnārnava*, and a commentary on the *Ṣoḍaśa-grantha*. There is another commentary by Jayagopāla Bhaṭṭa, the son of Cintāmaṇi Dīkṣita, the disciple of Kalyāṇarāja. He wrote a commentary on the *Taittirīya Upaniṣad*, on the *Kṛṣṇa-karṇāmṛta* of Bilvamaṅgala, and on the *Bhakti-vardhinī*.' There is also a commentary by Lakṣmaṇa Bhaṭṭa, grandson of Śrīnātha Bhaṭṭa and son of Gopīnātha Bhaṭṭa, and also two other anonymous commentaries.

Vallabha's *Bhakti-vardhinī* is a small tract of eleven verses, commented upon by Dvārakeśa, Giridhara, Bālakṛṣṇa Bhaṭṭa (son of the later Vallabha), by Lālu Bhaṭṭa, Jayagopāla Bhaṭṭa, Vallabha, Kalyāṇarāja, Puruṣottama, Gopeśvara, Kalyānarāja and Bālakṛṣṇa Bhaṭṭa; there is also another anonymous commentary.

The *Sannyāsa-nirṇaya*, the *Sevāphala* and the *Bhakti-vardhinī* are included in the *Sixteen Tracts* of Vallabha (the *Ṣoḍaśa-grantha*); the others are *Yamunāṣṭaka*, *Bālabodha*, *Siddhānta-muktāvalī*,

Puṣṭi-pravāha-maryādā, *Siddhānta-rahasya*, *Navaratna*, *Antaḥ-karaṇaprabodha*, *Vivekadhairyyāśraya*, *Kṛṣṇāśraya*, *Catuḥśloki*, *Bhakti-vardhinī*, *Jalabheda* and *Pañcapādya*. The *Yamunāṣṭaka* is a tract of nine verses in praise of the holy river Yamunā. *Bālabodha* is a small tract of nineteen verses, in which Vallabha says that pleasure (*kāma*) and extinction of sorrow (*mokṣa*) are the two primarily desirable things in the world; two others, *dharma* and *artha*, are desirables in a subsidiary manner, because through *artha* or wealth one may attain *dharma*, and through *dharma* one may attain happiness. *Mokṣa* can be attained by the grace of *Viṣṇu*. *Siddhānta-muktāvalī* is a small tract of twenty-one verses dealing with *bhakti*, which emphasize the necessity of abnegating all things to God. *Puṣṭi-pravāha-maryāda* is a small tract of twenty-five verses, in which Vallabha says that there are five kinds of natural defects, due to egotism, to birth in particular countries or times, to bad actions and bad associations. These can be removed by offering all that one has to God; one has a right to enjoy things after dedicating them to God. *Navaratna* is a tract of nine verses in which the necessity of abnegating and dedicating all things to God is emphasized. *Antaḥkaraṇa-prabodha* is a tract of ten verses which emphasize the necessity of self-inspection and prayer to God for forgiveness, and to convince one's mind that everything belongs to God. The *Vivekadhairyyāśraya* is a small tract of seventeen verses. It urges us to have full confidence in God and to feel that, if our wishes are not fulfilled by Him, there must be some reason known to Him; He knows everything and always looks to our welfare. It is therefore wrong to desire anything strongly; it is best to leave all things to God to manage as He thinks best. The *Kṛṣṇāśraya* is a tract of eleven verses explaining the necessity of depending in all matters on Kṛṣṇa, the Lord. *Catuḥśloki* is a tract of four verses of the same purport. The *Bhakti-vardhinī* is a tract of eleven verses, in which Vallabha says that the seed of the love of God exists in us all, only it is obstructed by various causes; when it manifests itself, one begins to love all beings in the world; when it grows in intensity it becomes impossible for one to be attached to worldly things. When love of God grows to this high intensity, it cannot be destroyed. The *Jalabheda* contains twenty verses, dealing with the different classes of devotees and ways of devotion. The *Pañcapādya* is a tract of five verses.

Viṭṭhaladīkṣita or Viṭṭhaleśa (1518–88), the son of Vallabha, is said to have written the following works: *Avatāra-tāratamya-stotra*, *Āryā*, *Kṛṣṇa-premāmṛta*, *Gīta-govinda-prathamāṣṭapadī-vivṛti*, *Gokulāṣṭaka*, *Janmāṣṭamī-nirṇaya*, *Jalabheda-ṭīkā*, *Dhruvāpada-ṭīkā*, *Nāma-candrikā*, *Nyāsādeśavivaraṇa-prabodha*, *Premāmṛta-bhāṣya*, *Bhakti-haṃsa*, *Bhakti-hetu-nirṇaya*, *Bhagavata-svatantratā*, *Bhagavadgītā-tātparya*, *Bhagavad-gītā-hetu-nirṇaya*, *Bhāgavata-tattva-dīpikā*, *Bhāgavata-daśama-skandha-vivṛti*, *Bhujaṅga-prayātāṣṭaka*, *Yāmunāṣṭaka-vivṛti*, *Rasasarvasva*, *Rāma-navamī-nirṇaya*, *Vallabhāṣṭaka*, *Vidvan-maṇḍana*, *Viveka-dhairyyāśraya-ṭīkā*, *Śikṣā-pattra*, *Śṛṅgārarasa-maṇḍana*, *Ṣaṭpadī*, *Sannyāsa-nirṇaya-vivaraṇa*, *Samayapradīpa*, *Sarvottama-stotra* with commentary, commentary on *Siddhānta-muktāvalī*, *Sevākaumudī*, *Svatantrālekhana* and *Svāmistotra*[1]. Of these *Vidyā-maṇḍana* is the most important; it was commented on by Puruṣottama and has already been noticed above in detail. A refutation of the *Vidyā-maṇḍana* and the *Śuddhādvaita-mārtaṇḍa* of Giridhara was attempted in 1868 in a work called *Sahasrākṣa* by Sadānanda, a Śaṅkarite thinker. This was again refuted in the *Prabhañjana* by Viṭṭhalanātha (of the nineteenth century) and there is a commentary on this by Govardhanaśarmā of the present century. From the *Sahasrākṣa* we know that Viṭṭhala had studied Nyāya in Navadvīpa and the Vedas, the *Mīmāṃsā* and the *Brahma-sūtra*, that he had gone to different countries carrying on his disputations and conquering his opponents, and that he was received with great honour by Svarūpasiṃha of Udaypur. Viṭṭhala's *Yamunāṣṭakavivṛti* was commented on by Harirāja; his commentary on Vallabha's *Siddhānta-muktāvalī* was commented on by Brajanātha, son of Raghunātha. The *Madhurāṣṭaka* of Vallabha was commented on by Viṭṭhala, and his work was further commented on by Ghanaśyāma. The *Madhurāṣṭaka* had other commentaries on it, by Harirāja, Bālakṛṣṇa, Raghunātha and Vallabha. Viṭṭhala also wrote commentaries on the *Nyāsadesa* and the *Puṣṭipravāha-maryādā* of Vallabha. His *Bhakti-hetu* was commented on by Raghunātha; in this work Viṭṭhala discusses the possible course of the rise of *bhakti*. He says that there are two principal ways; those who follow the *maryādā-mārga* follow their duties and attain God in course of time, but those who follow the *puṣṭi-mārga* depend entirely on the grace of God. God's grace is not conditioned by

[1] See Aufrechts' *Catalogus Catalogorum*.

good deeds, such as gifts, sacrifices, etc., or by the performance of the prescribed duties. The *jīvas* as such are the natural objects to whom God's grace is extended when He is pleased by good deeds. But it is more appropriate to hold that God's grace is free and independent of any conditions; God's will, being eternal, cannot be dependent on conditions originated through causes and effects. The opponents' view—that by good deeds and by prescribed duties performed for God, *bhakti* is attained, and through *bhakti* there is the grace of God and, through that, emancipation—is wrong; for though different persons may attain purity by the performance of good deeds, yet some may be endowed with knowledge and others with *bhakti*; and this difference cannot be explained except on the supposition that God's grace is free and unconditioned. The supposition that with grace as an accessory cause the purity of the mind produces *bhakti* is also wrong; it is much better to suppose that the grace of God flows freely and does not require the co-operation of other conditions; for the scriptures speak of the free exercise of God's grace. Those whom God takes in the path of *maryādā* attain their salvation in due course through the performance of duties, purity of mind, devotion, etc.; but those to whom He extends His special grace are accepted in the path of *puṣṭi-bhakti*; they attain *bhakti* even without the performance of any prescribed duties. The prescription of duties is only for those who are in the path of *maryādā*; the inclination to follow either the *maryādā* or the *puṣṭi* path depends on the free and spontaneous will of God[1], so that even in the *maryādā-mārga bhakti* is due to the grace of God and not to the performance of duties[2]. Viṭṭhala's view of the relation of God's will to all actions, whether performed by us or happening in the course of natural and material causes, reminds us of the doctrine of occasionalism, which is more or less of the same period as Viṭṭhala's enunciation of it; he says that whatever actions happened, are happening or will happen are due to the immediately preceding will of God to that effect; all causality is thus due to God's spontaneous will at the preceding

[1] *yeṣu jīveṣu yathā bhagavadicchā tathaiva teṣāṃ pravṛtter āvaśyakatvāt. Bhakti-hetu-nirṇaya*, p. 7.

[2] In the *Bhakti-haṃsa* (p. 56) of Viṭṭhala it is said that *bhakti* means affection (*sneha*): *bhaktipadasya śaktiḥ sneha eva.* Worship itself is not *bhakti*, but may lead to it; since *bhakti* is of the nature of affection, there cannot be any *viddhi* or injunction with reference to it.

moment[1]. The causality of so-called causes and conditions, or of precedent-negations (*prāg-abhāva*), or of the absence of negative causes and conditions, is thus discarded; for all these elements are effects, and therefore depend upon God's will for their happening; for without that nothing could happen. God's will is the ultimate cause of all effects or happenings. As God's will is thus the only cause of all occurrences or destructions, so it is the sole cause of the rise of *bhakti* in any individual. It is by His will that people are associated with different kinds of inclinations, but they work differently and that they have or have not *bhakti*. Viṭṭhala is said to have been a friend of Akbar. His other works were commentaries on *Puṣṭi-pravāha-maryādā* and *Siddhānta-muktāvalī*, *Aṇubhāṣya-pūrtti* (a commentary on the *Aṇubhāṣya*), *Nibandha-prakāśa*, *Subodhinī-ṭippaṇī* (a commentary on the *Subodhinī*), otherwise called *Sannyāsāvaccheda*. Vallabhācārya's first son was Gopināthaji Mahāraja, who wrote *Sādhanadīpaka* and other minor works, and Viṭṭhala was his second son. Viṭṭhala had seven sons and four daughters.

Pītāmbara, the great-grandson of Viṭṭhala, the pupil of Viṭṭhala and the father of Puruṣottama, wrote *Avatāravādāvalī*, *Bhakti-rasatvavāda*, *Dravya-śuddhi* and its commentary, and a commentary on the *Puṣṭi-pravāha-maryādā*. Puruṣottama was born in 1670; he wrote the following books; *Subodhinī-prakāśa* (a commentary on the *Subodhinī* commentary of Vallabha on the *Bhāgavata-purāṇa*), *Upaniṣad-dīpikā*, *Āvaraṇa-bhaṅga* on the *Prakāśa* commentary of Vallabha on his *Tattvārtha-dīpikā*, *Prārthanā-ratnākara*, *Bhakti-haṃsa-viveka*, *Utsava-pratāna*, *Suvarṇa-sūtra* (a commentary on the *Vidvanamaṇḍana*) and *Ṣoḍaśa-grantha-vivṛti*. He is said to have written twenty-four philosophical and theological tracts, of which seventeen have been available to the present writer, viz., *Bhedābheda-svarūpa-nirṇaya*, *Bhagavat-pratikṛti-pūjanavāda*, *Sṛṣṭi-bheda-vāda*, *Khyāti-vāda*, *Andhakāra-vāda*, *Brāhmaṇatvādi-devatādi-vāda*, *Jīva-pratibimbatva-khaṇḍana-vāda*, *Āvirbhāva-tirobhāva-vāda*, *Pratibimba-vāda*, *Bhaktyutkarṣa-vāda*, *Ūrddhva-puṇḍra-dhāraṇa-vāda*, *Mālādhāraṇa-vāda*, *Upadeśa-viṣaya-śaṅkā-nirāsa-vāda*, *Mūrti-pūjana-vāda*, *Śaṅkha-cakra-dhāraṇa-vāda*. He

[1] *yadā yadā yat yat kāryyaṃ bhavati bhāvi abhūd vā tat-tatkālopādhau kramikeṇaiva tena tena hetunā tat tat kāryyaṃ kariṣye iti tataḥ pūrvaṃ bhagavad-icchā asty āsīd vā iti mantavyam. Ibid.* p. 9.

also wrote commentaries on *Sevāphala*, *Sannyāsa-nirṇaya* and *Bhakti-vardhinī*, the *Bhāṣya-prakāśa* and the *Utsava-pratāna*. He wrote these commentaries also; *Nirodha-lakṣaṇa*, *Jalabheda*, *Pañca-pādya*, and the *Tīrtha* commentary on the *Bhakti-haṃsa* of Viṭṭhala on the *Siddhānta-muktāvalī* and the *Bāla-bodha*. He also wrote a sub-commentary on Viṭṭhala's *Bhāṣya* on the *Gāyatrī*, a commentary on *Vallabhāṣṭaka*, the *Vedānta-karaṇamāla* and the *Śāstrārtha-prakaraṇa-nibandha*, and a commentary on the *Gītā*. He is said to have written about nine hundred thousand verses, and is undoubtedly one of the most prominent members of the Vallabha school.

Muralīdhara, the pupil of Viṭṭhala, wrote a commentary on Vallabha's *Bhāṣya* called the *Bhāṣya-ṭīkā*; also the *Paratattvāñjana*, *Bhakti-cintāmaṇi*, *Bhagavannāma-darpaṇa*, *Bhagavannāma-vaibhava*. Viṭṭhala's great-grandson Vallabha, born in 1648, wrote the *Subodhinī-lekha*, a commentary on the *Sevāphala*, a commentary on the *Ṣoḍaśa-grantha*, the *Gītā-tattva-dīpanī*, and other works. Gopeśvaraji Mahārāja, the son of Kalyāṇarāja and the great-grandson of Viṭṭhala, was born in 1595, and wrote the *Raśmi* commentary on the *Prakāśa* of Vallabha, the *Subodhinī-bubhutra-bodhinī*, and a Hindi commentary on the *Śikṣāpatra* of Harirāja. The other Gopeśvara, known also as Yogi Gopeśvara, the author of *Bhakti-mārtaṇḍa*, was born much later, in 1781. Giridharji, born in 1845, wrote the *Bhāṣya-vivaraṇa* and other works.

Muralīdhara, the pupil of Viṭṭhala, wrote a commentary on Vallabha's *Aṇubhāṣya*, a commentary on the *Śāṇḍilya-sūtra*, the *Paratattvāñjana*, the *Bhakti-cintāmaṇi*, the *Bhagavannāma-darpaṇa* and the *Bhagavannāma-vaibhava*. Raghunātha, born in 1557, wrote the commentary *Nāma-candrikā* on Vallabha's *Bhakti-haṃsa*, also commentaries on his *Bhakti-hetu-nirṇaya* and *Vallabhāṣṭaka* (the *Bhakti-taraṅginī* and the *Bhakti-hetu-nirṇaya-vivṛti*). He also wrote a commentary on the *Puruṣottama-stotra* and the *Vallabhāṣṭaka*. Vallabha, otherwise known as Gokulanātha, son of Viṭṭhala, born in 1550, wrote the *Prapañca-sāra-bheda* and commentaries on the *Siddhānta-muktāvalī*, *Nirodha-lakṣaṇa*, *Madhurāṣṭaka*, *Sarvottamastotra*, *Vallabhāṣṭaka* and the *Gāyatrī-bhāṣya* of Vallabhācārya. Kalyāṇarāja, son of Govindarāja, son of Viṭṭhala, was born in 1571, and wrote commentaries on the *Jalabheda* and the *Siddhānta-muktāvalī*. His brother Gokulastava, born in 1580, wrote a commentary called *Trividhānāmāvalī-vivṛti*. Devakīnandana (1570), son of Raghunātha and grandson of Viṭṭhala, wrote the *Prakāśa* commentary on the *Bāla-bodha* of Vallabhācārya. Ghanaśyāma (1574), grandson of Viṭṭhala, wrote a sub-commentary on the *Madhurāṣṭaka-vivṛti* of Viṭṭhala. Kṛṣṇacandra Gosvāmi, son of Brajanātha and pupil of Vallabhācārya, wrote a short commentary on the *Brahma-sūtra*, the *Bhāva-prakāśikā*, in the fashion of his father Brajanātha's *Marīcikā* commentary on the *Brahma-sūtra*. This Brajanātha also wrote a commentary on *Siddhānta-muktāvalī*. Harirāja (1593), son of Kalyāṇarāja, wrote the *Śikṣā-patra* and commentaries on the *Siddhānta-muktāvalī*, the *Nirodha-lakṣaṇa*, *Pañcapādya*, *Madhurāṣṭaka*, and a *Pariśiṣṭa* in defence of Kalyāṇarāja's commentary on the *Jalabheda*. Gopeśa (1598), son of Ghanaśyāma, wrote commentaries on the *Nirodha-lakṣaṇa*, *Sevāphala* and *Sannyāsanirṇaya*. Gopeśvaraji Mahārāja (1598), brother of Harirāja, wrote a Hindi commentary on Harirāja's *Śikṣapātra*. Dvārakeśa, a pupil of Viṭṭhala, wrote a commentary on *Siddhānta-muktāvalī*. Jayagopāla Bhaṭṭa, disciple of Kalyāṇarāja, wrote commentaries on the *Sevāphala* and the *Taittirīya Upaniṣad*. Vallabha (1648), great-grandson of Viṭṭhala, wrote commentaries on the *Siddhānta-muktāvalī*, *Nirodha-lakṣaṇa*, *Sevāphala*, *Sannyāsa-nirṇaya*, *Bhakti-vardhinī*, *Jalabheda* and the *Madhurāṣṭaka*. Brajarāja, son of Śyāmala, wrote a commentary on the *Nirodha-lakṣaṇa*. Indiveśa and Govardhana Bhaṭṭa wrote respectively *Gāyatryartha-vivaraṇa* and *Gāyatryartha*. Śrīdharasvāmi wrote the *Bāla-bodhinī* commentary on the *Aṇubhāṣya* of Vallabha. Giridhara, the great-grandson of Viṭṭhala, wrote the *Siddhādvaita-mārtaṇḍa* and the *Prapañca-vāda*, following *Vidvāna-maṇḍana*. His pupil Rāmakṛṣṇa wrote the *Prakāśa* commentary on the *Siddhādvaita-mārtaṇḍa*, and another work, the *Śuddhādvaita-parikṣkāra*. Yogi Gopeśvara (1787) wrote the *Vādakathā*, *Ātmavāda*, *Bhakti-mārtaṇḍa*, *Caturthādhikaraṇamālā*, the *Raśmi* commentary on the *Bhāṣya-prakāśa* of Puruṣottama, and a commentary on Puruṣottama's *Vedāntādhikaraṇamālā*. Gokulotsava wrote a commentary on the *Trividhānāmāvalī* of Vallabha. Brajeśvara Bhaṭṭa wrote the *Brahmavidyā-bhāvana*, Haridāsa the *Haridāsa-siddhānta*, Icchārāma the *Pradīpa* on Vallabha's *Aṇubhāṣya* and Nirbhayarāma, the pupil of the *Adhikaraṇa-saṃgraha*.

Viṣṇusvāmin.

Viṣṇusvāmin is regarded by tradition as being the earliest founder of the *viśuddhādvaita* school which was regenerated by Vallabha. Śrīdhara, in his commentary on the *Bhāgavata-purāṇa*, also refers to Viṣṇusvāmin, and it is possible that he wrote a commentary on the *Bhāgavata-purāṇa*; but no such work is available. A brief account of Viṣṇusvāmin's views is available in the *Sakala-caryā-mata-saṃgraha* (by an anonymous writer), which merely summarizes Vallabha's views; there is nothing new in it which could be taken up here for discussion. This work, however, does not contain any account of Vallabha's philosophy, from which it may be assumed that it was probably written before the advent of Vallabha, and that the view of Viṣṇusvāmin contained therein was drawn either from the traditional account of Viṣṇusvāmin or from some of his works not available at the present time. It is unlikely, therefore, that the account of Viṣṇusvāmin in the *Sakalacaryā-mata-saṃgraha* is in reality a summary statement of Vallabha's views imposed on the older writer Viṣṇusvāmin. Vallabha himself, however, never refers to Viṣṇusvāmin as the originator of his system; there is a difference of opinion among the followers of Vallabha as to whether Vallabha followed in the footsteps of Viṣṇusvāmin. It is urged that while Vallabha emphasized the pure monistic texts of the Upaniṣads and regarded Brahman as undifferentiated, as one with himself, and as one with his qualities, Viṣṇusvāmin emphasized the duality implied in the Vedāntic texts[1]. Vallabha also, in his *Subodhinī* commentary on the *Bhāgavata-purāṇa* (III. 32. 37) describes the view of Viṣṇusvāmin as propounding a difference between the Brahman and the world through the quality of *tamas*, and distinguishes his own view as propounding Brahman as absolutely qualityless[2]. The meagre account of Viṣṇusvāmin given in *Sakalacaryā-mata-saṃgraha* does not lend us any assistance in discovering whether his view differed from that of Vallabha, and, if it did, in what points. It is

[1] Thus Nirbhayarāma, in *Adhikaraṇa-saṃgraha* (p. 1), says: *tasyāpi durbodhatvena vyākhyāna-sāpekṣatayā tasya vyākhyātāro Viṣṇusvāmi-madhva-prabhṛtayo brahmādvaita-vādasya sevya-sevaka-bhāvasya ca virodhaṃ manvānā abheda-bodhaka-śrutiṣu lakṣaṇayā bheda-paratvaṃ śuddhaṃ bhedam aṅgīcakruḥ.*

[2] *te ca sāmpratam Viṣṇusvāmyanusāriṇaḥ tattva-vādino Rāmānujaś ca tamo-rajah-sattvair bhinnā asmat-pratipāditāc ca nairguṇvādasya. Ibid.* p. 1.

also not impossible that the author of *Sakalacaryā-mata-saṃgraha* had not himself seen any work of Viṣṇusvamin and had transferred the views of Vallabha to Viṣṇusvāmin, who, according to some traditions, was the originator of the Śuddhādvaita system[1].

According to the *Vallabha-dig-vijaya* there was a king called Vijaya of the Pāṇḍya kingdom in the south. He had a priest Devasvāmin, whose son was Viṣṇusvāmin. Śukasvāmin, a great religious reformer of North India, was his fellow-student in the Vedānta; it is difficult to identify him in any way. Viṣṇusvāmin went to Dvārakā, to Bṛndāvana, then to Purī, and then returned home. At an advanced age he left his household deities to his son, and having renounced the world in the Vaiṣṇava fashion, came to Kāñcī. He had many pupils there, e.g., Śrīdevadarśaṇa, Śrīkaṇṭha, Sahasrārci, Śatadhṛti, Kumārapada, Parabhūti, and others. Before his death he left the charge of teaching his views to Śrīdevadarśaṇa. He had seven hundred principal followers teaching his views; one of them, Rājaviṣṇusvāmin, became a teacher in the Andhra country. Viṣṇusvāmin's temples and books were said to have been burnt at this time by the Buddhists. Vilva-maṅgala, a Tamil saint, succeeded to the pontifical chair at Śrīraṅgam, Vilva-maṅgala left the pontifical chair at Kāñcī to Deva-maṅgala and went to Bṛndāvana. Prabhāviṣṇusvāmin succeeded to the pontifical chair; he had many disciples, e.g., Śrīkaṇṭhagarbha, Satyavatī Paṇḍita, Somagiri, Narahari, Śrāntanidhi and others. He installed Śrāntanidhi in his pontifical chair before his death. Among the Viṣṇusvāmin teachers was one Govindācārya, whose disciple Vallabhacārya is said to have been. It is difficult to guess the date of Viṣṇusvāmin; it is not unlikely, however, that he lived in the twelfth or the thirteenth century.

[1] This tradition is found definitely maintained in the *Vallabha-dig-vijaya*, written by Jadunāthajī Mahārāja.

CHAPTER XXXII

CAITANYA AND HIS FOLLOWERS

Caitanya's Biographers.

CAITANYA was the last of the Vaiṣṇava reformers who had succeeded Nimbārka and Vallabha. As a matter of fact, he was a junior contemporary of Vallabha. So far as he is known to us, he did not leave behind any work treating of his own philosophy, and all that we can know of it is from the writings of his contemporary and later admirers and biographers. Even from these we know more of his character and of the particular nature of his devotion to God than about his philosophy. It is therefore extremely difficult to point out anything as being the philosophy of Caitanya. Many biographies of him were written in Sanskrit, Bengali, Assamese and Oriya and a critical study of the materials of Caitanya's biography in Bengali was published some time ago by Dr Biman Behari Mazumdar. Of the many biographies of Caitanya those by Murārigupta and Vṛndāvanadāsa deal with the first part of Caitanya's life, and the latter's work is regarded as the most authoritative and excellent treatment of his early life. Again, Kṛṣṇadāsa Kavirāja's Life, which emphasizes the second and third parts of Caitanya's life, is regarded as the most philosophical and instructive treatment of his most interesting period. Indeed, Vṛndāvanadāsa's *Caitanya-bhāgavata* and Kṛṣṇadāsa Kavirāja's *Caitanya-caritāmṛta* stand out as the most important biographical works on Caitanya. We have already mentioned Murārigupta, who wrote a small work in Sanskrit, full of exaggerations, though he was a contemporary. There are also biographies by Jayānanda and Locanadāsa, entitled *Caitanya-maṅgala*. Some Govinda and Svarūpa Dāmodara, supposed to have been personal attendants of Caitanya, were said to have kept notes, but these are apparently now lost. Kavi Karṇapūra wrote the *Caitanya-candrodaya-nāṭaka*, which may be regarded as the principal source of Kṛṣṇadāsa Kavirāja's work. Vṛndāvanadāsa was born in *śaka* 1429 (A.D. 1507); he had seen Caitanya during the first fifteen years of his life. Caitanya died in *śaka* 1455 (A.D. 1533) and the *Caitanya-bhāgavata* was written shortly after. Kṛṣṇadāsa Kavirāja's work, *Caitanya-caritāmṛta*, was written long afterwards. Though there is some dispute regarding the actual date of its completion, it is well-nigh certain that it was in *śaka* 1537 (A.D. 1616). The other date, found in *Prema-vilāsa*, is *śaka* 1503 (A.D. 1581), and this had been very well-combatted by Professor Rādhā Govinda Nath in his learned edition of the work. The *Caitanya-candrodaya-nāṭaka* was written by Kavi Karṇapūra in *śaka* 1494 (A.D. 1572). It would thus appear that for the most authentic account of Caitanya's life one should refer to this work and to Vṛndāvanadāsa's *Caitanya-bhāgavata*. Kavirāja Kṛṣṇadāsa's *Caitanya-caritāmṛta* is, however, the most learned of the biographies. There was also a *Caitanya-sahasra-nāma* by Sārvabhauma Bhaṭṭācārya, the *Govinda-vijaya* of Paramānandapurī, songs of Caitanya by Gauridāsa Paṇḍita, the *Gauḍarāja-vijaya* of Paramānanda Gupta, and songs of Caitanya by Gopāla Basu.

The Life of Caitanya.

I shall attempt here to give only a brief account of Caitanya's life, following principally the *Caitanya-bhāgavata*, *Caitanya-candrodaya-nāṭaka* and *Caitanya-caritāmṛta*.

There lived in Navadvīpa Jagannātha Miśra and his wife Śacī. On a full-moon day in Spring (the month of *Phālguna*), when there was an eclipse of the moon, in *śaka* 1407 (A.D. 1485), Caitanya was born to them. Navadvīpa at this time was inhabited by many Vaiṣṇavas who had migrated from Sylhet and other parts of India. Thus there were Śrīvāsa Paṇḍita, Śrīrāma Paṇḍita, Candraśekhara; Murārigupta, Puṇḍarīka Vidyānidhi, Caitanya-vallabha Datta. Thus the whole atmosphere was prepared for a big spark of fire which it was the business of Caitanya to throw into the combustible material. In Śāntipura, Advaita, a great Vaiṣṇava very much senior to Caitanya, was always regretting the general hollowness of the people and wishing for someone to create new fire. Caitanya's elder brother Viśvarūpa had gone out as an ascetic, and Caitanya, then the only son left to his parents, was particularly cherished by his widowed mother Śacī Devī, the daughter of Nīlāmbara Chakravarti.

Navadvīpa was at this time under Moslem rulers who had grown tyrannical. Sārvabhauma Bhaṭṭācārya, son of Viśārada

Paṇḍita and a great scholar, had gone over to Orissa to take refuge under the Hindu king there, Pratāparudra.

Caitanya studied in the Sanskrit school (*tol*) of Sudarśana Paṇḍita. His study in the school was probably limited to the Kalāpa grammar and some *kāvyas*. Some later biographers say that he had also read Nyāya (logic); there is, however, no proper evidence in support of this. He had, however, studied at home some *Purāṇas*, notably the great devotional work, *Śrīmad-bhāgavata*. As a student he was indeed very gifted; but he was also very vain, and always took special delight in defeating his fellow-students in debate. From his early days he had shown a strong liking for devotional songs. He took a special delight in identifying himself with Kṛṣṇa. Among his associates the names of the following may be mentioned: Śrīnivāsa Paṇḍita and his three brothers, Vāsudeva Datta, Mukunda Datta and Jagai, the writer, Śrīgarbha Paṇḍita, Murārigupta, Govinda, Śrīdhara, Gaṅgādāsa, Dāmodara, Candraśekhara, Mukunda, Sañjaya, Puruṣottama, Vijaya, Vakreśvara, Sanātana, Hṛdaya, Madana and Rāmānanda. Caitanya had received some instruction in the Vedas also from his father. He had also received instruction from Viṣṇu Paṇḍita and Gaṅgādāsa Paṇḍita. At this period of his life he became intimately acquainted with Haridāsa and Gadādhara.

Caitanya's first wife, Lakṣmī Devī, daughter of Vallabha Miśra, died of snake-bite; he then married Viṣṇupriyā. After his father's death he went to Gayā to perform the post-funeral rites; there he is said to have met saintly persons like Paramānanda Purī, Īśvara Purī, Raghunātha Purī, Brahmānanda Purī, Amara Purī, Gopāla Purī, and Ananta Purī. He was initiated by Īśvara Purī and decided to renounce the world. He came back, however, to Navadvīpa and began to teach the *Bhāgavata-purāṇa* for some time.

Nityānanda, an ascetic (*avadhūta*), joined him in Navadvīpa. His friendship further kindled the fire of Caitanya's passion for divine love, and both of them, together with other associates, began to spend days and nights in dancing and singing. It was at this time that through his influence and that of Nityānanda, two drunkards, Jagai and Madhai, were converted to his Vaiṣṇava cult of love. Shortly after this, with his mother's permission, he took the ascetic life and proceeded to Katwa, and from there to Śantipur to meet Advaita there. From this place he started for Purī with his followers.

Such is the brief outline of Caitanya's early life, bereft of all interesting episodes, and upon it there is a fair amount of unanimity among his various biographers.

Kṛṣṇadāsa Kavirāja's Bengali work, *Caitanya-caritāmṛta*, is probably one of the latest of his biographies, but on account of its recondite character has easily surpassed in popularity all other biographies of Caitanya. He divides Caitanya's life into three parts: *Ādilīlā* (the first part), *Madhya-līlā* (the second part) and *Antyalīlā* (the last part). The first part consists of an account of the first twenty-four years, at the end of which Caitanya renounced the world. He lived for another twenty-four years, and these are divided into two sections, the second and the last part of his life. Of these twenty-four years, six years were spent on pilgrimage; this marks the middle period. The remaining eighteen years were spent by him in Purī and form the final period, of which six years were spent in preaching the cult of holy love and the remaining twelve years in deep ecstasies and suffering pangs of separation from his beloved Kṛṣṇa, the Lord.

After his renunciation in the twenty-fourth year of his life, in the month of *Māgha* (January), he started for Bṛndāvana and travelled for three days in the Rāḍha country (Bengal). He did not know the way to Bṛndāvana and was led to Śāntipura by Nityānanda. Caitanya's mother, along with many other people, Śrīvāsa, Rāmai, Vidyānidhi, Gadādhara, Vakreśvara, Murāri, Śuklāmbara, Śrīdhara, Vyaya, Vāsudeva, Mukunda, Buddhimanta Khan, Nandana and Sañjaya, came to see him at Śāntipur. From Śāntipur Caitanya started for Purī with Nityānanda, Paṇḍita Jagadānanda, Dāmodara Paṇḍita and Mukunda Dutta by the side of the Ganges, by way of Bāleśvar (in Orissa). He then passed by Yājpur and Sākṣigopāla and came to Purī. Having arrived there, he went straight to the temple of Jagannātha, looked at the image and fell into a trance. Sārvabhauma Bhaṭṭācārya, who was then residing at Purī, brought him to his house; Nityānanda, Jagadānanda, Dāmodara all came and joined him there. Here Caitanya stayed for some time at the house of Sārvabhauma and held discussions with him, in the course of which he refuted the monistic doctrines of Śaṅkara[1].

[1] There is considerable divergence about this episode with Sārvabhauma; the Sanskrit *Caitanya-caritāmṛta* and the *Caitanya-candrodaya-nāṭaka* do not agree with the description in the *Caitanya-caritāmṛta* in Bengali of Kṛṣṇadāsa Kavirāja as given here.

After some time Caitanya started for the South and first came to Kūrmasthāna, probably a place in the Ganjam district (South Orissa); he then passed on by the banks of the Godāvarī and met Rāmānanda Ray. In a long conversation with him on the subtle aspect of the emotion of *bhakti* Caitanya was very much impressed by him; he passed some time with him in devotional songs and ecstasies. He then resumed his travel again and is said to have passed through Mallikārjuna-tīrtha, Ahobala-Nṛsiṃha, Skanda-tīrtha and other places, and later on came to Śrīraṅgam on the banks of the Kāverī. Here he lived in the house of Veṅkaṭa Bhaṭṭa for four months, after which he went to the Ṛṣabha mountain, where he met Paramānanda Purī. It is difficult to say how far he travelled in the South, but he must have gone probably as far as Travancore. It is also possible that he visited some of the places where Madhvācārya had great influence, and it is said that he had discussions with the teachers of the Madhva school. He discovered the *Brahma-saṃhitā* and the *Kṛṣṇa-karṇāmṛta*, two important manuscripts of Vaiṣṇavism, and brought them with him. He is said to have gone a little farther in the East up to Nāsika; but it is difficult to say to what extent the story of these tours is correct. On his return journey he met Rāmānanda Ray again, who followed him to Purī.

After his return to Purī, Pratāparudra, then King of Purī, solicited his acquaintance and became his disciple. In Purī Caitanya began to live in the house of Kāśī Miśra. Among others, he had as his followers Janārdana, Kṛṣṇadāsa, Śikhī Māhiti, Pradyumna Miśra, Jagannātha Dāsa, Murārī Māhiti, Candaneśvara and Siṃheśvara. Caitanya spent most of his time in devotional songs, dances and ecstasies. In A.D. 1514 he started for Bṛndāvana with a number of followers; but so many people thronged him by the time he came to Pāṇihāṭi and Kāmārahāṭi that he cancelled his programme and returned to Purī. In the autumn of the next year he again started for Bṛndāvana with Bālabhadra Bhaṭṭācārya and came to Benares; there he defeated in a discussion a well-known teacher, Prakāśānanda, who held monistic doctrines. In Bṛndāvana he met Śrī-rūpa Gosvāmī, Uddhavadāsa Mādhava, and others. Then he left Bṛndāvana and Mathurā and went to Allahabad by the side of the Ganges. There he met Vallabha Bhaṭṭa and Raghupati Upādhyāya, and gave elaborate religious instruction to

Śrī-rūpa. Later on Caitanya met Sanātana and imparted further religious instruction to him. He returned to Benares, where he taught Prakāśānanda; then he came back to Purī and spent some time there. Various stories are narrated in the *Caitanya-caritāmṛta*, describing the ecstatic joy of Caitanya in his moods of inspiration; on one occasion he had jumped into the sea in a state of ecstasy and was picked up by a fisherman. It is unfortunate, however, that we know nothing of the exact manner in which he died.

Emotionalism of Caitanya.

The religious life of Caitanya unfolds unique pathological symptoms of devotion which are perhaps unparalleled in the history of any other saints that we know of. The nearest approach will probably be in the life of St Francis of Assisi; but the emotional flow in Caitanya seems to be more self-centred and deeper. In the beginning of his career he not only remained immersed as it were in a peculiar type of self-intoxicating song-dance called the *kīrtana*, but he often imitated the various episodes of Kṛṣṇa's life as told in the *Purāṇas*. But with the maturity of his life of renunciation his intoxication and his love for Kṛṣṇa gradually so increased that he developed symptoms almost of madness and epilepsy. Blood came out of the pores of his hair, his teeth chattered, his body shrank in a moment and at the next appeared to swell up. He used to rub his mouth against the floor and weep, and had no sleep at night. Once he jumped into the sea; sometimes the joints of his bones apparently became dislocated, and sometimes the body seemed to contract. The only burden of his songs was that his heart was aching and breaking for Kṛṣṇa, the Lord. He was fond of reading the dramas of Rāmānanda Ray, the poems of Caṇḍidāsa and Vidyāpati, the *Kṛṣṇa-karṇāmṛta* of Vilva-maṅgala and the *Gīta-govinda* of Jayadeva; most of these were mystic songs of love for Kṛṣṇa in erotic phraseology. Nowhere do we find any account of such an ecstatic *bhakti* in the *Purāṇas*, in the *Gītā* or in any other religious literature of India—the *Bhāgavata-purāṇa* has, no doubt, one or two verses which in a way anticipate the sort of *bhakti* that we find in the life of Caitanya—but without the life of Caitanya our storehouse of pathological religious experience would have been wanting in one of the most fruitful harvests of pure emotionalism in religion. Caitanya wrote practically nothing, his instructions were few and we have no authentic record of the sort of discussions that he is said to have held. He gave but little instruction, his preaching practically consisted in the demonstration of his own mystic faith and love for Kṛṣṇa; yet the influence that he exerted on his contemporaries and also during some centuries after his death was enormous. Sanskrit and Bengali literature during this time received a new impetus, and Bengal became in a sense saturated with devotional lyrics. It is difficult for us to give any account of his own philosophy save what we can gather from the accounts given of him by his biographers. Jīva Gosvāmī and Baladeva Vidyābhūṣaṇa are probably the only persons of importance among the members of his faith who tried to deal with some kind of philosophy, as we shall see later on.

Gleanings from the Caitanya-Caritāmṛta on the subject of Caitanya's Philosophical Views.

Kṛṣṇadāsa Kavirāja, otherwise known as Kavirāja Gosvāmī, was not a contemporary of Caitanya; but he came into contact with many of his important followers and it may well be assumed that he was in possession of the traditional account of the episodes of Caitanya's life as current among them. He gives us an account of Vāsudeva Sārvabhauma's discussion with Caitanya at Purī, in which the latter tried to refute the monistic view. The supposed conversation shows that, according to Caitanya, Brahman cannot be indeterminate (*nirviśeṣa*); any attempt to prove the indeterminateness of Brahman would only go the other way, prove His determinate nature and establish the fact that He possesses all possible powers. These powers are threefold in their nature: the *Viṣṇu-śakti*, the *kṣetrajña-śakti*, and the *avidyā-śakti*. The first power, as *Viṣṇu-śakti*, may further be considered from three points of view, the *hlādinī*, *saudhinī* and *samvit*. These three powers, bliss, being, and consciousness, are held together in the transcendent power (*parā-śakti* or *Viṣṇu-śakti*) of God. The *kṣetrajña-śakti* or *jīva-śakti* (the power of God as souls of individuals) and the *avidyā-śakti* (by which the world-appearances are created) do not exist in the transcendent sphere of God. The Brahman is indeed devoid of all *prākṛta* or phenomenal qualities, but He is indeed full of nonphenomenal qualities. It is from this point of view that the Upaniṣads have described Brahman as *nirguṇa* (devoid of qualities) and also as devoid of all powers (*niḥśaktika*). The individual souls are within the control of *māyā-śakti*; but God is the controller of the *māyā-śakti* and through it of the individual souls. God creates the world by His unthinkable powers and yet remains unchanged within Himself. The world thus is not false; but, being a creation, it is destructible. The Śaṅkarite interpretation of the *Brahma-sūtra* is wrong and is not in consonance with the purport of the Upaniṣads.

In chapter VIII of the *Madhya-līlā* of the *Caitanya-caritāmṛta* we have the famous dialogue between Caitanya and Rāmānanda regarding the gradual superiority of the ideal of love. Rāmānanda says that devotion to God comes as the result of the performance of caste-duties. We may note here that according to the *Bhakti-rasāmṛta-sindhu bhakti* consists in attaching oneself to Kṛṣṇa for His satisfaction alone, without being in any way influenced by the desire for philosophic knowledge, *karma* or disinclination from worldly things (*vairāgya*), and without being associated with any desire for one's own interests[1].

The *Viṣṇu-purāṇa*, as quoted in the *Caitanya-caritāmṛta*, holds the view that it is by the performance of caste-duties and *āśrama*-duties that God can be worshipped. But the point is whether such performance of caste-duties and *āśrama*-duties can lead one to the attainment of *bhakti* or not. If *bhakti* means the service of God for His sake alone (*ānukūlyena Kṛṣṇānusevanam*), then the performance of caste-duties cannot be regarded as a necessary step towards its attainment; the only contribution that it may make can be the purification of mind, whereby the mind may be made fit to receive the grace of God. Caitanya, not satisfied with the reply of Rāmānanda, urges him to give a better account of *bhakti*. Rāmānanda in reply says that a still better state is that in which the devotee renounces all his interests in favour of God in all his performance of duties; but there is a still higher state in which one renounces all his duties through love of God. Unless one can renounce all thoughts about one's own advantage, one cannot proceed in the path of love. The next higher stage is that in which devotion is

[1] *anyābhilāṣitāśūnyaṃ jñāna-karmādy-anāvṛtam.*
ānukūlyena Kṛṣṇānusevanaṃ bhaktiruttamā.
Bhaktirasāmṛta-sindhu, I. I. 9.

impregnated with knowledge. Pure devotion should not have, however, any of the obstructive influences of knowledge; philosophical knowledge and mere disinclination obstruct the course of *bhakti*. Knowledge of God's nature and wisdom regarding the nature of the intimate relation of man with God may be regarded as unobstructive to *bhakti*. The natural and inalienable attachment of our mind to God is called *prema-bhakti*; it is fivefold: *śānta* (peaceful love), *dāsya* (servant of God), *sakhya* (friendship with God), *vātsalya* (filial attitude towards God), and *mādhurya* (sweet love, or love of God as one's lover). The different types of love may thus be arranged as above in a hierarchy of superiority; love of God as one's bridegroom or lover is indeed the highest. The love of the *gopīs* for Kṛṣṇa in the love-stories of Kṛṣṇa in Bṛndāvana typifies this highest form of love and particularly the love of Rādhā for Kṛṣṇa. Rāmānanda closes his discourse with the assertion that in the highest altitude of love, the lover and the beloved melt together into one, and through them both one unique manifestation of love realizes itself. Love attains its highest pitch when both the lover and the beloved lose their individuality in the sweet milky flow of love.

Later on, in *Madhya-līlā*, chapter XXIX, Caitanya, in describing the nature of *śuddhā bhakti* (pure devotion), says that pure devotion is that in which the devotee renounces all desires, all formal worship, all knowledge and work, and is attached to Kṛṣṇa with all his sense-faculties. A true devotee does not want anything from God, but is satisfied only in loving Him. It shows the same symptoms as ordinary human love, rising to the highest pitch of excellence.

In chapter XXII of *Madhya-līlā* it is said that the difference in intensity of devotion depends upon the difference of the depth of emotion. One who is devoted to Kṛṣṇa must possess preliminary moral qualities; he must be kind, truthful, equable to all, non-injurious, magnanimous, tender, pure, selfless, at peace with himself and with others; he must do good to others, must cling to Kṛṣṇa as his only support, must indulge in no other desires, must make no other effort than that of worshipping Kṛṣṇa, must be steady, must be in full control of all his passions; he should not be unmindful, should be always prepared to honour others, be full of humility and prepared to bear with fortitude all sorrows; he should indulge in association with true devotees—it is by such a course that love of Kṛṣṇa will gradually dawn in him. A true Vaiṣṇava should give up the company of women and of all those who are not attached to Kṛṣṇa. He should also give up caste-duties and *āśrama*-duties and cling to Kṛṣṇa in a helpless manner. To cling to Kṛṣṇa and to give oneself up to Him is the supreme duty of a Vaiṣṇava. Love of Kṛṣṇa is innate in a man's heart, and it is manifested under encouraging conditions. Love for God is a manifestation of the *hlādinī* power of God, and by virtue of the fact that it forms a constituent of the individual soul, God's attraction of individual souls towards Him is a fundamental fact of human life; it may remain dormant for a while, but it is bound to wake under suitable conditions.

The individual souls share both the *hlādinī* and the *samvit śakti* of God, and the *māyā-śakti* typified in matter. Standing between these two groups of power, the individual souls are called the *taṭastha-śakti*. A soul is impelled on one side by material forces and attractions, and urged upwards by the *hlādinī-śakti* of God. A man must therefore adopt such a course that the force of material attractions and desires may gradually wane, so that he may be pulled forward by the *hlādinī-śakti* of God.

Some Companions of Caitanya.

A great favourite of Caitanya was Nityānanda. The exact date of his birth and death is difficult to ascertain, but he seems to have been some years older than Caitanya. He was a Brahmin by caste, but became an *avadhuta* and had no caste-distinctions. He was a messenger of Caitanya, preaching the Vaiṣṇava religion in Bengal during Caitanya's absence at Purī; he is said to have converted to Vaiṣṇavism many Buddhists and low-caste Hindus of Bengal. At a rather advanced stage of life, Nityānanda broke the vow of asceticism and married the two daughters of Sūrjadās Sarkhel, brother of Gaurdāsa Sarkhel of Kalna; the two wives were Vasudhā and Jāhnavi. Nityānanda's son Vīrachand, also known as Vira-bhadra, became a prominent figure in the subsequent period of Vaiṣṇava history.

Pratāparudra was the son of Puruṣottamadeva, who had ascended his throne in 1478, and himself ascended the throne in 1503. He was very learned and took pleasure in literary disputes.

Mr Stirling, in his *History of Orissa* (published in 1891), says of him that he had marched with his army to Rameśwaram and took the famous city of Vijayanagara; he had also fought the Mahomedans and prevented them from attacking Purī. Caitanya's activities in Purī date principally between 1516 and 1533. Rāmānanda Ray was a minister of Pratāparudra, and at his intercession Caitanya came into contact with Pratāparudra, who became one of his followers. The influence of Caitanya together with the conversion of Pratāparudra produced a great impression upon the people of Orissa, and this led to the spread of Vaiṣṇavism and the collapse of Buddhism there in a very marked manner.

During the time of Caitanya, Hussain Shaha was the Nawab of Gaur. Two Brahmins, converted into Islam and having the Mahomedan names Sakar Malik and Dabir Khas, were his two high officers; they had seen Caitanya at Ramkeli and had been greatly influenced by him. Later in their lives they were known as Sanātana and Rūpa; they distributed their riches to the poor and became ascetics. Rūpa is said to have met Caitanya at Benares, where he received instruction from him; he wrote many Sanskrit works of great value, e.g., *Lalita-mādhava*, *Vidagdhamādhava*, *Ujjvalanīlamaṇi*, *Utkalikā-vallarī* (written in 1550), *Uddhava-dūta*, *Upadeśāmṛta*, *Kārpaṇya-puñjikā*, *Gaṅgāṣṭaka*, *Govindavirudāvali*, *Gaurāṅgakalpataru*, *Caitanyāṣṭaka*, *Dāna-keli-kaumudī*, *Nāṭaka-candrikā*, *Padyāvali*, *Paramārtha-sandarbha*, *Prīti-sandarbha*, *Premendu-sāgara*, *Mathurā-mahimā*, *Mukundamuktā-ratnāvalī-stotra-ṭīkā*, *Yāmunāṣṭaka*, *Rasāmṛta*, *Vilāpa-kusumāñjali*, *Brajavilāsa-stava*, *Śikṣādaśaka*, *Saṃkṣepa Bhāgavatāmṛta*, *Sādhana-paddhati*, *Stavamālā*, *Haṃsa-dūta-kāvya*, *Harināmāmṛta-vyākaraṇa*, *Hare-kṛṣṇa-mahāmantrārtha-nirūpaṇa*, *Chando'ṣṭādaśaka*.

Sanātana wrote the following works: *Ujjvala-rasa-kaṇā*, *Ujjvala-nīlamani-ṭīkā*, *Bhakti-bindu*, *Bhakti-sandarbha*, *Bhāgavata-krama-sandarbha*, *Bhāgavātamṛta*, *Yoga-śataka-vyākhyāna*, *Viṣṇu-toṣiṇī*, *Haribhakti-vilāsa*, *Bhakti-rasāmṛta-sindhu*. Sanātana had been put in prison by Hussain Shah when he heard that he was thinking of leaving him, but Sanātana bribed the gaoler, who set him at liberty. He at once crossed the Ganges and took the ascetic life; he went to Mathurā to meet his brother Rūpa, and returned to Purī to meet Caitanya. After staying some months in Purī, he went to Bṛndāvana. In the meanwhile Rūpa had also gone to Purī and he also returned to Bṛndāvana. Both of them were great devotees and spent their lives in the worship of Kṛṣṇa.

Advaitācārya's real name was Kamalākara Bhaṭṭācārya. He was born in 1434 and was thus fifty-two years older than Caitanya; he was a great Sanskrit scholar and resided at Śāntipur. He went to Nabadvīpa to finish his studies. People at this time had become very materialistic; Advaita was very much grieved at it and used to pray in his mind for the rise of some great prophet to change their minds. Caitanya, after he had taken to ascetic life, had visited Advaita at Śāntipur, where both of them enjoyed ecstatic dances; Advaita was then aged about seventy-five. It is said that he had paid a visit to Caitanya at Purī. He is said to have died in 1539 according to some, and in 1584 according to others (which is incredible).

Apart from Advaita and Nityānanda there were many other intimate companions of Caitanya, of whom Śrīvāsa or Śrīnivāsa was one. He was a brahmin of Sylhet who settled at Navadvīpa; he was quite a rich man. It is not possible to give his exact birth-date, but he had died long before 1540 (when Jayānanda wrote his *Caitanya-maṅgala*); he was probably about forty when Caitanya was born. As a boy Caitanya was a frequent visitor to Śrīvāsa's house. He was devoted to the study of the *Bhāgavata*, though in his early life he was more or less without a faith. He was also a constant companion of Advaita while he was at Navadvīpa. When Caitanya's mind was turned to God after his return from Gayā, Śrīvāsa's house was the scene of ecstatic dances. Śrīvāsa then became a great disciple of Caitanya. Nārāyaṇī, the mother of Bṛndāvanadāsa, the biographer of Caitanya, was a niece of Śrīvāsa.

Rāmānanda Ray, the minister of Pratāparudra and author of the *Jagannātha-vallabha*, was very much admired by Caitanya. He was a native of Vidyānagara, in Central India. The famous dialogue narrated in the *Caitanya-caritāmṛta* shows how Caitanya himself took lessons from Rāmānanda on the subject of high devotion. Rāmānanda Ray on his part was very fond of Caitanya and often spent his time with him.

CHAPTER XXXIII

THE PHILOSOPHY OF JĪVA GOSVĀMĪ AND BALADEVA VIDYĀBHŪṢAṆA, FOLLOWERS OF CAITANYA

Ontology.

JĪVA GOSVĀMĪ flourished shortly after Caitanya. He wrote a running commentary on the *Bhāgavata-purāṇa* which forms the second chapter (*Bhāgavata-sandarbha*) of his principal work, the *Ṣaṭ-sandarbha*. In this chapter he says that, when the great sages identify themselves with the ultimate reality, their minds are unable to realize the diverse powers of the Lord. The nature of the Lord thus appears in a general manner (*sāmānyena lakṣitam tathaiva sphurat*, p. 50), and at this stage the powers of Brahman are not perceived as different from Him. The ultimate reality, by virtue of its essential power (*svarūpasthhitayā eva śaktyā*), becomes the root support of all its other powers (*parāsām api śaktīnām mūlā-śrayarūpam*), and through the sentiment of devotion appears to the devotees as the possessor of diverse powers; He is then called Bhagavān. Pure bliss (*ānanda*) is the substance, and all the other powers are its qualities; in association with all the other powers it is called *Bhagavān* or God[1]. The concept of Brahman is thus the partial appearance of the total personality denoted by the word Bhagavān; the same Bhagavān appears as Paramātman in His aspect as controlling all beings and their movements. The three names Brahman, Bhagavān and Paramātman are used in accordance with the emphasis that is put on the different aspects of the total composite meaning; thus, as any one of the special aspects of God appears to the mind of the devotee, he associates it with the name of Brahman, Bhagavān or Paramātman[2].

The aspect as Brahman is realized only when the specific qualities and powers do not appear before the mind of the devotee.

[1] *ānanda-mātraṃ viśeṣyaṃ samastāḥ śaktayaḥ viśeṣaṇāni viśiṣṭo Bhagavān. Ṣaṭ-sandarbha*, p. 50.

[2] *tatraikasyaiva viśeṣaṇa-bhedena tad aviśiṣṭatvena ca pratipādanāt tathaiva tat-tad-upāsakapuruṣānubhava-bhedāc ca āvirbhāva-nāmnor bhedaḥ. Ibid.* p. 53.

In realizing the pure consciousness as the nature of the devotee's own self the nature of the Brahman as pure consciousness is also realized; the realization of the identity of one's own nature with that of Brahman is effected through the special practice of devotion[1]. In the monistic school of Vedānta, as interpreted by Śaṅkara, we find that the identity of the self with the Brahman is effected through the instruction in the Vedāntic maxim: "that art thou" (*tat tvam asi*). Here, however, the identity is revealed through the practice of devotion, or rather through the grace of God, which is awakened through such devotion.

The abode of Bhagavān is said to be *Vaikuṇṭha*. There are two interpretations of this word; in one sense it is said to be identical with the very nature of Brahman as unobscured by *māyā*[2]; in another interpretation it is said to be that which is neither the manifestation of *rajas* and *tamas* nor of the material *sattva* as associated with *rajas* and *tamas*. It is regarded as having a different kind of substance, being the manifestation of the essential power of Bhagavān or as pure *sattva*. This pure *sattva* is different from the material *sattva* of the Sāṃkhyists, which is associated with *rajas* and *tamas*, and for this reason it is regarded as *aprākṛta*, i.e., transcending the *prākṛta*. For this reason also it is regarded as eternal and unchanging[3]. The ordinary *guṇas*, such as *sattva*, *rajas* and *tamas*, are produced from the movement of the energy of *kāla* (time); but the *sattva-Vaikuṇṭha* is not within the control of *kāla*[4]. The *Vaikuṇṭha*, thus being devoid of any qualities, may in one sense be regarded as *nirviśeṣa* (differenceless); but in another sense differences may be said to exist in it also, although they

[1] *Ibid.* p. 54. *nanu sūkṣma-cid-rūpatvaṃ padārthānubhave kathaṃ pūrṇa-cid-ākāra-rūpa-madīya-brahma-svarūpaṃ sphuratu tatrāha, ananyabodhyā-tmatayā cid-ākāratā-sāmyena śuddha-tvaṃ padārthaikyabodhya-svarūpatayā. yady api tādṛg-ātmānubhavānantaraṃ tad-ananya-bodhyatā-kṛtau sādhaka-śaktir nāsti tathāpi pūrvaṃ tadartham eva kṛtayā sarvatrā'pi upajīvyayā sādhana-bhaktyā ārādhitasya śrī-bhagavataḥ prabhāvād eva tad api tatrodayate. Ibid.* p. 54.

[2] *yato vaikuṇṭhāt paraṃ Brahmākhyaṃ tattvaṃ paraṃ bhinnaṃ na bhavati. svarūpa-śakti-viśeṣāviṣkāreṇa māyayā nāvṛtaṃ tad ev tad-rūpam. Ibid.* p. 57.

[3] *yatra vaikuṇṭhe rajas tamaś ca na pravartate. tayor miśraṃ sahacaraṃ jaḍaṃ yat sattvaṃ na tad api. kintu anyad eva tac ca yā suṣṭhu sthāpayiṣyamāṇā māyātaḥ parā bhagavat-svarūpa-śaktiḥ tasyāḥ vṛttitvena cid-rūpaṃ śuddha-sattvākhyaṃ sattvam. Ibid.* p. 58.

[4] *Ibid.* p. 59. This view, that the *guṇas* are evolved by the movement of *kāla*, is not accepted in the ordinary classical view of Sāṃkhya, but is a theory of the Pañcarātra school. Cf. *Ahirbudhnya-saṃhitā*, chs. 6 and 7.

can only be of the nature of the pure *sattva* or the essential power of God[1].

The essential power (*svarūpa-śakti*) and the energy (*māyā-śakti*) are mutually antagonistic, but they are both supported in God[2]. The power of God is at once natural (*svābhāvika*) and unthinkable (*acintya*). It is further urged that even in the ordinary world the powers of things are unthinkable, i.e., neither can they be deduced from the nature of the things nor can they be directly perceived, but they have to be assumed because without such an assumption the effect would not be explainable. The word "unthinkable" (*acintya*) also means that it is difficult to assert whether the power is identical with the substance or different from it; on the one hand, power cannot be regarded as something extraneous to the substance, and, on the other, if it were identical with it, there could be no change, no movement, no effect. The substance is perceived, but the power is not; but, since an effect or a change is produced, the implication is that the substance must have exerted itself through its power or powers. Thus, the existence of powers as residing in the substance is not logically proved, but accepted as an implication[3]. The same is the case in regard to Brahman; His powers are identical with His nature and therefore co-eternal with Him. The concept of "unthinkableness" (*acintyatva*) is used to reconcile apparently contradictory notions (*durghaṭa-ghaṭakatvaṃ hy acintyatvam*). The internal and essential power (*antaraṅga-svarūpa-śakti*) exists in the very nature of the Brahman (*svarūpeṇa*) and also as its various manifestations designated by such terms as *Vaikuṇṭha*, etc. (*vaikuṇṭhādi-svarūpa-vaibhava-rūpeṇa*)[4]. The second power (*taṭasthaśakti*) is represented by the pure selves. The third power (*bahiraṅga-māyā-śakti*) is represented by the evolution of all cosmical categories and their root, the *pradhāna*. The analogy offered is that of the sun, its rays and the various

[1] *nanu guṇādy-abhāvān nirviśeṣa evāsau loka ity āśaṃkya tatra viśeṣas tasyāḥ śuddha-sattvātmikāyāḥ svarūpānatirikta-śakter eva vilāsa-rūpa iti. Ṣaṭ-sandarbha*, p. 59.

[2] *te ca svarūpa-śakti-māyā-śaktī paraspara-viruddhe, tathā tayor vṛttayaḥ sva-sva-gaṇa eva parasparāviruddhā api bahvyaḥ tathāpi tāsām ekaṃ nidhānaṃ tad eva. Ibid.* p. 61.

[3] *loke hi sarveṣāṃ bhāvānāṃ maṇi-mantrādīnāṃ śaktayaḥ acintya-jñāna-gocarāḥ acintyaṃ tarkāsahaṃ yaj-jñānaṃ kāryānyathānupapatti-pramāṇakaṃ tasya gocarāḥ santi. Ibid.* pp. 63–4.

[4] *Ibid.* p. 65.

colours which are manifested as the result of refraction. The external power of *māyā* (*bahiraṅga-śakti*) can affect the *jīvas* but not Brahman.

The *māyā* is defined in the *Bhāgavata* (as interpreted by Śrīdhara) as that which is manifested without any object and is not yet perceivable in its own nature, like an illusory image of darkness[1]. This is interpreted in a somewhat different form in the *Bhāgavata-sandarbha*, where it is said that *māyā* is that which appears outside the ultimate reality or Brahman, and ceases to appear with the realization of Brahman. It has no appearance in its own essential nature, i.e., without the support of the Brahman it cannot manifest itself; it is thus associated with Brahman in two forms as *jīva-māyā* and *guṇa-māyā*. The analogy of *ābhāsa*, which was explained by Śrīdhara as "illusory image," is here interpreted as the reflection of the solar light from outside the solar orb. The solar light cannot exist unless it is supported by the solar orb. But though this is so, yet the solar light can have an independent rôle and play outside the orb when it is reflected or refracted; thus it may dazzle the eyes of man and blind them to its real nature, and manifest itself in various colours. So also the analogy of darkness shows that, though darkness cannot exist where there is light, yet it cannot itself be perceived without the light of the eyes. The *prakṛti* and its developments are but manifestations or appearances, which are brought into being outside the Brahman by the power of the *māyā*; but the movement of the *māyā*, the functioning of the vital *prāṇas*, *manas* and the senses, the body, are all made possible by the fact that they are permeated by the original essential power of God (*antaraṅga-śakti*)[2]. Just as a piece of iron which derives its heat from the fire in which it is put cannot in its turn burn the fire or affect it in any manner, so the *māyā* and its appearances, which derive their essence from the essential power of God, cannot in any way affect God or His essential power.

The selves can know the body; but they cannot know the ultimate reality and the ultimate perceiver of all things. It is through *māyā* that different things have an apparently independent existence and

[1] *ṛte'rthaṃ yat pratīyeta na pratīyeta cātmani*
tad vidyād ātmano māyāṃ yathā bhāsaṃ yathā tamaḥ.

[2] *svarūpa-bhutākhyām antaraṅgāṃ śaktiṃ sarvasyāpi pravṛtty-anyathā-nupapattyā.* *Ibid.* p. 69.

are known by the selves; but the true and essential nature of Brahman is always one with all things, and, since in that state there is no duality, there is nothing knowable and no form separate from it. The ultimate reality, which reveals all things, reveals itself also—the heat rays of fire, which derive their existence from the fire, cannot burn the fire itself[1]. The *guṇas*—*sattva*, *rajas* and *tamas*—belong to the *jīva* and not to Brahman; for that reason, so long as the selves (*jīva*) are blinded by the power of *māyā*, there is an appearance of duality, which produces also the appearance of knower and knowable. The *māyā* is again described as twofold, the *guṇa-māyā*, which represents the material forces (*jaḍātmikā*), and the *ātma-māyā*, which is the will of God. There is also the concept of *jīva-māyā*, which is, again, threefold—creative (*Bhū*), protective (*Śrī*), and destructive (*Durgā*). The *ātma-māyā* is the essential power of God[2]. In another sense *māyā* is regarded as being composed of the three *guṇas*. The word *yoga-māyā* has also two meanings—it means the miraculous power achieved through the practice of the *yoga* when it is used as a power of the Yogins or sages; when applied to God (*parameśvara*), it means the manifestation of His spiritual power as pure consciousness (*cic-chakti-vilāsa*). When *māyā* is used in the sense of *ātma-māyā* or God's own *māyā*, it has thus three meanings, viz., His essential power (*svarūpa-śakti*), His will involving knowledge and movement (*jñāna-kriye*), and also the inner dalliance of His power as consciousness (*cic-chakti-vilāsa*)[3]. Thus, there is no *māyā* in *Vaikuṇṭha*, because it itself is of the nature of *māyā* or *svarūpa-śakti*; the *Vaikuṇṭha* is, thus, identical with *mokṣa* (emancipation).

Once it is admitted that the unthinkable power of God can explain all contradictory phenomena and also that by *yoga-māyā* God can directly manifest any form, appearance or phenomena, it was easy for the Vaiṣṇavas of the Gauḍiya school to exploit the idea theologically. Leaving aside the metaphysical idea of the non-Vaiṣṇava nature of the relation of God with His powers, they tried

[1] *svarūpa-vaibhave tasya jīvasya raśmi-sthānīyasya maṇḍalasthānīyo ya ātmā paramātmā sa eva svarūpa-śaktyā sarvam abhūt, anādita eva bhavann āste, na tu tat-praveśena, tat tatra itaraḥ sa jīvaḥ kenetareṇa karaṇa-bhūtena kaṃ padārthaṃ paśyet, na kenāpi kam api paśyet ity-arthaḥ; na hi raśmayaḥ svaśaktyā sūrya-maṇḍalāntargata-vaibhvaṃ prakāśayeyuḥ, na cārciṣo vahniṃ nirdaheyuḥ. Ṣaṭ-sandarbha*, p. 71.

[2] *mīyate anayā iti māyā-śabdena śakti-mātram api bhaṇyate. Ibid.* p. 73.

[3] *Ibid.* pp. 73–4.

by an extension of the metaphysical formula to defend their religious belief in the theological nature of the episodes of Kṛṣṇa in Vṛndāvana, as related in the *Bhāgavata*. Thus they held that Kṛṣṇa, including His body and all His dress and ornaments and the like, the *Gopīs*, with whom He had dalliance, and even the cows and trees of Vṛndāvana, were physically existent in limited forms and at the same time unlimited and spiritual as a manifestation of the essential nature of God. The Vaiṣṇavas were not afraid of any contradiction, because in accordance with the ingeniously-devised metaphysical formula the supra-logical nature of God's power was such that through it He could manifest Himself in all kinds of limited forms, and yet remain identical with His own supreme nature as pure bliss and consciousness. The contradiction was only apparent; because the very assumption that God's power is supra-logical resolves the difficulty of identifying the limited with the unlimited, the finite with the infinite[1]. The author of *Ṣaṭ-sandarbha* takes great pains to prove that the apparent physical form of Kṛṣṇa, as described in the *Bhāgavata-purāṇa*, is one with Brahman. It is not a case in which the identity is to be explained as having absolute affinity with Brahman (*atyanta-tādātmya*) or as being dependent on Brahman: if the Brahman reveals itself in pure mind, it must appear as one, without any qualitative difference of any kind; if, in associating Brahman with the form of Kṛṣṇa, this form appears to be an additional imposition, it is not the revelation of Brahman. It cannot be urged that the body of Kṛṣṇa is a product of pure *sattva*; for this has no *rajas* in it, and therefore there is no creative development in it. If there is any *rajas* in it, the body of Kṛṣṇa cannot be regarded as made up of pure *sattva*; and, if there is any mixture of *rajas*, then it would be an impure state and there can be no revelation of Brahman in it. Moreover, the text of the *Bhāgavata-purāṇa* is definitely against the view that the body of Kṛṣṇa is dependent only on pure *sattva*, because it asserts that the body of Kṛṣṇa is itself one and the same as pure *sattva* or pure

[1] *Ibid.* pp. 70–92. *satya-jñānānantānandaika-rasa-mūrtitvād yugapad eva sarvam api tat-tad-rūpaṃ vartata eva, kintu yūyaṃ sarvadā sarvaṃ na paśyatheti* (p. 87). *tataśca yadā tava yatrāṃśe tat-tad-upāsanā-phalasya yasya rūpasya prakāśanecchā tadaiva tatra tad-rūpaṃ prakāśate iti. iyaṃ kadety asya yuktiḥ. tasmāt tat tat sarvam api tasmin śrī-kṛṣṇa-rūpe'ntarbhūtam ity evam atrāpi tātparyam upasaṃharati* (p. 90). *tad ittham madhyamākāra eva sarvādhāratvāt bibhutvaṃ sādhitam. sarva-gatatvād api sādhyate. citraṃ vataitad ekena vapuṣā yugapat pṛthak gṛheṣu dvyaṣṭa-sāhasraṃ striya eka udāvahat.*

consciousness[1]. Again, since the body of Kṛṣṇa appears in diverse forms, and since all these forms are but the various manifestations of pure consciousness and bliss, they are more enjoyable by the devotee than the Brahman[2].

In the *Paramātma-sandarbha* the *jīva* or individual is described as an entity which in its own nature is pure and beyond *māyā*, but which perceives all the mental states produced by *māyā* and is affected by them. It is called *Kṣetrajña*, because it perceives itself to be associated with its internal and external body (*kṣetra*)[3]. In a more direct sense God is also called *Kṣetrajña*, because He not only behaves as the inner controller of *māyā* but also of all those that are affected by it and yet remains one with Himself through His essential power[4]. The *Kṣetrajña* should not be interpreted in a monistic manner, to mean only a pure unqualified consciousness (*nirviśeṣaṃ cid-vastu*), but as God, the supreme inner controller. The view that unqualified pure consciousness is the supreme reality is erroneous. Consequently a distinction is drawn between the *vyaṣṭi-kṣetrajña* (the individual person) and the *samaṣṭi-kṣetrajña* (the universal person)—God, the latter being the object of worship by the former. This form of God as the inner controller is called Paramātman.

God is further supposed to manifest Himself in three forms: first, as the presiding lord of the totality of selves and the *prakṛti*, which have come out of Him like sparks from fire—Saṅkarṣaṇa or Mahāviṣṇu; secondly, as the inner controller of all selves in their totality (*samaṣṭi-jīvāntaryāmī*)—*Pradyumna*. The distinction between the first and the second stage is that in the first the *jīva* and the *prakṛti* are in an undifferentiated stage, whereas in the second the totality of the *jīvas* has been separated outside of *prakṛti* and stands independently by itself. The third aspect of God is that in which He resides in every man as his inner controller.

The *jīvas* are described as atomic in size; they are infinite in number and are but the parts of God. *Māyā* is the power of God,

[1] *tasya śuddha-sattvasya prākṛtatvaṃ tu niṣiddham eva tasmāt na te prākṛta-sattva-pariṇāmā na vā tat-pracurāḥ kintu sva-prakāśatā-lakṣaṇa-śuddha-sattva-prakāśitā. Ṣaṭ-sandarbha*, p. 148, also pp. 147–8.

[2] *Ibid*. p. 149.

[3] *Ibid*. p. 209.

[4] *māyāyāṃ māyike'pi antar-yāmitayā praviṣṭo'pi svarūpa-śaktyā svarūpa-stha eva na tu tat-saṃsakta ity arthaḥ, vāsudevatvena sarva-kṣetra-jñātṛtvāt so'paraḥ kṣetrajña ātmā paramātmā. tad evam api mukhyaṃ kṣetrajñatvaṃ paramātmany eva. Ibid*. p. 210.

and the word is used in various senses in various contexts; it may mean the essential power, the external power, and it has also the sense of *pradhāna*[1].

The author of the *Ṣaṭ-sandarbha* denies the ordinary Vedāntic view that the Brahman is pure consciousness and the support (*āśraya*) of the objects (*viṣaya* or *māyā* or *ajñāna*). He regards the relation between *māyā* and Brahman as transcendental and supra-rational. Just as various conflicting and contradictory powers may reside in any particular medicine, so also various powers capable of producing manifold appearances may reside in Brahman, though the manner of association may be quite inexplicable and unthinkable. The appearance of duality is not due to the presence of *ajñāna* (or ignorance) in the Brahman, but through His unthinkable powers. The duality of the world can be reconciled with ultimate monism only on the supposition of the existence of the transcendent and supra-rational powers of God. This fact also explains how the power of God can transform itself into the material image without in any way affecting the unity and purity of God[2]. Thus both the subtle *jīvas* and the subtle material powers of the universe emanate from Paramātman, from whom both the conscious and the unconscious parts of the universe are produced. Paramātman, considered in Himself, may be taken as the agent of production (*nimitta-kāraṇa*), whereas in association with His powers He may be regarded as the material cause of the universe (*upādāna-kāraṇa*)[3]. Since the power of God is identical with the nature of God, the position of monism is well upheld.

On the subject of the relation between the parts and the whole the author of the *Ṣaṭ-sandarbha* says that the whole is not a conglomeration of the parts, neither is the whole the transformation of the parts or a change induced in the parts. Nor can the whole be regarded as different from the parts or one with it, or as associ-

[1] *tadevaṃ sandarbha-dvaye śakti-traya-vivṛtiḥ kṛtā. tatra nāmābhinnatā-janita-bhrānti-hānāya saṃgraha-ślokāḥ māyā syād antaraṅgāyāṃ bahiraṅgā ca sā smṛtā*

pradhāne'pi kvacid dṛṣṭā tad-vṛttir mohinī ca sā,
ādye traye syāt prakṛtiś cic-chaktis tvantaraṅgikā
śuddha-jīve'pi te dṛṣṭe tatheśa-jñāna-vīryayoḥ.
cinmayā-śakti-vṛtyos tu vidyā-śaktir udīryate
cic-chakti-vṛttau māyāyāṃ yoga-māyā samā smṛtā
pradhānāvyākṛtā-vyaktaṃ traiguṇye prakṛteḥ paraṃ
na māyāyāṃ na cic-chaktāv ityādyūhyam vivekibhiḥ. *Ibid.* p. 245.

[2] *Ibid.* p. 249.

[3] *Ibid.* p. 250.

ated with it. If the whole were entirely different from the parts, the parts would have nothing to do with the whole; if the parts were inherent in the whole, then any part would be found anywhere in the whole. Therefore the relation between the parts and the whole is of a supra-logical nature. From this position the author of the *Ṣaṭ-sandarbha* jumps to the conclusion that, wherever there is an appearance of any whole, such an appearance is due to the manifestation of Paramātman, which is the ultimate cause and the ultimate reality (*tasmād aikya-buddhyālambana-rūpaṃ yat pratīyate tat sarvatra paramātma-lakṣaṇaṃ sarvakāraṇam asty eva*, p. 252). All manifestations of separate wholes are, therefore, false appearances due to similarity; for wherever there is a whole there is the manifestation of God. In this way the whole universe may be regarded as one, and thus all duality is false[1].

Just as fire is different from wood, the spark and the smoke (though the latter two are often falsely regarded as being identical with the fire), so the self, as the separate perceiver called Bhagavān or Brahman, is also different from the five elements (the senses, the *antaḥkaraṇa* and the *pradhāna*) which together pass by the name of *jīva*[2].

Those who have their minds fixed on the Supreme Soul (Paramātman) and look upon the world as its manifestation thereby perceive only the element of ultimate reality in it; whereas those who are not accustomed to look upon the world as the manifestation of the supreme soul perceive it only as the effect of ignorance; thus to them the Paramātman, who pervades the world as the abiding Reality, does not show Himself to be such. Those who traffic in pure gold attach no importance to the various forms in which the gold may appear (bangles, necklaces and the like), because their chief interest lies in pure gold; whereas there are others whose chief interest is not pure gold, but only its varied unreal forms. This world is brought into being by God through His inherent power working upon Himself as the material cause; as the world is brought

[1] *tasmāt sarvaikya-buddhi-nidānāt pṛthag dehaikya-buddhiḥ sādṛśyabhramaḥ syāt, pūrvāparāvayavānusandhāne sati parasparam āśayaikatva-sthitatvenā'vayavatvsādhāraṇyena caikyasādṛśyāt praty-avayavam ekatayā pratīteḥ, so'yaṃ deha iti bhrama eva bhavatī'ty arthaḥ, prati-vṛkṣaṃ tad idaṃ vanaṃ itivat.*
Ṣaṭ-sandarbha, p. 253.

[2] *yatholmukāt viṣphuliṅgād dhūmād api svasambhavāt*
apy ātmatvena vimatād yathāgniḥ pṛthag ulmukāt
bhūtendriyāntaḥkaraṇāt pradhānāj-jīva-saṃjñitāt
ātmā tathā pṛthag draṣṭā bhagavān brahma-saṃjñitaḥ. *Ibid.* p. 254.

into being, He enters into it, controls it in every detail, and in the last stage (at the time of *pralaya*) He divests Himself of various forms of manifestation and returns to Himself as pure being, endowed with His own inherent power. Thus it is said in the *Viṣṇu-purāṇa* that the ignorant, instead of perceiving the world as pure knowledge, are deluded by perceiving it as the visible and tangible world of objects; but those who are pure in heart and wise perceive the whole world as the nature of God, as pure consciousness.

Status of the World.

Thus in the Vaiṣṇava system the world is not false (like the rope-snake), but destructible (like a jug). The world has no reality; for, though it is not false, it has no uninterrupted existence in past, present and future; only that can be regarded as real which is neither false nor has only an interrupted existence in time. Such reality can only be affirmed of Paramātman or His power[1]. The Upaniṣads say that in the beginning there existed ultimate Reality, *sat*; this term means the mutual identity of the subtle potential power of Brahman and the Brahman. The theory of *satkāryavāda* may be supposed to hold good with reference to the fact that it is the subtle power of God that manifests itself in diverse forms (*sūkṣmāvasthā-lakṣaṇa-tac-chaktiḥ*). Now the question arises, whether, if the world has the ultimate *sat* as its material cause, it must be as indestructible as that; if the world is indestructible, then why should it not be false (like the conch-shell-silver) and, consequently, why should not the *vivarta* theory be regarded as valid? The reply to such a question is that to argue that, because anything is produced from the real (*sat*), therefore it must also be real (*sat*) is false, since this is not everywhere the case; it cannot be asserted that the qualities of the effect should be wholly identical with the qualities of the cause; the rays of light emanating from fire have not the power of burning[2]. Śrīdhara, in his commentary on the *Viṣṇu-purāṇa*, asserting that Brahman has an unchangeable and a changeable form, explains the apparent incongruity in the possibility of the changeable coming out of the unchangeable on the

[1] *tato vivarta-vādinām iva rajju-sarpa-van na mithyātvaṃ kintu ghaṭa-van naśvaratvam eva tasya. tato mithyātvābhāve api tri-kālāvyabhicārā-bhāvāj jagato na sattvaṃ vivarta-pariṇāmāsiddhatvena tad-doṣa-dvayābhāvavaty eva hi vastuni sattvaṃ vidhīyate yathā paramātmani tacchaktau vā. Ibid.* p. 255.

[2] *Ibid.* p. 256.

basis of the above analogy of fire and the rays emanating from it. Again, in other cases an appearance like that of silver manifesting itself from the conch-shell is wholly false, as it has only appearance, but no utility; so there are many other things which, though they are believed to have a particular nature, are in reality quite different and have entirely different effects. Thus some wood poison may be believed to be dry ginger, and used as such; but it will still retain its poisonous effects. Here, in spite of the illusory knowledge of one thing as another, the things retain their natural qualities, which are not affected by the illusory notion.

The power a thing has of effecting any change or utility cannot be present at all times and places, or with the change of object, and so the power of effecting any change or utility, not being an eternal and all-abiding quality, cannot be regarded as the defining character of reality; so a false appearance like the conch-shell-silver, which has merely a perceivable form, but no other utility or power of effecting changes, cannot be regarded as real. Only that is real which is present in all cases of illusory objects or those which have any kind of utility; reality is that which lies as the ground and basis of all kinds of experience, illusory or relatively objective. The so-called real world about us, though no doubt endowed with the power of effecting changes or utility, is yet destructible. The word "destructible," however, is used only in the sense that the world returns to the original cause—the power of God—from which it came into being. The mere fact that we deal with the world and that it serves some purpose or utility is no proof that it is real; for our conduct and our dealings may proceed on the basis of blind convention, without assuming any reality in them. The currency of a series of conventions based on mutual beliefs cannot prove either their reality or their nature as knowledge (*vijñāna*) without any underlying substratum. Thus the currency of conventions cannot prove their validity. The world thus is neither false nor eternal; it is real, and yet does not remain in its apparent form, but loses itself in its own unmanifested state within the power of Brahman; and in this sense both the *satkārya* and the *pariṇāma* theories are valid[1].

It is wrong to suppose that originally the world did not exist at all and that in the end also it will absolutely cease to exist; for, since

[1] *Ṣaṭ-sandarbha*, p. 259.

absolute reality is altogether devoid of any other kind of experience, and is of the nature of homogeneous blissful experience, it is impossible to explain the world as an illusory imposition like the conch-shell-silver. It is for this reason that the world-creation is to be explained on the analogy of *pariṇāma* (or evolution) and not on the analogy of illusory appearances like the conch-shell-silver or the rope-snake. Through His own unthinkable, indeterminable and inscrutable power the Brahman remains one with Himself and yet produces the world[1]; thus it is wrong to think of Brahman as being the ground cause. If the world is eternally existent as it is, then the causal operation is meaningless; if the world is absolutely non-existent, then the notion of causal operation to produce the absolutely non-existent is also impossible. Therefore, the world is neither wholly existent nor wholly non-existent, but only existent in an unmanifested form. The jug exists in the lump of clay, in an unmanifested form; and causal operation is directed only to actualize the potential; the world also exists in the ultimate cause, in an unmanifested form, and is actualized in a manifest form by His natural power operating in a definite manner. It is thus wrong to suppose that the *māyā* of the *jīva*, from which comes all ignorance, is to be regarded as the cause of the majesty of God's powers; God is independent, all-powerful and all-creator, responsible for all that exists in the world. It is thus wrong to suppose that the *jīva* creates the world either by his own powers or by his own *ajñāna*; God is essentially true, and so He cannot create anything that is false[2].

The Vaiṣṇava theory thus accepts the doctrine of ultimate dissolution in *prakṛti* (*prakṛti-laya*). In the time of emancipation the world is not destroyed; for being of the nature of the power of God it cannot be destroyed; it is well known that in the case of *jīvan-mukti* the body remains. What happens in the stage of emancipation is that all illusory notions about the world vanish, but the world, as such, remains, since it is not false; emancipation is thus a state of subjective reformation, not an objective disappearance of the world. As the objective world is described as identical with

[1] *ato acintya-saṅkhyā-svarūpād acyutasyaiva tava pariṇāma-svīkāreṇa draviṇa-jātīnāṃ dravya-mātrāṇām mṛl-lohādīnāṃ vikalpā vedā ghaṭa-kuṇḍalādayas teṣāṃ panthāno mārgāḥ prakārās tair eva asmābhir upamīyate na tu kutrāpi bhṛama-rajatādibhiḥ. Ibid.* p. 260.

[2] *satya-svābhāvikācintya-śaktiḥ parameśvaras tuccha-māyikam api na kuryāt. Ibid.* p. 262.

God's powers, so also are the senses and the *buddhi*. When the Upaniṣad says that the *manas* is created by God, this merely means that God is identical with the cosmic *manas*, the *manas* of all beings, in His form as *Aniruddha*[1]. The ultimate cause is identical with the effect; wherever the effect is new (*apūrva*), and has a beginning and an end, it is illusory; for here the concept of cause and effect are mutually interdependent and not separately determinable. Until the effect is produced, nothing can be regarded as cause, and, unless the cause is determined, the effect cannot be determined[2]; so to validate the concept of causality the power as effect must be regarded as already existent in the cause. It is this potential existence of effect that proves its actual existence; thus the world exists as the natural energy of God, and as such it is eternally real. Even the slightest change and manifestation cannot be explained without reference to God or independently of Him; if such explanation were possible, the world also would be self-luminous pure consciousness.

It has been said that the *jīvas* are indeed the energy of God, but that still they may suffer from the defect of an obscuration of their self-luminosity. The *jīvas*, being of the nature of *taṭastha śakti*, are inferior to the essential power of God, by which their self-luminosity could be obscured[3]. This obscuration could be removed by God's will only through the spirit of enquiry regarding God's nature on the part of the *jīvas*. According to the *Ṣaṭ-sandarbha* the world is a real creation; but it refers with some approval to another view, that the world is a magical creation which deludes the *jīvas* into believing in a real objective existence of the world. This view, however, must be distinguished from the monistic view of Śaṅkara (which is that the real creator by His real power manifests the world-experience to a real perceiver)[4], and it also differs from the *Ṣaṭ-sandarbha* in that the latter regards the world as a real creation.

[1] *atas tan-mano'sṛjata manaḥ prajāpatim ity ādau manaḥ-śabdena samaṣṭi-mano'dhiṣṭhātā śrīmān aniruddha eva. Ṣaṭ-sandarbha*, p. 262.

antaḥ-karaṇa-bahiḥ-karaṇa-viṣaya-rūpeṇa paramātma-lakṣaṇaṃ jñānam eva bhātī tasmād ananyad eva buddhyādi-vastu ity-arthaḥ. Ibid. p. 263.

[2] *yāvat kāryaṃ na jāyate tāvat kāraṇatvaṃ mṛt-śuktyāder na siddhyati kāraṇatvāsiddhau ca kāryaṃ na jāyate eveti paraspara-sāpekṣatva-doṣāt. Ibid* p. 265.

[3] *Ibid.* p. 266.

[4] *satyenaiva kartā satyam eva draṣṭāraṃ prati satyaiva tayā śaktyā vastunaḥ sphuraṇāt loke api tathaiva dṛśyata iti. Ibid.* p. 268.

It must, however, be maintained that the main interest of the Vaiṣṇavas is not in these hair-splitting dialectical discussions; theirs is professedly a system of practical religious emotionalism, and this being so it matters very little to a Vaiṣṇava whether the world is real or unreal. His chief interest lies in the delight of his devotion to God[1]. It is further held that the ordinary experience of the world can well be explained by a reference to world-analogies; but the transcendental relation existing between God, the individual, the souls and the world can hardly be so explained. The Upaniṣad texts declare the identity of the *jīva* and *parameśvara*; but they only mean that *parameśvara* and the *jīva* alike are pure consciousness.

God and His Powers.

Returning to the *Ṣaṭ-sandarbha*, one stumbles over the problem how the Brahman, who is pure consciousness and unchangeable, can be associated with the ordinary *guṇas* of *prakṛti*. The ordinary analogy of play cannot apply to God; children find pleasure in play or are persuaded to play by their playmates; but God is self-realized in Himself and His powers, He cannot be persuaded to act by anybody, He is always dissociated from everything, and is not swayed by passions of any kind. As He is above the *guṇas*, they and their actions cannot be associated with Him. We may also ask how the *jīva*, who is identical with God, can be associated with the beginningless *avidyā*. He being of the nature of pure consciousness, there ought not to be any obscuration of His consciousness, either through time or through space or through conditions or through any internal or external cause. Moreover, since God exists in the form of the *jīvas* in all bodies, the *jīvas* ought not to be under the bondage of afflictions or *karma*. The solution of such difficulties is to be found in the supra-rational nature of the *māyā-śakti* of God, which, being supra-logical, cannot be dealt with by the apparatus of ordinary logic. The fact that the power of God can be conceived as internal (*antaraṅga*) and external (*bahiraṅga*) explains why what happens in the region of God's external power cannot affect His own internal nature; thus, though God in the form of *jīvas* may be under the influence of *māyā* and the world-experience arising therefrom, He remains all the time unaffected in His own internal

[1] *satyaṃ na satyaṃ naḥ kṛṣṇa-pādābjāmodam antarā*
jagat satyaṃ asatyaṃ vā ko'yaṃ tasmin durāgrahaḥ. *Ibid.* p. 269.

nature. The supra-logical and supra-rational distinction existing between the threefold powers (*svarūpa* or *antaraṅga*, *bahiraṅga*, and *taṭastha*) of God and their relation to Him explains difficulties which ordinarily may appear insurmountable. It is this supra-logical conception that explains how God can be within the sway of *māyā* and yet be its controller[1]. The *jīva* in reality is not under the sway of afflictions, but still he appears to be so through the influence of God's *māyā*; just as in dreams a man may have all kinds of untrue and distorted experiences, so also the world-experiences are imposed on the self through the influence of God's *māyā*. The appearance of impurity in the pure *jīva* is due to the influence of *māyā* acting as its *upādhi* (or condition)—just as the motionless moon appears to be moving on the ripples of a flowing river. Through the influence of *māyā* the individual *jīva* identifies himself with the *prakṛti* and falsely regards the qualities of the *prakṛti* as his own[2].

God's Relation to His Devotees.

The incarnations of God are also to be explained on the same analogy. It is not necessary for God to pass through incarnations or to exert any kind of effort for the maintenance of the world; for He is omnipotent; all the incarnations of God recounted in the *Purāṇas* are for the purpose of giving satisfaction to the devotees (*bhaktas*). They are effected by the manifestation of the essential powers of God (*svarūpa-śaktyāviṣkaraṇa*), out of sympathy for His devotees. This may naturally be taken to imply that God is affected by the sorrows and sufferings of His devotees and that He is pleased by their happiness. The essential function of the essential power of God is called *hlādinī*, and the essence of this *hlādinī* is *bhakti*, which is of the nature of pure bliss. *Bhakti* exists in both God and the devotee, in a dual relation[3]. God is self-realized, for

[1] *Ṣaṭ-sandarbha*, p. 270.

[2] *yathā jale pratibimbitasya eva candramaso jalopādhikṛtaḥ kampādi-guṇo dharmo dṛśyate na tvākāśa-sthitasya tadvad anātmanaḥ prakṛti-rūpopādher dharmaḥ ātmanaḥ śuddhasyāsann api aham eva so'yam ity āveśān māyayā upādhi-tādātmyāpannāhaṃkārābhāsasya pratibimba-sthānīyasya tasya draṣṭur ādhyātmikāvasthasya eva yady api syāt tathāpi śuddhaḥ asau tad-abhedābhimānena taṃ paśyati. Ibid.* p. 272.

[3] *parama-sāra-bhūtāyā api svarūpa-śakteḥ sāra-bhūtā hlādinī nāma yā vṛttis tasya eva sāra-bhūto vṛtti-viśeṣo bhaktiḥ sā ca raty-apara-paryāyā. bhaktir bhagavati bhakteṣu ca nikṣipta-nijobhaya-koṭiḥ sarvadā tiṣṭhati. Ibid.* p. 274.

the *bhakti* exists in the *bhakta*, and being a power of God it is in essence neither different from nor identical with Him. *Bhakti* is only a special manifestation of His power in the devotee, involving a duality and rousing in God a special manifestation of delight which may be interpreted as pleasure arising from the *bhakti* of the devotee. When God says that He is dependent on the *bhakta*, the idea is explicable only on the supposition that *bhakti* is the essence of the essential power of God; the devotee through his *bhakti* holds the essential nature of God within him. Now the question arises whether God really feels sorrow when the devotees feel it, and whether He is moved to sympathy by such an experience of sorrow. Some say that God, being all-blissful by nature, cannot have any experience of sorrow; but others say that He has a knowledge of suffering, not as existing in Himself, but as existing in the devotee. The writer of *Ṣaṭ-sandarbha*, however, objects that this does not solve the difficulty; if God has experience of sorrow, it does not matter whether He feels the pain as belonging to Himself or to others. It must therefore be admitted that, though God may somehow have a knowledge of suffering, yet He cannot have experience of it; and so, in spite of God's omnipotence, yet, since He has no experience of the suffering of men, He cannot be accused of cruelty in not releasing everyone from his suffering. The happiness of devotees consists in the experience of their devotion, and their sorrow is over obstruction in the way of their realization of God. God's supposed pity for His devotee originates from an experience of his devotion, expressing itself in forms of extreme humility (*dainyātmaka-bhakti*), and not from experience of an ordinary sorrow. When God tries to satisfy the desires of His devotee, He is not actuated by an experience of suffering, but by an experience of the devotion existing in the devotee. If God had experience of the sorrows of others and if in spite of His omnipotence He had not released them from them, He would have to be regarded as cruel; so also, if He had helped only some to get out of suffering and had left others to suffer, He would have to be regarded as being only a partial God. But God has no experience of the sorrows of others; He only experiences devotion in others. The efficacy of prayer does not prove that God is partial; for there is no one dear to Him or enemy to Him; but, when through devotion the devotee prays for anything to Him, He being present in his heart in one through the devotion, grants him the object of his desire; so it is not necessary for God to pass through stages of incarnation for the protection or maintenance of the world; but still He does so in order to satisfy prayers to God. All the incarnations of God are for the fulfilment of the devotee's desires. The inscrutability of God's behaviour in the fulfilment of His devotee's desires is to be found in the inscrutability of the supra-rational nature of the essential power of God. Though all the works of God are absolutely independent and self-determined, yet they are somehow in accord with the good and bad deeds of man. Even when God is pleased to punish the misdeeds of those who are inimical to his devotees, such punishment is not effected by the rousing of anger in Him, but is the natural result of His own blissful nature operating as a function of His *hlādinī*[1]. But the writer of the *Ṣaṭ-sandarbha* is unable to explain the fact why the impartial and passionless God should destroy the demons for the sake of His devotees, and he plainly admits that the indescribable nature of God's greatness is seen when, in spite of His absolute impartiality to all, He appears to be partial to some. Though He in Himself is beyond the influence of *māyā*, yet in showing mercy to His devotees He seems to express Himself in terms of *māyā* and to be under its sway. The transition from the transcendent *sattva* quality of God to His adoption of the ordinary qualities of *prakṛti* is supra-rational and cannot be explained. But the writer of the *Ṣaṭ-sandarbha* always tries to emphasize the facts that God is on the one hand actuated by His purpose of serving the interest of His devotees and that on the other hand all His movements are absolutely self-determined—though in the ordinary sense self-determination would be incompatible with being actuated by the interest of others. He further adds that, though it may ordinarily appear that God is moved to action in certain critical happenings in the course of world-events or in the life of His devotee, yet, since these events of the world are also due to the manifestation of His own power as *māyā*, the parallelism that may be noticed between world-events and His own efforts cannot be said to invalidate the view that the latter are self-determined. Thus

[1] *atha yadi kecit bhaktānām eva dviṣanti tadā tadā bhakta-pakṣa-pātāntaḥ-pātitvād bhagavatā svayaṃ taddveṣe api na doṣaḥ pratyuta bhakta-viṣayaka-tad-rateḥ poṣakatvena hlādinī-vṛtti-bhūtānandollāsa-viśeṣa evāsau. Ṣaṭ-sandarbha.* p. 278.

His own efforts are naturally roused by Himself through the impulsion of *bhakti*, in which there is a dual manifestation of the essential power of God, as existing in Himself and in the heart of the devotee. It has already been said that *bhakti* is the essence of the essential power of God which has for its constituents the devotee and God. The prompting or rousing of God's powers through world-events is thus only a mere appearance (*pravṛtyā bhāsa*), happening in consonance with the self-determining activity of God. It is further said that God's activity in creating the world is also motivated by His interest in giving satisfaction to His devotees. Time is the defining character of His movement, and, when God determines Himself to move forward for creation through time-movement, He wishes to create His own devotees, merged in the *prakṛti*, out of His mercy for them. But in order to create them He must disturb the equilibrium of the *prakṛti*, and for this purpose His spontaneous movement as thought separates the power (as *jīva-māyā*) from His essential power (*svarūpa-śakti*); thus the equilibrium of the former is disturbed, and *rajas* comes into prominence. The disturbance may be supposed to be created in an apparent manner (*tacchesatātmakaprabhāvenaivoddīpta*) or by the dynamic of *kāla*[1]. When God wishes to enjoy Himself in His manifold creation, He produces *sattva*, and, when He wishes to lie in sleep with His entire creation, He creates *tamas*. Thus all the creative actions of God are undertaken for the sake of His devotees. The lying in sleep of God is a state of ultimate dissolution. Again, though God exists in all as the internal controller, yet He is not perceived to be so; it is only in the mind of the devotee that He really appears in His true nature as the inner controller.

The author of the *Ṣaṭ-sandarbha* is in favour of the doctrine of three *vyūhas* as against the theory of four *vyūhas* of the Pañcarātras. He therefore refers to the *Mahābhārata* for different traditions of one, two, three and four *vyūhas*, and says that this discrepancy is to be explained by the inclusion of one or more *vyūhas* within the others. The *Bhāgavata-purāṇa* is so called from the fact that it accepts Bhagavān as the principal *vyūha*[2]. The enquiry (*jijñāsā*) concerning this Brahman has been explained by Rāmānuja as *dhyāna*, but according to the *Ṣaṭ-sandarbha* this *dhyāna* is nothing

[1] *Ibid.* p. 283.

[2] *Ibid.*

but the worship of God in a definite form; for it is not easy to indulge in any *dhyāna* (or worship of God) without associating it with a form on which one may fix his mind. Brahman is described as unchanging ultimate truth, and, as sorrow only is changeable, He is also to be regarded as wholly blissful. Brahman is also regarded as *satyam*, because He is the self-determiner, and His existence does not depend on the existence or the will of anything else. He, by his power as self-luminosity, dominates His other power as *māyā*, and is in Himself untouched by it. This shows that, though *māyā* is one of His powers, yet in His own nature He is beyond *māyā*. The real creation coming out of *māyā* consists of the three elements of fire, water and earth partaking of each other's parts. The Śaṅkarites say that the world is not a real creation, but an illusory imposition like the silver in the conch-shell; but such an illusion can only be due to similarity, and, if through it the conch-shell can be conceived as silver, it is also possible that the silver may also be misconceived as conch-shell. It is by no means true that the ground (*adhiṣṭhāna*) of illusion should be one and the illusion manifold; for it is possible to have the illusion of one object in the conglomeration of many; the collocation of many trees and hills and fog may produce the combined effect of a piece of cloud. The world of objects is always perceived, while the Brahman is perceived as pure self-luminosity; and, if it is possible to regard Brahman also as illusory, that will practically mean that Brahman cannot any longer be regarded as the ground of the world. The world therefore is to be regarded as real. The monistic view, that the Brahman is absolutely devoid of any quality, is false; for the very name Brahman signifies that He is supremely great. The world also has not only come out of Him, but stays in Him and will ultimately be dissolved in Him. Moreover, the effect should have some resemblance to the cause, and the visible and tangible world, of which God is the cause, naturally signifies that the cause itself cannot be absolutely devoid of quality[1]. Even on the supposition that Brahman is to be defined as that from which the world-illusion has come into being, the point remains, that this in itself is a distinguishing quality; and, even if Brahman be regarded as self-luminous, the self-luminosity itself is a quality which distinguishes

[1] *sādhya-dharmāvyabhicāri-sādhana-dharmānvita-vastu-viṣayatvān na tattv apramāṇam. Ṣaṭ-sandarbha*. p. 27.

Brahman from other objects. If self-luminosity is a distinguishing quality, and if Brahman is supposed to possess it, He cannot be regarded as qualityless[1].

Nature of bhakti.

The author of the *Ṣaṭ-sandarbha* discusses in the *Kṛṣṇa-sandarbha* the then favourite theme of the Vaiṣṇavas that Lord Kṛṣṇa is the manifestation of the entire Godhood. The details of such a discussion cannot pertinently be described in a work like the present one, and must therefore be omitted.

In the *Bhakti-sandarbha* the author of the *Ṣaṭ-sandarbha* deals with the nature of *bhakti*. He says that, though the *jīvas* are parts of God's power, yet through beginningless absence of true knowledge of the ultimate reality their mind is turned away from it, and through this weakness their self-knowledge is obscured by *māyā*; they are habituated to looking upon the *pradhāna* (the product of *sattva*, *rajas* and *tamas*) as being identical with themselves, and thereby suffer the sorrows associated with the cycles of birth and re-birth. Those *jīvas*, however, who by their religious practices have inherited from their last birth an inclination towards God, or those who through a special mercy of God have their spiritual eyes opened, naturally feel inclined towards God and have a realization of His nature whenever they listen to religious instruction. It is through the worship of God that there arise the knowledge of God and the realization of God, by which all sorrows are destroyed. In the Upaniṣads it is said that one should listen to the Upaniṣadic texts propounding the unity of Brahma and meditate upon them. Such a course brings one nearer God, because through it the realization of Brahma is said to be possible. The processes of *aṣṭāṅga-yoga* may also be regarded as leading one near to God's realization. Even the performance of *karma* helps one to attain the proximity of God; by performing one's duties one obeys the commands of God, and in the case of obligatory duties the performer derives no benefit, as the fruits of those actions are naturally dedicated to God. Knowledge associated with *bhakti* is also

[1] *jagaj-janmādi-bhramo yatas tad brahmeti svotprekṣā-pakṣe ca na nirviśeṣa-vastu-siddhiḥ bhrama-mūlam ajñānam ajñāna-sākṣi brahmeti upagamāt. sākṣitvaṃ hi prakāśaikarasatayā ucyate. prakāśatvaṃ tu jaḍād vyāvartakaṃ svasya parasya ca vyavahāra-yogyatāpādana-svabhāvena bhavati. tathā sati saviśeṣatvaṃ tad-abhāve prakāśataiva na syāt tucchataiva syāt. Ibid.* p. 291.

negatively helpful by detaching one's mind from objects other than God; yet *bhakti* alone, exhibited in chanting God's name and in being intoxicated with emotion for God, is considered to be of supreme importance. The two forms of *bhakti* have but one objective, namely, to afford pleasure to God; they are therefore regarded as *ahetukī*. The true devotee finds a natural pleasure in chanting the name of God and absorbing himself in meditation upon God's merciful actions for the sake of humanity. Though the paths of duty and of knowledge are prescribed for certain classes of persons, yet the path of *bhakti* is regarded as superior; those who are in it need not follow the path of knowledge and the path of disinclination from worldly things[1]. All the various duties prescribed in the *śāstras* are fruitful only if they are performed through the inspiration of *bhakti*, and, even if they are not performed, one may attain his highest only through the process of *bhakti*.

Bhakti is also described as being itself the emancipation (*mukti*)[2]. True philosophic knowledge (*tattva-jñāna*) is the secondary effect of *bhakti*. True *tattva-jñāna* consists in the realization of God in His three-fold form, as Brahman, Paramātman and Bhagavān in relation to His threefold powers, with which He is both identical and different. This reality of God can only be properly realized and apperceived through *bhakti*[3]. Knowledge is more remote than realization. *Bhakti* brings not only knowledge, but also realization (*jñāna-mātrasya kā vārttā sākṣād api kurvanti*); it is therefore held that *bhakti* is much higher than philosophic knowledge, which is regarded as the secondary effect of it. The true devotee can realize the nature of God either in association with His Powers or as divested of them, in His threefold form or in any one of His forms, according as it pleases him. The effect of one's good deeds is not the attainment of Heaven, but success in the satisfaction of God through the production of *bhakti*. The *nididhyāsana* of the Upaniṣads means the worship of God (*upāsanā*) by reciting the name and glory of God; when one does so with full attachment to God, all the bonds of his *karma* are torn asunder. The real difficulty however lies in the generation in one's mind of

[1] *bhajatāṃ jñāna-vairagyābhyāsena prayojanaṃ nāsti*. *Ṣaṭ-sandarbha*, p. 481.
[2] *niścalā tvayi bhaktir yā saiva muktir janārdana* (quotation from *Skanda-purāṇa, Revākhaṇḍa*). *Ibid.* p. 451.
[3] *Ibid.* p. 454.

a natural inclination for turning to God and finding supreme satisfaction in reciting His name and glories. By association with true devotees one's mind gradually becomes inclined to God, and this is further intensified by the study of religious literature like the *Bhāgavata-purāṇa*. As an immediate result of this, the mind becomes dissociated from *rajas* and *tamas* (desires and afflictions), and by a further extension of the attachment to God there dawns the wisdom of the nature of God and His realization; as a result, egoism is destroyed, all doubts are dissolved, and all bondage of *karma* is also destroyed. Through reciting God's name and listening to religious texts describing His nature one removes objective ignorance regarding the nature of God, by deep thought and meditation one dispels one's own subjective ignorance through the destruction of one's illusory views regarding God, and by the realization and direct apprehension of God the personal imperfection which was an obstacle to the comprehension of the nature of God is destroyed. The following of the path of *bhakti* is different from the following of the path of duties in this, that, unlike the latter, the former yields happiness both at the time of following and also when the ultimate fulfilment is attained[1]. Thus one should give up all efforts towards the path of obligatory or other kinds of duties (*karma*), or towards the path of knowledge or of disinclination (*vairāgya*)[2]. These are fruitless without *bhakti*; for, unless the works are dedicated to God, they are bound to afflict one with the bondage of *karma*, and mere knowledge without *bhakti* is only external and can produce neither realization nor bliss; thus neither the obligatory (*nitya*) nor the occasional (*naimittika*) duties should be performed, but the path of *bhakti* should alone be followed. If the ultimate success of *bhakti* is achieved, there is nothing to be said about it; but, even if the path of *bhakti* cannot be successfully followed in the present life, there is no punishment in store for the devotee; for the follower of the path of *bhakti* has no right to follow the path of knowledge or of duties (*bhakti-rasikasya karmā-nādhikārat*)[3]. God manifests Himself directly in the conscious processes of all men, and He is the world-soul[4]; and He alone is

[1] *karmānuṣṭhānavan na sādhana-kāle sādhya-kāle vā bhaktyanuṣṭhānaṃ duḥkha-rūpaṃ pratyuta sukha-rūpam eva*. *Ibid.* p. 457.

[2] *Ibid.* p. 457.

[3] *Ibid.* p. 460.

[4] *sarveṣāṃ dhī-vṛttibhiḥ anubhūtaṃ sarvaṃ yena sa eka eva sarvāntarātmā*. *Ibid.* p. 460.

to be worshipped. Since *bhakti* is in itself identical with emancipation, our ultimate object of attainment is *bhakti* (*bhaktir evābhidheyaṃ vastu*). A man who is on the path of *bhakti* has no need to undergo troublous efforts for self-concentration; for the very devotion would by itself produce self-concentration in a natural and easy manner through the force of the devotional emotion. The place of *bhakti* is so high that even those who have attained saintliness or the stage of *jīvan-mukti* and whose sins have been burnt away may have their fall, and their sins may re-grow through the will of God, if they are disrespectful to God[1]. Even when through *bhakti* the bondage of *karma* has been destroyed, there is scope for a still higher extension of *bhakti*, through which one attains a still purer form of his nature. Thus *bhakti* is a state of eternal realizations which may subsist even when the impurities of bondage are entirely removed. God is the supreme dispenser of all things; through His will even the lowest of men may be transformed into a god, and the gods also may be transformed into the lowest of men. The existence of *bhakti* is regarded as the universal dispeller of all evils; thus *bhakti* not only removes all kinds of defects, but even the impending evils of *karmas* which are on the point of fructification (*prārabdha-karma*) are destroyed through its power[2]. A true devotee therefore wants neither ordinary emancipation nor anything else, but is anxious only to pursue the path of *bhakti*.

To a devotee there is nothing so desired as God. This devotion to God may be absolutely qualityless (*nirguṇa*). The true knowledge of God must be the knowledge of the qualityless (*nirguṇa*), and therefore true devotion to Him must also be qualityless (*nirguṇa*); for, in whatever way *bhakti* may manifest itself, its sole object is the qualityless God. The meaning of the word "qualityless" (or *nirguṇa*) is that in itself it is beyond the *guṇas*. It has been explained before that *bhakti* is nothing but a manifestation of God's essential power, and as such it has God only as its constituent, and it must therefore be regarded as beyond the *guṇas*; but in its expression *bhakti* may appear both as within or without the *guṇas*. Knowledge of Brahman may also be regarded as occurring in a twofold form;

[1] *jīvan-muktā api punar bandhanaṃ yānti karmabhiḥ*
yady acintya-mahā-śaktau bhagavaty aparādhinaḥ.
Ṣaṭ-sandarbha, p. 505.

[2] *Ibid.* p. 516.

as identity between the self and God, as in the case of the so-called Brahma-vādins; and with a certain kind of duality, as in the case of devotees. For this reason, though *bhakti* consists of knowledge and action, it is to be regarded as *nirguṇa*, because it refers to God alone, who is beyond all *guṇas*. *Bhakti* is thus obviously a transcendental process. It is no doubt true that sometimes it is described as being associated with *guṇas* (*saguṇa*); but in all such cases such a characterization of *bhakti* can only be on account of its association with intellectual, volitional or emotional qualities of the mind[1]. *Bhakti* really means "to live with God"; since God Himself is beyond the *guṇas*, residence with or in God must necessarily mean a state beyond the *guṇas*. There are others, however, who distinguish *bhakti* as worshipful action and as God-realizing knowledge, and according to them it is only the latter that is regarded as being beyond the *guṇas* (*nirguṇa*). But, though the actual worshipping action is manifested in and through the *guṇas*, the spiritual action determining it must be regarded as outside the material influences[2].

A question may here naturally arise, that if God is always of the nature of pure bliss, how is it possible for the devotee to please Him by his *bhakti*? This has already been explained, and it may further be added that *bhakti* is a mode of the self-realization of God's own blissful nature; its mode of operation is such that here the *hlādinī* power of God works itself by taking in the devotee as its constituent and its nature is such that it is blissful not only to God, but also to the devotee[3]. The appearance of *bhakti* in a devotee is due to God's will manifesting His self-realizing power in him, and such a manifestation of His will is to be interpreted as His mercy. So God is the real cause of the appearance of *bhakti* in any individual. It is to be remembered that not only the rise of *bhakti* but even the functioning of the sense-powers is due to the influence of God; thus God realizes Himself through men in all their conduct, though in *bhakti* alone His highest and most blissful nature expresses itself for the highest satisfaction of the devotee, and this must therefore be regarded as an act of His special grace. It is said in the scriptures that even a short recitation of God's name is

[1] *yat tu śrī-kapila-devena bhakter api nirguṇa-saguṇāvasthāḥ kathitās tat punaḥ puruṣāntaḥkaraṇa-guṇā eva tasyām upacaryante iti sthitam. Ibid.* p. 520.
[2] *Ibid.* p. 522.
[3] *Ibid.* p. 523.

sufficient to satisfy God, and those who consider these texts as exaggeration (*arthavāda*) are punished by God. But the true devotee does not cease from reciting the name of God because a single recital has been sufficient to please Him; for the very recital of God's name fills him with thrills of great joy. But still there are cases in which a single recital is not sufficient to produce the realization of God; in such cases it is to be presumed that the devotee is a great sinner. To those who are great sinners God is not easily inclined to extend His mercy; such persons should continually recite the name of God until their sins are thereby washed away and the desired end is attained. The recital of God's name is by itself sufficient to destroy even the worst of sins; but insincerity of mind (*kauṭilya*), irreligiosity (*aśraddhā*), and attachment to those things which impede our attachment to God are the worst vices; for through their presence the revelation of the process of *bhakti* in the mind is obstructed, and such persons cannot attach themselves to God[1]. Thus much learning and consequent crookedness of heart may prove to be a much stronger impediment to the rise of *bhakti* than even the commission of the deadliest of sins or submersion in deep ignorance; for God is merciful to the latter but not to the former; such attitudes of mind can only be due to the existence of very grave long-standing sins. A single recital is sufficient for success only when there are no previous sins and when no serious offences are committed after the recital of the name[2]; but, if at the time of death one recites the name of God, then a single recital is sufficient to dispel all sins and bring about intimate association with God[3].

Without religious faith (*śraddhā*) it is not possible for a man to follow the path either of knowledge or of duties; but still religious faith is an indispensable condition for those who wish to follow the path of *bhakti*. Once the religious *bhakti* is roused one should give up the path of knowledge and of duties. *Bhakti* does not require for its fulfilment the following of any ritual process. Just as fire naturally by itself burns the straw, so the recital of God's name and His glories would by itself, without the delay of any intermediary process, destroy all sins. Religious faith is not in itself a part of *bhakti*, but it is a pre-condition which makes the

[1] *Ṣaṭ-sandarbha*, pp. 532–4. [2] *Ibid.* p. 536.
[3] *Ibid.* p. 536.

rise of *bhakti*[1] possible. In following the path of *bhakti* one should not try to follow also the path of knowledge or of duties; such a course will be a strong impediment to the acceleration of *bhakti*.

If *bhakti* produces proximity to God, then, since God has three powers—Brahman, Paramātman, and Bhagavān—it is possible to have three kinds of proximity; of these the third is better than the second, and the second is better than the first. The realization of God as endowed with forms is superior to His realization without any forms. The true devotee prefers his position as the servant of God to any other so-called higher position of power and glory[2]; he therefore wishes for pure *bhakti*, unassociated with any other so-called beneficial results. It is these devotees, who want God and God alone, that are called the *ekāntins*, who are superior to all other types of devotees; this kind of *bhakti* is called *ákiñcana-bhakti*. It may be argued, that since all individuals are parts of God, and since they are naturally attached to Him as parts to wholes, the *ákiñcana-bhakti* should be natural to them all; but to this the reply is that man is not a part of God so far as He is in His own essential nature, but he is a part of Him so far as He is endowed with His diverse powers, including His neutral powers (*taṭastha-śakti*). Man is a part of God in the sense that both externally and internally he is in direct connection with God; but still he has his own instincts, tendencies, habits and the like, and it is these that separate him from God. For this reason, though man shares in the life of God and has the same life as He, yet, being hidden in his own sheath of ideas and tendencies, he cannot indulge in his natural truth-right of devotion to God except through the grace of God[3]. When a man is not under the sway of great obstructive sins such as crookedness and the like, association with other devotees gives an occasion to God for extending His grace in rousing devotion in his mind. It cannot be said that all beings must necessarily attain salvation; the number of souls is infinite, and only those will attain salvation who may happen to awaken His grace. Man from beginningless time is

[1] *bhakti* is said to have nine characteristics, as follows:

śravaṇaṃ kīrtanaṃ viṣṇoḥ smaraṇaṃ pāda-sevanaṃ
arccanaṃ vandanaṃ dāsyaṃ saukhyam ātma-nivedanam.

Ibid. p. 541.

But it is not necessary that *bhakti* should be pursued in all these ninefold forms.

[2] *ko mūḍho dāsatāṃ prapya prābhavaṃ padam icchati.* *Ibid.* p. 551.

[3] *Ibid.* p. 553.

ignorant of God and is disinclined from Him; and this natural impediment can only be removed by association with true devotees (*sat-saṅga*); God descends into men through the grace of good devotees who have at some time or other suffered like other ordinary people and are therefore naturally sympathetic to them[1]. God Himself cannot have sympathy with men, for sympathy presupposes suffering; God is of the nature of pure bliss and could not have experienced the suffering of ordinary beings.

The best devotee is he who perceives God in all beings, and also perceives all beings as parts of himself and of God as He reveals Himself in him[2]. The second type of devotee is he who has love for God, friendship for His devotees, mercy for the ignorant and indifference with reference to his enemies[3]. The lower type of devotee is he who worships the image of God with faith and devotion, but has no special feeling for the devotees of God or other persons[4]. There are other descriptions also of the nature of the best devotee: thus it is said in the *Gītā* that he whose heart is pure and unafflicted by the tendencies of desire and deeds, and whose mind is always attached to God, is to be regarded as the best devotee[5]; it is further said that the best devotee is he who makes no distinction between himself and others, or between his own things and those of others, and is the friend of all persons and at absolute peace with himself[6]; and, further, that the best devotee is he whose heart is held directly by God and holds within it in bonds of love the lotus-feet of God[7].

From another point of view *bhakti* is defined as service (*sevā*) or as that by which everything can be attained; the former is called *svarūpa-lakṣaṇa* and the latter *taṭastha-lakṣaṇa*. *Bhakti* is again regarded as being of a threefold nature: as merely external (*āropa-*

[1] *Ṣaṭ-sandarbha*, p. 557.

[2] *sarva-bhūteṣu yaḥ paśyed bhagavad-bhāvam ātmanaḥ.*
bhūtāni bhagavaty ātmany eṣa bhāgavatottamaḥ. *Ibid.* p. 561.

[3] *īśvare tad-adhīneṣu bāliśeṣu dviṣatsv api*
prema-maitrī-kṛpopekṣā yaḥ karoti sa madhyamaḥ. *Ibid.* p. 562.

[4] *arccāyām eva haraye pūjāṃ yaḥ śraddhayeate*
na tad-bhakteṣu cānyeṣu sa bhaktaḥ prākṛtaḥ smṛtaḥ.
Ibid. p. 564.

[5] *na kāma-karma-bījānāṃ yasya cetasi sambhavaḥ*
vāsudevaika-nilayaḥ sa vai bhāgavatottamaḥ. *Ibid.* p. 564.

[6] *na yasya svaḥ para iti vitteṣv ātmani vā bhidā*
sarva-bhūta-suhṛc chāntaḥ sa vai bhāgavatottamaḥ. *Ibid.* p. 565.

[7] *Ibid.* p. 565.

siddha), as due to association with other devotees (*saṅga-siddha*), and as due to a sincere spirit of natural affection for God (*svarūpa-siddha*). In the first two cases the *bhakti* is called fictitious (*kitava*), and in the last it is called real (*akitava*)[1]. The most direct action to be performed in the path of *bhakti* is to listen to and recite the names and glories of God, but indirectly associated with it there is also the dedication of all actions to God. In doing this one includes even his bad deeds; a devotee not only dedicates the fruits of his religious duties, ordinary duties of life, but also those which are done through the prompting of passions. He confesses to God all the imperfections of his nature and all the bad deeds that he has performed, and prays to Him for His grace by which all his sins are washed away. The devotee prays to God that he may be intoxicated by love for Him in the same manner that a young woman is smitten with love for a young man or *vice versa*[2]. When a man performs an action through motives of self-interest, he may suffer through failures or through deficient results; but, when one dedicates his actions to God, he no longer suffers any pains through such failures. All actions and their fruits really belong to God; it is only through ignorance or false notions that we appropriate them to ourselves and are bound by their ties. But, if those very actions are performed in the true perspective, we cannot in any way be bound down by their effects; thus those actions which are responsible for our births and rebirths can destroy that cycle and free us from their bondage, when it is realized they belong not to us, but to God[3]. If it is argued that the performance of mandatory actions produces a new and unknown potency (*apūrva*) in the performer, then also it may be argued that the real performer in the man is his inner controller (*antar-yāmin*), which impels him to do the action, and so the action belongs to this inner controller—God; and it is wrong to suppose that the performer of the action is the real agent[4]. Thus all the Vedic duties can be performed only by God as the supreme agent, and so the fruits of all actions can belong only to Him.

The dedication of our actions to God may again be of a twofold nature: one may perform an action with the express object of

[1] *Ṣaṭ-sandarbha*, pp. 581–2.

[2] *yuvatīnāṃ yathā yūni yūnāñca yuvatau yathā*
mano'bhiramate tadvan mano me ramatāṃ tvayi.
Viṣṇu-purāṇam, *ibid.* p. 58

[3] *Ibid.* p. 584.

[4] *Ibid.* p. 585.

pleasing God thereby, or he may perform the action without any desire to reap their fruits, and may dedicate them to God—one is *karma-sannyāsa* and the other *phala-sannyāsa*. Actions may be motivated either through desires or for the sake of God, i.e., leaving the effects to God or for pleasing God, and this last is said to be due to pure *bhakti*. These three types of actions are classified as *kāmanā-nimitta*, *naiṣkarmya-nimitta* and *bhakti-nimitta*. True devotees perform all their actions for the sake of pleasing God and for nothing else[1]. *Bhakti* again may be regarded as associated with *karma*, and as such it may be regarded as *sakāma*, *kaivalya-kāma* and *bhakti-mātra-kāma*. When one becomes devoted to God for the fulfilment of ordinary desires, this is regarded as *sakāma-bhakti*. *Kaivalya-kāma-bhakti* may be regarded as associated with *karma* or with *karma* and knowledge (*jñāna*); this is to be found in the case of one who concentrates upon God and enters into the path of *yoga*, practises detachment, and tries to conceive of his unity with God, and through such processes frees himself from the bondage of *prakṛti*; through knowledge and action he tries to unify the *jīvātman* with the *paramātman*. The third type may be associated either with *karma* or with *karma* and *jñāna*. Of these the first class expresses their devotion by reciting God's name and glories, by continually worshipping Him, and by dedicating all their actions to God. The second class of devotees add to their duties of worship to God the continual pursuit of an enlightened view of all things; they think of all people as manifestations of God; they are patient under all exciting circumstances and detach themselves from all passions; they are respectful to the great and merciful to the humble and the poor, and friendly to their equals; they practise the virtues included within *yama* and *niyama*, destroy all their egotism, and continue to think of the glory of God and to recite His name. He who, however, has the highest type of *bhakti*—the *akiñcana-bhakti*—in him it is such that simply on hearing the name of God his mind flows to Him just as the waters of the Ganges flow into the ocean. Such a one does not accept anything that may be given to him; his only pleasure exists in being continuously immersed in God.

From another point of view *bhakti* can be divided into two classes, *vaidhī* and *rāgānuga*. The *vaidhī-bhakti* is of two kinds, leading him to devote himself to God, and to worship without any

[1] *Ṣaṭ-sandarbha*, p. 586.

ulterior motive. It is *vaidhī* because here the prompting to the course of *bhakti* comes from scriptural sources (otherwise called *vidhi*, or scriptural injunctions). The *vaidhī-bhakti* is of various kinds, such as seeking of protection (*śaraṇāpatti*), association with good teachers and devotees, to listen to God's name and to recite His name and glories[1]. Of these *śaraṇāgati* is the most important; it means seeking protection of God upon being driven to despair by all the dangers and sufferings of life. Thus in *śaraṇāgati* there must be a driving cause which impels one to seek the protection of God as the sole preserver. Those who turn to God merely out of deep attachment for Him are also impelled by their abhorrence of their previous state, when their minds were turned away from God. It also implies a belief either that there is no other protector, or a renunciation of any other person or being to whom one had clung for support. One should leave all hope in the Vedic or *smṛti* injunctions, and turn to God as the only support. *Śaraṇāpatti* may be defined as consisting of the following elements: (i) to work and think always in a manner agreeable to God, (ii) to desist from anything that may in any way displease God, (iii) strong faith that He will protect, (iv) clinging to Him for protection, (v) to throw oneself entirely into God's hands and to consider oneself entirely dependent on Him, and (vi) to consider oneself a very humble being waiting for the grace of God to descend on him[2]. Of all these the main importance is to be attached to the adoption of God alone as sole protector, with whom the other elements are only intimately associated. But next to the solicitation of the protection of God is the solicitation of help from one's religious teacher (*guru*) and devotion to his service, as well as to the service of great men, by whose association one may attain much that would be otherwise unattainable[3]. One of the chief forms in which the *vaidhī-bhakti* manifests itself is in regarding oneself as the servant of God, or in considering God as our best friend. The sentiments of service and friendship should be so deep and intense as to lead one to renounce

[1] *atha vaidhī-bhedāḥ śaraṇāpatti-śrī-gurv-ādi-sat-sevā-śravaṇa-kīrtanā-dayaḥ. Ṣaṭ-sandarbha*, p. 593.

[2] *śaraṇāpatter lakṣaṇaṃ vaiṣṇava-tantre,*
ānukūlyasya saṃkalpaḥ prātikūlya-vivarjanam
rakṣiṣyatīti viśvāso goptṛtve varaṇaṃ tathā
ātma-nikṣepa-kārpaṇye ṣaḍvidhā śaraṇāgatiḥ. *Ibid.* p. 593.

[3] *Ibid.* pp. 595–604.

one's personality entirely to God; this complete renunciation of oneself to God is technically called *ātma-nivedana*. The *rāgānuga*, or purely emotional type of *bhakti*, must be distinguished from *vaidhī-bhakti*; since the *rāgānuga-bhakti* follows only the bent of one's own emotions, it is difficult to define its various stages. In this form of *bhakti* the devotee may look upon God as if He were a human being, and may turn to Him with all the ardour and intensity of human emotions and passions; thus one of the chief forms in which this type of *bhakti* manifests itself is to be found in those cases where God is the object of a type of deep love which in human relation would be called sex-love. Sex-love is one of the most intense passions of which our human nature is capable, and, accordingly, God may be loved with the passionate intensity of sex-love. In following this course of love the devotee may for the time being forget the divinity of God, may look upon Him as a fellow-being, and may invest Him with all the possibilities of human relations and turn to Him as if He were his intimate friend or a most beloved husband. He may in such circumstances dispense entirely with the ritualistic formalities of worship, meditation, recital of His names or glories, and simply follow his own emotional bent and treat God just as may befit the tendency of his emotion at the time. There may however be stages where the *rāgānuga* is mixed up with *vaidhī*, where the devotee follows some of the courses of the *vaidhī-bhakti* and is yet passionately attached to God. But those who are simply dragged forward by passion for God are clearly above the range of the duties of *vaidhī-bhakti*; not only through such passionate attachment to God, but even when one's mind is filled with a strong emotion of anger and hatred towards God, so as to make one completely forget oneself and to render oneself entirely pervaded by God's presence—even as an object of hatred—one may, by such an absorption of one's nature in God, attain one's highest. The process by which one attains one's highest through *rāgānuga-bhakti* is the absorption of the nature of the devotee by God through an all-pervading intense emotion. For this reason, whenever the mind of a man is completely under the sway of a strong emotion of any description with reference to God, he is absorbed, as it were, in God's being and thus attains his highest through a complete disruption of his limited personality.

In the sixth section, the *Prīti-sandarbha*, the author of the *Ṣaṭ-sandarbha* deals with the nature of bliss (*prīti*) as the ultimate reality and object of the best of our human efforts. The ultimate object or end of man is the attainment of happiness and the destruction of sorrow; only when God is pleased can one secure the ultimate extinction of sorrow and the attainment of eternal happiness. God, the ultimate reality, is the ultimate and infinite bliss, though He may show Himself in diverse forms. The individual or the *jīva*, not having any true knowledge of God and being obscured by *māyā*, fails to know His true nature, becomes associated with many subjective conditions, and undergoes the sorrow of beginningless cycles of births and rebirths. The realization of the highest bliss consists in the realization of the ultimate reality; this can happen only through the cessation of one's ignorance and the consequent ultimate cessation of one's sorrows. Of these the former, though expressed in a negative form, is in reality positive, being of the nature of the self-luminosity of the ultimate reality and the self-manifestation of the same. The latter, being of the nature of a negation through destruction, is eternal and unchangeable—such that, when sorrows are once ultimately uprooted, there cannot be any further accretion of sorrow. The realization of God is thus the only way of attaining the highest happiness or bliss[1]. Emancipation (*mukti*) is the realization of God, accompanied as a consequence by that cessation of the bondage of egoism which is the same thing as existence in one's true nature. This existence in one's own nature is the same thing as the realization of one's own nature as the supreme soul (Paramātman). But in this connection it must be noted that the *jīva* is not identical with the supreme soul; for it is only a part of it; its nature as bliss is thus to be affirmed only because of the fact that its essence is derived from the essence of the supreme soul. The realization of God, the absolute whole, is only through the realization of His part as the supreme soul (*aṃśena aṃśi-prāpti*). This can be attained in two ways, first, as the attainment of Brahmahood by the revelation of His knowledge as constituting only His essential powers along with the destruction of individual ignorance (which is a state or function of *māyā* only);

[1] *nirastātiśayāhlāda-sukha-bhāvaika-lakṣaṇā*
bheṣajaṃ bhagavat-prāptir ekāntātyantikā matā.
Viṣṇu-purāṇa, *Ṣaṭ-sandarbha*, p. 674.

secondly, as the realization of God in His personal nature, as associated with His supra-rational powers in a personal manner. Emancipation (*mukti*) may be achieved both in life and after death; when one realizes the true nature of God, one's false apprehension of His nature vanishes and this is one's state of *mukti*; at death also there may be a revelation of God's true nature, and a direct and immediate realization of His nature as God.

Ultimate Realization.

The realization of the nature of ultimate reality may again be of a twofold nature: abstract, i.e., as Brahman, and concrete, i.e., as personal God or the supreme soul (Paramātman). In the latter case the richness of the concrete realization is further increased when one learns to realize God in all His diverse forms[1]. In this stage, though the devotee realizes the diverse manifold and infinite powers of God, he learns to identify his own nature with the nature of God as pure bliss. Such an identification of God's nature manifests itself in the form of the emotion of *bhakti* or joy (*prīti*); the devotee experiences his own nature as joy, and realizes his oneness with God through the nature of God as bliss or joy. It is through the experience of such joy that the ultimate cessation of sorrow becomes possible, and without it the devotee cannot realize God in association with all His diverse and infinite powers. By the intimate experience of the joyous nature of God His other attributes, characters and powers can also be revealed to him. Man naturally seeks to realize himself through joy; but ordinarily he does not know what is the true object of joy, and thus he wastes his energies by seeking joy in diverse worldly objects. He attains his true end when he realizes that God is the source of all joy, that He alone should be sought in all our endeavours, and that in this way alone can one attain absolute joy and ultimate liberation in joy. The true devotee wishes to attain *kaivalya*; but *kaivalya* means "purity," and, as the true nature of God is the only ultimate purity, *kaivalya* would mean the realization of God's nature. The joy of the realization of God and God alone should therefore be regarded as the true *kaivalya*, the ultimate nature of God.

In the state of *jīvan-mukti* the individual, through a true knowledge of himself and his relation to God, comes to realize that the

[1] *Ṣaṭ-sandarbha*, p. 675.

world is both being and non-being, and has therefore no real existence in its own true nature, but is only regarded as part of himself through his own ignorance (*avidyā*). The mere negation of the world is not enough; for there is here also the positive knowledge of the true nature of the individual as dependent on God. In this stage the individual realizes the falsity of associating world-experiences with his own nature, and learns to identify the latter as a part of God. In this state he has to experience all the fruits of his deeds which are on the point of yielding fruits, but he feels no interest in such experiences, and is no longer bound by them[1]. As a further culmination of this stage, the functioning of *māyā* in its individual form as ignorance (*avidyā*) ceases with the direct and immediate revelation of the true nature of God and with participation in His true nature as joy; the complete cessation of *māyā* should therefore be regarded as the final state of *mukti*[2].

It should be borne in mind that the *jīva* is a part of the ultimate reality in association with the energy of God as represented in the totality of the *jīvas*. The ultimate reality is like the sun and the *jīvas* are like the rays which emanate from it. From their root in God they have sprung out of Him, and, though seemingly independent of Him, are yet in complete dependence on Him. Their existence outside of Him also is not properly to be asserted; for in reality such an appearance of existence outside Him is only the effect of the veil of *māyā*. The comparison of the *jīvas* with the rays merely means that they have no separate existence from that body whose rays they are, and in this sense they are entirely dependent on God. When the *jīvas* are regarded as the power or energy of God, the idea is that they are the means through which God expresses Himself. As God is endowed with infinite powers, it is not difficult to admit that the *jīvas*, the manifestations of God's power, are in themselves real agents and enjoyers, and the suggestion of the extreme monist, that to assert agency or enjoyability of them is illusory, is invalid; for agency in an individual is a manifestation of God's power. It is through that that the *jīvas* pass through the cycle of *saṃsāra*, and it is through the operation of the essential power of God that they learn to perceive the identity of their own nature with God and immerse themselves in emotion towards Him. The view that there is

[1] *asya prārabdha-karma-mātrāṇām anabhiniveśenaiva bhogaḥ. Ibid.* p. 678.
[2] *Ibid.* p. 678.

no experience of joy in the state of emancipation is invalid; for in that case the state of emancipation would not be desirable. Moreover, the view that in the state of emancipation one becomes absolutely identical with Brahman, which is of the nature of pure joy, is also wrong; for no one wishes to become identical with joy, but to experience it. The extreme form of monism cannot therefore explain why the state of emancipation should be desirable; if emancipation cannot be proved to be an intensely desirable state, there will be no reason why anyone should make any effort to attain it. It may further be added that, if the ultimate reality be of the nature of pure bliss and knowledge, there is no way of explaining why it should be subject to the obscuring influence of *māyā*. The conception of whole and part explains the fact that, though the *jīvas* are not different from God, yet they are not absolutely identical, being indeed entirely dependent on Him. The proper way of regarding God is to recognize Him as presiding over all beings as they are associated with their specific conditions and limitations—as varied personalities and yet as one; this is the way to unify the concept of Paramātman with that of Bhagavan[1].

The Joy of bhakti.

Joy in God may be of a twofold nature. By an extension of meaning joy may be that attachment to God which produces the realization of the true conception of God (*bhagavad-viṣayānukulyātmakas tad-anugata-spṛhā dimayo jñāna-viśeṣas tat-prītiḥ*). But there is a more direct experience of joy in God which is directly of an intensely emotional nature; this type of *bhakti* is also called *rati*. This is also described as *bhakti* as love (*preman*). Just as one is attracted to physical objects by their beauty, apart from any notion of utility, so one may also be attracted by divine beauty and the diverse qualities of God, and fall into intense love with Him. It has already been said above that the joy of God manifests itself in the hearts of His devotees and produces their joyful experience of God.

[1] Apart from the higher kind of *mukti* reserved for the most superior type of *bhaktas* there are other kinds of inferior liberation described as *sālokya* (coexistence with God), *sārṣṭi* (the advantage of displaying the same miraculous powers as God), *sārūpya* (having the same form as that of God), *sāmīpya* (having the privilege of always being near God), *sāyujya* (the privilege of entering into the divine person of God). A true *bhakta*, however, always rejects these privileges, and remains content with his devotion to God. *Ṣaṭ-sandarbha*, p. 691.

This may be regarded as an active phase of God's joy as distinguished from His nature as pure joy. God's joy is said to be of two kinds: His nature as pure joy (*svarūpānanda*), and His nature in the active phases of the joy of His own powers (*svarūpa-śaktyānanda*). This last is again of two kinds, viz., *mānasānanda* and *aiśvaryānanda*, i.e., joy as the active operation of *bhakti*, and joy in His own majesty[1]. When a devotee is attached to God by a sense of His greatness or majesty, such a state of mind is not regarded as an instance of joy or *prīti*; but, when the *bhakti* takes a purely emotional form as the service of God, or as immediately dependent on Him, or as attached to Him through bonds of intense love (like those of a bride for her lover, of a friend for his friend, of a son for his father or of the father for his child), we have *bhakti* as *prīti*. *Prīti* or "joy" manifests itself in its most intense and elevated form when the attraction has all the outward appearance of physical love, and all the well-known exciting factors and modes of enjoyment of that emotion; but, as this emotion is directed towards God and has none of the biological or physiological accompaniments of physical love, it should be sharply distinguished from that love; but it has all the external expressions of erotic love. For this reason it can be properly described only in terms of the inward experience and the outward expressions of erotic love. Joy (*prīti*) is defined as an emotional experience constituting an inclination and attraction towards its object[2]. In ordinary emotions the objects to which they have reference are worldly objects of sense or ideas associated with them, but in godward emotions God is their only object. Such a joy in God flows easily (*svābhāvikī*) through God's grace, and is not the result of great efforts; it is superior to emancipation[3]. This joy may grow so much in intensity that the devotee may forget himself

[1] *Ibid*. p. 722

[2] *tatra ullāsātmako jñāna-viśeṣaḥ sukham; tathā viṣayānukūlyātmakas tad-ānukūlyānugata-tat-spṛhā-tad-anubhava-hetukollāsa-maya-jñāna-viśeṣa-priyatā. Ibid*. p. 718.

[3] The yearning implied in *bhakti* is almost a distressing impulse and is not only erotic in type. Thus it is said:

ajāta-pakṣā iva mātaraṃ khagāḥ
stanyaṃ yathā vatsatarāḥ kṣudhārtāḥ
priyaṃ priyeva vyuṣitaṃ viṣaṇṇo
mano'ravindākṣa didṛkṣate tvāṃ. *Ibid*. p. 726.

Two stages are sometimes distinguished according to the intensity of the development of joy, viz., *udaya*, *īṣad-udgama*; the latter has again two stages. The culminating stage is called *prakaṭodayāvasthā*.

completely and feel himself as one with God; this is technically called *mahābhāva*[1]. In a general sense *bhakti* may be said to produce a sense of unique possession (*mamatā*), and consequently great attachment of heart; this emotion may express itself in various forms. But there is also the other quieter form (*śānta*) of devotion, in which the devotee feels himself to be of God, but not that God is his, like Sanaka and other devotees of his type[2]. Here also there is a remote sense of God's possession, i.e., as master—as looking forward for His grace as a master (*bhṛtyatva*), protector (*pālyatva*), or as a fond parent (*lālyatva*). One may also enjoy God in himself, assuming the rôle of a parent and looking upon God as a dear child; this kind of emotion is called *vātsalya*. But, as has been said above, the most intense joy in God takes the conjugal form; the difference between eroticism (*kāma*) and this type of love (*rati*) is that the former seeks self-satisfaction, while the latter seeks the satisfaction of the beloved God; yearning is the common element in both. These devotees, through their dominant emotion of love, restrict their relation to God solely to His aspect of sweetness (*mādhurya*), as a great lover. The affection of Rādhā for Kṣṛṇa is said to illustrate the highest and intensest form of this love. The Vaiṣṇava writers frequently explain this love in accordance with the analysis of ordinary mundane love current in books of rhetoric (*alaṃkāra-śāstra*).

In treating of the subject of *bhakti* it is impossible not to make a short reference to the well known work of Rūpa Gosvāmī, *Bhakti-rasāmṛta-sindhu*. This work is divided into four books, *pūrva*, *dakṣiṇa*, *paścima*, and *uttara*, and each of these is divided into chapters called *laharīs*. In writing out the chapters of the *Bhakti-sandarbha* and the *Prīti-sandarbha* Jīva Gosvāmī, the nephew of Rūpa, was much indebted to the above work of the latter, on which he had also written a commentary, *Durgama-saṅgamana*, after the

[1] *Ṣaṭ-sandarbha*, p. 732. There occurs here a quotation from *Ujjvala-nīlamaṇi* to illustrate the situation:

rādhāyā bhavataśca citta-jatunī svedair vilāpya kramād
yuñjann adri-nikunja-kuñjara-pater nirdhūta-bheda-bhramam
citrāya svayam anvaranjayad iha brahmāṇḍa-harmyodare
bhūyobhir nava-rāga-hiṅgula-phalaiḥ śṛṅgāra-cāruḥ kṛtiḥ.

[2] *saty api bhedāpagame nātha tavāhaṃ na māmakīnas tvaṃ samudro hi taraṅgaḥ kvacana samudro na tāraṅgaḥ. Ibid.* p. 735. *harer guṇā dvividhāḥ bhakta-citta-saṃskāra-hetavas tadabhimāna-viśeṣya-hetavas'cānye...* (p. 733). *jñāna-bhaktir bhaktir vātsalyam maitrī kānta-bhāvaśca* (p. 738). Though all these different varieties of *bhakti* are mentioned, it is admitted that various other forms may arise from these simply by their mutual mixture in various degrees.

completion of the *Bhāgavata-sandarbha.* Superior (*uttama*) *bhakti* is here defined as the mental state and the associated physical actions for yielding satisfaction to Kṛṣṇa (*ānukūlyena kṛṣṇā-nuśīlanam*) without any further desire, motive or object of any description; such a *bhakti* must not be associated with any monistic philosophical wisdom, such as that of extreme monists like Śaṅkara, or the philosophical wisdom of Sāṃkhya, Yoga and other systems, nor with the performance of any obligatory or occasional duties as enjoined in the *smṛti* literature[1]. Such a *bhakti* has six characteristics. First, it destroys sins, their roots and ignorance. Sins are of two kinds, those which are not in a state of fruition (*aprārabdha*), and those which are (*prārabdha*); and *bhakti* removes them both. The roots of sins are evil tendencies of the mind, otherwise called the *karmāśayas*, and these too are destroyed by *bhakti*, which, as it is concrete wisdom, also destroys ignorance (*avidyā*). Secondly, it is described as holy or good (*śubhada*). Through *bhakti* one renders happiness to the world and is attached by bonds of friendship and love to all people; as a devotee is a friend of all, all beings are also his friends. Thirdly, a devotee is so much satisfied with his joy in *bhakti* that emancipation has no attractions for him. Fourthly, the attainment of *bhakti* is extremely difficult; for even with the utmost effort one may not attain it without the grace of God. Fifthly, the joy of *bhakti* is infinitely superior to the joy of emancipation through Brahma-knowledge. Sixthly, *bhakti* overcomes God to such an extent that He is completely drawn to the service of His devotee. Even a little *bhakti* is superior to much philosophical learning; philosophical and logical discussions lead to no certainty, and the thesis established by an able reasoner may easily be disproved by another who is abler; such logical discussions are only barren and ineffectual for true realization.

Rūpa distinguishes three kinds of *bhakti*: *sādhana*, *bhāva* and *preman*[2]. The *sādhana-bhakti* stands for the different means whose

[1] *anyābhilāsitā-śūnyaṃ jñāna-karmādy-anāvṛtam*
ānukūlyena kṛṣṇānuśīlanaṃ bhaktir uttamā.
Bhakti-rasāmṛta-sindhu, I. I. 9.

[2] *Ibid.* I. 2. I:
sa bhaktiḥ sādhanaṃ bhāvaḥ premā ceti tridhoditā.
In commenting upon this passage Jīva Gosvāmī says that *bhakti* is of two kinds, *sādhana* and *sādhya*; of these the second is of pure emotionalism and consists of five varieties: *bhāva*, *prema*, *praṇaya*, *sneha* and *rāga*. The author of *Ujjvala-nīla-maṇi* adds three more, *māna*, *anurāga* and *mahā-bhāva*. Rūpa has not mentioned these last because they are but variant forms of *prema*.

adoption enables the mental emotion to emerge in a natural way as *bhāva-bhakti* (also called *sādhya-bhakti*). But Rūpa further adds that the natural devotional emotion cannot be produced by any course of conduct or any effort; for *bhakti* is the highest good and as such is eternal. Nothing that is eternal can be produced; the true devotional emotion therefore cannot be created—it already exists in the heart, and the function of the *sādhana-bhakti* is merely to manifest it in the heart in the enjoyable form[1]. This *sādhana-bhakti* is of two kinds, *vaidhī* and *rāgānuga*[2]: these have already been described above. One is within the sphere of *vaidhī-bhakti* only so long as natural attachment to God does not reveal itself within one's heart. It is said that one who has a logical mind and is well read in the *śāstras*, and is also a man of firm conviction with a great faith in the Vaiṣṇava religion, is best fitted for *vaidhī-bhakti*[3]. Desire for worldly happiness or for emancipation is the greatest obstacle to the rise of *bhakti*. One following the path of *bhakti* incurs no demerit if he does not perform the obligatory and other duties as enjoined in the Vedas; but he is at fault if he does not perform the true duties of a Vaiṣṇava; but even in such cases a Vaiṣṇava need not perform any expiatory duties; for the mere recital of God's name is sufficient to remove all his sins. No injunctions of the *śāstras* have any reference to a devotee. The complete code of moral virtues and many ritualistic duties are counted as preliminary conditions for a person following the path of *bhakti*[4]. In many undeserving pupils too much learning or indulgence is regarded as a great obstruction of the path of *bhakti*[5]. A devotee of the *vaidhī* type should meditate upon the beauty of God and all His qualities and glories, and learn to regard himself as His servant; one of the conditions of meditation upon God as master is to train oneself in dedicating all one's actions to God. He should also try

[1] *kṛti-sādhyā bhavet sādhya-bhāvā sā sādhanābhidhā*
nitya-siddhasya bhāvasya prākaṭyaṃ hṛdi sādhyatā.
Bhakti-rasāmṛta-sindhu, I. 2. 2.

[2] *Ibid.* I. 2. 4.

[3] *śāstre yuktau ca nipuṇaḥ sarvathā dṛḍha-niścayaḥ*
prauḍha-śraddho'dhikārī yaḥ sa bhaktāvuttamaḥ mataḥ.
Ibid. I. 2. 11.

[4] *Ibid.* I. 2. 42, etc.

[5] *na śiṣyān anubadhnīta granthān naivābhyased bahūn*
na vyākhyām upayuñjīta nārambhān ārabhet kvacit.
Ibid. I. 2. 52.

to generate in himself the firm conviction that God is the greatest friend of His devotees; one should try to look upon God as one's best friend. The Śāstric duties should be performed only so long as there is no real inclination of the mind towards God, to recite His name, to listen to His glories, and to say them with joy. As soon as this stage comes, one is on the path of *vaidhī-bhakti* and must follow its specific duties, so that it may continually grow into a truly natural and irresistible emotion. Here begins the stage of *sādhya-bhakti* with *bhāva.* Even before we come to this there is another stage of *sādhana-bhakti*, the *rāgānuga.* It is only when one transcends this stage that one can come to a still higher stage of the *sādhya-bhakti* with its successive developments. *Rāgānuga-bhakti* is said to be an imitation of the *rāgātmikā*[1]. The *rāgātmikā-bhakti* is the *bhakti* as natural attachment; *rāga* means "attachment". This *rāgātmikā-bhakti* may be of the type of erotic emotion (*kāma*) or the assumption of other relationships[2], such as friendship, parenthood, etc. The *rāgānuga-bhakti* is that where there is no natural attachment, but where there is an effort to imitate the forms of natural emotional attachment, and it may be associated with the diverse steps taken for the furtherance of *vaidhī-bhakti.* The distinction of *prema* (spiritual love) and *kāma* has already been explained above. Though *kāma* is often used in connection with the intoxicating love of God, yet it is used in the sense of *prema*[3]. The *rāgānuga-bhakti* thus following the two kinds of subdivision of *rāgātmikā-bhakti* is itself also of two kinds, *kāmānuga* and *sambandhānuga.*

From the second stage of *sādhana-bhakti* as *rāgānuga* we come to the stage of *bhāva-bhakti*, which also evolves itself into ever more

[1] *virājantīm abhivyaktāṃ vraja-vāsi-janādiṣu*
rāgātmikām anusṛtā yā sā rāgānugocyate. *Ibid.* I. 2. 131.

[2] It is said that in the case of natural attachment, even when it takes the form of an inimical relationship to God, it is superior to any type of *vaidhī-bhakti* where there is no such natural attachment. Thus it is said in Jīva's *Durgama-saṅgamana*, I. 2. 135: *yathā vairānubandhena martyas tanmayatam iyāt na tathā bhakti-yogena iti me niścitā matiḥ tad api rāgamaya-kāmādy-upekṣayā vidhimayasya cittāveśa-hetutve'tyanta-nyūnatvam iti vyañjanārtham eva. yeṣu bhāvamayeṣu nindito'pi vairānubandho vidhimaya-bhakti-yogāc chreṣṭhāḥ.* The natural feeling of enmity towards God can be regarded as *bhāvātmikā* (or emotional) but not as *rāgātmikā.* It cannot also be regarded as *bhakti*, for there is no desire here to please God; it therefore stands on a separate basis; it is inferior to *rāgātmikā-bhakti* but superior to *vaidhī-bhakti.*

[3] *premaiva gopa-rāmāṇāṃ kāma ityagamat prathām.* *Ibid.* I. 2. 142, 143.

intense forms until it reaches the stage of *mahā-bhāva* already described. It is regarded as the manifestation of the pure transcendent *sattva* (the blissful nature of God). *Bhakti* has already been defined as behaviour that is intended to please God and which has no further object or end in view; as such it would involve some kind of effort (*ceṣṭā-rūpa*) on the part of the devotee. But here the meaning is modified to denote only the emotional condition of mind, including physiological and physical changes produced in the body by it, and as roused by emotive conditions such as the object of love, excitants of love, the feeding emotions, external manifestation determining and increasing the original dominant emotion[1]. The first stage of natural attachment to God as love is called *bhāva* and is associated with slight physiological effects like shedding tears or the rising of the hair on the body and the like[2]. This emotion is of a transcendental nature and of the nature of the power of God, involving consciousness and bliss; therefore it is on the one hand self-revealing (*svaprakāśa*) and self-enjoying, and on the other hand it reveals the nature of God, whose power it is, and to whom it refers. Being a power of God it appears in the mental states of the devotee, becomes identified with them, and manifests itself in identity with them. *Bhakti*, as it appears in the devotee, is thus an identity of the transcendent and the phenomenal, and reveals the dual function of enjoying the sweetness of the nature of God and the self-revealing sweet enjoyable nature of its own. It is thus cognitive with reference to its object, and involves a dual enjoyment of God's sweet nature as well as the sweet nature of *bhakti* itself. It is the root of all *rati* (or enjoyment) and is therefore also called *rati*[3]. An inferior amount of it is generally common to all,

[1] *śarīrendriya-vargasya vikārāṇāṃ vidhāyikāḥ*
bhāva-vibhāva-janitāś' citta-vṛttayaḥ īritāḥ.
Durgama-saṅgamana, I. 3. I.

[2] *premnas tu prathamāvasthā bhāva ity abhidhīyate*
sāttvikāḥ svalpa-mātrāḥ syuryatrāśru-pulakādayaḥ.
Bhakti-rasāmṛta-sindhu, I. 3. 3.

[3] *asau śuddha-sattva-viśeṣarūpa-rati-mūla-rūpatvena mukhya-vṛttyā tac-chabda-vācyā sā ratiḥ śrī-kṛṣṇādi-sarva-prakāśakatvena hetunā svayaṃ-prakāśa-rūpā'pi prapañcika-tat-priya-jananaṃ mano-vṛttau āvir-bhūya tat-tādātmyaṃ vrajantī tad-vṛttyā prakāśyavad bhāṣamānō brahmavat tasyāḥ sphurantī, tathā svasatkṛtena purvottarāvasthābhyām kāraṇa-kāryya-rūpeṇa śrī-bhagavadādi-mādhuryyānubhavena svāṃśena svāda-rūpā'pi yāni kṛṣṇādirūpāṇı teṣām āsvādasya hetutāṃ saṃvidaṃśena sādhakatamatāṃ pratipadyate hlādinyaṃśe tu svayaṃ hlādayantī tiṣṭhati.* *Durgama-saṅgamana*, I. 3. 4.

but the superior appearance which continues to grow is rare and comes only through the grace of God or His devotees. So even in the *vaidhī* and the *rāgānuga* also there is, no doubt, some amount of *bhāva* of the inferior type. The natural attachment to God of the superior type which arises without going through the ordinary prescribed path of *bhakti* (the *sādhana-bhakti*), is generally due to the grace of God.

In the first stage of the *bhāva-bhakti* the devotee manifests in himself a nature which remains absolutely unperturbed, even though there may be causes of perturbation; he always spends his time in reciting God's name with strong emotion; he is unattached to sense-objects, and, though great, he is always extremely humble, and has always the strong conviction of attaining the ultimate realization of God. He is also always extremely anxious to attain his end and always finds pleasure in the name of God[1]. The internal characteristic of *bhāva*, as *rati*, is extreme smoothness and liquidity of heart, but, wherever such a state is associated with other desires, even be it of emancipation, it should not be regarded as signifying the true state, and is called *ratyābhāsa*; for this is a state of absolute self-contentment, and it cannot be associated with any other desire of any kind.

When *bhāva* deepens, it is called *prema*; it is associated with a sense of possession in God and absolute detachment from all other things. This may rise from a direct development of *bhāva*, or through the immediate grace of God; it may be associated with a notion of the greatness of God or may manifest itself merely as an enjoyment of the sweetness of God. The development of *bhakti* depends on a special temperament derived in this life as a result of previous good deeds, and also on the efforts of this life. There is an elaborate description of the various characteristics of different kinds of joyous emotion with reference to God, and the various kinds of relationships on the assumption of which these may grow, but these can hardly be treated here.

Rūpa Gosvāmī wrote another work, *Saṃkṣepa-Bhāgavatāmṛta* which is a well recognized book in the Vaiṣṇava circle. It has at least two commentaries, one by Jīva Gosvāmī, and another, a later one, by Bṛindāvana Candra Tarkālaṅkāra; the latter was the pupil of Rādhācaraṇa Kavīndra. In this book Rūpa describes the various

[1] *Bhakti-rasāmṛta-sindhu*, I. 3. 11–16.

types of God's incarnation in accordance with the testimony of the *Purāṇas*: Kṛṣṇa is, of course, regarded as the highest God. His elder brother Sanātana also wrote a work, *Bṛhad-bhāgavatā-mṛta*, with a commentary on it, the *Dig-darśana*, in which he narrates the episodes of certain devotees in quest of God and their experiences.

The Philosophy of Baladeva Vidyābhūṣaṇa.

Baladeva was Vaiśya by caste and born in a village near Remuna in the Balesvar subdivision of Orissa; he was a pupil of *vairāgī* Pītāmvara Dāsa, and was generally known as Govinda Dāṣa. He was the disciple of a Kanouj Brahmin, Rādhā Dāmodara Dāsa, the author of *Vedānta-Syamantaka*. Rādhā Dāmodara was a disciple of Nayanānanda, the son of Rādhānanda, and a pupil of his grandfather, Rasikānanda Murāri, who was a disciple of Śyāmānanda, a junior contemporary of Jīva Gosvāmī. Śyāmānanda was a disciple of Hṛdaya Caitanya, who in his turn was a disciple of Gaurīdāsa Paṇḍita, a disciple of Nityānanda. Baladeva himself had two well known disciples, Nanda Miśra and Uddhava Dāsa; he wrote his commentary on Rūpa Gosvāmī's *Stava-mālā* in the Śaka era 1686 (or A.D. 1764). He is known to have written at least the following fourteen works: *Sāhitya-kaumudī* and its commentary, *Kṛṣṇānandī*; *Govinda-bhāṣya*; *Siddhānta-ratna*; *Kāvya-Kaustubha*; *Gītā-bhūṣaṇa*, a commentary on the *Gītā*; a commentary on Rādhā Dāmodara's *Chandaḥ-Kaustubha*; *Prameya-ratnāvalī* and its commentary, *Kānti-mālā*; a commentary on Rūpa's *Stava-mālā*; a commentary on Rūpa's *Laghu-bhāgavatā-mṛta*; *Nāmārtha-śuddhikā*, a commentary on *Sahasra-nāma*; a commentary on Jaya Deva's *Candrāloka*; *Siddhānta-darpaṇa*; a commentary on *Tattva-sandarbha*; a commentary on Rūpa's *Nāṭaka-candrikā*. He also wrote commentaries on some of the important Upaniṣads[1].

Baladeva's most important work is his commentary on the *Brahma-sūtra*, otherwise known as *Govinda-bhāṣya*. This has a sub-commentary on it called *Sūkṣma*; the name of the author of this commentary is not known, though it has been held by some to be a work of Baladeva himself. Baladeva has also summarized the

[1] M. M. Gopinath Kavirāja's introduction to *Siddhānta-ratna*, Part II. A. K. Sastri, in his introduction to *Prameya-ratnāvalī*, strongly criticizes the view that Baladeva was a *Vaiśya*. No satisfactory proofs are available on either side.

contents of his *Govinda-bhāṣya* in the *Siddhānta-ratna*, to which also there is a commentary. M. M. Gopinath Kavirāja says that the *Siddhānta-ratna* was written by Baladeva himself. There is nothing to urge in support of this assertion; the natural objection against it is that a Vaiṣṇava like Baladeva should not speak in glowing terms of praise of his own work[1]. *Siddhānta-ratna* is regarded by Baladeva not as a summary of *Govinda-bhāṣya*, but as partly a supplementary work and partly a commentary[2]. It is probable that the writer of the *Sūkṣma* commentary on the *Govinda-bhāṣya* is also the writer of the commentary on *Siddhānta-ratna*; for there is one introductory verse which is common to them both[3]. The *Siddhānta-ratna* contains much that is not contained in the *Govinda-bhāṣya*.

The eternal possession of bliss and the eternal cessation of sorrow is the ultimate end of man. This end can be achieved through the true knowledge of God in His essence (*svarūpataḥ*) and as associated with His qualities by one who knows also the nature of his own self (*sva-jñāna-pūrvakam*). The nature of God is pure consciousness and bliss. These two may also be regarded as the body of God (*na tu svarūpād vigrahasya atirekaḥ*). His spirit consists in knowledge, majesty and power[4]. Though one in Himself, He appears in many places and in the forms of His diverse devotees. These are therefore but modes of His manifestation in self-dalliance, and this is possible on account of His supra-logical powers, which are identical with His own nature[5]. This, however, should not lead us to suppose the correctness of the *bhedābheda* doctrine, of the simultaneous truth of the one and the many, or that of difference

[1] *sāndrānanda-syandi govinda-bhāṣyaṃ*
jīyād etat sindhu-gāmbhīryya-sambhṛt
yasmin sadyaḥ saṃśrute mānavānām
mohocchedī jāyate tattva-bodhaḥ.
Commentary on *Siddhānta-ratna*, p. 1.

[2] *Ibid.*

[3] *ālasyād apravṛttiḥ syāt*
puṃsāṃ yad grantha-vistare
govinda-bhāṣye saṃkṣipte
ṭippaṇī kriyate'tra tat.

Sukṣma commentary, p. 5, and the commentary on *Siddhānta-ratna*, p. 1.

[4] *Siddhānta-ratna*, pp. 1–13.

[5] *ekam eva sva-rūpam acintya-śaktyā yugapat sarvatrāvabhāty eko'pi san; sthānāni bhagavad-āvirbhāvāspadāni tad-vividha-līlā-śraya-bhūtāni vividha-bhāvavanto bhaktāś ca.* *Govinda-bhāṣya*, III. 2. 11.

and unity[1]; just as one actor, remaining one in himself, shows himself in diverse forms, so God also manifests Himself in diverse forms, in accordance with diverse effects and also in accordance with the mental plane and the ways in which diverse devotees conceive of Him[2]. On account of His supra-logical powers the laws of contradiction do not apply to Him; even contradictory qualities and conceptions may be safely associated in our notion of Him. So also His body is not different in nature from Him: He is thus identical with His body. The conception of a body distinct from Him is only in the minds of the devotees as an aid to the process of meditation; but, though this is imagination on their part, such a form is not false, but as a matter of fact is God Himself (*deha eva dehī* or *vigraha evātmā ātmaiva vigrahaḥ*). On account of the transcendent nature of God, in spite of His real nature as pure consciousness and bliss He may have His real nature in bodily form, as Kṛṣṇa. This form really arises in association with the mind of the devotee just as musical forms show themselves in association with the trained ears of a musician[3]. In this connection it may be observed that according to Baladeva even dream-creations are not false, but real, produced by the will of God and disappearing in the waking stage through the will of God[4]. These forms appearing in the minds of the devotees are therefore real forms, manifested by God through His will working in association with the minds of the devotees. In this connection it may also be pointed out that the *jīvas* are different from God. Even the imagined reflection of Brahman in *avidyā*, introduced by the extreme monists to explain *jīva* as being only a reflection of Brahman and as having no real existence outside it, is wrong; for the notion of similarity or reflection involves difference. The *jīvas* are atomic in nature, associated with the qualities of *prakṛti*, and absolutely dependent on God. Though Brahman is all-pervasive, yet He can be grasped by knowledge and devotion. A true realization of His nature and even a sensuous perception of Him is possible only through *sādhya-bhakti*,

[1] The *Sūkṣma* commentary on III. 2. 12 says that God's *māyā-śakti* has three functions: *hlādinī, sandhinī,* and *saṃvit*; it is through His *māyā-śakti*, i.e., the power as *māyā*, that He can manifest Himself in diverse ways.

[2] *dhyātṛ-bhedāt kāryya-bhedāc ca anekatayā pratīto'pi hariḥ svarūpaikyaṃ svasmin na muñcati. Govinda-bhāṣya,* III. 2. 13.

[3] *tan-mūrtatvaṃ khalu bhakti-vibhāvitena hṛdā grāhyaṃ gāndharvānuśīlitena śrotreṇa rāga-mūrtatvam iva. Ibid.* III. 2. 17.

[4] *Ibid.* III. 2. 1–5.

not through *sādhana-bhakti.* The consciousness and bliss of God may be regarded either as the substance of God or as His attributes. This twofold way of reference to God is due to the admission of the category of *viśeṣa*, by which, even in the absence of difference between the substance and the quality, it is possible to predicate the latter of the former as if such a difference existed. *Viśeṣa* is spoken of as the representative of difference (*bheda-pratinidhi*); that is, where no difference exists, the concept of *viśeṣa* enables us to predicate a difference; yet this *viśeṣa* is no mere *vikalpa* or mere false verbal affirmation. The ocean can be spoken of as water and waves by means of this concept of *viśeṣa*. The concept of *viśeṣa* means that, though there is no difference between God and His qualities, or between His nature and His body, yet there is some specific peculiarity which makes it possible to affirm the latter of the former; and by virtue of this peculiarity the differential predication may be regarded as true, though there may actually be no difference between the two. It is by virtue of this concept that such propositions as "Being exists," "Time always is," "Space is everywhere," may be regarded as true; they are neither false nor mere verbal assumption; if they were false, there would be no justification for such mental states. There is obviously a difference between the two propositions "Being exists" and "Being does not exist"; the former is regarded as legitimate, the latter as false. This proves that though there is no difference between "being" and "existence" there is such a peculiarity in it that, while the predication of existence to being is legitimate, its denial is false. If it were merely a case of verbal assumption, then the latter denial would also have been equally possible and justifiable. This peculiarity is identical with the object and does not exist in it in any particular relation. For this reason a further chain of relations is not required, and the charge of a vicious infinite also becomes inadmissible. If the concept of *viśeṣa* is not admitted, then the notion of "qualified" and "quality" is inexplicable[1]. The concept of *viśeṣa* in this sense was first introduced by Madhva; Baladeva borrowed the idea from him in interpreting the relation of God to His powers and qualities. This interpretation is entirely different from the view of Jīva and others who preceded Baladeva; we have already seen how Jīva interpreted the situation merely by the doctrine of the supra-logical

[1] *Ibid.* III. 2. 31.

nature of God's powers and the supra-logical nature of the difference and identity of power and the possessor of power, or of the quality and the substance. Baladeva, by introducing the concept of *viśeṣa*, tried to explain more clearly the exact nature of supra-logicality (*acintyatva*) in this case; this has been definitely pointed out in the *Sūkṣma* commentary[1].

The bliss of God is different from the bliss of the *jīvas*, both in nature and in quantity, and the nature of their knowledge is different. Brahman is thus different in nature both from the world and from the *jīvas*. All the unity texts of the Upaniṣads are to be explained merely as affirming that the world and the *jīvas* belong to God (*sarvatra tadīyatva-jñānārthaḥ*). Such a way of looking at the world will rouse the spirit of *bhakti*. The revelation of God's nature in those who follow the path of *vaidhī-bhakti* is different from that in those who follow the *ruci-bhakti*; in the former case He appears in all His majesty, in the latter He appears with all His sweetness. When God is worshipped in a limited form as Kṛṣṇa, He reveals Himself in His limited form to the devotee, and such is the supra-logical nature of God that even in this form He remains as the All-pervasive. It is evident that the acceptance of *viśeṣa* does not help Baladeva here and he has to accept the supra-logical nature of God to explain other parts of his religious dogmas.

God is regarded as being both the material cause of the world and as the supreme agent. He has three fundamental powers: the supreme power, *viṣṇu-śakti*, the power as *kṣetrajña*, the power as *avidyā*. In His first power Brahman remains in Himself as the unchangeable; His other two powers are transformed into the *jīvas* and the world. The Sāṃkhyist argues that, as the world is of a different nature from Brahman, Brahman cannot be regarded as its material cause. Even if it is urged that there are two subtle powers which may be regarded as the material cause of the world and the *jīvas*, their objection still holds good; for the development of the gross, which is different from the subtle, is not explained. To this the reply is that the effect need not necessarily be the same as or similar to the material cause. Brahman transforms Himself into the world, which is entirely different from Him. If there were absolute oneness between the material cause and the effect, then

[1] *tenaiva tasya vastvabhinnatvaṃ sva-nirvāhakatvaṃ ca svasya tādṛśe tad-bhāvojjṛmbhakam acintyatvaṃ sidhyati. Sūkṣma* on *Govinda-bhāṣya*, III. 2. 31.

one could not be called the cause and the other the effect; the lumpy character of the mud is not seen in the jug, which is its effect; in all cases that may be reviewed the effect must necessarily be different from the material cause. Such a modification does not in any way change the nature of Brahman. The changes are effected in His powers, while He remains unchanged by the modification of His powers. To turn to an ordinary example as an illustration, it may be pointed out that "a man with the stick" refers to none other than the man himself, though there is a difference between the man and the stick; so though the power of the Brahman is identical with Brahman in association with His powers, yet the existence of a difference between Brahman and His powers is not denied[1]. Moreover, there is always a difference between the material cause and the effect. The jug is different from the lump of clay, and the ornaments from the gold out of which they are made; also they serve different purposes and exist in different times. If the effect existed before the causal operation began, the application of the causal operation would be unnecessary; also the effect would be eternal. If it is held that the effect is a manifestation of that which was already existent, then a further question arises, whether this manifestation, itself an effect, requires a further manifestation, and so on; thus a chain of manifestations would be necessary, and the result would be a vicious infinite. Still, Baladeva does not deny the *pariṇāma* or the *abhivyakti* theory; he denies the Sāṃkhya view that even before the causal operation the effect exists, or that a manifestation (*abhivyakti*) would require a chain of manifestations. He defines effect as an independent manifestation (*svatantrābhivyaktimattvaṃ kila kāryatvam*), and such an effect cannot exist before the action of the causal operatives. The manifestation of the world is through the manifestation of God, on whom it is dependent. Such a manifestation can only happen through the causal operation inherent in God and initiated by His will. Thus the world is manifested out of the energy of God, and in a limited sense the world is identical with God; but once it is separated out of Him as effect, it is different from Him. The world did not exist at any time before it was manifested in its present form; therefore it is wrong to suppose that the world was at any stage identical with God, though God may always be regarded as the material cause of the

[1] *Ibid.* II. I. 13.

world[1]. Thus after all these discussions it becomes evident that there is really no difference of any importance between Baladeva's views and the Sāṃkhya view. Baladeva also admits that the world exists in a subtle form in God as endowed with His energies. He only takes exception to the verbal expression of the *kārikā* that the effect exists in the cause before the action of the causal operatives; for the effect does not exist in the cause *as effect* but in a subtle state. This subtle state is enlarged and endowed with spatio-temporal qualities by the action of the causal operatives before it can manifest itself as effect. The Sāṃkhya, however, differs in overstressing the existence of the effect in the cause, and in asserting that the function of the causal operatives is only to manifest openly what already existed in a covered manner. Here, however, the causal operatives are regarded as making a real change and addition. This addition of new qualities and functions is due to the operation of the causal will of God; it is of a supra-logical nature in the sense that they were not present in the subtle causal state, and yet have come into being through the operation of God's will. But, so far as the subtle cause exists in God as associated with Him, the world is not distinct and independent of God even in its present form[2]. The *jīvas* too have no independence in themselves; they are created by God, by His mere will, and having created the world and the *jīvas* He entered into them and remained as their inner controller. So the *jīvas* are as much under natural necessity as the objects of the physical world, and they have thus no freedom of action or of will[3]. The natural necessity of the world is but a manifestation of God's will through it. The spontaneous desire and will that is found in man is also an expression of God's will operating through man; thus man is as much subject to necessity as the world, and there is no freedom in man. Thus, though the cow which gives milk may seem to us as if it were giving the milk by its own will, yet the vital powers of the cow produce the milk, not the cow; so, when a person is perceived as doing a particular action or behaving in a particular manner or willing something, it is not he who is the

[1] *Govinda-bhāṣya*, II. I. 14.

[2] *tasmād ekam eva jīva-prakṛti-śaktimad brahma jagad-upādānam tadātmakaṃ ca iti siddham evam kāryāvasthatve'py avicintyatva-dharma-yogād apracyuta-pūrvāvasthaṃ cāvatiṣṭhate. Ibid.* II. I. 20.

[3] *cetanasyāpi jīvasyāśma-kāṣṭha-loṣṭravad asvātantryāt svataḥ kartṛtva-rūpānāpattiḥ. Ibid.* II. I. 23.

agent, but the supreme God, who is working through him[1]. But the question may arise, if God is the sole cause of all human willing and human action, then why should God, who is impartial, make us will so differently? The answer will be that God determines our action and will in accordance with the nature of our past deeds, which are beginningless. A further objection may be made, that if God determines our will in accordance with our past deeds, then God is dependent in His own determining action on the nature of our *karmas*; which will be a serious challenge to His unobstructed freedom. Moreover, since different kinds of action lead to different kinds of pleasurable and painful effects God may be regarded as partial. The reply to these objections is that God determines the *jīvas* in accordance with their own individual nature; the individual *jīvas* are originally of a different nature, and in accordance with their original difference God determines their will and actions differently. Though God is capable of changing their nature, He does not do so; but it is in the nature of God's own will that He reserves a preferential treatment for His devotee, to whom He extends His special grace[2]. God's own actions are not determined by any objective end or motive, but flow spontaneously through His enjoyment of His own blissful nature. His special grace towards His devotees flows from His own essential nature; it is this special treatment offered to His devotees that endears Him to them and that rouses others to turn towards Him[3].

Bhakti is also regarded as a species of knowledge (*bhaktir api jñāna-viśeṣo bhavati*)[4]. By *bhakti* one turns to God without any kind of objective end. *Bhakti* is also regarded as a power which can bind God to us[5]; this power is regarded as the essence of the *hlādinī* power of God as associated with consciousness. The consciousness here spoken of is identical with the *hlāda*, and its essence consists in a favourable outflow of natural inclination[6]. This is thus identical with God's essential nature as consciousness and bliss; yet it is not regarded as identical with Him, but as a power of

[1] *Ibid.* II. I. 24.

[2] *na ca karma-sāpekṣatvena īśyarsya asvātantryam;...anādi-jīva-svabhāvānusāreṇa hi karma kārayati sva-bhāvam anyathā-kartuṃ samartho'pi kasyāpi na karoti.* *Ibid.* II. I. 35.

[3] *Ibid.* II. I. 36.

[4] Commentary on *Siddhānta-ratna*, p. 29.

[5] *bhagavad-vaśīkāra-hetu-bhūtā śaktiḥ.* *Ibid.* p. 35.

[6] *hlāda-bhinnā saṃvid, yas tadānukūlyaṃśaḥ sa tasyāḥ sāraḥ.* *Ibid.* p. 37.

Him[1]. Though *bhakti* exists in God as His power, yet it qualifies the devotee also, it is pleasurable to them both, and they are both constituents of it[2]. It will be remembered that, of the three powers, *samvit* is superior to *sandhinī* and *hlādinī* is superior to *samvit*. God not only is, but He extends His being to everything else; *sandhinī* is the power by which God extends being to all. He is Himself of the nature of consciousness; *samvit* is the power by which His cognitive action is accomplished and by which He makes it possible for other people to know. Though He is of the nature of bliss, He experiences joy and makes it possible for others to have joyous experiences; the power by which He does this is called *hlādinī*.[3] True *bhakti* cannot have any object outside itself, simply for the reason that it is itself an experience of God as supreme bliss. That there is a kind of bliss other than sensuous pleasure is proved by our experience of our own nature as bliss during deep sleep. But, since we are but atoms of God's energy, it is necessarily proved that God's nature is supreme and infinite bliss; once that bliss is experienced, people will naturally turn away from worldly sensuous pleasure to God, once for all.

True knowledge destroys all merit and demerit, and so in the *jīvan-mukti* man holds his body only through the will of God. The effect of obligatory duties is not destroyed, except in so far as it produces meritorious results—admission to Heaven and the like—and it helps the rise of true knowledge; when the true knowledge dawns, it does not further show itself. It is also stated in the Kauṣītakī Upaniṣad that the merits of a wise man go to his friends and his demerits to his foes; so in the case of those devotees who are anxious to enter communion with God the meritorious effects of their deeds are distributed to those who are dear to Him, and the effects of their sinful actions are distributed to His enemies[4]. So, as the effects of the fructifying *karma* are distributed to other persons, the principle that all fructifying *karmas* must produce

[1] *svarūpānatirekiṇyapi tad-viśeṣatayā ca bhāsate'nyathā tasya śaktir iti vyapedeśa-siddheḥ. Siddhānta-ratna*, p. 38.

[2] *bhagavat-svarūpa-viśeṣa-bhūta-hlādinyādi-sārātmā bhaktir bhagavad-viśeṣaṇatayā bhakte ca pṛthag-viśeṣaṇatayā siddhā tayor ānandātiśayayo bhavati. Ibid.* p. 39.

[3] *tatra sadātmā'pi yayā sattaṃ dhatte dadāti ca sā sarva-deśa-kāla-dravya-vyāpti-hetuḥ sandhinī, saṃvid-ātmā'pi yayā saṃvetti saṃvedayati ca sā saṃvit, hlādātmā'pi yayā hlādate hlādayati ca sā hlādinī. Ibid.* pp. 39–40.

[4] *Govinda-bhāṣya*, IV. I. 17.

their effects is satisfied, and the devotee of God is released from them. The best way for true advancement can only be through the association of saintly devotees. Our bondage is real, and the destruction of the bondage is real and eternal. Even in the state of ultimate emancipation the *jīvas* retain their separate individuality from God.

In the sixth and seventh chapters of the *Siddhānta-ratna* Baladeva tries to refute Śaṅkara's doctrine of extreme monism; but as these arguments contain hardly anything new but merely repeat the arguments of the thinkers of the Rāmānuja and the Madhva Schools, they may well be omitted here. In his *Prameya-ratnāvalī* Baladeva gives a general summary of the main points of the Vaiṣṇava system of the Gauḍīya School. If one compares the account they give of Vaiṣṇava philosophy in the *Bhāgavata-sandarbha* with that given in Baladeva's *Govinda-bhāṣya* and *Siddhānta-ratna*, one finds that, though the fundamental principles are the same, yet many new elements were introduced by Baladeva into the Gauḍīya school of thought under the influence of Madhva, and on account of his personal predilections. The stress that is laid on the aspect of difference between Īśvara and the *jīva* and the world and the concept of *viśeṣa*, are definite traces of Madhva influence. Again, though Baladeva admires the *ruci-bhakti* as the best form of *bhakti*, he does not lay the same emphasis on it as is found in the works of Rūpa, Sanātana or Jīva. His concept of *bhakti* is also slightly different from that of Jīva; he does not use the older terminologies (*antaraṅga* and *bahiraṅga śakti*), and does not seek the explanation of his system on that concept. His *Prameya-ratna-mālā* has an old commentary, the *Kānti-mālā*, by one Kṛṣṇadeva Vedānta Vāgīśa. In the *Prameya-ratna-mālā* he pays his salutation to Ānanda-tīrtha or Madhva, whom he describes as his boat for crossing the ocean of *saṃsāra*. He gives also a list of the succession of teachers from whom he derived his ideas, and he thinks that by a meditation upon the succession of *gurus* one would succeed in producing the satisfaction of Hari. He further says that four *sampradāyas* or schools of Vaiṣṇavas, the *Śrī*, *Brahma*, *Rudra*, and *Sanaka*, will spring forth in Orissa (Utkala) in the Kali yuga, which may be identified with Rāmānuja, Madhva, Viṣṇusvāmin, and Nimbāditya. He enumerates the succession of his teachers, in the following order: Śrīkṛṣṇa, Brahmā, Devarṣi-

Bādarāyaṇa, Madhva, Padmanābha, Nṛhari, Mādhava, Akṣobhya, Jaya-tīrtha, Jñana-sindhu, Vidyānidhi, Rājendra, Jayadharma, Puruṣottama, Brāhmaṇya, Vyāsa-tīrtha, Lakṣmīpati, Mādhavendra, Iśvara, Advaita, Nityānanda and also Śrī Caitanya[1]. The system of thought represented by Baladeva may well be styled the Madhva-Gauḍīya system; we have had recently in Bengal a school of Vaiṣṇavas which calls itself Madhva-Gauḍīya.

[1] See an earlier list by Kavi-Karṇapūra, in his fanciful or legendary treatise *Gaura-gaṇoddeśa-dīpikā.*

INDEX

abhāva, 150, 294
abhāva-vikalpo, 183
abhijña, 297
Abhimāna, 41
Abhinava-candrikā, 62
abhivyakti, 143, 150, 443
Abnegation, 354
Absolute, 73
Absolute forgetfulness, 49
Absolute negation, 207
Accessories, 88
acchidra-sevā, 318*n.*
Accidental, 122
Account of the Madhva Gurus, 54
acintya, 16, 18, 19, 37, 398
acintya-śakti, 154
acintyatva, 398
acintya-viśeṣa-mahimnā, 19
Action, 3, 150
Acyutaprekṣa, 53
adharma, 4
adhikaraṇa, 129, 130, 134, 325, 326
Adhikaraṇa-saṃgraha, 381, 382*n.*
adhiṣṭhāna, 106, 119, 175, 250, 414
adhiṣṭhāna-caitanya, 242, 414
adhīna, 313
adhyasta, 119
adhyasyamāna, 299
Aditi, 132
adravya, 97
ddrśya, 135*n.*
adṛṣṭa, 201, 333
advaita, 125*n.*, 194, 385, 448
Advaita-siddhi, 63, 65, 208*n.*, 211, 214, 215, 216*n.*, 221, 223, 224, 227, 240*n.*, 242*n.*, 249*n.*, 252*n.*, 254, 269, 270*n.*, 275*n.*, 280*n.*, 302
advaya-tattva, 14
Affliction, 12, 44
After-image, 342
Agent, 299
Agni, 71
aham, 66, 159
aham-ajñaḥ, 265
aham-artha, 110, 264, 296, 297
ahaṃkāra, 24, 27, 31, 32*n.*, 40, 41, 47, 114, 150, 157, 158, 159, 314, 336
ahaṃ sphurāmi, 296
ahetuka, 190
ahetukī, 416
ahiṃsā, 9
Ahirbudhnya-saṃhitā, 36, 37, 39, 40, 42, 44, 45; categories, development of, 40–1; God in, 40; *puruṣa* in, 43; *śakti*, *myati*, *kāla*, etc., 44; time in, 40
Ahobala-Nṛsiṃha, 388
aikṣata, 135
aindrajālikasyeva avidyamāna-pradarśana-śaktih, 2
aindriya-vṛtti, 167
aiśvaryānanda, 431
Aitareya-Āraṇyaka, 55, 132*n.*
Aitareya-Brāhmaṇa, 55
Aitareya-upaniṣad-bhāṣya, 55
Aitareyopaniṣad, 90
Aitareyopaniṣad-bhāṣya-ṭippanī, 55
ajñāna, 63, 73, 83, 104, 106, 107, 117, 122, 152, 208, 215, 217, 218, 220, 221, 224, 237, 238, 239, 240, 243, 244, 245, 246, 247, 256, 257, 259, 261, 263, 264, 265, 266, 267, 268, 269, 270, 275, 276, 277, 278, 279, 281, 282, 283, 284, 285, 286, 288, 289, 290, 291, 292, 293, 294, 295, 297, 298, 305, 326, 403; criticism of, 261 ff.; inference of, 276 ff.; Madhusūdana's reply to the criticism of the view that *ajñāna* is egohood, refuted, 296 ff.; nature of its destruction discussed, 244 ff.; perception of, 264 ff.; relation to Brahman, 266; relation to dreamless sleep, 267; relation to egohood criticized, 294; relation to knowledge, 269; relation to negation, 270 ff.; relation to *vṛtti*, 267, criticized, 277; reply to Madhusūdana's criticism, 273; views of other Vedāntic authors refuted, 274
ajñāna-product, 287
ajñānatva, 217
akārpaṇya, 9
akārya-kāraṇānumāna, 201
Akbar, 379
akiñcana-bhakti, 421, 424
akitava, 423
akṣara, 135

Madhva (*cont.*)
184, 190, 203, 318, 319, 339, 346, 371, 388, 441, 447, 448; *Anubhāṣya* and commentaries thereon, 61; *Anuvyākhyāna*, account of, 62–3; *Anuvyākhyāna* with commentaries thereon, 62; *aprāmāṇya*, 163; *avidyā* doctrine, 159–60; *ākāśa* doctrine, 153–4; *bhakti*, view regarding, 58; *Bhāgavata-tātparya-nirṇaya* and commentary thereon, 59; *Bhāgavata-tātparya-nirṇaya*, manner of treatment in, 59; *bheda*, nature of, 178 ff.; discussion of the meaning of the word Brahman, 111–12 ff.; his interpretation of the *Brahma-sūtra* I. I. I, 102 ff.; interpretation of *Brahma-sūtra* I. I. 2, 121 ff.; interpretation of *Brahma-sūtra* I. I. 3–4, 127; his interpretation of the *Brahma-sūtras* elaborated by many other writers, 101; logical connection of the *Brahma-sūtras*, 87; monistic interpretation of Brahman, difficulties in, 125 ff.; other conditions of Brahma-knowledge are discarded, 110–11; what leads to Brahma enquiry, 102; a review of the important topics of the *Brahma-sūtras*, 129 ff.; *Brahma-sūtra-bhāṣya*, 61; Christianity, influence of, on, 92–3; concomitance in Madhva, 197 ff.; date of, 51; eternal damnation in, 58; definition of Brahman, discussions on, 121 ff.; difference (*bheda*), concept of, 73–4; view regarding five-fold differences, 57; difference, reality of, 178–9; difference as conceived by Śaṅkara criticized, 179–80; discussions, condition of, 115; discussion (*vāda*), nature of, 65; doubts defined, 176 ff.; his view regarding the emancipated, 57–8; emancipated souls, distinction among, 66; error, nature of, 118 ff.; falsehood, notion of, criticized, 84; falsity of the world, doctrine, discarded, 114; falsity of the world criticized in the *Tattvoddyota*, 67; *Gītā-tātparya*, account of, 59 ff.; *Gītā-tātparya*, manner of treatment in, 59; God as eternal perceiver of the world, 68; God's possession of many qualities defended, 71; God, collocation of *pramāṇas* leading to, 78; God, proof of existence, 76; God, nature of, 75; identity incomprehensible without difference, 79–80; identity, notion of, denied, 82; notion of absolute identity (*akhaṇḍārtha*) criticized, 73; identity of selves denied, 70; identity of the self and the world denied, 68; inference, 184 ff.; various kinds of inference in, 200–1; inference as *svārthānumāna* and *parārthānumāna*, 202; illusion defined, 173; illusion and doubt, 173 ff.; illusion, Mīmāṃsā view of, criticized, 174; illusion, Śaṅkara view criticized, 175; *karma*, *prārabdha* and *aprārabdha*, discussion of, 88; nature of *karma* in, 61; *karma-nirṇaya*, account of, 70 ff.; *kathā-lakṣaṇa*, account of, 65; intuitive knolwedge, 181; nature of knowledge discussed by Vyāsa-tīrtha as against Madhusūdana, 230 ff.; *kṛṣṇāmṛta-mahārṇava*, account of, 89; life of, 51 ff.; *Mahābhārata*, view regarding, 58; *Mahābhārata-tātparya-nirṇaya*, 57–8; *Mahābhārata-tātparya-nirṇaya*, commentary of, 59; *māyā* doctrine discarded, 113; *Māyāvāda-khaṇḍana* with commentaries thereon, 64; memory as *pramāṇa*, 162; *mithyā* and *anirvacanīya*, 80–1; *mithyātvānumāna-khaṇḍana* with commentaries thereon, 64; Mīmāṃsā doctrine of *karma* criticized, 71; *mokṣa* (liberation), nature described by the followers of Madhva, 315; *mokṣa*, different types of, 318; *mokṣa*, ways that lead to it, 316; the monism of Śaṅkara cannot be the basis of Brahma-enquiry, 103; monism, refutation of, by Vyāsa-tīrtha, 204 ff.; *nityānitya-viveka* cannot be a condition of Brahma-knowledge, 109; non-existence, nature of, 80; *Nyāya-vivaraṇa*, account of, 87; ontology, 150 ff.; criticism of, by Parakāla Yati, 95; perception, condition of, 182; perception, Nyāya definition and condition denied, 182–3; Prabhākara view discussed, 74; *prakṛti* doctrine, 156 ff.; *pramāṇas*, 160 ff.; *pramāṇas*, agreement with objects, 161; *pramāṇa*, criticism of other definitions of, 164; *pramāṇa*, Buddhist view of, considered, 167;